TEXTBOOK

Criminal Law

Second Edition

CONSULTANT EDITOR: LORD TEMPLEMAN

MICHAEL T MOLAN
BA, LLM (Lond), Barrister
Head of the Division of Law, South Bank University

INESSA · G · HADJIVAYANIS

OLD BAILEY PRESS

OLD BAILEY PRESS
200 Greyhound Road, London W14 9RY

First published 1997
Second edition 1999
Reprinted 2000

© The HLT Group Ltd 1999

ISBN 1 85836 310 1

British Library Cataloguing-in-Publication.
A CIP Catalogue record for this book is available from the British Library.

Acknowledgement
The publishers and author would like to thank the Incorporated Council of Law Reporting for England and Wales for kind permission to reproduce extracts from the Weekly Law Reports, and Butterworths for their kind permission to reproduce extracts from the All England Law Reports.

Printed and bound in Great Britain

Contents

Preface

Old Bailey Press textbooks are written specifically for students. Whatever their course they will find our books clear and concise, providing comprehensive and up-to-date coverage. Written by specialists in their field, our textbooks are reviewed and updated on a regular basis. A companion Casebook, Revision WorkBook and Statutes are also published.

This *Criminal Law* textbook is designed for use by any undergraduates who have Criminal Law within their syllabus. It will be equally useful for all CPE/LLDip students who must study criminal law as one of their compulsory subjects. In addition, those studying for certain professional examinations, such as those of the Institute of Legal Executives, will find this textbook gives them sufficient information for their appropriate examinations in criminal law.

The *Criminal Law* textbook provides the reader with a logical and accessible body of material, with related issues being covered together in discrete chapters, such as those dealing with the protection of life, accessorial liability and theft.

There have been many important developments since the last edition of this text in September 1997. The House of Lords has returned to the issue of the mens rea for murder, particularly the nature of intention based on evidence of foresight, in its decision in *R* v *Woollin*. The law relating to joint enterprise has been clarified to some extent by the important House of Lords' decision in *R* v *Powell and Daniels*; *R* v *English*, although there are certain aspects of the topic, notably accessorial liability for manslaughter, that still prove troublesome. The debate as to the extent to which the characteristics of the accused can be attributed to the reasonable man for the purposes of the objective test for self-control in the defence of provocation has reached a point where only a House of Lords' ruling can resolve the conflict between the Privy Council and the Court of Appeal, as evidenced by *R* v *Smith (Morgan)*. The problems caused by the House of Lords' decision in *Gomez* regarding theft where the owner consents to the transfer of property continue to reverberate, most significantly where the defendant acquires property following the making of a valid gift by the owner: see *R* v *Hinks*. Also noted in this edition are the changes to the substantive law consequent upon the enactment of the Crime and Disorder Act 1998, and the likely impact of the Human Rights Act 1998.

The law is stated as of 1 January 1999.

Table of Cases

Table of Statutes and Other Materials

1

Introduction to Criminal Law

1.1 The nature of criminal law

1.2 Sources of criminal law

1.3 The Human Rights Act 1998

1.4 Aspects of the criminal process

1.5 Preventing miscarriages of justice

1.6 The work of the Law Commission

1.1 The nature of criminal law

Let us start with two propositions. The first is that there is a basic human instinct to survive and, if possible, flourish. The second is that, however loosely arranged, humans tend to congregate together in societies. If these two propositions are accepted in broad terms it requires no great leap of imagination to see that societies themselves, as aggregations of the individuals comprising them, will have a collective instinct to survive and flourish. Human experience suggests that societies with a degree of structure and order, at least to the extent that this provides for efficient collectivism, are those most likely to flourish. It is from these imperatives that the criminal law of a state is usually born. What these imperatives are will change according to the needs of the society in question and, indeed, its cultural heritage. In most sophisticated and developed societies, however, one would expect to encounter prohibitions on actions that would otherwise threaten to imperil the safety of the state; activities that would otherwise imperil the health and safety of members of the society; and activities that would otherwise interfere with the possession, transfer and enjoyment of property whether personal or communal.

In terms of factors that historically go to shape the criminal law of a state most would cite natural law, perhaps as evidenced in a religious code, and the prevailing political ideology of the state as being of prime importance. The source of such laws in a modern secular society is, however, invariably referred to as 'the state', although this is not a term of art. For 'state' one might read 'those groups in society with a monopoly of power – whether economic, military or political'. In a dictatorship it might be the will of the dictator. In an idealised democracy it will be the will of the people as demonstrated through the democratic process.

Criminal law can thus be seen as a litany of prohibitions and duties: behaviour that the state considers to be unacceptable, or action that the state demands. Whilst it is possible to give a technical definition of crime, in terms of the elements that go to make up an offence (see Chapter 2), or the procedure followed in court in order to secure a conviction, it is much more difficult to define the concept of crime in theoretical terms. In some senses the answer would sound banal. An activity is a crime because the state has labelled it as a crime. On this basis, if the state decreed that it was an offence for men to grow beards, or for women to appear in public on Thursdays, those actions would become crimes, but they would not perhaps accord with our innate sense of what ought to be criminal and what should not. Addressing these issues brings to mind two fundamental points. What factors should lawmakers take into account when determining whether an activity should be criminalised? What characteristics should criminal offences have?

What principles should underpin the development of the criminal law?

Three key principles can be identified.

The first is that, in drafting criminal offences, the state should strive to strike the right balance between the principle of minimum criminalisation and social defence. The principle of minimum criminalisation is that there should be no more criminal prohibitions than are strictly necessary for society to function fairly and effectively. In a complex industrialised society, however, adherence to this principle is more theoretical than real, as evidenced by the mass of regulatory offences created every year. Governments also respond to public pressure for 'something to be done' about current problems, recent examples including joyriding, gun control, dangerous dogs and computer pornography. The social defence principle suggests that criminalisation is justified to some extent by the risk of harm to society's collective interests, or to the well being of individual citizens, that could be caused by an activity continuing unchecked. Underpinning the social defence argument to some extent is the notion that the criminal law also provides a moral yardstick in that it publicly proclaims certain activities to be unacceptable.

Second, the criminal law should be, and should be perceived to be, essentially fair in its content and operation. Hence, for example, the prohibition on retrospective criminal law, as enshrined in art 7 of the European Convention on Human Rights (see below). The principle of maximum (note not absolute) certainty (sometimes referred to as 'fair warning') suggests that the law should be clear, concise and intelligible. Given that ignorance of the law is no excuse citizens should be provided with as clear a statement of what is prohibited as is possible. In the United States criminal statutes can be declared void for uncertainty by the courts. Whilst that remains a constitutional impossibility in the United Kingdom, the enactment of the Human Rights Act 1998 (see below) raises the possibility of domestic legislation being challenged on the basis that the criminal prohibitions contained therein do not state clearly enough the nature of the offence being created, resulting in an incompatibility with the rights protected under the Act. The United Kingdom courts could also disapply domestic criminal law in favour of EC law, if the former were found to be irreconcilable with the latter.

Third, where criminal offences are created the principle of 'fair labelling' provides that they should distinguish properly between the types of harm prohibited and the elements to be established. For example an offence of homicide would be regarded as too broad. The law should set out separate offences of deliberate and non-deliberate killing and assign appropriate fault elements and punishments to both. Similarly, the fair labelling doctrine would require offences to make clear the distinction between activities such as theft and burglary, or rape and indecent assault. A fair and efficient system of criminal law provides for offences that distinguish between major and minor wrongdoings.

Should the criminal law be used to control certain activities?

Whether or not an activity is criminalised will depend on a number of factors, such as the harm caused, the harm risked; whether or not criminalisation will simply produce more crime; the social utility of the activity; the need to provide a moral lead; or the threat to economic and social stability posed by the activity.

Sometimes criminal liability is imposed because it provides a quick and cheap form of social control. Examples might include motoring offences, such as failing to display a car tax disc or having illegally low tyre tread depth. Similar thinking underpins offences such as not having a television licence, failing to file company accounts or not complying with data protection rules. These criminal offences are technical in nature, often require no proof of any intention to commit the offence, and can be processed quickly by the courts. The existence of the offences is highly publicised and the assumption is that citizens will conduct their affairs so as to avoid liability arising. There is a high degree of social utility in ensuring compliance. Citizens can see that there is a desirable social purpose in these laws being obeyed. Compliance contributes to the greater good.

The rationale for other offences is equally obvious. A capitalist society, or even one based on mixed economy principles, tends to have laws that protect the rights of private property owners. These rights are reflected in the laws relating to theft, robbery, burglary, deception and criminal damage. Offences against the person have a social order function, but are also designed to protect the weak from the strong, and to provide a form of indirect redress to the victim in situations where a civil action for damages would be pointless. Whilst for some these offences might also have a moral element, in that it is regarded as sinful to steal or assault others, they are essentially pragmatic. The economy functions more efficiently if private property rights are recognised; it is inefficient to have citizens who are injured through acts of violence and hence need treatment and are unable to work. The more the rights and wrongs of an activity are seen as being essential moral questions, however, the more contentious the criminalisation of that activity becomes.

To some extent criminal law can be seen as an embodiment or reflection of a society's mores. If a particular activity is regarded as morally offensive within a particular society, it may be prohibited by the criminal law and stigmatised by punishment, even though, in statistical terms, there may be only a very small number of individuals who would want to engage in that activity, eg incest or murder. For most of society's members such laws will simply be a reaffirmation of their beliefs. In a country such as England, which is at least nominally Christian, it is interesting to consider the extent to which the moral code laid down in the Ten Commandments (Exodus 20:1–17) is actually reflected in its criminal law. Inter alia, they provide:

1. Thou shalt have no other gods before me.
2. Thou shalt not worship graven images.
3. Thou shalt not take the name of the Lord thy God in vain.
4. Remember the Sabbath day, to keep it holy.
5. Honour thy father and thy mother.
6. Thou shalt not kill.
7. Thou shalt not commit adultery.
8. Thou shalt not steal.
9. Thou shalt not bear false witness against thy neighbour.
10. Thou shalt not covet thy neighbour's goods.

Of the prohibitions laid down in this list it is submitted that only those relating to murder and theft are clearly reflected in criminal law. The laws against blasphemy and Sunday trading do relate to certain aspects of the above, but these are both areas of law currently subject to criticism and calls for reform. Of the remaining Commandments, the absence of any parallel prohibition in criminal law perhaps indicates that such activities are either impossible to police, or ought to be left as matters of individual conscience. Society's views on such matters can be effected through the democratic process. The legislative enactments which liberalised the laws prohibiting abortion (Abortion Act 1967), and the laws relating to homosexual conduct in private between adults over the age of 21 (Sexual Offences Act 1967), were indicative of society's mood at that time, as reflected in the actions of its elected representatives. In more conservative times such laws might be subject to amendment or repeal if a government has a mandate for such action

Problems inevitably arise where there is a lack of consensus within society as to whether or not a particular matter should be brought within the scope of the criminal law. The issue of de-criminalisation has been raised in respect of so-called 'victimless crimes' such as the publication of obscene material, the possession of controlled drugs for personal consumption, and indulgence by adults in consensual sado-masochistic behaviour. On the one hand, there is the argument that the law must provide a form of moral yardstick by labelling such activities as criminal (see P

Devlin *The Enforcement of Morals* (1965)); on the other hand, it is argued that the law should not intervene in matters that relate essentially to personal morality (see H L A Hart *Law, Liberty and Morality* (1963)). To this it could be added that it is the very criminalisation of such activities that makes them a rich source of profit for those who trade in such commodities. Decriminalisation, it is contended, would release significant law-enforcement resources, remove the incentives for profiteering, and cause no appreciable harm to society. The American experience during the Prohibition period is instructive in this argument. Very often the question is whether individual autonomy, as opposed to welfarism, should be the overriding principle. If welfarism, it should be the product of the democratic process. Where society votes for 'welfare' or 'moral' legislation, the need for legitimacy demands that it should still have regard to the views of the minority, and be subject to review from time to time.

In this respect it is significant that, although juries are relied upon in criminal trials to determine issues of fact, in the course of doing so they are not infrequently called upon to determine issues that are essentially moral. The question of dishonesty in relation to the offence of theft is a good example. On the basis of *R* v *Ghosh* [1982] 1 QB 1053 a jury should consider whether a defendant's conduct was dishonest by the standard of ordinary decent people (ie themselves), and then consider whether or not the defendant realised that ordinary decent people would regard his actions as dishonest. Similarly, where members of a jury have to consider whether an assault was indecent, they will inevitably have regard to their own standards. It is in ways such as this that the link between law and current morality is maintained. As Lord Coleridge observed in *R* v *Dudley and Stephens* (1884) 14 QBD 273:

> 'Though law and morality are not the same, and many things may be immoral which are not necessarily illegal, yet the absolute divorce of law from morality would be of fatal consequence. ... We are often compelled to set up standards we cannot reach ourselves, and to lay down rules which we could not ourselves satisfy.'

Public law and private law

Criminal law is usually regarded as falling within sphere of public law. What does this mean, and how does public law differ from private law for these purposes? When an activity is referred to as being unlawful, one has to consider the sense in which that term is being used. An activity can be unlawful in that it involves a tortious act (a civil wrong), or because it is contrary to the criminal law, or both. How is the distinction between the law of torts and criminal law to be drawn?

Existing as it does in the sphere of private law, the law of torts is primarily concerned with resolving disputes between two parties, with a view to one being compensated for the wrongful actions of the other. By contrast, criminal proceedings, even private prosecutions, are instituted with a view to punishing the defendant if convicted. Magistrates do have limited powers to order a defendant to compensate the victim of his crime, but this is not always possible or appropriate.

As there is no compulsion upon one who has suffered loss as a result of a tortious act to commence civil proceedings for compensation, there may be many cases where the tortfeasor is never punished for his wrongdoing.

Even where damages are awarded, the defendant will frequently be supported by an insurance company, in which case the amount he is personally having to pay out, in the form of costs and increased premiums, bears little or no relation to the level of compensation actually awarded against him. How culpable must tortious behaviour be before the law steps in to label it as criminal? In *R* v *Bateman* (1925) 19 Cr App 8 Lord Hewart CJ explained that negligence should be regarded as criminal where:

> '... in the opinion of the jury, the negligence of the accused went beyond a mere matter of compensation between subjects and showed such disregard for the life and safety of others as to amount to a crime against the state and conduct deserving of punishment.'

What is being suggested here is that the label 'criminal' will be attached to behaviour that is so unacceptable that the state will punish it, regardless of whether those injuriously affected by it choose to pursue the matter or not. Similarly, in *R* v *Adomako* [1994] 3 WLR 288, Lord Mackay LC explained that, in cases where a lawful activity is performed in a negligent manner and death results, criminal liability can be imposed if the negligence is gross. For these purposes negligence becomes criminal if it involves such a departure from the proper standard of care incumbent upon the defendant that it should be judged to be criminal. The degree of circularity in such an approach is obvious, but his Lordship did not regard this as fatal to its being a correct as a test of how far conduct must depart from accepted standards to be characterised as criminal.

Frequently, the distinction between tortious and criminal behaviour rests upon the presence of some aggravating factor. Hence the tort of conversion can become the crime of theft if there is dishonesty and an intention to permanently deprive; trespass within a building can become burglary where it is accompanied by an intent to steal, rape, cause criminal damage, or to do some grievous bodily harm.

1.2 Sources of criminal law

Criminal offences exist either at common law, or are created by statute. Examples of common law offences include murder, manslaughter, certain assaults and incitement. Many important offences have been put on a statutory footing, these include offences under the Theft Acts 1968 to 1996, the Criminal Damage Act 1971 and the Criminal Attempts Act 1981. In addition, there may be cases where provisions of EC law are relevant, particularly if they suggest that domestic law may be inconsistent with EC law, and a defendant might also wish to rely on provisions of the European Convention on Human Rights, as incorporated by the Human Rights Act 1998 (see below and Chapter 15, section 15.4).

Common law

The judiciary have considerable powers to influence the development of criminal law through the 'discovery' of the common law. The prospect of the judiciary creating new forms of criminal liability at common law is abhorrent to many, involving as it does a breach of the separation of powers. Classically judges are there to apply the law, not to make it. The judges are aware of such criticisms and not surprisingly exercise this power with extreme caution, but will nevertheless act to supply the omission of the legislature where they see fit. As Viscount Simonds commented in *Shaw* v *DPP* [1961] 2 All ER 446, when dealing with the question of whether the courts could recognise a new offence of conspiring to corrupt public morals:

> 'Need I say my Lords, that I am no advocate of the right of judges to create new criminal offences? But, in the sphere of criminal law, I entertain no doubt that there remains in the courts of law a residual power to enforce the supreme and fundamental purpose of the law, to conserve not only the safety and order but also the moral welfare of the state, and that it is their duty to guard it against attacks which may be the more insidious because they are novel and unprepared for.'

Lord Reid, dissenting, stated:

> 'I think, or at least I hope, that it is now established that the courts cannot create new offences by individuals … when there is sufficient support from public opinion, Parliament does not hesitate to intervene. Where Parliament fears to tread it is not for the courts to rush in.'

It is sometimes hard to discern any consistency on the part of the courts regarding the extent to which judicial activism is to be regarded as inevitable or desirable. The House of Lords in *R* v *R* [1991] 3 WLR 767 rushed headlong into abolishing the husband's common law immunity from prosecution for raping a wife from whom he was not judicially separated, despite the frankly absurd approach to the interpretation of the relevant statute that was required to achieve this socially laudable result. A more cautious, and it is submitted, realistic approach was displayed by the House of Lords in *C (A Minor)* v *DPP* [1995] 2 WLR 383 where their Lordships refused to uphold the decision of the Divisional Court abolishing the 'mischievous discretion' rule requiring proof that a defendant between the ages of ten and 14 must have know that his or her actions were 'wrong' in order to be found guilty of a criminal offence. In assessing when it would be proper for the courts to intervene by way of judicial law-making, Lord Lowry suggested the following pointers:

1. Judges should be slow to impose their own remedies where the solution was doubtful.
2. Judges should be slow to act where Parliament had clearly declined to do so, or had legislated in the area without touching upon the difficulty raised in the instant case.
3. Fundamental legal doctrines should not be lightly overturned.

4. Issues of social policy should be left for determination by the legislature.
5. Judicial solutions should not be imposed unless finality was likely to result.

Significantly, perhaps, Parliament gave effect to the Divisional Court's ruling in enacting s34 of the Crime and Disorder Act 1998 which abolished the mischievous discretion rule.

Statutory offences

As regards the interpretation of criminal legislation, it is obviously the role of the judiciary to give effect to the intention of Parliament as expressed through such legislation. The rules of statutory interpretation relied upon are well known, but one rule, of particular significance here, is that any ambiguity in a statutory provision should be construed in favour of the defendant. Some observers might suggest that this principle is not applied by the judiciary as frequently as it might be.

There are three situations in which the judicial role in statutory interpretation will be of considerable importance. The first is where an older statute, using archaic terminology, has to be interpreted to deal with current-day problems. Section 23 of the Offences Against the Person Act 1861, for example, refers to a defendant acting 'maliciously'. It is inconceivable that Parliament would choose such an adverb today, yet judges have to attach some meaning to it which will be intelligible to juries: see *R* v *Cunningham* [1957] 2 QB 396. The second arises where the courts are invited to apply legislation to problems not contemplated by Parliament at the time when the legislation was enacted, eg nuisance telephone calls or stalking. Lord Steyn addressed both of these issues in the course of his speech in *R* v *Ireland*; *R* v *Burstow* [1997] 4 All ER 225. Regarding the question of whether psychiatric harm could be viewed as coming within the definition of grievous bodily harm for the purposes of s20 of the 1861 Act, he observed:

'... although out of considerations of piety we frequently refer to the actual intention of the draftsman, the correct approach is simply to consider whether the words of the Act of 1861 considered in the light of contemporary knowledge cover a recognisable psychiatric injury. It is undoubtedly true that there are statutes where the correct approach is to construe the legislation "as if one were interpreting it the day after it was passed" ... Bearing in mind that statutes are usually intended to operate for many years it would be most inconvenient if courts could never rely in difficult cases on the current meaning of statutes. Recognising the problem Lord Thring, the great Victorian draftsman of the second half of the last century, exhorted draftsmen to draft so that "An Act of Parliament should be deemed to be always speaking". ... In cases where the problem arises it is a matter of interpretation whether a court must search for the historical or original meaning of a statute or whether it is free to apply the current meaning of the statute to present day conditions. Statutes dealing with a particular grievance or problem may sometimes require to be historically interpreted. But the drafting technique of Lord Thring and his successors have brought about the situation that statutes will generally be found to be of the "always speaking" variety ... the Act of 1861 is a statute of the "always speaking" type: the statute must be interpreted in the light of the best current scientific appreciation of the link between the body and psychiatric injury.'

The third situation is where Parliament has simply failed to express itself clearly. Here the judges are left with the choice of construing any ambiguity in favour of the defendant, with the likely consequence of an acquittal, or of straining the wording of the provision to try to achieve the result Parliament originally intended. A clear example of this dilemma is provided by the House of Lords difficulties in applying s1(1), (2) and (3) of the Criminal Attempts Act 1981 in *Anderton* v *Ryan* [1985] AC 560 and *R* v *Shivpuri* [1987] AC 1. Parliament's intention in enacting the 1981 Act was to amend the law relating to the offence of attempt, so that a defendant could be guilty of attempting to commit a crime even though the facts were such (unknown to him) that the commission of the completed offence was impossible. If successful, the Act would produce some surprising results. The defendant who, intending to kill, fired a gun at a corpse believing it to be a live human being, could be guilty of attempted murder, even though the completed offence was clearly impossible. The language used in the 1981 Act to achieve this goal, particularly s1(3), is somewhat tortuous. In *Anderton* v *Ryan* Lord Roskill indicated that, notwithstanding the mischief rule of interpretation, whereby judges were expected to prefer the construction of a statute which enabled them to tackle the mischief Parliament had sought to combat, he could not allow his loyalty to that principle to lead him to a construction of the statute that would produce a result that he regarded as a manifest absurdity. Such an absurdity, in his view, would have been the conviction of Mrs Ryan, for attempting to handle what she believed to be a stolen video recorder, in the absence of proof by the prosecution that the item had been stolen. In short, his Lordship refused to give effect to the legislation as Parliament had intended. In *Shivpuri* the House of Lords found itself faced with the consequences of its previous decision. D had admitted to the police that he was a drugs courier, but examination of the parcel he had been paid to deliver revealed its contents to be a harmless vegetable matter. D was charged with attempting to deal in a proscribed drug, and the House of Lords had the option of either following *Anderton* v *Ryan*, a course of action which might have been construed as far too lenient given the nature of the activity involved, or of re-interpreting the legislation to cover D's behaviour. Not surprisingly, the latter course was adopted, despite the ambiguities of the legislation: see further Chapter 12.

1.3 The Human Rights Act 1998

The Human Rights Act 1998 has the effect of incorporating certain rights provided for in the European Convention on Human Rights into domestic law. When it comes into effect (late 1999 or early in the year 2000) this measure will make it unlawful for any public body to act in a way that is incompatible with one or more of the Convention rights. In effect it means that any defendant in a criminal trial will be able to raise a challenge to the proceedings on the basis that his Convention rights have been violated. Such a challenge might also form the basis of an appeal against conviction or sentence. Although the incorporation is likely to have more impact on procedural matters, such as arrest, detention, access to a lawyer etc, it should be noted that, as regards substantive criminal law, the courts will have to interpret statutes creating criminal liability (whether enacted prior to the incorporation of the Convention or afterwards), so as to give effect to the rights enshrined in the Convention. The government view, as expressed in para 2.8 of the White Paper *Rights Brought Home: The Human Rights Bill* (Cm 3782 (1997)), is that judges, in undertaking this task, will not be bound by previous interpretations of existing domestic legislation. Common law offences could be open to challenge under the new legislation on the basis that the ingredients of the offence are not sufficiently specified so as to enable a defendant to know exactly what conduct constituted an illegal act. As Brooke LJ observed in *D v DPP* [1998] 4 All ER 265:

> 'G K Chesterton told us how the rolling English drunkard made the rolling English road long before the importation to these islands of more efficient road-making techniques. The rolling English criminal law was not made by the rolling English drunkard – much though he has contributed to the overload of our criminal justice system – but to a student of history who is not concerned with the efficient and fair administration of the law, parts of it must have much the same old-fashioned charm as some of our winding country lanes. How the more incoherent parts of our criminal law will stand up to the rigorous standards required by the European Court of Human Rights, by which the citizen must have an adequate indication of the legal rules which are to be applied in any given case, remains to be seen as we prepare to receive the Convention for the Protection of Human Rights and Fundamental Freedoms ... into our national law in the millennium year.'

The Act does not expressly create a new procedure for raising alleged violations of Convention rights. Section 7(1) envisages that individuals will be able to bring proceedings (or a counterclaim) against a public body in the appropriate court or tribunal 'as may be determined in accordance with rules': s7(2). Section 7(9) provides that these rules are to be made by the Lord Chancellor. Alternatively, litigants will be allowed to 'rely on the Convention right or rights concerned in any legal proceedings' (s7(1)(b)), legal proceedings including, for these purposes 'proceedings brought by or at the instigation of a public authority; and ... an appeal against the decision of a court or tribunal': s7(6)(a) and (b). Criminal proceedings clearly come within this definition. Only the 'victim' of the alleged unlawful act is permitted to bring proceedings or rely on the Convention in legal proceedings: s7(1). It is clear that many of the cases involving reliance on Convention rights will take the form of applications for judicial review – given that the Act is of direct application to public bodies (see below). The result is that a narrower test for locus standi will be applied in applications alleging a breach of Convention rights, as compared to applications for review generally. As s7(3) makes clear: 'If the proceedings are brought on an application for judicial review, the applicant is to be taken to have a sufficient interest in relation to the unlawful act only if he is, or would be, a victim of that act.' 'Victim' for the purposes of s7 is defined as 'a victim for the purposes of art 34 of the Convention if proceedings were brought in the

European Court of Human Rights': s7(7). Section 7(5) provides for a time limit of 12 months for the bringing of proceedings where it is claimed that a public authority has acted in breach of Convention rights, time running from the date on which the act complained of took place. Beyond this a court or tribunal will have a discretion to allow proceedings outside this time limit if it considers it equitable to do so having regard to all the circumstances. This time limit would apply subject to any rule imposing a stricter time limit, hence, the three-month rule in relation to applications for judicial review would still apply.

Who can be the subject of these proceedings?

By virtue of s6(1) it becomes unlawful for a public authority to act (or fail to act in a way which is incompatible with a Convention right. A public body for these purposes includes a court or tribunal, and 'any person certain of whose functions are functions of a public nature, but does not include either House of Parliament or a person exercising functions in connection with proceedings in Parliament': s6(3). The term 'Parliament' as used in s6(3) does not include the House of Lords in its judicial capacity. A 'person is not a public authority by virtue only of subsection (3)(b) if the nature of the act is private.' It seems likely that the courts will be influenced by the jurisprudence built up in relation to applications for judicial review in determining whether non-statutory bodies can be regarded as public authorities for these purposes: see for example *R v Panel on Take-overs and Mergers, ex parte Datafin plc* [1987] 2 WLR 699; *R v Disciplinary Committee of the Jockey Club, ex parte The Aga Khan* [1993] 1 WLR 909; and *R v Insurance Ombudsman Bureau and the Insurance Ombudsman, ex parte Aegon Life* (1994) The Independent 11 January. The definition of public body would include statutory bodies empowered to instigate criminal proceedings, and other bodies such as the Criminal Cases Review Commission. Where the claim of unlawfulness under s6 is based upon a judicial act, proceedings under s7(1)(a) may only be brought by exercising a right of appeal, making an application for judicial review, or by following such procedure as may be laid down in rules made from time to time: s9(1).

What is required of a court considering a case involving an allegation that a Convention right has been violated?

A court or tribunal called upon to do so must interpret primary legislation and subordinate legislation 'in a way which is compatible with the Convention rights': s3(1). This duty applies whether the legislation was enacted before or after the coming into force of the Human Rights Act 1998.

Section 2(1) of the 1998 Act makes it clear that any court or tribunal determining a question arising in connection with a Convention right must take into account: any judgment, decision, declaration or advisory opinion of the European Court of Human Rights; any opinion of the Commission given in a report adopted under art

31 of the Convention; any decision of the Commission in connection with arts 26 or 27(2) of the Convention; or any decision of the Committee of Ministers taken under art 46 of the Convention, 'whenever made or given, so far as, in the opinion of the court or tribunal, it is relevant to the proceedings in which that question has arisen.' It may also be the case that the courts take into account rulings of the Privy Council in appeals concerning constitutional rights for those countries having written constitutions incorporating terms similar to those found in the Convention: see for example *DPP* v *Tokai* [1996] AC 856 and *Robinson* v *The Queen* [1985] AC 956.

It seems inevitable that the courts are going to have to adopt a new approach to statutory interpretation where Convention rights are concerned, rather than stick rigidly to the traditional 'rules' of interpretation. The tradition of the European Court of Human Rights is to be more flexible and evaluative in its exercise of its interpretative functions. Thus, domestic judges will have a more explicit role in assessing the merits of executive decision-making (ie its legitimacy within the context of the Convention), whereas their role to date, at least in theory, has been limited to scrutinising the legality of executive action by means of judicial review.

Judicial remedies

A court dealing with an application for judicial review of subordinate legislation (for example one creating criminal liability, providing for a procedural matter or dealing with rules of evidence) would be able to declare it to be ultra vires if it was found to incompatible with the Convention rights. The courts will have no such power in relation to primary legislation, however. Indeed s3(2)(b) expressly provides that the section 'does not affect the validity, continuing operation or enforcement of any incompatible primary legislation'. Further, the section cannot be relied upon to invalidate incompatible subordinate legislation if '(disregarding any possibility of revocation) primary legislation prevents removal of the incompatibility': s3(2)(c). Where an irreconcilable issue of compatibility arises before the House of Lords, the Judicial Committee of the Privy Council, the Courts-Martial Appeal Court, or the High Court or the Court of Appeal, that court will be empowered to grant a declaration of incompatibility. In relation to subordinate legislation the power to make such declarations will arise provided (disregarding any possibility of revocation) the primary legislation concerned prevents removal of the incompatibility. Where such a declaration is made it does not 'affect the validity, continuing operation or enforcement of the provision in respect of which it is given; and ... is not binding on the parties to the proceedings in which it is made': s4(6).

Whilst the 1998 Act does not provide for any new judicial remedies (other than the declaration of incompatibility), a court finding that a public authority as acted unlawfully within the terms of s6 'may grant such relief or remedy, or make such order, within its powers as it considers just and appropriate': s8(1). In the context of criminal proceedings it means that a court, persuaded to accept a defendant's argument based on alleged incompatibility of domestic law with the Convention rights, could: quash the indictment or summons; grant a stay of proceedings; exclude evidence prejudicial to the accused; direct a jury not to draw adverse inferences from the defendant's silence under questioning; allow a submission of no case; give a more favourable direction to the jury; or recognise the validity of a defence.

The right to liberty and security of the person

Article 5 of the Convention provides those rights designed to ensure a minimum level of security and liberty of the person. By virtue of this article no one should be deprived of their liberty save in the following circumstances: lawful detention of a person after conviction by a competent court; lawful arrest or detention for non-compliance with the lawful order of a court or in order to secure the fulfilment of any obligation prescribed by law; lawful arrest or detention effected for the purpose of bringing a person before the competent legal authority on reasonable suspicion of having committed an offence or when it is reasonably considered necessary to prevent his committing an offence or fleeing after having done so; detention of a minor by lawful order for the purpose of educational supervision or his lawful detention for the purpose of bringing him before the competent legal authority; lawful detention of persons for the prevention of the spreading of infectious diseases, of persons of unsound mind, alcoholics or drug addicts or vagrants; and the lawful arrest or detention of a person to prevent his effecting an unauthorised entry into the country or of a person against whom action is being taken with a view to deportation or extradition. In each case such deprivation should be in accordance with a procedure prescribed by law.

The wording of art 5(1) suggests that obscurely or vaguely worded criminal provisions of domestic substantive criminal law could be incompatible with the Convention rights because they do not satisfy the requirement that the deprivation of liberty should be 'prescribed by law'. This contention was tested in *Steel and Others* v *United Kingdom* (1998) The Times 1 October in respect of the common law power of police constable to arrest and detain in respect of alleged breaches of the peace (breach of the peace being treated as an offence for these purposes). The European Court of Human Rights held that where a defendant's actions clearly gave rise to a breach of the peace, or created an obvious possibility that a breach of the peace might occur, the common law was sufficiently clear so as not to amount to a breach of art 5. Where, however, powers to arrest for breach of the peace were used against peaceful demonstrators a violation of art 5 would occur, there being no grounds to justify the use of the power.

Article 5(2) provides that 'everyone who is arrested shall be informed promptly, in a language which he understands, of the reasons for his arrest and of any charge against him.' Under art 5(3) everyone arrested or detained in order that they be brought before the court on reasonable suspicion of having committed an offence has the right to be brought 'promptly before a judge or other officer authorised by law to exercise judicial power and shall be entitled to trial within a reasonable time or to release pending trial.' In *Brogan* v *United Kingdom* (1989) 11 EHRR 117, it was held that detention of terrorist suspects without charge for more than four days was in breach of art 5(3), but the United Kingdom successfully applied for a derogation in respect of art 5(3) in the light of the 'campaigns of organised terrorism connected with the affairs of Northern Ireland': see *Brannigan and McBride* v *United Kingdom* (1993) 17 EHRR 539. Although art 5(3) envisages conditions being attached to bail, the denial of bail (in murder or rape cases) as a matter of course, under s25 of the Criminal Justice and Public Order Act 1994, to defendants with previous convictions for murder or rape may come under closer scrutiny.

The right to contest the legality of detention before a court of law is enshrined in art 5(4). In *Hussain* v *United Kingdom* (1996) 22 EHRR 1, the court held unanimously that review of the applicants' detention by the Parole Board did not equate to the detention being reviewed by a court of law, because the Board did not provide for oral hearings and could not order the release of a prisoner wrongly detained. Neither was this deficiency cured by the prospect of an applicant being granted an oral hearing where he was permitted leave to apply for judicial review of the Parole Board's determination or that of the Home Secretary. Similarly, in *Chahal* v *United Kingdom* (1996) 23 EHRR 413, the determination of appeals against deportation orders by an advisory panel, where issues of national security were involved, was deemed to be a violation of article 5(4), because the panel did not provide sufficient procedural safeguards to amount to a 'court' as that term was used in the Convention.

Under art 5(5) everyone who has been the victim of arrest or detention in contravention of art 5 should have an enforceable right to compensation.

The right to a fair trial

Article 6 is effectively the 'due process' provision, dealing with aspects of a fair trial process. Article 6(1) provides (inter alia) for a fair and public hearing of criminal charges 'within a reasonable time by an independent and impartial tribunal established by law.' Subject to restrictions imposed in the interests of security or privacy, judgments are to be pronounced in public. Article 6(2) reflects the common law position to the extent that anyone charged with a criminal offence is presumed to be innocent until proved guilty. Questions may be raised in the future regarding the extent to which the discretion of the courts to withhold costs from a successful defendant in criminal proceedings can be seen as incompatible with art 6(2), such rulings being seen by some as an indication of the court's suspicions as to the defendant's innocence: see *Minelli* v *Switzerland* (1983) 5 EHRR 554.

The extent which the removal of the right to silence, pursuant to the introduction of the Criminal Evidence (Northern Ireland) Order (SI 1988/1987 (NI 20)), amounted to a violation of art 6 was contested in *Murray* v *United Kingdom* (1996) 22 EHRR 29, the European Court of Human Rights holding (by 14 votes to five) that although the right to remain silent under questioning, and the privilege against self-incrimination, were generally recognised international standards which lay at the heart of the notion of a fair procedure under art 6, they were not absolute rights. The matter had to be viewed in the light of the sufficiency of the procedural safeguards designed to prevent oppression, such as regular cautioning and access to legal advice, and the amount of evidence against the accused that was regarded as justifying the drawing of adverse inference in the event of his failing to refute it. The Court was satisfied that sufficient safeguards were in place to ensure that the objectives of art 6 could still be achieved, and that the drawing of reasonable inferences from the applicant's behaviour did not have the effect of shifting the burden of proof contrary to art 6(2). Note that in *Murray* there was clear evidence of guilt and the inferences were drawn by a single judge giving a reasoned judgment. These safeguards do not exist where the inferences are drawn by a jury, thus raising the prospect of a challenge to these procedures once the 1998 Act comes fully into force. By contrast, in *Saunders* v *United Kingdom* (1997) 23 EHRR 313, the use by the prosecution, during the applicant's trial for fraud, of statements made by him during investigations conducted by Department of Trade and Industry, was found to be a violation of art 6 because the applicant had faced the possibility of imprisonment for contempt of court if he refused to answer. Provisions of domestic law perceived as reversing the onus of proof are likely to come under close scrutiny once the Human Rights Act 1998 comes fully into force.

The specific due process requirements guaranteed under art 6(3) are that everyone charged with a criminal offence has the right to: 'be informed promptly, in a language which he understands and in detail, of the nature and cause of the accusation against him'; 'have adequate time and facilities for the preparation of his defence'; defend himself, or through a legal representative, and to be given free legal assistance 'when the interests of justice so require'; examine witnesses and 'obtain the attendance and examination of witnesses on his behalf under the same conditions as witnesses against him'; and have the free assistance of an interpreter if necessary. In a series of cases the European Court of Human Rights has confirmed that compliance with art 6 requires the provision of legal representation in any proceedings that could be regarded as punitive, for example proceedings for tax enforcement or proceedings that could result in the loss of liberty: see further *Benham* v *United Kingdom* (1996) 22 EHRR 293 and *Wynne* v *United Kingdom* (1994) 19 EHRR 333. In *Bonner* v *United Kingdom*; *Maxwell* v *United Kingdom* (1994) The Times 1 November, the Court held that the rights guaranteed by art 6 extended to the provision of legal aid to everyone charged with a criminal offence where the interests of justice so required, in light of the importance of the hearing (as regards the sentences imposed on the applicants), the limited scope for the unrepresented applicant to present his case competently, the nature of the proceedings, and clear evidence that the applicants lacked the financial resources to pay for their own lawyers. Similarly, the denial of access to a solicitor during the first 48 hours of police questioning has been held to be a violation of art 6(3)(c): see *Murray* v *United Kingdom* (above).

It remains to be seen whether or not the scheme for disclosure of prosecution and defence evidence created by the Criminal Procedure and Investigations Act 1996 accords with the requirements of art 6(3), in particular the right to have 'adequate facilities for the preparation of a defence'. Under the 1996 Act the prosecution is under no duty to make advance disclosure of its case in summary only trials: see Magistrates' Court (Advance Information) Rules 1995. The prosecution's duty of secondary disclosure only arises if the defence has made a disclosure, raising issues of self-incrimination.

No punishment without law

Article 7 is designed to ensure that the imposition of criminal, liability and punishment should be in accordance with accepted norms of the rule of law. In particular it outlaws retrospective criminal offences and the imposition of heavier penalties that those that were applicable at the time the criminal offence was committed. Article 7(2) specifically excludes from the scope of art 7(1) 'the trial and punishment of any person for any act or omission which, at the time when it was committed, was criminal according to the general principles of law recognised by civilised nations.'

Article 7(1) was successfully invoked by the applicant in *Welch* v *United Kingdom* (1995) 20 EHRR 247. Welch had been convicted of drug-related offences and sentenced to a long term of imprisonment. An order was made under the Drug Trafficking Offences Act 1986 (now the 1994 Act) which resulted in the confiscation of certain of the applicant's assets that could be regarded as the proceeds of drug dealing, even though the offences in question had been committed prior to the commencement of the Act. Granting the application, the Court held that the measure was clearly penal in nature and did violate art 7(1) by providing for a more severe penalty than could have been imposed when the drug-dealing offences were carried out. More generally, the way in which judges develop the principles of the common law within the English legal system has led to questions as to whether defendants are victims of retrospective law making. In *SW* v *United Kingdom* (1995) 21 EHRR 363, both applicants, who had been convicted of rape and attempted rape of their wives, claimed that there had been a violation of art 7(1) since, at the time the incidents giving rise to the convictions had occurred, there was, at common law, a rule that a husband could not be guilty of raping his wife. In rejecting the applicants' contention that the decision of the English court (see *R* v *R* [1991] 3 WLR 767) to disregard the common law rule and uphold the convictions amounted to the imposition of retrospective criminal liability, as their actions had not been contrary to the common law at the time they were committed, the Court held that art 7(1) did not prohibit the gradual clarification of the principles of criminal liability on a case by case basis provided the development could be reasonably foreseen. The gradual evolution of restrictions upon the husband's immunity from liability for marital rape, and the mounting criticism of the immunity, made the judicial development in the instant case reasonably foreseeable.

Effective remedies

Interestingly art 13 of the Convention, which provides that those complaining that their Convention rights have been violated should have the right to an effective remedy before a domestic authority, has not been incorporated into domestic law. This omission may not be as significant as it seems, however, given that the domestic courts are required, by s2 of the 1998 Act, to have regard to the jurisprudence of the European Court of Human Rights, and this includes the case law relevant to art 13. Of particular interest to criminal lawyers is the question of whether the Court of Appeal (Criminal Division) provides an effective remedy in criminal appeals, given the constrained nature of its powers under the Criminal Appeal Act 1995. As detailed in Chapter 4, the Court of Appeal is clearly of the view that it can only quash a conviction if it is unsafe. A conviction may be 'unsatisfactory' but the court will be powerless to act because it is not deemed to be 'unsafe': see *R* v *Chalkley* [1998] 2 All ER 155.

1.4 Aspects of the criminal process

Whilst this text is concerned with the mainstream substantive criminal offences of relevance to those undertaking an academic study of the subject, it is necessary to consider, at least in outline, the nature of the criminal process in which the substantive law is applied.

The decision to prosecute

Although a number of regulatory bodies are given specific powers as regards the bringing of prosecutions, in the vast majority of cases the decision to prosecute will rest with the Crown Prosecution Service (CPS), established under the Prosecution of Offences Act 1985. The CPS is headed by the Director of Public Prosecutions (DPP), and the minister responsible to Parliament for its operation is the Attorney-General. The DPP prepares an annual report for the Attorney-General on the operation of the system. Prior to the creation of the CPS the police were responsible for both the investigation and prosecution of offences. The rationale for the creation of the CPS was that these two functions ought, in the interests of justice, to be discharged by separate executive agencies.

A decision to prosecute will be made with reference to the Code for Crown Prosecutors, the most recent version of which was published in June 1994, pursuant to s10 of the Prosecution of Offences Act 1985. The purpose of the Code is to help ensure that prosecutors make fair and consistent decisions about prosecutions. The decision to prosecute follows the application of two tests to the given facts. First, the case is subjected to the evidential test whereby the prosecutor has to be satisfied that there is sufficient evidence to provide a realistic prospect of conviction (ie a properly directed bench or jury would be more likely than not to convict). For this first test to be satisfied the evidence would clearly need to be reliable and admissible. If, and only if, the evidential test is satisfied, the case will be subject to the 'public interest' test. Factors that suggest that a prosecution will be in the public interest include:

1. the likelihood of a substantial sentence being imposed on conviction;
2. the use of a weapon or violence during the offence;
3. the position of the victim (eg a person serving the public) and/or the position of the defendant (eg a person in a position of trust or authority;
4. evidence that the offence was premeditated, carried out by a group, or that the defendant was a 'ringleader';
5. the effect on the victim;
6. the likelihood of the offence being repeated;
7. the extent to which the offence, even though not serious, is a common occurrence in the area in which it has been committed.

Factors that suggest that a prosecution will not be in the public interest include:

1. the likelihood that only a nominal penalty will be imposed in the event of a conviction;
2. that the offence was the result of a genuine mistake or misunderstanding;
3. the lapse of time between the offence and the proceedings, except where the offence is serious, the delay has been caused by the defendant, the offence has only recently come to light, or the complexity of the offence has necessitated a lengthy inquiry;
4. where the defendant is elderly or was suffering from a form of mental illness at the time of the offence, unless there is a real possibility of the offence being repeated;
5. the defendant having put right the harm or loss caused;
6. the adverse effect of certain information being made public.

As a rider to the above, the Code adds that:

> '... Crown Prosecutors must always think very carefully about the interests of the victim, which are an important factor, when deciding where the public interest lies.'

In deciding what offence to charge, Crown Prosecutors should select charges that reflect the seriousness of the offence, give the courts adequate sentencing powers, and enable the case to be presented in a clear and simple way. As result the CPS will not always proceed with the most serious charge technically possible on the facts, nor necessarily all the possible offences to which the facts give rise.

Subject to certain statutory exceptions, it is open to individual citizens to bring private criminal prosecutions if the CPS declines to intervene or discontinues a prosecution prior to the case coming on for trial. The right to bring private prosecutions was expressly preserved by the 1985 Act. The individual wishing to commence a private prosecution must lay an information before a magistrate so that a summons can be issued. Practice suggests that magistrates will be reluctant to grant summonses in cases that are triable only in the Crown Court. A major disincentive for those wishing to pursue private prosecutions is that fact that legal aid is not available, hence some high profile cases have been backed by money raised by public donation: see the 'Stephen Lawrence' murder case etc. It should be noted that the CPS can intervene and adopt a private prosecution so that the cost is thereafter borne by the taxpayer, but equally the CPS can take over a case with the intention of then discontinuing proceedings, effectively putting an end to any chance of a prosecution.

The Law Commission has reviewed the system under which certain offences cannot be prosecuted without the consent of the law officers or Director of Public Prosecutions (see *Consents for Prosecution*: Consultation Paper No 149). Criticising the current arrangements as incoherent and illogical the Consultation Paper proposes that the right to bring a private prosecution should only be restricted in those circumstances where the public interest so dictates. It suggests that this might be the case in prosecutions involving: national security; foreign affairs; and freedom of expression. Consent might also be appropriate where 'it is particularly likely, given the availability of both criminal and civil proceedings in respect of the same conduct, that the public interest will not require a prosecution.'

The burden and standard of proof

In a criminal trial the burden of proving the charge rests with the prosecution. The standard of proof is beyond all reasonable doubt. In some situations a defendant will bear an evidential burden, ie will have to produce evidence upon which the trial judge can direct the jury (for example where the defence of provocation is raised, produce evidence that he was provoked to kill the victim). Alternatively, there are occasions when a defendant bears a legal burden of proof, such as the burden of proving diminished responsibility. In such cases the standard of proof that the defendant has to satisfy is the civil standard, ie on the balance of probabilities.

In affirming the common law position regarding burden and standard of proof, Lord Sankey LC, in *Woolmington* v *DPP* [1935] AC 462, stated:

'If at any period of a trial it was permissible for the judge to rule that the prosecution had established its case and that the onus was shifted on the prisoner to prove that he was not guilty, and that, unless he discharged that onus, the prosecution was entitled to succeed, it would be enabling the judge in such a case to say that the jury must in law find the prisoner guilty and so make the judge decide the case and not the jury, which is not the common law ... it is not till the end of the evidence that a verdict can properly be found and that at the end of the evidence it is not for the prisoner to establish his innocence, but for the prosecution to establish his guilt. Just as there is evidence on behalf of the prosecution so there may be evidence on behalf of the prisoner which may cause a doubt as to his guilt. In either case, he is entitled to the benefit of the doubt. But while the prosecution must prove the guilt of the prisoner, there is no such burden laid on the prisoner to prove his innocence, and it is sufficient for him to raise a doubt as to his guilt; he is not bound to satisfy the jury of his innocence. ... Throughout the web of the English criminal law one golden thread is always to be seen, that it is the duty of the prosecution to prove the prisoner's guilt subject to what I have already said as to the defence of insanity and subject also to any statutory exception. If, at the end of and on the whole of the case, there is a reasonable doubt, created by the evidence given by either the prosecution or the prisoner, as to whether the prisoner killed the deceased with a malicious intention, the prosecution has not made out the case and the prisoner is entitled to an acquittal. No matter what the charge or where the trial, the principle that the prosecution must prove the guilt of the prisoner is part of the common law of England and no attempt to whittle it down can be entertained.'

The classification of crime

Prior to the enactment of the Criminal Law Act 1967 crimes were classified as being either treasons, felonies or misdemeanours. In general terms felonies were the more serious offences, misdemeanours less serious. The distinction between felonies and misdemeanours was effectively abolished by the 1967 Act, which in turn introduced the concepts of the arrestable and non-arrestable offence. Arrestable offences are those falling within the provisions of s24 Police and Criminal Evidence Act 1984, in respect of which a police officer, and possibly a member of the public, can arrest without a warrant.

An alternative to classifying offences by reference to powers of arrest, is to classify them with reference to the procedure by which they are prosecuted. For these purposes offences are described as either being summary, indictable, or triable either way. The basis for this method of classification is to be found in the Magistrates' Court Act 1980.

Summary offences are those which are only triable summarily, ie before a magistrates' court. Such offences tend to be less serious in nature, which is hardly surprising given the limited powers of sentencing possessed by the magistrates' courts when compared to the Crown Court. Typical examples of such offences would be drunken driving, indecent exposure and assault upon a police officer in the execution of his duty. Common assault and battery are made summary only offences by the Criminal Justice Act 1988.

Indictable offences are the most serious offences in the criminal calendar – such as murder, treason and robbery which can only be tried on indictment in a Crown Court before a judge and jury. A number of offences can be tried either summarily before a magistrates court or on indictment before a Crown Court. Examples of such offences are handling stolen goods, theft, reckless driving and obtaining property by deception. The defendant will appear before the magistrates' court where the question of mode of trial will be considered, involving representations from the prosecution and the defence. A defendant cannot insist on a summary trial if the court considers trial on indictment more suitable, but if the court considers summary trial to be appropriate the defendant can still insist on his right to a trial on indictment, however unwise this may be. Certain offences only become triable either way where amount of damage involved exceeds a certain figure, eg criminal damage. Section 46 of the Criminal Justice and Public Order Act 1994 amends s22(1) of the Magistrates' Courts Act 1980 with the effect that magistrates must try summarily any criminal damage case where the value involved does not exceed £5,000 (an increase from £2,000). Similarly, the magistrates' court has no discretion where an offence triable either way is being prosecuted by the Attorney-General, Director of Public Prosecutions or Solicitor-General, and any of these officers requests trial on indictment.

Trial courts and rights of appeal

Despite the unglamorous nature of much of their work, magistrates' courts form the bedrock of the criminal justice system, dealing with over 90 per cent of all criminal cases. The vast majority of criminal offences are dealt with summarily, with lay or stipendiary magistrates determining questions of fact, law and sentence. As magistrates' courts are not courts of record, ie decisions of such courts have no value in terms of precedent, their deliberations are of little interest to the student of criminal law, but some consideration should be given to cases on appeal from magistrates' courts. A defendant convicted in the magistrates' court can appeal to the Crown Court against conviction and/or sentence. If the appeal is against conviction the Crown Court will effectively rehear the case before a Crown Court judge and two magistrates. In addition, under s11 of the Criminal Appeal Act 1995, the Criminal Cases Review Commission may refer a conviction following a trial in a magistrates' court to the Crown Court (see below). Note that decisions of the Crown Court in such a cases have no formal value as precedent.

A defendant convicted in the magistrates' court may wish to challenge a magistrate's ruling on a question of law, even though none of the facts as found are in dispute. In such a case a complete rehearing in the Crown Court is inappropriate, and the normal procedure would be to appeal by way of case stated to the Divisional Court of the High Court, requesting a ruling on the point of law in issue. If the Divisional Court rules in favour of the defendant the conviction will be quashed. It is also open to the prosecution to invoke this procedure where it feels that a defendant has been acquitted in the magistrates' court following a wrong ruling on a point of law. If the prosecution succeeds with such an appeal the Divisional Court can order the magistrates' court to enter a conviction against the defendant and consider the appropriate sentence.

A case can also be referred to the Divisional Court where a point of law arises in a case being considered by a Crown Court on appeal from a magistrates' court.

Again, this procedure is open to both prosecution and defence. The decisions of the Divisional Court are recorded, and in more important cases reported, and do have value as precedent. Appeal lies from a ruling on a point of law by the Divisional Court to the House of Lords. Note that such a procedure effectively 'leapfrogs' the Court of Appeal. Leave of either the Divisional Court or the House of Lords to appeal is required, and the case must be one involving a point of law of general public importance. The right of appeal is open to both prosecution and defence.

A defendant charged with an indictable offence must be tried in the Crown Court, and a defendant charged with an offence triable either way can opt for Crown Court trial, or the prosecution may insist on a Crown Court trial. Such a defendant will, however, make his first appearance before a magistrates' court where, in due course, a decision will be taken as regards committing him for trial at the Crown Court: see Part V of the Criminal Procedure and Investigations Act 1996.

Appeals by defendants tried on indictment in the Crown Court are heard by the Court of Appeal (Criminal Division), a procedure governed by the Criminal Appeal Act 1968, as amended by the Criminal Appeal Act 1995. The grounds for such an appeal, and the role of the Court of Appeal, are considered below at section 1.5. Both prosecution and defence can appeal against a ruling by the Court of Appeal within the terms of s33 of the Criminal Appeal Act 1968. Leave to appeal must be granted, either by the Court of Appeal or the House of Lords, on the basis that the case involves a point of law of general public importance that ought to be considered by the House. As regards sentencing decisions, the Court of Appeal's ruling is final.

It should be noted that, subject to the procedures for dealing with 'tainted acquittals' under ss54–57 of the Criminal Procedure and Investigations Act 1996, the prosecution cannot appeal against an acquittal in the Crown Court, although the Attorney-General has the power, under s36(1) of the Criminal Justice Act 1972, to refer any point of law arising during the trial for determination by the Court of Appeal. The ruling given by the Court of Appeal in such a case will be cited, for example, as *Attorney-General's Reference (No 1 of 1974)* [1974] QB 744 (the first such reference made under the 1972 Act). The nature of the Court's role in dealing with such a reference was summarised by Lord Mustill in *Attorney-General's Reference (No 3 of 1994)* [1997] 3 All ER 936, where he observed that:

'The courts have always firmly resisted attempts to obtain the answer to academic questions, however useful this might appear to be. Normally, where an appeal is brought in the context of an issue between parties, the identification of questions which the court should answer can be performed by considering whether a particular answer to the question of law might affect the outcome of the dispute. The peculiarity of a reference under the Act of 1972 is that it is not a step in a dispute, so that in one sense the questions referred are invariably academic. This peculiarity might, unless limits are observed, enable the Attorney-General, for the best of motives, to use an acquittal on a point of law to set in train a judicial roving commission on a particular branch of the law, with the aim of providing clear, practical and systematic solutions for problems of current interest. This is not the function of the court ... and the [wording of s36(1) was] ... designed to keep the proceedings in Attorney-General's references within proper bounds.'

Although the Court of Appeal may make a ruling that, had it been applied at the trial, would have resulted in the defendant's conviction, the acquittal will remain unaffected. Despite this, these rulings have the same status, in terms of precedent, as any other ruling of the Court of Appeal. The Court of Appeal may also refer the point further to the House of Lords.

Note also that, following the enactment of s36 of the Criminal Justice Act 1988, the prosecution may, with the leave of the Court of Appeal, appeal against what it regards as an unduly lenient sentence imposed by the Crown Court following trial on indictment.

Use of the civil courts

The Attorney-General can apply to the High Court for a declaration regarding an issue of criminal law, despite the fact that no criminal proceedings have been commenced. In *Attorney-General* v *Able* [1984] QB 795 the Attorney-General sought a declaration as to the legality of a booklet issued by *EXIT* which detailed various efficient methods of committing suicide. Woolf J indicated that the civil courts should not generally be used for determining issues of criminal law; to do so would be to usurp the functions of the criminal courts. Perhaps a further ground of objection is the difference in the standard of proof in civil as opposed to criminal proceedings.

1.5 Preventing miscarriages of justice

Any criminal justice system must make provision for remedying miscarriages of justice, not only to ensure that individual citizens receive fair treatment, but also to maintain confidence in, and respect for, the judicial process. Reference has already been made to the procedures that exist for challenging decisions of magistrates' courts, but the greatest concern about miscarriages of justice is likely to arise in relation to cases tried on indictment in the Crown Court, as the defendant will be at risk of receiving a much more significant punishment in the event of conviction.

The need for reform

During the 1980s the procedures for preventing and rectifying miscarriages of justice became the subject of much critical scrutiny, not least because of a number of cause celebres such as the cases of the 'Guildford Four' – see *R* v *Richardson and Others* (1989) The Times 20 October – and the 'Birmingham Six'. Aspects attracting particular criticism were the reluctance of Court of Appeal to overturn a jury's verdict in the absence of a procedural irregularity or error of law, even where the only evidence against the defendant was an uncorroborated confession; the unwillingness of the Court of Appeal to act simply because an appellant had been incompetently represented; the restrictive approach taken by the Court of Appeal to the admission of fresh evidence; and the reluctance of the Home Secretary to refer cases to the Court of Appeal (see below) – in the period 1989–92, of 700–800 applications, only 28 were referred to the Court of Appeal by the Home Secretary.

In March 1991 the Home Secretary announced the setting up of a Royal Commission, under Lord Runciman, to investigate every aspect of the criminal process, from pre-trial procedures to the handling of alleged miscarriages of justice by the Court of Appeal. The Commission delivered its report in July 1993, and a number of its key recommendations as regards reforming the machinery for dealing with alleged miscarriages of justice were, in substance, enacted in the Criminal Appeal Act 1995.

Appeal to the Court of Appeal

Under the Criminal Appeal Act 1968, as amended by the Criminal Appeal Act 1995, a defendant may appeal against conviction only if leave to do so is granted by the Court of Appeal, or the judge of the court of trial certifies that case is fit for appeal.

An appeal against conviction may be an appeal on a pure point of law, for example the interpretation of a word in a statute by the trial judge in his summing up to the jury, or a challenge to the jurisdiction of the English courts on the basis that the offence was committed abroad. In practice such appeals will be rare, as they involve the defendant in contending that, even if the jury had been correctly seized of all the evidence, it was not open to them to convict because the facts did not disclose an offence known to law, or at least not that with which the defendant was charged. Most appeals against conviction are in fact appeals involving mixed questions of fact and law. The vast majority of appeals from the Crown Court to the Court of Appeal are actually appeals against sentence, not conviction. In 1994, the Court received with 5,050 appeals against sentence. Leave to appeal is required, and the Court of Appeal can substitute any sentence that would have been available to the Crown Court at the time of trial; see also s36 of the Criminal Justice Act 1988 referred to above. Applications for leave are normally considered by a single judge of the Court, but appeal against a refusal of leave can be renewed before a full Court of Appeal hearing.

Grounds of appeal

Under s2(1) of the Criminal Appeal Act 1968, as amended by s2(1) of the 1995 Act, the Court of Appeal can only allow an appeal against conviction if satisfied that the conviction is unsafe. This replaces the old procedure under which appeals were allowed if the court was satisfied that the trial judge had made a wrong ruling on a point of law; or that there had been a procedural irregularity during the course of the trial; or that the conviction should be set aside because in all the circumstances of the case it was unsafe or unsatisfactory. A phrase often used was that the appeal would be allowed if there was a 'lurking doubt' that the conviction was unsafe or unsatisfactory. The powers of the court are now more limited. As was confirmed by the Court of Appeal in *R* v *Chalkley* [1998] 2 All ER 155, even if the court is uneasy about the course of events at the trial, in particular decisions regarding the obtaining and admission of evidence, there is no longer any scope to allow an appeal on the basis of some general 'unsatisfactoriness' unless this resulted in the conviction being 'unsafe' overall. The Court of Appeal in *R* v *Farrow* (1998) The Times 20 October has also confirmed that there is no longer any scope for the application of the old 'lurking doubt' test in evaluating whether or not a conviction should stand. The court should simply apply an unadorned test as to whether or not the conviction is safe. The decisions beg the question as to how far the course of proceedings adopted at the trial would have to depart from accepted standards of unfairness for an 'unsatisfactory' conviction to become an 'unsafe' one: see further *R* v *Simpson* [1998] Crim LR 481 and *R* v *Martin* [1998] 2 WLR 1.

Note also that, under the 1968 Act, the Court of Appeal was empowered to apply what was know as the 'proviso' to s2(1), by virtue of which it could decide an appeal in favour of the appellant, whilst dismissing the appeal against conviction, on the basis that no miscarriage of justice has actually occurred. Under the new s2(1) this option is no longer open to the court. In short, the revised formulation will give greater discretion to the Court of Appeal to allow appeals against conviction.

Where a defendant does decide to appeal against conviction his counsel needs to be mindful of the decision in *R* v *Leonard* [1998] 2 Cr App R 326. Section 18(2) of the Criminal Appeal Act 1968 requires that notice of appeal or application for leave to appeal against conviction be given within 28 days from the date of conviction, verdict or finding appealed against, or where an appeal against sentence, from the date the sentence was passed. This notice of application for leave to appeal must be given within 28 days of conviction notwithstanding there is a delay between conviction and sentence.

Appeals where the appellant has pleaded guilty

It may seem odd that the courts should allow a defendant who has freely admitted his guilt at trial to then seek to appeal against his inevitable conviction. There are, however, a number of situations where a possible miscarriage of justice can only be avoided by permitting such a course of action. A defendant may have pleaded guilty as a result of pressure from counsel, or the trial judge, ie plea bargaining. He may have pleaded guilty as a result of a wrong ruling in law by the trial judge, eg a trial judge rules that the only defence he will allow the defendant to put before the jury is that of insanity. The defendant prefers to plead guilty rather than be found not guilty by reason of insanity, then appeals against the judge's ruling. Much depends on what triggers the guilty plea. In *R* v *Chalkley* (above) the court confirmed that conviction following a guilty plea could be set aside where the plea had been tendered in error, had been tendered without any intention to admit the truth of the offence charged, or where a trial judge's direction left the accused with no legal basis for challenging the prosecution (for example a ruling that an offence is one of absolute liability where the accused's only argument is as to mens rea). A conviction could not be set aside, however, where the appellant had changed his plea for tactical reasons following a trial judge's ruling as to the admissibility of evidence, even if the evidence is wrongly admitted. In such cases the appellant is not contesting the material facts, only the evidence relied upon to establish them. The decision in *Chalkley* was followed by the Court of Appeal in *R* v *Kennedy* [1998] Crim LR 739 – conviction following guilty plea upheld despite allegations of entrapment to obtain statements from the appellant. In *R* v *Hewitson* (1998) (CA No 9705580/Y4) it was held that the ruling in *Chalkley* applies even where the prosecution accepts that without the contested evidence the appellant would not have had a case to answer.

Cases referred to the Court of Appeal

Prior to the enactment of the 1995 Act alleged miscarriages of justice could be brought to the attention of the Court of Appeal by the intervention of the Home Secretary acting under s17 of the 1968 Act. The power of referral was exercisable as the minister saw fit, and was particularly important in cases where the time limits for appealing against conviction had passed. In the light of criticisms of political intervention in the criminal process, and following recommendations made by the Royal Commission, the 1995 Act removed the Home Secretary's power of referral, and created a new independent body, the Criminal Cases Review Commission (CCRC), empowered to take over and enhance this role.

The CCRC has 14 members appointed by the Queen on the advice of the Prime Minister. At least one-third of the membership must be legally qualified. Under s9 of the 1995 Act the CCRC is empowered to refer any case that has been tried on indictment to the Court of Appeal. A reference in respect of any conviction following trial on indictment is to be treated, by the Court of Appeal, as an appeal under s1 of the 1968 Act. Similarly, where a person has been convicted of an offence by a magistrates' court, the CCRC may refer the case to the Crown Court. The basis for such a reference, as laid down in s13 of the 1995 Act, is that there is a real possibility that the conviction, verdict or finding would not be upheld if the reference were to be made, because of an argument or evidence not raised in the proceedings or, in the case of sentence, because of an argument on a point of law, or information, not so raised. Save in exceptional circumstances, the CCRC is not permitted to refer a case to the relevant court unless the convicted person has already appealed unsuccessfully.

Under s23A, added to the 1968 Act by s5 of the 1995 Act, the Court of Appeal can direct the CCRC to investigate a specific issue if it appears to the court that: it is relevant to the determination of a case and ought to be resolved before the case is determined; an investigation of the matter is likely to result in the court being able to resolve it; and the matter cannot be resolved by the court without an investigation being carried out by the CCRC. Once a case is referred to the CCRC it can ask the 'appropriate person' from the public body which carried out the original investigation to appoint officers to carry out an inquiry and report back. In most cases this means that the Chief Constable of the force that originally dealt with the case will appoint some of his or her officers to re-investigate the matter. Some have contended that this is a key weakness in the new machinery, although it has to be conceded that the cost of providing the CCRC with its own investigative branch would be prohibitive.

Cases where fresh evidence comes to light

By virtue of s23 of the 1968 Act, as amended by s4 of the 1995 Act, the Court of Appeal can here evidence that was not adduced at the original trial. In doing so it is required to have regard, inter alia, to whether the evidence is capable of belief (as opposed to 'likely to be credible' under the old law), the extent to which it affords any ground for appeal, the extent to which it would have been admissible if tendered at the trial, and whether there is any reasonable explanation for its not being so tendered. The court will expect an appellant to have co-operated with his lawyer at the time of the trial to ensure the availability of all relevant evidence, and in some cases to have employed an inquiry agent.

Powers of the Court of Appeal following an appeal

Having considered an appeal against conviction the Court of Appeal has a number of options. It can dismiss the appeal, leaving the sentence of the Crown Court to stand, or reduce the sentence. Alternatively, the appeal can be allowed and the conviction quashed, or the conviction can be quashed and a conviction for a lesser included offence substituted, eg reduce a conviction for murder to manslaughter: see further s3 of the 1968 Act. Under s7 of the 1968 Act the Court of Appeal can order a retrial, if it is in the interests of justice to do so. As a successful appeal in the Court of Appeal places the appellant in the same situation as if he had been acquitted by the jury, this has to be seen as a statutory exception to the autrefois acquit rule. Care must be taken to ensure that the same charge is brought, or a lesser included, or an alternative charge on the indictment. The power to order a retrial is rarely used, although in recent years there has been a significant increase, from 12 in 1992 to 51 in 1994.

Free pardon and compensation

A free pardon can be recommended by the Home Secretary where fresh evidence emerges that the defendant did not commit the offence for which he was convicted, and such a pardon has the effect of relieving the defendant from any penalty in connection with the conviction. Note that this by-passes the Court of Appeal altogether, but does not, however, quash the conviction as this is something only the Court of Appeal can do. The prisoner may also receive an ex gratia payment. Section 133 Criminal Justice Act 1988 has placed this power on a statutory basis, and in fact creates a duty to pay compensation where there has been a miscarriage of justice, but it offers no guidelines as to the basis upon which such compensation is to be paid. Unofficial guidelines indicate that about £10,000 per annum plus expenses and legal fees would be the normal level of payment.

1.6 The work of the Law Commission

Since the early 1980s the Law Commission has been involved in a programme aimed at codifying the criminal law of England and Wales. *The Report and Draft Criminal Code Bill for England and Wales*, published in 1989 (Law Com No 177), was described by the Law Commission as having as its purpose the task of addressing 'the question whether it is desirable to replace the existing fluctuating mix of legislation and common law by one codifying statute' (Vol I, para 1.4).

Volume I comprises recommendations and a Draft Criminal Code Bill and Appendices. Part I of the Bill deals with general principles of liability, whilst Part II deals with specific offences. Appendix B provides a series of illustrative examples of how the code might operate in given situations. Volume II provides a commentary on some of the Code provisions. Extracts from the commentary have been included, where appropriate, at various points in this textbook.

The origins of the Code can be traced back to 1981 when the preparatory work was started by a small group – the 'Code Team'. The team's terms of reference were to consider and

'... make proposals in relation to the aims and objects of a criminal code for England and Wales ... its nature and scope ... content, structure, lay-out and the interrelation of its parts ... the method and style of its drafting and ... to formulate, in a manner appropriate to such a code: (a) the general principles which should govern liability under it; (b) a standard terminology to be used in it; (c) the rules which should govern its interpretation.'

The 'Code Team' submitted its report to the Law Commission in November 1984, and it was published in March 1985. The Law Commission's Draft Code is based upon that produced by the Code Team, but reflects amendments and reforms suggested between 1985 and 1989, and expands Part II of the Draft Code which deals with specific offences. The Law Commission's report explains the background to the moves towards codification in the following terms:

'English criminal law is derived from a mixture of common law and statute. Most of the general principles of liability are still to be found in the common law, though some, for example, the law relating to conspiracy and attempts to commit crime have recently been defined in Acts of Parliament. The great majority of crimes are now defined by statute but there are important exceptions. Murder, manslaughter and assault are still offences at common law, though affected in various ways by statute. There is no system in the relative roles of common law and legislation. Thus, incitement to commit crime, though closely related to conspiracy and attempts is still a common law offence. Whether an offence is defined by statute has almost always been a matter of historical accident rather than systematic organisation. For example, rape is defined in the Sexual Offences (Amendment) Act 1976 because of the outcry which followed the decision in *DPP* v *Morgan* and led to the subsequent Heilbron Report. The legislation in force extends over a very long period of time. It is true that only a very small amount of significant legislation is earlier than the mid-nineteenth century, but that is quite long enough for the language of the criminal law and the style of drafting to have undergone substantial changes.' (Vol I, para 1.3)

The Law Commission cited a number of reasons in support of codification. At a fundamental level there are constitutional arguments to be considered. The criminal justice system should reflect the balance of power between the citizen and the state. The citizen should be presented with a rational and just system of laws. If the criminal law is a known and ascertainable body of rules, it promotes key aspects of due process , such as fair warning of potential liability. Professor A T H Smith viewed the introduction of a criminal code as significant because it involved the making of:

'... a symbolic statement about the constitutional relationship of Parliament and the courts, it requires a judicial deference to the legislative will greater than that which the courts have often shown to isolated and sporadic pieces of legislation.' (Vol I, para 2.2)

Codification was also seen as a means of promoting consistency, the Commission regarding inconsistency both in terminology and substance is a serious problem in English criminal law. A common definition of fundamental terms such as 'intention' or 'recklessness' can help to ensure that like cases are treated alike.

The Law Commission was well aware of the fact that legislation containing a criminal code would be subject to interpretation by the courts in the same way that any existing criminal legislation is, and that the result could be the emergence of a daunting body of case law; the experience of the Theft Acts 1968 and 1978 provides ample evidence. The Commission's report stated:

'Our objective ... has been to ensure that the Criminal Code Bill has been drafted with sufficient clarity to reduce difficulties of interpretation as far as is reasonably possible.' (Vol I, para 2.22)

The Commission's view was that problems of implementation were not to be confused with objections to codification in principle. Since the publication of the Draft Code the Commission has turned its attention to specific aspects of criminal law and has continued to invite submissions from parties with an interest in reform. The result has been a steady stream of consultation papers and reports on the key aspects of criminal law, such as compulsion, consent, non-fatal offences against the person, trade secrets, corruption, conspiracy to defraud, mentally incapacitated adults, accessorial liability and the 'year and a day' rule.

It is significant that, whilst most of the reports produced by the Commission generate praise from those involved in the criminal justice system, precious little parliamentary time has been found to give effect to its proposals for reform of the criminal law. In its report for 1993 the Commission expressed its grave concern on this matter, going as far as to suggest that its relationship with the House of Commons had all but broken down. Brooke J, Chairman of the Commission, singled out in particular the failure to reform substantial parts of existing criminal law as being 'a disgrace'. In the 1996 report Dame Mary Arden called for a 'fast track' procedure for implementing Law Commission Bills and re-emphasised the point that there was little point in the Law Commission issuing reports (at a cost of £4 million a year) if they were going to be ignored by legislators: see further the leading article 'Justice Delayed' (1997) The Times 14 March.

2

Actus Reus

2.1 Introduction

2.2 General considerations

2.3 Omissions

2.4 Involuntary acts

2.1 Introduction

It is common for criminal lawyers to talk of criminal offences having 'elements'. This is usually a shorthand reference to the actus reus and mens rea of an offence. In literal terms actus reus denotes a guilty act, mens rea denotes a guilty mind. The general basis for imposing liability in criminal law is that a defendant must be proved to have committed the guilty act whilst having had the guilty state of mind. As will be seen in the following chapters, criminal law throws up many exceptions to this general proposition, but as a method of approach to problems of criminal liability it has much to recommend itself to the newcomer to the subject.

When attempting to solve problems in criminal law it is logical to first ask whether the defendant has committed the prohibited act, or actus reus. If the answer to this question is in the affirmative, one can then ask whether the defendant possessed the requisite state of mind at the time of the act, in short whether he had mens rea. If the answer to this second question is also affirmative, one can ask a third question. Are there any defences available to the defendant in respect of his actions which might reduce or remove his criminal liability?

2.2 General considerations

Definition

Professor Glanville Williams has suggested the following approach:

> 'All that can truly be said, without exception, is that a crime requires some *external state of affairs* that can be categorised as criminal. What goes on inside a man's head is never enough in itself to constitute a crime, even though it be proved by a confession that it is fully believed to be genuine.' (*Textbook on Criminal Law*, 2nd ed, p146)

It might be wise, therefore, to proceed on the basis that the actus reus of an offence involves all the elements of the offence, with the exception of those that relate to the defendant's state of mind. Terms such as actus reus should be treated with caution, however. As Lord Diplock observed in *R* v *Miller* [1983] 1 All ER 978 at 980:

> 'My Lords, it would I think be conducive to clarity of analysis of the ingredients of a crime that is created by statute, as are the great majority of criminal offences today, if we were to avoid bad Latin and instead to think and speak ... about the conduct of the accused and his state of mind at the time of that conduct, instead of speaking of actus reus and mens rea.'

It should not be assumed that 'actus reus' and 'mens rea' are mutually exclusive concepts. Cases such as *R* v *Miller*, considered at section 2.3 below, illustrate the interrelationship between them.

In time the 'bad Latin' may come to be replaced by the more prosaic but accurate terminology preferred by the Law Commission in its Draft Code, which uses 'external elements of the offence' for actus reus, and 'fault element' for mens rea.

Types of actus reus

Offences can be classified on the basis of the type of actus reus involved.

Conduct

Some offences do not require proof of any result or consequence. The action of the defendant is all that has to be proved. A typical example is the offence of 'dangerous driving'. The prosecution does not have to prove that any harm was caused by this activity, or that life was endangered by it. Similarly the offence of perjury, under the Perjury Act 1911, requires the defendant only to make a statement that he knows or believes to be untrue whilst under oath. Liability can arise independently of whether the statement affects the outcome of the proceedings.

Circumstances

The actus reus of an offence can consist of elements which are almost entirely external to the physical actions of the defendant. For example, in *R* v *Larsonneur* (1933) 97 JP 206, D was a French national who had entered the United Kingdom lawfully, but was given only limited permission to remain in the country. Her passport stated that she had to leave the United Kingdom on 22 March 1933. On that day D left England, not to return to France but to travel to the Irish Free State. The Irish authorities made a deportation order against her, and she was forcibly removed from Ireland and returned to the United Kingdom mainland at Holyhead. On arrival at Holyhead D was convicted under the Aliens Order 1920, with being found in the United Kingdom whilst not having permission to enter the country. She appealed on the basis that her return to the United Kingdom had not been of her own free will, in that she had been forcibly taken to Holyhead by the immigration authorities. The Court of Appeal dismissed the appeal on the simple basis that the prosecution had proved the facts necessary for a conviction. On its face the decision does seem somewhat harsh and contrary to the theory that actus reus must be freely willed, but it can be explained, however, on the basis that the actus reus consisted of a 'state of affairs' which had to be found to exist, requiring little or no participation by D. The contention that her return to Holyhead was not freely willed (see section 2.4, below) could be countered by the observation that her travelling to the Irish Free State was, and it was this that led to her deportation.

The modern counterpart to *Larsonneur* is the decision of the Divisional Court in *Winzar* v *Chief Constable of Kent* (1983) The Times 28 March. D had been admitted to hospital on a stretcher. Upon examination he was found to be drunk and was told to leave. Later he was found in a corridor of the hospital and the police were called to remove him. The police officers took D outside onto the roadway, then placed him in a police car and drove him to the police station where he was charged with being found drunk in a public highway. D was convicted, and appealed on the ground that he had not been on the public road of his own volition. The Divisional Court upheld the conviction on the basis that all that was required for liability was that D should be perceived to be drunk whilst on a public highway. There was no need for the court to have any regard as to how he came to be there. It is submitted that, as in *Larsonneur*, the voluntary act leading to liability can be found at an earlier stage, in this case the defendant's voluntarily becoming intoxicated. As Goff LJ observed:

'In my judgment, looking at the purpose of this particular offence, it is designed to deal with the nuisance which can be caused by persons who are drunk in a public place. This kind of offence is caused quite simply when a person is found drunk in a public place or in a highway ... [A]n example ... illustrates how sensible that conclusion is. Suppose a person was found as being drunk in a restaurant or a place of that kind and was asked to leave. If he was asked to leave, he would walk out of the door of the restaurant and would be in a public place or in a highway of his own volition. He would be there of his own volition because he had responded to a request. However, if a man in a restaurant made a thorough nuisance of himself, was asked to leave, objected and was ejected, in those circumstances, he would not be in a public place of his own volition because he would have been put there either by a gentleman on the door of the restaurant, or by a police officer, who might have been called to deal with the man in question. It would be nonsense if one were to say that the man who responded to the plea to leave could be said to be found drunk in a public place or in a highway, whereas the man who had been compelled to leave could not.'

Result crimes

Offences such as homicide and assault require proof of a result as part of the actus reus. The defendant must be shown to have caused the death of the victim, or to have caused the injury suffered by the victim, as the case may be. Questions of causation can be very complex. It is not sufficient that the defendant's act can be shown to have been a factual cause of the prohibited act. It must be shown that the act is also a cause in law of the result. This matter is dealt with in more detail in Chapter 4, in the context of homicide.

An illustration

The statutory offence of theft provides a useful illustration of the various elements of a criminal offence. Section 1 of the Theft Act 1968 states:

> 'A person is guilty of theft if he dishonestly appropriates property belonging to another with the intention of permanently depriving the other of it ...'

If one deletes those expressions that relate to the mental state of the defendant, ie 'dishonesty' and 'intention to permanently deprive', what remains is the actus reus of the offence. The 'appropriation' could be regarded as the conduct of the defendant; the 'property belonging to another' constitutes the circumstances that must exist for the offence to be made out.

Actus reus must be proved

It is something of a truism in criminal law that there must be an actus reus for there to be any criminal liability. This is sometimes expressed by saying that 'actus reus must be proved'.

The case of *R* v *Deller* (1952) 36 Cr App R 184 illustrates the point. D sold a car which he wrongly believed to be the subject of a hire purchase agreement in respect of which payments were still outstanding. In fact the car was free from all encumbrances. He was charged with what is now the offence of obtaining property by deception. He appealed against his conviction on the basis that, as the car was free from all encumbrances, he had been telling the truth when he had told the purchaser this, even though he had thought he was lying. The Court of Appeal quashed his conviction. As the car was free from encumbrances D had not deceived the purchaser, hence the actus reus of deception was absent. The fact that D had thought he was committing an offence, ie he had mens rea, was insufficient on its own for liability.

The decision raises a number of interesting possibilities, such as the acquittal of the defendant who fires a gun at what he believes to be the sleeping figure of his enemy, intending to kill him, only to discover that in fact he was firing at a wax dummy. Again, the defendant has the mens rea, this time for murder, but has not committed the actus reus, indeed cannot, as there is no human being to be the victim.

It should be noted that Parliament has acted to bring such defendants within the scope of the criminal law. Were the same facts to arise today, Deller would almost certainly be guilty of attempting to obtain property by deception contrary to s1 of the Criminal Attempts Act 1981. Similarly, the would-be murderer could now be charged with attempted murder, even though he was only firing at a wax dummy. How such a result is achieved is detailed in Chapter 12.

Reform

Clause 15 of the Draft Code proposes the following:

> 'A reference in this Act to an "act" as an element of an offence refers also, where the context permits, to any result of the act, and any circumstance in which the act is done or the result occurs, that is an element of the offence, and references to a person's acting or doing an act shall be construed accordingly.'

In its commentary in Volume II of the Code Report, the Commission stated:

> 'Clause 15 ... is an interpretation clause. It does not define "act". It simply explains that where the Code refers to "an act" or to a person's "acting" or "doing an act", the reference embraces whatever relevant results and circumstances the context permits. This clarification of the use of the word "act" is not in fact essential; for we believe that no provision of the Code is on a fair reading truly ambiguous in its use of the term. But the clause may prove useful for the avoidance of doubt in those inexperienced in the reading of criminal statutes and as a protection against perverse reading or hopeless argument.' (Vol II, para 7.6)

2.3 Omissions

Introduction

It is customary to think of an actus reus as being the positive act of the defendant. In murder this might be the defendant's stabbing of the victim. In theft it might be the defendant's taking of money from a wallet. The matter to be considered here is whether a failure to act on the part of a defendant can form the basis of liability.

The general rule

The general rule in English criminal law is that there can be no liability for failing to act, unless at the time of the failure to act the defendant was under a legal duty to take positive action. A moral duty to act will not suffice here. Hence if D sees P, a blind man, walking towards the edge of a cliff from which there is a sheer drop of 300 feet onto jagged rocks below, he is under no legal duty to call out a warning. D is quite at liberty to watch P walk over the edge of the cliff top to his certain death. Similarly if D were to see a child P drowning in a swimming pool, D would be under no legal duty to prevent this. D could calmly stand at the pool side and film the tragedy if he so wished. The legal position rather reflects the saying that 'you are not your brother's keeper'. As will be explained below, the situation in the latter example would be markedly different were the child in the pool to be D's son, or if D was a pool attendant employed to ensure the safety of swimmers.

It should not be assumed that it is always a simple matter to differentiate between an act and an omission. In *R v Speck* (1977) 65 Cr App R 161, D was convicted of an offence under s1 of the Indecency with Children Act 1960. An eight-year-old girl had approached him and placed her hand on his penis. He allowed her hand to remain there for approximately five minutes, during which time he had an erection. He appealed against his conviction on the basis that he had not committed any 'act of gross indecency with or towards a child under the age of 14'. The Court of Appeal held, dismissing the appeal, that D's inactivity in failing to remove the hand of the little girl could amount to an invitation to the child to undertake the act.

As Lord Widgery CJ observed:

> 'Getting to the essential features of this problem, and accepting that for present purposes there was inactivity on the part of the appellant at all material times, we think that such inactivity can nevertheless amount to an invitation to the child to undertake the act. If a fair view of the facts be that the appellant has in any sense invited the child to do what she did, then the mere fact that the appellant himself remained inactive is no defence to it ...
>
> Since in our opinion the element of invitation is important, and that is an element which the jury ultimately would have to consider, the ruling in law should have been that the conduct described by the learned recorder could be an offence if the jury took the view that it amounted to an invitation from the male to the child, either to start, to stop, or to continue this activity.'

Unless it is accepted that D's demeanour towards the child constituted the positive act here, it is difficult to see on what basis his liability for failing to act could have been imposed, given the absence of any of the duties considered below.

Duty arising from statute

Liability for failing to act will be imposed where the defendant can be shown to have been under a statutory duty to take positive action. A leading example of such a provision is provided by the Children and Young Persons Act 1933, which creates the offence of wilfully neglecting a child. Hence by simply failing to provide food for a child, or failing to obtain appropriate medical care, a parent could be held criminally liable for any harm that results. At a more prosaic level, the Road Traffic Acts place motorists under various duties, such as the duty to report road accidents where persons have been injured, or the duty to provide breath test specimens. In these cases it is the failure to act that results in liability.

Duty arising from contract

Where a defendant is under an ascertainable contractual duty to act, his failure to perform the contractual duty in question can form the basis of criminal liability. Hence in the example detailed above, if D is employed as a swimming pool attendant, and he fails to help a child who appears to him to be drowning in the pool with the result that the child dies, D could be held criminally responsible for the death on the basis that he was under a contractual duty to help save the child. The fact that the child is not a party to the contract upon which the duty is based is not a relevant matter here. An authority for imposing liability on this basis is *R* v *Pittwood* (1902) 19 TLR 37. D was employed as a gate keeper at a railway crossing. One day he went for lunch leaving the gate open so that road traffic could cross the railway line. A hay cart crossing the line was hit by a train. One man was killed, another was seriously injured. D was convicted of manslaughter based on his failure to carry out his contractual duty to close the gate when a train approached. The case of *R* v *Benge* (1865) 4 F & F 594 provides a further illustration of such liability.

Duty arising at common law

In the absence of any statutory or contractual duty, the judiciary have seen fit to create a number of common law duties, where it has been felt that not to do so would be to wrongly relieve the defendant of all criminal liability.

Duties owed to family members

The common law recognises a duty that members of a family may owe to each other to care for each other's welfare. The problem with such common law duties is that their exact limits are rather difficult to define, hence it may be difficult to determine when liability is likely to arise. In *R* v *Gibbens and Proctor* (1918) 82 JP 287, the court recognised the common law duty that a parent owes towards his or her child, with the result that liability for murder can result if a parent deliberately fails to feed a child. Note however that this common law duty has largely been supplanted by the statutory duty under the Children and Young Persons Act 1933 referred to above. Similarly in *R* v *Instan* [1893] 1 QB 450, where D lived with her aunt, an elderly woman who developed gangrene in her leg and was unable to look after herself. D was the only person who knew of her condition, but failed to provide her aunt with food or medical assistance. After 12 days of suffering the aunt died. D was convicted of manslaughter and appealed, unsuccessfully, to the Court for Crown Cases Reserved. Lord Coleridge CJ expressed the view that English law would be hopelessly deficient if the judges were to be unable to base liability on the common duty of care owed by one relative to another.

Reliance

Partly because of the difficulties in determining the precise scope of a duty of care based on blood relationships, the courts have, in recent years, moved towards recognising the existence of a common law duty of care where there is a relationship of reliance between defendant and victim. In *R* v *Stone and Dobinson* [1977] QB 354, the defendants were convicted of the manslaughter of Stone's sister Fanny. Stone was an elderly man, having greatly impaired senses of sight, smell, and hearing. Dobinson, his common law wife, was described as 'weak and ineffectual'. It was accepted that both defendants were of low intelligence and not particularly 'worldly' in character. They were visited by Fanny who was a somewhat eccentric woman, described in court as being morbidly anxious about becoming overweight. The defendants took Fanny in and provided her with a bed, but over the following weeks Fanny's condition worsened. She did not eat properly, developed bed sores, and eventually died of blood poisoning as result of her untreated bed sores becoming infected. The defendants had not obtained any medical assistance for Fanny although they had known that she was unwell. In dismissing the appeal, the Court of Appeal held that the defendants had been under a common law duty to care for Fanny, the duty arising from their voluntarily assuming the responsibility for looking after her, and their knowledge that she was relying on them. The defendants' failure to discharge this duty was the cause of the victim's death. Whilst it is submitted that to base liability on reliance freely assumed, rather than blood relationships, is a more sensible approach, the result may be somewhat counter-productive. In the light of the above decision, surely Stone would have been well advised to turn his sister away when she arrived at his door needing somewhere to stay. By doing so he would have avoided any assumption of a duty to care for her.

The duty to limit harm caused by accidental acts

The instances of liability for failure to act considered above may not be a sufficient basis for imposing liability on a defendant who accidentally commits an act that causes harm, realises what has happened, but then does nothing to prevent further harm from occurring. The problem was considered by the House of Lords in *R* v *Miller* [1983] 2 AC 161. D, a vagrant, had been occupying an empty house. One evening he laid on a mattress and lit a cigarette. He fell asleep and the lighted cigarette set fire to the mattress. D was woken by the flames, but instead of putting the fire out, he got up and went into an adjoining room where he found another mattress, and went back to sleep. As a result, the house was substantially damaged by fire, and D was convicted of criminal damage. He appealed, contending that liability could not be based on his setting fire to the mattress as he had been asleep at the time, and that there could be no liability based on his failure to act (once he became aware of the fire) as he had not been under a legal duty to take any action. As the law then stood D's contentions were soundly based. A defendant will normally be able to plead the defence of automatism in respect of acts committed whilst asleep, and he was not under any statutory, contractual, or common law duty to put the fire out once he discovered it.

The Court of Appeal had dismissed his appeal, relying on the earlier Divisional Court decision in *Fagan* v *Metropolitan Police Commissioner* [1968] 3 All ER 442. The House of Lords, however, preferred to base liability on a new type of common law 'duty'. Lord Diplock accepted that D's initial setting fire to the mattress may not have been a culpable act in that he was asleep at the time, but his Lordship was of the opinion that once D awoke and realised what had happened, he came under a responsibility to limit the harmful effects of the fire (his Lordship deliberately avoided use of the word 'duty' for fear that it might confuse juries). D's failure to discharge this responsibility provided the basis for the imposition of liability.

Whilst the decision represents an important development of liability for failing to act at common law, there have been relatively few reported instances of its application since 1983. In *R* v *Ahmad* [1986] Crim LR 739, D (a landlord) agreed with a tenant that certain alterations would be carried out at a property, including the installation of a new stairway and bathroom. Once the work commenced disputes then arose between D and his tenant and work on the property ceased, leaving the tenant without a bathroom. D was convicted of doing acts calculated to interfere with the peace and comfort of one of his tenants, contrary to s1(3) of the Protection from Eviction Act 1977, but appealed successfully to the Court of Appeal on the basis that, as the Act required 'the doing of acts', he could not incur liability through mere inactivity. When he had removed the old bathroom, he had lacked the mens rea necessary for the offence. He may have intended the cessation of building work to interfere with the tenant's enjoyment of the property, but this was not accompanied by any 'acts' on the part of D as required by the statute. The Court felt that the House of Lords' decision in *Miller* was of no avail where a statute expressly stated that liability could only arise where positive acts were committed.

In *R* v *Khan (Rungzabe)* (1998) The Times 7 April the Court of Appeal noted, without deciding the point, that a drug dealer might incur liability where he supplied drugs to P and then failed to act when he became aware that the consumption of the drugs had resulted in P overdosing. Arguably, the imposition of liability in such cases would involve an extension of the *Miller* principle on the basis that the actions of P, in voluntarily consuming the drugs, can be seen as a novus actus interveniens. In *Miller* the defendant's falling asleep with the lighted cigarette in bed was the direct result of the ensuing fire.

Reform

The Code Team's draft published in 1985 did attempt to codify the law relating to liability for failing to act. For reasons outlined below, the Law Commission decided not to make any such provision in its 1989 report, restricting itself to codification of the law relating to 'supervening fault'. Clause 16 of the Draft Code provides:

'For the purposes of an offence which consists wholly or in part of an omission, state of affairs or occurrence, references in this Act to an "act" shall, where the context permits, be read as including references to the omission, state of affairs or occurrence by reason of which a person may be guilty of the offence, and references to a person's acting or doing an act shall be construed accordingly.'

The Commission commented upon the purpose of cl 16 as follows:

'In effect, it instructs the user of the Code that, when he is concerned with an offence of omission or with a situational offence, he should substitute a reference to the omission or situation in question (or to making that omission or being in that situation) for a Code provision referring to an act (or to acting or doing an act). He should do so, to be more precise, "where the context permits".' (Vol II, para 7.7)

Reference should also be made to cl 33(2) of the Draft Code, which deals with the liability of a defendant who fails to act due to physical incapacity.

Regarding the absence of any provision expressly creating liability for failing to act, the Commission's commentary on the code provides the following explanation:

> 'Criminal liability for failing to act is exceptional. Parliament sometimes makes it an offence to fail to do something (as with wilful neglect of a child, the failure of a motorist to exchange particulars after an accident or the failure of a company to make an annual return). Most other instances of liability for omissions depend upon judicial construction of statutory language as referring to omissions as well as to acts, or upon common law (that is, judicial) recognition, in limited and rather ill-defined circumstances, of a duty to act to prevent a particular kind of harm (notably certain harms to the person) or to prevent the commission of an offence.' (Vol II, para 7.9)

The commentary goes on to point out that previous efforts at law reform, such as that relating to offences against the person, failed to come up with any satisfactory solution to the problem (see Criminal Law Revision Committee *Fourteenth Report: Offences against the Person* (1980), Cmnd 7844, paras 254–255). Rather than specifying those offences that can be committed by omission and those that cannot, the Commission expresses its preference for a scheme under which terms such as 'act' and 'cause' can be construed as carrying with them the possibility of the offence in question being committed by omission. The existence or otherwise of a duty to act remaining a matter to be determined at common law. The Commission explains the consequence of this as follows:

> 'Clause 17(1) [of the draft code bill] makes it clear that, under the Code, results may be "caused" by omission. The draft Bill therefore defines homicide offences in terms of "causing death" rather than of "killing"; and other offences against the person similarly require the "causing" of relevant harms. It seems to us to be desirable to draft some other offences at least (most obviously, offences of damage to property) in the same way, in order to leave fully open to the courts the possibility of so construing the relevant (statutory) provisions as to impose liability for omissions. For to prefer "cause death" to "kill" while retaining "destroy or damage property" might be taken to imply an intention to exclude all liability for omissions in the latter case.' (Vol II, para 7.13)

In LCCP 122 the Law Commission expressed a preference for the approach demonstrated by the CLRC in its 14th Report (above), and this is re-affirmed in Law Com No 218. Clause 19(1) of the Draft Criminal Law Bill (DCLB), contained in Law Com No 218, states:

> 'An offence to which this section applies may be committed by a person who, with the result specified for the offence, omits to do an act that he is under a duty to do at common law. Where this section applies to an offence a person may commit an offence if, with the result specified for the offence, he omits to do an act that he is under a duty to do at common law; and accordingly references to acts include references to omissions.'

By virtue of cl 19(2) of the DCLB, cl 19(1) would apply to intentional serious injury, torture, unlawful detention, kidnapping, abduction and aggravated abduction. Note that the duty to act would have to be one recognised at common law, although the authors of the report describe this as a 'provisional conclusion' (para 6.13). The question remains as to whether or not breaches of statutory duty which are in themselves criminal offences, eg under the Health and Safety at Work Act 1974, should form the basis for prosecutions for serious physical harm or even homicide.

Despite its reluctance to provide expressly for liability for omissions, the Law Commission took the view that liability for failing to limit the scope of harm accidentally caused (ie the *Miller* principle) should be dealt with in the Draft Code, and its restatement and generalisation of the principle appeared in cl 23. The Commission was of the view that the principle should apply to all 'result crimes', although it conceded that the courts have not been willing to extend its application beyond this category of offences: see *Wings Ltd* v *Ellis* [1984] 1 WLR 731, *R* v *Ahmad* (above); and Vol II, paras 8.52, 8.53, of the Code Report. The commentary noted that:

'(i) Nothing in *Miller* limits the principle to a case in which the original act is blameworthy. Although the original act in that case (falling asleep with a lighted cigarette) was no doubt at least careless, the certified question answered in the affirmative by the House of Lords concerned liability for failure to take steps to extinguish, or prevent damage by, a fire started "accidentally" – which must mean (in the terms of clause 23) "[lacking] the fault required [for the offence]". The question was answered without comment upon this aspect.
(ii) For the principle to apply, the actor must become aware of what he has done and of the risk thereby created (paragraph (a)); the act that he then fails to do must be one that might prevent the occurrence or continuance of the result (paragraph (b)); and the result specified for the offence must occur, or (if it has already occurred) must continue, after the failure to act (paragraph (c)).' (Vol II, para 8.54)

Law Com No 218, in DCLB cl 31, restates cl 23 of the Draft Code, with minor modifications in the light of intervening consultation. It provides:

'Where it is an offence to be at fault in causing a result, a person who lacks the fault required when he does an act that may cause, or does cause, the result, he nevertheless commits the offence if –
(a) being aware that he has done the act and that the result may occur or, as the case may be, has occurred and may continue, and
(b) with the fault required,
he fails to take reasonable steps to prevent the result occurring or continuing and it does occur or continue.'

2.4 Involuntary acts

When considering the criminal liability of D in relation to an offence that requires some conduct on his part, or an act producing a particular prohibited consequence, it will be necessary to inquire into whether or not that conduct or act is freely willed. To a limited extent the common law recognises that there should be no criminal liability if D, through no fault of his own, is not in control of his actions when causing a prohibited consequence or engaging in prohibited conduct. Where such a condition arises as a result of mental illness it may be regarded as falling within the scope of the defence of insanity. Where there is no mental illness D may be able to raise the defence of automatism.

Definition

A defendant is regarded as being in a state of automatism when his actions are 'automatic' or, as Lord Denning stated in *Bratty* v *Attorney-General for Northern Ireland* [1963] AC 386, where something was done by the defendant's muscles without the control of his mind. He considered this definition to include such matters as spasms, reflex actions, sleepwalking, nightmares, fits and so on. Whilst this list is broadly descriptive of conditions that fall within the scope of automatism, care must be taken to identify the causes of such behaviour. In *R* v *Burgess* (1991) 93 Cr App R 41, the defendant claimed to have carried out a violent attack upon the victim whilst sleepwalking. In upholding the trial judge's refusal to allow the defence of automatism to go before the jury, Lord Lane CJ commented:

> 'We accept of course that sleep is a normal condition, but the evidence in the instant case indicates that sleep-walking, and particularly violence in sleep, is not normal.'

Automatism is generally associated with the operation of external factors upon the working of the brain, rather than inherent mental defects. In *R* v *Quick* [1973] QB 910, the defendant, a diabetic, was charged with assaulting a patient. The assault occurred whilst the defendant was in a state of hypoglycaemia (low blood sugar level due to an excess of insulin). Following the trial judge's direction that automatism would not be available as a defence, the defendant changed his plea to one of guilty, and then appealed. It was held that the defendant should have been acquitted on the ground of automatism. His unconscious state had been the result of external factors, the taking of insulin, and was of a transitory nature, therefore it could not properly be described as insanity.

The defence is not one of irresistible impulse, neither is it available where the defendant's mind is functioning, albeit imperfectly. This latter point is illustrated by the decision in *Broome* v *Perkins* [1987] RTR 321. The defendant, a diabetic, had lapsed into a hypoglycaemic state whilst driving along a familiar stretch of road, despite having taken a 'Mars Bar' to counteract the effect of insulin. Medical evidence was put forward at his trial that it was possible for the defendant to be in a hypoglycaemic state, and yet still be able to exercise some control over his car. He was charged with driving without due care and attention, but the justices dismissed the case against him on the basis that he had been in a state of automatism at the time of the alleged offence. The prosecution appealed successfully to the Divisional Court however, where it was held that the defendant should have been convicted, given that there was evidence that his mind had still been responding to 'gross stimuli', and thus he had been 'driving' at the time of the offence. Once the actus reus was established, the fault element required for this offence, ie carelessness, could be established objectively. Similarly, in *Attorney-General's Reference (No 2 of 1992)* [1993] 3 WLR 982, where the Court of Appeal rejected the appellant's contention that he had been in a state of automatism, referred to as 'driving without awareness', induced by 'repetitive visual stimulus experienced on long journeys on straight flat roads', Lord Taylor CJ observed:

> 'In our judgment, the "proper evidential foundation" was not laid in this case by ... [the] evidence of "driving without awareness". As the authorities ... show, the defence of automatism requires that there was a total destruction of voluntary control on the defendant's part. Impaired, reduced or partial control is not enough. Professor Brown [who gave expert evidence for the respondent] accepted that someone "driving without awareness" within his description, retains some control. He would be able to steer the vehicle and usually to react and return to full awareness when confronted by significant stimuli.'

The defendant bears an evidential burden in establishing the defence, which means that he must provide sufficient evidence of automatism for a jury to act upon. Whether or not he has done so is a matter of law for the trial judge, but it is apparent from the decided cases dealing with the defence that the defendant will normally need to produce some expert medical evidence as to his mental and physical state at the time of the offence.

In *R* v *T* [1990] Crim LR 256 (a decision of Southan J at Snaresbrook Crown Court), the defendant was a woman aged 23, who had been charged with robbery and actual bodily harm. On being arrested, there was evidence that the defendant was passive and indifferent to what was happening. During a subsequent interview, the defendant was only able to recollect some of the events during which the offences were alleged to have been committed. A week after her arrest the defendant was examined by a prison doctor and found to be suffering from a ruptured hymen and injuries posterior to the hymen. The defendant claimed that she had been raped three days prior to her arrest but had not told anyone about it. A psychiatrist subsequently diagnosed her as suffering from Post Traumatic Stress Disorder as a result of the rape, with the consequence that she had been in a Dissociative State at the time of the alleged offences, not acting with a conscious mind or will. On the basis of *Broome* v *Perkins* (above), the prosecution contended that the evidence showed that the defendant had had some awareness of what had happened, and therefore the only 'defence' open to the defendant was 'insane automatism' under the *M'Naghten* Rules. Southan J ruled that a proper foundation had been laid for the matter to go before the jury. It was his view that an incident such as rape could have an appalling effect on a young woman, however stable, and could satisfy the requirement laid down in *R* v *Quick* that there had to be evidence of 'an external factor' causing a malfunctioning of the mind. Post Traumatic Stress Disorder, involving, as the evidence suggested, a defendant acting as though in a 'dream', could therefore amount to automatism. It is submitted that the court may have been willing to adopt this lenient approach given the somewhat 'one-off' nature of the circumstances.

Availability of automatism as a defence

It is customary to describe automatism as a general defence in criminal law, meaning that it can be raised by way of defence to any criminal charge. Whilst this is broadly correct, there is some debate as to whether automatism can be raised as a defence to crimes of strict liability. The question arises because it is to some extent unclear whether a defence of automatism merely involves a denial of mens rea or whether it also involves a denial of actus reus. In simple terms the question hinges on the meaning given to the phrase 'voluntariness'. If automatism means that a defendant's actions were not voluntary, in that his mind was not controlling his body, then clearly the defence entails a denial of mens rea – this much is universally accepted. It can be argued, however, that an actus reus is only established where it is shown to have been freely willed, or voluntary, and hence a plea of automatism would involve not only a denial of mens rea, but also a denial of actus reus.

The question acquires a practical significance where the defendant is charged with an offence of strict liability, because if an offence requires proof only of actus reus, a defence which involves only a denial of mens rea will be of little significance; alternatively, if automatism does involve a denial of actus reus, then it is one of the few defences that a defendant can raise in respect of strict liability offences.

There are two points that can be made here. First, as is stated by the authors of Smith and Hogan *Criminal Law* (8th ed) p117, it is somewhat fallacious to assume that offences of strict liability require no proof of mens rea. Many so-called strict liability offences do require some mens rea in respect of some elements of the actus reus, hence even if automatism only amounts to a denial of mens rea, it will still afford a defence to such offences. The preferable view, however, is that automatism does negate the actus reus of an offence, on the basis that actus reus inevitably involves a mental element in the form of voluntariness. Not only does this approach have the virtue of recognising the artificiality of the actus reus/mens rea dichotomy (see Lord Diplock's comments in *R* v *Miller*), but it would also result in automatism being a defence to offences of 'absolute' liability, where arguably no mens rea whatsoever need be established on the part of the defendant.

The effect of automatism as a defence

Subject to the above comments concerning strict liability offences, automatism operates as a complete defence, in the sense that if the defendant succeeds in establishing it, he will be acquitted, and the court ceases to have any jurisdiction over him. It is this factor which perhaps explains the reluctance of the courts to recognise the defence of automatism in certain situations.

For example, in *R* v *Sandie Smith* [1982] Crim LR 531 the defendant, who had been charged with making threats to kill, sought to raise the defence of automatism based on the effects of her pre-menstrual tension. The Court of Appeal refused to recognise this as the basis for automatism because, if successful, it would result in the defendant being released into society without the courts being able to exercise any effective control over her. The evidence indicated that the defendant needed to have some medical supervision, and the court would only have the power to ensure this if she was convicted.

Where a defence of automatism is raised, the courts will have to consider whether the defendant should in fact be classified as criminally insane. The defence of insanity is considered below, but for present purposes it can be noted that the crude distinctions between insanity and automatism are that the former is associated with some 'internal' mental defect suffered by the defendant which manifests itself in violence and is prone to recur, whereas the latter is associated with some external factor operating on the mind of the defendant in circumstances that indicate that he is not otherwise a danger to society. Hence, a defendant who injures his wife by striking her in bed whilst he is having a nightmare, would normally be expected to succeed with a defence of automatism. If, however, there is evidence that this behaviour occurred because of some inherent defect on the part of the defendant and that it has happened in the past, or is likely to recur in the future, the jury may be directed to consider whether the defendant is criminally insane. Again the significance of the distinction lies in the fact that the courts have extensive powers of disposal over defendants found to be 'not guilty by reason of insanity', and can thus act to protect other members of society.

Self-induced automatism

A defendant may be prevented from raising the defence of automatism where there is evidence to show that he was in some way at fault in bringing about the state of automatism. Perhaps the most obvious instance of this arises where a defendant voluntarily consumes large amounts of alcohol or other drugs with the result that he ceases to be aware of his actions. Where this is the case, the defendant may be able to rely on the defence of intoxication (see Chapter 14), but not automatism. Similar problems can arise however, where a defendant becomes increasingly drowsy whilst driving his car, and instead of pulling over to the side of the road, he continues to drive, eventually falling asleep at the wheel, and causing an accident. Clearly he was in a state of automatism at the time of the crash, but equally we might say that it was his fault because he could have avoided the problem by ceasing to drive when he first became drowsy.

The principal authority on this point is the Court of Appeal decision in *R* v *Bailey* (1983) 77 Cr App R 76. The defendant, a diabetic, had felt unwell and had taken a mixture of sugar and water, but had not eaten anything. A short time after this he had struck a man on the head with an iron bar. At his trial the defendant faced charges under both ss18 and 20 of the Offences Against the Person Act 1861.

..e claimed that he had been unable to control his actions because he had been in a hypoglycaemic state at the time of the attack. The trial judge directed the jury that the defence of automatism was not available where it was 'self-induced', and the defendant was convicted of the s18 offence. On appeal, the Court of Appeal held that as s18 created a specific intent crime, even self-induced automatism could be relied upon as evidence that the defendant did not have the necessary mens rea for the offence (this is consistent with the availability of self-induced intoxication). In relation to the s20 offence, however, the court held that self-induced automatism would not provide a defence, where there was evidence that the defendant had been reckless in failing to eat after taking the insulin. The recklessness here would involve proof that the defendant had known that his failure to eat might make his actions more aggressive or uncontrollable. As Griffiths LJ stated:

> 'The question in each case will be whether the prosecution have proved the necessary element of recklessness.'

Does this mean, therefore, that if the defendant is charged with an offence involving *Caldwell*-type recklessness, such as criminal damage, he will not succeed with a defence based on self-induced intoxication where he gave no thought to an obvious and serious risk that he might damage property if he did not take certain steps to avoid entering into a state of automatism? See further *R* v *Marison* (1996) The Times 16 July.

Reform

The existing common law defence of non-insane automatism is restated by cl 33 of the Draft Code in the following terms:

> '(1) A person is not guilty of an offence if –
> (a) he acts in a state of automatism, that is, his act –
> (i) is a reflex, spasm or convulsion; or
> (ii) occurs while he is in a condition (whether of sleep, unconsciousness impaired consciousness or otherwise) depriving him of effective control of the act; and
> (b) the act or condition is the result neither of anything done or omitted with the fault required for the offence nor of voluntary intoxication.
> (2) A person is not guilty of an offence by virtue of an omission to act if
> (a) he is physically incapable of acting in the way required; and
> (b) his being so incapable is the result neither of anything done or omitted with the fault required for the offence nor of voluntary intoxication.'

The defence would be available, for example, where D, driving a car, has a sudden 'black-out', as a result of which the car mounts the kerb and comes to rest against a wall. D would not be guilty of driving without due care and attention (Vol I, Appendix B, example 33(i)). The commentary on cl 33(1) emphasises, however, the limited scope of the proposed provision:

> 'The main function of clause 33(1) is to protect a person who acts in a state of automatism from conviction of an offence of strict liability. It is conceded that he does

"the act" specified for the offence; but the clause declares him not guilty. One charged
with an offence requiring fault in the form of failure to comply with a standard of
conduct may also have to rely on the clause. On the other hand, a state of automatism will
negative a fault requirement of intention or knowledge or (normally) recklessness; so a
person charged with an offence of violence against another, or of criminal damage,
committed when he was in a condition of impaired consciousness, does not rely on this
clause for his acquittal but on the absence of the fault element of the offence.' (Vol II,
para 11.2)

References in cl 33(1) to spasms and reflex actions clearly derive from obiter
statements of Lord Denning in *Bratty* v *Attorney-General for Northern Ireland*
(above). The Law Commission felt, however, that inclusion of references to a
'condition (whether of sleep, unconsciousness, impaired consciousness or otherwise)'
depriving the defendant of effective control over his actions, was justified:

> '... both on principle and by some of the leading cases. The governing principle should be
> that a person is not guilty of an offence if, without relevant fault on his part, he cannot
> choose to act otherwise than as he does. The acts of the defendants in several cases have
> been treated as automatous although it is far from clear, and even unlikely, that they were
> entirely unconscious when they did the acts and although it cannot confidently be said
> that they exercised no control. in any sense of that phrase, over their relevant movements
> [eg *R* v *Kemp* [1957] 1 QB 399; *R* v *Quick* [1973] QB 910].' (Vol II, para 11.3)

The Commission was especially critical of decisions such as that in *Broome* v *Perkins*
(considered above), commenting that:

> '... it seems clear that D's condition was such that he could not choose to behave
> otherwise than as he did. Cases such as those we have mentioned above appear not to
> have been referred to. Finding it necessary to choose between the authorities, we propose
> a formula under which we expect (and indeed hope) that a person in the condition of the
> defendant in *Broome* v *Perkins* would be acquitted (subject to the question of prior fault).'
> (Vol II, para 11.4)

The doctrine of prior fault, developed at common law in decisions such as *R* v
Bailey (above), is incorporated in the Draft Code, as regards offences of strict
liability and negligence, at 33(1)(b), and (2)(b).

A defendant charged with an offence involving intention or recklessness who is
found to have been in a state of automatism at the time of the offence due to his
own prior fault would be dealt with under cl 22(6) of the Draft Code.

Clause 33(2) seeks to provide a defence where a person omits to act in a manner
required by law because of physical incapacity. For example, D's car passes a red
traffic light whilst he is in a state of automatism. D is not guilty of failing to comply
with a traffic sign. Similarly, D is involved in a traffic accident which he is under a
duty to report to the police within 24 hours. He is seriously injured in the accident
and spends more than a day in intensive care. He is not guilty of the offence of
failing to report the accident. (Vol I, Appendix B, examples 33(iv) and 33(v)).

For an explanation of references to voluntary intoxication as that phrase is used
in the Code, see cl 22.

3

Mens Rea

3.1 The nature of mens rea

As has been outlined above, mens rea is the term used to describe the state of mind that a defendant must be proved to have had at the time he committed the actus reus of an offence.

Why is mens rea necessary?

One might legitimately ask why mens rea should need to be proved. It would be far more straightforward in many ways if all offences were offences of strict liability, with the defendant's state of mind taken into account as a mitigating factor where necessary. If there is a simple answer, it perhaps lies in the fact that the existence of mens rea justifies punishment. With the notable exception of strict liability, the criminal law does not punish a man for his actions alone. The prohibited actions must be accompanied by a culpable state of mind. The mens rea that must be established can be discovered either by looking at past decisions, as in the case of common law offences such as murder, or by looking at the statute which creates the offence, such as the Criminal Damage Act 1971.

Some states of mind are regarded as being more culpable than others. Hence a defendant who deliberately commits a prohibited act should normally be punished more severely than one who recklessly or carelessly commits the same act.

48

Furthermore, there are some offences for which a defendant can only be punished if his actions can be shown to have been deliberate, recklessness or carelessness not being sufficient (see s18 Offences Against the Person Act 1861). It should be borne in mind that the allocation of a particular type of mens rea to an offence is a matter of judicial and legislative policy, not science. A question to bear in mind, when considering some of the judicial pronouncements on mens rea, is the extent to which the judges have given sufficient weight to the link between mens rea and punishment.

Subjective mens rea/objective mens rea

It is common to find criminal lawyers referring to a type of mens rea as 'objective' or 'subjective'. This jargon can be a little mystifying to the beginner, so a brief explanation is provided here. Subjective mens rea is based on what the defendant himself actually thought. One would ask questions such as: did the defendant foresee a particular consequence? Where subjective mens rea has to be established the jury must, so far as they possibly can, put themselves in the position of the defendant. They are not permitted to come to the conclusion that he had the necessary mens rea because he 'must have known' that something was going to happen. The question is whether he really did know that a particular consequence would occur.

Where the mens rea involved in an offence is objective, the jury can judge the defendant by the standard of the reasonable man. The defendant will be responsible for causing a particular result, such as criminal damage, if the jury members are convinced, beyond all reasonable doubt, that a reasonable person would have foreseen the consequence. In effect, if they themselves would have foreseen it. It should be obvious that it will be far easier for the prosecution to establish an objective type of mens rea than a subjective one. Such an analysis is, of necessity, simplistic. More complex formulations may be possible which are less easy to classify. An intermediate test might be, would a reasonable person, with the characteristics of the defendant, have been aware of the risks created by a particular activity?

Terminology

As has been mentioned above, one of the confusing aspects of any study of mens rea is the profusion of terms used to describe the different states of mind involved. Intention may seem like a straightforward concept, but one has to distinguish between 'purpose' intent and 'foresight' intent, 'direct' intent and 'oblique' intent, 'basic' intent and 'specific' intent. In addition there are states of mind which are not readily explained by the terms used, such as 'wilfully', and 'maliciously'. The various forms of intention and recklessness will be explored in some detail in the remainder of this chapter. Other expressions will be explained as and when they arise in the context of specific offences dealt with in subsequent chapters.

3.2 Intention

Judges are fond of describing intention as a perfectly ordinary English word that needs little in the way of explanation by a trial judge addressing a jury. If this were so, there would be very little case law on the matter. The truth is that the meaning of intention in English criminal law is somewhat unclear at present. One might go so far as to suggest that there is no legal definition of the concept, simply rules as to how juries are to go about the task of divining its existence. What follows is intended as a simple and generalised guide to the issues involved.

'Purpose' type intent

What the layman would readily recognise as intent is frequently referred to by lawyers as 'purpose' type intent. This involves a defendant not only foreseeing that his actions will bring about a particular consequence, but also a desire, or purpose, on his part that this consequence should occur. The typical example is that of the defendant, possibly an assassin, who places a bomb on a plane carrying passengers. He foresees that passengers will be killed and it is his purpose to cause death. There are relatively few offences requiring proof of 'purpose' type intent, possibly because of the heavy evidential burden that it throws onto the prosecution where it has to be established. At common law it was thought that the offence of attempt required this type of intent, but the statutory form of the offence that has supplanted it appears to be made out upon proof of intention based on foresight. See further s1(1) of the Criminal Attempts Act 1981, and *R* v *Walker & Hayles* (1990) 90 Cr App R 226.

The House of Lords had an opportunity to consider the meaning of purpose in *Chandler* v *DPP* [1964] AC 763. The appellants, who were demonstrators opposed to nuclear weapons, planned to demonstrate their opposition by occupying an RAF airfield and preventing aircraft from taking off. They were convicted of conspiring to enter a prohibited place for a purpose prejudicial to the interests of the state, contrary to s1 of the Official Secrets Act 1911. The appellants contended that their purpose had not been to prejudice the interests or safety of the state; on the contrary, they believed that the state would be safer without such weapons, and on that basis appealed against the conviction. It was held by the House of Lords, that a distinction had to be drawn between the 'aims' of the appellants and the 'purpose' with which the appellants had acted. The aim of their actions, or the motive behind them, might have been the perfectly laudable one of ridding the country of nuclear weapons, but the Act required evidence of purpose, which their Lordships took to mean 'immediate purpose' not the long term goals of the appellants. It was not disputed that the immediate purpose of the appellants had been to prevent aircraft from taking off; that having been established it was then a matter of evidence, as provided by the government of the day, as to whether such action would have been prejudicial to the interests of the state.

Intention based on proof of foresight

As indicated above, to require proof that it was the defendant's purpose to bring about a particular consequence may involve placing a very heavy evidential burden on the prosecution. It is possible that this may produce some anomalous results. Take the well known example of the defendant who insures an aircraft for many millions of pounds and plants bomb on board, timed to explode when the aircraft is in mid-flight. Suppose that the bomb explodes, destroying the aeroplane and killing all on board. It seems sensible enough to say that the defendant intended to kill the passengers, but in what sense is the word 'intended' being used here? If one asks what the defendant's purpose was, the answer must surely be the destruction of the aircraft, in order that he might recover the insurance monies. The defendant might even express the pious hope that he had wanted all the passengers to escape unharmed, as if by some miracle. Again, the response of the layman would be: 'He must have known that passengers were going to be killed', ie the defendant must have foreseen that passengers would be killed. The difficulty has been in determining whether the law should reflect the layman's view, or should adopt a narrower approach to foresight and intention.

What is foresight?

In *DPP* v *Smith* [1961] AC 290 the House of Lords, in considering the meaning of intention, adopted an objective approach to the concept of foresight, holding that a defendant could be presumed to have foreseen the natural and probable consequences of his actions. Hence, a defendant could be regarded as having intended a consequence if a reasonable person would have foreseen it. This decision was subject to much criticism, principally because it was at odds with the notion that mens rea should be the defendant's state of mind and no one else's, but it was not until Parliament enacted s8 of the Criminal Justice Act 1967 that the law was amended. Section 8 provides:

> 'A court or jury in determining whether a person has committed an offence –
> a) shall not be bound in law to infer that he intended or foresaw a result of his actions by reason only of its being a natural and probable consequence of those actions; but
> b) shall decide whether he did intend or foresee that result by reference to all the evidence, drawing such inferences from the evidence as appear proper in the circumstances.'

The section does not say when foresight is relevant, as that is an issue to be determined by looking at the nature of the mens rea required by the specific offence under consideration. What the section does make clear is that foresight is a subjective concept. The jury must have regard to what the defendant foresaw. They should not make assumptions based on what they as individuals would have foreseen, or on what they think a reasonable person would have foreseen. Additionally, it should be noted that, where a direction is given on intent, a failure to remind the jury that foresight is evidence of intent (and not to be equated with it) is likely to result in any subsequent conviction being quashed on the basis of a misdirection: see *R* v *Scalley* [1995] Crim LR 504.

When will the evidence of foresight justify a conclusion that the defendant intended a consequence?

This is a question that has troubled the higher courts on a number of occasions since 1975 although, as will be seen, the House of Lords may well have succeeded in settling the issue for the foreseeable future. In *Hyam* v *DPP* [1975] AC 55 the House of Lords (by a majority) held that foresight on the part of the defendant that his actions were likely, or highly likely, to cause death or grievous bodily harm was sufficient mens rea for murder. The decision was unsatisfactory for a number of reasons, not least because even amongst those Law Lords forming the majority there were conflicting reasons for arriving at this conclusion. Note that the test suggested in *Hyam* also suggested a relatively low level of foresight would suffice as evidence of intention.

The House of Lords returned to the matter on a number of occasions during the 1980s, notably in *R* v *Moloney* [1985] 1 All ER 1025 and *R* v *Hancock and Shankland* [1986] 2 WLR 257. In *Moloney* Lord Bridge indicated that the approach to intention in *Hyam* was too broad and that a jury (in a murder trial) should be directed to consider whether the death or grievous bodily harm was a natural consequence of the defendant's act. If it was they should consider whether the defendant foresaw it as such. If they were satisfied that he did have such foresight they could properly conclude that he intended death or grievous bodily harm. As regards the degree of foresight required, Lord Bridge observed (at p1036) that 'the probability of the consequence taken to have been foreseen must be little short of overwhelming before it will suffice to establish the necessary intent.'

In *Hancock* the defendants were miners taking part in a strike in South Wales. They had taken up position on a bridge over a motorway, knowing that miners who were not willing to come out on strike would be using the road and passing under the bridge. When a taxi carrying a working miner approached, the defendants dropped two large blocks of concrete over the bridge. One of the blocks fell through the windscreen of the car and killed its driver. The defendants were convicted of murdering the taxi driver, the trial judge having given the jury the *Moloney* guidelines on establishing intent. The defendants, who had been willing to plead guilty to manslaughter, appealed on the ground that their intention had been to block the road and frighten other miners into supporting the strike, not to cause death or serious injury. The Court of Appeal quashed the convictions, the Lord Chief Justice expressing considerable doubt as to the correctness of the *Moloney* guidelines.

The Crown appealed unsuccessfully to the House of Lords where it was held, Lord Scarman giving the main speech, that the *Moloney* guidelines on the relationship between foresight and intention were unsatisfactory in that they were likely to mislead a jury. His Lordship expressed the view that in the majority of cases juries should be left to determine for themselves whether a defendant intended a particular consequence, as it was a matter to which they could apply their own common sense. Where, however, a jury requested some guidance from the trial judge, he should explain to them that intention was not to be equated with foresight of consequences, but could be established if there was evidence that the defendant had foreseen a particular consequence. The stronger the evidence that he did foresee a consequence, then the greater the justification for the jury inferring that the defendant therefore intended the consequence. What Lord Scarman deliberately refrains from explaining is how much foresight is required for a jury to be justified in inferring that the defendant had the necessary intent. Does a defendant intend a consequence where he foresees it as probable, or must he foresee it as highly probable, or almost certain? It did little credit to English criminal law that such a basic concept as the meaning of intention should be shrouded in so much mystery, but in a practical, even cynical, sense, for as long as intention had no fixed meaning in law, there was less likelihood of judges misdirecting juries on the point, and thus creating opportunities for defendants to appeal against their convictions.

Notwithstanding Lord Scarman's reluctance to specify the nature of intention based on foresight, the Court of Appeal in *R v Nedrick* (1986) 83 Cr App R 267 took the opportunity to provide the type of guidance Lord Scarman had considered unnecessary. The defendant had been convicted of murder following a direction from the trial judge on the meaning of intention that was based largely on the, by now, discredited decision in *Hyam*. Quashing the conviction, and substituting it with a conviction for manslaughter, Lord Lane CJ summarised the position as follows at (p270):

'When determining whether the defendant had the necessary intent, it may therefore be helpful for a jury to ask themselves two questions: 1. How probable was the consequence that resulted from the defendant's voluntary act? 2. Did he foresee that consequence? If he did not appreciate that death or really serious harm was likely to result from his act, he cannot have intended to bring it about. If he did, but thought that the risk to which he was exposing the person killed was only slight, then it may be easy for the jury to conclude that he did not intend to bring about that result. On the other hand, if the jury are satisfied that at the material time the defendant recognised that death or serious harm would be virtually certain (barring some unforeseen intervention) to result from his voluntary act, then that is a fact from which they may find it easy to infer that he intended to kill or do serious bodily harm, even though he may not have had any desire to achieve that result. ... Where the charge is murder and in the rare cases where the simple direction is not enough, the jury should be directed that they are not entitled to infer the necessary intention, unless they feel sure that death or serious bodily harm was a virtual certainty (barring some unforeseen intervention) as a result of the defendant's actions and that the defendant appreciated that such was the case. Where a man realises that it is for all practical purposes inevitable that his actions will result in death or serious harm, the inference may be irresistible that he intended that result, however little he may have desired or wished it to happen. The decision is one for the jury to be reached upon a consideration of all the evidence.'

Note that there is a subtle but significant shift here, from the jury being entitled to infer intent from evidence of foresight, to their not being entitled to do so unless the evidence discloses a minimum level of foresight, ie that of virtual certainty, that requires further scrutiny.

Given that it provides some helpful clarification, is Lord Lane's approach inconsistent with that of Lord Scarman in *Hancock*? The House of Lords has now made clear that the answer to that question is 'no'.

In *R v Woollin* [1998] 4 All ER 103 the House of Lords considered an appeal by a defendant who had been convicted of murder having thrown his three-month-old son on to a hard surface, causing fatal head injuries. At the trial the issue arose as to whether the defendant had intended to cause grievous bodily harm. The trial judge gave the jury a *Nedrick* direction, but went on to advise them that they could nevertheless convict if they were sure that the defendant had recognised that there was a substantial risk of grievous bodily harm resulting from his actions. Following conviction the Court of Appeal dismissed the defendant's appeal, holding that a *Nedrick*-type direction was only required where the evidence of intent was limited to the admitted actions of the accused – it was unnecessary where there was other evidence. Allowing the appeal, and substituting a conviction for manslaughter, the House of Lords held that the conviction was unsafe as the trial judge had, by his direction, blurred the distinction between intention and recklessness. The House of Lords confirmed that the approach of the Court of Appeal in *Nedrick* was correct, and the use of the *Nedrick* direction was not limited in its application as had been suggested by the Court of Appeal. Addressing the fact that in *Hancock* Lord Scarman had been reluctant to provide much in the way of guidance for juries regarding the task of determining whether or not there was evidence of intention, Lord Steyn observed (at p110b–c):

'... imagine that in a case such as *R v Hancock* the jury sent a note to the judge to the following effect:

"We are satisfied that the defendant, though he did not want to cause serious harm, knew that it was probable that his act would cause serious bodily harm. We are not sure whether a probability is enough for murder. Please explain."

One may alter the question by substituting "highly probable" for "probable". Or one may imagine the jury asking whether a foresight of a "substantial risk" that the defendant's act would cause serious injury was enough. What is the judge to say to the jury? *R v Hancock* does not rule out an answer by the judge but it certainly does not explain how such questions are to be answered. It is well known that judges were sometimes advised to deflect such questions by the statement that "intention" is an ordinary word in the English language. That is surely an unhelpful response to what may be a sensible question. In these circumstances it is not altogether surprising that in *R v Nedrick* the Court of Appeal felt compelled to provide a model direction for the assistance of trial judges.'

Turning to the Crown's submission that *Nedrick* was in conflict with *Hancock*, Lord Steyn observed (at p111f–h):

> 'Counsel [for the Crown] argued that in order to bring some coherence to the process of determining intention Lord Lane CJ [in *Nedrick*] specified a minimum level of foresight, namely virtual certainty. But that is not in conflict with the decision in *R v Hancock*, which, apart from disapproving Lord Bridge's "natural consequence" model direction, approved *R v Moloney* in all other respects. And in *R v Moloney* ... Lord Bridge said that if a person foresees the probability of a consequence as little short of overwhelming, this "will suffice to establish the necessary intent" (my emphasis). Nor did the House in *R v Hancock* rule out the framing of model directions by the Court of Appeal for the assistance of trial judges. I would therefore reject the argument that the guidance given in *R v Nedrick* was in conflict with the decision of the House in *R v Hancock*.'

Having expressed a preference for trial judges directing juries in terms of being entitled to 'find' intention rather than infer it from evidence of foresight, Lord Steyn concluded by observing that the model direction in *Nedrick* was now a tried and tested formula that trial judges ought to continue to use. Note the reference to the jury being entitled to find that there was intent. If there is evidence that D foresaw death of grievous bodily harm as virtually certain ought they not be bound to find that there was intent?

Specific and basic intent

In simple terms, basic intent is the mens rea that relates to the actus reus committed by the defendant. For example, in the 'simple' offence of criminal damage, the actus reus comprises the damage or destruction of another's property; the mens rea need not go beyond an intention to do criminal damage. An offence of specific intent is one where the mens rea goes beyond the actus reus in the sense that the defendant has some ulterior purpose in mind. An example is provided by the offence of 'aggravated' criminal damage. This offence is committed where a defendant causes damage or destruction to property with the intention of thereby endangering life. The actus reus, it will be noted, is almost identical to that of the simple offence; the differentiating factor is the further or specific intent that the defendant must possess to endanger life. This issue is considered in more depth in the context of intoxication: see Chapter 14.

Reform

Clause 18 of the Draft Code proposed a definition of intent encompassing the situations where the defendant hoped or knew that a circumstance existed or would exist, or where he acted to bring about a result or was aware that it would occur as a result of his actions in the ordinary course of events.

Despite the evidence that the senior judiciary did not favour a settled definition for intention, as indicated by comments in both *R v Moloney,* and *R v Hancock and*

Shankland, the Law Commission, in the Code Report, sought to justify the position taken by asserting:

> 'We remain of the opinion that it is in the interest of clarity and the consistent application of criminal law to define intention; and that justice requires the inclusion of the case where the defendant knows that his act will cause the relevant result, "in the ordinary course of events" … It is possible that, under the Code, juries will, in a few cases, find intention to be proved where, under the existing law, they might not have done so.' (para 8.16)

The basis provided by cl 18 of the Draft Code has been exploited by the Law Commission in Law Com No 218, with the result that cl 1(a) of the DCLB provides that a defendant acts 'intentionally' with respect to a result when:

> '(i) it is his purpose to cause it, or
> (ii) although it is not his purpose to cause it, he knows that it would occur in the ordinary course of events if he were to succeed in his purpose of causing some other result …'

The commentary in Law Com No 218 envisages that the vast majority of cases where intent has to be proved will fall within 1(a)(i), but accepts that it is the formulation of intent in 1(a)(ii) that is likely to attract most academic discussion. The use of the phrase 'in the ordinary course of events' was to ensure that the proposed definition of intention covered the defendant who knows that the achievement of his purpose will *necessarily* involve the causing of some further event in the absence of some wholly unforeseeable supervening event. The preference for the requirement that the defendant should have to know of the risk of the result occurring, rather than merely be aware of the risk, is designed to prevent any possible overlap between recklessness and intent. The definition treats the defendant as intending a consequence if he knows that it is a necessary concomitant of achieving his main purpose if that purpose is to be achieved. For example, the terrorist cannot be sure that his bomb will go off, but he knows that it must if he is to achieve the destruction of the police station where he has planted it. Clause 1(a)(ii) also excludes the possibility of liability where it is the defendant's intention to avoid harm. Law Com No 218 (para 7.13) gives the example of a father throwing his child from a blazing building to avoid certain death, in the knowledge that the child will be injured on hitting the ground. As the commentary explains:

> 'In the example … the father … has as his purpose to prevent injury to the child. He acts to achieve that purpose, however difficult or unlikely that may be in the circumstances. If, applying clause 1(a)(ii), he were to succeed in his purpose, injury to the child would, of necessity and by definition, not occur. Clause 1(a)(ii) therefore excludes any suggestion that in a (hypothetical) case [such as in the example given] injuries that in fact occur, though sought to be avoided, were inflicted intentionally.'

3.3 Recklessness

Perhaps the majority of significant offences in criminal law require proof of either intention or recklessness on the part of the defendant. The result is that the prosecution can secure a conviction for an offence without going as far as proving that the defendant intended to commit it, recklessness being sufficient. Central to the concept of recklessness is the fact that the defendant is, in reality, being punished for taking an unjustified risk. Clearly many human activities involve risk of injury to person or property, but a distinction is drawn between those that have some social utility and those that do not. Hence the brain surgeon performing a delicate operation is taking the risk that the patient might not survive the operation, but the risk here would normally be regarded as justifiable on the basis that there is a high degree of social utility associated with it. By contrast, the vandal throwing a brick over a high wall is taking the risk that there may be a person on the other side who may be injured, or some property that may be damaged. His actions would be labelled as reckless in the sense that they have no apparent social utility.

Subjective recklessness

If it is accepted that recklessness is concerned with the taking of unjustifiable risks, the second issue that arises is the basis upon which liability for recklessness is to be imposed. Should a defendant have to be aware of the risk that he is taking, or should it be sufficient that a reasonable man would have realised that the risk involved was obvious?

Until the House of Lords' decision in *Commissioner of Police of the Metropolis* v *Caldwell* (considered below), recklessness was widely understood to be a subjective concept, based on what the defendant foresaw. The leading modern authority was the decision of the Court of Appeal in *R* v *Cunningham* [1957] 2 QB 396. The defendant had entered the basement of a building and ripped a gas meter from the wall in order to remove the money that it contained. In his efforts the defendant ruptured the gas supply pipes with the result that gas escaped and seeped through the porous basement wall into an adjoining property, which was occupied. He was convicted of maliciously administering a noxious substance, contrary to s23 of the Offences Against the Person Act 1861, following a direction from the trial judge that the jury were to convict if they were satisfied that the defendant's action had been 'wicked'. The Court of Appeal, allowing the defendant's appeal, held that for a defendant to have acted 'maliciously' as was required by this offence, there had to be proof that he had intended to cause the harm in question, or had been reckless as to whether such harm would be caused. In this context recklessness involved the defendant in being aware of the risk that his actions might cause the prohibited consequence.

Objective recklessness

In *Commissioner of Police of the Metropolis* v *Caldwell* [1982] AC 341 a majority of Law Lords endorsed the introduction of a new form of recklessness into English criminal law – a recklessness based not simply on the defendant's foresight of a risk, but one that encompassed also his failure to consider a risk that would have been obvious to the reasonable man. In *Commissioner of Police of the Metropolis* v *Caldwell*, the defendant, who had been sacked from his employment at a hotel, became drunk and returned at night to the hotel, setting it on fire. There were ten people resident in the hotel at the time, but the fire was discovered and extinguished before any serious harm could be caused. The defendant pleaded guilty to a charge under s1(1) of the Criminal Damage Act 1971, but pleaded not guilty to the more serious charge under s1(2) of the 1971 Act, which alleged criminal damage with intent to endanger life or recklessness as to whether life would be endangered. His contention was that due to his drunken state it had never crossed his mind that lives might be endangered by his actions, he had simply set fire to the hotel because of his grudge against his former employer. On appeal, one of the questions certified for consideration by the House of Lords was that of whether or not the defendant had been reckless as to whether the life of another would be endangered, within the meaning of s1(2)(b) of the 1971 Act. The House of Lords held, inter alia (Lords Wilberforce and Edmund-Davies dissenting), that a defendant was to be regarded as reckless where he created an obvious risk of a particular type of harm occurring, and either went on to take that risk, or failed to give any thought to its existence.

The House of Lords in this case did not overrule *Cunningham*; far from it – the speeches of the majority re-affirm its existence as a form of recklessness in criminal law. The significance of the decision is the introduction of an alternative form of recklessness based upon the defendant's failure to advert to a risk that would have been obvious to the reasonable person. How did Lord Diplock (who gave the leading speech on behalf of the majority) justify this extension of liability? His Lordship noted that the *Cunningham* definition of recklessness had come about in the course of attempting to define the term 'maliciously' as it appeared in the Offences Against the Person Act 1861. He felt that in that particular context the form of recklessness identified by the courts would of necessity have to be somewhat restricted, requiring some reference to the foresight of consequences on the part of the accused. He further noted, however, that the Criminal Damage Act 1971 had replaced the Malicious Damage Act of 1861, and that Parliament had chosen to use the word 'reckless' to denote the mens rea rather than 'maliciously'. In Lord Diplock's view this lead to the conclusion that *Cunningham* was not an appropriate authority for use in the interpretation of recklessness as used in the context of a modern statute. As he expressed it, the restricted meaning given to recklessness in *Cunningham*:

> '... was not directed to and consequently has no bearing on the meaning of the adjective "reckless" in section 1 of the Criminal Damage Act 1971. To use it for that purpose can, in my view, only be misleading.'

Lord Diplock concluded by summarising his view in the following terms:

'In my opinion, a person charged with an offence under section 1(1) of the Criminal Damage Act 1971 is "reckless as to whether any such property would be destroyed or damaged" if (1) he does an act which in fact creates an obvious risk that property will be destroyed or damaged and (2) when he does the act he either has not given any thought to the possibility of there being any such risk or has recognised that there was some risk involved and has nonetheless gone on to do it. That would be a proper direction to the jury; cases in the Court of Appeal which held otherwise should be regarded as overruled.'

Lord Diplock firmly rejected the use of 'jargon' such as 'objective' or 'subjective' to describe the type of mens rea involved, stating that mens rea must by definition be the state of mind of the accused as opposed to the state of mind of some mythical reasonable man, but subsequent cases have emphasised the objective nature of what has come to be known as *Caldwell* recklessness.

In *R* v *Lawrence* [1981] 2 WLR 524, where the defendant motor cyclist, who had collided with and killed a pedestrian, was charged with causing death by reckless driving contrary to s1 of the Road Traffic Act 1972, Lord Diplock stated that:

'Recklessness on the part of the doer of an act does presuppose that there is something in the circumstances that would have drawn the attention of an ordinary prudent individual to the possibility that his act was capable of causing the kind of serious harmful consequences that the section which creates the offence was intended to prevent ...'

Despite Lord Diplock's protestations to the contrary it is submitted that this points clearly to an objective basis for liability. Once a risk that would have been obvious to a reasonable man is shown to have existed, all that is needed is evidence that the defendant never thought about it. It is almost as if omitting to think has been elevated to the status of mens rea. Such criticisms have not gone unanswered by the House of Lords. In *R* v *Reid* [1992] 3 All ER 673, where their lordships confirmed their support for Lord Diplock's view of recklessness as illustrated in *R* v *Lawrence*, with reference to the debate as to the subjective/objective nature of the mens rea involved, Lord Keith stated (p674h–j):

'Absence of something from a person's state of mind is as much part of his state of mind as is its presence. Inadvertence to risk is no less a subjective state of mind than is disregard of a recognised risk.'

This decision also gave the House of Lords the opportunity to assess the alleged inconsistency in Lord Diplock's dictum to the effect that inadvertent recklessness required awareness of an obvious and serious risk, whilst advertent recklessness required evidence that the driver had failed to think about 'some' risk. Rejecting the contention that any such anomaly existed, Lord Keith stated (p675h–j):

'"Any such risk" is not referring to obvious and serious risk but merely to the risk of causing physical injury or substantial damage to property. "Some risk" means some risk of the same thing. There is thus no inconsistency.'

Lord Goff, whilst agreeing with this analysis, went on to add (at p691j):

> '... Lord Diplock's requirement that the risk be obvious must logically relate only to his first category of recklessness; it cannot be relevant where the defendant is in fact aware that there is some risk of the relevant kind.'

If one accepts that there is at least some sound public policy basis for punishing a 'thoughtless' defendant, does this extend to punishing a defendant to whom the risk of harm could never have occurred? The question arose for consideration in *Elliot* v *C* [1983] 1 WLR 939. The defendant, an educationally subnormal 14-year-old schoolgirl, had entered a neighbour's garden shed, poured white spirit on the floor and ignited it. The defendant had then fled as the shed burst into flames. The magistrates dismissed a charge under s1(1) of the Criminal Damage Act 1971, on the basis that the defendant would not have been aware of the risk of damage to property even if she had given thought to the matter. The prosecution appealed by way of case stated to the Divisional Court where it was held, allowing the appeal, that there was no room for importing a subjective element into the definition of recklessness propounded by Lord Diplock in *Caldwell* and *Lawrence*. Robert Goff LJ acknowledged the obvious unfairness in judging someone such as the defendant by the standard of the reasonable adult, but felt constrained to follow the House of Lords' decisions. The House of Lords subsequently refused a petition for leave to appeal, and the decision was subsequently confirmed by the Court of Appeal in *R* v *Stephen Malcom R* (1984) 79 Cr App R 334, and more recently in *R* v *Coles* [1994] Crim LR 820. There might still be a case for arguing that an exception could be made in the case of an educationally sub-normal defendant, on the basis of views expressed by Lord Goff in *R* v *Reid*, to the effect that a defendant might not be regarded as reckless where his ability to appreciate risk was adversely affected by illness, although it is conceded that in *Coles* there was little evidence to justify such a conclusion.

The lacuna argument

In the course of his speech in *Lawrence* (above), Lord Diplock expressed the view that, once a jury was satisfied that a defendant had, by his actions, created an obvious and serious risk of harm, a jury would be entitled to infer either that he had given no thought to it, or that he had been aware of the risk, unless the defendant gave an explanation as to his state of mind that displaced the inference. In other words, a finding of recklessness on the part of the defendant was an automatic consequence of the jury's finding that he had created an obvious and serious risk of harm, unless the defendant put forward evidence of some other state of mind.

It has since been contended that this 'other' state of mind might arise where the defendant considered whether there was a risk of harm and, for quite plausible reasons, wrongly concluded that there was no risk. The contention is that such a defendant is not *Cunningham* reckless because he does not think that he is taking a risk, yet neither is he *Caldwell* reckless because, far from having given no thought to the risk, he has given considerable thought to it, albeit coming to the wrong conclusion as to its significance. The possibility that such a gap or *lacuna* existed between the two established concepts of recklessness was adverted to by the Divisional Court *Chief Constable of Avon and Somerset* v *Shimmen* (1987) 84 Cr App R 7. The defendant had broken a shop window whilst demonstrating his martial arts skills to his friends. He had made as if to kick at the shop window intending to stop with his foot a fraction away from the glass, thus displaying his self-control. Confirming his liability on a charge of criminal damage, the court held that, whilst on the facts there was evidence that the defendant had been reckless in that he had been aware of the risk of damage to the window, there was at least scope for the argument that a defendant might not be reckless where he genuinely believed he had taken sufficient precautions to preclude harm from occurring. See further *R* v *Crossman* [1986] Crim LR 406 where the lacuna was not considered but perhaps should have been.

More significant recognition of the lacuna theory has been granted by the House of Lords in *Reid* (above). The appellant was driving a car with a passenger in the front seat. He attempted to overtake another car whilst still in the nearside lane. A taxi drivers' rest hut protruded some six feet into the nearside lane. The appellant's car struck the hut whilst he was attempting the overtaking manoeuvre, the collision resulting in the death of his passenger. The appellant was convicted of causing death by reckless driving, contrary to s1 Road Traffic Act 1972 (as amended by the Road Traffic Act 1988). Their Lordships recognised that there were three situations where the exact form of words used by Lord Diplock may require some alteration to take account of the unusual facts of a particular case: first, where the driver acted under some understandable or excusable mistake of fact. Lord Ackner appeared to accept counsel for the Crown's example of such a case where the driver of a left hand drive car overtaking on the brow of a hill is misinformed as to the safety of doing so by his passenger. His Lordship added an example of his own where the driver of a powerful car attempts an apparently safe manoeuvre that becomes dangerous because of a wholly unexpected fuel line blockage. Lord Goff accepted that:

'... if the defendant is addressing his mind to the possibility of risk and suffers from a bona fide mistake as to specific fact which if true would have excluded the risk, he cannot be described as reckless.'

The second situation was where the driver's capacity to appreciate risk had been adversely affected by some condition (illness or shock, per Lord Goff at p690 h–j) arising otherwise than through the fault of the driver, and the third where the driver acted under duress.

A possible grey area remains in cases where the defendant creates an obvious and serious risk of harm, but does not regard it as a danger because of steps that he is about to take to nullify it. An example arose in *R* v *Merrick* [1996] 1 Cr App R 130, with D offering a 'service' to householders whereby he would remove television cabling attached to their properties where the owners of the cables (with whom D was in dispute) had not been granted permission to run the cables or refused to make wayleave payments in respect of the cable runs. In response to a charge of criminal damage (being reckless as to whether life would be endangered – the allegation being that, in the course of removing a piece of equipment, he had left a live mains cable exposed for approximately five minutes before cementing it underground), D contended that he knew that leaving a live wire exposed would represent a danger, but he had come prepared to deal with the danger and would not have undertaken the work unless he had felt competent to leave the installation in a safe condition. The Court of Appeal, upholding the conviction, held that if D were to avail himself of the lacuna doctrine, he had to show that he had taken precautions to prevent any risk from arising, rather than acting to limit the risk once he had caused a danger to arise. As Hidden J observed (at p137):

> 'There is a clear distinction to be drawn between the avoiding of a risk and the taking of steps to remedy a risk which has already been created. If an accused person is successfully to contend that the taking of certain steps has prevented him from falling within the definition then those steps must be ones directed towards preventing the risk at all, rather than remedying it once it has arisen. The appellant in this case was unable to do that. He accepted that he had created a risk by exposing the cable and further that the cable was exposed for six minutes before he dealt with it. Though he said that he took reasonable precautions to eliminate the danger using the materials that he had brought with him for that purpose, by then he was inevitably remedying a risk that he had already created rather than preventing the risk which arose when the live wire was exposed.'

This conclusion may, with respect, be open to question. Assuming that, by cutting the cable, D intentionally damaged property belonging to another, it seems perverse to contend that it was his intention thereby to endanger life, given that he intended to render the site safe before leaving it. Similarly, whilst D was well aware of the danger to life presented by the live wire per se, he would not have foreseen any risk of life being endangered, because the live wire was under his supervision whilst exposed, and was subsequently buried. In other words D thought about the risk and decided there was no (significant) risk. To deny D the opportunity to pray in aid the lacuna argument because his steps to minimise the risk occured after it had been created seems unsustainable.

Examples of cases illustrating the lacuna issue may be very rare, but the existence of the lacuna is vital if the automatic inference of recklessness mentioned above is not to prevail.

Cunningham *or* Caldwell *recklessness?*

A situation now exists whereby there are two distinct concepts of recklessness in criminal law: what might be broadly termed subjective, or *Cunningham* recklessness; and (with all due respect to Lord Diplock) what might be termed objective, or *Caldwell* recklessness. Will proof of either justify a conviction wherever the mens rea of a crime is satisfied by proof of recklessness? It is obvious from the above that *Caldwell* recklessness is sufficient in respect of criminal damage and was sufficient for causing death by reckless driving (now replaced with causing death by dangerous driving: Road Traffic Act 1991). In *R* v *Seymour* [1983] 2 AC 493, Lord Roskill expressed the view that *Caldwell* recklessness should be applied by the courts wherever the mens rea of the offence required proof of recklessness, unless Parliament had expressly ordained otherwise, and in the course of that decision *Caldwell* was applied to the common law offence of manslaughter. It is submitted, however, that Lord Roskill's obiter statement may constitute a somewhat sweeping generalisation. In *R* v *Satnam*; *R* v *Kewal* (1983) 78 Cr App R 149, the Court of Appeal expressly rejected the application of *Caldwell* recklessness to the offence of rape, Bristow J stating that *Caldwell* and *Lawrence* were concerned with recklessness in different contexts under different statutes.

Similarly in *W (A Minor)* v *Dolbey* [1983] Crim LR 681, the Divisional Court held that the recklessness involved in the offence of malicious wounding under s20 of the Offences Against the Person Act 1861, was *Cunningham* recklessness. Robert Goff LJ expressed the view that nothing said by Lord Diplock in *Caldwell* was intended to have any impact on the interpretation of the word 'malicious' under the 1861 Act. This view was endorsed by the House of Lords in *R* v *Parmenter* [1991] 3 WLR 914, where it was also confirmed that *Cunningham* recklessness applied to assault.

It is further submitted that *Caldwell* recklessness would have no application to offences of fraud or deception. Some support for this is provided by the decision of the Divisional Court in *Large* v *Mainprize* [1989] Crim LR 213. The respondent, a fisherman required by statute to furnish details of the size of his catch, had understated the quantity of a catch by some 50 per cent. He claimed that this was the result of an error in the use of his calculator. He was charged with recklessly furnishing false information as to his catch, contrary to reg 3(2) of the Sea Fishing (Enforcement of Community Control Measures) Regulations 1985. The justices dismissed the information against him and the prosecutor appealed unsuccessfully from this decision. The Divisional Court expressed the view that recklessness, in the context of the offence under consideration, required evidence of some conscious indifference to truth or falsity, or foresight of consequences without desire for them, but with either indifference, or willingness to run the risk. The court concluded that the justices had been entitled to find that the defendant had merely been guilty of a simple error, ie he had given no thought to the possibility of his statement being false. In conclusion, therefore, the scope for the application of *Caldwell* is severely limited. At present it applies to criminal damage and reckless manslaughter only. What of the future? In *R* v *Reid* the House of Lords was happy to reaffirm Lord Diplock's approach to recklessness in relation to causing death by reckless driving, but it should be borne in mind that this aspect of the case is somewhat academic given that the offence no longer exists. Does the decision supply support for continued application of *Caldwell* in its current form? It is not without significance that Lord Browne-Wilkinson observed (at p694a–d):

> 'My first comment is that, in the absence of a general statutory definition of the word "reckless", I do not accept that the constituent elements of recklessness must be the same in all statutes. In particular the following factors may lead to the word being given different meanings in different statutes. First, the history of the legislation. Lord Goff has demonstrated the statutory derivation of the phrase "driving recklessly" in the road traffic legislation. That history is markedly different from that of s1 of the Criminal Damage Act 1971 which was under consideration in *R v Caldwell* [1981] 1 All ER 961, [1982] AC 341. Second, the statutory provision (as in s1 of the Criminal Damage Act 1971) may require proof of recklessness as to a special consequence or, as in the present case, the word may be used on its own simply as a description of the prohibited act. It is not apparent to me that these two different uses of the word necessarily postulate the same ingredients in the mens rea of the offence. Third, the single word "recklessness" may be used as in the Road Traffic Act, to describe both the nature of the actus reus – the type of driving – and also the mental state of the defendant in driving in that manner. This is to be contrasted with cases such as those under the Criminal Damage Act 1971, where the word is directed only to the mental state of the accused not to the act itself. Finally, the word 'reckless' may be used in relation to the doing of one or more isolated acts, as in the Criminal Damage Act 1971, or as in the present case in relation to a continuous course of action (driving) which is part of life for nearly everybody and which, although capable of being done safely, is inherently dangerous. For these reasons, I propose to deal with the decision in *R v Lawrence* alone and, despite the close link between the two cases, express no view on the decision in *R v Caldwell*.'

Reform

Clause 1(b) of the DCLB proposes that a defendant acts recklessly with respect to:

1. a circumstance when he is aware of a risk that it exists or will exist;
2. a result when he is aware of a risk that it will occur;

and it is unreasonable, having regard to the circumstances known to him, to take that risk.

Save for minor modifications this is effectively the definition proposed in the Draft Code. As the Code Report observed:

> 'The modern English criminal law tradition tends to require a positive state of mind with respect to the various external elements of an offence of any seriousness … [A]lthough this "subjectivist" tradition is not without its critics, we are proposing a Code that stays within the mainstream of English criminal law. But in doing so we do not exclude the possibility that Parliament may hereafter wish to create offences constructed upon a different foundation of liability. The group of House of Lords' cases led by *R v Caldwell* [above] can, indeed, be interpreted as having placed some serious offences upon such a different foundation. It will, of course, be open to Parliament to pursue the line followed by those cases by rejecting or modifying the fault requirements proposed for particular offences by providing further key terms to supplement [those] … that we have defined.' (Vol II, para 8.20)

Presumably the defendant who considers a risk, but discounts it as unlikely to materialise, such as the driver of the left hand drive car referred to by Lord Ackner in *Reid*, would not be reckless under clause 1(b) on the basis that, having regard to the circumstances known to him, it was not unreasonable to overtake on the brow of the hill.

It is interesting to note that the Code Team's draft of 1985 included a fault element referred to as 'heedlessness' which equated to the objective form of recklessness expounded in *R* v *Caldwell*. Of its non-appearance in the Draft Code bill the Code Report states:

'We have not found occasion to use that expression in the definitions of offences in Part II of our Bill … but it remains available if there should prove to be a use for it.' (Vol II, para 8.21)

3.4 Negligence

Negligence, in the sense that the defendant falls below the standard to be expected of the reasonable man, is clearly sufficient to justify liability in civil law. Whether it should also constitute the fault element for a criminal offence is more questionable. In a civil matter the defendant may suffer financially, but there is no question of his being imprisoned, or acquiring a criminal record in respect of his negligence. In criminal proceedings such consequences are possible, and the criticisms levelled at the imposition of strict liability, to the effect that a criminal conviction should not be possible in the absence of fault, can to a limited extent be applied to the imposition of criminal liability on the basis of negligence. Unlike strict liability offences, however, negligence has been used as the basis for serious offences, such as manslaughter. Despite the decision in *Kong Cheuk Kwan* v *R* (1985) 82 Cr App R 18, where Lord Roskill, on behalf of the Privy Council expressly approved of the obiter statement of Watkins LJ (delivering the judgment of the Court of Appeal) in *R* v *Seymour* (1983) 76 Cr App R 211, to the effect that:

'… [the court is] … of the view that it is no longer necessary or helpful to make reference to compensation and negligence …'

the House of Lords in *R* v *Adomako* [1994] 3 WLR 288 has confirmed that liability for killing by gross negligence still exists at common law: see further Chapter 4, section 4.10.

3.5 Strict liability

Strict liability is the term used to describe the imposition of criminal liability without proof of fault on the part of the defendant. As such it represents an exception to one of the basic principles of criminal liability, that actus reus and mens rea must be proved. It was suggested earlier that it is the presence of the defendant's mens rea or 'fault' that can be said to justify the punishments imposed under the criminal law. If this is correct, then it would appear that to punish a defendant for the commission of a strict liability offence is, per se, unjust. Some reported cases do indeed give this impression, see *R v Larsonneur* (1933) 24 Cr App R 74, but as will be seen from what follows, the courts rarely interpret an offence as being one of truly absolute liability (ie requiring no mens rea whatsoever), and where liability without fault is imposed, it tends to be for quasi-criminal, or 'regulatory' offences, the punishment for which rarely involves loss of liberty.

The rationale of strict liability

The purpose of imposing strict liability is to place the onus upon those who engage in a particular activity to ensure that they do not transgress the prohibitions laid down by the law. In simple terms, the law is suggesting that those who are in any doubt as to whether their actions will fall foul of the law should avoid such activities. It was observed by Lord Hailsham in *Smedleys Ltd v Breed* [1974] AC 839 that if the imposition of strict liability caused injustice to the defendant, one way for him to avoid it was to desist from the activity that involved him in the commission of offences, and that this might be the view taken by the courts where the activity was viewed as unnecessary or inefficient. Hence the person selling food to the public must accept that the onus is upon him to ensure that it is fit for consumption. If this increases the cost of his product, then that should be passed on to all his consumers. Should he not be able to comply with the law and operate as a commercially viable outfit, then he should cease trading. The man attracted to a young girl is taking the risk that, although she consents to sexual intercourse with him, she may be below the age of consent. He can avoid this risk, ultimately, by remaining celibate. Similarly, the individual asked to carry another's bag through customs without having the opportunity to ascertain its contents can avoid liability by refusing to act as a courier. One of the factors behind the court's decision in *Kirkland v Robinson* (considered below) was that there was no social utility in the defendant's possession of wild birds: see further *R v Blake* [1997] 1 Cr App R 209.

Statutory interpretation

Given that strict liability offences are almost invariably created by statute, the manner in which they will operate rests to a large extent on how the courts decide to interpret them.

One of the basic rules of statutory interpretation is the presumption in favour of mens rea. Where a statutory provision creates a criminal offence but no reference is made to the mens rea that must be established, the courts will nevertheless assume that Parliament intended the offence to involve the proof of some degree of mens rea, unless there is sufficient evidence to the contrary. Some of the factors considered by a court in deciding whether an offence is one of strict liability are considered below, but before turning to them it should be understood that a court's finding that an offence does require proof of some mens rea does not necessarily mean that mens rea will have to be proved in relation to every element of the actus reus.

A comparison of the decisions in *R* v *Prince* (1875) LR 2 CCR 154 and *R* v *Hibbert* (1869) LR 1 CCR 184 is illustrative of this point. The defendants in both cases were charged with offences under s55 of the Offences Against the Person Act 1861 (now repealed), namely the unlawful removal of a girl below the age of 16 from the custody of her father against his will. Hibbert had abducted a girl below the age of 16, but had been ignorant of the fact that she was living with her parents. Prince had similarly abducted a girl below the age of 16 who was living with her parents, but he had claimed that he honestly believed her to be older than 16. Hibbert was acquitted, but Prince was convicted. An explanation for the contrasting results in these cases is that whereas the courts 'read in' a requirement of mens rea as regards certain elements of the actus reus, in other words the defendant had to be aware that he was abducting a girl, and that she was in the custody of her parents, no mens rea was required as regards the girl's age. In other words, liability was absolute as regards this element, and Prince's defence of honest and reasonable mistake was of no avail. The main purpose of the provision under which he was charged was to protect girls under the age of 16, not necessarily those roaming the streets.

The statute must be read as a whole
In determining whether the presumption in favour of mens rea is to be displaced, the courts are required to have reference to the whole statute in which the offence appears.

In *Cundy* v *Le Cocq* (1884) 13 QBD 207 the defendant was convicted of unlawfully selling alcohol to an intoxicated person, contrary to s13 of the Licensing Act 1872. On appeal, the defendant contended that he had been unaware of the customer's drunkenness and thus should have been acquitted. The Divisional Court interpreted s13 as creating an offence of strict liability since it was itself silent as to mens rea, whereas other offences under the same Act expressly required proof of knowledge on the part of the defendant. The conclusion was that where Parliament had intended mens rea to be proved under the Act it had stated such.

A similar approach may be taken by the courts when dealing with an offence which is silent as to mens rea, but in relation to which Parliament has enacted a specific statutory defence. In *Kirkland* v *Robinson* [1987] Crim LR 643 the defendant's conviction for unlawfully possessing four wild goshawks was upheld, despite his honest belief that they had been bred in captivity. Not only did the statute in question, the Wildlife and Countryside Act 1981, create other offences which expressly required proof of knowledge, but it provided a statutory defence to the offence with which the defendant had been charged, under s1(3). The Divisional Court concluded, therefore, that Parliament had intended there to be an absolute prohibition on the possession of such birds, subject only to the defendant bringing himself within the terms of the statutory defence.

Even the statutory defence may be construed in very narrow terms where the courts sense this is warranted by the context. Hence in *Smedleys Ltd* v *Breed* (above) the House of Lords upheld the defendant's conviction under s2(1) of the Food and Drugs Act 1955 ('selling food not of the substance demanded by the purchaser'), which had resulted from complaints that four tins of peas produced by the defendants had contained caterpillars. The 1955 Act had contained a statutory defence in s3(3), where it could be shown that the presence of the extraneous matter was an *unavoidable* consequence of the manufacturing process, but it was held, interpreting the provision literally, that the defence was of no avail to the defendants, as the presence of the caterpillars could have been detected by means of a visual check of every tin. Neither were their Lordships moved by the submission that there had been only four complaints in respect of approximately 3,500,000 tins. The paramount purpose of the legislation was seen as being the protection of the public, which would be respected even where it led to the imposition of impossibly high standards upon the defendants; see further *Alphacell Ltd* v *Woodward* [1972] AC 824 (imposition of strict liability for river pollution despite the taking of all reasonable precautions).

There is, arguably, a greater tendency on the part of the courts to regard a statute as imposing strict or absolute liability where the offence created is viewed as being 'regulatory' or 'quasi-criminal' in nature. As Lord Evershed observed in *Lim Chin Aik* v *R* [1963] AC 160:

> 'Where the subject-matter of the statute is the regulation for the public welfare of a particular activity – statutes regulating the sale of food and drink are to be found among the earliest examples – it can be and frequently has been inferred that the legislature intended that such activities should be carried out under conditions of strict liability. The presumption is that the statute or statutory instrument can be effectively enforced only if those in charge of the relevant activities are made responsible for seeing that they are complied with. When such a presumption is to be inferred, it displaces the ordinary presumptions of mens rea. Thus sellers of meat may be made responsible for seeing that the meat is fit for human consumption and it is no answer for them to say that they were not aware that it was polluted ... the distribution of bad meat (and its far-reaching consequences) would not be effectively prevented.'

Other areas where the courts have adopted this approach are offences created under building regulations: *Gammon Ltd* v *Attorney-General for Hong Kong* (1984) 80 Cr App R 194; supplying controlled medicines without a valid prescription: *Pharmaceutical Society of Great Britain* v *Storkwain* [1986] 1 WLR 903; carrying out unauthorised work on a listed building: *R* v *Wells Street Metropolitan Stipendiary Magistrate, ex parte Westminster City Council* (1986) The Times 22 May; and breach of an enforcement notice: *R* v *Collet* [1994] 1 WLR 475.

There must be some purpose in imposing strict liability
The courts will be reluctant to construe a statute as imposing strict liability upon a

defendant, where there is evidence to suggest that despite his having taken all reasonable steps, he cannot avoid the commission of an offence.

In *Sherras* v *De Rutzen* [1895] 1 QB 918 the defendant was convicted of selling alcohol to a police officer whilst on duty, contrary to s16(2) of the Licensing Act 1872. The police officer had not been wearing the arm band that would have indicated that he was on duty. The Divisional Court held that the conviction should be quashed, despite the absence from s16(2) of any words importing proof of mens rea as an element of the offence. Wright J expressed the view that the presumption in favour of mens rea would only be displaced by the wording of the statute itself, or its subject matter. In this case the latter factor was significant, in that no amount of reasonable care by the defendant would have prevented the offence from being committed.

This approach was approved by the Privy Council in *Lim Chin Aik* v *R* [1963] AC 160, where the defendant had been convicted of contravening an order prohibiting, in absolute terms, his entry into Singapore, despite his ignorance of the order's existence. In allowing the defendant's appeal, Lord Evershed expressed the view that the imposition of strict liability could only really be justified where it would actually succeed in placing the onus to comply with the law on the defendant. As he explained:

'... it is not enough ... merely to label the statute as one dealing with a grave social evil and from that to infer that strict liability was intended. It is pertinent also to inquire whether putting the defendant under strict liability will assist in the enforcement of the regulations. That means that there must be something he can do, directly or indirectly, by supervision or inspection, by improvement of his business methods or by exhorting those whom he may be expected to influence or control, which will promote the observance of the regulations. Unless this is so, there is no reason in penalising him, and it cannot be inferred that the legislature imposed strict liability merely in order to find a luckless victim ... [w]here it can be shown that the imposition of strict liability would result in the prosecution and conviction of a class of persons whose conduct could not in any way affect the observance of the law, their Lordships consider that, even where the statute is dealing with a grave social evil, strict liability is not likely to be intended ... [i]t seems to their Lordships that, where a man is said to have contravened an order or an order of prohibition, the common sense of the language presumes that he was aware of the order before he can be said to have contravened it.'

Similar considerations motivated the House of Lords in *Sweet* v *Parsley* [1970] AC 132 to quash the conviction of a defendant who, following a police raid on a house which she had let out to students, had been prosecuted under s5(b) of the Dangerous Drugs Act 1965 of 'being concerned in the management of premises used for the smoking of cannabis'. The defendant had not known that drugs were being consumed there. As Lord Reid observed:

'If this section means what the Divisional Court have held that it means, then hundreds of thousands of people who sublet part of the premises or take in lodgers or are concerned in the management of residential premises or institutions are daily incurring a risk of being convicted of a serious offence in circumstances where they are in no way to blame. For the greatest vigilance cannot prevent tenants, lodgers or inmates or guests whom they bring in from smoking cannabis cigarettes in their own rooms. It was suggested in argument that this appellant brought this conviction on herself because it is found as a fact that when the police searched the premises there were people there of the "beatnik fraternity". But surely it would be going a very long way to say that persons managing premises of any kind ought to safeguard themselves by refusing accommodation to all who are of slovenly or exotic appearance, or who bring in guests of that kind. And unfortunately drug taking is by no means confined to those of unusual appearance.'

See also *Gammon Ltd* v *Attorney-General for Hong Kong* (above).

By contrast, in *R* v *Bezzina*; *R* v *Codling*; *R* v *Elvin* [1994] 1 WLR 1057, where the appellants were each convicted, at separate trials, of being the owner of a dog which, whilst dangerously out of control in a public place, had injured a person contrary to s3(1) of the Dangerous Dogs Act 1991, the court was persuaded that the imposition of absolute liability would serve a useful purpose. In dismissing the appeals against conviction, the court held that the presumption against strict liability was rebutted by the fact that: (a) the Dangerous Dogs Act 1991 addressed a matter of social concern and public safety; (b) the court was satisfied that the imposition of strict liability would encourage greater vigilance by owners in seeking to prevent the commission of prohibited acts, ie the court felt that it was proper to put the onus on the dog owner to prevent the occurrence of harm; and (c) the statute, when read as a whole indicated that s3(1) imposed absolute liability, since s3(2) afforded a defence where D left the dog in the charge of a fit and proper person, and s3(3) impliedly required mens rea where it referred to an owner 'allowing' a dog to be in a non-public place. Note that the court declined to deal with one of the more interesting points argued on appeal, ie what would the appellant's liability have been if a properly secured dog, released from the appellant's premises following a burglary, had caused injury to a member of the public whilst loose? Clearly such a question goes to the heart of the issue as to whether or not it was the intention of Parliament to incriminate 'blameless' dog owners.

Public danger posed by defendant's conduct: drugs and guns

As a general rule, the more serious the criminal offence created by statute, the less likely the courts are to view it as an offence of strict liability. However, the courts are sometimes persuaded to impose strict liability after concluding that the possible unfairness that this might involve for the defendant is outweighed by the potential harm to the public posed by his conduct. Hence in *R* v *Howells* [1977] 3 All ER 417 the defendant was convicted of possessing an unlicensed firearm, contrary to s58(2) Firearms Act 1968, despite his honest belief that it was an antique and thus exempt from the provisions of the Act. As Browne LJ observed:

'... the danger to the community resulting from the possession of lethal firearms is so obviously great that an absolute prohibition against their possession without proper authority must have been the intention of Parliament when considered in conjunction with the words of the section ... to allow a defence of honest and reasonable belief that the firearm was an antique and therefore excluded would be likely to defeat the clear intentions of the Act.'

The balancing of priorities that has to be carried out, in a sense, raises the same issue; what knowledge, if any, must a defendant have in order for the court to conclude that he was in possession of the drugs or guns?

In *Warner* v *MPC* [1969] 2 AC 256, an authority from which it is extremely difficult, if not impossible, to extract a clear ratio, a majority of their Lordships appeared to hold that s1 of the Drugs (Prevention of Misuse) Act 1964, under which it was an offence to be in unlawful possession of a prohibited drug, did create an offence of strict liability as regards the nature of the substance in the defendant's possession, but it nevertheless had to be proved that he knew he was in possession of 'something'. Hence, if drugs were slipped into a defendant's pocket without his knowledge he could not be guilty under s1 because he would not have known he was in possession of anything. If, however, he was knowingly in possession of a package of some sort, but was ignorant of the fact that it contained cocaine powder, it became necessary to look at the defendant's knowledge as to the nature and quality of the package's contents. Where he was mistaken as to the nature of its contents, for example where he honestly believed it to contain boiled sweets, it would appear from the speeches of the majority that he was to be acquitted, although this may have been subject to such factors as the defendant's opportunity to check the contents, and the existence of any factors that should have made him suspect that it might contain drugs. Where, on the other hand, he knew the nature of the contents but was mistaken as to its quality, for example, where he believed the package to contain sherbet powder, it would appear that he could be convicted: see further *R* v *Fernandez* [1970] Crim LR 277.

If the controlled drug is not in a container of any sort, it is submitted that knowledge on the part of the defendant that he is in possession of 'something' will suffice. Applying these principles, the defendant in *R* v *Marriot* [1970] 1 All ER 595, was convicted of unlawful possession of a prohibited drug, when he was found to have two milligrams of cannabis smeared on the blade of a penknife in his possession. The conviction was upheld, on the ground that although he had not known the substance to be cannabis, he had known that there was something smeared on the blade of the knife.

With a view to removing some of the complexities introduced into this branch of the law by *Warner* v *MPC*, Parliament enacted the Misuse of Drugs Act 1971. Section 5 of the 1971 Act creates the offence of possessing a controlled drug, but s28(3)(b)(i) goes on to provide that a defendant should be acquitted if:

'... he proves that he neither believed nor suspected nor had reason to suspect that the substance ... in question was a controlled drug.'

The Court of Appeal in *R* v *McNamara* (1988) 87 Cr App R 246 held that as far as the 'container' cases were concerned, Parliament, in enacting s28, had not intended to relieve the Crown of the initial burden of proving that the defendant had known he was in possession of a container holding 'something', and that it in fact held a controlled drug. Once the prosecution had established these matters, however, the onus was then upon the defendant to bring himself within the terms of s28(3)(b)(i). With respect this is a helpful clarification of the law, but the point still appears to cause difficulty. In *R* v *Lewis* (1987) 87 Cr App R 270, the Court of Appeal held that a defendant could be in possession of drugs where they were found in his house, despite the fact that he had not known that they were there, because he had had an opportunity to find them. The difficulty with this ruling is that it is not analogous to the case of the defendant who has a box which he knows to contain *something*, but who fails to inquire as to what it is; Lewis did not discover the drugs because he did not know there was anything in the house to go searching for! See further *R* v *Conway and Burke* [1994] Crim LR 826.

In *R* v *Bradish* (1990) 90 Cr App R 271 the appellant was convicted of possessing a prohibited weapon (a CS gas canister) contrary to s5(1) of the Firearms Act 1968, despite his assertion that he had not known that the canister contained CS gas. Auld J, on behalf of the Court of Appeal, rejected the assertion that, unlike most of the authorities on possession of firearms, the appellant's was a 'container' case, and as such the authorities dealing with possession of dangerous drugs should be applied. The court noted the social dangers presented by offensive weapons; the absence of any mental element in the wording of the offence; the reference to the defendants state of mind in *other* sections of the Act; and the provision of specific defences in analogous legislation, but not in the 1968 Act. In particular the court refused to follow the 'half-way house' approach to mens rea and possession adopted by the majority in *Warner*, because it was decided before the enactment of the 1968, and it was thus significant that the legislature, when passing that Act, made no provision clarifying the position as to the need or not to prove mens rea in relation to possession. As Auld J observed:

> '... the possibilities and consequences of evasion would be too great for effective control, even if the burden of proving lack of guilty knowledge were to be on the accused. The difficulty of enforcement, when presented with such a defence, would be particularly difficult where there is a prosecution for possession of a component part of a firearm or prohibited weapon, as provided for by sections 1 and 5 when read with section 57(1) of the 1968 Act. It would be easy for an accused to maintain, lyingly but with conviction, that he did not recognise the object in his possession as part of a firearm or prohibited weapon. To the argument that the innocent possessor or carrier of firearms or prohibited weapons or parts of them is at risk of unfair conviction under these provisions there has to be balanced the important public policy behind the legislation of protecting the public from the misuse of such dangerous weapons. Just as the Chicago-style gangster might plausibly maintain that he believed his violin case to contain a violin, not a sub-machine gun, so it might be difficult to meet a London lout's assertion that he did not know an unmarked plastic bottle in his possession contained ammonia rather than something to drink.'

Reform

The difficulties in ascertaining whether a statutory provision creates liability without fault are adverted to in the commentary that accompanies the Code Report:

'An enactment creating an offence should ordinarily specify the fault required for the offence or expressly provide that the offence is one of strict liability in respect of one or more identified elements. It is necessary, however, to have a general rule for the interpretation of any offence the definition of which does not state, in respect of one or more elements, whether fault is required or what degree of fault is required. The absence of a consistent rule of interpretation has been a regrettable source of uncertainty in English law. Clause 20 [set out below] provides such a rule. It would implement a policy that we recommended in our Report on the Mental Element in Crime [(1978) Law Com No 89], though in a manner a good deal less complex than that suggested in the draft Bill appended to that Report. The proposal to include this provision was well supported on consultation.' (Vol II, para 8.25)

The proposed clause states:

'(1) Every offence requires a fault element of recklessness with or respect to each of its elements other than fault elements, unless otherwise provided.
(2) Subsection 1 does not apply to pre-Code offences as defined in section 6 (to which section 2(3) applies).'

The clause would apply to offences in the Draft Code and to offences subsequently created; the interpretation of existing legislation would not be affected. The clause would create a presumption that mens rea, in at least the form of recklessness as defined elsewhere in the Code, would be required in relation to each element of an offence, unless otherwise provided. As the commentary states:

'We considered a suggestion that the clause should seek to make the presumption displaceable only by *express* provision requiring some fault other than recklessness, or stating that no fault is required, with respect to an element of an offence. We do not think that this would be appropriate. We are mindful of the "constitutional platitude" pointed out by Lord Ackner in *Hunt* [1987] AC 352 at 380 that the courts must give effect to what Parliament has provided not only "expressly" but also by "necessary implication". If the terms of a future enactment creating an offence plainly implied an intention to displace the presumption created by clause 20(1), the courts would no doubt feel obliged to give effect to that intention even if the present clause were to require express provision for the purpose.' (Vol II, para 8.28)

The intended effect of the clause is illustrated in the examples provided in Appendix B to Volume 1:

'Under clause 147 a person commits burglary if he enters a building as a trespasser intending to steal in the building. Nothing is said as to any fault required in respect of the fact that the entrant is a trespasser. The offence is committed only if the entrant knows that, or is reckless whether, he is trespassing.' (example 20(i))

'An offence of causing polluting matter to enter a watercourse is enacted after the Code comes into force. In the absence of provision to the contrary the offence requires (a) an intention to cause the matter to enter the watercourse or recklessness whether it will do so, and (b) knowledge that the matter is a pollutant or recklessness.' (example 20(ii))

3.6 Mistake and mens rea

To talk of mistake in terms of it being a substantive defence in criminal law is somewhat misleading, as a defendant who seeks to rely on a mistake of fact or law by way of defence is in truth denying that he had the mens rea for the crime with which he is charged. Thus where D fires a gun at P, causing his death, and D claims that he honestly believed he was firing at a wax figure, D might be said to have the defence of mistake, but in reality his defence will simply be a denial of mens rea; he intended to damage a wax figure, not to kill a human being.

Mistake can be raised by a defendant to any charge provided that the offence is one requiring some degree of fault on his part. Whilst there is always an evidential burden on the defendant to put evidence before the jury that he did actually make the mistake upon which he relies, the legal burden always rests with the Crown to establish beyond reasonable doubt that the defendant was not mistaken and therefore did have the requisite mens rea for the offence with which he is charged. As is the case in any trial where the prosecution fails to establish mens rea, if the defendant succeeds with his 'defence' of mistake he must be acquitted.

Mistake of law

It might be assumed that, since ignorance of the law is not supposed to provide a defence, there can be no scope for the operation of a defence based on mistake of law. There are, however, a limited number of situations where it can operate to prevent the imposition of criminal liability. A defendant who murders a victim is not normally permitted to raise by way of defence the contention that he mistakenly thought homicide to be lawful, but where his ignorance of the law's restraints arises from a disease of the mind that manifests itself in violence and is likely to recur, such a defence could operate so as to relieve him of liability for murder. The defendant would not, however, be regarded as raising the defence of mistake as such, but the defence of insanity: see *M'Naghten's Case* (1843) 10 C & F 200 considered in Chapter 14.

By way of contrast to mistake of criminal law, mistake of civil law can provide a defence to a criminal charge, in that it might lead D to rely on a claim of right. In *R v Smith* [1974] QB 354, D's conviction for criminal damage was quashed by the Court of Appeal, because he had honestly (although as a matter of civil law incorrectly) thought that the fittings he had removed from his rented flat belonged in law to him and not his landlord. As stated above, however, this decision does little more than state the obvious; D did not have the intention to damage property belonging to another, only that which he honestly believed was his. Similarly, under s2(1)(a) of the Theft Act 1968, a defendant is not to be regarded as dishonest for the purposes of theft when he takes property in the honest belief that he has the right in law to do so. The result might be that where D enters into a contract to purchase goods from P under which property in the goods is not to pass to D until two weeks later, but D, misconstruing the contract, honestly believes he has an immediate right to deal in the goods, D could rely on his honest mistake of contract law as evidence that he honestly believed he had the right in law to treat the goods as his own.

Mistake of fact

The extent to which mistake of fact will be permitted to operate as a denial of mens rea rather depends upon the nature of the offence with which the defendant is charged. If it is an offence of absolute liability, a defence such as mistake, which is simply a denial of mens rea, will not avail the defendant. Where, however, some mens rea is required, there will normally be some correlation between the type of mens rea that has to be proved and the type of mistake that will successfully negative evidence of mens rea.

Strict liability offences

As discussed in section 3.5, a statute creating criminal liability may be silent as to the mens rea necessary for a conviction, yet the courts will nevertheless presume that some fault must be established on the part of the defendant unless there is evidence to rebut the assumption. Hence, there may be scope for the operation of a defence of mistake in relation to such offences, although in a somewhat limited form. Much depends on how the courts view the offence as a whole.

In *B* v *DPP* [1998] 4 All ER 265, the defendant was convicted of inciting P, a 13-year-old girl, to commit an act of gross indecency contrary to s1(1) of the Indecency with Children Act 1960. He appealed unsuccessfully on the ground that, as he had honestly believed P to be over the age of 14, he should have been acquitted. In concluding that mistake as to the age of the victim would not afford a defence the court was mindful of the legislative history of the 1960 Act, in particular the fact that it had been enacted to close a loophole in the law created by the Sexual Offences Act 1956. Adopting the view that the 1960 Act should be construed on the same basis as the 1956 Act, Rougier J noted that some provisions in the 1956 Act expressly required proof of mens rea, as denoted by reference to the defendant acting 'knowingly' in regard to some aspect of the actus reus. Elsewhere there were provisions in the 1956 Act that were silent as to mens rea, but in relation to which Parliament had created statutory defences. In particular, he noted that s5 of the 1956 Act (sexual intercourse with a girl under the age of 13) provided for no excuses as to a mistaken belief that the girl might be older, whilst the less serious offence under s6 (sexual intercourse with a girl under the age of 16) did provide for the so-called 'young man's defence' (ie a man under 24 could contend that he had reasonably believed the girl to be older than 16). As Rougier J observed (at p274e–h):

'To my mind, the inclusion of the specific statutory defence in the two sections which I have mentioned demonstrates conclusively that Parliament did not intend that defence to be available to those other offences where there is no such provision. For instance, the comparison between the terms of ss5 and 6 to my mind is deadly. How could it possibly be said that, having expressly provided for a limited defence to the less serious offence, Parliament must be assumed to have intended that a similar defence should be available for the more serious without express provision? And this takes no account of the fact that if the appellant's contention is right, the suggested implied defence would be available to a person of any age with a number of previous convictions for similar offences behind him, whether or not there were reasonable grounds for his mistaken belief. If I am correct in believing that the principles governing the construction of the 1956 Act apply also to s1 of the 1960 Act, then it follows that there is no room for implying what I have called the, basic principle defence founded on a mistaken belief or lack of knowledge of the victim's age.'

Hence the absence of any express mens rea requirement under s1(1) of the 1960 Act, and the absence of any statutory defence, persuaded him to the conclusion that a mistake as to the age of the victim under s1(1) would be irrelevant, regardless of whether it was honest or reasonable. Tucker J agreed with Rougier J, and referred to a range of other offences where mistake as to age would not be regarded as providing any defence, notably incest and possession of indecent pictures of children. He added, somewhat tellingly (at p276e–f):

'I deduce from all these statutory provisions that it is the clear intention of Parliament to protect young children and to make it an offence to commit offences against children under a certain age, whether or not the defendant knows of the age of the victims, and that it was intended that, save where expressly provided, a mistaken or honest belief in the victim's age should not afford a defence. In my judgment it is not open to the courts to create a defence in circumstances such as the present where Parliament clearly intended that no such defence should be available. The effect of [counsel for the appellant's] submissions would be that a defendant charged with an offence under s1(1) of the Indecency with Children Act 1960 would be in a better position than if he were charged with an offence under s6(1) of the Sexual Offences Act 1956 [unlawful sexual intercourse with a girl below the age of 16 – mistake as to age only available to men under 24]. This is because, according to [his] submission, in the first case the onus of proof would be on the prosecution, whereas in the second case proof of the exception lies on the person relying on it. Such a result would offend common sense, and cannot have been intended by Parliament.'

Where the social dangers attaching to the defendant's actions are not so grave, and the defendant is seen as having acted in a morally blameless fashion, the courts are likely to be more lenient. For example, in *R v Tolson* (1889) 23 QBD 168, D's husband left her in 1881 and she heard nothing of him for the next five years. In 1887, wrongly believing her husband to have drowned at sea, D remarried. When her husband returned D was charged with bigamy, contrary to s57 of the Offences Against the Person Act 1861, a provision that has no express mens rea requirement. On appeal against her conviction, it was held, by a majority, that she should be acquitted. Her honest and reasonable belief that she was a widow provided a good defence or, as it might be expressed, she was permitted to rely on an honest mistake that a reasonable woman would have made in the circumstances. As Lord Diplock observed in *Sweet v Parsley* [1970] AC 132, when analysing the decision in *Tolson* (at p163):

'Where penal provisions are of general application to the conduct of ordinary citizens in the course of their everyday life, the presumption is that the standard of care required of them in informing themselves of facts which would make their conduct unlawful, is that of the familiar common law duty of care. But where the subject-matter of a statute is the regulation of a particular activity involving potential danger to public health, safety or morals, in which citizens have a choice as to whether they participate or not, the court may feel driven to infer an intention of Parliament to impose, by penal sanctions, a higher duty of care on those who choose to participate and to place on them an obligation to take whatever measures may be necessary to prevent the prohibited act, without regard to those considerations of cost or business practicability which play a part in the determination of what would be required of them in order to fulfil the ordinary common law duty of care.'

In the course of submissions made on behalf of the appellants in *DPP* v *Morgan* [1975] AC 182, the House of Lords was invited to reconsider the status of *Tolson*, but the majority felt that it remained unaffected by the outcome of the appeal before them. Lord Hailsham expressed the view that it was something of a special case in that it was 'a narrow decision based on the construction of a statute'. Lord Fraser adopted the view that the approach of the court in *Tolson* was one peculiar to statutory offences which were 'absolute' in nature (ie contained no express requirement of mens rea). It follows, therefore, that a defendant would not be guilty of bigamy if he honestly and reasonably believed his first marriage to have been void, annulled, or dissolved: see further *R* v *Gould* [1968] 2 QB 65.

Offences requiring proof of fault
If D is charged with an offence, the definition of which expressly or impliedly requires proof of mens rea, then the principles enunciated by the majority in *Morgan* apply to the operation of mistake as a denial of mens rea. In *Morgan* the defendants had been convicted of rape, despite their contentions that they had believed P to have been consenting to sexual intercourse. They appealed against the trial judge's direction that D's mistake as to P's consent would only provide a defence if it was both honest and reasonable. The Court of Appeal dismissed the appeal, but the House of Lords, by a majority of three to two, held that a defendant was to be judged on the facts as he honestly believed them to be, and thus a mistake of fact would afford a defence no matter how unreasonable it might be, provided it was honestly made. The rationale behind the majority view is illustrated by a passage in the speech of Lord Hailsham where he observed:

'I believe that "mens rea" means "guilty or criminal mind", and if it be the case, as seems to be accepted here that [the] mental element in rape is ... intent, to insist that a belief [in the consent of the victim] must be reasonable to excuse is to insist that either the accused is to be found guilty of intending to do that which in truth he did not intend to do, or that his state of mind, though innocent of evil intent, can convict him if it be honest but not rational ...'

This does not, of course, give a defendant carte blanche to raise quite spurious defences based on supposed mistakes of fact. An important controlling factor is the part played by the jury. The more unreasonable the mistake a defendant claims to have made, the less likely the jury is to believe that it was honestly made.

The position where a defendant makes a mistake regarding the availability of a defence is considered further in Chapter 6, section 6.4 and Chapter 15, section 15.3.

Reform

Clause 21 of the Draft Code restates the oft cited maxim that ignorance of the law is no excuse, but admits exceptions where the mistake of law negatives the fault element required for an offence. The purpose of the general prohibition upon such a defence is, as the Code Report commentary on this clause indicates:

> '... to preclude any attempt to stimulate judicial recognition of exceptions to the general rule by reliance on clause 45(c), under which common law defences can be developed, but only if they are not inconsistent with other Code provisions.' (Vol II, para 8.29)

The Draft Code does not deal directly with mistake of fact as a 'defence' as, given the construction of the Code, it is unnecessary to do so. Clause 14 provides:

> 'A court or jury, in determining whether a person had, or may have had, a particular state of mind, shall have regard to all the evidence including, where appropriate, the presence or absence of reasonable grounds for having that state of mind.'

The clause thus states what should be obvious, that mistake of fact relating to an element of an offence is actually a denial of mens rea. The defendant is entitled to be judged on the facts as he believes them to be; thus a defendant who stabs to death a victim in the belief that he was stabbing a wax dummy should be acquitted of murder, but, in assessing whether or not the defendant genuinely believed himself to be stabbing a wax dummy, the jury will be entitled to take into account the existence of any reasonable grounds for such belief.

3.7 Infancy

It is generally taken to be a hallmark of a civilised system of criminal justice that those who are not fully responsible for their actions should not be tried and punished as those who are. Within this principle, there is also general acceptance that children in particular need to be protected by the law and cannot be expected to show the same powers of rationalisation and self-control as adults. Beyond those points, it becomes a matter of conjecture as to when the criminal law ought to apply to young persons and, when it does, whether the emphasis should be treatment or punishment.

The position of children as defendants in English criminal law is governed by a mixture of statute and common law. Under s16 of the Children and Young Persons Act 1963 a child under the age of ten cannot incur criminal responsibility, there being an irrebuttable presumption against mens rea. Where an adult uses such a child in order to commit offences, for example sending a child into a house via a small open window in order to steal, the adult should normally be charged as the principal offender on the basis of innocent agency, although this may not be suitable in respect of certain offences, eg rape: see further *DPP* v *K and C* [1997] 1 Cr App R 36.

Prior to the enactment of s34 of the Crime and Disorder Act 1998 a defendant between the ages of ten and 14 could not be convicted of a criminal offence unless there was sufficient evidence to rebut the presumption that he was doli incapax, the presumption being rebuttable by clear and positive evidence that he knew that his actions were 'seriously wrong', such evidence not consisting merely in the evidence of the acts amounting to the offence itself.

The House of Lords in *C (A Minor)* v *DPP* [1995] 2 WLR 383 declined the opportunity to abolish the presumption offered by the grounds of appeal in that case. Lord Lowry was, at the time, persuaded to reject the argument for judicial reform of the law as it stood by the fact that in its White Paper *Crime, Justice and Protecting the Public* (Cm 965) the (then Conservative) government had confirmed its support for the retention of the doli incapax rule. Given that the issue involved arguments based on social policy it was, in his Lordship's view, a classic case for parliamentary investigation, deliberation and legislation. As indicated above, that legislation has now been enacted, s34 providing that:

'The rebuttable presumption of criminal law that a child aged ten or over is incapable of committing an offence is hereby abolished.'

The law as it stands following the enactment of s34 is open to criticism on the basis that it results in the imposition of criminal liability at too young an age. In some jurisdictions juvenile offenders are dealt with in the civil courts, so that the emphasis is on treatment and supervision rather than punishment. Even within the United Kingdom the law varies, with the age of criminal responsibility in Scotland and Northern Ireland being eight. Across Europe most countries have a higher starting age, typically 14 or 15, with some countries not imposing full liability until 18. Exceptions are Ireland, Cyprus and Switzerland where the starting age is seven.

3.8 Transferred malice

Under the doctrine of transferred malice, where a defendant fires a gun intending to kill X, but misses and instead kills Y, he will not be able to escape liability for the murder of Y simply because it was his intention was to kill X. The defendant has still committed the actus reus that he intended, namely to cause the death of a human being. In this sense it might be said that the 'malice' against X can be transferred to Y. As Lord Mustill observed in *Attorney-General's Reference (No 3 of 1994)* [1997] 3 All ER 936:

'The effect of transferred malice, as I understand it, is that the intended victim and the actual victim are treated as if they were one, so that what was intended to happen to the first person (but did not happen) is added to what actually did happen to the second person (but was not intended to happen), with the result that what was intended and what happened are married to make a notionally intended and actually consummated crime. The cases are treated as if the actual victim had been the intended victim from the start. To make any sense of this process there must, as it seems to me, be some compatibility between the original intention and the actual occurrence, and this is, indeed, what one finds in the cases.'

The basis for this principle is the decision of the Court for Crown Cases Reserved in *R v Latimer* (1886) 17 QBD 359, in which D struck a blow with his belt at Horace Chapple which glanced off him, severely injuring an innocent bystander, Ellen Rolston. D was convicted of maliciously wounding the woman, and appealed on the ground that it had never been his intention to hurt her. The court upheld the conviction on the basis that D had committed the actus reus of the offence with the necessary mens rea, ie he had acted maliciously. There was no requirement in the relevant act that his mens rea should relate to a named victim. The limitation placed on the doctrine of transferred malice is that the mens rea can only be 'transferred' from one victim to another, or one item of property to another, within the same offence. Hence in *R v Pembliton* (1874) LR 2 CCR 119, where D threw a stone at another person during an argument, and missed, breaking a nearby window instead, a conviction for malicious damage to property was quashed, the court holding that the doctrine of transferred malice was inapplicable where the defendant's intention had not been to cause the type of harm that actually materialised. His intention to assault another person could not be used as the mens rea for the damage that he had caused to the window.

Again Lord Mustill observed in *Attorney-General's Reference (No 3 of 1994)* that:

'The court in *Latimer* was, I believe, entirely justified in finding a distinction between their statutory backgrounds and one can well accept that the answers given, one for acquittal, the other for conviction, would be the same today. But the harking back to a concept of general malice, which amounts to no more than this, that a wrongful act displays a malevolence which can be attached to any adverse consequence, has long been out of date. And to speak of a particular malice which is "transferred" simply disguises the problem by idiomatic language. The defendant's malice is directed at one objective, and when after the event the court treats it as directed at another object it is not recognising a "transfer" but creating a new malice which never existed before. As Dr Glanville Williams pointed out (*Criminal Law*, the General Part 2nd Ed (1961), p184) the doctrine is "rather an arbitrary exception to general principles". Like many of its kind this is useful enough to yield rough justice, in particular cases, and it can sensibly be retained notwithstanding its lack of any sound intellectual basis. But it is another matter to build a new rule upon it.'

Thus, in *Attorney-General's Reference (No 3 of 1994)*, the House of Lords held that the doctrine of transferred malice could not be extended to impose liability on a defendant who had attacked a pregnant woman, intending to cause her grievous bodily harm, where the attack was a causative factor in the eventual death of the

child that she had been carrying, the child dying four months after being bor
prematurely. The basis for this refusal was that it would involve a double 'transfe
of intent. First from the mother to the foetus and then from the foetus to the chi
as yet unborn. As Lord Mustill explained:

> 'The defendant intended to commit and did commit an immediate crime of violence to
> the mother. He committed no relevant violence to the foetus, which was not a person,
> either at the time or in the future, and intended no harm to the foetus or to the human
> person which it would become. If fictions are useful, as they can be, they are only
> damaged by straining them beyond their limits. I would not overstrain the idea of
> transferred malice by trying to make it fit the present case.'

Hence, whilst D could be guilty of murder if he shot at P, but missed and killed Z,
the inference is that D could not be guilty of murder if he shot at P intending to do
grievous bodily harm, but missed and killed Z.

Reform

Clause 32 of the DCLB provides:

> '(1) In determining whether a person is guilty of an offence, his intention to cause, or his
> awareness of a risk that he will cause, a result in relation to a person or thing capable of
> being the victim or subject-matter of the offence shall be treated as an intention to cause
> or, as the case may be, an awareness of the risk that he will cause, that result in relation
> to any other person or thing affected by his conduct.
> (2) Any defence on which a person might have relied on a charge of an offence in relation
> to a person or thing within his contemplation is open to him on a charge of the same
> offence in relation to a person or thing not within his contemplation.'

Save for the necessary amendment in relation to recklessness, cl 32 effectively
replicates the original proposal in cl 24 of the Draft Code.

The explanation provided in Law Com No 218 for the provision of a general
statement on transferred fault states:

> 'Where a person intends to affect one person or thing (X) and actually affects another (Y),
> he may be charged with an offence of attempt in relation to X; or it may be possible to
> satisfy a court or jury that he was reckless with respect to Y. But an attempt charge may
> be impossible (where it is not known until trial that the defendant claims to have had X
> and not Y in contemplation); or inappropriate (as not describing the harm done
> adequately for labelling or sentencing purposes). Moreover, recklessness with respect to Y
> may be insufficient to establish the offence or incapable of being proved. The rule stated
> by [clause 32] overcomes these difficulties.' (para 42.1)

4

The Protection of Life

4.1 The range of offences

English criminal law provides a range of offences that recognise the sanctity of life by prohibiting the unlawful killing of a human being. The generic term 'homicide' covers offences such as murder, manslaughter, and causing death by dangerous driving. What all homicides have in common is the unlawful killing of a human being; what distinguishes them is either the state of mind of the defendant who has caused death, or the defences available. For these purposes a human being comes into existence at the moment of birth, provided that the child has had an existence independent of its mother. Such independent existence need only be momentary. There are some old authorities on the point, although they may need to be treated with caution, which suggest that whilst the child's body must have been expelled from the mother's womb (see *R v Poulton* (1832) 5 C & P 329), the cord between mother and child does not have to have been cut: see *R v Reeves* (1839) 9 C & P 25.

82

In *R* v *Brain* (1834) 6 C & P 349, Parke J directed the jury that a baby could be the victim of homicide, even though it had not started breathing: see further *R* v *Enoch* (1833) 5 C & P 539 and *R* v *Handley* (1874) 13 Cox CC 79.

Regarding the point at which life ceases for the purposes of homicide, doctors frequently refer to a patient as being 'brain dead', indicating that, whilst he can be kept alive on a life support machine, there is no chance of his ever recovering consciousness. For the purposes of criminal law such a patient would not be regarded as 'legally dead', in the sense that if D were to enter a hospital ward and deliberately switch off a machine maintaining the vital functions of such a patient, he could still nevertheless be charged with murder or manslaughter: see further on this point *R* v *Malcherek and Steel* (below).

In addition the criminal law extends a degree of protection to the unborn child.

Abortion and child destruction

Sections 58 and 59 of the Offences Against the Person Act 1861

Section 58 of the 1861 Act creates the offence of unlawfully procuring a miscarriage. The offence can be committed by anyone who unlawfully administers any poison or noxious substance, or uses any means to procure a miscarriage. Where the defendant is a woman who has administered such substances to herself, or used such means upon herself, the prosecution must prove that she was actually pregnant at the time. In the case of any other defendant, there can be liability under s58 regardless of whether the woman concerned is pregnant or not.

Note that s58 distinguishes between poison and other noxious substances. It has been held that where the substance administered is not a recognised poison, it must be taken in such quantities that it becomes harmful to health: see *R* v *Marlow* (1964) 49 Cr App R 49.

Where a woman, who wrongly believes herself to be pregnant, persuades another person to commit an offence under the section, she may still be guilty of conspiring to commit the offence or of being an accomplice to the offence, notwithstanding the fact that she herself is not pregnant: see *R* v *Whitchurch* (1890) 24 QBD 420 and *R* v *Sockett* (1908) 72 JP 428.

An important limitation on the scope of the offence is the requirement that the defendant should be proved to have acted unlawfully. In *R* v *Bourne* [1939] 1 KB 687, the defendant doctor performed an abortion upon a 14-year-old girl who had been raped. He performed the operation in a hospital, with the consent of the parents, and did not receive any fee. He had formed the view that if the girl was allowed to give birth she might not survive. The defendant was acquitted by the jury of a charge under s58, following a direction from MacNaghten J to the effect that such conduct was not to be viewed as unlawful where the defendant acted in good faith, to save the life of the mother. Were the situation to arise today, the doctor might well be protected from a prosecution under s58 by the provisions of the Abortion Act 1967, considered below. The direction in *R* v *Bourne* can also be seen as an indirect recognition of the defence of necessity, although the common law still refuses to permit this as a general defence.

Under s59 of the 1861 Act liability is extended to those who knowingly supply the means for procuring a miscarriage, regardless of whether or not the woman upon whom they are to be used, or to whom they are to be supplied, is pregnant or not.

Infant Life (Preservation) Act 1929
Section 1(1) of this Act provides that any person who intentionally causes the death of a child capable of being born alive shall, following conviction, be liable to life imprisonment. The Act expressly provides that no one who commits such acts in good faith, to preserve the life of the mother, shall be guilty of the offence.

The Act contains a rebuttable presumption in s1(2) that a child is capable of being born alive once 28 weeks of pregnancy has passed. Given that this provision was enacted some 60 years ago, since when the skill of doctors in keeping alive premature babies has increased out of all recognition, there has been considerable pressure for the '28 week rule' to be altered. As stated above it is actually a rebuttable presumption, not a rule, so it is always open to the prosecution to bring a charge under the 1929 Act even though an abortion has been performed on a woman who was less than 28 weeks pregnant, provided it can be proved beyond all reasonable doubt that the baby would have survived had it been born at that stage of the pregnancy. The matter was considered by the Court of Appeal in *C* v *S* [1987] 2 WLR 1108, where the defendant was a single woman, between 18 and 21 weeks pregnant, who wished to have an abortion. The father applied for an injunction to prevent the abortion, on the ground, inter alia, that if carried out it would constitute an offence under the 1929 Act, since in his view the child was by now a viable foetus, or child capable of being born alive. The court held that whilst a foetus of this age might display rudimentary signs of life, the medical evidence established on a balance of probabilities that such a foetus was not a child capable of being born alive for the purposes of the 1929 Act. The evidence of the foetus' viability was much clearer, however, in *Rance* v *Mid Downs Health Authority* [1991] 1 All ER 801. The plaintiff sought damages for the alleged failure of the defendant's radiographer to identify a foetus as having spina bifida. The plaintiff's contention was that if the condition had been correctly identified she would have sought an abortion. The court found as a fact that if the abortion had taken place, the foetus would have been 27 weeks old, and thus protected by the terms of the 1929 Act. The '28 week rule' was clearly rebutted by the evidence that if the child had been born after 27 weeks it would have been capable of sustaining an independent existence. In those circumstances the court refused to allow the plaintiff to pursue a cause of action based on the failure of the health authority to carry out an abortion which would in any event have been an offence under the 1929 Act.

Abortion Act 1967
The 1967 Act, as amended by the Human Fertilisation and Embryology Act 1990,

provides that doctors carrying out abortions will not incur liability under s58 of the 1861 Act or the Infant Life (Preservation) Act 1929, provided the conditions laid down in s1 of the 1967 Act are complied with.

Such abortion will be lawful if carried out within the first 24 weeks of the pregnancy, where two registered medical practitioners, acting in good faith, are of the opinion that the continuation of the pregnancy would involve risk, greater than if pregnancy were terminated, of injury to the physical or mental health of the pregnant woman or any existing children of her family.

Beyond 24 weeks there are three grounds for permitting a termination. First the doctors must have formed the view that a termination is required to prevent grave permanent injury to the mother's mental or physical health. Secondly, because pregnancy would involve risk to the mother's life greater than if the pregnancy were terminated. Thirdly, because it is necessary due to the substantial risk of the child being born with serious physical or mental handicaps.

Section 5(1) of the 1967 Act, as amended by the 1990 Act, has the further effect of removing the possibility of liability under the Infant Life (Preservation) Act 1929 where an abortion is carried out within the terms of the 1967 Act.

It remains a matter of some doubt as to whether a doctor performing an abortion not permitted by the 1967 Act could nevertheless rely on the decision in *R* v *Bourne* (above) by way of defence.

Abortion and homicide

What is the liability of D who, perhaps attempting to carry out an abortion, inflicts injuries on the foetus which is subsequently born alive but then dies as a result of the pre-natal injuries inflicted by D? Clearly D could be charged with attempting to commit an offence under the 1861 or 1929 legislation outlined above, but could he, as an alternative, be charged with murder or manslaughter? Except under statute an embryo or foetus in utero cannot be the victim of a crime of violence. A child 'en ventre sa mere' does not have a distinct human personality, the termination of which could give rise to any liability at common law: see further *Kelly* v *Kelly* (1997) The Times 5 June. Violence towards a foetus, however, which results in harm suffered after the baby has been born alive can give rise to criminal responsibility, notwithstanding that the harm would not have been criminal (at common law) if it had been suffered in utero. The fact that there might be an interval in time between the doing of an act by D (with the necessary mens rea) towards the foetus and its impact on the child when subsequently born does not in itself prevent the intent, the act and the death from together amounting to murder, so long as there is an unbroken causal connection between the act and the death.

More problematic is the situation where D's acts are directed at the woman carrying a child, with the result that the child dies sometime after birth as a result of the effects of the attack. In *Attorney-General's Reference (No 3 of 1994)* [1997] 3 All ER 936 the House of Lords considered the case of D who had stabbed P, his girlfriend, who was in the 23rd week of her pregnancy. D was convicted of causing grievous bodily harm with intent. As a result of the stabbing P underwent an operation to repair a cut in the wall of her uterus. The doctors performing the operation wrongly concluded that there had been no injury to the foetus, but it later transpired that it had suffered damage to its abdomen. Three weeks after the operation P went into labour and gave birth to a daughter. Some weeks later P died. The child died 120 days after being born. There was no evidence directly linking the injury to the child with its death. The medical evidence indicated that she had died as a result of the premature birth and its attendant complications. D was charged with the murder of the child but acquitted following a direction from the trial judge to the jury that there could be no conviction for murder or manslaughter. The House of Lords held that (even assuming a chain of causation could be established linking the stabbing of the mother with the death of the baby) a conviction for murder would not be possible, but a conviction for manslaughter would be sustainable where D intentionally committed a dangerous and unlawful act upon a pregnant woman that resulted in her giving birth to a child who subsequently died as a result of prenatal injuries sustained in the attack upon the mother.

A key factor in the House of Lords' ruling regarding liability for murder was its rejection of the Crown's submission that, in law, the mother was to be regarded as being the same legally entity as the foetus, and vice-versa. Lord Mustill rejected this notion on the basis that he believed it to be:

> '... wholly unfounded in fact. ... There was, of course, an intimate bond between the foetus and the mother, created by the total dependence of the foetus on the protective physical environment furnished by the mother, and on the supply by the mother through the physical linkage between them of the nutriments, oxygen and other substances essential to foetal life and development. ... But the relationship was one of bond, not of identity. The mother and the foetus were two distinct organisms living symbiotically, not a single organism with two aspects. The mother's leg was part of the mother; the foetus was not.'

This finding forced the Crown to fall back on the notion that the doctrine of transferred malice could be invoked to transfer the 'malice' directed at the mother to the foetus and, in turn, to the child once born. Lord Mustill explained that the House of Lords' refusal to accept this argument was based upon a recognition that it involved:

> '... a double "transfer" of intent: first from the mother to the foetus and then from the foetus to the child as yet unborn. Then one would have to deploy the fiction (or at least the doctrine) which converts an intention to commit serious harm into the mens rea of murder. For me, this is too much. If one could find any logic in the rules I would follow it from one fiction to another, but whatever grounds there may once have been have long since disappeared. I am willing to follow old laws until they are overturned, but not to make a new law on a basis for which there is no principle ...'

Lord Hope, who dealt at more length with the issue of liability for manslaughter, explained why a distinction would be made between the two forms of homicide in this situation, and why liability for manslaughter was a possibility:

> '[In unlawful act manslaughter] The intention which must be discovered is an intention to do an act which is unlawful and dangerous. In this case the act which had to be shown to be an unlawful and dangerous act was the stabbing of the child's mother. There can be no doubt that all sober and reasonable people would regard that act, within the appropriate meaning of this term, as dangerous. It is plain that it was unlawful as it was done with the intention of causing her injury. As the defendant intended to commit that act, all the ingredients necessary for mens rea in regard to the crime of manslaughter were established, irrespective of who was the ultimate victim of it. The fact that the child whom the mother was carrying at the time was born alive and then died as a result of the stabbing is all that was needed for the offence of manslaughter when actus reus for that crime was completed by the child's death. The question, once all the other elements are satisfied, is simply one of causation. The defendant must accept all the consequences of his act, so long as the jury are satisfied that he did what he did intentionally, that what he did was unlawful and that, applying the correct test, it was also dangerous. The death of the child was unintentional, but the nature and quality of the act which caused it was such that it was criminal and therefore punishable. In my opinion that is sufficient for the offence of manslaughter. There is no need to look to the doctrine of transferred malice for a solution to the problem raised by this case so far as manslaughter is concerned.'

Reform

The offence of unlawfully procuring a miscarriage set out in s58 of the 1861 Act (with the exception of passages relating to a woman procuring her own miscarriage) would be replaced by cl 66 of the Draft Code which provides:

> 'A person is guilty of an offence if he intentionally causes the miscarriage of a woman otherwise than in accordance with the provisions of the Abortion Act 1967.'

Self abortion is provided for separately in cl 67, which states that a pregnant woman is guilty of an offence if she intentionally causes her own miscarriage otherwise than in accordance with the provisions of the Abortion Act 1967.

Interestingly, the Code envisages a departure from the usual rules relating to impossibility in that it goes on to provide that a woman who is not pregnant cannot be guilty of an attempt to commit an offence under the Draft Code. Clause 68 proposes an offence of supplying or procuring an article or substance knowing that it is to be used with the intention of causing the miscarriage of a woman otherwise than in accordance with the provisions of the Abortion Act 1967, whether the woman concerned is pregnant or not. Clause 69 reproduces the effect of s1 of the Infant Life (Preservation) Act 1929 in Code style. Subsection (3) goes on to provide for the situation where a child is killed whilst being born. It states:

> 'A person who is found not guilty of murder or manslaughter (or attempted murder or manslaughter) of a child by reason only of the fact that the jury is uncertain whether the child had been born or whether he had an existence independent of his mother when his death occurred (or, in the case of an attempt, when the act was done) shall be convicted of child destruction (or attempted child destruction).'

4.2 Causation

Homicide is a 'result crime' in the sense that the defendant must be proved to have caused the victim's death. Two matters have to be considered. Did the defendant in fact cause the victim's death, and if so, can he be held to have caused it in law?

Causation in fact

This can be resolved by the application of the 'but for' test. In the majority of situations proof of causation in fact is almost a formality as it will be self evident; however, the case of *R* v *White* [1910] 2 KB 124 illustrates how problems can arise. The defendant placed two grains of potassium cyanide in a glass containing his mother's drink. She drank the contents of the glass, but died of heart failure before the poison could take effect. The defendant was charged with murder, and convicted of attempted murder, a finding against which he appealed unsuccessfully. As regards causation in fact, the defendant's act in placing the poison in his mother's drink did not in any way cause her death. If one were to ask, 'But for the defendant's act would his mother have died?', the answer would obviously have to be in the affirmative; she would have died anyway, thus disproving causation in fact. In such cases the appropriate charge would then be one of attempting to commit the substantive offence, provided that the defendant has taken sufficient steps towards its commission.

The passage of time

At common law, by virtue of what was known as the 'year and a day rule', D would not have been guilty of either murder or manslaughter if P had died more than 366 days from the date upon which D inflicted harm upon P. The basis for this rule, the origins of which could be traced back over 800 years, was that if P had survived for more than a year after being attacked by D there would be great uncertainty, if P subsequently died, as to whether D's act was the cause of death or whether some other supervening cause was responsible. For comparatively recent illustrations of the rule being applied see *R* v *Dyson* [1908] 2 KB 454, and *R* v *Coroner for Inner West London, ex parte De Luca* [1988] 3 WLR 286. It was open to the courts to convict D of a non-fatal offence, such as grievous bodily harm with intent and, if P died within 366 days of D's attack, charge D with murder or manslaughter. The 'autrefois convict doctrine' was not applicable because D had never been in jeopardy of being convicted for murder or manslaughter at his first trial: see *R* v *Golding* (1994) The Times 28 April.

Unsuccessful attempts were made to introduce an amendment to what became the Criminal Justice and Public Order Act 1994 when it was before the House of Commons so as to include a clause abolishing the 'year and a day' rule, proponents of change pointing out that in this respect English law was out of step with that of other comparable countries, the rule never having been part of Scots law, and no longer forming part of the law in any European country other than Cyprus. The argument that the rule was needed because of the evidential difficulty in determining whether D's act caused P's death no longer bore close scrutiny, given the state of modern forensic science. Particularly difficult moral and ethical questions arose where the victim of a criminal attack was left in a persistent vegetative state as a result of injuries inflicted by D. Given the technical ability to sustain patients in this condition for many years, it was seen as absurd that D should escape liability for murder or manslaughter simply because the decision to disconnect a life support system was effected more than 366 days after his unlawful act. The rule was also open to criticism on the ground that it presented problems to prosecutors considering manslaughter charges against companies where unsafe working practices resulted in the deaths of employees some years after being exposed to health dangers in the workplace.

In its report *Legislating the Criminal Code: The Year and a Day Rule in Homicide* (Law Com No 230), the Law Commission recommended the abolition of the rule, and these proposals have since been enacted, with some amendments, in the form of the Law Reform (Year and a Day Rule) Act 1996. Under the 1996 Act, which has the effect of abolishing the year and a day rule, there are two situations where the Attorney-General's consent will be required if any person is to be prosecuted for a 'fatal offence'. The first is where the death of the victim occurs more than three years after the injury alleged to have caused the death is sustained, and the second is where the person to be prosecuted has already been convicted of an offence committed in connection with the offence. The Act, which applies in England, Wales and Northern Ireland, came into effect on 17 August 1996.

Causation in law

Simply because a chain of causation in fact can be established, it should not be assumed that legal liability will necessarily follow. The principles of causation in law exist to prevent D from being convicted where his acts are too remote from the death, or where his acts are only a minimal cause of death. The general test to be applied in order to establish causation in law is whether D's act has accelerated P's death to an extent that is more than merely negligible? D's act does not necessarily need to be a substantial cause of P's death, but must be more than de minimis. Assuming that, prima facie, D's act is a cause in law of P's death, D may be able to contend that there has been a novus actus interveniens, or break in the chain of causation, that relieves him of liability for the completed offence.

Novus actus interveniens: the acts and omissions of the victim

Whilst the duty resting upon the victim to mitigate the harmful effects of any wrongful action is a well developed concept in the law of torts, there appears to be no corresponding duty resting upon the victim of an unlawful criminal assault. Hence, if D attacks P, causing injuries that are potentially life-threatening, and P neglects to attend to the injuries or seek competent assistance, with the result that P dies, D may be unable to contend that P's failure to obtain medical treatment broke the chain of causation. In *R v Holland* (1841) 2 Mood & R 351, D struck P's hand with an iron bar, causing it to be badly cut. P decided not to seek treatment, developed lockjaw, and later died. The court held that D had caused the death of P in fact and in law: see further *R v Wall* (1802) 28 State Tr 51. Whilst these decisions might seem justifiable given the somewhat crude state of medical treatment at the time, the principle is still applicable today, the leading modern authority being the decision of the Court of Appeal in *R v Blaue* (1975) 61 Cr App R 271. D had stabbed P, who was a Jehovah's Witness, and she was admitted to hospital where doctors diagnosed that she would need an immediate blood transfusion if her life was to be saved. P refused the necessary transfusion, because it was against her religious beliefs, and died of her wounds shortly after. D appealed against his conviction for manslaughter on the ground that P's refusal of treatment had broken the chain of causation, but the court held that he had to take his victim as he found her, meaning not just her physical condition but also her religious beliefs. In a sense what the court was doing in this case was extending the so-called 'thin skull rule' to encompass not just the physical peculiarities of the victim but also the victim's mental state. As Lawton LJ observed:

> 'It has long been the policy of the law that those who use violence on other people must take their victims as they find them. This in our judgment means the whole man, not just the physical man. It does not lie in the mouth of the assailant to say that his victim's religious beliefs which inhibited him from accepting certain kinds of treatment were unreasonable.'

Whilst *Blaue* suggests that no peculiarities of P can be relied upon by D to contend that the chain of causation was broken by P's action or inaction, a slightly different analysis emerges from those cases dealing with so-called 'escape' situations: those where P dies in his or her efforts to escape from an attack threatened or perpetrated by D. Early cases on this point establish that such a defendant can be charged with murder or manslaughter, provided that P's fear was well grounded: see *R v Pitts* (1842) Car & M 248. More recently, in *R v Mackie* (1973) 57 Cr App R 453, the Court of Appeal upheld the manslaughter conviction of D whose three-year-old son fell downstairs and died in trying to escape from a beating, the court endorsing the trial judge's direction to the jury which had invited them to consider, first, whether the boy had been in fear, secondly whether that fear had caused him to try to escape, thirdly whether the fear was well founded, and if so, whether it was caused by the unlawful conduct of D. In *DPP v Daley* [1980] AC 237, Lord Keith summarised what, in their Lordships' view, the prosecution had to establish in such cases, namely:

1. P, immediately before he sustained his injuries, was in fear of being hurt physically.
2. P's fear was such that it caused him to try to escape.
3. Whilst P was trying to escape, and because he was trying to escape, he met his death.
4. P's fear of being hurt there and then was reasonable and was caused by the conduct of D.
5. D's conduct which caused the fear was unlawful.
6. D's conduct was such as any sober and reasonable person would recognise as likely to subject the victim to at least the risk of some harm resulting from it, albeit not serious harm.

Despite the detailed nature of these guidelines, it may still be necessary, in some cases, to give a jury further guidance on the issue of causation, particularly where there is evidence that P's reaction was disproportionate to D's threat. In *R* v *Roberts* (1971) 56 Cr App R 95 Stephenson LJ suggested that the correct approach is to ask:

> 'Was [the victim's reaction] the natural result of what the assailant said and did, in the sense that it was something that could reasonably have been foreseen as the consequence of what he was saying or doing? As it was said in one of the old cases, it had got to be shown to be his act, and if of course the victim does something so "daft", in the words of the appellant in this case, or so unexpected, [such] ... that this particular assailant did not actually foresee it [and] ... that no reasonable man could be expected to foresee it, then it is only in a very remote and unreal sense a consequence of his assault, it is really occasioned by a voluntary act on the part of the victim which could not be reasonably foreseen and which breaks the chain of causation between the assault and the harm or injury.'

In short, if P's response to D's threats is reasonably foreseeable, it will not constitute a novus actus interveniens; see further *R* v *Corbett* [1996] Crim LR 594. Is it true to say, therefore, that an unforeseeable or 'daft' action by P, by way of response to D's threats or attack, will result in the chain of causation being broken?

In *R* v *Dear* [1996] Crim LR 595, D was convicted of the murder of P, having attacked P and stabbed him several times with a 'Stanley' knife. D appealed on the basis that P had effectively committed suicide, and thus broken the chain of causation in law, either by reopening wounds inflicted by D, or by failing to seek medical attention for wounds inflicted by D that had subsequently reopened of their own accord. Dismissing the appeal, the Court of Appeal took the view that P had died of wounds inflicted by D, and that D's liability should not depend on distinctions between P's acting negligently or with gross negligence in respect of his injuries. A jury would be entitled to find that D's stabbing of P was a cause in law of P's death even if P had deliberately reopened the wounds. On the basis that the wounds inflicted by D were an operating and substantial cause of death, the decision is uncontroversial, indeed unremarkable. The decision does, however, raise questions as to the limits of liability. If P's wounds were well on the way to being healed and he chose, for whatever reason, to pick at them, causing them to reopen, with fatal consequences, would D still be regarded as having caused the death? At what point does such activity fall outside the scheme of foreseeable actions referred to in *Roberts*, and become 'daft'? Alternatively, does D, on the basis of *Blaue*, have to take the victim as he finds him, including his 'daft' behaviour in respect of his injuries?

The solution might lie in distinguishing between cases where the original injury inflicted by D is the cause of death, and those in which D's unlawful acts are merely the background explaining why P took action that amounted to an independent and supervening cause of death. Two cases illustrate this point. First, in *R v Dalby* [1982] 1 WLR 425, where P voluntarily consumed a large quantity of proscribed drugs supplied by D, the Court of Appeal allowed D's appeal against his conviction for manslaughter on the basis, as Waller LJ observed, that:

> 'In this case the supply of drugs would itself have caused no harm unless the deceased had subsequently used the drugs in a form and quantity which was dangerous.'

This suggests that P's voluntary act in consuming the drugs was an independent and operating cause of death, a view subsequently confirmed in *R v Goodfellow* (1986) 83 Cr App R 23. Second, in *R v Armstrong* [1989] Crim LR 149, D, a drug addict, supplied P, who had already taken large amounts of alcohol, with heroin and drug-taking paraphernalia. P died shortly after self-injection of a large quantity of the heroin. Owen J (at first instance) upheld defence counsel's submissions that either there was, on the facts, no or no sufficient evidence that heroin had been a substantial cause of death, or alternatively that if heroin did cause death, P's self-injection was a novus actus interveniens. It is submitted that *Dalby* and *Armstrong* may mark the point at which the defendant is no longer responsible for the actions of the victim.

On this basis, for example, where P, having been indecently assaulted by D, commits suicide by shooting himself in the head because of an overwhelming sense of shame or depression, it is submitted that P's action should be regarded as a novus actus interveniens, notwithstanding the ratio of *Blaue*. The matter has been examined by the civil courts in *Pigney v Pointers Transport Services* [1957] 2 All ER 807, where it was held that the chain of causation was not broken by P's suicide which was induced by an anxiety neurosis developed following an accident caused by D's negligence. It is submitted, however, that caution should be exercised in seeking to relying on decisions concerned with claims for compensation, when considering the imposition of criminal liability.

To date, the only significant attempt to reconcile *Blaue* and *Roberts* is the Court of Appeal's decision in *R v Williams* [1992] 1 WLR 380, where D had jumped to his death from a moving car in order to escape from a robbery. Stuart-Smith LJ stated:

> '... the nature of the threat is of importance in considering both the foreseeability of harm to the victim from the threat and the question of whether the deceased's conduct was proportionate to the threat; that is to say that it was within the ambit of reasonableness and not so daft as to make his own voluntary act one which amounted to a novus actus interveniens and consequently broke the chain of causation ... It should of course be

borne in mind that a victim may in the agony of the moment do the wrong thing ... [T]he jury should bear in mind any particular characteristics of the victim and the fact that in the agony of the moment he may act without thought and deliberation.'

The difficulty with this approach, however, is that it simply begs the question: if P is 'daft' and attempts an escape that a sensible person would realise was foolhardy, does P's escape break the chain of causation, or does D have to take his victim as he finds him?

Novus actus interveniens: the acts of a third party

The principle of reasonable foreseeability is equally applicable to those situations where the intervention of a third party is a factor in causing the death of P. In *R* v *Pagett* (1983) 76 Cr App R 279, D had armed himself with a shot-gun and taken a P, a pregnant girl, hostage in a block of flats. The police besieged the building, calling on him to come out, which he eventually did, holding P in front of him as a human shield. D fired the shot-gun at the police officers who returned fire, striking and killing P. D was convicted of manslaughter, the conviction being upheld by the Court of Appeal which held that the reasonable actions of a third party, by way of self-defence, could not be regarded as a novus actus interveniens. In this case the police officers had instinctively returned D's fire; the need for them to act in self-defence had been caused by D's firing of his own gun, and their actions were reasonable in the circumstances. As Robert Goff LJ observed:

> 'There can, we consider, be no doubt that a reasonable act performed for the purpose of self-preservation, being of course itself an act caused by the accused's own act, does not operate as a novus actus interveniens ... for present purposes, we can see no distinction in principle between an attempt to escape the consequences of the accused's act, and a response which takes the form of self-defence. Furthermore, in our judgment, if a reasonable act of self-defence against the act of the accused causes the death of a third party, we can see no reason in principle why the act of self-defence, being an involuntary act caused by the act of the accused, should relieve the accused from criminal responsibility for the death of the third party.'

Novus actus interveniens: the acts of a third party – medical treatment

In what circumstances can the medical treatment received by P, following an attack by D, relieve D of liability for homicide if P subsequently dies? Perhaps a simple and logical response would be to contend that whilst it is reasonably foreseeable that the victim of an attack will require medical attention, the chain of causation should be broken if that medical attention is unforeseeably poor or incompetent. As will be seen, however, there are broader policy considerations to take into account. Should D's liability depend upon the quality of health care available to P? To what extent should the courts take into account the pressures under which doctors providing public health care have to operate?

A useful starting point is the Court of Appeal's decision in *R* v *Jordan* (1956) 40

Cr App R 152. D had stabbed P who was admitted to hospital, where he died some eight days later. D was convicted of murder, but appealed when new evidence came to light that, whilst in hospital, the victim had been given a drug to which he was allergic. The conviction was quashed on the ground that the medical treatment had been 'palpably wrong', with the result that it broke the chain of causation between the stabbing and the death. The evidence was that the original stab wound was well on the way to being healed at the time of death, and thus it could be said to be merely the setting within which another cause of death operated. As Hallett J observed:

> '... we are disposed to accept it as the law that death resulting from any normal treatment employed to deal with a felonious injury may be regarded as caused by the felonious injury, but we do not think it necessary to examine the cases in details or to formulate for the assistance of those who have to deal with such matters in the future the correct test which ought to be laid down with regard to what is necessary to be proved in order to establish causal connection between the death and the felonious injury. Not only one feature, but two separate and independent features, of treatment were, in the opinion of the doctors, palpably wrong and these produced the symptoms discovered at the post-mortem examination which were the direct and immediate cause of death, namely, the pneumonia resulting from the conditions of oedema which was found.'

Whilst *Jordan* clearly establishes that wrongful medical treatment can constitute a novus actus, subsequent decisions confirm that it is, to some extent, a decision that rests upon its own peculiar facts, and, more generally, that the courts are reluctant, as a matter of policy, to permit D to escape liability on the basis of P receiving inadequate treatment. In *R v Smith* [1959] 2 QB 35, D had been involved in a barrack-room fight with P, a fellow soldier, during the course of which he had stabbed P several times with a bayonet, which resulted in P being taken to a medical post where he died approximately one hour later. On being convicted of murder D contended that the chain of causation between the stabbing and the death had been broken by the way in which P had been treated, in particular the fact that he had been handled roughly whilst being carried to the medical post, and that there had been a delay in providing P with treatment because of the number of other cases being dealt with. Upholding the conviction, Lord Parker CJ observed:

> '... if at the time of death the original wound is still an operating cause and a substantial cause, then the death can properly be said to be the result of the wound, albeit that some other cause of death is also operating. Only if it can be said that the original wounding is merely the setting in which another cause operates can it be said that the death did not result from the wound. Putting it another way, only if the second cause is so overwhelming as to make the original wound merely part of the history can it be said that the death does not flow from the wound ...'

In cases where the evidence suggests that medical treatment may amount to a supervening event such as to break the chain of causation, there is no onus on the Crown to establish that the medical treatment was *not* a substantial cause of death. As Schiemann LJ observed in *R v Mellor* [1996] 2 Cr App R 245:

'In homicide cases, where the victim of the alleged crime does not die immediately, supervening events will occur which are likely to have some causative effect leading to the victim's death; for example, a delay in the arrival of the ambulance, a delay in resuscitation, the victim's individual response to medical or surgical treatment, and the quality of the medical, surgical and nursing care. Sometimes such an event may be the result of negligence or mistake or bad luck. It is a question of fact and degree in each case for the jury to decide, having regard to the gravity of the supervening event, however caused, whether the injuries inflicted by the defendant were [nevertheless] a significant cause of death.'

The emphasis on the original wound inflicted by D as the cause of death also underpins the approach of the courts in those cases where doctors have decided to withdraw treatment from the victim of an assault, with the result that the victim dies. In *R* v *Malcherek*; *R* v *Steel* (1981) 73 Cr App R 173, both defendants had, in separate incidents, attacked women, causing injuries that were so severe that their victims had to be placed on life support machines in hospital. In both cases doctors decided to switch off the machines after determining that the victims were 'brain dead' and that there was no prospect of recovery. Both defendants were convicted of murder. The common ground of appeal in both cases was that the doctors had broken the chain of causation between the defendants' attacks and the deaths of the victims by deliberately switching off the life support machines. The Court of Appeal, dismissing the appeals, held that in both cases the operating and substantial cause of death had been the original wounds inflicted by the defendants. The effect of the life support machine was merely to hold the effect of those injuries in suspension; as soon as the machine was switched off the original wounds would continue to cause the death of the victim, even if death ensued within seconds of the machine's disconnection. On a broader policy basis, the Lord Chief Justice expressed the view that nothing done by a doctor in the ordinary course of medical treatment could be regarded as a novus actus interveniens. As he put it:

'... if treatment is given bona fides by competent and careful medical practitioners, then evidence will not be admissible to show that the treatment would not have been administered in the same way by other medical practitioners. In other words the fact that the victim has died, despite or because of medical treatment for the initial injury given by careful and skilled medical practitioners, will not exonerate the original assailant from responsibility for the death.'

It is tempting, in the light of the above, to talk in terms of medical treatment breaking the chain of causation only if it is reckless or grossly negligent, suggesting perhaps that liability for the death is thereby transferred to the medical practitioners treating the victim. The Court of Appeal's decision in *R* v *Cheshire* (1991) 93 Cr App R 251, however, suggests that a clear distinction should be maintained between the actions of medical practitioners, which may break the chain of causation, and the state of mind that accompanies such actions. Beldam LJ noted that:

'Even though negligence in the treatment of the victim was the immediate cause of his death, the jury should not regard it as excluding the responsibility of the accused unless the negligent treatment was so independent of his acts, and in itself so potent in causing death, that they regard the contribution made by his acts as insignificant ... [E]ven if more experienced doctors than those who attended the deceased would have recognised the rare complication in time to have prevented the deceased's death, that complication was a direct consequence of the appellant's acts which remained a significant cause of his death.'

Coincidence of mens rea and actus reus

It is a general principle in criminal law that for liability to be established it must be shown that the defendant possessed the necessary mens rea at the time the actus reus was committed. For example, D sets off in his car to visit P at his house intending to stab him to death and on the way accidentally runs over and kills a pedestrian who steps into the road without looking. D cannot be charged with murder when he subsequently discovers that the pedestrian he has accidentally killed is in fact P. D had the necessary mens rea when he set out on his journey, and committed the actus reus of murder when he ran P over, killing him. There was, however, no coincidence of the two. At the time of the accident D was not driving his car intending to kill another human being.

Whilst the principle is clearly correct, a strict application of it can produce difficulties for the prosecution, as illustrated by the Privy Council decision in *Thabo Meli* v *R* [1954] 1 WLR 228. The defendants had taken their intended victim to a hut and plied him with drink so that he became intoxicated. They then hit the victim around the head, intending to kill him. In fact the defendants only succeeded in knocking the victim unconscious but, believing him to be dead, they threw him over a cliff. The victim died of exposure some time later. The defendants were convicted of murder, and appealed to the Privy Council on the ground that there had been no coincidence of the mens rea and actus reus of murder, in the sense that when they had acted with the intention of killing the victim by striking him on the head, they had failed to kill him. On the other hand, when they did actually cause his death, by throwing him over the cliff, they lacked the mens rea for murder as they believed he was already dead. The Privy Council held that the correct view of what the defendants had done was to treat the chain of events as a continuing actus reus. The actus reus of causing death started with the victim being struck on the head and continued until he died of exposure. It was sufficient for the prosecution to establish that at some time during that chain of events the defendants had acted with the requisite mens rea for murder. See also on this point *R* v *Church* [1966] 1 QB 59.

It is perhaps more accurate to regard the 'coincidence' rule as but an aspect of the wider principles of causation. In both *Thabo Meli* and *Church* the courts were in effect expressing the view that nothing done by the defendants broke the chain of causation between the first violent act and the victim's death. As pointed out in *Smith & Hogan's Criminal Law* (8th ed (1996) p347), the matter would be otherwise if, for example D, having wounded P, visited him in hospital and accidentally infected him with smallpox thus causing his death. In such a case liability for the death could not be traced back to the original unlawfully inflicted injury.

It would appear that D's actions will be regarded as falling within the same series of events even where there is a considerable gap in time between the original injury and the act causing death. In *R* v *Le Brun* [1991] 3 WLR 653, the defendant had punched his wife on the chin and later caused her death when attempting to move her body. Lord Lane CJ commented:

> 'It seems to us that where the unlawful application of force and the eventual act causing death are part of the same sequence of events, the same transaction, the fact that there is an appreciable interval of time between the two does not serve to exonerate the defendant from liability. That is certainly so where the appellant's subsequent actions which caused death, after the initial unlawful blow, are designed to conceal his commission of the original unlawful assault … [T]he original unlawful blow to the chin was a causa sine qua non of the later actus reus. It was the opening event in a series which was to culminate in death: the first link in the chain of causation, to use another metaphor. It cannot be said that the actions of the appellant in dragging the victim away with the intention of evading liability broke the chain which linked the initial blow with the death.'

Reform

The complex issue of causation, which is relevant to all 'result' crimes, is dealt with by cl 17 of the Draft Code. This is a matter which, to date, has not received consideration by the Criminal Law Revision Committee. The purpose of cl 17 is to restate the principles to be found in the common law. Clause 17(1) provides:

> '17(1) Subject to subsections (2) and (3), a person causes a result which is an element of an offence when:
> (a) he does an act which makes a more than negligible contribution to its occurrence; or
> (b) he omits to do an act which might prevent its occurrence and which he is under a duty to do according to the law relating to the offence.

As regards cl 17(1)(a), the Code Report commentary states:

> 'Under existing law a person's act need not be the sole, or even the major, cause of a harmful result. It is enough that the act is a "substantial" [*R* v *Smith*] or "significant" [*Pagett*] cause of the result, and in this context this means merely that the defendant's contribution must be outside the de minimis range. Accordingly it is wrong, for example, to direct a jury that the defendant is not liable if he is less than one-fifth to blame [*R* v *Hennigan* [1971] 3 All ER 133].' (Vol II, para 7.15)

The commentary goes on to point out that under the test put forward there may be more than one cause of a result where two persons are independently liable in respect of the same harm. The test reflects the existing common law in not taking account of a victim s peculiar susceptibility to harm. Clause 17(1)(b) deals with the issue of causation in relation to omissions. The way in which it would operate is indicated in the example given in Appendix B, Volume I, example 17(ii):

> 'E's mistress lives with E and P, E's child by his wife. While E is away P falls seriously ill. D, wishing P to die fails to call a doctor. P dies. P's life might have been prolonged by

medical attention. If D was under a duty to obtain medical attention for P she is guilty of murder. She has caused P's death intending to cause death.'

The possibility of a novus actus interveniens breaking the chain of causation is dealt with by cl 17(2), which states:

'A person does not cause a result where, after he does such an act or makes such an omission, an act or event occurs –
(a) which is the immediate and sufficient cause of the result;
(b) which he did not foresee, and
(c) which could not in the circumstances reasonably have been foreseen.'

As the commentary upon this subsection states, this is essentially a restatement of the common law:

'[The clause] appears to restate satisfactorily for criminal law the principles which determine whether intervening acts or events are sufficient to break the chain of causation between the defendant's conduct and the result, as it is sometimes put, whether in the circumstances the defendant's conduct is a cause in law of the result. According to this provision a person will still be liable if his intended victim suffers injury in trying to escape from the threatened attack unless the victim has done something so improbable that it can properly be said not to have been reasonably foreseeable. Equally, liability for homicide will be unaffected if the victim refuses medical treatment for a wound caused by the defendant. Even if the refusal could be said to unforeseeable, it is not sufficient in itself to cause the victim's death – in such a case, to use the language of the cases, the original wound is still the ioperatingî and substantial causeî of death.' (Vol II, para 7.17)

Clause 17(3) deals with the application of the proposals for causation to accomplices. This will be considered in more detail in Chapter 13.

4.3 The mens rea of murder

In a memorable passage in *Attorney-General's Reference (No 3 of 1994)* [1997] 3 All ER 936 Lord Mustill observed that, on the basis that murder was widely thought to be the gravest of crimes:

'One could expect a developed system to embody a law of murder clear enough to yield an unequivocal result on a given set of facts, a result which conforms with apparent justice and has a sound intellectual base. This is not so in England, where the law of homicide is permeated by anomaly, fiction, misnomer and obsolete reasoning.'

As the following will demonstrate this is certainly a fair critique of the law in so far as it relates to the development of the mens rea for murder.

Homicide Act 1957

Prior to the enactment of s1 of the Homicide Act 1957, 'constructive malice' was sufficient mens rea for murder. The result was that if D killed in the course of committing a felony, such as burglary, he would be charged with murder because the necessary mens rea would be construed from his having committed the felony. This 'felony murder' rule as it was known operated in a spectacularly harsh fashion. Where, for example, D burgled P's house wrongly thinking it to be unoccupied, and P, on disturbing D in the process of stealing goods, died of shock, D could be charged with P's murder, even though he might not have actually had the intention of injuring anyone.

The 1957 Act abolished constructive malice, but did not replace it with a statutory definition of murder, s1(1) simply providing that:

'Where a person kills another in the course or furtherance of some other offence, the killing shall not amount to murder unless done with the same malice aforethought (express or implied) as is required for the killing to amount to murder when not done in the course or furtherance of another offence.'

Whilst it is true that Coke's classic definition of murder refers to D acting with 'malice aforethought', and that this is widely understood by the layman as the mental element required for murder, it is submitted that in modern terms the expression is inaccurate, and the perpetuation of it by Parliament in s1(1) of the 1957 Act is at best unhelpful. The term is likely to mislead the unwary in that it suggests some element of planning on the part of D is required, when in truth murder can be quite spontaneous. Further, it suggests that D must act with some degree of ill will against P, when again no such evidence is required by the law. As Lord Mustill further observed in *Attorney-General's Reference (No 3 of 1994)* when considering the example of the terrorist who hides a bomb in an aircraft intending to cause an explosion in flight:

'This is not a case of "general malice" where under the old law any wrongful act sufficed to prove the evil disposition which was taken to supply the necessary intent for homicide. Nor is it transferred malice, for there is no need of a transfer. The intention is already aimed directly at the class of potential victims of which the actual victim forms part. The intent and the actus reus completed by the explosion are joined from the start, even though the identity of the ultimate victim is not yet fixed. So also with the shots fired indiscriminately into a crowd. No ancient fictions are needed to make these cases of murder.'

Shortly after the 1957 Act came into effect the Court of Appeal in *R* v *Vickers* [1957] 2 QB 664 held that D could be convicted of murder if it was established that he had intended to kill, or had intended grievous bodily harm. This was effectively a re-introduction of a form of constructive liability. In *Hyam* v *DPP* [1975] AC 55 a majority of their Lordships extended the mens rea somewhat further by holding that it was sufficient for D to have foreseen that death or grievous bodily harm was a probable, or highly probable, consequence of his actions. This 'heretical' confusion of foresight with mens rea was compounded in the subsequent House of Lords' decision in *R* v *Cunningham* [1982] AC 566. It was not until the House of Lords' decision in *R* v *Moloney* [1985] AC 905 that the law was placed on something resembling a sound footing, in that their Lordships held that foresight of consequences on the part of D was not a form of mens rea, but evidence of it. Lord Bridge went on to suggest that where a jury in a murder trial sought some assistance from the trial judge as to the meaning of intention to kill or intention to do grievous bodily harm, they should be directed to ask themselves whether the death or grievous bodily harm was the natural consequence of D's act, and further whether D had foreseen death or grievous bodily harm as the natural consequence of his act. If the jury answered both questions in the affirmative they were entitled to infer that D had intended the consequences of his acts: see further Chapter 3, section 3.2. Notwithstanding Lord Scarman's reluctance in *R v Hancock* [1986] AC 455 to provide much in the way of guidance for juries regarding the task of determining whether or not there was evidence of intention, the House of Lords in *R v Woollin* [1998] 4 All ER 103 has endorsed the approach of the Court of Appeal in *R v Nedrick* [1986] 3 All ER 1. Hence, if a jury seeks guidance on the right approach to intent in a murder trial, it should be made clear to them that they are entitled to find that the defendant intended to kill or do grievous bodily harm if they are sure that he foresaw death or grievous bodily harm as a virtually certain consequence of his actions.

A rough and ready rationale for accepting intention to cause grievous bodily harm as being sufficient mens rea for murder is that if D is willing to inflict grievous bodily harm, how is he to know that P might not die? An intention to cause grievous bodily harm at least evidences a willingness to accept a substantial risk that P might die. The problem with this approach, however, is that it introduces an element of risk-taking as part of the mental element for an offence which should require proof of intent. The problem is further exacerbated by the fact that conviction for murder carries with it a mandatory penalty of life imprisonment. Lord Mustill recognised as much in his speech in *Attorney-General's Reference (No 3 of 1994)*. Whilst accepting that there was clear authority for the rule, he refused to extend it to apply to the novel facts before the court in that case. As he observed:

> '... in a system based on binding precedent there could be no ground for doubting a long course of existing law, and certainly none which could now permit this House even to contemplate such a fundamental change as to abolish the grievous harm rule. ... But when asked to strike out into new territory it is, I think, right to recognise that the grievous harm rule is an outcropping of old law from which the surrounding strata of rationalisations have weathered away. It survives but exemplifies no principle which can be applied to a new situation.'

Further, in *R v Powell and Daniels; R v English* [1997] 4 All ER 545 Lord Steyn observed:

> 'In English law a defendant may be convicted of murder who is in no ordinary sense a murderer. ... This rule turns murder into a constructive crime. The fault element does not correspond to the conduct leading to the charge, ie the causing of death. A person is liable to conviction for a more serious crime than he foresaw or contemplated ... This is a point of considerable importance. The Home Office records show that in the last three years for which statistics are available mandatory life sentences for murder were imposed

in 192 cases in 1994; in 214 cases in 1995; and in 257 cases in 1996. Lord Windlesham, writing with great Home Office experience, has said that a minority of defendants convicted of murder have been convicted on the basis that they had an intent to kill: "Responses to Crime," vol 3 (1996), at 342, n29. That assessment does not surprise me. What is the justification for this position? There is an argument that, given the unpredictability whether a serious injury will result in death, an offender who intended to cause serious bodily injury cannot complain of a conviction of murder in the event of a death. But this argument is outweighed by the practical consideration that immediately below murder there is the crime of manslaughter for which the court may impose a discretionary life sentence or a very long period of imprisonment. Accepting the need for a mandatory life sentence for murder, the problem is one of classification. The present definition of the mental element of murder results in defendants being classified as murderers who are not in truth murderers. It happens both in cases where only one offender is involved and in cases resulting from joint criminal enterprises. It results in the imposition of mandatory life sentences when neither justice nor the needs of society require the classification of the case as murder and the imposition of a mandatory life sentence.'

Punishment

A defendant convicted of murder will be sentenced to life imprisonment. The punishment is mandatory, in the sense that it is the only sentence that can be imposed, but the trial judge does have the discretion to make a recommendation as to the minimum period of imprisonment that the defendant should serve before being considered for release on parole. The death penalty was abolished as a sentence for murder by Parliament in 1965, leaving only treason and piracy with violence as capital offences. The United Kingdom has, in the past, declined to ratify Protocol 6 to the European Convention on Human Rights, which prohibits the death penalty, on the basis that 'the issue is not one of basic constitutional principle but is a matter of judgement and conscience to be decided by Members of Parliament as they see fit.' (See *Rights Brought Home: The Human Rights Bill* (Cm 3782).) The Human Rights Act 1998, which incorporates the Convention into domestic law, does however contain a provision obliging the government to sign, ratify and incorporate the Protocol.

Reform

Clause 54 of the Draft Code states that a person 'is guilty of murder if he causes the death of another: intending to cause death; or intending to cause serious personal harm and being aware that he may cause death [subject to certain defences]'. In the light of the subsequent proposals in the DCLB, the reference to 'serious personal harm' would now presumably be replaced with a reference to 'serious injury'. For these purposes cl 53(a) of the Draft Code provides that 'another' means 'a person who has been born and has an existence independent of his mother and, unless the context otherwise requires, "death" mean[s] the death of ... such a person.' As the commentary on cl 53(a) observes:

inition of "another" in clause 53(a) effectively defines the person against whom
nces ... may be committed. Though, following Coke, the definition of a person "in
is traditionally discussed only in relation to homicide, it is clear that, in principle,
ime definition must apply to offences against the person generally. This is achieved
,aragraph (a). That paragraph also makes it clear that a person who intends to cause
ι. death of ... an unborn child does not intend to commit murder and is not, by reason
of that intention, guilty of murder if the child is born alive and then dies of the injury.
This settles a matter of doubt in the present law in accordance with, as we think, sound
principle. A person who intended to kill the mother would be guilty of murder of the
child if the injuries he inflicted with that intent caused the child to die after it had been
born alive: see ... (transferred fault).' (Vol II, para 14.2)

The House of Lords continues to emphasis the need for legislative intervention to
reform the law in this area. As Lord Mustill observed in *R* v *Powell and Daniels*; *R* v
English (above):

'Once again, an appeal to this House has shown how badly our country needs a new law
of homicide, or a new law of punishment for homicide, or preferably both. The judges
can do nothing about this, being held fast by binding authorities on the one hand and a
mandatory statute on the other. Only Parliament has the powers, if it will choose to
exercise them. It may not be a popular choice, but surely it is justice that counts.'

In the same case, Lord Steyn added:

'... in *R* v *Cunningham* ... the House of Lords declined to rationalise and modernise the
law on this point. Only Lord Edmund-Davies expressed the hope that the legislature
would undertake reform. ... In my view the problem ought to be addressed. There is
available a precise and sensible solution, namely, that a killing should be classified as
murder if there is an intention to kill or an intention to cause really serious bodily harm
coupled with awareness of the risk of death: 14th Report of the Law Revision Committee,
(1980), para 31, adopted in the Criminal Code, for England and Wales, (Law Com No
177), (1986), clause 54(1). This solution was supported by the House of Lords Select
Committee on Murder and Life Imprisonment, HL Paper 78-1, 1989, para 68.'

4.4 Voluntary manslaughter: provocation

When a defendant has caused a victim's death, and has been proved to have had the
necessary mens rea for murder, he may still be able to avoid a conviction for murder
by establishing that he comes within the scope of one of the four defences which are
only available to a defendant charged with murder. The four defences are:
provocation; diminished responsibility; infanticide; and suicide pact. In each case, if
the defendant succeeds with the defence, his liability is reduced from murder to
manslaughter, the significance of this being that for murder the punishment is a
mandatory life sentence, whereas for manslaughter the sentence is at the discretion
of the trial judge. This form of manslaughter is described as 'voluntary' because
there will have been evidence that the defendant did intend to kill or cause grievous
bodily harm.

Provocation is a common law defence that can only be raised in relation to a charge of murder. Its origins can be traced back over several centuries, and its evolution reflects the common law's attempts to make concessions to the frailty of the human spirit. The defence is based upon an acceptance that a reasonable, even-tempered person might be so provoked by certain incidents that he is driven to kill. Broadly the defence operates thus: if there is evidence that can be left to the jury indicating that D was provoked so as to lose his self-control and kill, the question then becomes one of whether the reasonable person would have acted in a like fashion.

Although the defence will almost always be raised by the principal offender whose actions are the direct cause of the victim's death, there is no rule of common law or under statute to prevent the defence being raised by one who is an accomplice to murder, whether as counsellor, procurer, aider or abettor: see further *R* v *Marks* [1998] Crim LR 676. Note that in cases where the killing results from a pre-arranged plan it might be difficult for a defendant charged as an accomplice to discharge the evidential burden of proving that the killing resulted from a sudden and temporary loss of self-control.

What can amount to provocation?

Historically, the common law has taken a somewhat restrictive view in respect of what could provide the basis for the defence of provocation, limiting the defence to instances where D was attacked, encountered his spouse committing adultery, or discovered another man sodomising his son. For many years it was doubted whether words alone could ever constitute provocation. Although the defence is still based on the common law, a major liberalisation of its scope was achieved with the enactment of s3 Homicide Act 1957, which provides:

> 'Where on a charge of murder there is evidence on which the jury can find that the person charged was provoked (whether by things done or by things said or by both together) to lose his self-control, the question whether the provocation was enough to make a reasonable man do as he did shall be left to be determined by the jury; and in determining that question the jury shall take into account everything both done and said according to the effect which, in their opinion, it would have on a reasonable man.'

The effect of this provision is that it is now possible for *anything* to constitute provocation, including words spoken by another, the actions of third parties, and provocation directed at third parties (this latter point was confirmed in *R* v *Pearson* [1992] Crim LR 193). Hence in *R* v *Doughty* [1986] Crim LR 625, it was held to be a misdirection for a trial judge to tell a jury that the persistent crying of a 17-day-old baby could not constitute provocation.

As indicated below, the focus is no longer so much upon what can constitute provocation, but more on the issues of whether there is evidence of provocation, and how the reasonable man would have responded. In this sense, circumstances may fail to give rise to the defence of provocation, not because there is any rule to that effect, but because they do not provide direct evidence of any provoking event. In *R* v *Acott* [1997] 1 WLR 306, for example, Lord Steyn suggested that loss of self-control brought on by panic, fear, sheer bad temper, or circumstances such as being caught in slow traffic, would not provide a sufficient evidential basis for the defence, although he was also at pains to add that each case was to be judged on its own facts. On this basis there must be considerable doubt as to the rectitude of the Privy Council's decision in *Edwards* v *R* [1973] AC 648, where it was held that self-induced provocation (ie where D induces P to provoke him) could not be allowed as a defence, the rationale being that the defendant should not be permitted to escape liability where he has instigated the incident.

It is submitted that the better view of self-induced provocation is that expressed by the Court of Appeal in *R* v *Johnson* [1989] 2 All ER 839, where it was again emphasised that, under s3 of the 1957 Act, anything could amount to provocation including actions provoked by the accused. The appellant in that case had been deprived of the opportunity of having his defence considered properly by the jury, following the trial judge's ruling that he was bound to follow *Edwards* v *R*.

Leaving the defence to the jury

Section 3 places an evidential burden on D, in the sense that there must be sufficient evidence of provocation to justify the trial judge leaving the defence to the jury. If, as was the case in *R* v *Cocker* [1989] Crim LR 740 for example, the evidence is that when D killed P he was aware of his actions, and had killed in cold blood, the trial judge will be justified in omitting any reference to provocation in his directions to the jury. It is not enough that the circumstances suggest that D may have been provoked.

The House of Lords has confirmed, in *R* v *Acott* (above), that before a judge is required to leave the defence of provocation to the jury there had to be some evidence of specific acts or words of provocation resulting in D's loss of self-control. Such evidence could come from any source, and need not be relied upon directly by D himself, but should be such as to show that the killing might have resulted from D's uncontrolled reaction to the provocation. The speculative possibility that such evidence existed, for example on the basis that provoking act may have been the 'last straw' is not a sufficient ground for leaving the defence to the jury. Such an approach is surely right given that there must be some evidence of what provoked D before a jury can apply the objective test and assess what the reaction of the reasonable person would have been.

The judge's role in determining whether the jury should be directed on provocation was usefully summarised by Lord Taylor CJ in *R* v *Cambridge* [1994] 1 WLR 971, where he observed:

> 'The starting point, therefore, is whether there is evidence on which the jury can find the defendant was in fact provoked to lose his self-control. That is a question for the judge. In our judgment, therefore, there must be evidence on the first limb from which a reasonable jury might properly conclude that the defendant was in fact provoked to lose

his self-control or may have been so by some words or acts or both together. If the judge decides that there is not such evidence, he ought not to leave provocation to the jury. If, on the other hand, he concludes that there is such evidence on the first limb of the two-stage test, the statute obliges him to leave provocation to the jury, even if he himself believes the circumstances to be such that no reasonable man would have reacted as the defendant did.'

In the event that the trial judge feels uncertain as to whether or not D has discharged the evidential burden, decisions of the Court of Appeal such as that in *R v Rossiter* [1994] 2 All ER 752 suggest that he should be given the benefit of the doubt. D killed her husband during a domestic quarrel, the evidence indicating that she had been exposed to physical and verbal abuse by the deceased. She maintained that the killing had either been accidental or had occurred whilst she had been defending herself, and denied ever having had the intention to kill the deceased or cause grievous bodily harm. Her counsel was thus not able to put the defence of provocation before the jury. Allowing her appeal, the Court of Appeal held that, despite her assertions to the contrary, it was possible to infer from the evidence that D had lost her self-control and killed; hence the jury should have been directed to consider the defence of provocation. On the question of provocation, however, Russell LJ observed:

'We take the law to be that whenever there is material which is capable of amounting to provocation, however tenuous it may be, the jury must be given the privilege of ruling upon it.'

This approach seems to hold even where the defence of provocation would be inconsistent with the manner in which D has seen fit to contest the charge against him or her. In *Cambridge* (above) the Court of Appeal held that the trial judge had erred in not leaving the issue of provocation to the jury, even though D's 'defence' had been one of alibi, because witnesses gave evidence at the trial that he had been involved in an altercation with the deceased shortly before he was found dead, hence there was evidence that D might have been provoked (albeit that it would also have meant that his alibi was false!).

The tactical implications of this are significant. If D, charged with murder, simply pleads not guilty, members of the jury harbouring a reasonable doubt as to guilt might acquit. Where jury members are presented with the possibility of convicting of manslaughter on the grounds of provocation they may opt for this rather than an outright acquittal. Clearly this is a less advantageous result as far as D is concerned.

On the basis of *R v Burgess and McLean* [1995] Crim LR 425 and *R v Dhillon* [1997] Crim LR 295, however, a trial judge should not accede to defence counsel's submission that the defence of provocation be withheld from the jury if there is nevertheless prima facie evidence of provocation that a reasonable jury can act upon. The effect is that a defendant should be allowed the chance of benefiting from a perverse verdict in his favour even if the trial judge believes that no reasonable person would have been provoked to kill in the circumstances in question. It seems unlikely that a defendant convicted of 'voluntary' manslaughter in such a case could ever successfully appeal against his conviction because the trial judge erred in his favour! See further on this point *R* v *Cox* [1995] Crim LR 741 and *R* v *Stewart* [1995] 4 All ER 999.

Was the defendant provoked?

In the course of formulating his well known definition of provocation in *R* v *Duffy* [1949] 1 All ER 932 Devlin J referred to the need for evidence that D, at the time of the killing, had been suffering from 'a sudden and temporary loss of self-control, rendering him so subject to passion as to make him, at that moment, no longer the master of his own mind.' *R* v *Richens* [1993] Crim LR 384, however, suggests that it would be unwise for a trial judge to embellish this requirement by suggesting to the jury that the appellant should provide evidence of having completely lost his self-control, to the extent that he did not realise what he was doing.

If the jury, when considering whether or not D suffered a sudden and temporary loss of self-control, focuses on the last incident which causes D to lose his self-control and kill, a somewhat distorted picture may emerge. In some cases the incident that provokes D is the proverbial 'last straw'. Taken alone this incident may be somewhat trifling, and lead the jury to conclude that D could not have been acting under provocation. Increasingly, however, the courts are showing themselves willing to consider the history of events leading up to the defendant's outburst. In *R* v *Dryden* [1995] 4 All ER 987, for example, where D had shot dead local planning authority's principal planning officer following a dispute about planning permission for D's bungalow, Lord Taylor CJ, adverting to the need to have regard to the history behind the incident indicated that: 'It was in regard to his obsession with his property and this dispute that the [threatened demolition of D's bungalow] was "the last straw" in the build-up of stress upon the appellant.'

Further, in *R* v *Humphreys* [1995] 4 All ER 1008, a case where the deceased had abused the defendant, both physically and verbally, over a period of time and encouraged her to continue her prostitution, Hirst LJ observed:

> '... we ... do not think that on the facts of this case a mere historical recital, devoid of any analysis or guidance, ... sufficient. ... This tempestuous relationship was a complex story, with several distinct and cumulative strands of potentially provocative conduct building up until the final encounter. Over the long term there was continuing cruelty, represented by the beatings and the continued encouragement of prostitution, and by the breakdown of the sexual relationship. On the first part of the night in question there was the threatened "gang bang", and the drunkenness. Immediately before the killing, quite apart from the wounding verbal taunt, there was [the deceased's] appearance in an undressed state, posing a threat of sex which [the appellant] did not want and which he must have known she did not want, thus demonstrating potentially provocative conduct immediately beforehand not only by words but also by deeds. Finally of course there is the taunt itself, which was put forward as the trigger which caused the appellant's self-

control to snap ... we consider that ... guidance in the form of careful analysis of these strands should have been given by the judge so that the jury could clearly understand their potential significance.'

That a jury should be encouraged to look at the whole chain of events was also confirmed by Lord Goff in *R* v *Morhall* (considered below) where he observed:

'... in an appropriate case, it may be necessary to refer to other circumstances affecting the gravity of the provocation to the defendant which do not fall strictly within the description of "characteristics" as for example the defendant's history or the circumstances in which he is placed at the relevant time ...'

Finally, note the observation of Lord Taylor CJ in *R* v *Thornton (No 2)* [1996] 2 All ER 1023 at 1030 to the effect that:

'A jury may more readily find there was a sudden loss of control triggered by even a minor incident, if the defendant has endured abuse over a period, on the "last straw" basis.'

How swiftly must the killing flow from the provocation?

The use, by Devlin J of the word 'sudden' introduces the issue of 'cooling time', in the sense that where there is a gap in time between the provocation and the killing, the defendant may encounter evidential difficulties in trying to establish the defence. In *R* v *Hayward* (1833) 6 C & P 157 the judge directed the jury to consider whether there had been time between the alleged provocation and killing, 'for the blood to cool, and for reason to resume its seat'. The difficulties that a defendant can encounter were illustrated in *R* v *Ibrams and Gregory* (1981) 74 Cr App R 154. The defendants and a young woman had been terrorised and bullied over a period of time by the deceased, a man called Monk. Believing that police protection would be ineffective, they devised a plan that involved the woman enticing the deceased to her bed, whereupon the defendants would burst into the room and attack him. The plan was carried out as arranged, resulting in the death of Monk. The defendants were convicted of murder following the trial judge's decision to withdraw the defence of provocation from the jury and the defendants appealed unsuccessfully to the Court of Appeal. Lawton LJ expressed the view that the gap of seven days between the last act of provocation and the killing refuted any evidence that it had been carried out by defendants suffering from a sudden and temporary loss of self-control as envisaged by Devlin J in *R* v *Duffy* (above).

In *R* v *Brown* [1972] 2 All ER 1328 the Court of Appeal approved a direction to the jury that to find provocation they had to find it in something done on the morning of the killing. By contrast, in *R* v *Davies* (1974) Cr App R 253 the same court thought it too generous to the defendant to direct the jury that they could consider the whole of the deceased's conduct throughout the turbulent years preceding the death.

Finally, in *R* v *Ballie* [1995] 2 Cr App R 31, the appellant had killed the victim having gone to the attic of his house to retrieve a gun, and having driven several miles to the deceased's house (stopping off for petrol on the way). The Court of Appeal criticised the trial judge's refusal to allow the defence of provocation to be left to the jury as 'too austere', Henry LJ observing that 'there was arguably no "natural break" between [D receiving information] which caused him to go up into the attic to find the shotgun hidden there, and the shooting itself'.

To ask whether or not there had been a 'natural break' between the provoking event and the killing is possibly more helpful that any attempt to determine specific time limits within which a defendant must kill in order to come within the defence of provocation. As noted above, if there is any evidence of provocation that a jury can act upon the safest course of action for the trial judge is to give a direction on the defence.

The 'reasonable person' test

Once the defendant has discharged the burden of establishing evidence of provocation upon which a jury can be directed, the jury will have to engage in the task of applying the objective test, ie determining whether or not a reasonable person, sharing certain characteristics of the accused would have reacted as the defendant did. In *Mancini* v *DPP* [1942] AC 1 the House of Lords held that, as a matter of law, there had to be a reasonable relationship between the mode of provocation and the acts of the defendant, in the sense that a defendant would be expected to answer words with words, stones with stones and knives with knives. With the enactment of s3 of the Homicide Act 1957, however, this must now be seen as nothing more that a guideline. The important question is whether the defendant's actions were such as could have been expected from the reasonable person, and this is a matter for each jury to determine.

For many years the reasonable man test was applied somewhat inflexibly, in the sense that he was not thought to possess any peculiar characteristics. For example, in *Bedder* v *DPP* [1954] 2 All ER 801, where the defendant killed after being taunted regarding his impotence, the court refused to take this characteristic into account. The reasonable man was not impotent.

Over the years, however, the law has become more humane. In the landmark decision of the House of Lords in *DPP* v *Camplin* [1978] 2 All ER 168, Lord Diplock was at pains to stress that the jury should be told that the reasonable man was a person having the power of self-control to be expected of an ordinary person of the sex and age of the accused, but in other respects sharing such of the accused's characteristics as they think would affect the gravity of the provocation to him.

The effect of this change was plain to see in *Camplin* itself. Camplin, a 15-year-old-boy had been raped by a man named Khan. Khan had then taunted Camplin about this, prompting Camplin to beat Khan to death. In trying to assess the seriousness or gravity of that provocation it would have been meaningless to ask how the reasonable 15-year-old (who had not been raped) would have responded to such taunts. The reasonable 15-year-old who had not been raped would not have even understood why he was being taunted in this manner. The circumstances (ie having been raped) have to be taken in to account to show why the provocation is wounding.

In *R v Morhall* [1995] 3 WLR 330 D had killed P following an argument over D's addiction to glue sniffing. Allowing D's appeal against his conviction for murder, the House of Lords held that D's glue-sniffing habit was of 'particular relevance' as the words of P were directed to that condition, and there was nothing in the speeches in *Camplin* to suggest that such a characteristic ought to be excluded from consideration. Lord Goff expressed the view that the Court of Appeal had misunderstood the nature of the reasonable person test because, as he explained, the test:

> '... is concerned not with ratiocination, nor with the reasonable man whom we know so well in the law of negligence ... nor with reasonable conduct generally. The function of the test is only to introduce, as a matter of policy, a standard of self-control which has to be complied with if provocation is to be established in law ... to speak of the degree of self-control attributable to the ordinary person ... perhaps is more apt, and certainly less likely to mislead, than to do so with reference to the reasonable person ... [I]ndeed, by exploiting the adjective "reasonable" it is easy to caricature the law as stated in s3 of the 1957 Act by talking of the test of, for example, the reasonable blackmailer or ... the reasonable glue sniffer ... [T]his however is misleading. In my opinion it would be entirely consistent with the law as stated in s3 of the 1957 Act, as properly understood, to direct the jury simply with reference to a hypothetical person having the power of self-control to be expected of an ordinary person of the age and sex of the defendant, but in other respects sharing such of the defendant's characteristics as they think would affect the gravity of the provocation to him ...'

Lord Goff endorsed the view expressed by Lord Diplock in *Camplin* to the effect that the jury should be directed to consider circumstances affecting the gravity of the provocation that may not fall within the strict definition of characteristics, such as the defendant's background and his current situation (sometimes referred to as 'the entire factual situation'). On this basis a defendant who killed having been taunted about his paedophiliac tendencies could contend that he should be judged by the standard of the *ordinary* person of the age and sex of the defendant, having the defendant's inclinations. Such characteristics are simply evidence that provide an explanation as to why the defendant found the taunts to be so provocative.

Indeed, the current position can be summarised by saying that a characteristic can be taken into account for the purposes of assessing the gravity of the provocation to the defendant:

1. even though the characteristic is not permanent – as Lord Goff observed in *Morhall* – some physical conditions, such as eczema, may be transitory in nature and yet can surely be taken into account if the subject of taunts;
2. even though the provocation is not directly related to the characteristic;
3. even though the characteristics are factors such as the defendant's history or the

circumstances in which he is placed at the time of the provocation, for example being unemployed, lacking education, being spurned in love, being sent to prison or being a sexual deviant.

It is, however, vital to bear in mind that these observations relate to characteristics taken into account for the purpose of assessing the gravity of the provocation. The essential issue, on which judicial opinion is somewhat divided at present, is the second stage of the objective test, the extent to which these matters might also be characteristics for the purposes of assessing the degree of self-control to be expected of the reasonable person.

What test should be used for assessing the desired standard of self-control?

Should the law adopt an entirely objective test, or should it attribute to the reasonable man any characteristics of the accused that suggest he has difficulty in exercising self-control?

Certain basic issues seem to be settled, largely as a result of *DPP* v *Camplin*. The so-called 'universal' characteristics of the accused can be attributed to the reasonable man for the purposes of the self-control test. These are age and sex. Hence, in *Camplin*'s case the test became: Would the reasonable 15-year-old boy have been provoked to lose his self-control and kill? Camplin was, of course, provoked by the taunts of the deceased who had just raped him. He was not taunted about his age. However, his age was a characteristic to be attributed to the reasonable man, simply because it would have been manifestly unfair to expect a 15-year-old boy to display the self-control expected of a reasonable adult.

At what age a young defendant is to be judged by the standard of an adult is unclear, but in *R* v *Ali* [1989] Crim LR 736 the Court of Appeal dismissed the appeal of the 20-year-old appellant who had contended that a 20-year-old might not be expected to display the self-control of a more mature man.

Similarly, according to the House of Lords in *Camplin*, sex will be taken into account, regardless of the nature of the provocation, although one might well ask why. The House of Lords seems to have been hinting at some difference in the degree of self-control to be expected of a woman as opposed to a man. Are women generally, more reasonable creatures than men? If they are, they would find it more difficult to satisfy the objective test (ie a greater degree of self-control would be expected). Conversely, is the House of Lords suggesting that women are less able to control their emotions than men? In which case women should find it easier to satisfy the objective test. If neither generalisation is true, then why take sex into account, other than to avoid the linguistic incongruity of asking the jury to consider whether a reasonable man would have lost his self-control when the defendant is in fact a woman? Suppose, for example, that a woman claims that she lost her self-control and killed because she was suffering from extreme PMT, or post-natal depression, at the time of the provocation. It may sound ludicrous to judge her by the standard of the reasonable man, but to make allowances because she is a woman would directly conflict with the notion (clearly stated in *Camplin*) that the reasonable person is even-tempered and able to exercise reasonable control over his or her emotions. In severe cases the proper course of action would be to raise the defence of diminished responsibility based on the medical evidence of PMT or post-natal depression: see further section 4.5 below.

So much for age and sex. What other characteristics are attributed to the reasonable man or woman in assessing whether that reasonable person would have been provoked to kill? Lord Diplock, in *DPP* v *Camplin*, saw the reasonable person as being sober, not exceptionally excitable or pugnacious, and possessed of such powers of self-control as everyone is entitled to expect from his fellow citizens. As he expressed it:

> "The public policy that underlay the adoption of the reasonable man test in the common law doctrine of provocation was to reduce the incidence of fatal violence by preventing a person relying on his own exceptional pugnacity or excitability as an excuse for loss of self-control ... for purposes of the law of provocation the reasonable man has never been confined to the adult male. It means an ordinary person of either sex, not exceptionally excitable or pugnacious, but possessed of such powers of self-control as everyone is entitled to expect that his fellow citizens will exercise in society as it is today.'

This approach involves a degree of rough justice, but has much to commend it.

Under this approach evidence of intoxication becomes irrelevant for the purposes of assessing self-control, because the reasonable person is not a drunkard (see *R* v *Wardrope* [1960] Crim LR 770) or an addict, and there is in any event a separate defence of intoxication. As has been seen in *Morhall*, if the defendant is taunted about his glue-sniffing addiction, that characteristic can be taken into account to explain the gravity of the provocation, but the test would still be whether a sober person, with the power of self-control possessed of an ordinary person (ie not a glue sniffer), would have been provoked to kill. Similarly, under the *Camplin* approach, evidence of pugnacity or bad temper becomes irrelevant for the purposes of the self-control test, because to allow either as a characteristic would, in theory, permit those with 'shorter fuses' greater scope to plead the defence of provocation. Finally, under the *Camplin* approach, and subject to the views expressed in a number of more recent Court of Appeal decisions, it could be argued that evidence of mental abnormality should go to support a defence of diminished responsibility, not provocation.

The move towards greater subjectivity

The Court of Appeal, in a process starting with that court's decision in *R* v *Newell* (1980) 71 Cr App R 331, has tended to the view that the mental peculiarities of the accused can be attributed to the reasonable person when applying the objective test for self-control. In *Newell* a male friend of the defendant made disparaging remarks about the defendant's former girlfriend, and then made homosexual advances towards him. The defendant, a chronic alcoholic who also suffered from depression, thereupon killed his friend. The Court of Appeal determined that alcoholism and drug taking could not be taken into account when applying the objective control test (because they were inconsistent with assumptions made about the reasonable person). It also expressed agreement with the view that moodiness, depression and irascibility would also be excluded. The Court went on, however, to cite with approval the decision of North J in *R* v *McGregor* [1962] NZLR 1069, to the effect that the objective test of self-control could be modified to take into account permanent characteristics of the defendant that were significant and marked the defendant out as being different from the ordinary run of mankind.

Thus, the actual decision as such in *Newell* was unremarkable, but the obiter statements expressing support for the more liberal approach to the attribution of characteristics to the reasonable person were highly significant, as four subsequent Court of Appeal decisions demonstrate.

Perhaps significantly, the first three of these are all cases of domestic violence. In *R* v *Ahluwalia* [1992] 4 All ER 889 Lord Taylor CJ, albeit obiter, made it clear that amongst the characteristics that could be taken into account for the purposes of the objective self-control test, he would include 'battered-woman syndrome', post-traumatic stress disorder and learned helplessness. More recently the Court has re-confirmed this approach in *R* v *Thornton (No 2)*. In *R* v *Humphreys* [1995] 4 All ER 1008 another case involving abuse of a woman by a male partner, the Court of Appeal ruled that dyslexia, anorexia, immaturity and a tendency to engage in attention-seeking by wrist-slashing, were all factors that could be taken into account when applying the objective control test. As Hirst LJ observed:

> '... Mr Milmo [counsel for the Crown] ... accepted and indeed suggested, that, for example, dyslexia and anorexia would qualify as eligible characteristics. We think that there is much force in Mrs Grindrod's [counsel for the appellant] submission in her reply that the appellant's tendency to attention-seeking by wrist-slashing is closely comparable to the latter, and, like the latter, can in truth be regarded as a psychological illness or disorder which is in no way repugnant or wholly inconsistent with the concept of the reasonable person. It is also a permanent condition which ... was abnormal and therefore set the appellant apart from that concept. Furthermore, it was clearly open to the jury to conclude that the provocative taunt relied upon as the trigger inevitably hit directly at this very abnormality, and was calculated to strike a very raw nerve. Immaturity is clearly in no way repugnant; indeed it suggests that the appellant was unduly young for her comparatively young age, and thus brings the case on this ground into close comparison with *DPP* v *Camplin*. We therefore consider that the judge should have left for the jury's deliberation these two relevant characteristics as eligible for attribution to the reasonable woman, it being for them to decide what if any weight should be given to them in all the circumstances ...'

Finally, in *R* v *Dryden* [1995] 4 All ER 987, the defendant shot dead a planning officer in full view of the TV cameras. This was the culmination of a long-running dispute over planning permission. The defendant was unsuccessful in his appeal against his conviction for murder because the Court felt there was evidence that he had planned the killing. What is significant, however, is the Court's willingness to accept that the defendant's eccentricity, his depressive illness and his paranoid thinking were significant traits that marked him out from the run of mankind, and ought to have been put to the jury as characteristics to be attributed to the reasonable man in their assessment of whether a reasonable man would have been provoked to lose his self-control and kill.

All four decisions suggest that the mental peculiarities of the defendant can now be taken into account when assessing how reasonable it was for the defendant to have lost his or her self-control and killed.

The Privy Council view

Some members of the House of Lords and the Privy Council appear to see things differently and want to hold the line on objectivity. For example, in *Morhall*, Lord Goff was at pains to point out that, whilst glue-sniffing was a characteristic that could be taken into account for the purposes of assessing the gravity of the provocation, the defendant was to be otherwise assessed by the standard of the '... hypothetical person having the power of self-control to be expected of an ordinary person of the age and sex of the defendant'.

Strictly speaking those comments of Lord Goff in *Morhall* were obiter, as he was not addressing the point of law raised in that appeal, but he returned to the issue when the Privy Council considered the appeal in *Luc Thiet Thuan* v *R* [1996] 2 All ER 1033. Here the appellant was convicted of murdering his former girlfriend and sentenced to death. He had advanced a defence of provocation – based on her claim that his performance as a lover left a lot to be required – and appealed on the ground that his mental instability (irritability arising from an old head injury) should have been taken into account when assessing whether the provocation would have caused a reasonable man to lose his self-control and kill.

The Privy Council, by a majority (Lord Steyn dissenting), ruled that this characteristic had been rightly excluded. As Lord Goff saw it the key distinction was between individual peculiarities relevant to the gravity of the provocation that should be taken into account and those individual peculiarities, related to the accused's level of self-control, that should not. The head injury fell within the latter category.

In arriving at this conclusion he was extremely critical of the Court of Appeal's approach to the problem, and observed that the opinions expressed in *Newell* had exercised an unhappy influence upon the reasoning in subsequent decisions such as *Ahluwalia*, *Dryden* and *Humphreys*.

Which view is correct?

In terms of the law applicable in our Crown Courts, the position is reasonably clear. Privy Council decisions are not binding and neither are obiter statements in the House of Lords. The Court of Appeal has recently made this clear in *R* v *Campbell (No 2)* [1997] 1 Cr App R 199. The appellant, who had been convicted of murder, was diagnosed as suffering from frontal lobe epilepsy and appealed against his conviction, for a second time, in 1996. Part of the argument advanced on his behalf was that the trial judge's direction on provocation should be looked at again, given the subsequent changes in the law, as the jury may have been inclined to exclude evidence of mental abnormality when applying the self-control test. Lord Bingham CJ, observing that the Court of Appeal regarded itself as bound by its own previous decisions and not those of the Privy Council, agreed that a retrial should be granted. He went on:

> 'We are, however, conscious that the body of Court of Appeal authority which is in doubt represents a judicial response, born of experience in criminal trials up and down the country, to what fairness seems to require. If the concept of the reasonable man expressed in section 3 were accepted without qualification, successful pleas of provocation would be rare indeed, since it is not altogether easy to imagine circumstances in which a reasonable man would strike a fatal blow with the necessary mental intention, whatever the provocation ... if there is an effective retrial in this case, and provocation is an issue, it will be the duty of the trial judge to apply the law binding upon him as it then stands.'

Similarly, in *R* v *Parker* [1997] Crim LR 760, the Court of Appeal, refusing to follow *Luc Thiet Thuan*, ordered a retrial in the case of an appellant who had been denied the opportunity, when putting forward the defence of provocation, to adduce expert evidence that his chronic alcoholism had resulted in brain damage making him more susceptible to provocation. In *R* v *Smith (Morgan)* [1998] 4 All ER 387 the Court of Appeal again refused to follow Lord Goff's lead in *Luc Thiet Thuan*, this time holding that severe depression could be taken into account for the purposes of applying the objective self-control test. Potts J expressed the view that this conclusion was not inconsistent with the speech of Lord Diplock in *Camplin*; in particular he cited Lord Diplock's comments to the effect that the question was not merely whether such a reasonable person would in like circumstances have been provoked to lose his self-control but also whether he would have reacted to the provocation as the accused did. Potts J also sought support from the dissenting advice of Lord Steyn in *Luc Thiet Thuan*, who in turn cited from Lord Simon's speech in *Camplin* where (at pp724–725) he (Lord Simon) had observed that:

> '... it is one thing to invoke the reasonable man for the standard of self-control which the law requires; it is quite another to substitute some hypothetical being from whom all mental and physical attributes (except perhaps sex) have been abstracted.'

Potts J agreed with the view expressed by Lord Steyn in *Luc* to the effect that Lord Simon's views were inconsistent with the notion that youthful immaturity was the only mental characteristic that could be taken into account when applying the objective limb of the test for provocation.

Having referred to the line of Court of Appeal decisions from *R* v *Ahluwalia* [1992] 4 All ER 889 to *R* v *Thornton (No 2)* [1996] 2 All ER 1023, Potts J continued:

'In our judgment, Lord Taylor CJ in *R* v *Thornton (No 2)* did no more than adapt Lord Diplock's formulation in *Camplin*'s case to the facts of the case then under appeal. In our opinion, the decisions of the Court of Appeal cited are in accordance with, and are a logical extension of, the decision in *DPP* v *Camplin*. They are binding on this court. In origin, the defence of provocation saved from the gallows those who would otherwise have been guilty of murder. Its incremental development over the years has been marked not by logic but by a slowly changing sense of what is fair. Words have been added to conduct as a possible trigger and the number of characteristics with which a reasonable man is deemed to be endowed, when having his theoretical response assessed by a jury, have been increased. The essential question raised by this appeal is whether, on the authorities binding on this court, any distinction can now properly be drawn, when attributing such characteristics for the purposes of the objective part of the test imposed by s3 of the Homicide Act 1957, between their relevance to the gravity of the provocation to a reasonable man and his reaction to it. It seems to us that in *Camplin*'s case Lord Diplock drew no such distinction, nor did other divisions of this court in the cases to which reference has been made. In our judgment the minority advice of Lord Steyn in *Luc Thiet Thuan* ... accurately states the law of England. We emphasise here that we have not overlooked the speech of Lord Goff in *R* v *Morhall*. But the House of Lords in *Morhall* was, as Lord Steyn pointed out in *Luc Thiet Thuan*, concerned with a different problem altogether – the characteristic supplying the sting of provocative conduct. There is nothing in Lord Goff's speech in that case inconsistent with Lord Taylor CJ's reasoning in *R* v *Thornton (No 2)* or of this court in the other decisions cited.'

See Chapter 16, section 16.1, for further details.

In policy terms it is submitted that the Court of Appeal's approach is questionable. Lord Bingham CJ in *Campbell*, observed that:

'If the concept of the reasonable man expressed in section 3 [of the Homicide Act 1957] were accepted without qualification, successful pleas of provocation would be rare indeed, since it is not altogether easy to imagine circumstances in which a reasonable man would strike a fatal blow with the necessary mental intention, whatever the provocation ...'

In other words he is suggesting that, if the law adopts an objective approach to self-control, it would be difficult to make out the defence of provocation, but one might ask what hardship is done by denying the defence where the accused fails to show the self-control to be expected of the ordinary reasonable person. It could be argued that the defence of diminished responsibility (considered at section 4.5 below) should be invoked when the defendant seeks to rely on his mental peculiarities to excuse his actions.

There are a number of compelling reasons for this conclusion. First, where diminished responsibility is raised as a defence the burden of proof rests upon the defendant. He has to establish the condition on the balance of probabilities. In short, without medical evidence he will not succeed. This provides a proper safeguard against spurious factors being raised as excuses. By contrast a defendant raising the defence of provocation merely has to provide evidence upon which a jury can act. The possibility arises, therefore, that a defendant seeking to rely on his mental peculiarities as the excuse for having committed murder might fail, on the balance of probabilities, to establish the defence of diminished responsibility, but might nevertheless succeed with the defence of provocation because he creates a reasonable doubt in the minds of the jury as to whether or not the defence of provocation is made out. Such a result seems incongruous.

The second reason for concluding that the approach of the Court of Appeal is misguided involves looking again at the inspiration for its line of reasoning. As indicated earlier this was the New Zealand case of *McGregor* (above). In that case the court was interpreting a provision similar in terms to s3 of the Homicide Act 1957, but with one crucial difference. At the time there was no statutory defence of diminished responsibility in New Zealand. Hence it is not surprising that the New Zealand courts sought to interpret their law of provocation liberally, to include any defendant labouring under mental peculiarities affecting his ability to exercise normal self-control. To import that approach into the English law of provocation, however, was unnecessary, given the fact that the defence of diminished responsibility had already been created by the Homicide Act 1957.

There is one situation that does appear to present some difficulty for critics of the Court of Appeal's approach. How should the law treat the adult defendant, with the mental age of a child, who is provoked to kill? If the provocation takes the form of taunts regarding mental age, that factor can be taken into account to explain the gravity of the provocation to the defendant, but what of self-control? The rationale of *Camplin*, however, is that in applying the objective self-control test it would be wrong to put an old head on young shoulders. Logically, therefore, an adult with a mental age of nine, who is provoked to kill, should be judged by the standard of the reasonable adult with a mental age of nine, the view taken by the Court of Appeal in *R v Raven* [1982] Crim LR 51. So how could such a defendant be catered for in a defence of provocation if mental peculiarities were to be excluded from the self-control test? The answer lies, again, in such a defendant being brought within the scope of diminished responsibility, on the basis that his responsibility for his actions has been substantially impaired by his retarded development.

The matter needs to be resolved once and for all by the House of Lords and in this respect it is worth noting that leave to appeal to the House of Lords was granted by the Court of Appeal in *R v Smith* (above), on the basis of the following certified point of law of general public importance: 'Are characteristics other than age and sex, attributable to the reasonable man, for the purpose of section 3 of the Homicide Act 1957, relevant not only to the gravity of the provocation to him but also to the standard of self-control to be expected?'

Reform

Clause 55 of the Draft Code envisages a single offence of manslaughter, covering what is at present dealt with at common law under the offences of voluntary and involuntary manslaughter. It provides (inter alia) that a person is guilty of manslaughter if he is not guilty of murder by reason only of the fact that a defence is provided by cl 58 (provocation). The defence of provocation, which would be available to both principals and accessories, is defined in cl 58 as being available to a defendant who:

> '(a) acts when provoked (whether by things done or by things said or by both and whether by the deceased person or by another) to lose his self-control; and
> (b) the provocation is, in all the circumstances (including any of his personal characteristics that affect its gravity), sufficient ground for the loss of self-control.'

This provision is largely a restatement of the existing law, with the defendant being judged on the facts as he honestly believes them to be.

4.5 Voluntary manslaughter: diminished responsibility

The defence of diminished responsibility was introduced by s2(1) of the Homicide Act 1957, which provides:

> 'Where a person kills or is party to a killing of another, he shall not be convicted of murder if he was suffering from such abnormality of mind (whether arising from a condition of arrested or retarded development of mind or any inherent causes or induced by disease or injury) as substantially impaired his mental responsibility for his acts and omissions in doing or being a party to the killing.'

The defence is only available where D's acts or omissions cause death, hence it will not avail a defendant charged with attempted murder: see *R* v *Campbell* [1997] Crim LR 495. Where D succeeds with the defence he will be convicted of manslaughter on the grounds of diminished responsibility. Section 2(2) of the 1957 Act states clearly that the burden of proving the defence rests upon the defendant, there being no duty upon the trial judge to do so on his behalf: see *R* v *Campbell* [1987] Crim LR 257. Given that the standard of proof which the defendant has to achieve is the balance of probabilities, he will have to obtain cogent medical evidence as to his condition, and trials involving claims of diminished responsibility frequently result in the unedifying spectacle of expert psychiatrists putting forward contradictory views as to the defendant's mental state.

When the defence was enacted murder was still a capital offence, and for many defendants the only way of avoiding this consequence was to try and raise the defence of insanity. As will be seen (Chapter 14), insanity is a somewhat limited defence of mental abnormality, in that it does not excuse the defendant who knows what he is doing, and who quite possibly knows that it is wrong, but is nevertheless unable to restrain himself. Hence, many defendants charged with murder were unable to avail themselves of an appropriate defence. Since the introduction of diminished responsibility nearly all of those who would formerly have raised the defence of insanity, as a defence to murder, now rely on the statutory defence.

Abnormality of the mind

The meaning of this phrase was considered by the Court of Appeal in *R v Byrne* [1960] 2 QB 396, where the defendant had strangled a young woman, and there was evidence that he was a sexual psychopath, and could exercise but little control over his actions. The defence of diminished responsibility was rejected by the trial judge, and the defendant was convicted of murder. He appealed on the basis that the defence should have been put to the jury. The Court of Appeal allowed the appeal on the basis that the trial judge had been wrong to exclude from the scope of the defence situations where a defendant was simply unable to exercise any self-control over his actions. Lord Parker CJ explained that an abnormality of the mind was simply a state of mind that the reasonable person would find abnormal, and that this was essentially a matter of fact for the jury to determine. Whilst it would be a misdirection for a trial judge to direct a jury that diminished responsibility was to be equated with 'borderline insanity' (see *R v Seers* [1985] Crim LR 85), it is generally accepted that conditions such as schizophrenia, manic depression and senile dementia could provide a basis for the defence. More recently the courts have accepted that conditions such as battered woman syndrome might also provide evidence supporting the defence: see *R v Ahluwalia* (above) and *R v Hobson* (1997) The Times 25 June.

The Court of Appeal, in *R v Brown* [1993] Crim LR 961, has confirmed that whilst it is desirable for a trial judge, directing a jury as to the meaning to be given to 'abnormality of the mind', to embellish the provisions of s2(1) of the 1957 Act by adverting to *Byrne*, it would not necessarily amount to a miscarriage of justice if this course of action was not followed. Clearly juries would be influenced by the medical evidence, but they were entitled to come to their own conclusions as to whether an abnormality resulted in a substantial impairment of the defendant's self-control. The danger with this approach, it is submitted, is that it may leave the jury in the position of having to adjudicate between conflicting expert evidence. What of the situation where the expert witnesses are unanimous in finding that the defendant was suffering from diminished responsibility? *R v Sanders* (1991) 93 Cr App R 245 suggests that in such cases the jury should be directed to accept the evidence and return a verdict of guilty of manslaughter. Watkins LJ points out, however, that if there are other circumstances, such as the history of the accused's conduct before and after the killing, the jury should consider the medical evidence in the light of this and may decide to reject it. The fact that the jury reject uncontroverted medical evidence is not of itself a ground of appeal provided they have been directed properly: see *Walton v R* [1978] 1 All ER 542; *R v Matheson* (1958) 42 Cr App R 145; and *R v Kiszko* (1979) 68 Cr App R 62. In *R v Egan* [1992] 4 All ER 470, the Court of Appeal considered the word 'substantial' as used in s2(1) of the 1957 Act, as being descriptive of the degree to which the accused's mental responsibility should be impaired in order for the defence to be made out. The court expressed agreement with the decision in *R v Lloyd* [1967] 1 All ER 107, to the effect that 'substantial' should be approached by the jury in a commonsense way as meaning:

'... more than some trivial degree of impairment which does not make any appreciable difference to a person's ability to control himself, but it means less than total impairment.'

Diminished responsibility and intoxication

The fact that a defendant might have been drunk or under the influence of drugs at the time of committing a murder is largely irrelevant to the issue of diminished responsibility, as it will not constitute an 'inherent cause' within s2. Similarly, the courts will not normally be prepared to accept the transient effect of drugs as amounting to an injury for the purposes of s2: see *R* v *O'Connell* [1997] Crim LR 683. The Court of Appeal in *R* v *Fenton* (1975) 61 Cr App R 261, acknowledged however, that intoxication could become a relevant factor, where it amounted to chronic alcoholism, in that the defendant's responsibility for his actions became substantially impaired because of his craving for drink. In *R* v *Gittens* [1984] QB 698, the Court of Appeal suggested that where the jury had to deal with both diminished responsibility and intoxication, they should be directed to consider, first whether the defendant would have killed as he did without having been intoxicated, and if the answer to that was affirmative, the second question would be whether he would have been suffering from diminished responsibility when he did so. This approach has subsequently been approved by the Court of Appeal in *R* v *Atkinson* [1985] Crim LR 314 and *R* v *Egan* (above). A distinction must be drawn, however, between a craving for drink which is caused by an abnormality of the mind, and an abnormality of the mind which is caused by a craving for drink. In *R* v *Tandy* [1989] 1 All ER 267, the Court of Appeal accepted that where a defendant could show that she was suffering from an abnormality of the mind at the time she killed, that it was induced by disease, namely alcoholism, and that it was such as substantially impaired her responsibility for her actions, then the defence of diminished responsibility would be made out. It would fail, however, where the evidence was that the defendant's first drink had been taken voluntarily, in that she had simply not resisted an impulse to drink alcohol and had subsequently ceased to have responsibility for her actions: see further *R* v *Inseal* [1992] Crim LR 35. The principles developed in *Tandy* in respect of alcoholism and diminished responsibility have been extended to other areas of substance abuse. In *R* v *Sanderson* (1994) 98 Cr App R 325 the appellant sought to raise the defence of diminished responsibility based on evidence of his long-term use of heroin and cocaine, although there was a conflict of expert medical evidence as to the relevance of the drug taking. For the appellant it was contended that he suffered from an abnormality of the mind, namely paranoid psychosis, that arose from inherent causes, such as the appellant's upbringing, and had been exacerbated by his drug taking. For the Crown it was contended that the appellant did suffer from a form of paranoia that was related to drug use and that he would not suffer from any paranoia if the drug taking ceased. Allowing his appeal and substituting a conviction for manslaughter on the grounds of diminished responsibility, the Court of Appeal held that although, if the jury believed the evidence of the expert witness for the

Crown, it would have been open to them to hold that the appellant had not been suffering from diminished responsibility, the trial judge should have directed them that the evidence advanced for the appellant, if correct, did disclose a mental illness that could constitute an abnormality of the mind, which arose from an inherent cause, thus satisfying the requirements of s2(1) of the Homicide Act 1957. In the circumstances the court did not feel that the proviso could be applied. Note that although the matter did not arise directly for consideration, the court appeared to accept the proposition that 'abnormality of the mind' encompassed not only physical or organic disorders, but also mental illness that manifested itself in a functional sense.

Reform

As noted above, cl 55 of the Draft Code provides that a defendant charged with murder and found to be suffering from diminished responsibility should be convicted of manslaughter.

Clause 56 goes on to provide that to bring himself within the terms of the defence, a defendant must be shown to have been suffering from such mental abnormality (at the time of the act causing death) that it amounted to a substantial enough reason to reduce his offence to manslaughter. Mental abnormality is further defined as 'mental illness, arrested or incomplete development of mind, psychopathic disorder, and any other disorder or disability of mind, except intoxication'. The intoxicated defendant wishing to avail himself of the defence will only be permitted to do so where it would have applied even if he were not intoxicated. Whether evidence indicates mental abnormality is to be regarded as a question of law. Mental abnormality is, for the purposes of this clause, to be taken to have the meaning attributed to it in s4 of the Mental Health Act 1959 (now s1(2) of the Act of 1983).

The clause does not attempt to codify the Court of Appeal's decision in *R* v *Tandy* (above) (in which it was held that intoxication may found diminished responsibility if the defendant is suffering from alcoholism, which renders the taking of 'the first drink' involuntary) as this was seen as raising issues which were conceptually over-complex.

4.6 Voluntary manslaughter: infanticide

The Infanticide Act 1938 provides that where a woman kills her child before it reaches 12 months in age, and there is evidence to show that at the time of the killing the balance of her mind was disturbed by the effect of giving birth, or the effect of lactation consequent upon giving birth to the child, a jury is entitled to find her not guilty of murder, but guilty instead of infanticide. The defence is clearly designed to cater for women who may be very seriously affected by post-natal depression. Note that it would not afford a defence to a woman suffering from post-natal depression who killed one of her older children, but it is arguable that she would raise diminished responsibility in such circumstances.

Reform

Clause 64 of the Draft Code provides:

'(1) A woman who, but for this section, would be guilty of murder or manslaughter of her child is not guilty of murder or manslaughter, but is guilty of infanticide, if her act is done when the child is under the age of twelve months and when the balance of her mind is disturbed by reason of the effect of giving birth or of circumstances consequent upon the birth.

(2) A woman who in the circumstances specified in subsection attempts to cause the death of her child is not guilty of attempted murder but is guilty of (1) attempted infanticide.

(3) A woman may be convicted of infanticide (or attempted infanticide) although the jury is uncertain whether the child had been born or whether it had an existence independent of her when its death occurred (or, in the case of an attempt, when the act was done).

As the commentary upon this clause indicates, it incorporates the recommendations of the Criminal Law Revision Committee's Fourteenth Report *Offences Against the Person* (1980) Cmnd 7844 in relation to infanticide. Note in particular the comments concerning the overlap between infanticide and child destruction:

'Subsection (3) provides for the case where the jury is satisfied that the defendant is guilty of either infanticide or child destruction but not satisfied that it was the one rather than the other. If the jury was uncertain, either whether the child had been born, or whether he had an existence independent of the defendant when his death occurred, it would be bound to acquit of murder or manslaughter and it would be impossible to say whether the defendant was guilty of infanticide or of child destruction. Though satisfied that it was either the one offence or the other, the jury would be bound, at least in theory, to acquit of both offences. The Committee [CLRC] thought that there should be provision for cases of this kind. The subsection enables the jury to convict of infanticide. Infanticide is chosen rather than child destruction because, under the Code, infanticide is the less serious offence. We have followed the recommendation of the Committee to reduce the maximum penalty for infanticide to five years but, like the Committee, propose no change in the penalty for child destruction. To do so would inevitably involve reconsideration of the penalty for abortion which would be controversial and could not be undertaken without consultation. If the penalties for the three offences were rationalised, this subsection might require reconsideration.

The subsection provides only for the case where the jury is uncertain. If the jury is satisfied, either that the child had not been born at the material time, or that he did not then have an existence independent of his mother, it would have to acquit of murder, manslaughter and infanticide. The defendant would be guilty of child destruction but it would be wrong to allow conviction of an offence punishable with life imprisonment on a charge of an offence punishable only with a maximum of five years.' (Vol II, paras 14.27, 14.28)

4.7 Voluntary manslaughter: suicide pact

Section 4 of the Homicide Act 1957 introduces the defence of suicide pact. It would be used in a situation where A and B agree to end their lives by each injecting the other with a massive drug overdose at the same time. The plan is carried out, and A dies, but B is found by C and rushed to hospital, and is saved. B caused the death of A deliberately and is prima facie guilty of murdering him, but B would be able to avail himself of s4, provided that he can show the purpose of the agreement with A was that they should both die, and that when he injected A with the drug, he himself was under a 'settled expectation' of dying. See further *R* v *McShane* (1978) 66 Cr App R 97.

Reform

The Draft Code contains, in cl 62, proposals for a new offence of 'suicide pact killing', in line with the recommendations of the Criminal Law Revision Committee's Fourteenth Report *Offences Against the Person* (1980) Cmnd 7844. The offence would be punishable with a maximum of seven years' imprisonment. As the Code Report commentary explains:

> 'It applies to the case of a party to a suicide pact who kills another party to the pact or who procures, assists or encourages a third person to kill a party to the pact. It does not apply to the case of a person who procures the other to take his own life. He is not a person "who, but for this section, would be guilty of murder", because suicide is no longer self-murder, or any offence. He will, however. be guilty of an offence under [cl 63 which deals with complicity in suicide]. Subsection (3) [of cl 62], implementing the Committee's recommendation, provides that it is a defence to a charge of attempted murder that the defendant attempted to kill in pursuance of a suicide pact; but the defendant will be guilty of an attempt to commit the offence.' (Vol II, paras 14.23, 14.24)

As indicated above, cl 63 provides that a person is guilty of an offence if he '... procures, assists or encourages suicide or attempted suicide committed by another'. The commentary states:

> 'This clause reproduces the effect of s2 of the Suicide Act 1961 but with the reduced maximum penalty of seven years' imprisonment ... It is made clear that the offence is committed only when the suicide is committed or attempted. A person who attempts to procure the suicide of another will be guilty of an offence under clause 49(1): clause 49(6) does not apply because this is not a case of an attempt to procure the commission of an offence.' (Vol II, para 14.25)

4.8 Death from excessive force

In addition to codifying the existing forms of involuntary manslaughter, cl 55 of the Draft Code seeks to introduce a new head of manslaughter where death results

from the use of excessive force by the defendant. The matter is d
detail by cl 59 which provides:

> 'A person who, but for this section, would be guilty of murder is not guil'
> the time of his act, he believes the use of the force which causes death t'
> reasonable to effect a purpose referred to in section 44 (use of force in public ...
> defence), but the force exceeds that which is necessary and reasonable in the circumstances
> which exist or (where there is a difference) in those which he believes to exist.'

As the commentary notes, this clause implements the recommendations of the
Criminal Law Revision Committee's Fourteenth Report *Offences Against the Person*
(1980) Cmnd 7844 (paras 95 and 96). The recommendation:

> '... adopted a principle then accepted in some parts of the Commonwealth, particularly
> Australia ... Recently, however, the High Court of Australia, in *DPP* v *Zekelic* (1987) 61
> ALJR 375 has overruled its previous decisions on the use of excessive force and followed
> *Palmer* v *R* [1971] AC 814, bringing Australian law into line with the present law of
> England: the intentional use of deadly force in self-defence or the prevention of crime is
> either justified, in which case no crime is committed, or it is not, in which case the killer
> is guilty of murder. The Australian High Court overruled its previous decisions not
> because they thought the principle applied was unsound but because of the complexity
> which had arisen from the courts' attempts to state the law in a form which took account
> of the burden of proof. The Australian law was changed not because it was thought to be
> wrong in principle, but because it was too difficult for juries to understand and apply. We
> do not believe that these difficulties will arise under the Code. Applying clauses 13 (proof)
> and 44 (use of force in public or private defence), the judge should be able to direct the
> jury in readily comprehensible terms. *DPP* v *Zekelic* does not, in our opinion, affect the
> soundness of the Committee's recommendation.' (Vol II, para 14.19)

4.9 Involuntary manslaughter: unlawful act/constructive manslaughter

In common with murder and voluntary manslaughter, involuntary manslaughter
involves the defendant in causing the death of the victim, but unlike those two
forms of homicide the defendant will not have had any intention to kill or do
grievous bodily harm; indeed the defendant will probably not have contemplated the
death of the victim at all. At present there are three forms of involuntary
manslaughter; that which is based on an unlawful act which causes death; that based
upon recklessness which causes death; and that based upon killing by gross
negligence. As with voluntary manslaughter, if a defendant is convicted of
involuntary manslaughter the sentence is at the discretion of the trial judge and can
range between life imprisonment and an unconditional discharge.

Manslaughter based upon an unlawful act, or constructive manslaughter as it is
sometimes known, requires proof that the defendant committed a dangerous criminal
act, accompanied by the requisite mens rea, which resulted in the death of the
victim. Causation has already been considered above, so it is the remaining elements
of the offence that are considered here.

ιnlawful act

An act can be described as 'unlawful' where it involves a breach of either civil or criminal law. Formerly it was accepted that the unlawful act in unlawful act manslaughter could be something that was merely tortious and not necessarily criminal. For example in *R* v *Fenton* (1830) 1 Lew CC 179, the defendant's liability for manslaughter was based on his tortious act of trespass to property, namely throwing stones down a mine shaft, causing a corf carrying miners to overturn, killing them.

Since the decision in *R* v *Franklin* (1883) 15 Cox CC 163, however, it has been settled law that unlawful act manslaughter must be based on a criminal act. In that case, Field J stated that:

> '... the mere fact of a civil wrong committed by one person against another ought not to be used as an incident which is a necessary step in a criminal case. I have a great abhorrence of constructive crime.'

It follows from the above that if the prosecution cannot establish a criminal act on the part of the defendant, there can be no liability on his part for unlawful act manslaughter. There is more recent authority for this proposition in the Court of Appeal's decision in *R* v *Arobieke* [1988] Crim LR 314, where the defendant had been convicted of manslaughter on the basis that his presence at a railway station had caused the victim, whom he knew to be terrified of him, to attempt an escape by crossing the railway tracks, with the result that he was electrocuted. In quashing the conviction, the Court of Appeal held that there had been no criminal act by the defendant, as the evidence did not show that the defendant had physically threatened or chased the deceased. Similar difficulties resulted in the quashing of the defendant's conviction for manslaughter in *R* v *Evans* [1992] Crim LR 659.

On the basis of *R* v *Lowe* [1973] QB 702 and *R* v *Khan (Rungzabe)* (1998) The Times 7 April, it would appear that unlawful act manslaughter cannot be based on an omission. The appropriate basis for liability will be killing by gross negligence: see section 4.10 below.

Any criminal act?

As unlawful act manslaughter is a serious offence against the person, must the criminal act upon which it is based also be an offence against the person, or will any criminal offence suffice provided it is the cause of death? Provided the criminal act satisfies the test for 'dangerousness' (as to which see below), it would appear that the courts are willing to adopt a liberal approach to the type of criminal act upon which this form of manslaughter will be based. In *R* v *Cato* [1976] 1 WLR 110, the defendant and the deceased agreed to inject each other with heroin. The deceased (Farmer) had consented to a number of such injections during the course of an evening. The following morning he was found to have died from the effects of the drug-taking. The defendant was convicted of maliciously administering a noxious substance contrary to s23 of the Offences Against the Person Act 1861, and of manslaughter, either on the basis that his unlawful act had caused death, or on the basis that he had recklessly caused Farmer's death. The defendant appealed against his convictions on the grounds, inter alia, that there had been no unlawful act since the deceased had consented to the injection of heroin, and that the consent should have been taken into account in determining whether or not the defendant had acted recklessly. The Court of Appeal held that the defendant had been properly convicted on both counts. Lord Widgery CJ expressed the view of the court that heroin was a noxious substance on the basis that it was likely to injure in common use, and that the defendant had administered it knowing of its noxious qualities. The victim's consent to suffer harm of this nature could never relieve the defendant of his liability, or destroy the unlawfulness of the defendant's act. Even if this was wrong, his Lordship would be willing to base liability for unlawful act manslaughter on the defendant's unlawful possession of heroin at the time he injected the deceased.

The decision has been criticised because, whilst no one would deny the criminality of unlawful possession of heroin, it could not be said that this was an offence that was 'directed at' the victim, any more than the illegal possession of a firearm could be. This point was subsequently considered by the Court of Appeal in *R* v *Dalby* [1982] 1 WLR 425. The defendant had been in lawful possession of a controlled drug which he had supplied to his friend, the deceased. The deceased had consumed a large quantity of the drug in one session, and subsequently injected himself with other substances. The following morning he was found to have died of a drug overdose. The defendant was convicted of unlawful act manslaughter, based on his unlawful supply of the controlled drug, and he appealed on the basis that his supply of the drug was not a dangerous act which had operated as the direct cause of death. He contended that the death was due to the deceased's act in consuming such a large dose of the drug in such a short space of time. The Court of Appeal allowed the appeal, Waller LJ holding that the defendant's act had not in any event been the direct cause of death, but had merely made it possible for the deceased to kill himself. His Lordship went on to state that where manslaughter was based on an unlawful and dangerous act, it had to be an act directed at the victim which was likely to cause immediate injury, albeit slight.

The decision suggested several important limitations upon the scope of unlawful act manslaughter, in that it seemed to exclude the possibility of basing liability on offences against property, or regulatory offences such as those under the Misuse of Drugs Act 1971, and also in that it seemed to introduce an extra element of mens rea into the offence by requiring the defendant to 'direct' his action against the victim. The potential significance of *R* v *Dalby* was greatly reduced, however, following *R* v *Goodfellow* (1986) 83 Cr App R 23. The defendant had deliberately fire bombed his own council house in the hope that he would be rehoused by the council. His wife and children, who had been in the house, were killed in the ensuing blaze. He appealed against his conviction for manslaughter on the ground, inter alia, that his unlawful act (criminal damage) had not been directed at the victims as required by *R* v *Dalby*. The Court of Appeal held that this latter authority should not be construed as requiring proof of an intention on the part of the defendant to harm the victims. It was to be viewed primarily as an authority on causation, in that the prosecution had to establish that there had been no fresh intervening cause between the defendant's act and the death. Clearly that had been an issue in *R* v *Dalby*, but was not an issue on the facts of the present case. The court seems to have been satisfied to accept that any dangerous criminal act causing the death of the victim would provide the basis for an unlawful act manslaughter charge. Further, in *Attorney-General's Reference (No 3 of 1994)* [1997] 3 All ER 936, Lord Hope also rejected the notion that the unlawful and dangerous act had to be directed at the person who actually died as a result of the defendant's actions, distinguishing *R* v *Dalby* on its facts. He preferred the view expressed in *DPP* v *Newbury* (considered below) to the effect that it was enough that D's act was dangerous because it was likely to injure some person.

In other respects *R* v *Goodfellow* is a decision that has some welcome aspects. For example there is no good reason why an offence such as aggravated criminal damage, given that it involves an intention to endanger life, or recklessness as to whether life is endangered, should not provide the unlawful act in this type of manslaughter. Further, there is clear authority that the defendant's act need not be the direct cause of death. In *R* v *Mitchell* [1983] 2 WLR 938, the Court of Appeal upheld the conviction for manslaughter of a defendant who, having become involved in an altercation whilst queuing in a busy post office, pushed an elderly man, causing him to fall accidentally onto the deceased, an elderly woman, who subsequently died in hospital from her injuries. Staughton J expressed the view of the court that it was sufficient for the jury to be satisfied that the defendant's intentional act had caused the victim's death. The actions of the elderly man in falling on the victim were entirely foreseeable and did not break the chain of causation between the defendant's assault and the victim's death. *R* v *Dalby* was distinguishable on its facts as a case where the victim was not injured as a direct and immediate result of the defendant's act. See further the commentary to *R* v *Ball* [1989] Crim LR 730 at 731–2.

A dangerous criminal act

A point made repeatedly in a number of the authorities cited above is the requirement that the unlawful act upon which constructive manslaughter is based must be dangerous. In *R* v *Larkin* [1943] 1 All ER 217, Humphreys J explained this in terms of the unlawful act being one which was likely to injure another person. In *R* v *Church* [1966] 1 QB 59, Edmund Davies J provided a slightly more elaborate definition of dangerousness where he stated:

> '... the unlawful act must be such as all sober and reasonable people would inevitably recognise must subject the other person to, at least, the risk of some harm resulting therefrom, albeit not serious harm.'

This is clearly an objective test, but it leaves open the question as to the type of harm that has to be reasonably foreseeable. Following the more recent Court of Appeal decision in *R* v *Dawson* (1985) 81 Cr App R 150, it would appear that the jury must be directed to consider the possibility of physical harm as opposed to merely emotional disturbance. Hence if D, dressed as a ghost, jumps out in front of P, who suffers a heart attack and dies, it may be the case that D cannot be convicted of unlawful act manslaughter because the only harm that was reasonably foreseeable as a result of his action was that the victim would be frightened. Compare this with the situation where D loads a sawn-off shot-gun, holds it P's head and crooks his finger around the trigger. If P dies of a heart attack brought on by his fear of dying, D should be guilty of unlawful act manslaughter, on the basis that the reasonable person would not only foresee P being scared, but would have foreseen P being so scared as to suffer physical harm.

The real problem, it is submitted, concerns the victim who has some physical peculiarity, unknown to the defendant, that makes the victim more vulnerable in the event of an attack. On the basis of *R* v *Blaue* it might be thought that the defendant who frightens a victim, only to find that the victim dies because he has a weak heart, should be required to take his victim as he finds him. Note however that in *R* v *Dawson*, where the defendants had attacked a petrol filling station attendant who had a weak heart, Watkins LJ, referring to the test for determining whether or not the unlawful act was dangerous, stated:

> '... this test can only be undertaken upon the basis of the knowledge gained by a sober and reasonable man as though he were present at the scene of the crime and watched the unlawful act being performed ... he has the same knowledge as the man attempting to rob and no more.'

This seems to suggest that if the accused makes a reasonable mistake as to the fortitude and strength of the victim, it has to be taken into account in assessing the dangerousness of his unlawful act. Since the decision in *R* v *Dawson*, the matter has been considered on two occasions by the Court of Appeal. In *R* v *Watson* [1989] 1 WLR 684, the appellant had burgled a house occupied by an 87-year-old man who suffered from a heart condition. The appellant disturbed the occupant, and abused him verbally, but made off without stealing anything. The police were called shortly afterwards, and a local council workman arrived to repair the windows broken by the appellant in gaining entry. An hour and a half after the burglary the occupant had a heart attack and died. The appellant was convicted of manslaughter but appealed successfully on the ground that his counsel had been denied a sufficient opportunity to address the jury on the issue of whether the excitement caused by the arrival of the police and the council workman could have taken over as the operating and substantial cause of death. As to the nature of the unlawful act however, the court recognised that, following *R* v *Dawson*, and applying the test established by Watkins LJ, the unlawful act had to be dangerous in the sense that all sober and reasonable persons would foresee that it created a risk of some physical harm occurring to the victim, but added that in applying this test, the reasonable person was to be imbued with all the knowledge that the defendant had gained throughout his burglarious trespass (ie his realisation of the occupant's frailty) and not just the appellant's limited or non-existent knowledge at the moment he first entered the property. On this basis, therefore, the burglary did constitute a dangerous unlawful act, but only because it is assumed by the court that the appellant was aware of the frailty of the victim. Lord Lane CJ stated (at p687) that:

> '... the appellant ... during the course of the unlawful act must have become aware of [the victim's] frailty and approximate age.'

What if the defendant makes an honest but unreasonable mistake as to circumstances? What if Watson had honestly but mistakenly thought that his victim was a much younger and fitter man, even though it would have been obvious to a reasonable man that this was not the case? The Court of Appeal's decision in *R* v *Ball* [1989] Crim LR 730 may go some way towards providing a solution.

The appellant had been involved in a long-running dispute with his neighbour, G, over her parking her vehicle on his land. Eventually the appellant had the vehicle sold whilst it was still parked on his land. G, accompanied by two men, called on the appellant to investigate the disappearance of the vehicle. An altercation developed, which culminated in the appellant grabbing a handful of cartridges, loading his shotgun, and firing at G from approximately 12 yards. G was killed in the attack. The appellant was acquitted of murder, on the basis that he had honestly believed that he had loaded the gun with blank cartridges, and had only intended to frighten G, but was convicted of constructive manslaughter. The appellant appealed on the basis that the trial judge had erred in directing the jury as to how they should have assessed the 'dangerousness' of his unlawful act, in that they had not been told to bear in mind the appellant's mistaken belief that he was firing blanks, when applying the *Dawson* test. In dismissing the appeal, the court held that once it was established that the appellant had intentionally committed an unlawful act, the question of its dangerousness was to be decided by applying the objective test (as in *R* v *Dawson*). The court refused to impute to the reasonable man the appellant's mistake of fact (ie believing the live cartridges to be blanks).

Although the decision in *R* v *Ball* was delivered some three days before that in *R* v *Watson*, the approach taken by the Court of Appeal in the latter case can be relied upon to explain the decision in the former. In *R* v *Watson* the court stressed the need to look at the whole of the defendant's actions in assessing their 'dangerousness', which in that case meant looking at the burglarious trespass in its entirety. In *R* v *Ball*, therefore, the whole of the appellant's actions should be considered, not just his firing of the gun, but also his grabbing a handful of cartridges in order to load them, without checking to see if any were live. It is perhaps to be assumed that the reasonable person would have realised the dangerousness of such behaviour.

The test for dangerousness will also be satisfied, even though the eventual victim was not a life in being at the time of D's unlawful act. As Lord Hope observed, in *Attorney-General's Reference (No 3 of 1994)* (the facts of which are considered in section 4.1 above):

> 'I consider that it is sufficient that at the time of the stabbing the defendant had the mens rea which was needed to convict him of an assault on the child's mother. That was an unlawful act, and it was also an act which was dangerous in the sense indicated by Humphreys J in *R v Larkin* ... in the passage which was quoted with approval by Lord Salmon in *DPP v Newbury* ... Dangerousness in this context is not a high standard. All it requires is that it was an act which was likely to injure another person. As "injury" in this sense means "harm" the other person must also be a living person. ... It is enough that the original unlawful and dangerous act, to which the required mental state is related, and the eventual death of the victim are both part of the same sequence of events.'

On this basis, because D knew that the person he was stabbing was pregnant, that knowledge could be imputed to the reasonable person in assessing whether his unlawful act satisfied the test for dangerousness. It is presumed that the reasonable person would foresee not only harm to the pregnant woman but that the foetus might suffer harm as a result of the attack, after being born.

The mens rea of unlawful act manslaughter

As mentioned above, the most striking difference between murder and unlawful act manslaughter lies in the mens rea. Whilst the former requires proof that D intended to kill or do grievous bodily harm, the latter does not require any proof that D foresaw death at all. As Lord Hope explained in *Attorney-General's Reference (No 3 of 1994)*:

> '... the accused must be proved to have intended to do what he did, it is not necessary to prove that he knew that his act was unlawful or dangerous. So it must follow that it is unnecessary to prove that he knew that his act was likely to injure the person who died as a result of it. All that need be proved is that he intentionally did what he did. ... As Lord Salmon put it in *DPP v Newbury* ... manslaughter is one of those crimes in which only what is called a basic intention need be proved – that is, an intention to do the act which constitutes the crime.'

The term 'intention ought not to be taken too literally here, as it is presumed that if the unlawful act can be committed recklessly, for example assault or criminal damage, then proof of the relevant form of recklessness will suffice.

It should perhaps, be noted, however, that the courts are not always entirely scrupulous in identifying precisely what unlawful act (ie which crime) the allegation of manslaughter is based on: see *Cato* (above) and *DPP v Newbury and Jones* [1976] AC 500.

Clearly, where the prosecution is unable to establish the mens rea for the unlawful act, D cannot be liable. This statement of the obvious is neatly illustrated by *R v Lamb* [1967] 2 QB 981, where D, as a joke, pointed a revolver at his friend (P) and pulled the trigger. The gun fired, killing P. D had previously checked to ensure that the chamber facing the firing-pin of the gun was empty, and thus did not expect the gun to fire. What D had not known was that his pulling the trigger made the chamber of the gun rotate, so as to present a loaded chamber to the firing-pin. D appealed successfully against his conviction for manslaughter, the Court of Appeal ruling that even if it was assumed that P had apprehended immediate physical violence, if D thought that it was all a joke he could not have had the mens rea for the unlawful act of assault, and thus could not be guilty of unlawful act manslaughter. Similarly, in *R* v *Jennings* [1990] Crim LR 588, the Court of Appeal allowed the appellant's appeal against his conviction for manslaughter, on the basis that establishing of the unlawful act upon which the prosecution had sought to rely (the offence of carrying an offensive weapon contrary to s1 Prevention of Crimes Act 1953) required evidence of the appellant's intention in relation to the use of the weapon, since it had not been made or adapted for use for causing injury to the person. The issue of intention had not been left to the jury as it should. See also *R* v *Slingsby* [1995] Crim LR 570.

Where there is doubt as to mens rea, the prosecution might be well advised to add an alternative count alleging killing by gross negligence, considered below.

4.10 Involuntary manslaughter: killing by gross negligence

The origins of the modern law

In addition to manslaughter based on an unlawful and dangerous act that causes death, the common law has traditionally recognised that liability for manslaughter can arise from a grossly negligent act or omission that causes death. Not infrequently juries are invited to consider both types of manslaughter as alternative bases for liability arising out of the same set of facts. Hence in *Cato*, and *Lamb*, considered above, the juries were invited to consider the defendant's liability for manslaughter, either on the basis that he had committed a dangerous unlawful act which had resulted in death, or on the basis that the death had been caused by the defendant's gross negligence.

It is possible to trace the emergence of killing by gross manslaughter to cases where death resulted from medical treatment. The courts took the view that it was unjust and could possibly be counter-productive to hold that liability for manslaughter could flow from mere inadvertence on the part of a medical practitioner, particularly where he found himself having to deal with a pre-existing danger not of his own making. Lord Hewart CJ, in *R* v *Bateman* (1925) 94 LJKB 791, sought to identify the determinants of liability in such cases. The appellant had operated on a woman who subsequently died. His appeal against his conviction for manslaughter was allowed on the ground that the trial judge had failed to distinguish between the degree of negligence required for civil liability and that required for manslaughter. Lord Hewart CJ held that, to secure a conviction in such cases, the Crown had to prove: (a) that D <u>owed</u> P a <u>duty of care</u>; (b) that D had <u>breached</u> that <u>duty</u> of care; (c) that the <u>breach</u> had <u>caused</u> the <u>death</u> of P; and (d) that D's <u>negligence</u> was <u>gross</u> in that it went <u>beyond</u> a mere <u>matter of compensation</u> between subjects. Whilst *Bateman* was followed in subsequent cases, there emerged a tendency on the part of the courts to <u>conceptualise</u> the <u>fault element required</u> for this head of manslaughter by <u>characterising</u> it as a form of '<u>recklessness</u>'. Hence in *Andrews* v *DPP* [1937] AC 576, where the defendant appealed unsuccessfully against his conviction for manslaughter arising out of a 'hit and run' incident, Lord Atkin, observing that a <u>very high degree of negligence</u> was required to <u>secure a conviction</u>, stated:

'... of all the epithets that can be applied "reckless" most nearly covers the case ... but it is probably not all embracing, for "<u>reckless</u>" suggests an <u>indifference to risk</u>, whereas the <u>accused</u> may have appreciated the risk, and <u>intended to avoid</u> it, and yet <u>shown</u> in the means <u>adopted to avoid the risk</u> such a degree of <u>negligence</u> as would <u>justify a conviction</u>.'

Similarly in *R* v *Stone and Dobinson* [1977] QB 354, Geoffrey Lane CJ, describing the <u>fault element</u> required for <u>killing by gross negligence</u>, stated:

'Mere inadvertence is not enough. The defendant must be <u>proved</u> to have been <u>indifferent</u> to a <u>obvious risk</u> of <u>injury</u> to <u>health</u>, or actually to have <u>foreseen</u> the risk but to have <u>determined nevertheless</u> to <u>run it</u>.'

Decisions such as *Andrews* and *Stone and Dobinson* were somewhat problematic in that there was no clear indication of what was meant by indifference. Did it imply that D had never thought about the risk (as in *Caldwell* recklessness where D gives no thought etc), or did it imply that D was aware of the possible outcomes but did not care whether the risk materialised or not?

Killing by gross negligence eclipsed

During the 1980s the tide of judicial opinion turned away from the further development of manslaughter based on killing by gross negligence, and towards the creation of what was arguably a new head of common law manslaughter based on <u>Caldwell/Lawrence</u> recklessness. In *R* v *Seymour* [1983] 2 AC 493 the defendant, in the course of his <u>efforts</u> to <u>move</u> the victim's car <u>out of the way</u> by <u>pushing it</u> with <u>his truck</u>, <u>jammed her body</u> between his <u>truck</u> and her <u>car</u>, as a result of which she <u>sustained fatal injuries</u>. Although he could (at the time) have been charged with causing death by reckless driving contrary to the Road Traffic Act 1972, the prosecution pursued a charge of common law manslaughter (which gave the judge a discretion to impose a higher sentence upon conviction), and the defendant was convicted. The trial judge had directed the jury that they should convict if they were satisfied that the defendant had caused death, and had been reckless in so doing, recklessness here having the meaning attributed to it in *Lawrence*. The House of Lords held that the conviction should stand, Lord Roskill stating that 'objective', or *Caldwell* type, recklessness applied equally to common law manslaughter and the statutory offence of motor manslaughter under the Road Traffic Act 1972. Hence D could be guilty of reckless manslaughter where he, by his conduct, created an obvious and serious risk of physical harm, and either he had given no thought to it or had been aware of it and determined to take it. In *Kong Cheuk Kwan* v *R* (1985) 82 Cr App R 18, the Privy Council (Lord Roskill giving the judgment of the Board) applied the 'new' form of reckless manslaughter to a case involving a collision between two hydrofoils in Hong Kong harbour which had resulted in the deaths of two passengers. Citing Lord Atkin's preference for the epithet 'reckless' to describe the degree of fault required in killing by gross negligence, Lord Roskill promulgated the notion that as *Caldwell/Lawrence* now provided the model definition of recklessness applicable wherever recklessness was involved as a fault element, it should be used as the basis for the trial judge's direction to the jury in cases where formerly an explanation of gross negligence would have been provided. Indeed, Lord Roskill went so far as to expressly endorse the comments of Waller LJ when *Seymour* was before the Court of Appeal, to the effect that, in relation to manslaughter '... it is no longer necessary or helpful to make references to compensation or negligence'.

See further *R* v *Slingsby* [1995] Crim LR 570.

Killing by gross negligence reinstated

In the wake of the decisions of the House of Lords and Privy Council in *Seymour* and *Kong Cheuk Kwan* respectively, many commentators concluded that killing by gross negligence had perhaps disappeared as a head of manslaughter, although there were clearly some members of the Court of Appeal who did not know this or at least thought otherwise: see *R* v *Ball* [1989] Crim LR 730. The reinstatement of killing by gross negligence arose out of a number of appeals against conviction for manslaughter that were heard together on the basis that they raised identical or sufficiently similar points of law: *R* v *Prentice*; *R* v *Sulman*; *R* v *Adomako*; *R* v *Holloway* [1993] 3 WLR 927. Prentice and Sulman were junior hospital doctors required to carry out a lumbar puncture and other procedures in relation to a patient suffering from leukaemia. The injections were not conducted properly and a drug which should have been administered by injection in the patient's arm was injected into his spine. The patient died despite the efforts of the doctors to rectify the error. Holloway was a qualified electrician who was contracted to fit a central heating programmer in a residential dwelling. The programmer was incorrectly wired by the appellant with the result that, during the operation of certain programmes, the metal parts of the heating system became live. Five months after the installation of the programmer, one of the occupants was killed as a result of electrocution, the death being caused by the incorrect wiring of the programmer. All three appellants were convicted, following directions at first instance in terms of reckless manslaughter, and appealed successfully.

The Court of Appeal held that where death was caused by a breach of duty on the part of the defendant, a prosecution on the basis of reckless manslaughter might be appropriate where the situation was one involving motor manslaughter, as the risk of harm was created by the accused himself. Where, however, the defendant had been under a duty to act in a situation where there was a pre-existing risk of harm to others not of his making, such as a doctor treating a sick patient, it was appropriate to apply a standard of fault that allowed the court to ask questions as to why the defendant might have made errors having fatal consequences. In this regard the Lord Chief Justice observed:

> 'It might well be unnecessary to ask such questions when the issue is simply as to whether the speed of a person's driving was reckless, but they are central questions when examining the degree of negligence of a skilled man exercising his trade. They are questions which obviously must be asked once the issue is defined as gross negligence, but might well not be asked under the *Lawrence* direction of recklessness.'

It might be observed that the distinction drawn between one who creates a risk, such as a motorist who decides to overtake on the brow of a hill, and one who is presented with a dangerous situation, such as a doctor attending an patient, seems to be sustainable in respect of Prentice and Sulman, but can it really be extended to an electrician contracted to fit a central heating programmer?

In the view of the Court of Appeal, a further distinction between reckless manslaughter and killing by gross negligence related to the assessment of the risk involved. As the Lord Chief Justice explained:

> '... the "obvious risk" of Lord Diplock's formulation in *Caldwell* ... meant obvious to "the ordinary prudent individual". Everyone knows what can happen when you strike a match, and practically everyone, whether as a driver or a passenger, knows the risks of the road. But in expert fields where duty is undertaken, be it by a doctor or an electrician, the criteria of what the ordinary prudent individual would appreciate can hardly be applied in the same way.'

The fourth appellant, Adomako, a locum tenens anaesthetist employed at a hospital, was assisting in an operation on a patient for a detached retina. During the operation the tube from the patient's ventilator became detached. By the time the appellant became aware that something had gone wrong the damage caused to the patient had become irreversible and he died. The appellant was convicted of manslaughter following a direction from the trial judge, in terms of gross negligence as the basis for liability rather than recklessness, and his appeal was rejected by the Court of Appeal, which certified the following point of law of general public importance for consideration by House of Lords ([1994] 3 WLR 288):

> 'In cases of manslaughter by gross negligence not involving driving but involving a breach of duty is it a sufficient direction to the jury to adopt the gross negligence test set out by the Court of Appeal in the present case following *R v Bateman* (1925) 19 Cr App R 8 and *Andrews v DPP* [1937] AC 576 without reference to the test of recklessness as defined in *R v Lawrence* [1982] AC 510 or as adapted to the circumstances of the case?': see *R v Adomako* [1994] 1 WLR 15.

Dismissing the appeal, and answering the certified question in the affirmative, Lord Mackay LC expressed the view that *Andrews* v *DPP* was a decision of the House of Lords that had not been overruled, and was thus still binding. In his view the ordinary principles of negligence should be invoked, and liability imposed where a grossly negligent breach of duty could be shown to have caused death. He observed:

> 'The jury will have to consider whether the extent to which the defendant's conduct departed from the proper standard of care incumbent upon him, involving as it must have done a risk of death to the patient, was such that it should be judged criminal. It is true that to a certain extent this involves an element of circularity, but in this branch of the law I do not believe that it is fatal to its being correct as a test of how far conduct must depart from accepted standards to be characterised as criminal.'

In his Lordship's view the variety of fact situations that could give rise to a charge of manslaughter was so great that it was unwise to attempt a more specific direction. Interestingly, in *R* v *Khan (Rungzabe)* (above), the Court of Appeal noted, without deciding the point, that a drug dealer might incur liability where he supplied drugs to another and then failed to act when he became aware that the consumption of the drugs had resulted in the recipient overdosing. Does the supplier of illegal drugs owe a duty of care to the consumer? If the answer is yes, does the supplier of an unlicensed firearm owe a duty of care to the recipient who turns it on himself and commits suicide? See also *R* v *DPP, ex parte Jones* (1996) The Independent 12 June. In *R* v *Litchfield* [1998] Crim LR 507 the Court of Appeal held that the owner and master of a schooner that broke up on rocks off the cost of Cornwall with the loss of three crew members had owed the victims a duty of care upon which liability for killing by gross negligence could be based. On the facts, the plotting of a dangerous course and setting out with contaminated fuel in the fuel tanks provided the evidence of gross negligence.

Although in cases of manslaughter cased by breach of duty it was not necessary for the trial judge to refer to *R* v *Lawrence*, it was open to the trial judge to use the word 'reckless' in its ordinary meaning (ie as used in *R* v *Stone and Dobinson* [1977] QB 354) as part of his exposition of the law if he deemed it appropriate. The Lord Chancellor went on to explain that *Seymour* (above) and *Kong Cheuk Kwan* (above) should no longer be followed as the underlying statutory provisions (ie Road Traffic Act 1972) had been repealed, and because there were problems in distinguishing between cases where death resulted from driving and those where death resulted from the navigation of a craft.

Motor manslaughter

Many cases of death resulting from the use of a motor vehicle are classified as 'accidents' and do not result in criminal proceedings as regards the death. Until 1956, if criminal proceedings were brought, drivers who caused death were indicted for manslaughter, but in many cases juries showed themselves reluctant to convict 'fellow motorists' for homicide. As a response to this problem, the Road Traffic Act

1956 introduced the offence of causing death by reckless or dangerous driving, an offence carrying up to five years' imprisonment. In 1977 the law was amended by the Criminal Law Act so that the offence became one of causing death by reckless driving alone. In due course the offence of causing death by reckless driving was consolidated in the Road Traffic Act 1988. Difficulties persisted, however, not least in relation to the correct interpretation of recklessness within this particular statutory context: see *R* v *Lawrence* [1982] AC 510 and *R* v *Reid* [1992] 1 WLR 793, considered at Chapter 3, section 3.3. *The Road Traffic Law Review Report* (1988) (the 'North Committee' report) concluded that an entirely objective type of fault was required, and the reformulation of the offence was effected by the Road Traffic Act 1991, amending the Road Traffic Act 1988, so that s1 now provides:

'A person who causes the death of another person by driving a mechanically propelled vehicle dangerously on a road or other public place is guilty of an offence.'

Dangerous driving is further defined in s2(1)(a) as driving that falls below what would be expected of a competent and careful driver, in that it would be obvious to such a person that driving in the manner in question would be dangerous. The danger can relate either to injury to another, or serious damage to property. The new offence carries a maximum penalty of five years' imprisonment and/or a fine.

4.11 Corporate criminal liability for causing death

The concept of the company as an artificial legal person is a legal fiction born out of the need to allow individuals to create commercial enterprises without, necessarily, putting their own capital at risk, and to permit others to participate in the ownership and control of the company by the purchase and sale of shares. The doctrine of corporate legal personality is also useful when issues of civil liability arise, in ensuring that the liability of those who have invested in the company is limited to the extent of their share holdings. The imposition of criminal liability on companies, however, poses a number of problems, principally because the common law has developed on notions of the individual responsibility of natural legal persons.

Why do we need to impose criminal liability on companies? Two broad reasons can be identified. First, the activities of companies need to be regulated in the public interest, for example in relation to health and safety, pollution etc. It will often be the case that criminal liability offers the only effective sanction, given that prosecutions are brought by the state and not (normally) at the behest of private individuals. With many of theses 'regulatory' offences liability is strict, hence no fault has to be shown. The second reason is that many deaths and injuries are caused in the pursuit of commercial activities, for example in factories, building sites, or in the transportation of passengers by road, air, sea and rail. In each case the question arises as to whether or not the company concerned should itself be charged in relation to the death.

How is criminal liability to be imposed?

It has to be accepted at the outset that there are certain offences in respect of which an artificial legal person such as a corporation cannot incur liability, for example: murder, because of the mandatory penalty; rape, because of the nature of the actus reus. Beyond this, however, the notion of imposing criminal liability on companies per se is now so commonplace as to hardly merit comment. There is a vast panoply of regulatory or quasi-criminal' offences created under statute, where liability is strict or absolute (ie no mens rea is required). Provided the company can be shown to have caused the commission of the offence through those acting on its behalf there should be no particular difficulty in upholding a conviction: see further *Griffiths v Studebakers Ltd* [1924] 1 KB 102; *Coppen v Moore (No 2)* [1898] 2 QB 306; *Alphacell Ltd v Woodward* [1972] AC 824; and *National Rivers Authority v Alfred McAlpine Homes East Ltd* [1994] 4 All ER 286 – all considered at Chapter 13, section 13.8.

Mens rea offences

More difficult is the problem of imposing criminal liability upon a company where the offence in question clearly requires proof of mens rea. Given that a company is an artificial legal entity it becomes necessary to engage in a legal fiction as to where this mens rea might be located, ie whose mens rea is to be equated with that of the company? The traditional approach of the English courts has been to require the prosecution to prove that those who can be regarded as the 'directing minds' of the company had the necessary mens rea. The modern origin of this doctrine is the speech of Lord Haldane LC in *Lennard's Carry Co Ltd v Asiatic Petroleum* [1915] AC 705 where he opined that the knowledge of someone who was the directing mind and will or the ego and centre of the personality of the corporation could be attributed to the company. The doctrine was relied also upon, to some extent, by the House of Lords in *Tesco Supermarkets Ltd v Natrass* [1972] AC 153, where Lord Diplock observed:

'... what natural persons are to be treated in law as being the company for the purpose of acts done in the course of its business, including the taking of precautions and the exercise of due diligence to avoid the commission of a criminal offence, is to be found by identifying those natural persons who by the memorandum and articles of association or as a result of action taken by the directors, or by the company in general meeting pursuant to the articles, are entrusted with the exercise of the powers of the company ... [t]here has been in recent years a tendency to extract from Denning LJ's judgment in *H L Bolton (Engineering) Co Ltd v T J Graham & Sons Ltd* [1957] 1 QB 159 ... his vivid metaphor about the "brains and nerve centre" of a company as contrasted with its hands, and to treat this dichotomy, and not the articles of association, as laying down the test of whether or not a particular person is to be regarded in law as being the company itself when performing duties which a statute imposes on the company. In the case in which this metaphor was first used Denning LJ was dealing with acts and intentions of directors of the company in whom the powers of the company were vested under its articles of association. The decision in that case is not authority for extending the class of persons whose acts are to be regarded in law as the personal acts of the company itself, beyond those who by, or by action taken under, its articles of association are entitled to exercise the powers of the company.'

Lord Reid took a less legalistic approach, identifying those who could be the embodiment of the company in terms of constituting its directing mind as being the directors, and possibly other senior officers of the company carrying out functions of management. Viscount Dilhorne found it useful to talk in terms of those who were in actual control of the operations of the company in the sense that they were not answerable to others in the company regarding the manner in which they discharged their duties. Presumably if those who constitute the directing will of the company delegate their functions to employees further down the chain of command, liability can still be imposed on the basis of a 'quasi-delegation' principle: see further *Moore v I Bressler Ltd* [1944] 2 All ER 515 and *R v ICR Haulage Ltd* [1944] KB 551.

The 'directing mind and will' doctrine identified by Lord Haldane LC was appropriate, on its facts, for the case that he had before him, and more generally satisfies the attempts to employ a doctrine based on assumptions about choices made by individuals (mens rea) to bodies that are clearly artificial legal entities (companies), but it is fraught with difficulty in application. Even if a senior manager or director can be shown to have had some mens rea, it may be that he lacks sufficient knowledge, when viewed in isolation, for proof of mens rea to be made out. It may be that the required degree of fault can only be proved by aggregating the knowledge of a number of directors or managers. It by no means clear that such an approach is permissible: see *ex parte Spooner* (below).

Meanwhile evidence of a more liberal approach to the 'directing mind and will' doctrine can be identified in the Privy Council's decision in *Meridian Global Funds Management Asia v Securities Commission* [1995] 3 WLR 413. Two investment managers (Koo and Ng) employed by Meridian used the company's funds to acquire a controlling interest in Euro-National Corporation Ltd. Under s20 of the (New Zealand) Securities Amendment Act 1988 any person becoming a substantial security holder in a public issuer had to give notice of the fact. Meridian accepted that its funds had been used to acquire such an interest and that no such notification had been given. At first instance the court, acting at the behest of the Commission, held that the knowledge of Koo and Ng could be attributed to Meridian, and thus it had been in breach of its duty under s20 of the 1988 Act. The Court of Appeal upheld this ruling but did so on the basis that Koo's knowledge was attributable to Meridian under the 'directing mind and will' doctrine (ie that the act had been carried out by an employee who could be thus described). Dismissing Meridian's appeal, the Privy Council observed that there was a clear need for rules by which acts could be attributed to a company or persona ficta. The rules of attribution to be applied in any given case were to be arrived at by reference to the company's articles of association and the principles of company law – the primary rules of attribution; and the principles of agency, vicarious liability and estoppel – the general rules of attribution. By application of these rules the actions of a company's servants and agents could be attributed to the company itself. Noting that the difficulty in applying the principles of criminal law to companies arose from the fact that it normally only created personal liability, and was thus not readily susceptible to the application of the rules of attribution, possible solutions were identified as:

1. refusing to impose criminal liability on a corporation on the basis that it was not meant to be applied to corporate bodies, eg offences such as rape;
2. imposing criminal liability only where the activity was specifically authorised by the shareholders and/or the board of directors;
3. in situations where (1) and (2) did not provide the solution, interpreting the relevant criminal provision to determine, with reference to its underlying policy, how it was meant to apply to a company, in particular whose act would be attributable to the company.

Lord Hoffmann expressed the view that the decision in *Lennard's Carrying Co Ltd* v *Asiatic Petroleum Co Ltd* (above) was explicable on the basis that the relevant legislation, the Merchant Shipping Act 1894, was drafted with individual shipowners in mind, and because the company in that case was engaged in only one type of activity – hence the directing mind and will of the company could be equated with an individual shipowner when assessing the attribution of liability for the prohibited act. In his view confusion had been caused by later cases adopting an overly literal interpretation of the concept of 'directing mind and will'. The policy of the (New Zealand) Securities Amendment Act 1988 was that notice should be given once a substantial interest in a public company was acquired. Rather than attributing knowledge only if it could be found on the part of the directing mind and will of Meridian, it was more appropriate to look at the organisation of the company's business and ask who had the authority to acquire such interests. Koo had been given such authority and hence his knowledge was attributable to the company. Note that Lord Hoffmann rejected the contention that the knowledge of Koo was unattributable to Meridian because his actions had been unauthorised – presumably on the basis that his actions had been within the scope of the ostensible authority delegated to him by Meridian.

So, can a company be guilty of manslaughter?

In *R* v *Coroner for East Kent, ex parte Spooner* (1989) 88 Cr App R 10 Bingham LJ was prepared to accept that a corporate body could be guilty of manslaughter where both the mens rea and actus reus could be established against those who were the 'embodiment of the corporate body itself'. On the facts, however, he was not satisfied that there was a sustainable case against the directors of Townsend Car Ferries Ltd in respect of the deaths resulting from the capsizing of the *Herald of Free Enterprise*. His doubts were realised when a prosecution for manslaughter was actually brought against the ship owners in *R* v *P & O European Ferries (Dover) Ltd*

(1991) 93 Cr App R 72. At the trial at the Central Criminal Court, Turner J ultimately felt constrained to withdraw the case from the jury due to lack of evidence against the senior employees involved, despite the fact that the Sheen Inquiry into the tragedy had concluded that there were serious shortcomings in the management of the company's ferry operations, and that ships had, in the past, left port with their bow doors open. The trial did involve at least a theoretical victory for the prosecution and proponents of corporate liability for manslaughter, in that in the course of argument the trial judge ruled that a company could incur liability for manslaughter. He stated (at p88):

'... if it be accepted that manslaughter in English law is the unlawful killing of one human being by another human being (which must include both direct and indirect acts) and that a person who is the embodiment of a corporation and acting for the purposes of the corporation is doing the act or omission which caused the death, the corporation as well as the person may also be found guilty of manslaughter.'

In 1995 OLL, a company that operated an outdoor activity centre was convicted on four counts of manslaughter after a group of teenagers died in a canoeing accident in Lyme Bay (*R* v *Kite and OLL Ltd*, Winchester Crown Court, 8 December 1994). The company was fined £60,000 and the managing director sentenced to three years' imprisonment. It is perhaps significant that this case involved a small company where knowledge of the risk on the part of the managing director could be established. In cases involving more complex business organisations there may be greater evidential difficulties. An employee may be responsible for safety, but may not be sufficiently senior to be identified with the 'mind' of the company.

Hybrid offences

In addition to strict liability and mens rea offences, there is a third category, sometimes referred to as hybrid offences. In most cases liability is strict subject to some sort of due diligence provision where the onus is placed on the defendant to establish that the employer (typically a company) took all reasonable steps to prevent the prohibited consequence from occurring. For example, s2(1) of the Health and Safety at Work Act 1974 creates an offence of failing to ensure, so far as is reasonably practicable, the safety and welfare at work of employees; and s3 creates a similar offence in relation to the safety of other persons at the workplace. The key question here is how far the duty to take such reasonable steps extends within the company's hierarchy. For example, if one adopts the notion, as in *Tesco Supermarkets Ltd* v *Natrass*, that the company was to be equated only with senior management, such a defence would be made out if it could be shown that the failure to take all reasonable steps etc had been as a result of the failings of a junior manager. Hence, in *Tesco Supermarkets Ltd* v *Natrass*, the company escaped liability because the mis-pricing of goods on display, contrary to s11 of the Trade Descriptions Act 1968, had resulted from the act or default of 'another person', namely one of its store managers, ie someone who was not the embodiment of the company. In the light of the Privy Council's decision in *Meridian*, it would appear that the concept of those employees regarded as the manifestation of the company is likely to be extended, but the question arises as to whether a company should be convicted if it can be shown that any employee has failed to take the reasonable steps required to prevent a prohibited outcome. It is submitted that much may depend on what the courts feel is necessary to ensure that the legislation in question operates as Parliament intended. Hence, in *Tesco Stores* v *Brent London Borough Council* [1993] 2 All ER 718 the company was charged with selling an '18' classified video to a customer who was known to the cashier to be under that age. The offence was subject to a defence that the defendant had reasonable grounds to believe that the purchaser was over 18. Tesco Stores contended that those who were the directing mind and will of the company (ie the senior managers) could not possibly know the ages of customers buying videos in the company's stores, and that the cashier selling the video on behalf of the company, who did have knowledge as to the purchaser's age, could not be regarded as the embodiment of the company for the purposes of imposing criminal liability. Rejecting these contentions, the court held that Parliament cannot have intended that the directors of a company should be able to represent the company in such cases and plead ignorance as to the circumstances in which goods were sold, as to do so would render the relevant law unenforceable. In effect the court took the view that as the offence fell between the two traditional categories of absolute liability on the one hand and full mens rea on the other, the principles of vicarious ability would be invoked to impose liability on the defendant company for the actions of its employee. Further support for the notion that a company will not be able to raise a 'due diligence' defence if any employee has failed to comply with it, is to be found in *R* v *British Steel* [1995] 1 WLR 1356. In *R* v *Gateway Foodmarkets Ltd* [1997] Crim LR 512, however, the Court of Appeal adopted the approach that the defendant company, which owned a national chain of supermarkets, failed to satisfy the due diligence provisions of s2(1) of the 1974 Act, where one of its store managers had turned a blind eye to a dangerous working practice in one of their stores that resulted in the death of an employee. The implication of this ruling is that if the failure to ensure a safe system of work had been the fault of a more junior employee, the company might have escaped liability. It is submitted that the more rational approach is to hold that the need to show due diligence should extend to all those for whom the company is vicariously liable in civil law. If a death were to result from the actions of an employee who was 'off on a frolic of his own' a company would still be able to invoke a due diligence defence provided other employees had taken reasonable steps: see further *R* v *Associated Octel Co Ltd* [1996] 1 WLR 1543.

The enforcement problem

It is clear that many people have been killed in transport accidents over the past 15 years in circumstances suggesting that the cause went beyond mere employee error. Further, there were more than 10,000 workplace deaths between 1986 and 1996, and in many of these cases there will have been evidence of culpability on the part of the employer. Why is it, therefore, that prosecutions for corporate manslaughter are so rare? One answer, of course, is that, given the technical difficulties in establishing the requisite fault, as outlined above, there is an understandable reluctance on the part of prosecuting authorities to 'waste' public money on prosecutions doomed to failure. Equally significant, however, is the policy adopted by the Health and Safety Executive (HSE) which investigates workplace deaths. Critics argue that there is a reluctance on the part of the HSE to carry out through investigations and refer appropriate cases to the Crown Prosecution Service. To some extent this may reflect an underfunding of the HSE, but may also reflect a culture in which liability for manslaughter is seen as an unusual and exceptional sanction, rather than the norm where there is evidence of death resulting from an employer's gross negligence.

The punishment problem

The question of appropriate punishment also requires proper consideration. Where the employees or customers of a company are killed as a result of its commercial activities, damages will be recoverable in civil law if fault can be established. The imposition of criminal sanctions is not designed to provide compensation. It is a mark of society's disapproval of the wrongful act. But what is the point of this? The obvious penalty in the form of a large fine may only serve to harm a company's shareholders, who will normally be innocent parties in the case. Where individual managers are found to have caused death or injury through their actions or omissions, and are found to have had the requisite mens rea, they may incur personal liability, but that is an issue distinct from the company's liability. It may be that more imaginative forms of punishment need to be considered, such as the supervision of spending by the company on retraining employees, product development and safety procedures. These could include a requirement that companies above a certain size have a director responsible for customer safety who could be held personally responsible for injuries and deaths if he failed to take necessary steps to ensure an adequately safe level of operating. To ensure that he did not become a 'director with responsibility for going to prison', statute could provide that other directors also became criminally liable if it could be shown that they had failed to act upon his previous safety recommendations.

4.12 Reform of unlawful act manslaughter

The Law Commission's Consultation Paper No 135 *Criminal Law – Involuntary Manslaughter* proposed:

1. the abolition of unlawful act manslaughter;
2. the introduction of a form of reckless manslaughter where D is reckless (in the subjective sense) as to whether death or serious personal injury would result from his actions, the offence carrying the possibility of life imprisonment;
3. a) the abolition of common law 'motor-manslaughter', leaving such cases to be dealt with by either the statutory offence of causing death by dangerous driving or the proposed new offence of reckless manslaughter; or
   b) the disapplication of *Commissioner of Police for the Metropolis* v *Caldwell* [1982] AC 341; [1981] 1 All ER 961 to the common law form of 'motor-manslaughter' established in *R* v *Seymour* [1983] 2 AC 493; [1983] Crim LR 742; (1983) 77 Cr App R 215; (1983) 76 Cr App R 211 so as to amalgamate such offences within the proposed offence of (subject) reckless manslaughter;
4. the introduction of a new head of involuntary manslaughter, not based on conscious risk-taking, where liability would arise where D ought reasonably to have been aware of a significant risk that his conduct could result in death or serious injury, and his conduct fell seriously and significantly below what could be reasonably have been expected of him in preventing that risk from occurring or in preventing risk, once in being, from resulting in the prohibited harm.

The Commission favoured the application of the new offence of manslaughter based on unconscious risk-taking to corporations. As the Consultation Paper states at para 5.77:

'It is in our view much easier to say that a *corporation*, as such, has failed to do something, or has failed to meet a particular standard of conduct than it is to say that a corporation has done a positive act, or has entertained a particular subjective state of mind. The former statements can be made directly, without recourse to the intermediary step of finding a human mind and a decision making process on the part of an individual within or representing the company; and thus the need for the identification theory, in order to bring the corporation within the subjective requirements of the law, largely falls away.'

Following a period during which interested parties made submissions on these proposals, the Law Commission published its report *Legislating the Criminal Code: Involuntary Manslaughter* (Law Com No 237) in May 1996. This criticises the existing common law on involuntary manslaughter as being too broad, lacking clarity in the wake of the House of Lords decision in *R* v *Adomako* [1994] 3 WLR 288; [1994] 1 WLR 15, and for being anomalous in its treatment of death caused by omission. Under the scheme proposed in the report, the current structure of manslaughter offences based on unlawful act manslaughter and killing by gross negligence would be replaced by three offences:

1. reckless killing;
2. killing by gross carelessness;
3. corporate killing.

A verdict of reckless killing would arise where D caused death and at the time was aware of the risk of death or grievous bodily harm and it was unreasonable for him to take the risk. The offence would be punishable with life imprisonment.

A verdict of killing by gross carelessness would arise where there was an obvious risk of death or grievous bodily harm (that is, obvious to the reasonable person in D's position), and D was capable of appreciating that risk, and his conduct fell far below what could be expected of him. The offence envisages judges being able to resort to an alternative formulation where appropriate where D, capable of appreciating the risk, kills in the course of causing injury by conduct that constitutes an offence. The offence would be one that could be committed by omission provided that D was under a common law duty to act. The report envisages a likely maximum sentence of ten years' imprisonment.

The proposed new offence of corporate killing would be one that could only be committed by a body corporate. The prosecution would have to prove that the death was caused by failings in the organisation of the company's activities such as to amount to neglecting the health and safety of its employees or those affected by its actions. The fault element, as for the gross carelessness offence outlined above, would be that the company's conduct fell far below what could be expected, although there would be no need to prove that the risk in question was obvious or that the company was capable of appreciating it. The offence would be punishable by a fine, or by an order to undertake rectification of company procedures.

5

Non-fatal Offences Against the Person

5.1 Assault and battery

5.2 Stalking

5.3 Offences Against the Person Act 1861 s47

5.4 Offences Against the Person Act 1861 s20

5.5 Offences Against the Person Act 1861 s18

5.6 Offences Against the Person Act 1861 ss23 and 24

5.7 False imprisonment, kidnapping, abduction and hostage-taking

5.8 Offences against police constables

5.9 Reform

5.1 Assault and battery

Introduction

Assault and battery exist as torts actionable in civil law and as criminal offences. In terms of criminal liability there is some dispute as to whether or not there is still an offence of assault contrary to common law (see below), but the term is used to describe elements of more serious statutory offences, such as assault occasioning actual bodily harm (see s47 of the Offences Against the Person Act 1861), indecent assault (considered at Chapter 6, section 6.3) and assault upon a police officer in the execution of his duty (see s89(1) of the Police Act 1996).

Assault: the narrow concept

When used in the narrow sense, the term common assault involves D intentionally or recklessly causing P to apprehend immediate and unlawful personal violence. No physical contact is required: see comments of Lord Lane CJ in *R v Mansfield Justices, ex parte Sharkey* [1985] QB 613 at 627. Hence, it can be committed by D shaking his fist in P's face, or thrusting a knife towards him. The emphasis is on the reaction of P. Even if D meant his threats as a joke, an assault is nevertheless

144

committed if P is sufficiently frightened: see *Logdon* v *DPP* [1976] Crim LR 12, where D was convicted of assault notwithstanding that his pointing an imitation gun at P had been intended as a joke. If such a threat is made to P who is asleep then it seems no offence is committed. P does not apprehend immediate physical violence, and D cannot be charged with attempting to commit a summary offence: s1(4) Criminal Attempts Act 1981.

It is a statement of the obvious to say that D need not physically threaten P in order to cause fear of violence. Mere words can clearly induce fear, as where D tells P that he is about to stab him with a knife. Notwithstanding this, however, English law was, for many years, unclear as to whether or not such words could amount to a criminal assault. On the one hand there was the dictum of Holroyd J in his direction given to the jury in *R* v *Meade & Belt* (1823)1 Lew CC 184 at 185, to the effect that no words or singing could ever constitute an assault. On the other there was the obiter statement of Lord Goddard CJ in *R* v *Wilson* [1955] 1 All ER 744 at 745, where he stated that the phrase 'get out knives', when spoken by D, constituted an assault. The matter now appears settled by the House of Lords' decision in *R* v *Ireland; R* v *Burstow* [1997] 4 All ER 225. In answering the first of the two certified questions, the Law Lords confirmed that, whilst there was no question of assault, in the form of a battery, being committed by means words alone or silent telephone calls, there was no reason why, on an appropriate set of facts, a defendant could not be charged with 'narrow' assault on the basis that he had, by his words or telephone calls, caused the victim to apprehend immediate physical violence. Reviewing the authorities relied upon to support the contention that words alone could amount to an assault, Lord Steyn dismissed *R* v *Meade & Belt* as being 'the slenderest authority' and went on to observe that:

'The proposition that a gesture may amount to an assault but that words can never suffice is unrealistic and indefensible. A thing said is also a thing done. There is no reason why something said should be incapable of causing an apprehension of immediate personal violence eg a man accosting a woman in a dark alley saying "come with me or I will stab you." I would therefore reject the proposition that an assault can never be committed by words.'

Lord Steyn went on to confirm that silent telephone calls might also amount to assaults provided that the victim anticipated immediate physical violence as a result of it. As he explained:

'... there is no reason why a telephone caller who says to a woman in a menacing way "I will be at your door in a minute or two" may not be guilty of an assault if he causes his victim to apprehend immediate personal violence. Take now the case of the silent caller. He intends by his silence to cause fear and he is so understood. The victim is assailed by uncertainty about his intentions. Fear may dominate her emotions and it may be the fear that the caller's arrival at her door may be imminent. She may fear the possibility of immediate personal violence. As a matter of law the caller may be guilty of an assault: whether he is or not will depend on the circumstance and in particular on the impact of the caller's potentially menacing call or calls on the victim.'

The decision should be seen as a welcome rationalisation of the common law. Given that s12 of the Criminal Law Act 1977 creates the offence of making threats to kill, it was always somewhat anomalous that threatening to break another's legs did not amount to an offence. If such was the case a situation could arise in which D could be convicted of unlawful act manslaughter if he threatened to kill P, causing P to become so frightened that he suffered a fatal heart attack, but not if P died of fright following a threat by D to break P's arm: see further *R* v *Constanza* (1997) The Times 31 March.

Although the ruling in *R* v *Ireland; R* v *Burstow* makes it clear that words, and even silence, can amount to an assault, there is no indication of how the courts should deal with the conditional verbal threat, eg 'Be quiet or I'll pull the trigger of this loaded gun and blow your brains out'.

It is submitted that a defendant can still escape liability where his threat is couched in terms that indicate that it will not be carried out there and then. Hence, in *Tuberville* v *Savage* (1669) 1 Mod Rep 3 there was held to be no assault when D placed his hand on his sword and said to P: 'If it were not assize time I would not take such language from you.' D was in fact saying that he was not going to strike P. Perhaps more questionable is the assertion that D does not commit an assault where he tells P that he will be shot if he does not remain silent. Although the words suggest that D is not going to assault P, it is here conditional on P's own behaviour, as opposed to some external factor, such as the presence of judges in the town in *Tuberville* v *Savage*. See further on this point *Blake* v *Barnard* (1840) 9 C & P 626 and *Read* v *Coker* (1853) 13 CB 850.

Immediacy

The requirement of immediacy in the crime of assault is generally understood to mean that P must perceive the threat as one which can be carried out 'there and then' by D. This raises the interesting possibility that D might not be guilty of assault where he waves his fist angrily at P who is on the other side of a counter behind a toughened glass screen, if the evidence is that there is no way that D can actually make contact with P. Of course, if P knows this then he is unlikely to apprehend any physical violence in any event. Similarly, if D sits in the public gallery of a court room looking at a jury member in an intimidatory manner, a charge of assault may not be sustainable in the face of the argument that any threat of force involved in this conduct could not have been carried out until the jury member had left the court building.

In *Smith* v *Superintendent of Woking Police Station* (1983) 76 Cr App R 234 D was convicted of being on enclosed premises for an unlawful purpose, namely assault. He had terrified P, a woman occupying a ground-floor flat, by staring in through the window at her. The Divisional Court was satisfied that, even though D was outside the building, there was evidence to suggest that P was terrified by the prospect of some immediate violence. Note also that the court here stated that it was not necessary for the prosecution to establish precisely what P feared would happen. A general apprehension of violence was sufficient. Hence, even if the threat is not actually of immediate violence, the requirement is satisfied if P believes the threat to be immediate. See further *R* v *Ireland*; *R* v *Burstow* (above) where the House of Lords confirmed that the requirement of immediacy was satisfied where D's use of the telephone had put him into immediate contact with P, causing her there and then to apprehend violence. Presumably the prosecution will have to adduce evidence of where P thought the calls were being made from. If D were to telephone P and inform him that a bomb had been placed in P's house and was about to explode, P would doubtless apprehend immediate physical violence (assuming he believed what he was told). Where the prosecution rests upon the cumulative effect of a series of telephone calls there is also the problem of identifying which call caused the harm – assuming the psychological damage is something that develops over a series of calls.

In *R* v *Constanza* (1997) The Times 31 March the Court of Appeal confirmed that a threat to inflict harm at sometime in the future can be an assault provided the concept of the future (in the victim's mind) encompasses the idea of the harm being caused immediately. Hence, a threat of significant physical violence issued by D against P can be an assault if P genuinely believes that the threat is constant and that D is willing to carry it out at any moment.

The broader concept: assault and battery

Instances of D assaulting P without there being any physical contact are, it is assumed, comparatively rare. There is usually some physical contact between P and D that will constitute a battery. Battery is defined in *Cole* v *Turner* (1705) 6 Mod Rep 149 as involving the least touching of another person in anger. If D pushes P out of the way so as to get to the front of a queue, D would have committed a battery, but it should be remembered that there is a certain degree of physical contact that everyone is deemed to have consented to as part of everyday life, such as might occur between respectable passengers on a crowded train or bus. Further, there is no need to establish that the victim of a battery apprehended immediate physical violence, even though this is nearly always involved where the offence is committed. Hence, where D approaches P from the rear and hits him on the back of the head, D will have committed a battery, but not necessarily an assault.

Despite the foregoing, it would be regarded as archaic, if not odd, for a victim to describe himself as having been battered; hence the modern trend to use the term assault in a broad sense to include both assault and battery. As James J stated in *Fagan* v *MPC* [1969] 1 QB 439 at p444:

> 'Although "assault" is an independent crime and is to be treated as such for practical purposes today "assault" is generally synonymous with the term "battery", and is a term used to mean the actual intended use of unlawful force to another person without his consent.'

Similar comments are made by Lord Lane LJ in *R v Williams (Gladstone)* (1983) 78 Cr App R 276 at 279.

This confusion as to the nature of assault and battery does little credit to the law, and can cause problems of a highly technical nature. For example, if a defendant is charged with assault, could he contend that the charge is bad for duplicity on the ground that it alleges two offences, namely assault and battery?

Mann LJ, adverting to the issue in *DPP v Taylor* [1992] 2 WLR 460, expressed his preference for the use of the phrase 'assault by beating' in indictments alleging assault in the broad sense. It remains to be seen what the impact of this ruling will be on other offences involving an allegation of assault, eg sexual offences, and offences against police officers. Will indictments for indecent assault have to specify whether there was physical contact?

A further difficulty was illustrated by *R v Lynsey* [1995] 3 All ER 654. D had been charged with a number of offences including common assault contrary to s39 of the Criminal Justice Act 1988. At the suggestion of the trial judge the indictment had been amended to allege battery instead of assault, and the appellant was convicted. He appealed on the ground that s40 of the Criminal Justice Act 1988, which permitted certain summary offences to be charged on indictment, included a reference to common assault but not battery. The Court of Appeal held, dismissing the appeal, that in order to provide a rational approach to this area of law the term 'common assault' had to be interpreted widely to include the offence of battery. Henry LJ, observing that 'The present appeal ... is yet another example of how bad laws costs money and clog up courts with better things to do ...', continued:

> 'Where the narrow meaning of the phrase "common assault" makes no sense in the context of s40 and cannot possibly reflect any rational policy, it is entirely permissible as a matter of construction, in our view, to prefer the wider meaning of the same phrase, which makes good sense and reflects a rational policy. Draftsmen after all sometimes make mistakes ... for the reasons we have given ... the [trial] judge was right, and the appeal fails and the draftsman is saved from the mess which in our judgment he contributed to. The law, however, remains in the state it is; the remedy is with Parliament. They have the Law Commission's paper and its draft Bill before them, and have had it since November 1993. That would have dealt with this problem as the broad definition of assault is included in s6 of the draft Bill, and an amendment to s40(3)(a) of the 1988 Act incorporates that broad definition as a summary offence which can be included in an indictment where the provisions of s40(1) are complied with.'

It is possible to envisage other situations where this confusion as to the identity of the wider offence of assault could give rise to difficulty. For example, can exposing a victim to noise amount to an assault? Where the noise is meant to frighten P into apprehending immediate physical violence the logical answer would seem to be that it can. Difficulties could arise, however, where the noise is intended simply to cause annoyance or injury. D may put his hands around P's ear and shout at the top of his voice, causing P to suffer from tinnitus thereafter. D has no intention to frighten as such, but he clearly intends to do P some harm. Presumably the essence of the 'assault' charge against D would be battery, but it would be very odd if it was framed in terms of 'assault by beating' as suggested above. Similarly, where D causes damage to P's retina by shining a laser pen in his eye there is no doubt that, if permanent harm is suffered by P, D could be found to have caused actual bodily harm. However, as is explained below, that offence requires proof of an assault on the part of D. It is assumed that the courts will take a sufficiently flexible approach to the concept of battery to take account of threats created by new technology.

Is there an offence of assault at common law?

That an offence of assault contrary to common law existed until 1861 is not seriously disputed, but in *R* v *Harrow Justices, ex parte Osaseri* [1986] QB 589, May LJ expressed the view that the effect of s47 of the Offences Against the Person Act 1861 had been to place the common law offence on a statutory basis. He based this assertion on the wording of s47, which creates the offence of assault occasioning actual bodily harm, and goes on to provide that 'whosoever shall be convicted upon an indictment for a common assault shall be liable to be imprisoned for any term not exceeding one year.' Whilst May LJ left open the possibility that there might still be a remaining common law offence of assault by beating, the existence of the 'remnant' of an offence at common law was later denied by Mann LJ in *DPP* v *Taylor* (above). Mann LJ was of the opinion that both common assault and battery had become subsumed in the statutory offence under s47, and went on to hold that the offences (of assault and battery) should now be charged under s39 of the Criminal Justice Act 1988, which provides:

'Common assault and battery shall be summary offences and a person guilty of either of them shall be liable ... to imprisonment for a term not exceeding six months.'

The difficulty with this view is that s39 could be seen as a purely procedural provision. It does not create any offences, but merely prescribes the procedure by which they are enforced. This leads inevitably to the same questions being asked as to the effect of s47 of the 1861 Act. Again it can be argued that the provisions of s47 relating to punishment for common assault do not make the offence statutory, but merely indicate the penalty to be applicable following conviction. Statutory provision of punishments for common law offences is not unknown; consider the position relating to murder and life imprisonment.

Mens rea for common assault and battery

The mens rea required for common assault is intention to cause the victim to apprehend immediate physical violence, or recklessness on the part of the defendant as to whether this will occur. Authority for this proposition is to be found in the Court of Appeal's decision in *R* v *Venna* (1975) 61 Cr App R 310, a decision concerned with a charge under s47 of the 1861 Act. It seems clear that in *Venna* the type of recklessness the Court had in mind was *Cunningham*, or subjective recklessness. The Court referred approvingly to the earlier case of *R* v *Bradshaw* (1878) 14 Cox CC 83 where recklessness in relation to assault and battery had been defined in terms consistent with *Cunningham*. The acceptance by the Divisional Court in *DPP* v *Khan* (1990) 91 Cr App R 29 that *Caldwell* recklessness applied to offences of assault was overruled by the Court of Appeal in *R* v *Spratt* (1990) 91 Cr App R 362, where the Court expressed its preference for the subjective approach. Nothing said in *R* v *Savage*; *R* v *Parmenter* [1991] 3 WLR 914 casts any doubt upon this. Similarly, in relation to battery, the mens rea would appear to be intention to cause some impact upon the body of another, or at least an awareness on the part of the defendant that he may cause such impact.

Racially motivated assault

The Crime and Disorder Act 1998 introduces a number of racially aggravated offences, including, by virtue of s29, racially aggravated assault. An assault is 'racially aggravated' for these purposes if the terms of s28 are satisfied. The prosecution must establish that:

1. at the time of committing the offence or immediately before or after doing so, the offender demonstrates towards the victim of the offence hostility based on the victim's membership (or presumed [by the offender] membership) of a racial group; or
2. the offence is motivated (wholly or partly) by hostility towards members of a racial group based on their membership of that group. For the purposes of s28 'racial group' means 'a group of persons defined by reference to race, colour, nationality (including citizenship) or ethnic or national origins'.

The whole point of creating these aggravated offences is to provide the courts with greater sentencing powers to reflect the aggravating factor of racial hatred. Hence a conviction on indictment for racially motivated assault carries the possibility of two years' imprisonment, as opposed to the maximum six months where it is tried summarily.

5.2 Stalking

Although stalking has never been legally defined it is generally agreed to cover the obsessive behaviour of those who follow their victims about in public places, make nuisance telephone calls, send offensive or suggestive mail, take items of clothing from washing lines, peer in through the windows of dwellings and generally intrude upon the privacy of the victim. In certain extreme cases victims have suffered various forms of psychological distress causing lasting damage. Certain technical offences, such as the sending of indecent, offensive or threatening mail contrary to the Malicious Communications Act 1988, or the making of indecent, obscene or menacing calls contrary to the Telecommunications Act 1984, can be invoked to tackle such behaviour but they tend not to carry penalties truly reflective of the harm caused. The mainstream non-fatal offences against the person are frequently inappropriate in the absence of some direct assault – although see *R* v *Ireland*; *R* v *Burstow* (above) as evidence of the courts' willingness to extend these offences to tackle harassment. The civil law provides some protection for those who are the victims of violence perpetrated by their spouses or other members of their families – see the Domestic Violence and Matrimonial Proceedings Act 1976 and the Family law Act 1996 – but in most cases stalkers are unrelated to their victims.

In recognition of these problems with the existing law Parliament enacted the Protection from Harassment Act 1997. The Act creates two new criminal offences. Section 2(1) makes it an offence to pursue a course of conduct which amounts to a breach of the prohibition laid down in s1, where it is provided that:

> '(1) A person must not pursue a course of conduct –
> a) which amounts to harassment of another, and
> b) which he knows or ought to know amounts to harassment of the other.
> (2) For the purposes of this section, the person whose course of conduct is in question ought to know that it amounts to harassment of another if a reasonable person in possession of the same information would think the course of conduct amounted to harassment of the other.
> (3) Subsection (1) does not apply to a course of conduct if the person who pursued it shows –
> a) that it was pursued for the purpose of preventing or detecting crime,
> b) that it was pursued under any enactment or rule of law or to comply with any condition or requirement imposed by any person under any enactment, or
> c) that in the particular circumstances the pursuit of the course of conduct was reasonable.'

The offence created by s2(1) is arrestable within the terms of s24(2) of the Police and Criminal Evidence Act 1984, and is triable on a summary basis only.

A more serious offence is introduced by s4, which provides:

> '(1) A person whose course of conduct causes another to fear, on at least two occasions, that violence will be used against him is guilty of an offence if he knows or ought to know that his course of conduct will cause the other so to fear on each of those occasions.
> (2) For the purposes of this section, the person whose course of conduct is in question ought to know that it will cause another to fear that violence will be used against him on any occasion if a reasonable person in possession of the same information would think the course of conduct would cause the other so to fear on that occasion.
> (3) It is a defence for a person charged with an offence under this section to show that–
> a) his course of conduct was pursued for the purpose of preventing or detecting crime,
> b) his course of conduct was pursued under any enactment or rule of law or to comply with any condition or requirement imposed by any person under any enactment, or
> c) the pursuit of his course of conduct was reasonable for the protection of himself or another or for the protection of his or another's property.'

The offence is triable either way, carrying a maximum sentence of five years' imprisonment upon conviction. A jury may find a defendant not guilty under s4, but instead return a verdict of guilty of the offence under s2.

In relation to either offence the courts are empowered, by virtue of s5, to grant a restraining order for the purpose of protecting the victim of the offence, or any other person mentioned in the order, from further conduct which amounts to harassment, or will cause a fear of violence. By virtue of s5(5), a defendant who, without reasonable excuse, does anything which he is prohibited from doing by an order under the section, will be guilty of an offence, for which the maximum penalty (following trial on indictment) is five years' imprisonment.

The Act also creates a civil remedy by providing, in s3, that an actual or apprehended breach of s1 may be the subject of a claim in civil proceedings by the person who is or may be the victim of the course of conduct in question. Damages may be awarded for (among other things) any anxiety caused by the harassment and any financial loss resulting from the harassment. An injunction may also be granted for the purpose of restraining the defendant from pursuing any conduct which amounts to harassment, and failure to observe the terms of any such injunction will be an offence.

It is significant that the Act does not actually provide a definition of what is meant by stalking or, indeed, harassment, concentrating instead on the effect on the victim. The rationale for this is that the offence under s2 will remain flexible and could be employed in a wide range of circumstances.

Whilst the damage done by those who engage in activities generically referred to as stalking is not to be underestimated, the danger is that these proposed offences may impinge upon other activities hitherto regarded as legitimate, such as investigative journalism, door-to-door selling and even debt collection. Much depends upon the interpretation of s1(3)(c), whether or not 'in the particular circumstances the pursuit of the course of conduct was reasonable.' Conversely, it may be that in some respects the law does not go far enough. It could, for example, be argued that the proposed law ought to extend to situations where the defendant sets out to cause public embarrassment to the victim, perhaps by publishing letters or photographs.

The Act also attracted some criticism from Lord Steyn in the course of his speech in *R v Ireland; R v Burstow*, where he observed that:

> '[Under the Act] The maximum custodial penalty is six months' imprisonment. This penalty may ... be inadequate to deal with persistent offenders who cause serious psychiatric injury to victims. Section 4(1) of the Act of 1997 which creates the offence of putting people in fear of violence seems more appropriate. It provides for maximum custodial penalty upon conviction on indictment of five years' imprisonment. On the other hand, section 4 only applies when as a result of a course of conduct the victim has cause to fear, on at least two occasions, that violence will be used against her. It may be difficult to secure a conviction in respect of a silent caller: the victim in such cases may have cause to fear that violence may be used against her but no more. In my view, therefore, the

provisions [the 1997 Act] ... are not ideally suited to deal with the significant problem [of malicious telephone calls] ... which I have described.'

Aggravated forms of the offences created by ss2 and 4 of the Protection from Harassment Act 1997 have been introduced by s32 of the Crime and Disorder Act 1998 which creates offences of racially aggravated harassment. The maximum sentences of imprisonment that can be imposed where the aggravated offences are tried on indictment are two and seven years respectively.

5.3 Offences Against the Person Act 1861 s47

Section 47 provides:

> 'Whosoever shall be convicted on indictment of any assault occasioning actual bodily harm shall be ... [liable to punishment].'

Where it is tried on indictment, s47 carried the possibility of five years' imprisonment. As with assault, the Crime and Disorder Act 1998 introduces a racially aggravated form of the offence, the concept of racially aggravated being as explained above in the context of assault. The aggravated nature of the offence is reflected in the higher maximum penalty of seven years' imprisonment.

Actus reus

The actus reus of the offence requires proof of three elements: an assault; causation; and actual bodily harm.

Assault

The meaning of assault has already been considered in section 5.1, above. It only needs to be reiterated here that the assault upon which liability for s47 is based can be either 'narrow' or 'broad'. Hence the offence would be made out if D were to rush into a room waving a poker threateningly at P, causing P to jump out of the window to escape, with the result that P sustains a twisted ankle in his fall to the ground. More commonly, the offence will involve direct physical contact between D and P, resulting in some minor harm to P.

Occasioning

The word 'occasioning' as used in s47 can be taken to mean causing. The section provides an example of what is sometimes called a 'result' crime, in that it must be shown that D's actions have caused the prohibited result. It is first necessary to ascertain whether or not D is the cause in fact of the injury. This can be resolved by applying the so-called 'but for' test; but for D's actions would the victim have suffered the injury? Assuming that causation in fact can be established, it is then necessary to consider whether or not D was the cause in law of the victim's injury?

R v *Notman* [1994] Crim LR 518, applying *R* v *Hennigan* (1971) 55 Cr App R 262, confirms that, whilst a trial judge should make it clear to the jury that the defendant's actions have to be more than a de minimis cause of the injury in question, the expression 'substantial cause' is suitable for most purposes in describing the test for causation in law that has to be applied.

Where more complex issues of remoteness do arise, ie because the defendant contends that there is some novus actus interveniens that breaks the chain of causation, the court should invoke the test explained by Stephenson LJ in *R* v *Roberts* (1971) 56 Cr App R 95. Here the defendant had given a lift to the victim, a young woman, and during the journey he made a number of improper suggestions to her, and at one stage touched her breasts. The victim jumped from the car whilst it was moving (the speed was variously stated as being between 20 and 40 miles per hour), and suffered grazing and concussion in her fall. The defendant was convicted under s47, and appealed on the ground that the victim's action in jumping from the car had broken the chain of causation, thus relieving him of liability for the harm. In dismissing the appeal, his Lordship explained that the correct test for causation in law was to ask: Were the actions of the victim the natural result of what the alleged assailant said and did, in the sense that it was something that could reasonably have been foreseen as the consequence of what he was saying or doing? Only if there was some voluntary act on the part of the victim that could be regarded as 'daft' or unexpected, in the sense that no reasonable man could be expected to foresee it, would the chain of causation in law be broken.

On this basis it might be argued that the victim s actions would have broken the chain of causation had she jumped from a car travelling at 70 miles per hour, but this conflicts with the ratio of *R* v *Blaue* [1975] 1 WLR 1411 which holds that a defendant should have to take his victim as he finds him or her. Thus, if the victim is 'daft' enough to try and escape from an indecent assault by jumping from a speeding car should not the defendant be responsible for the consequences? For a more detailed consideration of causation see Chapter 4, section 4.2.

Actual bodily harm

Actual bodily harm was defined by Lynskey J, when addressing a jury at Hampshire Assizes in *R* v *Miller* [1954] 2 QB 282, where he explained that the expression covered any hurt or injury likely to interfere with the health or comfort of the victim. For example, in *R* v *Roberts* (above), the actual bodily harm was grazing and concussion. It is submitted that actual bodily harm would also encompass injuries such as bruising (see *R* v *Reigate Justices, ex parte Counsell* (1983) 148 JP 193), sprained joints, and, possibly, concussion, nausea and vomiting. On the facts of *Miller* the jury concluded that inducing a nervous hysterical condition in the victim came within the definition, but this should now be seen in the light of the decision of the Court of Appeal in *R* v *Chan Fook* [1994] 1 WLR 689. Hobhouse J, whilst confirming that psychiatric injury could come within the scope of actual bodily harm, provided there was medical evidence to show that the harm was more than mere emotional disturbance, rejected the notion that it could encompass conditions such as fear, distress, panic or other hysterical or nervous conditions. Confirming the correctness of the decision in *Chan Fook*, Lord Steyn, in the course of his speech in *R v Ireland; R v Burstow* (above) observed:

'The victims in [in these two cases] ... did not develop psychotic or psychoneurotic conditions ... they developed mental disturbances of a lesser order, namely neurotic disorders. For present purposes the relevant forms of neurosis are anxiety disorders and depressive disorders. Neuroses must be distinguished from simple states of fear, or problems in coping with everyday life. Where the line is to be drawn must be a matter of psychiatric judgment. But for present purposes it is important to note that modern psychiatry treats neuroses as recognisable psychiatric illnesses ... Moreover, it is essential to bear in mind that neurotic illnesses affect the central nervous system of the body, because emotions such as fear and anxiety are brain functions ... I would ... point out that, although out of considerations of piety we frequently refer to the actual intention of the draftsman, the correct approach is simply to consider whether the words of the Act of 1861 considered in the light of contemporary knowledge cover a recognisable psychiatric injury. ... The proposition that the Victorian legislator when enacting sections 18, 20 and 47 of the Act 1861, would not have had in mind psychiatric illness is no doubt correct. Psychiatry was in its infancy in 1861. But the subjective intention of the draftsman is immaterial. The only relevant enquiry is as to the sense of the words in the context in which they are used. Moreover the Act of 1861 is a statute of the "always speaking" type: the statute must be interpreted in the light of the best current scientific appreciation of the link between the body and psychiatric injury. For these reasons I would, therefore, reject the challenge to the correctness of *Chan-Fook*. ... In my view the ruling in that case was based on principled and cogent reasoning and it marked a sound and essential clarification of the law.'

R v Morris (1997) The Times 13 November confirms that a charge of occasioning actual bodily harm contrary to s47 should not be left to a jury, where non-physical assault is alleged, unless there is psychiatric evidence to support the prosecution's case.

Mens rea

It is notable that s47 does not expressly state any mens rea requirement – yet it has never been contended that the offence is one of absolute or strict liability. The courts have always 'read in' some mens rea requirement, the basis of the modern interpretation being the Court of Appeal's decision in *R v Venna* (1975) 61 Cr App R 310, where it was held that the prosecution would have to establish intention or recklessness on the part of the accused. Despite the views expressed in decisions such as *DPP v Khan* (1990) 91 Cr App R 29, the issue as to the type of recklessness that has to be established under s47 seems now to have been conclusively resolved in favour of *Cunningham*: see *R v Savage; R v Parmenter* [1991] 3 WLR 914.

What is the extent of the mens rea?

In *R* v *Cunningham* (1957) 41 Cr App R 155, Byrne J referred to a concept of recklessness involving the defendant being:

> '... recklessness as to whether such harm should occur or not (ie the accused has foreseen that the particular kind of harm might be done and yet has gone on to take the risk of it).'

Applied to s47, this would require proof that the defendant foresaw the risk of actual bodily harm resulting from his assault yet went on to take that risk, but does the mental element have to extend beyond the causing of the assault? The matter was addressed by the Court of Appeal in two separate cases which, by coincidence, were before different sittings of that court at exactly the same time. In *R* v *Savage* (1990) 91 Cr App R 317, the appellant was charged with unlawful wounding contrary to s20 of the Offences Against the Person Act 1861, the prosecution having alleged that the appellant had approached the victim and thrown the contents of an almost full pint glass of beer at her, and that she had let go of the glass which broke, with the result that the victim suffered cuts. The appellant admitted that it had been her intention to throw the beer over the victim but denied any intention to cut her with the glass. The appellant appealed successfully against her conviction under s20 because of the trial judge's misdirection as to the mental element for that offence, but the court substituted a conviction for s47, on the basis that the offence did not require proof of recklessness or 'maliciousness' in relation to the 'occasioning' of the actual bodily harm. The appellant had deliberately thrown the beer over the victim, an act which was obviously an assault, and that 'assault' had undoubtedly occasioned the actual bodily harm which occurred. The court effectively relegated the issue of the resulting harm to one of causation, to be assessed objectively. In the second of these cases, *R* v *Spratt* (above), the appellant had fired an air pistol from the window of his dwelling into a courtyard below. He claimed that he had been aiming at a sign. A pellet from the gun struck a child playing in the yard. The appellant denied any knowledge that children were in the vicinity of the sign. The appellant pleaded guilty to a s47 offence following his counsel's advice that *Caldwell* recklessness now applied to the offence. As has been indicated above, the Court of Appeal held that *Cunningham* should have been applied, but it is notable that in the headnote to the report it is stated that:

> 'A defendant could not be guilty of an offence under s47 ... where he failed to give thought to the possibility that his action might give rise to a risk of causing bodily harm to another person.'

This clearly required a further element of mens rea not specified in *Savage* and the two decisions were clearly irreconcilable as to this issue. The Court of Appeal attempted to resolve the problem in the course of its decision in *R* v *Parmenter* (1991) 92 Cr App R 68. Having reviewed the two decisions, Mustill LJ stated (at p74):

> 'It seems to us that they are not in conflict as regards a case where the defendant neither intends nor adverts to the possibility that there will be any physical contact at all. (This

case is governed by *Spratt* and not by *Savage*). Nor is there any conflict where the defendant does advert to the possibility of harm, albeit not necessarily of the kind which actually happened.

But in the intermediate case we are driven to conclude that there is a conflict, for if the glass slipped from the defendant's hand in *Savage* [above] by mistake, there would not (even under the wide interpretation given by *Mowatt*) have been the mental element as regards the physical harm which is called for by *Spratt* [above]. We are obliged to resolve this conflict in order to decide the present appeal, and after careful consideration must prefer *Spratt* [above] which was founded on a line of authority leading directly to the conclusion there expressed: whereas these authorities are not mentioned in *Savage*, and cannot have been brought to the attention of the court.'

This analysis was, however, firmly rejected by Lord Ackner by the time the appeals in *R* v *Savage*; *R* v *Parmenter* (above) were considered by the House of Lords. Lord Ackner noted that s47 did not expressly require any mens rea as regards the causing of actual bodily harm, and felt unable to conclude that any was required by necessary implication. In his Lordship's view, the words 'occasioning actual bodily harm' were descriptive of the word 'assault' by reference to a particular kind of consequence. In support of this conclusion, Lord Ackner cited *R* v *Roberts* (above), and the finding in that case that the mens rea for s47 was the same as the mens rea required for common assault.

It now seems settled, therefore, that once an assault is established, the only remaining question under s47 is that of whether or not the actual bodily harm was a consequence of that assault. This matter can be resolved by applying an objective test. It will not be necessary to investigate the defendant's degree of awareness of consequences.

5.4 Offences Against the Person Act 1861 s20

Section 20 of the Offences Against the Person Act 1861 in effect creates two offences: 'malicious wounding'; and 'maliciously inflicting grievous bodily harm'. Both offences carry the possibility of five years imprisonment.

A defendant convicted under s20 following trial on indictment can be imprisoned for five years. The Crime and Disorder Act 1998 introduces a racially aggravated form of s20, the aggravating element being as explained in relation to assault above. The aggravated offence carries a maximum penalty of seven years' imprisonment.

Malicious wounding

Actus reus
A wounding requires there to have been a break in the surface of the victim's skin. A graze may not be sufficient to satisfy this. The dermis and the epidermis must have been broken. Similarly, where the defendant's action causes internal bleeding only, this will not be held to constitute wounding. The authority for these

propositions is the decision of the Divisional Court in *JJC (A Minor)* v *Eisenhower* [1984] QB 331, where it was held that broken blood vessels in the victim's eye, caused by pellets fired from an air gun by the defendant, did not amount to a wounding within s20. A defendant in such a case might, however, still be guilty of actual bodily harm, or even grievous bodily harm in extreme cases. As this is a 'result crime' it will be necessary to establish that the defendant's act is a sufficiently proximate cause of the victim's wound. Complications may arise where the defendant's act is the indirect cause of the wound, eg ordering a dog to bite a victim: see *R* v *Dume* (1987) The Times 16 October.

Mens rea

The mens rea required for the offence is denoted by the word 'malicious'. The basis for the modern interpretation of this somewhat archaic expression is the decision of the Court of Appeal in *R* v *Cunningham* (1957) 41 Cr App R 155. The defendant was charged with unlawfully and maliciously causing a person to take a noxious thing, namely coal gas, so as to endanger her life, contrary to s23 of the Offences against the Person Act 1861, an offence which also has the word 'maliciously' to denote the mens rea required. In the course of his judgment, Byrne J referred (at p159) to:

> '... the following principle which was propounded by the late Professor C S Kenny in the first edition of his *Outlines of Criminal Law* published in 1902 and repeated at page 186 of the sixteenth edition edited by Mr J W Cecil Turner and published in 1952. "In any statutory definition of a crime, malice must be taken not in the old vague sense of wickedness in general but as requiring either (1) an actual intention to do the particular kind of harm that in fact was done; or (2) recklessness as to whether such harm should occur or not (ie the accused has foreseen that the particular kind of harm might be done and yet has gone on to take the risk of it). It is neither limited to nor does it indeed require any ill will towards the person injured". The same principle is repeated by Mr Turner in his tenth edition of *Russell on Crime* at p1592: "... in our opinion the word 'maliciously' in a statutory crime postulates foresight of consequence."'

Note that for these purposes maliciousness was equated with intention or recklessness, the recklessness being subjective (requiring proof of foresight on the part of the accused), and the consequence the accused must have been proved to have been aware of, was the harm specified in the offence. For the purposes of s20, therefore, the defendant would at least have to be aware of the risk of causing grievous bodily harm or wounding. A gloss was placed upon the definition in *Cunningham* by Diplock LJ in the later case of *R* v *Mowatt* (1967) 51 Cr App R 402 at 406 where, having referred to the facts of *Cunningham* he stated:

> 'No doubt upon these facts the jury should be instructed that they must be satisfied before convicting the accused that he was aware that physical harm to some human being was a possible consequence of his unlawful act in wrenching off the gas meter [the act that caused the coal gas to escape]. In the words of the court, "maliciously in a statutory crime postulates foresight of consequence", and upon this proposition we do not wish to cast any doubt. But the court in that case also expressed approval obiter of a more general

statement by Professor Kenny [Kenny's *Outlines of Criminal Law*, extracted above] …
[T]his generalisation is not in our view, appropriate to the specific alternative statutory
offences described in ss18 and 20 of the Offences against the Person Act 1861. In the
offence under s20, and in the alternative verdict which may be given on a charge under
s18, for neither of which is any specific intent required, the word "maliciously" does
import upon the part of the person who unlawfully inflicts the wound or other grievous
bodily harm an awareness that his act may have caused the consequence of causing some
physical harm to some other person. That is what is meant by "the particular kind of
harm" in the citation from Professor Kenny. It is quite unnecessary that the accused
should have foreseen that his unlawful act might cause physical harm of the gravity
described in the section, ie, a wound or serious physical injury. It is enough that he
should have foreseen that some physical harm to some person, albeit of a minor character,
might result.'

Clearly the interpretation offered by Diplock LJ represents a significant 'watering
down' of the mens rea requirement for s20. A defendant could now be guilty of the
offence if he punches P foreseeing that he might cause bruising, but actually cuts his
face with the force of the blow. Despite Diplock LJ's reference to 'should have
foreseen', it would appear that, following the enactment of s8 of the Criminal Justice
Act 1967, the defendant must at least foresee some physical harm. Foresight that the
victim will be frightened is not of itself sufficient. Hence in *R* v *Sullivan* [1981] Crim
LR 46 the defendant, who had swerved his car towards a group of pedestrians
intending to scare them, was acquitted of a charge under s20, when he lost control of
the vehicle and subsequently collided with the pedestrians causing injury. As he had
only foreseen the risk of 'psychic harm' his liability was reduced to s47.

Any remaining doubts as to the validity of the reasoning in *R* v *Mowatt* have
since been swept aside by the House of Lords decision in *R* v *Savage*; *R* v
Parmenter [1991] 3 WLR 914, in which Lord Ackner confirmed that the gloss placed
upon *Cunningham* by *Mowatt* was correct. His Lordship rejected the criticism that
the mens rea should extend to the actus reus specified. Consistent with his analysis
of s47, considered above, he cited *R* v *Roberts* (above) and the offence of murder,
where a defendant can be convicted even though he only foresees grievous bodily
harm. In short, he rejected that there was any hard and fast principle in criminal law
that the mens rea of an offence should necessarily extend to the actus reus. See
further *R* v *Rushworth* (1993) 95 Cr App R 252, where Mann LJ suggested that an
accurate statement of what was required when directing a jury as to the meaning of
the word 'maliciously' would be the following:

'In order to establish an offence under section 20 the prosecution must prove either that
the defendant intended to, or that he actually foresaw his act might cause physical harm
to some person albeit harm of a minor character.'

There is one issue of principle that remains unresolved by the decision in *R* v
Savage; *R* v *Parmenter*. Both s47 and s20 carry the same maximum penalty, ie five
years imprisonment, yet they are now distinguished to the extent that the former
requires no mens rea as to consequences, whilst the latter requires at least an
awareness that some physical harm might occur. The distinction can, of course, be

reflected in the exercise of judicial discretion when sentencing, but it is submitted that either the maximum punishment for s47 should reflect the lower degree of mens rea required, or alternatively it should be seen as an offence that does require some mens rea as to consequences, thus placing it on the same footing as s20. Lord Ackner was not unaware of these criticisms, but explained the situation as being the result of 'piecemeal legislation'. He cited with approval J C Smith's view that the 1861 Act was:

> '... a ragbag of offences brought together from a wide variety of sources with no attempt, as the draftsman frankly acknowledged, to introduce consistency as to substance or as to form'.

Maliciously inflicting grievous bodily harm

Actus reus: grievous bodily harm

Grievous bodily harm was defined by the House of Lords in *DPP* v *Smith* [1961] AC 290 as 'really serious harm'. More recently, the Court of Appeal in *R* v *Saunders* [1985] Crim LR 230, held that it is sufficient for a trial judge to direct a jury that grievous bodily harm simply means 'serious harm': see also *R* v *Janjua* [1998] Crim LR 675. A fractured limb will thus satisfy the definition, as would permanent disablement of the victim, a fractured skull or the rupturing of internal organs. On the basis of *R* v *Brown and Stratton* [1998] Crim LR 485 it would be a misdirection for a trial judge to direct a jury to decide whether or not the harm caused amounted to grievous bodily harm by considering how they would classify it if they were the victims. Whether or not harm amounts to grievous bodily harm is to be determined objectively, with particular regard being had to the medical evidence: see further *R* v *Ireland* (above).

R v *Gelder* (1994 unreported, but see news report in *The Times* 25 May 1994) suggests that a 'psychological battering' caused by repeated obscene telephone calls can amount to grievous bodily harm, there being evidence that the harm manifested itself in insomnia, diarrhoea and sickness.

Actus reus: inflicting

Whilst s18 of the 1861 Act refers to D 'causing' grievous bodily harm, and s47 refers to D 'occasioning' actual bodily harm, s20 has given rise to difficulty because of the draftsman's use of the word 'inflicting' to denote the actions of D that have to be proved. Taken on its own the word is perhaps suggestive of direct harm, but the courts have for many years taken a broader view. For example, in *R* v *Martin* (1881) 8 QBD 54, D blocked the exit doors of a theatre, put out the lights in a passageway and shouted 'Fire!', causing theatre-goers leaving the performance in panic to be severely injured by being crushed against the locked doors. In confirming his conviction under s20, the Court for Crown Cases Reserved impliedly accepted that the battery causing the harm could be indirect (ie no physical contact between D and P).

Rather than simply take the view that the word 'inflict' denoted a need to prove causation, however, the courts embarked upon a rather tortuous course of reasoning, as exemplified in *R v Clarence* (1888) 22 QBD 23 where D was acquitted of inflicting grievous bodily harm on his wife (having infected her with venereal disease during consensual sexual intercourse), on the basis that, although there had been physical contact, an 'assault' as such could not be identified (the wife had consented to the intercourse and did not apprehend any immediate physical violence).

The matter is not merely one of academic interest. Under s6(3) of the Criminal Law Act 1967 a jury can acquit a defendant as charged, but substitute a conviction for a lesser offence, provided the lesser offence is one encompassed by the more serious offence. Hence, a defendant can be acquitted on a murder charge but convicted of manslaughter, the lesser-included offence. In the scheme of the 1861 Act this begged the question of whether s20 was an alternative to s18, ie whether causing under s18 was wide enough to encompass the notion of inflicting under s20. In *R v Mandair* [1994] 2 WLR 700, a case in which the jury had acquitted the defendant of the s18 offence, but returned a verdict of guilty of 'causing grievous bodily harm' contrary to s20 of the 1861 Act, a majority of their Lordships held that the causing of grievous bodily harm (the defendant had thrown sulphuric acid at his wife causing severe facial burns) had been contrary to s20 in that it had consisted of inflicting grievous bodily harm. The term 'causing' under s18 was wide enough to encompass any manner of 'inflicting' under s20, hence a conviction for inflicting grievous bodily harm contrary to s20 was available as an alternative to causing grievous bodily harm contrary to s18. It would indeed be illogical if s18, the more serious offence, required less in terms of proof of causation, than the lesser offence under s20.

Similarly, the question arose as to whether s47 was a lesser-included offence within s20. Logically, if the infliction of harm contrary to s20 did not necessarily require proof of an assault it would not be open to a jury to acquit D of the s20 charge and exercise the power, granted by s6(3) of the 1967 Act, to find D guilty of the lesser offence under s47. In *R v Wilson; R v Jenkins* [1983] 3 WLR 686 the House of Lords, noting that the broad approach to s6(3) was to ask if the more serious charge against D should expressly or impliedly amount to, or include, the lesser offence, concluded, somewhat unsatisfactorily, that a defendant acquitted under s20 could nevertheless be convicted under s47, although this did not mean that proof of an assault was a precondition of establishing the infliction of harm. Lord Roskill went further in citing with approval the decision of the Supreme Court of Victoria in *R v Salisbury* [1976] VR 452, wherein it was held that the infliction of harm did not require an assault but did require proof of force being applied violently to the body so that the victim suffered grievous bodily harm: see further *R v Savage; R v Parmenter* (above) and *R v Brown* [1993] 2 WLR 556. In the latter case Lord Jauncey, rejecting the contention that the consent of the victim might be a defence to a charge under s47 but not s20, bases his argument on the fact that complications would arise precisely because s47 is an alternative verdict where D is charged with maliciously inflicting grievous bodily harm contrary to s20.

The House of Lords has considered that matter most recently in *R* v *Ireland; R* v *Burstow* (above), where one of the two certified questions was whether an offence of inflicting grievous bodily harm under s20 of the Offences Against the Person Act 1861 could be committed where no physical violence was applied directly or indirectly to the body of the victim. The House confirmed that the word 'inflicting' in s20 of the 1861 Act was to be approached on the basis that it had the same meaning as 'cause'. The divergence in terminology between ss47, 20 and 18 was not to be regarded as significant where, as was the case with the 1861 Act, the statute was comprised of clauses drawn from a disparate collection of earlier statutes. As Lord Steyn explained, the framers of the 1861 Act did not have consistency of expression as one of their aims. Reviewing the authorities, he observed that *R* v *Wilson; R* v *Jenkins* (above) was at best neutral as to the meaning of the word 'inflict' in the context of s20, given that Lord Diplock had expressed himself as willing to accept that there could be an infliction of harm under s20 without an assault being committed. Similarly, the decision of the House in *Mandair* suggested no great divergence in meaning between 'cause' and 'inflict'. *Clarence* (above) was not regarded as being of any great assistance because the judges in that case had clearly not contemplated the possibility of psychiatric harm being caused without physical contact. Lord Steyn added:

'The problem is one of construction. The question is whether as a matter of current usage the contextual interpretation of "inflict" can embrace the idea of one person inflicting psychiatric injury on another. One can without straining the language in any way answer that question in the affirmative. I am not saying that the words cause and inflict are exactly synonymous. They are not. What I am saying is that in the context of the Act of 1861 one can nowadays quite naturally speak of inflicting psychiatric injury. Moreover, there is internal contextual support in the statute for this view. It would be absurd to differentiate between sections 18 and 20 in the way argued on behalf of *Burstow*. As the Lord Chief Justice observed in *Burstow* [in the court below], this should be a very practical area of the law. The interpretation and approach should so far as possible be adopted which treats the ladder of offences as a coherent body of law.'

Mens rea

The mens rea requires proof that the defendant acted maliciously: see above.

5.5 Offences Against the Person Act 1861 s18

Section 18 of the 1861 Act provides (inter alia):

'Whosoever shall unlawfully and maliciously ... wound or cause any grievous bodily harm to any person ... with intent to do some grievous bodily harm to any person ... shall be guilty of an offence ...'

Actus reus

The actus reus of the offence, wounding or causing grievous bodily harm, has been considered above at section 5.4

Mens rea

The main distinguishing factor separating s18 from s20 is the mens rea required. Again the defendant must be malicious, as to which see section 5.2 above, but in addition he must be proved to have had a further specific intent, in that it must have been the defendant's intention to do some grievous bodily harm to the victim. The principal authority on this point is the Court of Appeal's decision in *R* v *Belfon* [1976] 1 WLR 741. The defendant had slashed the victim with a razor causing severe wounds to his face and chest, and was convicted under s18. The trial judge's direction to the jury was that they could convict if they were satisfied that the defendant had foreseen grievous bodily harm as something that would probably result from his actions. The conviction was quashed by the Court of Appeal, Wein J holding that the prosecution had to establish that it was the defendant's purpose to do some grievous bodily harm. Recklessness as to consequences was certainly not sufficient.

It is logical to assume that the meaning given to intent under s18 should be the same as that given to intent in the context of murder, not least because intention to do grievous bodily harm will suffice for murder: see Chapter 4, section 4.3. On this basis a defendant should not be convicted of causing grievous bodily harm contrary to s18 unless there is evidence that he foresaw grievous bodily harm as a virtually certain consequence of his actions: see *R* v *Hancock* [1986] AC 455 and *R* v *Woollin* [1998] 4 All ER 103. It should be noted that, in the course of his speech in the latter case, Lord Steyn (at p108) expressed the view that his comments on intent were confined to the context of murder, and that it should not be assumed that 'intent' should have the same meaning throughout criminal law, but he did not elaborate on this. Quite what 'other' meaning intention might have outside the confines of murder is, therefore, unclear. See also *R* v *Bryson* [1985] Crim LR 669.

Charging standards

Following the publication of the revised Code for Crown Prosecutors, the police and the Crown Prosecution Service have co-operated in the development of charging standards on (non-sexual and non-fatal) offences against the person to ensure greater consistency.

An assault involving a battery that results in harm that technically constitutes actual bodily harm contrary to s47 of the Offences Against the Persons Act 1861 should be charged as a common assault contrary to s39 of the 1861 Act where the injury amounts to no more than a graze, scratch, abrasion, bruise (including a 'black eye'), swelling, reddening of the skin, or a superficial cut. Where such injuries are the result of an assault upon a constable in the execution of his duty a charge under s51(1) of the Police Act 1964 is to be preferred.

The following injuries should normally be charged under s47 of the 1861 Act: loss or breaking of a tooth or teeth; temporary loss of sensory functions; extensive or multiple bruising; displaced broken nose, minor fractures; cuts requiring stitches; and psychiatric injury which goes beyond fear and panic, supported by appropriate expert evidence.

Section 20 of the 1861 should be reserved for those wounds considered to be serious, ie on a par with grievous bodily harm. Injuries that should be equated with grievous bodily harm include those resulting in: permanent disability or loss of a sensory function; more than minor permanent visible disfigurement; broken or displaced limbs or bones; injuries causing substantial loss of blood (ie necessitating a transfusion); and injury resulting in lengthy treatment or incapacitation.

5.6 Offences Against the Person Act 1861 ss23 and 24

Section 23 of the 1861 Act creates the offence of 'maliciously administering a noxious substance so as to endanger life, or inflict grievous bodily harm'. Section 24 also involves the malicious administering of a noxious substance, but requires a further intent, namely that this should 'injure, aggrieve, or annoy' the victim.

Actus reus

Both ss23 and 24 require the administering of a noxious substance.

Noxious substance

In *R* v *Cato* (1976) 62 Cr App R 41 the Court of Appeal stated that a substance was noxious for the purposes of these offences if it was likely to injure in common use. In *R* v *Marcus* [1981] 1 WLR 774, however, a preferable approach was suggested, where it was held that whether or not a substance was noxious would depend on the circumstances in which it was taken. Such circumstances would involve the quality and quantity of the substance, and the characteristics of the person to whom it was being given.

Administering

The term 'administration' was thought to carrying with it some quasi-medical meaning, with the result that a defendant could not be guilty under s23 where he squirted a noxious substance in the face of his victim: see *R* v *Dones* [1987] Crim LR 682. The correct view is that advanced by the Court of Appeal in *R* v *Gillard* (1988) 87 Cr App R 189, where McNeill J observed that the trial judge had erred in holding that 'administering' and 'taking' were to be treated effectively as synonymous or as conjunctive words. He continued:

'The word "takes" postulates some ingestion by the victim; "administer" must have some other meaning and there is no difficulty in including in that meaning such conduct as spraying the victim with noxious fluid or vapour, whether from a device such as a gas canister or, for example, hosing down with effluent. There is no necessity when the word "administer" is used to postulate any form of entry into the victim's body, whether through any orifice or by absorption; a court dealing with such a case should not have to determine questions of pathology such as, for example, the manner in which skin irritation results from exposure to CS gas or the manner in which the eye waters when exposed to irritant. The word "ingest" should be reserved to its natural meaning of intake into the digestive system and not permitted to obscure the statutory words. In the view of this Court, the proper construction of "administer" in section 24 includes conduct which not being the application of direct force to the victim nevertheless brings the noxious thing into contact with his body. While such conduct might in law amount to an assault, this Court considers that so to charge it would tend to mislead a jury.'

Mens rea

Both offences require proof of the defendant acting maliciously, as to which see section 5.4 above, but note particularly that the defendant in *R* v *Cunningham* [1957] 2 QB 396, was charged under s23.

Section 24 clearly requires proof of a further intent to injure aggrieve or annoy the victim. This means that D's purpose in administering the noxious substance must be examined. In *R* v *Weatherall* [1968] Crim LR 115 the trial judge directed a jury that the necessary mens rea had not been established where the defendant had given his wife sleeping tablets so that he could look through her handbag for letters revealing details of her adultery whilst she was asleep.

The nature of the ulterior intent was also considered by the House of Lords in *R* v *Hill* [1986] Crim LR 815. The defendant, a homosexual man, admitted giving some slimming tablets, which were normally only available on prescription, to a number of small boys. He had hoped that the effect of the tablets would be to lower the boys' inhibitions and make them more susceptible to his advances. The Court of Appeal had quashed his conviction on the ground that the trial judge might have misdirected the jury into assuming that an intention to keep the boys awake amounted to a sufficient ulterior intent for a conviction under s24. The question certified for consideration by their Lordships was:

'Whether the offence of administering a noxious substance with intent to injure … is capable of being committed when a noxious thing is administered to a person without lawful excuse with the intention only of keeping that person awake.'

The House of Lords restored the conviction on the basis that there was overwhelming evidence that the defendant had intended the administration of the tablets to injure the metabolisms of the boys who took them. In answer to the certified question, it was held that (in so far as it could be answered on the facts of this case) the matter had to be approached by looking at the object that the defendant had in mind. To keep a pilot awake by plying him with stimulants so that he could safely land an aircraft would not involve the commission of an offence, whereas to deprive him of sleep for the purposes of interrogation might well do so. Similarly, it was suggested that to keep a child awake in order to greet the arrival of a relative late at night, or view a fireworks display, would fall outside s24.

By implication, a man who secretly gives a woman sleeping pills with a view to sexually assaulting her whilst she is asleep would come within s24, but not where he does so in order to ensure that he has an uninterrupted night's sleep when sharing a bed with her.

In theory the offences created by s23 and s24 of the 1861 Act could be used to prosecute those who knowingly infect other persons with viruses. This possibility begs the further question of whether a charge could be brought where D has sexual intercourse with P whilst knowingly being HIV positive. Although a person suffering from AIDS can be detained pursuant to a magistrates' order issued under the Public Health Control of Diseases Act 1984 and the Infectious Diseases Regulations 1985, it would appear that this power could only be used prospectively, where there was a risk to other people, and not retrospectively where deliberate transmission had taken place. In 1992 Roy Cornes, a haemophiliac who was HIV positive, was accused of having sexual intercourse with four women, knowing or being reckless as to whether any of them would thereby develop the condition. No action was taken against him prior to his death in 1994. In August 1997 the government announced its intention to act upon the Law Commission's proposals for the reform of the law relating to offences against the person (considered at section 5.10 below) to make it easier to secure convictions in cases of deliberate or reckless transmission of disease. Even if these measures see the light of day three difficulties will remain. First, the evidential problem of establishing that it was contact with D that caused P to become HIV positive; second, the need to prove D's awareness of his condition and the consequences of unprotected sexual contact; and third, there will be the moral issue of punishing defendants who may in any event not have long to live.

5.7 False imprisonment, kidnapping, abduction and hostage-taking

In addition to the common law and statutory offences dealing with direct physical assaults, there is a range of offences designed to protect the individual from being detained against his will, or alternatively being taken against his will. Under the Taking of Hostages Act 1982 it is an offence for any person to detain another in order to compel a state or international organisation, or indeed another person, to perform certain acts, or abstain from any course of conduct, by means of threatening to kill, injure or further detain the person or persons taken hostage. Reflecting the nature of international terrorism, the offence is triable in the English courts regardless of the nationality of the defendant or the place where the hostage-taking is alleged to have taken place. The offence is punishable with life imprisonment.

False imprisonment

At common law it is an offence to restrain another's freedom of movement, provided the necessary mens rea is established. In the same way as assault and battery exist as both torts and crimes, false imprisonment can give rise to both civil and criminal liability. In *R* v *James* (1997) The Times 13 March the Court of Appeal confirmed that the actus reus of false imprisonment arose where D placed unlawful restrictions on P's freedom of movement, the mens rea requiring proof that D intended to cause such restrictions or was reckless as to whether or not he did so, the recklessness being as defined in *R* v *Cunningham* [1957] 2 QB 396.

The detention can occur in a dwelling, office, shop or other building or in an unconfined area if P submits to the detention. Imprisonment for these purposes encompasses the legal concept of arrest: see *R* v *Rahman* (1985) 81 Cr App R 349. Subject to the de minimis principle, the imprisonment need only be fleeting or momentary for the offence to be made out. In most cases P will be aware of the restraints being placed on his freedom of movement, but in theory criminal liability could arise where D locks the door of the room in which P has fallen asleep, notwithstanding that P is, at the time, unaware of his confinement. The imprisonment will normally result from a positive act by D, but in cases where he is under a positive legal duty to act, his failure to do so could give rise to liability, for example where D, a bus driver, refuses to open the doors of the bus to allow passengers off at the end of a bus route.

The requirement that the imprisonment should be 'false' or 'wrongful' involves proof that there was no legal basis for the detention. Hence, in the above example, a bus driver might escape liability for false imprisonment if he refused to allow passengers off the bus at a place other than a recognised bus stop. As to the powers given to both citizens and police constables to restrict the movements of others by exercising powers of arrest, see further ss24 and 25 of the Police and Criminal Evidence Act 1984.

In cases where P was restrained by fear of what D might do if she tried to escape, rather than being physically restrained, the jury should be directed to consider D's mens rea very carefully. If the evidence is that P's fear arose merely as a by-product of D's words or actions, rather than as a result of intentional or reckless assault by D, he should be acquitted. Hence if D says to P, 'I'll break our neck if you try to escape', with the result that P is too frightened to leave, there will be strong evidence that D intended to restrain P's freedom of movement by intimidating her. Note that, notwithstanding House of Lords' ruling in *R* v *Ireland; R* v *Burstow* (above), to the effect that words can amount to an assault, false imprisonment does not require proof of an assault: *R* v *Linsberg* (1905) 69 JP 107.

More subtle cases will provide evidential difficulties. Suppose that P visits D's house and is attacked by D. P may feel unable to leave for fear that she will be attacked again. The problem here is that P will feel restrained, but it may not be D's intentions that P should feel so restrained. Unless the prosecution can show that

D was at least aware of the risk that P would feel unable to leave because of the fear of further assaults it will not be possible to secure a conviction. A similar case would be where P1 and P2 visit D, and D assaults P1 who tries to escape. P2 may feel that she too will be assaulted if she tries to escape. Again, a prosecution of D for the false imprisonment of P2 will require proof of his awareness of the effect of his actions on P2.

Kidnapping

Kidnapping is essentially an aggravated form of false imprisonment. As the House of Lords made clear in *R* v *D* [1984] AC 778, it is a common law offence that requires proof that D, by force or fraud, carried away P without his or her consent, and without any lawful excuse. Although cases of kidnapping may also involve the removal of the victim to a secret destination this is not an element of the offence that has to be proved. Notwithstanding that the offence is known as 'kidnapping' there may be evidential difficulties where the victim is a young child. The absence of consent may be a necessary inference given the age of the victim, but small children can frequently be removed without D having to exercise any fraud or indeed use any force. In such cases the prosecution would have to resort to a charge of false imprisonment. The concept of lawful excuse is not entirely clear in the context of this offence, but it is submitted that it should at least mirror the emerging common law doctrine of necessity. Thus D could escape liability if he took P into custody for fear that P was in physical danger. Whether fears for P's moral welfare would also provide a lawful excuse is a moot point: see *R* v *Henman* [1987] Crim LR 333. A prosecution of a parent for kidnapping a child will require the consent of the DPP.

Where a child is removed from the United Kingdom by a person connected with the child (eg a parent, guardian or other person having custody of the child) without the appropriate consent, an offence may be committed contrary to s1 of the Child Abduction Act 1984, as amended by the Children Act 1989. Note that the offence does not require proof of the absence of consent on the part of the child concerned. Section 2 of the 1984 Act also creates an offence of removing a child from the control of the person having lawful control over the child.

5.8 Offences against police constables

Assault upon a police officer in the execution of his duty

This offence, originally enacted as s51(1) of the Police Act 1964, now to be found in s89(1) Police Act 1996, states:

> 'Any person who assaults a constable in the execution of his duty, or a person assisting a constable in the execution of his duty, shall be guilty of an offence ...'

For the purposes of this offence, assault bears both its narrow and its broad meaning, as considered above. Thus, as was stated by James J in *Fagan* v *MPC* (above), a constable can be assaulted, even where he does not apprehend immediate physical harm. A police officer is any person who has been lawfully sworn as such.

In the execution of his duty

Ascertaining the scope of a constable's duties is a matter which has given the courts some considerable difficulty, yet it is a matter which is crucial to the offence under s89(1), in that if a police officer is not acting within the execution of his duty, an element of the actus reus is absent and there can be no liability. The offence certainly extends beyond those situations where a police officer is exercising some positive statutory duty. In the majority of situations a police officer will in fact be exercising powers not duties, but it would be nonsense to therefore suggest that he was no longer acting in the execution of his duty. As a very general statement of the law it might be said that provided a police officer can point to some legal authority for his actions, he is acting within the scope of his duties. This reflects the view adopted by the Divisional Court in *Coffin* v *Smith* (1980) 71 Cr App R 221, where D assaulted a police officer who had been called to deal with a group of gatecrashers at a youth club disco. It was accepted that no offences had been committed by D up to this point, but he was nevertheless charged with assaulting a police officer in the execution of his duty. The justices upheld a submission of no case to answer on the basis that the police officer had not been under any duty to compel D to leave the scene. Donaldson LJ regarded this approach as totally wrong. In his view a police officer was acting within the execution of his duty where he was taking steps that were necessary to keep the peace, and was not committing any act which was prima facie an unlawful interference with a person's liberty or property.

On the basis of the above, and decisions such as *Weight* v *Long* [1986] Crim LR 746 and *Mepstead* v *DPP* [1996] Crim LR 111, therefore, it would appear a police officer will be acting within the scope of his duty where he acts to keep the peace, to prevent the commission of an offence, and to investigate offences already committed, provided the force he uses is within the bounds of what is reasonably necessary in the circumstances. In effect it means that D has to produce some evidence that a police officer has exceeded his powers before he will be able to succeed with a submission that the officer is not acting in the execution of his duty, a view supported by a number of decisions.

In *R* v *Waterfield* [1964] 1 QB 164, the Court of Appeal held that D was not guilty of an offence under (what was then) s51(1), where he had assaulted a police officer who had detained his car, the officer not having any specific power to do so. In *Lindley* v *Rutter* [1980] Crim LR 729 a police officer had removed some clothing from an inebriated detainee, but only had power to do this if there was evidence that failure to do so might result in harm to the detainee or others. The detainee resisted the officer's attempts to remove the clothing and was charged under s51(1) of the 1964 Act. The Divisional Court held that the officer had not been acting in the execution of her duty, as there were no grounds to justify her removal of the detainee's clothing, hence the offence of assault was not made out. Finally, *Kerr* v *DPP* [1995] Crim LR 394 confirmed that D will not be guilty of the offence under what is now s89(1), where he resists force used against him by a constable who wrongly believes that the defendant is under arrest. A charge of common assault always remains a possibility in such cases, but presumably D will be able to raise the defence that he was entitled to use reasonable force.

Mens rea
D must have the intention to assault, as to which (see above). The difficult issues here are whether D must know that a police officer is acting in the execution of his duty, and further whether he must know that the person he is assaulting is a police officer. As regards the first matter, the venerable case of *R* v *Forbes and Webb* (1865) 10 Cox CC 362 is still good authority for the proposition that the offence is not assault *knowing* the police officer to be in the execution of his duty, but assault upon a police officer who *is* in the execution of his duty. This rather suggests that liability as to this element of the actus reus is strict, but it is a view which has received implicit approval (albeit in relation to a quite different offence) in subsequent cases such as *R* v *Prince* (1875) LR 2 CCR 154. The decisions in *McBride* v *Turnock* [1964] Crim LR 456 and *Albert* v *Lavin* [1981] 1 All ER 628 also both support the view that a D cannot rely on the contention that he honestly believed the person he was assaulting was not a police officer, although the latter case admits of the possibility that D might be permitted to rely on an honest and reasonable mistake that the victim was not a police officer. It might now be the case, however, following the decision of the Court of Appeal in *R* v *Williams* [1987] 3 All ER 411, which was approved by the Privy Council in *Beckford* v *R* [1987] 3 All ER 425 (see further Chapter 15, section 15.3), that the courts would look more favourably on D who seeks to rely on an honest belief that the victim of his assault was not a police officer.

Both of the decisions referred to approve the principle that where D makes an honest, although not necessarily reasonable mistake as to the existence of an attack by an assailant from which he must defend himself, he should be judged on the facts as he honestly believes them to be, thus justifying the use of reasonable force by way of self-defence. Applying these authorities to a situation under s89(1), D, who honestly believed that a plain clothed police officer making an arrest was in reality a robber attacking an innocent victim, would not be guilty under the section if he used reasonable force on the police officer to prevent the perceived attack. This conclusion is also supported by the obiter statements of Widgery LJ in *R* v *Fennell* [1970] 3 All ER 2 15, where he suggests that D who honestly believes that his child is being unlawfully detained by a police officer, and who further honestly believes that the child is in imminent danger of injury, would be justified in using reasonable force in order to secure his child's release, although there might still be liability under s89(2), considered below.

Wilful obstruction of a police officer in the execution of his duty

Originally enacted as s51(3) of the Police Act 1964, s89(2) of the Police Act 1996 now provides:

'Any person who resists or wilfully obstructs a constable in the execution of his duty, or a person assisting a constable in the execution of his duty, shall be guilty of an offence ...'

Obstruction

Essentially obstruction is any act or omission that makes it appreciably more difficult for an officer to execute his duty: see *Rice* v *Connolly* [1966] 2 QB 414 and *Bennett* v *Bale* [1986] Crim LR 404. Hence to warn drivers that there is a police speed trap in operation so that they slow down from unlawful to lawful speeds can constitute obstruction: see *Betts* v *Stevens* [1910] 1 KB 1. Similarly, to deliberately consume alcohol so as to prevent the administration of a valid breathalyser test has been held to amount to obstruction: see *Dibble* v *Ingleton* [1972] 1 QB 480. Clearly a balance has to be struck between the demands of public policy and the freedom of the individual. In *Rice* v *Connolly* (above) it was held that D was not guilty of obstruction simply on the basis of his refusal to answer questions when stopped by a police officer in the street. Note that in such cases there is no duty to answer police questions. Where a duty does exist, failure to perform that duty could amount to obstruction. Hence, in *Lunt* v *DPP* [1993] Crim LR 534, D, who had refused to admit police officers to his home after being traced following a traffic accident, was convicted of wilful obstruction, on the basis that, under the Road Traffic Act 1988, he had been under a duty to admit the officers.

The obstruction must be something done without lawful excuse, not a lawful omission as in this case. It would not amount to obstruction to advise a burglar not to burgle a particular house because the owner has had an alarm fitted, whereas it would be an offence to warn a burglar, who was in the act of breaking into the house, of the impending arrival of the police. Further, the fact that D intends to obstruct is not sufficient unless there is some evidence that his actions have actually impeded the police: see *Bennett* v *Bale* (above).

Police constable in the execution of his duty

This expression has the same meaning here as it does in relation to the offence of assault upon a police constable considered above.

Mens rea

In addition to the matters considered above, the prosecution has to establish that D's obstruction of the police officer was wilful. In general terms an obstruction is wilful if D intends that his action should make the police officer's execution of his duty more difficult. Uncertainties have arisen, however, with the well meaning member of the public who intervenes to help the police, but who in fact only succeeds in making the situation worse. In *Willmott* v *Atack* [1977] QB 498, D was present at the scene of an arrest at which the police officers concerned were having some difficulty in carrying out. Believing he could help resolve the situation more effectively, D interposed himself between the arresting officers and the suspect, action that resulted in his being convicted under s51(3). The Divisional Court, quashing the conviction, held that D only obstructed wilfully where he acted with some hostility towards the police, and that had not been the situation here, as D had intended to positively assist. This decision was not followed, however, in the subsequent Divisional Court decision in *Hills* v *Ellis* [1983] QB 680, where D had witnessed a fight outside a football ground and intervened when he saw the innocent party in the fight being arrested by a police officer. He grabbed the arresting officer's elbow and shouted at him in order to alert the officer to what D feared would be a miscarriage of justice. Upholding D's conviction under s51(3), the Divisional Court held that, looking at the matter objectively, D had in fact obstructed the police officer and had intended to do so. The 'hostility' referred to in *Willmott* v *Atack* as being a necessary element of the mens rea was held to be satisfied here by evidence that D's actions were 'aimed at' the police officers. The court stressed that D's motive in acting as he had was irrelevant. It seems clear that the court viewed it as being contrary to public policy to encourage members of the public to intervene wherever they thought a police officer to be making an error of judgment. The Divisional Court appears to have extended this strict approach further still in *Lewis* v *Cox* [1984] Crim LR 756, by removing any requirement that D's act be aimed at the police officers in the literal sense. D, whose friend had been placed under arrest in the back of a police van, opened the back door of the van to enquire which police station the friend was being taken to, and thereby prevented the van from being driven away. The magistrates had dismissed the obstruction charge brought on the basis that D's action in opening the van doors had not been directed against the police. The Divisional Court, allowing the prosecutor's appeal, held that it was sufficient for a conviction that D had known that his actions would make it more difficult for the police to drive away.

5.9 Reform

In its report *Legislating the Criminal Code: Offences Against the Person and General Principles* (1993) Law Com No 218, the Law Commission proposed that the principle statutory and common law offences against the person should be replaced by new statutory offences. Building upon this work, the government published a Consultation Paper, *Violence: Reforming the Offences Against the Person Act 1861* in March 1998. A draft Bill was also published indicating the form that the changes would take.

As the Consultation Paper states:

'Reforming the law on violence against the person is not just an academic exercise – criminal cases involving non-fatal offences against the person make up a large part of the work of the courts and cost a great deal of taxpayers money. In 1996 83,000 cases came before the courts. It is therefore particularly important that the law governing such behaviour should be robust, clear and well understood. Unclear or uncertain criminal law risks creating injustice and unfairness to individuals as well as making the work of the police and courts far more difficult and time-consuming ... the law should be set out in clear terms and in plain, modern language.' (para 1.2)

The proposals are not intended to make the law tougher or more lenient, simply to introduce much needed clarity of expression and consistency in the use of terms.

Clauses 1 to 3 propose new offences to replace ss18, 20 and 47 of the 1861 Act. They provide as follows:

'1(1) A person is guilty of an offence if he intentionally causes serious injury to another.
(2) A person is guilty of an offence if he omits to do an act which he has a duty to do at common law, the omission results in serious injury to another, and he intends the omission to have that result.
(3) An offence under this section is committed notwithstanding that the injury occurs outside England and Wales if the act causing injury is done in England and Wales or the omission resulting in injury is made there.
(4) A person guilty of an offence under this section is liable on conviction on indictment to imprisonment for life.

2(1) A person is guilty of an offence if he recklessly causes serious injury to another.
(2) An offence under this section is committed notwithstanding that the injury occurs outside England and Wales if the act causing injury is done in England and Wales.
(3) A person guilty of an offence under this section is liable –
(a) on conviction on indictment, to imprisonment for a term not exceeding 7 years;
(b) on summary conviction, to imprisonment for a term not exceeding 6 months or a fine not exceeding the statutory maximum or both.

3(1) A person is guilty of an offence if he intentionally or recklessly causes injury to another.
(2) An offence under this section is committed notwithstanding that the injury occurs outside England and Wales if the act causing injury is done in England and Wales.
(3) A person guilty of an offence under this section is liable –
(a) on conviction on indictment, to imprisonment for a term not exceeding 5 years;
(b) on summary conviction, to imprisonment for a term not exceeding 6 months or a fine not exceeding the statutory maximum or both.'

The concept of injury is further clarified in cl 15, which provides:

'15(1) In this Act "injury" means –
(a) physical injury, or
(b) mental injury.
(2) Physical injury does not include anything caused by disease but (subject to that) it includes pain, unconsciousness and any other impairment of a person's physical condition.
(3) Mental injury does not include anything caused by disease but (subject to that) it includes any impairment of a person's mental health.
(4) In its application to section 1 this section applies without the exceptions relating to things caused by disease.'

There is no definition of what constitutes a 'serious' injury, hence there might still be some scope for litigation on this point. The provisions are significant in that they would see the introduction of criminal liability for the deliberate passing on of diseases and viruses, notably HIV. As the Consultation Paper explains:

'In LC 218 the Law Commission were unequivocal that the Offences Against the Person Act 1861 could be used to prosecute the transmission of disease, and recommended that the proposed new offences should enable the intentional or reckless transmission of disease to be prosecuted in appropriate cases. The Government has not accepted this recommendation in full ... There are few decided cases on this point, so the position in the criminal law is not entirely clear. The most commonly cited case, that of *Clarence* (1888), seems to indicate that the 1861 Act could not be successfully used to prosecute the reckless transmission of disease. However, it is now accepted that the judgement related to one specific offence and to the issue of consent, and that in principle it may well be possible to prosecute individuals for transmitting illness and disease at least when they do so intentionally. Although this has not been tested in the courts in recent years, in *Ireland* and *Burstow* the House of Lords held that the 1861 Act could be used to prosecute the infliction of psychiatric injury. In reforming the law, the issue of whether and if so how the transmission of disease should fall within the criminal law needs the most careful consideration. ...The Government recognises that this is a very sensitive issue. The criminal law deals with behaviour that is wrong in intent and in deed. The Law Commission's original proposal, which included illness and disease in the definition of injury, would have resulted in the intentional or reckless transmission of disease being open to prosecution. They argued that the width of their proposal would be balanced by the fact that prosecution would only be appropriate in the most serious cases. The Government has considered their views very carefully, but is not persuaded that it would be right or appropriate to make the range of normal everyday activities during which illness could be transmitted potentially criminal. We think it would be wrong to criminalise the reckless transmission of normally minor illnesses such as measles or mumps, even though they could have potentially serious consequences for those vulnerable to infection. ... An issue of this importance has ramifications beyond the criminal law, into the wider considerations of social and public health policy. The Government is particularly concerned that the law should not seem to discriminate against those who are HIV positive, have AIDS or viral hepatitis or who carry any kind of disease. Nor do we want to discourage people from coming forward for diagnostic tests and treatment, in the interests of their own health and that of others, because of an unfounded fear of criminal prosecution. ...The Government therefore considered whether it should exclude all transmission of disease from the criminal law, and concluded that that too would not be appropriate. The existing law extends into this area, even though it has not been used. There is a strong case for arguing that society should have criminal sanctions available for use to deal with evil acts. It is hard to argue that the law should not be able to deal with the person who gives a disease causing serious illness to others with intent to do them such harm. That is clearly a form of violence against the person. Such a gap in the law would be difficult to justify. ... The Government therefore proposes that the criminal law should apply only to those whom it can be proved beyond reasonable doubt had deliberately transmitted a disease intending to cause a serious illness. This aims to strike a sensible balance between allowing very serious intentional acts to be punished whilst not rendering individuals liable for prosecution for unintentional or reckless acts, or for the transmission of minor disease. The Government believes that this is close to the effect of the present law, and that it is right in principle to continue to allow the law to be used in those rare grave cases where prosecution would be justified. This proposal will clarify the present law which, because it is largely untested is unclear; by doing so the effect of the law will be confined to the most serious and culpable behaviour. ... It is important to emphasise that this proposal does not reflect a significant change in the law. Prosecutions for the transmission of disease are very rare for very good reasons. Any criminal charge has to be supported by evidence and proved to a court beyond reasonable doubt. It is very difficult to prove both the causal linkage of the transmission and also to prove that it was done intentionally. To do so beyond reasonable doubt is even more difficult. The Government does not expect that the proposed offence will be used very often, but considers that it is important that it should exist to provide a safeguard against the worst behaviour.' (paras 3.12–3.19)

The proposals leave open the question of whether the reckless transmission of disease could amount to common law manslaughter if death were to result therefrom. Liability for killing by gross negligence could not be ruled out. Clause 16 provides for a statutory formulation of the supervening fault principle in *R* v *Miller*, to the effect that a defendant would incur liability for failing to take measures to prevent the harmful consequences of their actions once they become aware that such harm might result.

The fault terms adopted in the draft Bill are further defined in cl 14 which provides:

'14(1) A person acts intentionally with respect to a result if –
(a) it is his purpose to cause it, or
(b) although it is not his purpose to cause it, he knows that it would occur in the ordinary course of events if he were to succeed in his purpose of causing some other result.
(2) A person acts recklessly with respect to a result if he is aware of a risk that it will occur and it is unreasonable to take that risk having regard to the circumstances as he knows or believes them to be.
(3) A person intends an omission to have a result if –
(a) it is his purpose that the result will occur, or
(b) although it is not his purpose that the result will occur, he knows that it would occur in the ordinary course of events if he were to succeed in his purpose that some other result will occur.
(4) A person is reckless whether an omission will have a result if he is aware of a risk that the result will occur and it is unreasonable to take that risk having regard to the circumstances as he knows or believes them to be.
(5) Related expressions must be construed accordingly.
(6) This section has effect for the purposes of this Act.'

These definitions are said to only apply for the purposes of this Act. If it were enacted, however, a defendant charged with murder would have to be proved to have had either the intent to kill, intention here having its common law meaning, or to have had intention to cause serious injury, in relation to which the statutory definition would presumably apply. Significantly, the proposals embrace the subjective concept of recklessness. Clause 17 codifies the principle of transferred malice as regards the draft Bill offences.

The draft Bill seeks to abolish common assault and common battery, and replace them both with a new statutory offence defined in cl 4 as follows:

'4(1) A person is guilty of an offence if –
(a) he intentionally or recklessly applies force to or causes an impact on the body of another, or
(b) he intentionally or recklessly causes the other to believe that any such force or impact is imminent.
(2) No such offence is committed if the force or impact, not being intended or likely to cause injury, is in the circumstances such as is generally acceptable in the ordinary conduct of daily life and the defendant does not know or believe that it is in fact unacceptable to the other person.
(3) A person guilty of an offence under this section is liable on summary conviction to imprisonment for a term not exceeding 6 months or a fine not exceeding level 5 on the standard scale or both.'

The government's aim is that the courts should be able to apply this definition of assault wherever the term occurs as an element of an offence (eg indecent assault, and assaults on police officers and others specified persons).

Other new offences proposed in the draft Bill include making threats to cause death or serious injury (cl 10 replacing s16 of the 1861 Act); administering a substance capable of causing injury to the other (cl 11 replacing ss23 and 24 of the 1861 Act); and torture (cl 12, a revised restatement of s134 Criminal Justice Act 1988).

The offence of assaulting a police officer in the execution of his duty, currently found in s89(1) of the Police Act 1996, is restated in cl 5, with additional offences provided by cls 6 and 7. They provide:

5(1) A person is guilty of an offence if he assaults –
(a) a constable acting in the execution of his duty, or
(b) a person assisting a constable acting in the execution of his duty.
(2) For the purposes of this section a person assaults if he commits the offence under section 4.
(3) A reference in this section to a constable acting in the execution of his duty includes a reference to a constable who is a member of a police force maintained in Scotland or Northern Ireland when he is executing a warrant, or otherwise acting in England and Wales, by virtue of an enactment conferring powers on him in England and Wales.
(4) For the purposes of subsection (3) each of the following is a police force –
(a) a police force within the meaning given by section 50 of the Police (Scotland) Act 1967;
(b) the Royal Ulster Constabulary and the Royal Ulster Constabulary Reserve.
(5) A person guilty of an offence under this section is liable on summary conviction to imprisonment for a term not exceeding 6 months or a fine not exceeding level 5 on the standard scale or both.

6(1) A person is guilty of an offence under this section if he causes serious injury to another intending to resist, prevent or terminate the lawful arrest or detention of himself or a third person.
(2) The question whether the defendant believes the arrest or detention is lawful must be determined according to the circumstances as he believes them to be.

(3) A person guilty of an offence under this section is liable on conviction on indictment to imprisonment for life.

7(1) A person is guilty of an offence if he assaults another intending to resist, prevent or terminate the lawful arrest or detention of himself or a third person.
(2) The question whether the defendant believes the arrest or detention is lawful must be determined according to the circumstances as he believes them to be.
(3) For the purposes of this section a person assaults if he commits the offence under section 4.
(4) A person guilty of an offence under this section is liable –
(a) on conviction on indictment, to imprisonment for a term not exceeding 2 years;
(b) on summary conviction, to imprisonment for a term not exceeding 6 months or a fine not exceeding the statutory maximum or both.'

In relation to defences, cl 18 provides that, subject to cl 19 which deals with voluntary intoxication, all existing defences shall continue to be available in relation to the proposed offences, including consent, duress and self-defence.

Under cl 19, for the purposes of the draft Bill, a person who was voluntarily intoxicated at any material time must be treated: (a) as having been aware of any risk of which he would have been aware had he not been intoxicated; and (b) as having known or believed in any circumstances which he would have known or believed in had he not been intoxicated. In this respect the proposals are perhaps open to criticism for ascribing to D beliefs that he may not have actually had at the time of the offence.

Voluntarily intoxication will be made out if D takes an intoxicant otherwise than properly for a medicinal purpose, is aware that it is or may be an intoxicant, and takes it in such a quantity as impairs his awareness or understanding.

Intoxication will be presumed to have been voluntary unless there is adduced such evidence as might lead the court or jury to conclude that there is a reasonable possibility that the intoxication was involuntary. For these purposes an intoxicant is any alcohol, drug or other thing which, when taken into the body, may impair the awareness or understanding of the person taking it. A person must be treated as taking an intoxicant if he permits it to be administered to him.

Note that the Law Commission has already produced its recommendations regarding placing the rules on intoxication and criminal liability on a statutory footing (see *Intoxication in the Criminal Law* – Law Com No 122 considered at Chapter 14, section 14.2). These changes were considered to be too complex for the purposes of this draft Bill, however.

6

Sexual Offences and Consent

6.1 Rape

6.2 Unlawful sexual intercourse

6.3 Indecent assault

6.4 The defence of consent

6.1 Rape

The statutory basis for the offence of rape is s1(1) of the Sexual Offences Act 1956, as amended by s1(2) of the Sexual Offences (Amendment) Act 1976 and s142 of the Criminal Justice and Public Order Act 1994. In its amended form s1 of the 1956 Act now states:

'(1) It is an offence for a man to rape a woman or another man.
(2) A man commits rape if–
a) he has sexual intercourse with a person (whether vaginal or anal) who at the time of the intercourse does not consent to it; and
b) at the time he knows that the person does not consent to the intercourse or is reckless as to whether that person consents to it.
(3) A man also commits rape if he induces a married woman to have sexual intercourse with him by impersonating her husband.
(4) Subsection (2) applies for the purpose of any enactment.'

Actus reus of rape

The Criminal Justice and Public Order Act 1994, by virtue of s142, has substantially redrawn the offence of rape by introducing the concept of male rape, ie non-consensual buggery committed by one man upon another. The revised offence retains the generic term 'sexual intercourse' to cover both vaginal and anal intercourse, thus creating the possibility that a man could be guilty of raping a woman, even though he has sodomised her, and not had vaginal intercourse. The term 'sexual intercourse' is defined further in s44 of the Sexual Offences Act 1956 which provides:

'Where, on the trial of any offence under this Act, it is necessary to prove sexual intercourse (whether natural or unnatural), it shall not be necessary to prove the

178

completion of the intercourse by the emission of the seed, but the intercourse shall be deemed complete upon proof of penetration only.'

There are still certain forms of violent sexual assault that can be traumatic for the victim that fall outside the scope of rape, eg the penetration of the vagina or anus by means of objects such as bottles or sticks. Similarly, the penetration of other orifices, particularly the mouth in cases of forced oral sex, would have to be charged as indecent assault; see further *R* v *Kowalski* (1987) 86 Cr App R 339.

Although s1(1) refers to a man committing the offence, it is possible for any male over the age of 10 to be charged with rape, following the enactment of the Sexual Offences Act 1993, which abolishes the presumption that a boy below the age of 14 cannot perform sexual intercourse for the purposes of offences where that is an element. Clearly, it is technically possible for a woman to be charged with rape, but only as an accomplice.

Prior to the reforms effected by s142 of the Criminal Justice and Public Order Act 1994, the prosecution were required to prove that the sexual intercourse in question was 'unlawful'. For centuries this had been taken to mean that the sexual intercourse had to be between parties who were not lawfully man and wife, on the basis that the wife's consent to intercourse was presumed from her having entered into the marriage. As Hale stated (*Pleas of the Crown* Vol 1, p629):

> '... by their mutual matrimonial consent and contract the wife hath given up herself in this kind unto her husband which she cannot retract.'

Limits were set upon the rule in relation to married persons no longer living together as man and wife, eg *R* v *Clarke* (1949) 33 Cr App R 216, where it was held that a husband could be guilty of rape upon his wife where a separation order was in force, the wife's consent to intercourse being revoked by the order; and *R* v *Steele* (1976) 65 Cr App R 22, where a husband was convicted of rape having given the court an undertaking that he would not molest his wife from whom he was living apart. See further *R* v *Miller* [1954] 2 QB 282. The House of Lords took the lead in abolishing the common rule against marital rape, however, in *R* v *R* [1991] 3 WLR 767, where Lord Keith noted that:

> 'By the second half of the twentieth century the status of a husband and wife are now for all practical purposes equal partners in marriage and both husband and wife are tutors and curators of their children. A wife is not obliged to obey her husband in all things nor to suffer excessive sexual demands on the part of her husband. She may rely on such demands as evidence of unreasonable behaviour for the purposes of divorce. A live system of law will always have regard to changing circumstances to test the justification for any exception to the application of a general rule. Nowadays it cannot seriously be maintained that by marriage a wife submits herself irrevocably to sexual intercourse in all circumstances. It cannot be affirmed nowadays, whatever the position may have been in earlier centuries, that it is an incident of modern marriage that a wife consents to intercourse in all circumstances, including sexual intercourse obtained only by force. There is no doubt that a wife does not consent to assault upon her person and there is no plausible justification for saying today that she nevertheless is to be taken to consent to intercourse by assault.'

Although their Lordships' ruling was widely applauded as being enlightened and dynamic, the problem remained that the offence of rape, as defined under statute at the time, still required proof that the sexual intercourse was 'unlawful'. At the time Lord Keith dealt with this issue by asserting:

> '... it is clearly unlawful to have sexual intercourse with any woman without her consent, and that the use of the word in the [statute] adds nothing ... it should be treated as being mere surplusage in this enactment ...'

Whilst this reasoning was, with respect, somewhat questionable, the new formulation of the offence of rape provided by s1(1) of the 1956 Act puts the matter beyond doubt by omitting any reference to the intercourse having to be unlawful.

The consent of the victim, to the commission of what would otherwise be an unlawful act, is normally raised as a defence by the defendant. The offence of rape is somewhat unusual in this respect in that the absence of consent on the part of the victim is an element of the crime that has to be positively established by the prosecution. In *R* v *Olugboja* (1981) 73 Cr App R 344 it was held that there should be no need to prove submission on the part of the woman; the simple question for the jury was now one of, did the woman consent?

The evidence that consent was not given can simply be the complainant's testimony. There is no need for any direct evidence of threats, deceit or force being used by the defendant, or resistance from the complainant, although these might be factors that would influence a jury one way or another: see *R* v *Malone* [1998] Crim LR 834. Some cases may present no factual or evidential problem, as where D uses force on P without offering P any choice as to what is to happen. Similarly, if P makes consent conditional upon D wearing a condom during intercourse, D will be guilty of rape if he refuses to comply with that condition and nevertheless proceeds to have intercourse: see further *Attorney-General's Reference (No 28 of 1996)* (1997) The Times 27 January.

More difficult are those cases where P only 'consents' to sexual intercourse because he or she views himself or herself as having no option, perhaps because D has a knife at his or her face, or because D has indicated that he will report P to the police for a crime he or she has committed unless he can have sexual intercourse with P. The first example is perhaps readily identifiable as rape, but the latter is less likely to be so viewed. In both cases it could be claimed that P has considered his or her predicament and decided that he or she prefers to have intercourse rather than deal with the consequences of not doing so, yet in both cases it could be claimed there is an absence of free and voluntary consent. In reality the matter depends upon the jury's conception of what looks like rape and what does not. Where the threats or inducements are not such as to remove any suggestion that P had a real choice, D may nevertheless be convicted of the lesser offence under s2(1) of the 1956 Act, namely procuring a person by threats or intimidation to have sexual intercourse. Even as regards this lesser offence, however, the prosecution would have to prove that P would not have consented but for the threats. Where the threats are of a less serious nature, such as where D indicates that P will not get a part in a film unless D can have sexual intercourse with P, it would seem that no offence whatsoever is committed: see further the commentary on *R* v *McAllister* [1997] Crim LR 233 at 234. As Dunn LJ (in *Olugboja*) expressed the matter:

> 'Although "consent" is [a] common word it covers a wide range of states of mind in the context of intercourse between a man and a woman, ranging from actual desire on the one hand to reluctant acquiescence on the other. We do not think that the issue of consent should be left to a jury without some further direction. What this should be will depend on the circumstances of each case. The jury ... should be directed that consent, or the absence of it, is to be given its ordinary meaning and if need be, by way of example, that there is a difference between consent and submission; every consent involves a submission, but it by no means follows that a mere submission involves consent ... In the less common type of case where intercourse takes place after threats not involving violence or the fear of it ... a jury will have to be ... directed to concentrate on the state of mind of the victim immediately before the act of sexual intercourse, having regard to all the relevant circumstances; and in particular, the events leading up to the act and her reaction to them showing their impact on her mind. Apparent acquiescence after penetration does not necessarily involve consent, which must have occurred before the act takes place ... the dividing line ... between real consent on the one hand and mere submission on the other may not be easy to draw. Where it is to be drawn in a given case is for the jury to decide, applying their combined good sense, experience and knowledge of human nature and modern behaviour to all the relevant facts of that case.'

Although the court in *Olugboja* was concerned with the offence of rape as defined under the pre-1994 law, it is submitted that the general principles stated above in relation to the absence or otherwise of consent on the part of the victim should apply equally whether the victim is male or female.

Consent and fraud

The effect of fraud on the consent of the victim will depend on the nature and circumstances of the deception. By virtue of s1(3) of the 1956 Act (as amended), a man who induces a married woman to have sexual intercourse with him by impersonating her husband commits rape, although liability would not extend to a situation where D fraudulently induced P into thinking that they had just been through a marriage ceremony and proceeded to have intercourse with her. If the ceremony was bogus, then P would not be a 'married woman', *R* v *Papadimitropoulos* (1957) 98 Crim LR 249, although D might nevertheless be guilty of procurement contrary to s3(1) of the 1956 Act (below).

The scope of the offence of rape has since been extended to other instances of impersonation by the Court of Appeal in *R* v *Elbekkay* [1995] Crim LR 163. D had sexual intercourse with P, having entered her room pretending to be E, her long standing sexual partner. On appeal against his conviction for rape D contended that, whilst the facts of the case could give rise to liability under s3(1) of the 1956 Act, there could be no liability for rape as s1(3) provided that instances of 'impersonation' could only result in a conviction for rape where the defendant had pretended to be the complainant's husband. Dismissing the appeal, the court held that s4 Criminal Law Amendment Act 1885, which s1(3) of the 1956 Act simply re-enacted, had been merely declaratory of the common law. Hence when s4 of the 1885 Act was introduced the position of an unmarried woman consenting to sexual intercourse with a man she believed to be her regular partner had not been considered. The court regarded it as very unlikely that Parliament, in enacting s1(3) of the 1956 Act, had meant to exclude the possibility of liability for rape arising where a defendant procured intercourse by impersonating the long-standing sexual partner of an unmarried woman. In arriving at this conclusion the court was persuaded by the words of Lord Keith in *R* v *R* (above) at p 616C, to the effect that:

'... the common law is ... capable of evolving in the light of changing social, economic and cultural developments ...'

The decision, whilst welcome, begs the question of the extent to which it could be applied to cases involving more short-lived relationships.

It is possible that other types of fraud might also negate P's consent where P's mistake as to what D is proposing is sufficiently fundamental. In *R* v *Williams* (1923) 17 Cr App R 56, D, a singing master, told P, his pupil, that she needed an operation to improve her singing voice, to which she agreed. The operation consisted of him having sexual intercourse with her. When charged with rape he contended that she had consented to his actions. The court held that there was no consent in this case. What P had thought she was consenting to was something fundamentally different from that which occurred. In this respect the decision followed earlier authorities such as *R* v *Flattery* (1877) 2 QBD 410.

Situations where D succeeds in persuading P to have sexual intercourse with him by resort to some lesser, or non-fundamental, deception are likely to fall within the scope of s3(1) of the 1956 Act, which creates the offence of procuring a woman to have sexual intercourse by false pretences or false representations, rather than the offence of rape. The nature of the offence created by s3(1) is usefully illustrated by the facts of *R* v *Linekar* [1995] 3 All ER 69. D had sexual intercourse with P, who had been working as a prostitute. P alleged that, prior to sexual intercourse, D had promised to pay her £25 for sex, but later refused to do so. On a charge of rape the trial judge directed the jury to the effect that, if P's consent to intercourse had been obtained by fraud she could not properly be regarded as having given her consent. Allowing the appeal, and noting that D should have been charged with procuring sexual intercourse by false pretences contrary to s3(1), Morland J cited with approval the dictum of Wills J in *R* v *Clarence* (1888) 22 QBD 23 to the effect that the only types of fraud that would destroy the effect of a woman's consent to sexual intercourse were frauds as to the nature of the act being performed, or fraud as to the identity of the person performing the act. Examples given by Wills J of situations where fraud would not vitiate P's consent to intercourse included that of D giving a prostitute counterfeit coins in payment for sex, and where D falsely presents himself as an honest virtuous person without a criminal record, in order to persuade P to have sex with him. In both cases P still knows that she is consenting to sexual intercourse. Morland J also drew further support from *R* v *Papadimitropoulos* (above), where the view was expressed that it was not the fraud producing the mistake that was material but the effect of the mistake itself. On this basis the court was satisfied that D's fraud as to payment was not such as could be said to vitiate P's consent. It is perhaps worth noting that P said that she had only consented to intercourse on the basis that D would be wearing a condom, which he did not do. Could it be argued in such cases that P has not consented to intercourse, on the basis that with the obvious danger of AIDS consent to 'safe' sex is consent to an act that is materially different from unprotected sex? It is submitted that an alternative would have been to charge him with obtaining services by deception contrary to s1 Theft Act 1978: see Chapter 8, section 8.5.

The mens rea of rape

D must intend to have vaginal or anal intercourse (as defined above), and must know that P does not consent to it, or he must at least be reckless as to whether P consents. The key decision in this regard is that of the House of Lords in *DPP* v *Morgan* [1975] 2 All ER 347. Morgan, an RAF NCO, persuaded three junior members of the force to come back to his house to have sexual intercourse with his wife. Although the men were initially incredulous, Morgan assured them that his wife derived sexual satisfaction from being forced to have sex with strangers, and that if she protested they should ignore her and assume it was part of play acting. Mrs Morgan was dragged from her bed by the men and each of them had sexual intercourse with her in turn, her husband being the last to do so. Morgan was convicted of aiding and abetting rape, and his three colleagues where convicted of rape. The trial judge had directed the jury that they should convict the three younger men, even if they had believed Mrs Morgan to be consenting, if they were of the view that there were no reasonable grounds for that belief. Although the appeals were dismissed by application of the proviso to the Criminal Appeal Act 1968, the House of Lords held, by a majority, that a man could not be guilty of rape if he honestly, albeit mistakenly, believed that a woman was consenting to sexual intercourse. The mens rea involved is subjective in that regardless of what the reasonable man may have thought or believed, the prosecution must prove that the defendant knew the victim not to be consenting, or that he was at least reckless as to this circumstance.

The decision in *Morgan* produced much (it is submitted misplaced) criticism, being described in some quarters as amounting to a 'Rapists' Charter'. By way of response Parliament enacted s1(2) of the Sexual Offences (Amendment) Act 1976 Act (now amended by the Criminal Justice and Public Order Act 1994), which to a large extent states the obvious by providing that:

'... if at a trial for a rape offence the jury has to consider whether a man believed that a woman or man was consenting to sexual intercourse, the presence or absence of reasonable grounds for such a belief is a matter to which the jury is to have regard, in conjunction with any other relevant matters, in considering whether he so believed.'

This does nothing to alter mens rea required for rape as a matter of substantive law. The issue remains one of what D believed. It is simply a reminder to the jury to consider the plausibility of D's claim that he believed P to be consenting in the light of the evidence.

Given the nature of the offence, and the opportunity for a man to ascertain whether or not his sexual partner is consenting to sexual intercourse, it could be argued that there should either be a positive duty on a man to obtain express consent prior to sexual intercourse, or that an objective test should be introduced based on whether the reasonable man would have believed P to have been consenting. Neither suggestion is without difficulty. Regarding the first, it cannot be assumed that simply because P gives his or her express consent that the consent is therefore freely given and unambiguous. P may still agree because of some perceived threats. As regards the second, the effect would be to reduce the role played by D at a rape trial to that of a bystander, with the exception of those cases where he is denying that intercourse took place. Only P would be able to give evidence as to whether he or she was consenting, and it will be for the jury to determine whether a reasonable person would have realised that P was not consenting to the sexual intercourse: see further Helen Reece 'When a woman says "No" she means "No" ...' [1997] NLJ 1616.

Given that recklessness as to consent will suffice, the question arises as to whether the *Cunningham* or *Caldwell* model should apply. The Court of Appeal decision in *R v Satnam and Kewal* (1983) 78 Cr App R 149 indicates that *Caldwell* recklessness should not be relied upon on a charge of rape as it would have the effect of importing an objective element into the mens rea of the crime, where it seems clear that Parliament intended this to be subjective. A defendant who fails to advert to an obvious risk that a person is not consenting to sexual intercourse will not, therefore, be guilty of reckless rape. One who has sexual intercourse not caring whether a person consents will be guilty.

Reform

Clause 89 of the Draft Code, which deals with the definition of rape, has been largely overtaken by the reforms outlined above. To the extent that it addresses the issue of consent, however, it is still worthy of consideration, provided that it is borne in mind that the offence is no longer gender specific. The Draft Code addresses the difficult problems of distinguishing between consent and submission, and determining the extent to which consent can be vitiated by deception. Clause 89(2) states:

'For the purposes of this section a woman shall be treated as not consenting to sexual intercourse if she consents to it –

(a) because a threat, express or implied, has been made to use force against her or another if she does not consent and she believes that, if she does not consent, the threat will be carried out immediately or before she can free herself from it; or
(b) because she has been deceived as to –
(i) the nature of the act; or
(ii) the identity of the man.'

The Code Report commentary upon this provision states:

'[S]ubsection (2) makes it clear that a man is guilty of rape where he obtains the woman's consent by a threat to use force against her or another. The [Criminal Law Revision] Committee thought that "it should not be rape if, taking a reasonable view, the threats were not capable of being carried out immediately." The Committee made no recommendation to require the woman's belief to be based on reasonable grounds. Detention, in itself, would not negative the effect of consent but the Committee thought that it should be rape where a woman is confined by a man for the purpose of sexual intercourse and there is an express or implied threat to use force against her should she try to escape. But, if the woman knows that she can free herself from the effect of the threat and does not do so, her consent to sexual intercourse will negative rape. The effect of the subsection is that consent obtained by other threats – for example, to break off an engagement or to dismiss from employment – will negative rape but the man will be guilty of an offence under clause 90 [procurement of a woman by threats].' [Vol II para 15.13]

As to deception, the commentary goes on to state:

'Subsection (2), again following the Committee, specifies the circumstances in which it will be rape if consent is obtained by deception. There is authority at common law [*R* v *Williams* [1923] 1 KB 340] that it is rape if the woman is deceived as to the nature of the act and the Sexual Offences Act 1956, s1(2), provides that a man who induces a woman to have sexual intercourse with him by impersonating her husband commits rape; but it is by no means clear that intercourse obtained by other deceptions as to identity constitutes rape. The subsection provides that it does. The effect is that consent obtained by any other deception – for example, that the man is not married or that he intends to marry the woman – will negative rape, as under the present law, but the man will be guilty of an offence under clause 91 [procurement of a woman by deception].' [Vol II para 15.15]

6.2 Unlawful sexual intercourse

Intercourse with a girl under thirteen

Section 5 of the 1956 Act states:

'It is [an offence] for a man to have unlawful sexual intercourse with a girl under the age of thirteen.'

The offence is punishable by life imprisonment. Sexual intercourse carries the meaning provided by s44 of the 1956 Act.

The offence would appear to be one of strict liability, hence the defendant will not be able to rely on the defence that he honestly believed the girl in question to be above 13 years of age, no matter how reasonable his belief: see *R* v *Prince* (1875) LR 2 CCR 154 and *B* v *DPP* [1998] 4 All ER 265.

Intercourse with a girl under sixteen

Section 6 of the 1956 Act states that it is an offence (subject to certain exceptions) for a man to have unlawful sexual intercourse with a girl under the age of 16. Section 6(2) provides for an exception where D, having contracted a marriage which is invalid by virtue of s2 of the Marriage Act 1949, or s1 of the Age of Marriage Act 1929, has intercourse with P whom he honestly and reasonably believes to be his wife in law. For the purposes of this offence 'sexual intercourse' carries the meaning given above.

Like s5, this offence is one of strict liability, and the decision in *R* v *Prince* applies with full force as regards the woman's age, except in the case of a defendant below the age of 24. Section 6(3) provides that a defendant under 24 will not be guilty of an offence if he has consensual intercourse with a girl under 16 provided he has not previously been charged with the offence, and honestly and reasonably believed her to be older than 16.

Buggery and bestiality

Section 12(1) of the Sexual Offences Act 1956 provides that it is an offence for a person to commit buggery with another person or with an animal. In this the statute does little more than restate the common law, there being no further elaboration on the elements of the offence.

At common law the offence is committed by a man who has anal intercourse with another man or woman, or by any person who has sexual intercourse, whether vaginal or anal, with an animal. To some extent the ambit of the offence has been restricted by the amendments made to the offence of rape by s142 of the Criminal Justice and Public Order Act 1994 (detailed above at section 6.1), as a result of which rape now encompasses cases of non-consensual anal intercourse where the victim may be male or female. The offence of buggery will now, therefore, be charged in those situations where the anal intercourse is consensual, but nevertheless unlawful. Because consent is regarded as irrelevant at common law, both parties are charged with the offence of buggery as co-principals. The party undertaking the act of buggery is referred to as 'the agent' and the party allowing himself, or herself, to be penetrated anally is referred to as 'the patient'.

The law relating to homosexual conduct has, of course, been liberalised during the latter part of the twentieth century. By virtue of the Sexual Offences Act 1967, anal intercourse between consenting male adults (over the age of 21) in private was declared not to be an offence. More recently, s143 of the Criminal Justice and Public Order Act 1994 reduced the age of consent for anal intercourse to 18. The significance of this latter change was that it applied to any anal intercourse between two persons, whether homosexual or heterosexual. For these purposes anal intercourse between two men does not take place in private if two or more persons are present or take part, or if it takes place in a lavatory to which the public are permitted access. In theory, therefore the act could be committed 'in private' by two men, or a man and a woman, in a secluded part of a public park at night. The offence of buggery with an animal can be charged regardless of whether the act took place in public or private.

The effect of these modifications is, therefore, that a charge of buggery will be effectively restricted, in the normal course of events, to cases of D having consensual anal intercourse with P, where P is aged between 16 and 18, or cases where D has sexual connection with an animal. A case of a woman having sexual connection with an animal requires evidence of her having been penetrated by the animal: see *R* v *Bourne* (1952) 36 Cr App Rep 125.

As with the offence of rape, where the defendant (agent) is male, the offence is complete upon proof of penetration, there being no need to prove emission of seed. The presumption that a boy under the age of 14 could not commit the offence was removed by the Sexual Offences Act 1993.

A person under the age of 18 convicted of buggery can be sentenced to two years' imprisonment. Where the defendant is over 21 the maximum increases to five years. Buggery with an animal carries the possibility of life imprisonment.

6.3 Indecent assault

Section 14(1) of the 1956 Act provides: 'It is an offence ... for a person to make an indecent assault upon a woman.' Similarly, s15 creates the offence of indecent assault on a man. Where the s15 offence is committed by a man, an offence under s13 of the 1956 Act, indecency between men, may be committed. Although s46 of the 1956 Act extends the meaning of man and woman to encompass 'boy' and 'girl' respectively, if the victim is under the age of 14, a defendant may instead be charged under the Indecency with Children Act 1960, considered below.

Actus reus

The assault required by the offence has been construed so as to include assault in the strict sense, ie causing another to apprehend immediate physical contact, and assault in the broad sense, ie encompassing actual physical contact see *R* v *Rolfe* (1952) 36 Cr App R 4 and *R* v *Sargeant* [1997] Crim LR 50. In this latter case the Court of Appeal confirmed that there was no need to prove that the violence apprehended by P should of itself have been indecent in nature. Hence D was guilty under s15 where he threatened violence to P, under threat of which P acceded to D's order that he should masturbate into a condom for D's sexual gratification.

Following the rulings in *R* v *Constanza* [1997] Crim LR 576 and *R* v *Ireland*; *R* v *Burstow* [1997] 4 All ER 225, to the effect that words alone can constitute an assault, there is also the theoretical possibility of an indecent assault being committed where the threats are of an indecent nature, although other offences may be more appropriate, eg insulting behaviour contrary to s4 of the Public Order Act 1986.

If there is physical contact it is not necessary to prove the victim's awareness of the contact or his awareness of the circumstances of indecency. Where there is no such contact, the complainant must be shown to have apprehended the assault and to have been aware of the circumstances giving rise to indecency. Problems may arise where D plays a passive or non-hostile role in the incident, such as where P, young girl, places her hand on D's penis and he does nothing to avoid or discontinue the contact. Decisions such as *Fairclough* v *Whipp* [1951] 2 All ER 834 suggested that no assault would be committed by D in such cases; similarly *Williams* v *Gibbs* [1958] Crim LR 127 and *DPP* v *Rodgers* (1953) 37 Cr App R 137. More recently in *R* v *M'Cormack* [1969] 2 QB 442 the Court of Appeal held that an indecent act committed upon a 15-year-old girl was an offence notwithstanding that it was done without hostility. In the case of children under 14 many of these incidents would now be dealt with under the Indecency with Children Act 1960, considered below, where the problem of proving an assault does not arise. Where P is over 16, it is submitted that an assault is committed where he or she apprehends physical contact to which he or she does not consent. This leaves the problem of victims between the ages of 14 and 16 who by law cannot consent to indecent assault. In such cases the decision in *R* v *M'Cormack* should prevail.

Indecency is not defined by the 1956 Act, but to secure a conviction the prosecution must prove that the assault in question was committed in circumstances of indecency. In *R* v *Court* [1989] AC 28 the House of Lords confirmed the view of the Court of Appeal that indecency involved a contravention of standards of decent behaviour in regard to sexual modesty or privacy. Clearly this is a flexible concept which will vary from case to case. What one jury regards as indecent, another may find amusing and acceptable. Where an assault is objectively incapable of being regarded as indecent, the fact that D derived a secret sexual ratification from the activity cannot provide evidence of the indecent circumstances: see *R* v *George* [1956] Crim LR 52 as affirmed in *Court*. Alternatively, an act that gives rise to an irresistible inference of indecency, such as where D rips off P's dress in a public place, will be regarded as indecent, devoid of any further explanation or justification, eg that D had noticed that the back of P's dress had caught fire. Similarly, a doctor carrying out an intimate examination of a patient is, in principle, committing an indecent assault, but would point to both the necessity of the act and the patient's informed consent in order to rebut any assertions of indecency. In cases where D's actions are ambivalent, in the sense that the act could be regarded as indecent, the jury should be directed to come to a conclusion based on all the relevant evidence, which might include the relationship between D and P, how D had come to act in the way he had, and the reason for his actions. In particular, the House of Lords in

Court confirmed, by a majority, that for these purposes, the motivation behind D's actions could be relevant, where it is evident from statements put before the court. In that case D had spanked a 12-year-old girl on the buttocks. He later admitted to police that he had done so because of his 'buttock fetish', and the jury were directed to take this into account in assessing whether or not D's assault had been indecent. It is submitted that if D's secret sexual gratification is irrelevant where his act is not overtly indecent, it seems odd that it should be admissible as evidence to justify holding that his equivocal act could be regarded as indecent.

Mens rea

The assault must be committed intentionally or recklessly: see *R* v *Venna* [1976] QB 421. The recklessness involved is subjective as in *R* v *Cunningham* [1957] 2 QB 396. The majority of their Lordships in *Court* were also of the opinion that, in cases where D's actions were merely capable of being regarded as indecent, some mens rea in respect of the indecent circumstances was also required. As Lord Ackner observed:

> 'For the defendant to be liable to be convicted of the offence of indecent assault, where the circumstances of the alleged offence can be given an innocent as well as an indecent interpretation, without the prosecution being obliged to establish that the defendant intended to commit both an assault and an indecent one, seems to me quite unacceptable and not what Parliament intended.'

In *R* v *C* [1992] Crim LR 642, D was found to have inserted his fingers into the vagina of a young girl. In response to a charge of indecent assault he indicated that he had been drinking and could not remember the incident. The trial judge directed the jury that the offence was one of basic intent and D was duly convicted. On appeal, the court rejected the contention that, following *Court*, the offence required proof of a specific intent, preferring the view that the admission of evidence relating to D's purpose in *Court* was permissible given the ambiguous nature of the assault in that case. Where, on the other hand, the assault in question was unequivocally indecent, there was no need to inquire into D's intention or motive. Provided D had not been in a state of automatism (through no fault of his own) the necessary elements of liability would have been present. This perhaps raises the question of whether D could rely on evidence of self-induced intoxication in a case where the indecent act is ambiguous in nature. If so, it would presumably reduce D's liability to common assault (ie battery): see further *R* v *Parsons* [1993] Crim LR 792.

Indecency with Children Act 1960

Section 1(1) of the 1960 Act provides:

> 'Any person who commits an act of gross indecency with or towards a child under the age of fourteen, or who incites a child under that age to such an act with him or another, shall be liable on conviction on indictment to imprisonment for a term not exceeding two years,

or on summary conviction to imprisonment for a term not exceeding six months, to a fine not exceeding [the prescribed sum] or to both.'

There is no need to prove any action upon the part of the child, the offence being complete if an incitement is proved. Mere inactivity on the part of D will suffice if the court concludes that the inactivity amounted to an invitation to a child to continue with an act of gross indecency: see *R v Speck* (1977) 65 Cr App R 161. There is no specific statutory provision for any defence based on a genuine misapprehension as to the age of the child. Hence, even if D honestly believes P to be over the age of 14 he can still incur liability: see *B v DPP* [1998] 4 All ER 265 at Chapter 16, section 16.2.

Reform

Clause 111 of the DCCB provides that;

'A person is guilty of an indecent assault if he assaults another in such a manner, of which he is aware, or in such circumstances, of which he is aware, as are : (a) indecent, whatever the purpose with which the act is done; or (b) indecent only if the act is done with an indecent purpose and he acts with such a purpose.'

The clause amalgamates the existing offences dealing with men and women, and also takes account of the House of Lords' decision in *Court* with its reference to D's purpose.

6.4 The defence of consent

Whilst the general defences in criminal law are dealt with in Chapters 14 and 15, the defence of consent is considered in detail at this juncture, given its especial relevance to the offences based on assault. In deciding whether or not to allow the victim's consent to affect the criminal liability; of the defendant, and if so to what extent, the criminal law draws a broad distinction between offences against property and offences against the person. In relation to offences against property, the consent of the victim will usually nullify any potential criminal liability, thus consent can be the difference between theft and the giving of a gift: although see *R v Gomez* [1992] 3 WLR 1067, considered in Chapter 7, section 7.4. Similarly, the consent of the occupier of premises can nullify what would otherwise be a trespass, and thus a burglary; the consent of the owner can nullify what would otherwise be criminal damage.

In relation to offences against the person the law takes a somewhat more paternalistic approach, permitting the individual a degree of autonomy (for example, adults are permitted to consent to sexual intercourse) but drawing the line at activities that could be regarded as anti-social, or contrary to public policy.

On the basis of decisions such as *R v Donovan* [1934] 2 KB 498 and *Attorney-*

General's Reference (No 6 of 1980) [1981] QB 715 the basic common law position is that, subject to a number of significant exceptions, the consent of a victim to suffer harm inflicted by the defendant can only provide the defendant with a defence if the harm inflicted does not amount to actual bodily harm, or worse. For these purposes Swift J in *Donovan* took as the meaning of 'bodily harm' anything that was calculated to interfere with the health or comfort of the victim. The exceptions to this rule were listed by Lord Lane CJ in *Attorney-General's Reference (No 6 of 1980)* as:

> '... properly conducted games and sports, lawful chastisement or correction, reasonable surgical interference, dangerous exhibitions etc ...'.

Most of these exceptions have some basis in utilitarianism, that is they can be justified as securing some greater public good. In the case of medical treatment this is fairly self-evident, although there may be questions raised as regards some fringe medical activities connected with cosmetic surgery. The origins of the exception related to games and sport can be traced through decisions such as *Donovan*, where the court took that view that for men to engage in 'manly diversions' such as '... cudgels, foils, and wrestling' was in the public interest, to encourage individuals to take up sport and maintain physical fitness. It is assumed that this exception covers organised sports, played according to recognised rules, with appropriate supervision from a referee or umpire, but would not extent to prize-fighting, or indeed a situation where two individuals simply agreed to have a fight to settle their differences: see *Attorney-General's Reference (No 6 of 1980)*.

Exactly how much harm a participant in a sporting activity can be assumed to have consented to is a matter for debate. It seems doubtful whether a footballer who suffers a sprained ankle following a heavy tackle during a game could launch a private prosecution for assault against his opponent, because he will be assumed to have consented to suffering the type of harm that can be reasonably foreseen as a consequence of playing the game. An injury inflicted by an opponent deliberately flouting the rules ought, on the other hand, at least to provide the basis for a criminal prosecution; see cases such as *R v Billinghurst* [1978] Crim LR 553. Despite calls for it to be banned, boxing remains lawful, presumably because it is a properly regulated activity, where the aim is to demonstrate pugilistic skills. Given the regrettable fact, however, that boxers do die in the ring, or as a direct consequence of injuries inflicted therein, it could be asked why this particular activity is granted such licence by the law. A boxer does not actually consent to his own death at the hands of his opponent when he enters the ring, but he clearly consents to a more than negligible risk of this occurring. The question is whether the law should permit him to do so.

Consent has also been recognised as a defence to injuries caused during the course of rough horseplay or practical jokes, provided that there is no intention to do harm: see *R v Jones (Terence)* (1986) 83 Cr App R 375, cited with approval in *R v Aitken and Others* [1992] 1 WLR 1066. In this latter case, the victim's participation in practical jokes played on companions was accepted as evidence suggesting that he realised that he too could become a victim and consented to this.

Notwithstanding the decision in *R* v *Donovan*, the extent to which an adult should be given the right to consent to actual bodily harm in the pursuit of sexual gratification is a question that has still not be satisfactorily settled at common law. In *R* v *Boyea* [1992] Crim LR 575, for example, D inserted his fist into P's vagina and twisted it around, causing her injury. Whilst his conviction for indecent assault was upheld on the basis that the harm caused to the complainant exceeded the level of injury to which she could have consented, the court appeared willing to accept that the degree of harm to which a complainant could be said to have validly consented during heterosexual congress may be greater now than was the case at the time that *Donovan* (above) was decided.

At present a distinction appears to be drawn by the courts between 'healthy' (ie heterosexual) sexual activity on the one hand, and harm inflicted to satisfy depraved and perverted desires on the other. In *R* v *Brown* [1993] 2 WLR 556 the majority upheld convictions, under ss47 and 20 of the Offences Against the Person Act 1861, in respect of appellants who belonged to a homosexual sado-masochistic group, whose members inflicted pain on each other for mutual sexual pleasure. Their activities included the nailing of a 'willing victim's' foreskin or scrotum to a board; the insertion of hot wax into a victim's urethra, followed by the burning of his penis with a candle; and the incising of a victim's scrotum with a scalpel, causing loss of blood. Lord Templeman, rejecting the contention that every person has a right to deal with his body as he pleases, observed that :

> 'Although the law is often broken, the criminal law restrains a practice which is regarded as dangerous and injurious to individuals and which if allowed and extended is harmful to society generally ... Society is entitled and bound to protect itself against a cult of violence. Pleasure derived from the infliction of pain is an evil thing.'

Lord Jauncey regarded the matter as one requiring parliamentary intervention if the law was to be liberalised. Lord Lowry appeared to regard the criminal law as having an important role to play in the promotion of activities conducive to the enhancement or enjoyment of family life and the welfare of society. His Lordship was unable to recognise sado-masochistic homosexual activity as furthering such aims, nor was he willing to recognise an exception in respect of such acts on the basis that they constituted a 'manly diversion'. Lord Mustill, dissenting, explained that for him the guiding principle was that:

> '... the state should interfere with the rights of an individual to live his or her life as he or she may choose no more than is necessary to ensure a proper balance between the special interests of the individual and the general interests of the individuals who together comprise the populace at large.'

On this basis he felt unable to conclude that the denial of the defence of consent in the circumstances of the case was justified.

The position adopted by the majority in the House of Lords has subsequently been supported by the European Court of Human Rights: see *Laskey, Jaggard and Brown* v *United Kingdom* (1997) 24 EHRR 39. In a unanimous judgment the Court expressed the view that the determination of the level of harm to which the victim of an assault could validly consent was unquestionably a matter for the state to decide, and that the criminal sanctions imposed represented an interference in the private lives of the applicants that was necessary in a democratic society for the preservation of health or morals.

By contrast the courts have tended to take an indulgent view of physical mutilation born of vanity, religious observance, or fashion-consciousness, provided that the consent of the victim has been freely given on a fully informed basis. Hence in *Brown* Lord Templeman observed that '... ritual circumcision, tattooing, ear-piercing ... are all lawful activities'. In *R* v *Wilson* [1996] 3 WLR 125 this permissiveness was even extended to the case of D who, with his wife's consent, had burnt his initials onto her buttocks. Two bases can be identified for the decision in the judgment of Russell LJ. On the one hand he regarded the case as coming within the 'tattooing' exception in *Brown*; secondly, taking a broader policy based view, his Lordship thought it relevant that D's wife had instigated the activity; that there was no aggressive intent on the part of D; that D was motivated by his wife's '... desire ... to assist her in what she regarded as the acquisition of a desirable piece of personal adornment ...'; and finally that consensual activity between husband and wife in the privacy of the matrimonial home was not a matter for criminal investigation. Whilst the decision seems entirely sensible and justifiable, given the observations of the majority in *Brown*, some of the observations of Russell LJ seem, with respect, a little questionable. 'Aggressive' intent has never been part of the mens rea of assault. On the contrary, in cases of indecent assault the intent may be quite the opposite of aggressive. Neither should D's motivation have any bearing on the issue of mens rea. To rely upon the fact that P instigated the activity as a reason for permitting the defence of consent seems dubious. Would it have made any difference if the complainant in *R* v *Donovan* had instigated the caning? Further, is the Court of Appeal seriously seeking to distinguish between what happens in the matrimonial home, and activities that take place in premises occupied by couples living in sin, or indeed in hotel rooms booked out to adulterous couples? It is also interesting to speculate on what view the court would have taken of D had he been a homosexual carrying out a similar branding operation on the buttocks of his male partner.

Consent vitiated by mistake

It may well be the case that P consents to physical contact with D because he or she is labouring under some mistake as to what D is doing, why D is doing it, whether D is qualified to do it, or even possibly as to who D is. As far as the offence of rape is concerned that matter has already been considered at section 6.1 (above). It would appear that similar principles apply in relation to assaults generally. In *R* v

Richardson (1998) The Times 6 April a dentist, who had continued to treat patients despite having been suspended from practice as a registered dental practitioner by the General Dental Council, was acquitted on appeal because the defence of consent had not been considered at her trial. The Court of Appeal held that the consent of her patients could provide a good defence to charges under s47 of the 1861 Act, because they had not been mistaken as to the nature of the actions she was performing upon them, and they were not mistaken as to her identity. Interestingly the Court rejected the contention that there was any place in criminal law for the civil law doctrine of 'informed' or 'real' consent. Is the approach of the Court of Appeal satisfactory? How would the Court have approached the case of a defendant who had no dental qualifications whatsoever masquerading as a qualified dentist? Alternatively, what if a qualified dentist continued to practice knowing that she was HIV positive, withholding this information from her patients? Can it really be said that the 'mistake' on the part of the patient in each case is immaterial as regards consent?

Where the defendant is mistaken as to the victim's consent

Provided D honestly believes P to be consenting to physical contact, and provided the physical contact is of a type to which P's consent (if given) would have provided a defence, D should be able to rely on the defence of consent: see *R* v *Kimber* [1983] 1 WLR 1118. D's belief that P is consenting does not have to be reasonable, provided the belief is honestly held. Obviously, the more unlikely the defendant's mistake, the less likely it is that the jury will believe that D honestly made it. The approach of the court in this case has been confirmed by subsequent decisions such as *Beckford* v *R* [1987] 3 All ER 425: see Chapter 15, section 15.3.

7

Theft

7.1 Introduction to theft

The Theft Act 1968 is largely the result of preparatory work carried out by the Criminal Law Revision Committee (CLRC) and is based upon the CLRC's Eighth Report (Cmnd 2977). The aim of the Act was to sweep away many of the unnecessarily complex aspects of the existing law, based as it was on the Larceny Act 1916 and common law. In particular the aim of the CLRC was to introduce a new statutory framework, based on concepts, and using language, that ordinary men and women, of average literacy, could comprehend. To some extent this aim has been realised, but two factors should be borne in mind. First, that the criminal law of theft does not exist in a legal vacuum. It rests upon civil law concepts of ownership, property, contract and so on. Not only are such concepts complex in themselves, but they are constantly evolving. Secondly, since the enactment of the Theft Act 1968 a considerable body of case law has developed indicating the way in which the courts interpret the provisions of the Act. Not only does the volume of the caselaw increase complexity, but the contradictory nature of some decisions introduces uncertainty and confusion. Further, it rapidly became evident that some provisions of the 1968 Act were unworkable, and that significant loopholes existed, necessitating the enactment of the Theft Act 1978 and the Theft (Amendment) Act 1996.

Reform

Whereas the Draft Code encompasses significant reforms of some general principles of criminal liability, it has no major recommendations in respect of the mainstream offences of dishonesty. As the commentary indicates:

'Chapter III of Part II of the Code contains the offences currently to be found in the Theft Act 1968, the Theft Act 1978, Part I of the Forgery and Counterfeiting Act 1981 and s9 of the Criminal Attempts Act 1981 (vehicle interference). It brings together, that is to say, those statutory offences which share (in broad terms) an element of dishonest conduct or intention and which will be conveniently located in the Code. The two Theft Acts obviously belong in this Chapter ... Unlike Chapters I and II, which for the most part implement modern law reform proposals, Chapter III offers no new law. It consists of a restatement of the existing offences, with (in general) only such changes as are required for consistency with the general content and style of the Code. The result, we believe, is that some of the offences are stated a good deal more simply and clearly. Very few amendments with more than merely stylistic significance – and these only minor ones – have been thought to be justifiable. They have been made in order to eliminate manifest error or inconsistency in the existing statutes or to improve clarity without risk of substantive change.' (Vol II, paras 16.1 and 16.3)

A consequence of this approach is that the Theft Acts remain largely unreformed by the Draft Code Bill. As the Commission conceded:

'Some will be disappointed by such restraint in the treatment of the Theft Acts. The law penalising dishonest conduct is of central importance and offences under these Acts account for a very large proportion of all the indictable offences with which the courts have to deal. It is a matter for some concern that both the Acts themselves (especially that of 1968) and the substantial case law that they have generated are regarded by some critics as seriously defective. This is not, however, a matter that it would be appropriate to pursue here. Our task at this point is to include in the draft Code the law of criminal dishonesty in its existing statutory condition.' (Vol II, para 16.4)

It is likely that some more concrete proposals will emerge in the next few years, given the Commission's undertaking to embark on a 'comprehensive review of dishonesty offences' (*Criminal Law: Conspiracy to Defraud* (Law Com No 228)). Such a review will be necessary if the offence of conspiracy to defraud is abolished, as it might leave some unacceptable loopholes in the law. Proposals for reform are, therefore, considered at appropriate points throughout this chapter.

7.2 The offence of theft

Section 1(1) of the Theft Act 1968 creates the offence of theft. It provides:

'A person is guilty of theft if he dishonestly appropriates property belonging to another with the intention of permanently depriving the other of it; and "theft" and "steal" shall be construed accordingly.'

Besides being an offence in its own right, it should be remembered that the elements of theft may need to be established in order to prove liability for other offences, such as robbery (s8), burglary (s9) and, to a lesser extent, going equipped (s25). Whilst s1(1) creates an offence, ss2–6 provide complete or partial definitions of the elements of theft. As s1(3) states:

> 'The five following sections of this Act shall have effect as regards the interpretation and operation of this section (and, except as otherwise provided by this Act, shall apply only for purposes of this section).'

The maximum punishment that can be imposed where a defendant has been convicted of theft following a trial on indictment, was reduced from ten years to seven by s26 of the Criminal Justice Act 1991.

7.3 What can be stolen?

Section 4(1) provides a general definition of property for the purposes of theft, where it states:

> ' "Property" includes money and all other property, real or personal, including things in action and other intangible property.'

This seemingly wide definition is limited however, by the provisions that follow in ss4(2) to 4(4). Before considering those, a number of points need to be considered.

Section 4(1) expressly refers to 'things in action and other intangible property'. Thus the law of theft is extended to protect patents, copyright, shares, and debts. Intangible property may, for example, take the form of a bank account in credit. The balance is owed to the customer by the bank. Where a defendant (D), takes the victim's (P) cheque book and forges P's signature on cheques resulting in a reduction or extinction of P's bank balance, D can be said to have appropriated P's property within s4(1). The Court of Appeal accepted this reasoning in *R* v *Kohn* (1979) 69 Cr App R 395. Similarly, it is submitted, where P is granted an overdraft facility and D draws on the account using P's cheques, D is 'using up' P's intangible property, namely the right to draw money out up to a certain limit. See further *Chan Man-Sin* v *R* [1988] Crim LR 319, which provides support for this submission. The phrase 'other intangible property' has been held by the Privy Council to extend to things such as export quotas, which could be traded for value: see *Attorney-General for Hong Kong* v *Nai-Keung* [1988] Crim LR 125.

Notwithstanding that s4(1) covers intangible property, confidential information has been held to fall outside the definition of property. The Divisional Court in *Oxford* v *Moss* [1979] Crim LR 119 upheld a decision of the justices that a student, who had obtained a proof of an examination paper he was due to sit, was not guilty of theft on the basis that information could not be stolen. Clearly the paper on which the examination questions were typed was property belonging to the University, but there was no evidence that the defendant intended to permanently deprive the University of it. The implication of the decision is that trade secrets would not be property capable of being stolen either. An agreement to obtain such information might amount, however, to a common law conspiracy to defraud.

In its Consultation Paper *Misuse of Trade Secrets* (Law Com No 150 (1997)), the Law Commission provisionally proposes that the deliberate misuse of trade secrets should become a criminal offence. In support of this proposition it cites the following arguments: that the harm done by theft of property and that done by one who misuses information can be indistinguishable; that investment in research and development should be protected by the criminal law; that it is inconsistent to protect copyright and trade marks but not trade secrets; and civil remedies remain an inadequate way of discouraging wrongdoers. The proposed offence would operate subject to a number of defences that would permit disclosure of information for the prevention of crime, to protect public health, or which was otherwise in the public interest.

Electricity is not property that can be stolen, see *Low* v *Blease* (1975) 119 SJ 695, but the dishonest abstraction of electricity is covered by s13 of the 1968 Act.

At common law there is no property in a human corpse. The issue is not dealt with by the 1968 Act, hence it would appear that a human corpse cannot be stolen: see *R* v *Sharpe* (1857) Dears & B 160. This statement does, however, require some qualification. Grave robbers can be charged with theft of items from the grave, including the coffin and winding sheet. The executors or administrators of the deceased have the right to possession of the corpse for the purposes of ensuring that it is appropriately interred or buried. Further, a person might acquire property rights over a human corpse where some skill and effort has been exercised, eg mummification. Hence a human skeleton could be property, as could the preserved foetus of a two-headed child: see *Doodeward* v *Spence* (1908) 6 CLR 406. As Griffith J observed at p413:

> '... when a person has by the lawful exercise of work or skill so dealt with a human body or part of a human body in his lawful possession that it has acquired some attributes differentiating from a mere corpse awaiting burial, he acquires a right to retain possession of it, at least as against any person not entitled to have it delivered to him for the purpose of burial.'

In *R* v *Kelly* [1998] 3 All ER 741 the Court of Appeal held that body parts in the possession of the Royal College of Surgeons for anatomical research could be property for the purposes of s4(1) of the Theft Act 1968. Rose LJ observed (at pp749–750):

> '... in our judgment, parts of a corpse are capable of being property within s4 of the Theft Act, if they have acquired different attributes by virtue of the application of skill such as dissection or preservation techniques, for exhibition or teaching purposes. ... Furthermore, the common law does not stand still. It may be that if, on some future occasion, the question arises, the courts will hold that human body parts are capable of being property for the purposes of s4, even without the acquisition of different attributes, if they have a use or significance beyond their mere existence. This may be so if, for

example, they are intended for use in an organ transplant operation, for the extraction of DNA or, for that matter, as an exhibit in a trial.'

See Chapter 16, section 16.3, for further details; and see also *Dobson* v *North Tyneside Health Authority* [1997] 1 WLR 596.

Less doubt surrounds the status of products of the body. In *R* v *Rothery* [1976] RTR 550 the Court of Appeal held that a human blood sample could be stolen, while in *R* v *Welsh* [1974] RTR 478 the defendant was convicted of stealing a sample of urine that he himself had provided for analysis by the police. It seems reasonable to suggest that human organs donated for transplant operations, and human sperm deposited in sperm banks, would also be regarded as property for the purposes of theft.

Theft of land is dealt with by s4(2) which provides that a person cannot steal land, or things forming part of land and severed from it by him or by his directions, except in the following cases:

'a) when he is a trustee or personal representative, or is authorised by power of attorney, or as liquidator of a company, or otherwise, to sell or dispose of land belonging to another, and he appropriates the land or anything forming part of it by dealing with it in breach of the confidence reposed in him; or
b) when he is not in possession of the land and appropriates anything forming part of the land by severing it or causing it to be severed, or after it has been severed; or
c) when, being in possession of the land under a tenancy, he appropriates the whole or part of any fixture or structure let to be used with the land.'

The subsection further provides that:

'For purposes of this subsection "land" does not include incorporated hereditaments. The term "tenancy" means a tenancy for years or any less period and includes an agreement for such a tenancy, but a person who after the end of a tenancy remains in possession as statutory tenant or otherwise is to be treated as having possession under the tenancy, and ìletî shall be construed accordingly.'

It may in some situations be difficult to determine whether property forms part of the land upon which it is sited or not. In *Billing* v *Pill* [1954] 1 QB 70 it was held that an army hut bolted onto a concrete base did not form part of the land, and was therefore a chattel capable of being stolen (under the Larceny Act 1916). Lord Goddard CJ had no doubt that the concrete base itself had become part of the land.

The question of the extent to which plants constitute property for the purposes of theft is provided for by s4(3) which provides that a person who picks mushrooms growing wild on any land, or who picks flowers, fruit or foliage from a plant growing wild on any land, does not (although not in possession of the land) steal what he picks, unless he does it for reward or for sale or other commercial purpose. The term 'mushroom' includes any fungus, and 'plant' includes any shrub or tree. Presumably a defendant must intend to sell the produce when he picks it, and would fall outside the section were he to pick mushrooms growing wild and then later decide to sell them. Reference to 'other commercial purpose' suggests that the picking of wild plants should be on an organised basis in order for liability to arise.

Animals are covered by s4(4) which provides that wild creatures, tamed or untamed, will be regarded as property, subject to the proviso that a person 'cannot steal a wild creature not tamed nor ordinarily kept in captivity, or the carcass of any such creature unless either it has been reduced into possession by or on behalf of another person and possession of it has not since been lost or abandoned, or another person is in course of reducing it into possession.' Animals in zoos, safari parks, and domestic pets can all be stolen, even if they are appropriated having escaped from captivity. Wild animals are obviously protected by other legislation. Interestingly, the Court of Appeal held in *R* v *Howlett* [1968] Crim LR 222 that mussels in a mussel bed were wild animals at large and could not be stolen.

7.4 Appropriation

The concept of appropriation lies at the heart of theft. It replaces the more complex notions such as 'trespassory taking' and 'carrying away' that were features of the former law of larceny. Whilst it may have been the intention of Parliament to use the word 'appropriates' on the basis that it was a term readily understandable by literate men and women, there continues to be considerable debate as to its precise meaning.

The starting point is the definition provided by s3(1) of the Theft Act 1968, which provides:

> 'Any assumption by a person of the rights of an owner amounts to an appropriation, and this includes, where he has come by the property (innocently or not) without stealing it, any later assumption of a right to it by keeping or dealing with it as owner.'

Although the House of Lords' decision in *R* v *Morris* [1983] 3 All ER 288 appears to add a gloss to the effect that any assumption of any right will suffice, taken to its logical conclusion such an approach would lead to an absurdly wide offence – does D appropriate P's property by looking at it, given that one of P's rights is to look at his own property? The point may be largely academic, as D would not incur any liability for theft unless it could be shown that his assumption of P's rights was accompanied by dishonesty, but nonetheless it is submitted that a more sensible approach would have been to limit the scope of appropriation to an assumption of those rights exclusive to the owner: see further commentary on *R* v *Hilton* [1997] Crim LR 761 at 764. In *R* v *Ngan* (1997) The Times 24 July Legatt LJ observed that the presentation of a cheque by D amounted to an appropriation because it was an assertion of a right adverse to P, the true owner of amount credited to the account. Quite what his Lordship meant by the use of the word 'adverse' in these circumstances is unclear. As is explained below, D can assume the rights of P in respect of P's property without adversely affecting them.

The problem of consent

Does a charge of theft require proof that D acted without the consent of P? This question has arguably provoked the greatest difficulty in the interpretation of appropriation. Nowhere in s3 is it provided that the appropriation must be proved to have been without P's consent, although in the majority of cases it will have been. If, however, it is accepted that D can appropriate with P's consent, the division between s1 theft, and s15 obtaining by deception, as explained below, becomes blurred to the point of invisibility.

The issue was addressed for the first time by the House of Lords in its decision in *Lawrence* v *MPC* [1972] AC 626. P, an Italian student who spoke very little English, took a taxi ride for which the proper fare was 52p. He offered D, the taxi driver, a £1 note, but D indicated that more money was needed and proceeded to take a further £1 note and a £5 note from P's open wallet. The question of P's consent to this taking was never satisfactorily determined because he had to give his evidence through an interpreter. D was convicted of theft and appealed unsuccessfully to the House of Lords. Viscount Dilhorne rejected D's contention that he should have been charged under s15 and not s1. Not only did his Lordship take the view that D could appropriate the £6, notwithstanding that the student might have consented to its taking, but that D could appropriate the £6 as he became the owner of it. As mentioned above, an inescapable conclusion that results from this ruling is that the distinction between theft and obtaining property by deception, for all practical purposes, disappears. Nearly all cases of the latter would be chargeable as the former.

The problems created by *Lawrence* were not merely academic. Subsequent decisions of the lower courts indicated a reluctance to accept Viscount Dilhorne's approach. The decisions in *R* v *McPherson* [1973] Crim LR 191; *R* v *Meech* [1974] QB 549; *R* v *Skipp* [1975] Crim LR 114; and *Eddy* v *Niman* [1981] Crim LR 502, all turned upon a concept of appropriation which recognised the need for some unauthorised act on the part of D. It is submitted that unauthorised in this context meant without the consent of the owner.

For example, in *Skipp*, D collected three separate loads of produce intending not to return to Leicester with them, but to divert to another destination and sell them dishonestly. He argued that he had committed theft each time he collected a load intending not to deliver it to its correct destination, and thus the indictment was bad for duplicity. The Court of Appeal held that D had been rightly charged with one theft of the three loads on the back of his lorry. The theft took place when he diverted from the authorised route back to Leicester with dishonest intent; this was D's first unauthorised act. Similarly, it appeared that a shopper, even one having an intention to steal, did not do so simply by placing goods in the wire basket provided by the store, as these actions were authorised: see *Eddy* v *Niman* [1981] Crim LR 502. By contrast, a customer was regarded as having appropriated goods in a store by placing them in her own bag, instead of the wire basket provided, because this was unauthorised: see *McPherson* (above).

In *Morris* (above) the House of Lords was presented with an opportunity to reflect on these difficulties, and possibly provide some degree of clarification. Their Lordships had to consider the extent to which label switching in supermarkets constituted theft. As Lord Roskill explained, the switching of price labels amounted to appropriation because it was an assumption by D of the owner's right to determine what price the goods were to be sold at. If accompanied by mens rea it would be theft. Further, where D committed theft by label switching, he might then proceed to commit the offence of obtaining property by deception where he paid the lower price for the goods at the checkout. In this sense label switching could also be seen as an attempt to commit s15. In so far as it dealt with the facts of the appeal, the decision was unobjectionable. Difficulties were caused, however, by Lord Roskill's obiter statements on appropriation. His Lordship began by referring to *Lawrence* and re-affirming it as the guiding authority on appropriation. He then proceeded to deliver a speech somewhat at odds with what was decided therein. Lord Roskill envisaged appropriation as any assumption of any right of the owner, which had not been expressly or impliedly authorised by the owner, but which amounted to adverse interference with, or usurpation of, the owner's rights. The exclusion of expressly or impliedly authorised acts from the concept of appropriation was widely interpreted as excluding those acts to which the owner has consented, in direct contradiction to *Lawrence*.

In the wake of *Morris*, judges, practitioners and students of criminal law were left with two House of Lords' decisions on appropriation which were in many respects irreconcilable. Generally the academic view was that *Morris* was to be preferred to *Lawrence*. There was considerable doubt as to whether the victim in Lawrence's taxi actually consented to the defendant taking the £6, in which case it is one of the most unremarkable examples of theft to have arisen in any magistrates' court. If he was 'fooled' into allowing Lawrence to take the extra money then it might be said with some persuasion that Lawrence was wrongly charged with theft and should have been charged with obtaining the money by deception. The Court of Appeal remained divided on the issue. In *R v Philipou* (1989) 89 Cr App R 290 it was held that where a defendant and his co-accused were the sole directors and shareholders of a company, he could be guilty of theft by removing funds from one of the company's bank accounts. O'Connor LJ expressed the view that it was obvious that Lord Roskill in *Morris* had not intended to insert the words 'without the consent of the owner' into the definition of appropriation under s3(1). His Lordship went on to suggest that it was the dishonesty with which an act was done that could operate so as to make the act relied upon an adverse appropriation of the owner's rights. It is submitted that the issue of appropriation need not have given rise to any difficulty in this case, since it is clear from *Attorney-General's Reference (No 2 of 1982)* [1984] 2 All ER 216 that where the shareholders and directors of a company act dishonestly in relation to the company, their consent to the dishonest acts cannot be imputed to the company, hence it cannot be contended that the company consents to these actions. In that sense D's acts could easily have been regarded as an appropriation; the withdrawal of funds from the company's account was not an act which it expressly or impliedly authorised.

Conversely in *R* v *Fritschy* [1985] Crim LR 745 it was held that, as theft required proof of some overt unauthorised act on the part of D, he could not be guilty of stealing within the jurisdiction of the English courts where he had collected Krugerrands in London as directed, even though he intended to make off with them once he reached continental Europe. The case is very much a re-affirmation of the approach in *Skipp* (above). Fritschy's unauthorised act would have occurred at the point at which he deviated from the delivery instructions, ie after leaving England. Matters were further complicated by the contribution of the Court of Appeal (Civil Division) in *Dobson* v *General Accident Fire and Life Assurance Corporation plc* [1989] 3 All ER 927, a case concerning an action for breach of contract brought against the defendant insurance company which had refused to compensate the plaintiff under his household contents insurance policy. The plaintiff had advertised a gold watch and diamond ring for sale. A rogue, posing as a bona fide purchaser, visited his house to examine the goods, and agreed to buy them at the asking price of £5,950, payment to be by means of a building society cheque. It subsequently transpired that the cheque had been stolen and was worthless, but by this time the purchaser had disappeared. The plaintiff made a claim against the defendant insurers under his house contents policy, which provided cover for his possessions in respect of theft. The defendants refused to make any payment contending that what had occurred could not amount to theft within s1(1) of the Theft Act 1968 because, inter alia, there could have been no appropriation of the property since the owner had consented to the purchaser taking the items. At first instance it was held that the plaintiff had been the victim of a theft, and this decision was upheld on appeal. In dismissing the insurance company's appeal, the Court held that the plaintiff had only intended to pass property in the goods in return for a valid building society cheque, hence when the goods were handed to the purchaser they were still property belonging to another as against him. Further, there could be an appropriation of the plaintiff's property even if he appeared to consent to its being taken by another, since the House of Lords' decision in *Lawrence* made it clear that there was no need, in proving theft, to establish that the taking had been without the owner's consent.

The House of Lords revisits the issue

Inevitably the whole question, of whether or not appropriation involves an act done without the consent of the owner, had to be reconsidered by the House of Lords, and the opportunity was not long in coming. In *R* v *Gomez* [1992] 3 WLR 1067 D obtained electrical equipment in exchange for worthless building society cheques. During the course of his trial he submitted that he should not have been charged with theft, as there had been no appropriation of the goods. This submission was based on the proposition that any such appropriation had to be without the consent of the owner, and that the owner in this case, through its agent, had expressly consented to the delivery of the goods. The trial judge rejected this submission, and the defendant changed his plea to guilty. Significantly, the Court of Appeal allowed his appeal, Lord Lane CJ commenting that since the transfer of the goods had been with the consent and express authority of the owner, there was no lack of authorisation and therefore no appropriation. The question certified for consideration by the House of Lords was stated as follows:

> 'When theft is alleged and that which is alleged to be stolen passes to the defendant with the consent of the owner, but that has been obtained by a false representation, has (a) an appropriation within the meaning of section 1(1) of the Theft Act 1968 taken place, or (b) must such a passing of property necessarily involve an element of adverse inference with or usurpation of some right of the owner?'

The choice for the House of Lords was, therefore, starkly laid out. *Lawrence* or *Morris*? That a majority of their Lordships should have opted for *Lawrence* in preference to *Morris* is a source of disappointment but not great surprise. Lord Keith confirmed that the defendant in *Morris* had committed an appropriation when he switched price labels, but went on to express the view that Lord Roskill's dictum, to the effect that appropriation involved an act not expressly or impliedly authorised by the owner, was not be construed so as to suggest that only an unauthorised act would satisfy the requirements of s3(1). Lord Keith opted to expressly approve *Lawrence*, in particular Viscount Dilhorne's dictum that theft could be committed even where the owner consented to the defendant's taking of the property. His Lordship also expressed his full agreement with the views of Parker CJ in *Dobson*, to the effect that *Morris* could not be taken to have overruled *Lawrence*. As Lord Keith put it:

> 'The actual decision in *Morris* was correct, but it was erroneous, in addition to being unnecessary for the decision, to indicate that an act expressly or impliedly authorised by the owner could never amount to an appropriation. There is no material distinction between the facts in *Dobson* and those in the present case. In each case the owner of the goods was induced by fraud to part with them to the rogue. *Lawrence* makes it clear that consent to or authorisation by the owner of the taking by the rogue is irrelevant.'

The alternative view

Lord Lowry's powerful dissent in *Gomez* is worthy of close attention. He explains with admirable clarity the significance of the Criminal Law Revision Committee's report that presaged the enactment of the Theft Act 1968, and the sense in which the report supports his assertion that the intention of Parliament had been to maintain a fundamental distinction between theft and obtaining property by deception. This writer has considerable sympathy with the view that Parliament did intend s1 and s15 to have at least distinct, if not mutually exclusive, spheres of operation. As Lord Lowry concluded:

'To simplify the law, where possible, is a worthy objective but, my Lords, I maintain that the law, as envisaged in the [CLRC] report, is simple enough: there is no problem (and there would have been none in *Lawrence*, *Morris* and the present case) if one prosecutes under section 15 all offenders involving obtaining by deception and prosecutes theft in general under section 1. In that way some thefts will come under section 15, but no 'false pretences' will come under section 1.'

With respect, Lord Keith's reasons for not consulting the CLRC report are less than convincing. He stated:

'In my opinion it serves no useful purpose at the present time to seek to construe the relevant provisions of the Theft Act by reference to the report which preceded it. ... [T]he decision in *Lawrence* was a clear decision of this House upon the construction of the word "appropriate" in section 1(1) of the Act, which had stood for 12 years when doubt was thrown upon it by obiter dicta in *Morris*. *Lawrence* must be regarded as authoritative and correct, and there is no question of it now being right to depart from it.'

What is the effect of **Gomez**?

The majority of their Lordships accept that the effect of the ruling in *Gomez* is to create a situation in which nearly every case of obtaining property by deception can be charged as such under s15, or alternatively as theft under s1(1). Lord Browne-Wilkinson admits as much although he attempts to defend this conclusion by observing that there may still be exceptions:

'Take for example a man who obtains land by deception. Save as otherwise expressly provided, the definitions in sections 4 and 5 of the Act apply only for the purposes of interpreting section 1 of the Act: see section 1(3). Section 34(1) applies subsection (1) of section 4 and subsection (1) of section 5 generally for the purposes of the Act. Accordingly the other subsections of section 4 and section 5 do not apply to section 15. Suppose that a fraudster has persuaded a victim to part with his house: the fraudster is not guilty of theft of the land since section 4(2) provides that you cannot steal land. The charge could only be laid under section 15 which contains no provisions excluding land from the definition of property.'

One can perhaps be forgiven for speculating on how many such cases have come before the courts since 1968. With great respect it is submitted that this remaining exclusive role for s15 identified by his Lordship is in reality negligible. An interesting indication of parliamentary intent may be the change introduced by s26 of the Criminal Justice Act 1991, whereby the maximum sentence for theft was reduced to seven years' imprisonment, whilst that for obtaining property by deception remained at ten. If the view of the majority is that nearly all cases under s15 can be charged as theft why should there be such a disparity in possible punishment? Is there something peculiarly culpable about obtaining land by deception that would warrant an extra three years' incarceration?

Gomez also indicates the view to be adopted in respect of certain earlier Court of Appeal decisions. According to Lord Keith, both *Skipp* and *Fritschy* are now to be regarded as having been wrongly decided. Interestingly this means that he thinks that Skipp's conviction should have been quashed, whilst that of Fritschy should have been upheld. The approach adopted in *Phillipou* (above) to abstraction of money from a limited company by a person in a position to give the consent of the company to the abstraction, was approved by both Lord Keith and Lord Browne-Wilkinson. It is a matter for speculation as to what extent, if at all, their Lordships were influenced by decisions such as that of Tucker J, during the trial of Asil Nadir, where charges against the ex-chairman of Polly Peck International alleging theft totalling £119,000,000 were dropped because of the confusion as to whether his transfer of funds from a Polly Peck account to that of a subsidiary had the consent of the company. Lord Browne-Wilkinson did observe, however, that in his view:

> 'The pillaging of companies by those who control them is now all too common. It would offend both common sense and justice to hold that the very control which enables such people to extract the company s assets constitutes a defence to a charge of theft from the company. The question in each case must be whether the extraction of the property from the company was dishonest, not whether the alleged thief has consented to his own wrongdoing.'

The position of shoppers in self-service stores is also worthy of note. Any assumption of any right of the owner can now be an appropriation of property, regardless of the intentions of either party. As Lord Browne-Wilkinson observed:

> 'For myself ... I regard the word "appropriation" in isolation as being an objective description of the act done irrespective of the mental state of either the owner or the accused.'

As a result, the honest shopper selecting goods in a supermarket now appropriates them, even though the goods cannot be placed in the trolley as requested by the store without such action by the shopper. What of the customer who selects underpriced goods in a supermarket, intending to purchase them at the lower price if allowed to do so, and knowing the goods to be underpriced? When the matter came before the Divisional Court in *Dip Kaur* v *Chief Constable for Hampshire* [1981] 1 WLR 578, Lord Lane CJ held that there could be no theft until the defendant committed some act that only the owner would be allowed to perform, such as taking the shoes from the store. In that case the defendant had taken the shoes to the checkout and paid the lower, incorrect, price for them, and had been arrested on leaving the store. The Lord Chief Justice was of the view that by the time of her arrest property in the shoes had passed to the defendant, following the transaction at the checkout. That transaction had been vitiated by the cashier's mistake as to price, but in his Lordship's view the mistake could only render the contract voidable, and up to the time of the arrest the transaction had not been avoided. A few years later, however, the Lord Chief Justice was to change his views on this matter. When *Morris* came before him in the Court of Appeal, he expressed the view that, on reflection, *Dip Kaur* had been wrongly decided. It was now his Lordship's view that the defendant had appropriated the shoes when she had selected them. In the House of Lords, Lord Roskill stated that he was disposed to agree with the learned Lord Chief Justice, but went further, however, and expressed his distaste for the tendency to try and resolve issues of criminal liability by way of reference to:

> '... questions whether particular contracts are void or voidable on the ground of mistake or fraud or whether any mistake is sufficiently fundamental to vitiate a contract. These difficult questions should so far as possible be confined to those fields of law to which they are immediately relevant, and I do not regard them as relevant questions under the Theft Act 1968.'

The resolution of this problem, following *Gomez*, would now seem to lie in accepting that the selection of a wrongly priced item is an appropriation, shifting attention instead to the state of mind of the shopper. Any defendant with a passing knowledge of contract law would be tempted to claim that the price label is in any event no more than an invitation to treat, and that the customer is at liberty to select an item with the intention of making any offer he wishes to at the checkout. Section 2(1)(a) of the 1968 Act (D's honest belief in a legal right) would seem relevant here. Failing that, would ordinary decent people consider such action dishonest (see section 7.6, below)?

Has **Gomez** *settled all arguments on appropriation and consent?*

Despite the strength of the argument that, at the third attempt, the House of Lords has, in its decision in *Gomez*, put an end to the debate on the nature of appropriation, it is submitted that there is still room to argue that the decision can be regarded as limited in its effect.

In *R v Mazo* [1997] 2 Cr App R 518 D received cheques totalling £37,000, apparently as gifts from P, her employer. The prosecution case was that P had been mentally unstable at the time of the transfers and that D was thus guilty of theft of the money. Allowing the appeal because of the inadequate direction from the trial judge as to the validity of the transfers, the Court of Appeal held that if P was of sound mind the gifts were valid and there could be no theft; conversely if P was of unsound mind, the gifts were invalid and the issue then became one of D's mens rea (as to which see further *R v Hopkins; R v Kendrick* [1997] 2 Cr App R 524). The court went on to hold that the taking of a gift could be theft if P was induced to confer it as a result of D's deception, a conclusion that is consistent with *Gomez* in as much as it applies the rule that there can be appropriation even where the donor consents to D's taking the property. The correctness of the finding in *Mazo*, that a valid inter vivos gift of property was a bar to any charge of theft of that property by the recipient, was noted but not accepted by a differently constituted Court of Appeal some ten months later in *R v Hopkins; R v Kendrick*, Ebsworth J observing that:

> 'It is not for these purposes, we find, necessary to consider whether or not that apparent gloss on *Gomez* is well-founded.'

Ebsworth J appeared to prefer the view that there could be an appropriation, even if a gift was valid, on the basis that the key issue was, in any event, the dishonesty of the recipient. The Court of Appeal also preferred this approach in *R v Hinks* [1998] Crim LR 904 where the appellant had befriended P, a 53-year-old man of limited intelligence, who transferred £60,000 into the appellant's bank account. Dismissing her appeal against a conviction of theft of the money, the Court held that a defendant could appropriate property notwithstanding that the donor consented to his receiving it, and notwithstanding the fact that the transfer took the form of a valid gift. Indeed, in the Court's view, s1 of the Theft Act 1968 did not require the jury to examine the validity or otherwise of any gift, and the state of mind of the donor was irrelevant. Belief that the owner consented to the transfer might be relevant to dishonesty, but had no bearing on appropriation.

It is submitted, however, that the approach in *R v Hopkins*; *R v Kendrick* and *R v Hinks* could produce intolerable uncertainty – it could mean that D could be convicted of theft of the property received as a matter of criminal law, but would be able to resist moves to recover it as a matter of civil law, because in civil law the transfer would be valid and he would have an absolute title to the property. Suppose that P, believing his stamp collection to be of little value, gives it to D who knows that it is worth £10,000. D is aware that P may regret this rash gift in the future, but decides nevertheless to exploit the opportunity by accepting the gift. Assuming for the moment that D's actions might be regarded as dishonest, would a court really regard D as having appropriated the property even though P fully and freely agreed to D having it? By ignoring the validity of the transfer the courts are also paying insufficient regard to the issues of whether or not the property involved could still be regarded as property belonging to another for the purposes of s5 of the 1968 Act. If one accepts for the sake of argument that there can be an appropriation, even though the donor consents to D having the property, it must still be an appropriation of property belonging to another. Suppose that D befriends P and expresses admiration for P's Rolex watch. P leaves the watch on the table with a note addressed to D stating 'I relinquish all legal rights over the watch – now the watch is yours'. When D picks up the watch surely it is his property. He is not assuming the rights of the owner, he is the owner – hence he cannot be guilty of theft. If the ruling in *Hinks* is correct P, in this example, could himself be committing the actus reus of theft if he were to change his mind and retrieve his watch from D's coat pocket. Further, although according to the court in *Hinks* there has been a theft, the property in question would not be 'stolen' for the purposes of s22 of the Theft Act 1968 (handling stolen goods), as the property will throughout have been in the lawful custody of the owner (as a matter of civil law) – either P, or the recipient, D.

There is some academic support for the view that the *Gomez* approach to appropriation may not be applied where there has been no fraud (a notion as yet unsupported by any express authority, but see *Smith & Hogan* (8th ed, 1996) pp518–519. To this end it is, perhaps, not without significance that all the key cases supporting the proposition that D can appropriate even with the owner's consent, ie *Lawrence* v *MPC*, *Dobson* v *General Accident Fire and Life Assurance Corporation plc* and *Gomez*, all involve situations where D deceived P into parting with the property in question. Hence the argument that cases where there is no deception might fall outside the *Gomez* principle.

Beyond this, the only post-*Gomez* authority to suggest that an unauthorised act may still be required to establish an appropriation is the decision of the Court of Appeal in *R* v *Gallasso* (1994) 98 Cr App R 284. D, a nurse caring for mentally disturbed adults, was entrusted with looking after the financial affairs of her patients, and in particular was authorised to withdraw money from their accounts in order to pay for their day-to-day requirements. When J, one of her patients, received a cheque for £4,000, D opened a second account in his name and paid the cheque into that account, subsequently transferring £3,000 from this second account to J's first account, and £1,000 from J's second account to her own account. Some time later D used a cheque for £1,800, that had been sent to J, to open a cashcard account in his name. D, who was convicted of theft in respect of the transfer of £1,000 to her own account, and in respect of the cheque for £1,800 that she used to open the cashcard account, appealed successfully against conviction in respect of the cheque for £1,800 on the ground that she had not committed an appropriation. The Court of Appeal held that in opening the cashcard account D was acting in a proper manner in relation to the cheque, in the sense that she was confirming J's right to the money rather than usurping it. Whatever D's secret dishonest intent, it could not convert her actions into an appropriation. The decision seems to be almost totally at odds with the rationale of *Gomez* as to the nature of appropriation, in that the Court seems to be requiring some evidence of an overt act of adverse interference with the owner's rights for appropriation to be made out. The Court of Appeal was either being subversive or its decision is per incuriam.

Clearly, if the acquittal in *Gallasso* is correct, the decision in *Fritschy* cannot be wrong. The fact that Gallasso was paying in the cheque, intending to divert funds later, whilst Fritschy had no intention of going to Switzerland with the Krugerrands, cannot be the basis of any sensible distinction. If the Court of Appeal is seriously seeking to reintroduce the distinction between those cases where the defendant carries off the property and those where he does not, Parliament may as well repeal the 1968 Act and start again, as these are the very problems it was designed to address. With respect it is submitted that, following *Gomez*, Gallasso appropriated the cheque when she took possession of it, regardless of her intent. If she had the mens rea for theft at the time, then the offence was made out. Perhaps a charge of attempted theft would have avoided these difficulties.

Appropriation by D not in possession of P's property

Given that appropriation can now take the form of any assumption of any of the owner's rights it is clearly the case that D can appropriate goods without being in possession of them, or indeed without the owner being aware that any usurpation of rights has taken place. Although the defendant in *R* v *Bloxham* (1943) 29 Cr App R 37, who purported to sell a refrigerator belonging to the local authority, was acquitted of attempted theft, J C Smith contends (*The Law of Theft* 7th ed para 29) that such behaviour could now be theft under the 1968 Act. The refrigerator was property belonging to another, D dishonestly appropriated it by assuming the right of the owner to sell it, and it may be argued that he had intention to permanently deprive within s6(1) by virtue of his treating the property as his own to dispose of (see section 7.7, below). Further support is provided by *R* v *Pitham and Hehl* (1976) 65 Cr App R 45, in which the Court of Appeal held that D could appropriate another's goods where he purported to sell them even though he was not in possession of the goods at that time, although the decision has been criticised on the basis that, in contrast to *Bloxham*, the purchaser knew that the goods did not belong to D, and that the situation really involved an agreement to steal P's property. In any event, it is submitted that where the putative purchaser of the goods is unaware of D's dishonesty the appropriate charge would be obtaining by deception contrary to s15.

Appropriation of funds held in bank accounts

Where D takes P's cheque book and draws cheques drawn on P's account by forging P's signature, he will probably incur liability under the Forgery and Counterfeiting Act 1981, and also liability for various deception offences. As to whether such actions can give rise to liability for theft, the contents of an account (or the overdraft facility available) will clearly be property belonging to another as against the defendant (see *R* v *Kohn* (1979) 69 Cr App R 395), but is the act of making out the cheque and signing in the name of the account holder to be regarded as an appropriation of P's right to draw money out? Although the debiting of an account which occurs as a consequence of a forged cheque having been honoured is a nullity, since the bank only has authority to pay out against valid orders, and the account holder loses nothing (see *Tai Hing Cotton Mill Ltd* v *Liu Chong Hing Bank Ltd* [1986] AC 80), the current authorities indicate that a charge of theft might be sustainable. In *Chan Man-Sin* v *R* [1988] 1 WLR 196, wherein it was held that the drawing, presenting, or negotiating of forged cheques could amount to a usurpation of the account holder's rights, Lord Oliver stressed that, following the House of Lords' decision in *Morris*, it was not necessary for the prosecution to prove that D had usurped all the rights of P, but simply that he had committed any assumption of any of P's rights. Precisely when the appropriation occurred in this case was not made clear. One view is that it could have occurred when D made out the cheques and presented them; another is that it may not have occurred until the bank honoured them. In *Kohn* the Court of Appeal expressed the view that the theft did not occur until the transaction had gone through to completion, and in *R* v *Hilton* (above), that the theft did not occur until a transfer of funds from the account had been made, albeit that the transaction would be a nullity. It is submitted, however, that the correct approach is that adopted in *Re Osman* [1988] Crim LR 611, where the Divisional Court held that theft (ie appropriation) occurred when D dishonestly dispatched a telex instructing a New York bank to transfer funds from the bank account belonging to the company, of which he was the chairman, to the bank account of another unconnected company, from whom he was to receive corrupt payments. The decision of the Court of Appeal in *R* v *Ngan* (above), also supports the notion that appropriation of funds in a bank account occurs as soon as D presents a cheque for payment.

The theft is complete in law at the moment the telex is dispatched, and thus can be said to have been committed in the country from which the telex is dispatched. A distinction can be drawn between the situation in *Osman* and that where D merely sends instructions via a computer keyboard from one country to another with a view to fraudulently misappropriating funds via the computer to which the instructions are sent. As Beldam LJ explained, in *R* v *Governor of Brixton Prison, ex parte Levin* [1997] 1 Cr App Rep 335;

> 'Until the instruction is recorded on the disc, there is in fact no appropriation of the rights of [the defrauded bank] ... in the case of a virtually instantaneous instruction intended to take effect where the computer is situated it seems to us artificial to regard the insertion of an instruction as having been done only at the remote place where the keyboard is situated ... [although] there was an appropriation of the right of the client to gain access to the computer [that was] a different right of property which ... had been appropriated by the applicant many times before he actually set about entering the computer for the purpose of giving any instructions.'

It might also be added that a more straightforward solution would have been to regard the appropriation as a continuing act that started where the instructions were keyed in and continued where they were received.

If D makes unauthorised use of a cheque book to draw cheques on an account which is not in credit, and in respect of which there is no overdraft facility, he cannot be charged with theft in relation to the account, for the simple reason that there is no property to appropriate: see *Kohn* (above). A charge of theft of the cheque itself may be considered, but this would not be without its complexities: see those aspects of *R* v *Duru* [1973] 3 All ER 715 not overruled by the House of Lords' decision in *R* v *Preddy* [1996] 3 All ER 481.

If D draws cheques on his own account where he does not have authority to do so, for example where he is overdrawn and has no agreed overdraft facility, it would appear that he does not commit theft. In *R* v *Navvabi* (1986) 83 Cr App R 271 where D had drawn cheques on his account supported by his cheque guarantee card, when there were insufficient funds in his account to meet the cheques, the Court of Appeal allowed his appeal against his conviction for theft on the basis that the use of the cheque card and delivery of the cheque did no more than give the payee a contractual right to payment as against the bank, and as such there was no usurpation of the bank's rights in relation to its funds, either at the time the cheque was made out, or at the time the funds were transferred to the payee. It would appear that the payment of the money by the bank to the payee could only be regarded as an appropriation by D if the bank was in some way acting as his agent. Clearly the bank was transferring the funds to the payee because of the contractual obligations arising from the use of the cheque card, and not because it wished to respond to D's instructions.

Can a defendant appropriate property where he comes by it innocently?

Section 3(1) specifically provides that appropriation includes situations where D comes by property innocently and later assumes the rights of the owner. A simple illustration would be where D agreed to collect property belonging to P in order to deliver it to X. Having collected the goods D then decides to keep them for himself. He would have come by the goods innocently, but would have subsequently stolen them. The precise moment at which theft occurs would depend upon one's view of *Gomez*. On the basis that any assumption of the rights of the owner can be an appropriation, D appropriates as soon as he takes possession of the goods, but does not commit theft until his appropriation is accompanied by mens rea. Alternatively, if one contends that *Gomez* only applies to situations where D obtains possession by deception, the theft might not be regarded as occurring until D fails to take the goods to X (see again *Skipp* etc, above). If *Gomez* is applied regardless of whether or not there is any deception by D, it is difficult to see what the purpose of the reference in s3(1) to 'later appropriation' might be, because even if D is 'innocent' any assumption by him of the rights of the owner will, in any event, be an appropriation: see further *Pilgrim* v *Rice-Smith* [1977] 1 WLR 671. If D found property in the street, and on later discovering that it belonged to his neighbour resolved to keep it, he would be regarded as having appropriated it the moment he picked it up. There would be no scope for contending that he came by it innocently and subsequently appropriated it.

The bona fide purchaser for value without notice

Some protection from a prosecution for theft is offered to the bona fide purchaser for value without notice by s3(2), which provides:

> 'Where property or a right or interest in property is or purports to be transferred for value to a person acting in good faith, no later assumption by him of rights which he believed himself to be acquiring shall, by reason of any defect in the transferor's title, amount to theft of the property.'

Where, therefore, P buys stolen property from D, unaware that it is stolen, and he gives value for it, he will not be guilty of theft if he later discovers the truth and resolves to keep the property; neither will he incur any liability for handling stolen goods: see Chapter 10.

The duration of appropriation

In *R* v *Atakpu; R* v *Abrahams* [1993] 3 WLR 812 the Court of Appeal considered two issues: first, could property that had been appropriated by D be appropriated again each time he assumed the rights of the owner?; and, second, was appropriation a continuous act? The appellants had hired cars in Germany using false documents, planning to sell the cars on returning to the United Kingdom, but were detained at customs on returning to the United Kingdom, and in due course charged with conspiring to steal the cars. Following a direction from the trial judge that an appropriation of the vehicles occurred within the United Kingdom, the appellants were convicted and subsequently appealed. The Court of Appeal, allowing the appeals, held that, applying *Gomez*, the appropriation of the cars took place in Germany even though the hire company was deceived into parting with the possession of them, and they had thus been stolen outside the jurisdiction. The theft was complete before the appellants returned. The Court recognised that decisions such as those in *Meech* (above) and *Pitham and Hehl* (above), provided support for the proposition that there could not be a fresh appropriation every time the appellants subsequently dealt with the cars on their return to the jurisdiction. By contrast cases such as *R* v *Hale* (1978) 68 Cr App R 415 identified theft as a continuing act. Attempting to reconcile these various approaches Ward J, giving the judgment of the court, observed:

> '... it would seem (1) theft can occur in an instant by a single appropriation but it can also involve a course of dealing with property lasting longer and involving several appropriations before the transaction is complete; (2) theft is a finite act – it has a beginning and it has an end; (3) at what point the transaction is complete is a matter for the jury to decide upon the facts of each case; (4) though there may be several appropriations in the course of a single theft or several appropriations of different goods each constituting a separate theft as in *Skipp*, no case suggests that there can be successive thefts of the same property (assuming of course that possession is constant and not lost or abandoned, later to be assumed again).'

Although the court regarded theft as a finite act, it recommended a flexible approach whereby the question of whether or not the theft was still taking place should be left to the jury, properly directed. The test of whether or not the defendants were still 'on the job', as propounded by *Smith and Hogan* (8th ed, 1996) p527, was endorsed by the court.

Presumably if the appellants had sold the cars in the United Kingdom they could have been indicted for handling stolen goods as, under s24 of the 1968 Act, it matters not where the theft producing the goods was committed, and they would no longer have been 'in the course of stealing'.

7.5 Property belonging to another

Section 5(1) of the Theft Act 1968 provides an extended meaning for the phrase 'belonging to another'. It states:

'Property shall be regarded as belonging to any person having possession or control of it, or having in it any proprietary right or interest (not being an equitable interest arising only from an agreement to transfer or grant an interest).'

Clearly the section does not require that property should be owned by the person from whom it is appropriated, mere possession is sufficient. As Potter LJ observed in *R* v *Arnold* [1997] 4 All ER 1 (at p9d–e):

'It is plain from the wording [of s5(1)] that an equitable proprietary interest will suffice, so that beneficiaries of a trust, properly so-called, are protected, albeit the question of whether particular property is indeed the subject of a trust may not be straightforward …'

Difficult questions may also arise where D is charged with theft of property of which he is the legal owner. For example, in *R* v *Turner (No 2)* [1971] 2 All ER 441, D removed his car from outside the garage at which it had been repaired, intending to avoid having to pay for the repair. The Court of Appeal held that the car could be regarded as 'property belonging to another' as against the defendant owner, since it was in the possession and control of the repairer. Were the same facts to present themselves today, a charge of making off without payment contrary to s3 Theft Act 1978 would be more appropriate. The repairer might be regarded as having a right to retain goods until the repairs are paid for (a repairer's lien), but the trial judge had directed the jury not to consider the case on this basis. See further *R* v *Bonner* [1970] 1 WLR 838 – a partner can be convicted of theft of partnership property.

R v *Meredith* [1973] Crim LR 253 suggests that where the custodian of goods has no right to retain them as against the owner they will not be regarded as property belonging to another, the defendant in that case being held by a Crown Court judge to have no case to answer on a charge of theft, where he had removed his car from a police station yard. This seems to be a doubtful proposition. In *R* v *Kelly* (considered above in relation to property capable of being stolen) Rose LJ observed that the question of whether or not the Royal College of Surgeons had the right to retain the body parts that the defendant was alleged to have stolen was irrelevant to the issue of whether or not they constituted property belonging to another. As he explained:

'So far as the question of possession by the Royal College of Surgeons is concerned, in our judgment the learned judge was correct to rule that the college had possession, sufficiently for the purposes of and within s5(1) of the Theft Act 1968. We are unable to accept that possession, for the purposes of that section, is in any way dependent on the period of possession, ie whether it is for a limited time, or an indefinite time. In our judgment, the evidence, so far as it was material, before the jury, was to the effect that factually, the parts were in the custody of the Royal College of Surgeons. They were, as it seems to us, in their control and possession within the meaning of s5(1). That conclusion is, as it seems to us, reinforced by the judgment of the Court of Appeal in *R* v *Turner (No 2)*. We do not accept that the passage in Lord Parker CJ's judgment which we have read is to be regarded as limited to the facts of that particular case. In expressing the view that no other word such as 'lawful' was to be read into s5(1), by reference to possession, that court was construing s5 entirely consonantly with the construction which we now place upon it for the purposes of this appeal ... it was not necessary for the judge to direct the jury that the college was in lawful possession rather than merely in possession.'

See Chapter 16, section 16.3, for further details.

On the basis of this decision it seems clear that D can be guilty of theft where he steals property from P that P has just stolen from X. The lawfulness of P's possession is irrelevant – he is in possession as a matter of fact.

Lost and abandoned property

For the purposes of theft the distinction between lost and abandoned property is of significance. Where P loses a £10 note in the street and has no idea of its whereabouts, it still remains property belonging to another as against D who picks it up. Whether or not D will be guilty of theft will depend upon whether or not he is found to have had the necessary mens rea. On the other hand, where P deliberately leaves his newspaper on a train and it is picked up by D who occupies the seat after him, the newspaper would not be regarded as property belonging to another as against D. The vital distinction between the two situations is that in the latter, P intends to relinquish his rights of ownership (he has animus revocandi), and if property is ownerless it cannot be stolen. Caution should be exercised, however, before the conclusion that P has relinquished his rights of ownership is reached. On the basis of the Divisional Court's decision in *Williams* v *Phillips* (1957) 41 Cr App R 5, refuse put out for collection by local authority workers remains property belonging to the householder until collected, whereupon property passes to the local authority. Hence, refuse workers helping themselves to such property could be convicted of theft, on the basis that, as against them, the property is at all times property belonging to another.

Those who go searching for valuable items with metal detectors can incur liability for theft if they decide to keep what they find. Under the Treasure Act 1996 (which replaced the old common law of 'treasure trove'), valuable items of at least a minimum antiquity are designated as 'treasure' provided a number of conditions are satisfied. If D were to find an item of treasure and decided to keep it he would be committing the actus reus of theft, but would not have mens rea (ie, would not be dishonest) unless he was aware of his obligations in respect of the Crown's interests. If an item falls outside the statutory definition of treasure, the courts are likely to favour the interests of the owner of the land where the item was found, rather than the interests of the finder: see *Waverley Borough Council* v *Fletcher* [1996] QB 334. This is particularly so if the finder has had to commit some sort of trespass to discover the item, eg digging up a playing field or dredging the lake of a golf course at night: see *Hibbert* v *McKiernan* [1948] 2 KB 142.

Property subject to a trust

Section 5(2) provides:

> 'Where property is subject to a trust, the persons to whom it belongs shall be regarded as including any person having a right to enforce the trust, and an intention to defeat the trust shall be regarded accordingly as an intention to deprive of the property any person having that right.'

As noted above, s5(1) covers the situation where property is held on trust, the trust property belonging to those entitled to enforce the trust. There is, therefore, a large overlap between s5(1) and s5(2), save that s5(2) would cover the situation where there are no readily identifiable beneficiaries to enforce the trust, such as may be the case with charitable trusts.

Section 5(3)

Section 5(3), along with s5(4) (below), has the effect of extending the definition of 'belonging to another' to situations in which, at common law, property would normally pass from P to D. Section 5(3) provides:

> 'Where a person receives property from or on account of another, and is under an obligation to the other to retain and deal with that property or its proceeds in a particular way, the property or proceeds shall be regarded (as against him) as belonging to the other.'

This provision, at least superficially, seems to be describing a relationship between the transferor and transferee of property that closely resembles the creation of a trust. If this were the case, however, s5(3) would be redundant because, as indicated above, trust property is protected by both s5(1) and s5(2). Logic dictates, therefore, that s5(3) can apply to situations where P entrusts property to D in circumstances falling short of the creation of a trustee/beneficiary relationship. As Potter LJ observed in *R* v *Arnold* (above) (p9f–h):

> '... we see no good reason to introduce words of limitation in relation to the interest of the transferor, save that at the time of handing over the property to the recipient he should lawfully be in possession of it in circumstances which give him a legal right vis-à-vis the recipient to require that the property be retained or dealt with in a particular way for the benefit of the transferor. ... Nor do we consider that the position must be different where the recipient is throughout the "true owner" if by agreement ... he recognises a legal obligation to retain or deal with the property in the interest and/or for the benefit of the transferor, but subsequently, in knowing breach of that obligation, misappropriates it to his own unfettered use.'

For example, suppose P enters into a contract with D under which D is to paint P's house and is given an advance of £100 to buy materials, D could be guilty of theft if he subsequently spends that money dishonestly on other items. Section 5(3) would operate so as to prevent property passing, with the result that D would be spending money belonging to P.

The section requires the defendant to be under an obligation to retain the property or its proceeds. *R v Gilks* [1972] 3 All ER 280 is authority for the proposition that this obligation must be a legally enforceable one. The obligation is not that any property received should be retained in its original form, but that a separate fund, equal to the value of the property originally received, should be maintained. The court in *R v Hayes* (1977) 64 Cr App R 82 proceeded on the basis that the question of whether or not a legal obligation arose for the purposes of s5(3) was one for the jury to determine, whilst in *R v Mainwaring* (1981) 74 Cr App R 99, it was held that the trial judge should direct the jury as to what could give rise to a legal obligation and then leave it to them to determine whether one arose on the facts. Following *R v Dubar* [1994] 1 WLR 1484, it would appear that the latter approach is to be preferred. The Courts-Martial Appeal Court observed that there were irreconcilable differences between the approach of Lawton LJ in *Mainwaring* (above), and the approach of Edmund-Davies LJ in *R v Hall* [1973] QB 126, which had in turn been approved by Lord Widgery CJ in *Hayes* (above). The court held that the judge advocate had correctly expressed the law by directing the court that if it found certain facts to be made out then, *as a matter of law*, an obligation arose to which s5(3) applied: see further *R v Breaks and Huggan* [1998] Crim LR 349.

The question is clearly one of civil law, and one has to examine the transaction to determine whether or not the parties intend that there should be legal consequences. In *R v Cullen* ((1974) unreported), the defendant, who was P's mistress, was convicted of theft of £20 that he had given her to buy food, when she dishonestly spent it for her own purposes. The decision has been criticised on the basis that in terms of contract law it may have been a domestic agreement: see *Balfour v Balfour* [1919] 2 KB 571. Where money is given by persons sharing a house to the defendant so that a communal bill can be paid, the argument that there is a legal obligation to deal with the money in that way seems more plausible: see *Davidge v Bunnett* [1984] Crim LR 296.

Whether an obligation exists or not, and if it does, the nature of the obligation, is to be determined by construing the express and implied terms of the contract between the parties. In *R v Hall* [1973] 1 QB 126, the Court of Appeal held that a travel agent, who had accepted money for securing airline tickets for customers, was not under an obligation within s5(3). Once the money was paid over to the defendant he was free to use it as he pleased, and was therefore not guilty of theft when he was later unable to provide the tickets required. See also *R v Klineberg* (1998) The Times 19 November. Similarly, in *Attorney-General's Reference (No 1 of 1985)* [1986] Crim LR 476, the Court of Appeal held that a publican who, contrary to his agreement with a brewery, sold his own beer over the counter of the tied public house of which he was the manager, could not be guilty of theft of the proceeds by keeping them. He was not under an obligation to hand over the proceeds to the brewery within s5(3) (thus they did not become property belonging to another), because he did not receive the proceeds on account of the brewery. See

Lee Cheung Wing v *R* [1992] Crim LR 440 for possible alternative charges under s17 of the 1968 Act.

Conversely in *R* v *Brewster* (1979) 69 Cr App R 375, it was held that an insurance broker could be guilty of theft of insurance premiums collected by him for which he had to account to the insurance company. A determining factor was that the contract between the defendant and the insurance company stated that at all times the premiums were to be the property of the company. In assessing the scope of the obligation, it is important to note that s5(3) applies to both the property received and its proceeds.

In *R* v *Wain* [1995] 2 Cr App R 660, D, who had arranged a number of events in order to raise money for a charity, opened a separate bank account, in the name of the charity, in order to deposit the money. With the consent of the charity D was permitted to transfer the sums credited to the charity to his own account and drew a cheque in favour of the charity for the sum due. The cheque was dishonoured, as were subsequent cheques, and D was convicted of theft of the sums collected. He appealed on the ground that the trial judge had erred in rejecting his contention that, following the decision of the Divisional Court in *Lewis* v *Lethbridge* [1987] Crim LR 59, there was no legal obligation to deal with the sums raised in any particular way with the consequence that s5(3) Theft Act 1968 could not operate. The Court of Appeal, dismissing his appeal, held that, applying *Davidge* v *Bunnett* [1984] Crim LR 297, D was under an obligation to retain at least the proceeds of the sums collected, if not the actual notes and coins. The sums credited to his own account remained property belonging to another by virtue of s5(3). The decision of the Divisional Court in *Lewis* v *Lethbridge* [1987] Crim LR 59 was disapproved, McGowan LJ observing that:

> '... we feel obliged to comment that [Macpherson J in *Lewis* v *Lethbridge*] ... was forgetting that s5(3) ... referred not merely to dealing with that property but also its proceeds.'

His Lordship continued:

> 'It seems to us that the approach of the court in the *Lethbridge* case was a very narrow one based, apparently, on the finding by the justices that there was no requirement of the charity that the appellant hand over the same notes and coins. Neither was there in the present case. But what the Divisional Court does not appear to have considered in that case was the true aspect. It was either not argued or the court felt, for some reason, that it could not be considered because of that finding of the justices. We are unable to agree with them about that ... we feel that in deciding, as they did in the *Lethbridge* case, the Divisional Court was not following the decision in *Davidge* v *Bunnett*. There the obligation on the defendant was "to keep in existence a fund sufficient to pay the bill". So also in the *Lethbridge* case, and so also in the present case.
>
> Leaving aside all the authorities, it seems to us that by virtue of s5(3), the appellant was plainly under an obligation to retain, if not the actual notes and coins, at least their proceeds, that is to say the money credited in the bank account which he opened for the trust with the actual property. When he took the money credited to that account and moved it over to his own bank account, it was still the proceeds of the notes and coins

donated which he proceeded to use for his own purposes, thereby appropriating them ...
Whether a person in the position of the appellant is a trustee is to be judged on an
objective basis. It is an obligation imposed on him by law. It is not essential that he
should have realised that he was a trustee, but of course the question remains as to
whether he was acting honestly ...'

The court seemed to accept the argument that, regardless of the terms of the
agreement entered into by the appellant with the telethon organisers, the appellant
became a trustee of the sums donated by those contributing to the charitable cause
at the events he had organised. If this is correct, is recourse to s5(3) strictly
necessary, given that s5(2) provides that property which is subject to a trust can be
regarded as belonging to those who have the right to enforce the trust? The question
of whether or not D hands over exactly the same notes and coins collected may be
relevant to the issue of intention to permanently deprive: see *R* v *Velumyl* [1989]
Crim LR 299. McGowan LJ's comment that '... by virtue of s5(3), the appellant
was plainly under an obligation ...' is, with respect, questionable, given that s5(3)
can only operate if the defendant *is* under an obligation to retain and deal with the
property in a particular way. The subsection does not create the obligation, the
obligation must exist before the subsection can bite. See further *R* v *Rader* [1992]
Crim LR 663.

In the absence of any formal contractual relationship between the parties, proof
of the type of legal obligation required for the purposes of s5(3) is likely to be
fraught with difficulty. In *DPP* v *Huskinson* [1988] Crim LR 620, the respondent
was charged with theft of the proceeds of a cheque for housing benefit which he
had, in part, spent on himself. The Divisional Court held that the only possible
basis for the legal obligation required under s5(3) was the legislation under which
the benefit had been paid, the Social Security and Housing Benefit Act 1982, and
the court was unable to determine any express or implied obligation in those
provisions to the effect that the respondent was compelled, as a matter of law, to use
the housing benefit to pay off his arrears of rent.

In addition to establishing the legally binding nature of the obligation, the
prosecution must establish that the defendant knew that he was under a legal
obligation to deal with the property in a particular way. This was the basis for the
appellant's successful appeal in *R* v *Wills* (1991) 92 Cr App R 297 where
Farquharson LJ commented that:

'Whether a person is under an obligation to deal with property in a particular way can
only be established by proving that he had knowledge of that obligation. Proof that the
property was not dealt with in conformity with the obligation is not sufficient in itself.'

In this particular case it is tempting to ask whether or not the appellant could have
denied that he was dishonest in dealing with the proceeds of the cheques. If he was
unaware of the transactions creating the obligation he would have believed that the
money belonged to his firm to be used as he thought fit. As explained in section 7.6
below, s2(1)(a) of the 1968 Act provides that a defendant is not to be regarded as
dishonest if he honestly believes he has the right in law to appropriate property.

Section 5(4)

Section 5(4) deals with the complex problems that arise where a defendant receives property by mistake. It states:

> 'Where a person gets property by another's mistake, and is under an obligation to make restoration (in whole or in part) of the property or its proceeds or of the value thereof, then to the extent of that obligation the property or proceeds shall be regarded (as against him) as belonging to the person entitled to restoration, and an intention not to make restoration shall be regarded accordingly as an intention to deprive that person of the property or proceeds.'

An initial difficulty is the subsection's reliance on the concept of mistake. The purpose of the provision is clearly to stop property passing to the defendant where it otherwise would do at common law, but in what circumstances can property pass where a transaction is vitiated by mistake? The subsection can have no relevance in those situations where the mistake is fundamental, because no property can pass under a void transaction (assuming that one accepts that the effect of a fundamental mistake is to render a transaction void). The property in question would remain, as against the defendant, property belonging to another by virtue of s5(1). The subsection can, therefore, only sensibly apply where the transaction is vitiated by a non-fundamental mistake which renders it voidable. If this analysis is correct, one would then have to ask which situations will involve a *legal* obligation to restore the property received by mistake, since, as with s5(3), the defendant must be under such an obligation, to make restoration of the property, its proceeds, or the value thereof: see *R* v *Gilks* (above).

Arguably, where P by mistake gives D ten loaves of bread instead of nine, D is not under any obligation to return the extra loaf of bread to P even though he is aware of the mistake. It could be contended that no obligation to return the extra loaf arises until P 'avoids' the transaction by pointing out the error to D (see *Car and Universal Finance Co Ltd* v *Caldwell* [1965] 1 QB 525), at which point the property in the extra loaf would re-vest in P and by definition would be 'property belonging to another' as against D, quite independently of s5(4).

It would appear that in suggesting a provision in the nature of s5(4), the CLRC intended to bring within the scope of theft behaviour such as that of the defendant in *Moynes* v *Cooper* [1956] 1 QB 439, where an employee received a wage packet containing money which should have been deducted to take account of advance payments that had already been made to him during the previous week. The overpayment was discovered by the defendant employee some time later when he was at home, and he proceeded to spend the money. As the law then stood he had to be acquitted of theft. It is envisaged that he would now be within the scope of s5(4), as where there is an overpayment of money, D will be under a quasi-contractual obligation to repay the sum. In civil law it could be recovered by way of an action for money had and received. This would be sufficient to create the legal obligation required by the subsection. Hence the provision could be relied upon where D receives too much change in a shop or from a bank clerk.

Following the decision in *Chase Manhattan Bank NA* v *Israel-British Bank London Ltd* [1981] Ch 105, to the effect that a party transferring money by mistake retains an equitable interest in it where an action will lie to recover sums paid under a mistake of fact, and thus it can be regarded a property belonging to another as against the transferor within s5(1), s5(4) could be regarded as redundant. The courts have extended its operation, however, to encompass bank giro credits made in error, and cheques erroneously drawn in favour of payees.

In *Attorney-General's Reference (No 1 of 1983)* [1985] QB 182, the defendant had been overpaid, the amount being credited directly to her current account. The evidence suggested that having discovered the overpayment, the defendant simply allowed the money to remain in the account, but she was acquitted on a charge of theft of the overpayment. The Court of Appeal offered guidance by suggesting that the defendant had 'got' a chose in action by mistake and was under an obligation to restore 'the value' of the overpayment to her employer. The nature of the obligation was not discussed at length, but Lord Lane CJ suggested it was based on the employer's right to restitution. He further suggested that s5(4) only started to operate from the moment the defendant became aware of the overpayment, implying that, as with s5(3), D will not incur liability unless aware of the obligation to make restoration. Does this mean that the defendant who receives too much money by way of change in a shop, and honestly believes that he does not have to return it unless asked, could escape liability on the basis of his ignorance regarding the obligation? It is submitted that knowledge of the overpayment and knowledge of the obligation to restore are quite different issues.

Note that the subsection extends to proceeds of property and its value. If D receives £5 too much in change from a shopkeeper, buys a book with the £5, and then realises what has happened, the book becomes property belonging to the shopkeeper as against D. Should D resolve to keep it, he could be guilty of theft; see further *R* v *Stalham* [1993] Crim LR 310.

Chase Manhattan Bank NA v *Israel-British Bank London Ltd* was applied in *R* v *Shadrokh-Cigari* [1988] Crim LR 465, where the appellant, who was the guardian of a child to whose bank account $286,000 had been credited in error instead of $286, persuaded the child to sign authorities instructing the bank to issue banker's drafts, in favour of the appellant. The appellant subsequently credited a number of his own accounts with the sums indicated on the drafts, and was convicted of theft of the drafts on the basis that they remained property belonging to another, namely the issuing bank. The Court of Appeal expressed the view that the conviction for theft was sustainable on two grounds. One view was that as the appellant had obtained the drafts as a result of a fundamental mistake of fact on the part of the bank, he was under an obligation to restore them to the bank, and this gave rise to the bank having an equitable interest in the drafts. Under s5(1) of the Theft Act 1968, therefore, the drafts could still be regarded as property belonging to the bank.

Alternatively, the situation could be regarded as one falling within s5(4) of the 1968 Act, in that the appellant had obtained the drafts as a result of the bank's mistake, and was under an obligation to restore the property or its proceeds. There may be a difficulty in asserting that the appellant was under an obligation to restore the intangible property represented by the drafts to the bank, as the bank had never had the right to enforce the drafts (as they had never been made out in favour of the bank or assigned to them), but the appellant clearly had obtained the drafts, as documents, and these had been owned by the bank before being transferred to him by mistake. The problem of cheques made out by mistake was also considered by a differently constituted Court of Appeal in *R* v *Davis* [1988] Crim LR 762, where the appellant, who had been in receipt of housing benefit, was sent duplicate cheques in respect of the benefit, as a result of a computer error, and continued to receive some cheques after he had ceased to be eligible for benefit. In relation to two of the six counts of theft upon which the appellant had been convicted (where there was evidence that he had endorsed cheques in favour of his landlord in order to pay his rent) the Court of Appeal allowed his appeal as there was no evidence that the appellant had received cash in return for the cheques. The court upheld the convictions on the remaining counts however, expressing the view that although the appellant could not be guilty of stealing the intangible property represented by the cheques (ie the right to payment) as this was not, and never had been, a type of property belonging to another as against the appellant, he could be guilty of stealing the proceeds of the cheques obtained by mistake, namely the cash received in return for the endorsing of the cheques. The court further expressed the view that the prosecution did not have to indicate which of the cheques the appellant had been entitled to receive and which he had obtained by mistake. Section 5(4) referred to the obligation to restore the whole or part of property got by another's mistake. Liability for theft attached to the 'surplus', ie the extent to which property that the appellant had obtained by mistake exceeded property to which the appellant had been entitled.

7.6 Dishonesty

A defendant can only be convicted of theft where his actions are found to be dishonest. It is this element in theft that results in any defendant charged with the offence having the right to trial by jury, regardless of how trivial the value of the property involved may be. A conviction for theft inevitably carries with it a slur on the defendant's character. It should be remembered that a defendant can be dishonest even where he does not act with a view to making a gain for himself or another. It is sufficient that he acts with a view to causing loss to the victim, this being the effect of s1(2) of the 1968 Act. Dishonesty is dealt with in s2 of the Theft Act 1968, but it only provides a partial, or negative, definition, and that this only applies to dishonesty in the context of theft, not deception or handling.

Section 2(1)(a)

Section 2(1)(a) provides that a person's appropriation of property belonging to another is not to be regarded as dishonest:

'… if he appropriates the property in the belief that he has in law the right to deprive the other of it, on behalf of himself or of a third person.'

The test is subjective. The defendant's belief that he has in law the right to deprive another of property merely has to be honestly held, it does not have to be reasonable. This is confirmed by the Court of Appeal's decision in *R v Holden* [1991] Crim LR 478. As with all such subjective tests, the more outlandish the defendant's honest belief, the less likely the justices, or the jury, are to believe him. Further, the belief must relate to a legal right to deprive; hence if D wrongly thought property had passed to him from P under the terms of a contract, and he purported to sell the property on to X, his assumption of the rights of the owner would not be dishonest, provided his belief in the legal right to sell was genuine. In effect the defendant can rely on a mistake of civil (contract) law as a defence. It remains to be seen whether a defendant who believes he has a moral right to take property could bring himself within this subsection. It is submitted that it is more likely that he would be found not to have been dishonest under *R v Ghosh* [1982] 1 QB 1053 (below).

Section 2(1)(b)

Section 2(1)(b) provides that a person's appropriation of property belonging to another is not to be regarded as dishonest:

'… if he appropriates the property in the belief that he would have the other's consent if the other knew of the appropriation and the circumstances of it.'

The subsection might apply where D's car has run out of petrol, and D takes a can of fuel from his next-door neighbour P's garden. D has clearly appropriated property belonging to another and has intention to permanently deprive P of the petrol, but may be able to argue that he honestly believed P would have consented had he known. Again the test is subjective.

Section 2(1)(c)

Section 2(1)(c) provides that a person's appropriation of property belonging to another is not to be regarded as dishonest:

'… (except where the property came to him as trustee or personal representative) if he appropriates the property in the belief that the person to whom the property belongs cannot be discovered by taking reasonable steps.'

The subsection will be of particular significance where the defendant finds property that has been lost by the owner (property that has been deliberately abandoned ceases to be property belonging to another within s5). Again, the test for the defendant's belief is subjective. As regards the question of what might be required by taking reasonable steps to discover ownership, this will depend partly on the identification available, the location in which it is found, and the value of the property. A defendant finding a £10 note in the street may well come within s2(1)(c), unless he has just seen it fall from the wallet of P who is walking in front of him. Similarly, if the defendant finds a suitcase containing £1,000,000 in the street, one would expect him to make considerable efforts to locate the owner. Nevertheless it should be kept in mind that the subsection is concerned with what the defendant views as reasonable steps: see further *R* v *Small* [1987] Crim LR 777 which affirms this latter point.

Section 2(2)

Section 2(2) provides:

> 'A person's appropriation of property belonging to another may be dishonest notwithstanding that he is willing to pay for the property.'

This subsection is included for the avoidance of doubt. Where D sees P's newspaper poking out of his letterbox, pulls out the newspaper, and leaves its price on P's doormat, D could still be guilty of theft. He has appropriated property belonging to another with intention to permanently deprive, and s2(2) states that he can still be regarded as dishonest; whether he is or not falls to be determined by the jury.

Dishonesty beyond s2

Should a defendant, who appropriates property belonging to another, intending to permanently deprive the other of it, knowing he has no legal right to do so, knowing that the owner does not consent, and knowing how to return the goods to the owner, nevertheless be able to escape liability for theft on the basis that he is not dishonest? The question is really asking whether a defendant who is unable to escape liability under s2(1), should nevertheless be able to contend that he is not dishonest. The answer must be yes. Whether certain behaviour is dishonest or not is a mixed question of law and morality, and one that has engendered considerable academic and judicial discussion. It is clear, however, that a defendant unable to bring himself within s2(1) may nevertheless escape liability because the jury do not regard his actions as blameworthy. Following *R* v *Feely* [1973] 1 QB 530, it is no longer permissible for a trial judge to withdraw the issue of dishonesty from a jury by directing them that, as a matter of law, the defendant's actions were dishonest. In cases where the defendant cannot avail himself of s2(1), and where there is nevertheless some debate as to whether or not his actions were dishonest, the matter should be left to the jury to determine, applying their own standards of common decency. The criticism of such an approach is that it may tend to play down the subjective element of dishonesty where the defendant contends that he believed he was behaving honestly. In this respect the Court of Appeal's decision in *R* v *Ghosh* [1982] 1 QB 1053, despite the fact that it was concerned with obtaining property by deception, may provide the 'model direction' for theft cases. The court held that in cases of doubt the jury should be directed in the following terms:

> 'Was the defendant dishonest according to the standards of ordinary decent people? If yes, did the defendant realise that what he was doing was dishonest by these standards?'

There is a rider to this test in *Ghosh* to the effect that the defendant is to be regarded as dishonest even where he believes his actions to be morally justified, if he nevertheless realises that ordinary decent people would regard it as wrong. A possible loophole in this new test is that a defendant may not have thought about whether ordinary decent people would have regarded his actions as dishonest, or even if he had, he may not have been able to tell. Further, the test does not remove the possibility of inconsistencies between juries, although it must be said that this latter problem is not the exclusive preserve of theft: see further *R* v *Forrester* [1992] Crim LR 79.

7.7 Intention to permanently deprive

The requirement that the prosecution must establish an intention to permanently deprive on the part of D is, in simple terms, what distinguishes borrowing from theft. Note that P does not, in fact, have to be permanently deprived of his property; it is sufficient that D intended him to be so deprived. Where such intention is lacking, liability might still be imposed, subject to other conditions being met, under s11 or s12 of the Theft Act 1968, considered at section 7.8 below.

The 1968 Act does not provide a definition of intention to permanently deprive. It was clearly the view of the framers of the Act that the existence or otherwise of such an intention was a matter that a jury or bench of magistrates could determine using their common sense, and in the vast majority of thefts that come before the courts this is no doubt the case.

Section 6 exists, therefore, for the avoidance of doubt. It is essentially a deeming provision. If D comes within its terms he can be deemed to have had the necessary intention to permanently deprive, despite the fact that, as a matter of strict logic, it could be argued that such intention was lacking. On numerous occasions the Court of Appeal has stressed that it should be the last resort of those seeking to determine whether or not a defendant has intention to permanently deprive, not the first. The first limb of s6(1) provides that:

> 'A person appropriating property belonging to another without meaning the other permanently to lose the thing itself is nevertheless to be regarded as having the intention of permanently depriving the other of it if his intention is to treat the thing as his own to dispose of regardless of the other's rights ...'

Hence D can be deemed to have an intention to permanently deprive by reference to what he does with P's property. If D takes P's property intending to sell it back to P the subsection would be satisfied. D is treating P's property as if it were his to sell. The fact that P will get the property back if he agrees to buy it is irrelevant: see *R* v *Hall* (1848) 1 Den 381 (D took fat from a candle-maker and then offered it for sale to the owner). The same applies if D takes P's property on the basis that he will only let P have it back at a given price, although here there may be an alternative charge of blackmail available to the prosecution: see s21(1) Theft Act 1968. A fortiori if D takes P's property and sells it to a third party. In *R* v *Marshall; R* v *Coombes; R* v *Eren* (1998) The Times 10 March the Court of Appeal upheld convictions for theft where the appellants had collected London Underground tickets from passengers exiting stations and sold them on to other members of the public seeking to travel on London Underground. The appellants argued that the issuing of the ticket by London Underground was analogous to the issuing of a cheque. Property was created in the form of the right of the purchaser to travel on the London Underground system that was subsequently transferred to the appellants. At no time did any such right belong to London Underground, hence there could be no intention to permanently deprive it of that right. As regards the actual ticket, the appellants contended that there could be no intention to permanently deprive London Underground as the ticket would, in the normal course of events, be returned to it anyway. Rejecting these arguments Mantell LJ expressed the Court's preference for the view that when a traveller purchased a ticket a contract came into existence that created rights on both sides. The purchaser acquiring the right to travel, London Underground acquiring the right to insist that the ticket should only be used by the person to whom it was originally issued. It was that right that the appellants could be said to have been disregarding. The charge related to theft of tangible property, the actual tickets, however, and the Court was of the view that, on the basis of *R* v *Fernandes* (considered below), the appellants had treated the tickets as their own to dispose of regardless of the rights of London Underground. The fact that London underground might get the tickets back when their usefulness to travellers was extinguished was not relevant on this point.

How would the Court have dealt with an appellant who obtained tickets from those leaving London Underground stations because he was a collector of old tickets? Would he escape liability simply on the basis that he is not dishonest? Mantell LJ suggests that the Court's ruling could have implications for all ticket touts, and even for an ordinary motorist passing on the benefit of an unexpired parking ticket to another motorist. If D acquires, legitimately, a ticket for a major sporting occasion and sells it on for a profit it seems hard to imagine a court concluding that his actions were dishonest, even if the ticket does remain the property of the issuing body throughout (which is questionable). Unlike the facts of *Marshall and Others*, where essentially London Underground lost out on ticket sales, the promoter of the sporting occasion can only sell each seat once. As regards the common practice of motorists passing on unexpired 'pay and display' type parking tickets, again dishonesty would be difficult to establish. This case does have more in common with the London Underground problem, in that the car park operator could sell the parking space many times over, and he is cheated out of a sale if a ticket is transferred. There is the further issue, however, that the ticket is never returned to the car park operator. Liability could only attach to the theft of the rights vested in the issuer of such a ticket at the point of sale, thus bringing into sharp focus the question of whether or not the right to not have tickets transferred is a type of property protected under the Theft Act 1968.

D can also be regarded as satisfying the subsection where he abandons property belonging to P if the circumstances are such that there is little likelihood of P ever having the property returned to him. For example, D takes P's book and leaves it in a dustbin. D may hope that it is returned to P, but it is likely to be regarded as a disposal regardless of P's rights. Similarly, if D takes P's money and invests it in a high-risk enterprise. He may hope that P will recoup more than the sum invested, but the circumstances might indicate that, realistically, D sees little chance of any return. In *R* v *Fernandes* [1996] 1 Cr App R 175 the Court of Appeal (Auld LJ) observed:

> 'In our view, section 6(1), which is expressed in general terms, is not limited in its application to the illustrations given by Lord Lane CJ in *Lloyd* [considered below]. Nor, in saying that in most cases it would be unnecessary to refer to the provision, did Lord Lane [in *Lloyd*] suggest that it should be so limited. The critical notion, stated expressly in the first limb and incorporated by reference in the second, is whether a defendant intended "to treat the thing as his own to dispose of regardless of the other's rights". The second limb of subsection (1), and also subsection (2), are merely specific illustrations of the application of that notion. We consider that section 6 may apply to a person in possession or control of another's property who, dishonestly and for his own purpose, deals with that property in such a manner that he knows that he is risking its loss.'

The meaning to be attributed to the phrase 'to dispose of' as it is used in s6(1) is not entirely clear. In *DPP* v *Lavender* [1994] Crim LR 297, where D took two doors from a council property that was under construction, and used them to replace the damaged doors in his girlfriend's property, which was also owned by the same local authority, the Divisional Court upheld his conviction for theft on the basis that first limb of s6(1) was satisfied because D had manifested an intention to treat the doors as his own by hanging them in a different property from that for which they were intended. The difficulty with this approach is that D was not, for example, offering the doors for sale to the authority, or anyone else, and the authority never lost possession of the doors. It is submitted that the approach of the Court of Appeal in *R* v *Cahill* [1993] Crim LR 141 is to be preferred, where it was held that 'to dispose of' implied a getting rid of the property by destroying or selling it.

The second limb of s6(1) provides that:

> '... a borrowing or lending of it may amount to so treating it [ie may amount to D treating the thing as his own to dispose of regardless of the other's rights] if, but only if, the borrowing or lending is for a period and in circumstances making it equivalent to an outright taking or disposal.'

Hence it countenances circumstances where borrowing or lending can be regarded as an intention to permanently deprive P of his property. As Lord Lane CJ explained in *R* v *Lloyd* [1985] QB 829:

> 'This half of the subsection ... is intended to make it clear that a mere borrowing is never enough to constitute the necessary guilty mind unless the intention is to return the thing in such a changed state that it can truly be said that all its goodness or virtue has gone: for example: *R* v *Beecham* (1851) 5 Cox CC 181, where the defendant stole railway tickets intending that they should be returned to the railway company in the usual way only after the journeys had been completed. ... [T]he learned judge in the present case gave another example, namely the taking of a torch battery with the intention of returning it only when its power is exhausted.'

Thus, the second limb would be satisfied where D borrows P's video recorder and uses it for five years. D may have intended all along to return the machine to P, but at the end of five years it may be of little practical use to P, given the wear and tear it has suffered, and its resale value will only be a fraction of what it was at the time it was taken. Similarly, if D, at the beginning of the season, were to take P's season ticket that allowed P to attend all of his football team's home games. If D were to keep the ticket until the end of the season and then return it to P he would, it is submitted, be guilty of theft, by virtue of s6(1), on the basis that the ticket has lost its value. Perhaps more uncertain is the situation where D takes the ticket to get into one or two of (say) 18 home games; in such a case P has hardly been deprived of his complete interest in the ticket. It may be more appropriate to charge D with theft of the chose in action that is represented by the ticket, ie the right to enter the grandstand for that game. The whole problem can be avoided if D is charged with obtaining services by deception contrary to s1(1) Theft Act 1978 when he uses the ticket to gain admission to the ground

The requirement that the borrowing or lending of the property should result in its losing virtually all of its value before a defendant could be deemed to have intention to permanently deprive, was reaffirmed by the Court of Appeal in *Lloyd* (above). The appellants had taken prints of first run feature films from cinemas, copied them onto video tapes and returned the films to the cinemas in time for the next showing to the public. There was no evidence that the cinemas were ever prevented from showing the films at the advertised times. The convictions for conspiracy to steal the films were quashed on the basis that there was insufficient evidence of intention to permanently deprive. As Lord Lane CJ explained:

> 'The goodness, the virtue, the practical value of the films to the owners has not gone out of the article. The film could still be projected to paying audiences, and, had everything gone according to the conspirators' plans, would have been projected in the ordinary way to audiences at the Odeon Cinema, Barking, who would have paid for their seats. Our view is that those particular films which were the subject of this alleged conspiracy had not themselves diminished in value at all. What had happened was that the borrowed film had been used or was going to be used to perpetrate a copyright swindle on the owners whereby their commercial interests were grossly and adversely affected. ... [T]hat

borrowing, it seems to us, was not for a period, or in such circumstances, as made it equivalent to an outright taking or disposal. There was still virtue in the film.'

This emphasis on the property losing its virtue or value was also relied upon to secure the conviction of the defendant in *R* v *Arnold* [1997] 4 All ER 1, where the appellant had been charged with theft of a number of bills of exchange. On the basis that, once negotiated, the bills of exchange would be returned to the owners, he contended that he could not have had any intention to permanently deprive the owners of their property (ie the pieces of paper constituting the bills). In rejecting this contention, Potter LJ, on behalf of the Court of Appeal explained (at p15a–b):

'It seems to us that, in a case where a defendant has appropriated a valuable security handed over on the basis of an obligation that he will retain or deal with it for the benefit or to the account of the transferor, there is good reason for the application of s6(1) if the intention of the transferee at the time of the appropriation is that the document should find its way back to the transferor only after all the benefit to the transferor has been lost or removed as a result of its use in breach of such obligation.'

In theory the Court could have relied on a aspect of an earlier decision in *R* v *Duru* [1973] 3 All ER 715, not overruled by the later House of Lords' decision in *R* v *Preddy* [1996] 3 All ER 481, to the effect that D can be deemed to have intention to permanently deprive P, the drawer of a cheque, of the actual piece of paper on which the cheque is written, notwithstanding that it is eventually returned to P, because once it has been through the clearing process it ceases to be a negotiable instrument and therefore ceases to be 'in substance, the same thing as it was before'. That the Court opted not to adopt this reasoning is perhaps explained by the academic criticism that it has encountered (see *Smith & Hogan* (8th ed, 1996) p582 where it is described as 'unconvincing'), and it is interesting to note that, in concluding his judgment in *Arnold*, Potter LJ observed that:

'... there is good reason, where the factual situation permits, to give effect to the rationale behind *R* v *Duru* that the "substance" of a cheque or valuable security lies in the right to present it and obtain the benefit of the proceeds, rather than in its character as a mere piece of paper with a message on it.'

For the position as regards the obtaining of cheques by deception: see now s15A of the Theft Act 1968, as inserted by the Theft (Amendment) Act 1996.

Finally, s6(2) provides:

'Without prejudice to the generality of subsection (1) above, where a person, having possession or control (lawfully or not) of property belonging to another, parts with the property under a condition as to its return which he may not be able to perform, this (if done for purposes of his own and without the other's authority) amounts to treating the property as his own to dispose of regardless of the other's rights.'

This provision is designed to cater for situations such as that where D takes P's property and pledges it with a pawnbroker without P's permission. In such a case D has parted with the property subject to a condition that he might not be able to perform, namely redeem the pledge by the appointed date. Similarly, if D uses P's money for gambling purposes without P's permission. Again the effect is that D is deemed to have intended to permanently deprive P of his property. Consideration should perhaps be given to the possibility that, where D is nevertheless positive that he will be able to redeem the pledge, a jury might be persuaded to the view that his taking was not dishonest.

Motor vehicles

Special considerations apply where the property taken is a registered motor vehicle. Given the ease with which the ownership of abandoned vehicles can be traced, intention to permanently deprive may be virtually impossible to establish, hence the existence of the offence of taking a conveyance contrary to s12 of the 1968 Act: see section 7.8 below.

Conditional intent

Does D commit theft where he takes a painting because it might be valuable, intending to keep it if it is, but discovers it is of little value and returns it to the owner? It might be argued that he has only a conditional intention to steal the painting, and as that condition is never fulfilled, he never has a present unconditional intention to permanently deprive the owner. Two decisions of the Court of Appeal, *R v Easom* [1971] 2 QB 315 and *R v Husseyn* (1977) 67 Cr App R 131, established that a conviction for theft was only sustainable where there was clear evidence that D had a present intention to permanently deprive P. Problems were compounded by the fact that as the law then stood D could not be charged with attempted theft where there was no property that he wanted to steal. Recourse was had to tortuous reasoning and dubious indictments in order to circumvent these difficulties, see *R v Bayley and Easterbrook* [1980] Crim LR 503 and *Scudder v Barrett* [1979] 3 WLR 591, but the major problems were removed by the enactment of the Criminal Attempts Act 1981 as interpreted by the House of Lords in *R v Shivpuri* [1986] 2 All ER 334. D can now be charged with attempting to steal property he believed to be in existence, or of value. Although problems may yet remain where the full offence of theft is charged, the prosecution can avoid many difficulties if the charge does not particularise the property D is alleged to have attempted to steal.

Intention to permanently deprive and dishonesty

It is clear that although D might have intention to permanently deprive P of his property, he may not necessarily be dishonest. For example, if D takes money from P, intending to repay it at a later date, he is still to be regarded as having an intention to permanently deprive the owner of the money, since it is to be assumed that he will not be returning exactly the same notes and coins: see *R v Velumyl*

[1989] Crim LR 299. D will, however, contend that he was not dishonest, given his intention to replace the money with an equivalent fund. Clearly difficulties could arise if the particular notes and coins taken by D had some rarity or sentimental value. Similarly, in a situation such as arose in *Fernandes* (above), if D takes P's money without permission and invests it in what he genuinely believes will be a short-term profitable venture, he may escape liability on the basis that he was not dishonest: see s2(1)(b) Theft Act 1968. The only problem for D lies in explaining why he did not inform P of his intentions prior to withdrawing the money. Other possibilities are that D may take an item of P's property because there is property belonging to D that has not been returned to him by P. Again, the intention to permanently deprive P will be apparent, but D may seek to rely on s2(1)(a) Theft Act 1968 and/or *Ghosh*.

7.8 Theft related offences not requiring an intention to permanently deprive

Theft Act 1968 s11

The Criminal Law Revision Committee envisaged the offence created by s11 as covering situations where a defendant removes an item, from a public exhibition or an art gallery to which the public has access, but lacks any intention to permanently deprive the owner of the item. The Committee sought to avoid extending theft to include temporary deprivation, or creating a general offence of temporary deprivation.

Section 11(1) provides:

> 'Subject to subsections (2) and (3) below, where the public have access to a building in order to view the building or part of it, or a collection or part of a collection housed in it, any person who without lawful authority removes from the building or its grounds the whole or part of any article displayed or kept for display to the public in the building or that part of it or in its grounds shall be guilty of an offence.'

The maximum sentence available following conviction on indictment is five years imprisonment. Note that the offence may be a suitable alternative charge where the elements necessary for s1 theft, or s9 burglary cannot be made out. A defendant who removes items from a public exhibition and refuses to return them unless the owner or some other person fulfils a condition (such as payment of a sum of money to charity) could be charged with theft, contrary to s1, on the basis (inter alia) that he can be deemed to have intention to permanently deprive within s6(1), or blackmail contrary to s21, on the basis that he is making a demand that is unwarranted, accompanied by menaces, with a view to gain or another's loss.

'Building to which the public have access in order to view ...'

The building must be one that the general public have been invited to enter, and not simply some section of the public. The owner's purpose in inviting the public must be to enable them to view the building itself or a collection housed in it. Section 11(2) provides:

> 'It is immaterial for purposes of subsection (1) above, that the public's access to a building is limited to a particular period or particular occasion; but where anything removed from a building or its grounds is there otherwise than as forming part of, or being on loan for exhibition with, a collection intended for permanent exhibition to the public, the person removing it does not thereby commit an offence under this section unless he removes it on a day when the public have access to the building as mentioned in subsection (1) above.'

As to the meaning of 'collection' s11(1) further provides:

> '..."collection" includes a collection got together for a temporary purpose, but references in this section to a collection do not apply to a collection made or exhibited for the purpose of effecting sales or other commercial dealings.'

Where the public are admitted to a commercial gallery, therefore, an offence would not be committed within s11, where one of the paintings on display is 'borrowed'.

Clearly an offence is not committed where a defendant borrows items from a building which is open to the public but not for the purposes listed in s11(1). In *R* v *Barr* [1978] Crim LR 244, therefore, no offence under s11 was committed by a defendant who removed a cross which was on display in a church for devotional purposes.

Provided that articles are exhibited within a building, liability extends to the removal of articles from the grounds of the building which also form part of the exhibition.

Mens rea

The defendant must intend to remove the article in question, knowing he does not have the consent of the owner, or other lawful authority to do so; in this regard s11(3) provides:

> 'A person does not commit an offence under this section if he believes that he has lawful authority for the removal of the thing in question or that he would have it if the person entitled to give it knew of the removal and the circumstances of it.'

Note that there is no requirement that the prosecution prove the defendant to have acted dishonestly.

Taking a conveyance

Section 12 replaces the old offence of 'taking and driving away' with a wider offence of 'taking a conveyance'. In common with ss11 and 13, no intention to permanently deprive the owner need be proved on the part of the defendant. Where a defendant is charged with theft of a conveyance contrary to s1, the jury may return a verdict of 'not guilty as charged' and substitute a verdict of guilty in respect of the lesser included offence under s12 (see s12(4)). Section 12(1) provides:

'Subject to subsections (5) and (6) below, a person shall be guilty of an offence if, without having the consent of the owner or other lawful authority, he takes any conveyance for his own or another's use or, knowing that any conveyance has been taken without such authority, drives it or allows himself to be carried in or on it.'

In the majority of situations a defendant charged with the offence will simply have been 'stealing a ride', in that he takes a conveyance from point 'A' without the owner's consent and leaves it at point 'B'. One of the difficulties in making such conduct theft in respect of motor vehicles is proof of any intention to permanently deprive. Even where D takes the victim's vehicle in Cornwall and leaves it in Newcastle-upon-Tyne, he will still deny intention to permanently deprive on the basis that he knew the vehicle would be returned to the owner once its registration number was traced on computer records held at the DVLA. A charge of theft might be more viable where the defendant takes a vehicle and destroys it, ships it out of the country, or changes its chassis number and registration plates, and sells it.

Section 12(5) makes separate provision in respect of pedal cycles where it states:

'Subsection (1) above shall not apply in relation to pedal cycles; but, subject to subsection (6) below, a person who, without having the consent of the owner or other lawful authority, takes a pedal cycle for his own or another 's use, or rides a pedal cycle knowing it to have been taken without such authority, shall on summary conviction be liable to a fine not exceeding fifty pounds.'

The maximum punishment available for the offence under s12(1) following trial on indictment is three years' imprisonment.

'Conveyance'
Section 12(7)(a) provides:

' "Conveyance" means any conveyance constructed or adapted for the carriage of a person or persons whether by land, water or air, except that it does not include a conveyance constructed or adapted for use only under the control of a person not carried in or on it, and "drive" shall be construed accordingly.'

This definition would seem to exclude goods vehicles where no provision is made for the person controlling the vehicle to sit on it. A goods trailer might fall within this category, as might some electric milk floats which are operated by a person walking alongside. *Neal* v *Gribble* [1978] RTR 409 is authority for the proposition that a horse is not a 'conveyance' within s12, although a horse-drawn vehicle would seem to be within the definition.

'Takes ... drives ... or allows himself to be carried'
Whilst a defendant will incur liability by driving another's conveyance without consent, it is clear that liability does not depend upon the conveyance being 'taken away'. For a 'taking' within the section there must be some movement of the conveyance, even if only for a short distance. The decision to prosecute should be based, it is submitted, on whether an owner has suffered some, albeit temporary,

deprivation of his property. Where there is no movement of the conveyance, a charge of attempt may still be appropriate: see *R* v *Bogacki* [1973] QB 832. Similarly, where a defendant is charged under s12 on the basis that as a passenger, he 'allowed himself to be carried', some movement of the vehicle must be established: see *R* v *Miller* [1976] Crim LR 147 and *R* v *Diggin* [1980] Crim LR 656.

'For his own or another's use ...'

Where the charge alleges a taking of the conveyance by the defendant, the prosecution must prove that this was for his own, or another's use. Notwithstanding the questionable decision of the Court of Appeal in *R* v *Pearce* [1973] Crim LR 321, it is submitted that the prosecution must prove that the defendant has used the vehicle in question as a conveyance, ie he has been transported by it, or has enabled another person to be transported on it. This view is supported by a number of authorities.

In *R* v *Bow* (1976) 64 Cr App R 54 the Court of Appeal held that the appellant had taken a conveyance for his own use, when he had sat in the driver's seat, released the handbrake, and steered it downhill for 200 yards in order to prevent it from causing any further obstruction to a road across which it had been parked. Despite his motives, and the fact that he had not started the engine, the defendant had used the vehicle as a conveyance. Where a defendant pushed a woman's car around a corner as a practical joke, the intention being to give the impression that it had been stolen, the Court of Appeal held that the defendant was not guilty within s12. He had not actually sat in the car and used it as a conveyance: see *R* v *Stokes* [1982] Crim LR 695. Finally, in *R* v *Dunn and Derby* [1984] Crim LR 367, a judge directed a jury at Snaresbrook Crown Court to acquit, where a defendant who was charged under s12 admitted wheeling a motor-cycle 40 yards without the owner's consent so that he could inspect it more closely under a street light. The Crown conceded that by pushing the motorbike and not riding on it the defendant had not used the vehicle as a conveyance.

'Without the consent of the owner ...'

In general terms, where a defendant takes a vehicle without permission he will not have the consent of the owner. If a defendant removes a victim's car from outside his house and drives it to a spot five miles away without first having secured the owner's consent, he will be liable under s12. Similarly where a defendant has limited permission to take a conveyance, for example to deliver his employer's goods and then return the vehicle to his place of work, a deviation from the permitted route could be a taking without consent. In this latter example it may be argued that the employer impliedly consents to some reasonable deviation – it will be a matter of degree in each case. That such activity can amount to an offence within s12 is evidenced by two authorities. First, *R* v *Phipps and McGill* [1970] RTR 209, a defendant was given permission to drive the owner's car to a London station. The defendant did so, but then decided to drive to a south coast resort in the car without obtaining any further permission. The Court of Appeal held this second taking to be without the owner's consent. Secondly, in *McKnight* v *Davies* [1974] RTR 4 the defendant lorry driver was held to have taken his employer's lorry without consent when, instead of returning it to his employer's place of business at the end of the working day, he drove to a public house. As Lord Widgery CJ observed:

> 'The difficulty ... is in defining the kind of unauthorised activity on the part of the driver, whose original control is lawful, which will amount to an unlawful taking for the purpose of section 12. Not every brief, unauthorised diversion from his proper route by an employed driver in the course of his working day will necessarily involve a "taking" of the vehicle for his own use. If, however, as in *R* v *Wibberley* [1966] 2 QB 214, he returns to the vehicle after he has parked it for the night and drives it off on an unauthorised errand, he is clearly guilty of the offence. Similarly, if in the course of his working day, or otherwise while his authority to use the vehicle is unexpired, he appropriates it to his own use in a manner which repudiates the rights of the true owner, and shows that he has assumed control of the vehicle for his own purposes, he can properly be regarded as having taken the vehicle within section 12.'

Deception and consent

A difficulty arises where the defendant obtains consent from the owner to his taking a vehicle, as a result of some deception he has exercised on the owner. For example, D rushes into his neighbour's house and asks to borrow his neighbour P's car to take his sick wife to hospital. P agrees. In fact D intends to use the car to drive himself to the cinema, and he does so. Has D taken the car without consent? Two authorities seem to suggests that there would be no liability under s12. In *R* v *Peart* [1970] 2 QB 672 the defendant had asked the owner of a car for permission to drive it to Alnwick, a nearby town, and this was granted. The defendant drove the car to Burnley, as he had always intended, and did not return the car until the following day. The Court of Appeal allowed his appeal against conviction under s12, holding that no offence was committed where a defendant obtained consent by deception. This seemingly odd decision is explained by reference to the court's reluctance to create an offence of obtaining property by deception without intention to permanently deprive the owner. It was felt that to do so would both unnecessarily complicate the offence, and to go against the wishes of the legislature. Secondly, in *Whittaker* v *Campbell* [1983] 3 WLR 676, the Divisional Court developed this view further by holding that provided the owner had given de facto consent to the taking of his vehicle, it mattered not that the consent was obtained by deception or even fraud. The defendant in this case had hired a vehicle after producing another man's driving licence to the owner. In allowing the appeal against conviction under s12, Robert Goff LJ contended that there could be no liability, even where the defendant's deception induces the owner to make a 'fundamental mistake', for example as to identity. Again the underlying reasoning is the reluctance to create an offence of obtaining property by deception in the absence of any intention to permanently deprive the owner.

A conclusion can thus be reached, that where a defendant simply takes a vehicle without asking for permission, or has permission to use it in a particular way and having done so he decides, without seeking further permission, to make some different use of the vehicle, he may well incur liability under s12. Where, on the other hand, the defendant deliberately exercises some fraud or deception from the outset and obtains some de facto consent from the owner, he does not incur liability because he does have some 'consent' – despite the fact that many might regard the latter behaviour as more dishonest.

Mens rea

The defendant must know that the owner does not consent to the taking, or know that the conveyance has been taken without the owner's authority. The owner, for these purposes, being defined by s12(7)(b):

> ' "Owner" in relation to a conveyance which is the subject of a hiring agreement or hire-purchase agreement, means the person in possession of the conveyance under that agreement.'

Section 12(6) provides further in relation to mens rea:

> 'A person does not commit an offence under this section by anything done in the belief that he has lawful authority to do it or that he would have the owner's consent if the owner knew of his doing it and the circumstances of it.'

In relation to this latter provision, the Court of Appeal held in *R* v *Clotworthy* [1981] Crim LR 501, that the test to be applied was subjective. What was vital was that the defendant believed he had lawful authority, or would have had the consent of the owner, not that he actually had such authority or would have had such consent. The more unreasonable the defendant's belief, the less likely the jury are to accept his evidence. It would appear that a drunken mistake by a defendant that the car he is driving is his own will not provide the basis for a defence under s12(6): see *R* v *Gannon* (1988) 87 Cr App R 254.

Aggravated vehicle taking

The Aggravated Vehicle Taking Act 1992 was Parliament's response to the problem of cars being taken without the consent of the owner, and used to cause serious injury or damage to property. The offence builds upon the elements of s12 of the Theft Act 1968, by introducing a new s12A.

Under the aggravated offence, a person will incur liability if he commits the basic offence under s12 and it is proved, at any time after the vehicle was unlawfully taken and before it was recovered, the vehicle was driven dangerously in a public place, damage was caused to the vehicle, or due to such driving accidental injury occurred to any person or harm was caused to any property other than the vehicle. Hence in *Dawes* v *DPP* [1994] Crim LR 604, the appellant was convicted of the aggravated offence where he had unknowingly taken a vehicle adapted by police to trap 'joyriders', the vehicle having been fitted with devices that caused the engine to cut out after it had been driven 30 yards and activated the central locking, thus trapping the appellant within. He caused damage whilst trying to break out of the car. The court held that his detention within the car had not been unlawful, thus he had not been entitled to use force in order to free himself. Where D causes accidental injury to another he will be guilty of the offence regardless of whether his driving was at fault or not: see *R* v *Marsh* [1997] Crim LR 205 which confirms that the effect of s12A(2)(b) is to introduce a form of strict liability, in the sense that the 'causing' of the accident does not require proof of any fault on D's part. Provided the 'but for' test is satisfied the offence is made out – even if the evidence is that the victim deliberately runs out and throws herself in front of D's car. Presumably if D suffers some form of blackout prior to the accident he can contend that he was not 'driving': see Chapter 2, section 2.4. The Act provides for a maximum penalty of five years' imprisonment following conviction.

A defendant can escape liability, the burden of proof being upon him, by establishing either that the dangerous driving, accident or harm was caused prior to the unlawful taking under s12, or that he was neither in, nor in the vicinity of, the vehicle when these events occurred.

It should be borne in mind that any defendant causing damage to property, or injury to others could, in any event, be charged under the Criminal Damage Act 1971, or with a range of common law and statutory assaults, as appropriate.

Dishonestly abstracting electricity

The offence of abstracting electricity is created by s13 of the Theft Act 1968 which states:

> 'A person who dishonestly uses without due authority, or dishonestly causes to be wasted or diverted, any electricity shall on conviction on indictment be liable to imprisonment for a term not exceeding five years.'

Such activity cannot be brought within the scope of theft because electricity is not property within the definition provided by s4 of the 1968 Act: see *Low* v *Blease* (1975) 119 Sol Jo 695. It would appear that the electricity can come from a mains supply or from a battery. Dishonest use of a private telephone line could arguably be within the scope of the offence under s13, as could the insertion of foreign coins of little value in a washing machine or car wash. Similarly, unauthorised use of a photocopier would involve liability, and possibly a charge of theft of the paper obtained. Following *R* v *McCreadie and Tume* [1992] Crim LR 872, it would appear that the test for abstraction is to ask whether but for the defendants' actions the electricity would have been consumed? If the answer is 'no' the actus reus is made out.

The result is that in the not infrequent case of squatters consuming electricity on a metered supply in a dwelling, the prosecution does not have to provide proof of any tampering with the meter.

The mens rea required would appear to be that the defendant knows he is abstracting electricity, and is dishonest at the time he does this. It is submitted that the meaning of dishonesty here is that provided by the Court of Appeal in *R v Ghosh* [1982] QB 1053. In *R v McCreadie* (above), the Court of Appeal, approving the use of *Ghosh* in the context of this offence, felt that the appellants' defence (that they were intending to pay the bill when it arrived), was undermined by the evidence that they had not notified the electricity company of their occupation, that they were moving out when the police arrived, and that they had not notified the electricity company of their impending departure.

7.9 Making off without payment

Section 3(1) of the Theft Act 1978 creates the offence of making off without payment. It provides:

> 'Subject to subsection (3) below, a person who, knowing that payment on the spot for any goods supplied or service done is required or expected from him, dishonestly makes off without having paid as required or expected and with intent to avoid payment of the amount due shall be guilty of an offence.'

The offence is aimed at the defendant who, for example, drives to a petrol station and fills the tank of his car, intending all the time to pay, but having taken the petrol decides not to pay, and drives off without exercising any deception as to his intentions. He cannot be guilty of theft because his appropriation of the petrol was not dishonest, and when he drives from the petrol station property in the petrol has passed to him. Neither does he obtain the petrol by deception. Clearly, however, he will have committed an offence contrary to s3.

Actus reus

The offence applies equally to goods and services for which payment has not been made. However a restriction is introduced by s3(3) which provides:

> 'Subsection (1) above shall not apply where the supply of the goods or the doing of the service is contrary to law, or where the service done is such that payment is not legally enforceable.'

Hence if D were to run out of a brothel without paying for the sexual intercourse he has just had with a prostitute P he would not incur any liability under s3(1). Similarly where D is under no liability to pay P for a service performed or goods supplied, because P is in breach of contract, no liability under s3(1) can arise. This latter point was reaffirmed by the Divisional Court in *Troughton* v *Metropolitan Police* [1987] Crim LR 138, when the defendant's conviction for making off without paying for a taxi journey was quashed on the basis that payment for the journey was unenforceable under s3(3) because the taxi driver was in breach of a contract of complete obligation, having failed to take the defendant to his required destination.

There must be evidence of D having 'made off'. The phrase suggests a departure at high speed, but obviously this is not necessary for conviction. The most effective departure by one seeking to avoid payment is likely to be one that is quiet and unobtrusive. Although the statute does not make clear exactly where the making off must occur, it should be noted that D must be shown to have made off knowing that payment on the spot is required, thus it will normally arise after a service has been provided (as is made clear by s3(2)) or after goods have been supplied (eg food in a restaurant or petrol at a filling station). In *R v McDavitt* [1981] Crim LR 843, where D ran from his table at a restaurant without having paid for his meal, the court held that for the completed offence there would have to be evidence that D had left the premises altogether. Where, as in *R v McDavitt*, a defendant is apprehended before exiting from the premises, the appropriate charge could be one of attempt.

The issue was considered in *R v Aziz* [1993] Crim LR 708, where the appellant was one of two men who had called a taxi to take them to a nightclub. On arrival at the destination the driver asked for the correct fare, which was £15, but the appellant and his companion contested the amount due, and offered to pay £4. The driver surmised that his passengers were was not going to pay and started to drive them back to the point from which they had been collected, but en route decided to drive them to a police station. The appellant and his companion began to damage the car's fittings, and the driver pulled into a petrol station and asked the attendant to call the police, at which the appellant made off. Upholding his conviction under s3, the Court of Appeal noted that the phrase 'knowing that payment on the spot ... is expected' was a reference to the defendant's state of mind, and not to a specific location. It was sufficient that the requirement to pay had come into existence, and that the defendant was shown to have made off from the place where payment would normally be made. In the case of a taxi journey, the place for payment could be inside the cab, or standing outside the cab. Presumably the requirement to pay did not come into existence until the driver in this case had taken the appellant to his requested destination, see *Troughton* v *Metropolitan Police* (above), but at any time after that, payment could be demanded, hence making off at any time after reaching the destination could form the basis of the offence.

The defendant must have made off 'without having paid as required and expected', an expression that may be somewhat ambiguous now. Failing to make any payment at all would clearly satisfy this requirement, as would the leaving of an inadequate amount, foreign currency, or counterfeit notes. It is submitted that the phrase also encompasses the defendant who pays for goods or services using another person's cheques or credit card, although there may be other more appropriate offences in such cases. More questionable is the situation where the defendant uses his own cheques supported by his cheque guarantee card, or his own credit card knowing he does not have authority to do so because he has reached or already exceeded his overdraft or credit limit. It could be argued on the basis of *MPC* v *Charles* [1976] 1 All ER 659 and *R v Lambie* [1981] 1 All ER 332 that the retailer would not accept the cheque or credit card in payment if he knew that the defendant had no authority to use these items, but s3 is not a deception offence, and given that payment is guaranteed, it is submitted that a defendant who acts in this way does pay as required and expected. The same probably cannot be said of the defendant who draws a cheque on his own account to pay for goods or services, which is not supported by a cheque guarantee card and which he knows will not be honoured when presented for payment. A worthless cheque is not payment as required and expected, and there should be liability under s3; see further *R v Brooks and Brooks* (1982) 76 Cr App R 66.

Mens rea

The defendant must know that payment on the spot for any goods supplied or service done is required or expected from him, and in this respect s3(2) provides that 'payment on the spot' includes payment at the time of collecting goods on which work has been done or in respect of which service has been provided. D will escape liability therefore, if he leaves a restaurant without paying in the honest belief that his companions who remain at the table will pay his share of the bill, or where he believes that the goods or services are provided free of charge, or where he believes that the goods or services are being supplied on credit, and that payment will not be due until some later date: see further *R v Brooks and Brooks* (1982) 76 Cr App R 66. The defendant must be dishonest at the time of his making off; where necessary the test in *R v Ghosh* [1982] QB 1053 is applicable.

The House of Lords, in *R v Allen* [1985] AC 1029, ruled that the requirement in s3(1), that D should be proved to have intended to avoid payment, should be interpreted so as to require proof of an intention to permanently avoid payment. The defendant had stayed at a hotel for nearly a month and left without paying the bill, but contacted the hotel a few days later and explained he was in financial difficulties and would return to the hotel to collect his belongings and leave his passport as security. When he did so he was arrested and charged with an offence contrary to s3(1). The trial judge directed the jury that the intent to avoid payment merely referred to the time when payment should have been made 'on the spot' and the defendant was convicted. Lord Hailsham was content to endorse the reasoning adopted by Boreham J in the court below, to the effect that, if intent to avoid payment meant no more than an intention to delay or defer payment of the amount due, it added little to the other elements. Anyone who knew that payment on the spot was expected or required of him and who dishonestly made off without paying as required or expected must have had at least an intention to delay or defer payment. Thus the conjoined phrase 'and with intent to avoid payment of the amount due' added a further ingredient: an intention to do more than delay or defer, an intention to evade payment altogether. Lord Hailsham was also of the view that if Parliament had intended to create an offence involving intention only to delay payment it would have said so in more explicit terms. Support for the House of

Lords' view is provided by the Criminal Law Revision Committee's Thirteenth Report (*Section 16 of the Theft Act 1968*) (Cmnd 6733 (1977)), which led to the passing of the 1978 Act. Paragraphs 18 states:

> '... there was general support for our suggestion that where the customer knows that he is expected to pay on the spot for goods supplied to him or services done for him it should be an offence for him dishonestly to go away without having paid and intending never to pay.'

Whilst it is encouraging to see the House of Lords construing the ambiguity in the statute in favour of the accused, the ruling does reveal the limited protection that s3 offers to taxi drivers, restauranters and owners of filling stations, as anyone making off without payment, if subsequently apprehended, can claim that they *did* intend to pay at some later date. Liability may well then depend upon the plausibility of the defendant's evidence.

8

Deception and Related Offences

8.1 Section 15

Section 15(1) creates the offence of obtaining property by deception. It provides:

> 'A person who by any deception dishonestly obtains property belonging to another, with the intention of permanently depriving the other of it, shall on conviction on indictment be liable to imprisonment for a term not exceeding ten years.'

Prior to the House of Lords' decision in *R v Gomez* [1993] AC 442, it was possible to identify quite distinct roles for the offences of theft and obtaining property by deception, on the basis that the former required proof of an unauthorised assumption of the owner's rights (as was suggested by Lord Roskill in *R v Morris*), whilst the latter involved the owner consenting to the property being taken, but only because of the defendant's deception. As explained in Chapter 7, following *Gomez* the offence of theft can now cover the vast majority of situations that would previously have only fallen within s15, as there is no need for the prosecution to prove that the defendant's appropriation of the property was without the owner's consent.

'Property belonging to another'

Section 34(1) states that ss4(1) and 5(1) relating to property belonging to another should apply generally for the purposes of the 1968 Act. Property for the purposes of s15(1) has, therefore, a meaning broadly similar to that provided in s4 for the purposes of theft, with some extension as regards land. The requirement that the property should, as against D, be property belonging to another at the time of the obtaining may be more problematic. If D exercises a deception that induces P to part merely with possession of goods, this element of the offence should cause no difficulty. The property remains property belonging to another under s5(1) by virtue of P's remaining proprietary rights and interests in the property. More difficult, perhaps, is the situation where D exercises a deception that induces P to part with both possession and ownership in favour of D. It could be contended in such cases that, at the time of the obtaining, property had passed to D, and had thus ceased to be property belonging to another at the moment. There are a number of reasons, however, why such an argument would be likely to fail. First, s15(2), considered below, makes it clear that D can commit the offence where he obtains, amongst other things, ownership of the property in question. Secondly, the House of Lords in *Lawrence* v *MPC* [1972] AC 626 expressly rejected D's contention that because he had been made the owner of the money by P he could not be appropriating property belonging to another. Viscount Dilhorne effectively ruled that D could appropriate or obtain property *whilst* becoming the owner of it. Thirdly, it could be contended that if D has exercised a deception in order to obtain ownership, P retains some proprietary right in respect of the property (see s5(1)), because the contract, if there is one, is voidable. Lastly, it could be contended that D's deception renders any contract void, thus making it impossible for ownership to pass to D, in which case the property would remain property belonging to another.

Note that since s5(1) applies to s15, a situation analogous to that in *R* v *Turner (No 2)* [1971] 2 All ER 441 could arise if D were to obtain his own property by deception from P, who has lawful possession of it.

Loopholes did start to appear, however, in respect of the electronic transfer of funds and payments by cheque induced by deception. In *R* v *Preddy; R v Slade* [1996] 3 WLR 255 the appellants were charged with obtaining property by deception on the basis that they had made over 40 applications to building societies for mortgage advances in order to purchase properties. The applications contained deliberate falsehoods intended to deceive the lenders into granting the applications. The same solicitor acted for both the lenders and the appellants and the transfer of funds was executed electronically via 'CHAPS' (Clearing House Automated Payments System). Allowing the appeals, Lord Goff explained that, whilst the sums standing to the credit of the lending institutions in their bank accounts were undoubtedly property within s4 of the 1968 Act, being choses in action (debts owed by the bank where the accounts were maintained), the real question was whether they represented property belonging to another at the time the appellants' accounts were credited. The difficulty for the prosecution lay in the fact that when the lending institution's account was debited, its chose in action was extinguished (or reduced *pro tanto*). When the appellants' accounts were credited, a new chose in action, belonging to the defendant, was created. The same reasoning applied where funds obtained by deception were transferred by cheque. The chose in action created when a cheque was drawn up belonged to the payee. It had never existed as property belonging to another as against the payee; thus a charge under s15 could not succeed. Given its ruling in this case, the House of Lords confirmed that *R* v *Danger* (1857) 7 Cox CC 303 was correctly decided, and that *R* v *Duru* [1974] 1 WLR 2 and *R* v *Mitchell* [1993] Crim LR 788 were no longer to be followed.

It could be argued that, at common law, where the electronic transfer of funds is procured as a result of D's fraud, the chose in action that it is created (ie the balance created in favour of D in his account) can still be regarded as property belonging to P on the basis that equity will impose a constructive trust on D: see *R* v *Governor of Brixton Prison, ex parte Levin* [1996] 4 All ER 350 and comments of Lord Browne-Wilkinson in *Westdeutsche Landesbank Girozentrale* v *Islington London Borough Council* [1996] 2 All ER 961 at 996. For an illustration of similar problems in relation to bills of exchange: see *R* v *Caresana* [1996] Crim LR 667. Where a cheque is obtained by deception, the actual piece of paper is normally property belonging to another as against D (although this was not the case in *Danger*), hence a conviction under s15 is technically possible on this basis: see further J C Smith 'Obtaining Cheques by Deception or Theft' [1997] Crim LR 396. In *R* v *Graham and Others* [1997] Crim LR 340 the Court of Appeal, whilst allowing the appeals of a number of defendants who had been convicted of *Preddy*-type frauds prior to the House of Lords' ruling in that case, held that where D had obtained cheques by deception, a conviction for procuring the execution of a valuable security contrary to s20(2) of the Theft Act 1968 could be substituted: considered further at section 8.4 below.

Parliament has now acted to shore up the law in this area with the enactment of the Theft (Amendment) Act 1996. Section 1(1) of this creates a new offence of obtaining a money transfer by deception. It does so by adding a s15A to the 1968 Act that provides:

'(1) A person is guilty of an offence if by any deception he dishonestly obtains a money transfer for himself or another.
(2) A money transfer occurs when –
a) a debit is made to one account,
b) a credit is made to another, and
c) the credit results from the debit or the debit results from the credit.
(3) References to a credit and to a debit are to a credit of an amount of money and to a debit of an amount of money.
(4) It is immaterial (in particular) –
a) whether the amount credited is the same as the amount debited;
b) whether the money transfer is effected on presentment of a cheque or by another method;
c) whether any delay occurs in the process by which the money transfer is effected;
d) whether any intermediate credits or debits are made in the course of the money transfer;
e) whether either of the accounts is overdrawn before or after the money transfer is effected.'

Deception has the same meaning as in s15 of the 1968 Act. The offence carries a maximum penalty of imprisonment for a term not exceeding ten years.

The 1996 Act further creates a new offence of dishonestly retaining a wrongful credit by inserting a new s24A in the 1968 Act, and by s4(1) makes it clear that s1(1) of the Theft Act 1978 does encompass the obtaining of a loan where it is made on the understanding that payment (whether by way of interest or otherwise) will be or has been made in respect of the loan.

'Obtains'

Subsection 15(2) provides:

> 'For the purposes of this section a person is to be treated as obtaining property if he obtains ownership, possession or control of it and "obtains" includes obtaining for another or enabling another to obtain or to retain.'

It is clear from the above that the offence is committed where D induces P to loan property, make a gift of it, or sell it to D, provided that D has the necessary mens rea at the time. Further, it would be an offence for D to deceive P into giving property to a third party, or allowing a third party to retain such property. It is submitted that were D to deceive P into permitting D to retain property of which D already had possession or control, the appropriate charge would be one of theft, by virtue of s3(1). Where D already has ownership (albeit a voidable title) and he deceives P into allowing him to retain it, the situation is less clear. Theft may be inappropriate on the basis that the property no longer belongs to another, unless it can be argued that P retains an equitable interest within s5(1). A charge under s15 may be impossible on the basis that subs(2) does not contemplate such a situation.

Jurisdictional problems can arise where a deception is exercised in one country in order to obtain property in another. Where D is abroad and he communicates his deception to persons within the jurisdiction of the English courts, an offence, or an attempt, will have been committed within the jurisdiction. See *R* v *Baxter* [1972] QB 1; *DPP* v *Stonehouse* [1978] AC 55. The English courts will also normally have jurisdiction where D in England communicates a deception to P who is abroad, and as a result receives property belonging to P in England; see *R* v *Tirado* (1974) 59 Cr App R 80, which the Court of Appeal stated was to be preferred to *R* v *Harden* [1963] 1 QB 8.

Given the above, the Court of Appeal decision in *R* v *Thompson* [1984] 1 WLR 962 seems rather difficult to support. The defendant, whilst employed as a computer operator at a bank in Kuwait, had instructed the bank's computer to transfer amounts from customers' accounts to a savings account he had opened for himself at another Kuwaiti bank. On his return to England, the defendant requested that the balance of his savings account should be transferred by telex to his accounts in England. The Court of Appeal, applying the proviso to s2(1) Criminal Appeal Act 1968, upheld the defendant's conviction under s15, rejecting his contention that if there had been an obtaining it occurred in Kuwait. The decision has been criticised on the basis that when the money was transferred in Kuwait from the defendant's employer to his own account, he obtained a chose in action, but not by deception as machines cannot be deceived. Further, when the request was made from England, to transfer the money from Kuwait, the defendant may have been exercising a deception, but what he was obtaining was a chose in action (bank balance) that belonged to himself. The Court of Appeal insisted, however, that a debt brought about by fraud could not be regarded as a chose in action, a finding which raises the broader question as to what the defendant did obtain.

'By deception ...'

Deception is in part defined by s15(4) which provides:

> 'For purposes of this section "deception" means any deception (whether deliberate or reckless) by words or conduct as to fact or as to law, including a deception as to the present intentions of the person using the deception or any other person.'

Where the deception is in the form of words, the statement must obviously be untrue, and the burden of proving this rests upon the prosecution. In some instances the truthfulness or otherwise of a statement can only be established by reference to facts known to the defendant, for example, the defendant's statement to prospective purchasers that certain goods are 'the cheapest in town'. In such a case the onus is on the defendants to prove something within their personal knowledge: see *R* v *Mandry and Wooste*r [1973] 3 All ER 996.

A statement alleged to constitute a deception must be one of fact or law, whether this is the case is a matter to be determined by the jury: see *R* v *Banaster* [1979] RTR 113. On this basis, it would appear that a statement of opinion by the defendant cannot constitute a deception, even though it may result in a victim parting with his property at an undervalue. Distinguishing between a statement of fact and one of opinion can clearly cause difficulty. The decision of Nottingham Crown Court in *R* v *King* [1979] Crim LR 122 suggests that a defendant who knows a representation, such as the odometer reading on a motor car, to be untrue, but who states that it 'may be incorrect' implies that as far as he knows it is correct, and thus commits a deception. The Court of Appeal's decision in *R* v *Silverman* [1987] Crim LR 574 suggests that a relevant factor may be the nature of the relationship existing between the parties. Clearly if a defendant presenting a grossly excessive quotation accompanies it with an assertion to the effect that he will only be making a modest profit, he will be perpetrating a misrepresentation of fact. If, as in *Silverman*'s case, a relationship of mutual trust had been built up over a long period of time, the court may conclude that the appellant's silence as to the excessive nature of the charges comprises part of the deception inducing payment.

It is submitted that an expression of opinion which is not genuinely held should be regarded as a misrepresentation of the present intentions of the persons expressing the opinion: see further *R* v *Jeff and Bassett* (1966) 51 Cr App R 28.

There is no clear authority under the 1968 Act as to whether silence, or as J C

Smith puts it, 'an omission to undeceive', can constitute deception. As a matter of civil law, silence can amount to a misrepresentation.

In any event, the conduct accompanying silence can amount to a deception. In so providing, s15(4) affirms much older decisions such as that in *R v Barnard* (1837) 7 C & P 784, where the defendant obtained goods on credit by false pretences (deception) in that he dressed up as an undergraduate in a fellow-commoner's cap and gown.

The significance of conduct as a deception rests with what the conduct implies. In *DPP v Ray* [1974] AC 370, the defendant had ordered a meal in a restaurant and had consumed it with an honest state of mind. He then discovered his inability to pay for the meal and remained silent as to this change in circumstances. The defendant waited until the dining area was clear of waiters before running out. The House of Lords held that the defendant had exercised a deception by remaining seated in the restaurant having decided not to pay. His remaining in this position created the implied and continuing representation that he was an honest customer who intended to pay the bill, thus inducing the waiters to leave the dining area unattended, giving him the opportunity to run off without paying. What can be implied from any given conduct clearly depends upon the facts of each case. In *R v Williams* [1980] Crim LR 589, where the defendant had been tendering obsolete Yugoslavian dinar notes at a bureau de change and obtaining sterling in exchange, the Court of Appeal held that implicit in the tendering of the notes was the representation that it was valid currency having an equivalent sterling value.

If a defendant makes a statement of fact or law, which he believes to be untrue, but which unknown to him is truthful, he could, despite the fact that there is in reality no deception, be convicted of attempting to obtain property by deception, on the basis that he has taken steps that he believes to be more than merely preparatory to obtaining property by deception; see s1(1) Criminal Attempts Act 1981, as interpreted in *R v Shivpuri* [1986] 2 WLR 988. In this respect it is submitted that the defendant in cases such as *R v Deller* (1952) 36 Cr App R 184, (wherein it was held that the defendant could not be guilty of obtaining by false pretences because the car he was selling was, unknown to him, free from encumbrances), would now be guilty of an attempt; but see further *R v Wheeler* (1990) 92 Cr App Rep 279.

The deception must be operative

The deception must cause the obtaining of property, hence the deception must precede the obtaining of property. In *R v Collis-Smith* [1971] Crim LR 716, D, who had put petrol into his car, and then falsely told the attendant that his employer would be paying for the petrol, was successful in his appeal against conviction under s15(1) on the basis that his deception did not arise until after the property in the petrol had passed to him; on virtually identical facts see also *R v Coady* [1996] Crim LR 518. For a conviction under s15 the prosecution needed to show:

1. that by driving onto the forecourt and selecting a pump D was, impliedly,

asserting that he was honest and had valid means to pay (see *DPP* v *Ray* [1974] AC 370);

2. that this representation operated on the mind of the cashier and induced him to permit the petrol to flow from the pump; and

3. that D knew or was reckless as to the impression created by his behaviour and its consequences.

Alternative charges that might be pursued include theft – the fact that the cashier consents to the appellant receiving the petrol is irrelevant (see *R* v *Gomez* [1993] AC 442); making off without payment (see s3 Theft Act 1978) on the basis that D has not paid as required and expected; or, under s2(1)(b) of the 1978 Act, inducing a creditor to wait for or forgo payment with intent to make permanent default.

Assuming that the deception does arise prior to the obtaining of the property, the question of causation necessitates the application of a 'but for' test. But for the deception would D have obtained the property? If the answer is 'no' the deception is operative, if 'yes' then the deception is not operative because D would have obtained the property anyway. Hence in *R* v *Talbot* [1995] Crim LR 396, D's conviction under s15 was upheld where she gave false information in order to obtain housing benefit, even though she was, in any event, entitled to make the claim. The court adopted the view that the deception was nevertheless operative, given that the local authority officers had given evidence to the effect that they would not have paid the appellant housing benefit if they had known the truth, as she was deliberately making false statements on her application forms. Even where a deception is found not to be operative, the defendant might nevertheless be guilty of an attempt provided that the required mens rea is present.

As a matter of law a machine cannot be deceived; hence a deception can only be operative where it operates on a human mind: see *Davies* v *Flackett* (1972) 116 SJ 526. Where D places a worthless token in a machine and extracts a bar of chocolate he cannot therefore be charged under s15, but can be charged with theft: see further *R* v *Hands* (1887) 16 Cox CC 188 (larceny where D used a brass disc to obtain cigarettes from a machine) and *R* v *Goodwin* [1996] Crim LR 262, where the Court of Appeal upheld D's conviction for going equipped to steal where he used foreign coins in gaming machines. More difficult is the situation where D uses a worthless token to operate a machine that provides a service, such as a car wash, a weighing machine or a washing machine. He cannot be charged with obtaining services by deception because of the rule that deception must operate on a human mind. He cannot be charged with theft because he does not obtain any property. The only possible charge in such cases would appear to be one of dishonestly abstracting electricity contrary to s13 of the 1968 Act.

The rule that there must be evidence of the deception operating on the mind of a natural person can also cause technical difficulties where D is alleged to have obtained property by deception from a company. On the basis of *R* v *Rozeik* [1996] 1 WLR 159 (a case involving an allegation that cheques were obtained by deception from loan companies), the prosecution must show that an employee or officer whose state of mind stands for that of the company (eg a manager with authority to sign cheques) has been deceived. Thus, if an authorised company officer is aware of D's fraudulent request for the cheque, his knowledge of the fraud is attributed to the company, and the company cannot, therefore, be regarded as having been deceived. Although a company officer who is aware of D's fraudulent behaviour, but who nevertheless proceeds to issue a cheque payable to D, will almost invariably be a party to the fraud being perpetrated by D, a safer course for the prosecution on such facts is to bring a charge of conspiracy to defraud.

In some cases, however, the facts themselves reveal that the deception can have been the only reason for the defendant being given the property; hence in *Etim* v *Hatfield* [1975] Crim LR 234, where the defendant had made a false statement to a Post Office clerk in order to obtain supplementary benefit, the court held that it was a necessary inference from the facts that the deception induced the payment, there being no other conceivable reason. Ultimately the question of whether the deception has been operative is one of fact for the jury: see *R* v *King and Stockwell* [1987] Crim LR 398.

In *R* v *Hamilton* [1990] Crim LR 806, the Court of Appeal considered the case of an appellant who had forged the authorising signature on a number of stolen company cheques, paid them into a building society account, and withdrawn cash by signing withdrawal slips. He was convicted of, inter alia, obtaining or attempting to obtain property by deception, on the basis that he had falsely represented that the balance in the building society account was genuine and that he was entitled to withdraw the sums therefrom. On appeal, counsel for the appellant contended that there had been no representation, and therefore no false representation, ie deception, since the completion of a withdrawal slip effectively involved the appellant in saying nothing more than 'give me the money', and that there had been no representations as to the source of funds credited to the account; neither was there any representation as to his entitlement to the sum claimed. In dismissing his appeal, the court held that, given that the appellant had dishonestly induced the bank to make the credit entries in his favour by using the stolen cheques, the primary question was as to what representations, if any, should be inferred from his act of presenting the withdrawal slip. It rejected the submission that presentation of the withdrawal slip meant no more than 'give me the money'. The money in the account was identified by means of the number on the slip, and the appellant's presentation of it was a representation to the bank that he was the person entitled to withdraw funds from the account. A jury could infer from his conduct that he was representing that he was the person to whom the bank was indebted in respect of the account, and by demanding withdrawal of a stated sum he necessarily represented that the bank owed him that amount. In arriving at this conclusion the court relied upon passages from *Joachimson* v *Swiss Bank Corp* [1921] 3 KB 110 at p127, to the effect that the relationship between a bank and its customers, in regard to deposit and current accounts, was that of debtor and creditor, with a condition that the debt only became payable by the bank upon a proper demand being made at the branch where the amount was held. The appellant had no right to demand payment of any money from the account. When the building society had received payment in respect of the cheques from the drawer's bank, it had done so under a mistake of fact, on discovery of which the money became repayable to the paying bank. The court further expressed its view that although the authorities dealing with representations made by those drawing cheques could be distinguished, because of the involvement of a third party, the present situation was analogous to that of an individual seeking to withdraw cash from his own account by means of a cheque payable to 'self' or cash.

The decision raises a number of interesting questions. Suppose that D steals £1,000 and places it in a deposit account at a bank. Does he commit an offence of deception when he requests the bank to deliver up the money? Can this example be distinguished from the above case? How would the situation differ, if at all, if D forged £1,000 in £10 notes and paid them into a deposit account? What offence would he commit in requesting the withdrawal of an equivalent sum? Note that the appellant had also sought to challenge his conviction on two further grounds. First, the contention that the bank clerk had not been induced to hand over money in response to the withdrawal slip, but by checking D's balance on a VDU screen. The court held that a representation only has to be a cause of the obtaining, not the sole cause, and that the presentation of the slip at least caused the clerk to check the screen. Secondly, the appellant pointed to the fact that the clerk had not been called to give evidence to the effect that he would not have paid out if he had known the true situation. In rejecting this contention it would appear that the court regarded it as an irresistible inference, following *R* v *Lambie* (considered below), that the clerk would not have paid out funds had he known the truth.

Deception, cheques and credit cards

If a defendant uses his own cheque book and cheque card to buy goods costing less than £50, having been informed by his bank that he must not write any cheques because he is overdrawn, he will be guilty of deception. He has represented that he has authority to write cheques when in fact he does not. The difficulty lies in establishing that this deception induces the retailer to part with the goods, because he knows (provided the conditions of use are met) that he will be reimbursed by the defendant's bank in accordance with the bank guarantee inscribed on the cheque card. Reimbursement by the bank is in no way dependent on there being any funds in the defendant's account. The defendant may thus argue that it is not his deception that induces the retailer to accept the cheque in return for goods, but the guarantee offered by the bank. The same problem arises in respect of defendants charged with 'going equipped to cheat': see *R* v *Rashid* [1977] 2 All ER 237 and *R* v *Doukas* [1978] 1 All ER 1061.

The problem was addressed by the House of Lords in *Metropolitan Police Commissioner* v *Charles* [1977] AC 177. The appellant had drawn cheques, supported by his cheque guarantee card, on his current account for amounts in excess of his agreed overdraft. The cheques had been exchanged for gaming chips in a casino. He was convicted on a number of counts alleging that he had obtained a pecuniary advantage (being allowed to borrow by way of overdraft) by deception, contrary to s16(1) of the Theft Act 1968, and appealed unsuccessfully to the House of Lords. Lord Edmund-Davies identified the representations made by the drawer of a cheque, using a cheque guarantee card as follows:

> 'By drawing the cheque the accused represented that it would be met, and by producing the card so that the number thereon could be endorsed on the cheque he in effect represented, "I am authorised by the bank to show this to you and so create a direct contractual relationship between the bank and you that they will honour this cheque." The production of the card was the badge of the accused's ostensible authority to make such a representation on the bank's behalf.'

Notwithstanding that the appellant's representations were false, as he had no such authority, it was contended that his deception was not operative, as the manager of the casino would have accepted the cheques in any event, because payment by the bank was guaranteed through use of the card.

Despite the casino manager's assertions that where a cheque guarantee card was used no inquiries were made as to the client's credit-worthiness, and that the relationship between the client and his bank was 'irrelevant', Lord Edmund-Davies sought to stress that:

> '... [the manager] made clear that the accused's cheques were accepted *only* because he produced a cheque card, and he repeatedly stressed that, had he been aware that the accused was using his cheque book and cheque card "in a way in which he was not allowed or entitled to use [them]" no cheque would have been accepted. The evidence of that witness, taken as a whole, points irresistibly to the conclusions (a) that by this dishonest conduct the accused deceived [the manager] in the manner averred in the particulars of the charges and (b) that [the manager] was thereby induced to accept the cheques because of his belief that the representations as to both cheque and card were true.'

The deception, therefore, became operative because the House of Lords concluded that the casino would not have accepted the cheques supported by the cheque card had the truth been known. The problem, of course, is that on the facts there was no evidence that the casino manager was aware of the lack of authority. The decision therefore rests upon an assumption as to how the payee would have responded. The decision is also questionable in the sense that the relationship between the defendant and his bank is entirely private. Were a retailer to enquire of a customer whether or not he had permission to use his cheque card, the customer could quite understandably refuse to answer. It is submitted that the inference drawn in *Charles* is a necessary one in order to make the section effective.

The corresponding difficulty in relation to credit cards arose in *R* v *Lambie* [1981] Crim LR 712. The appellant used her own credit card to buy goods totalling less than £50, knowing she was in excess of her spending limit. Despite the shop assistant's evidence that she had made no assumptions whatsoever as regards the appellant's authority to use the card, the appellant's conviction under s16(1) (the charges were based on events taking place before the 1978 Act came into force) was upheld by the House of Lords on the basis that if the shop assistant had known the truth she would not have accepted the credit card in payment, hence the use of the card was an operative deception. Again the problem here is that the shop assistant did not know of the lack of authority, so the House of Lords had to resort to assumptions as to how she would have acted in order to make the deception operative. The defendant in such a case could, of course, call the retailer or shop assistant to give evidence that he was prepared to accept the credit card in full knowledge of the D's lack of authority, but the retailer is unlikely to want to run the risk of becoming an accomplice to the D's fraud on the credit card company.

It is clear from *Charles* that a defendant who uses a cheque book and a cheque card without authority commits an offence under s16, by obtaining a pecuniary advantage (being allowed to borrow by way of overdraft) by deception. It matters not that the deception is exercised on the retailer, and the pecuniary advantage obtained from the bank. As Lawton LJ observed in *R* v *Kovacks* [1974] 1 WLR 370 at p373:

> 'Section 16(1) does not provide either expressly or by implication that the person deceived must suffer any loss arising from the deception. What does have to be proved is that the accused by deception obtained for himself or another a pecuniary advantage. What there must be is a causal connection between the deception used and the pecuniary advantage obtained.'

What other offences might such a defendant commit? Prima facie he also obtains property by deception from the retailer, or possibly services contrary to s1(1) of the 1978 Act, yet the defendant might well contend that, since the cheque was bound to be honoured by the bank, he was not dishonest vis-à-vis the retailer, as he knew he would not suffer any financial loss. In reality, the retailer is unlikely to be interested in pressing a charge under s15, if indeed he ever learns of the defendant's criminality.

Lambie was charged with an offence contrary to s16 of the 1968 Act which has since been abolished, thus raising the question as to which offence would now be appropriate should the circumstances recur. It seems inappropriate to describe a credit card account as an overdraft, thus rendering a charge under the remaining sections of s16 impossible. Perhaps the answer is to charge the defendant with obtaining the services of the credit card company by deception, but it would have to be established that the service was one in respect of which payment was required. One remaining possibility is that of charging the defendant with dishonestly, by deception, securing the remission of a liability, contrary to s2(1)(a) of the 1978 Act, but again the problem of dishonesty may arise as the defendant is using his or her own credit card.

Remoteness

There will be no liability under s15(1) where the deception is too remote from the obtaining of property. If D gives false details that enable him to enter a race which he then wins, as a result of which he is awarded a prize, he will not be guilty of obtaining the prize by deception. The prize is obtained as a result of winning the race, not the deception by which he gained entry to it: see *R* v *Button* [1900] 2 QB 597. Similarly where D deceives P into allowing him to place bets on horses which subsequently win. D receives the winnings because the horses he backed have won, not because of his deception: see *R* v *Clucas* [1949] 2 KB 226. Whilst s16 of the 1968 Act (see below) does cover some of these problems, difficulties can arise in cases such as *R* v *Miller* [1992] Crim LR 744, where the appellant, having posed as an authorised taxi driver, charged passengers ten times the normal rate for a journey from airports to central London. Despite the Court of Appeal's assertion that the convictions for obtaining the fares by deception could stand as long as the various deceptions alleged in the indictment could be said to be the cause of the money being handed over, there remained the point that the passenger paying the money at the end of the journey may have done so knowing that he was being swindled. Following the House of Lords' decision in *R* v *Gomez*, it might be the case that a charge of theft would be more appropriate in circumstances such as these.

Mens rea

The mens rea required for s15 involves proof of dishonesty and deception.

Deception

Section 15(4) states that the defendant must intend to deceive or be reckless as to whether he deceives. In *R* v *Staines* (1974) 60 Cr App R 160 the Court of Appeal accepted that reckless in this context involved more than simple carelessness, or negligence on the part of the defendant, and amounted to indifference as to whether a statement was true or false. It is submitted that the *Cunningham* test for recklessness should continue to be used, that is, a defendant should only be found to have been reckless where he is aware of the risk that he may deceive another, but goes on to take that risk. In any event, it seems unlikely that a defendant could have failed to realise that there was an obvious risk that he might be deceiving another and yet at the same time be dishonest. This view is supported by *Large* v *Mainprize* [1989] Crim LR 213. Simply because the evidence reveals an intentional or reckless deception does not mean that the jury would therefore be entitled to assume dishonesty. The two matters must be assessed independently: see *R* v *Feeny* (1992) 94 Cr App R 1, and the commentary on *R* v *Goldman* [1997] Crim LR 894, at p895.

Dishonesty

Unlikely dishonesty in theft, to which s2(1) of the 1968 Act applies, there is no negative definition of dishonesty applicable to deception offences. In cases of doubt the Court of Appeal's decision in *R* v *Ghosh* [1982] 1 QB 1053 should be referred to, although a *Ghosh*-type direction is not necessary in every case. In *R* v *Price* (1990) 90 Cr App R 409, the appellant's defence to a number of deception charges was that he believed himself to be the beneficiary of a trust fund, and shortly expected to receive £100,000. In directing the jury as to dishonesty the trial judge had not referred to the direction set out in *Ghosh*, but had invited the jury to draw an analogy between the appellant and Billy Bunter, on the basis that the latter had always been depicted as persuading others to lend him money on the strength of a postal order which was always going to arrive but which never materialised. Dismissing the appeal, the court expressed the view that in cases such as the present the *Ghosh* direction was unnecessary, as there was no evidence that the appellant believed that what he was alleged to have done was in accordance with the ordinary person's idea of honesty. The judge's references to the Billy Bunter stories were not unfair given the hopelessness of the defence case. Where it is necessary to resort to *Ghosh* a trial judge would be wise to use the ipsissima verba of Lord Lane CJ in *Ghosh*, rather than resorting to a paraphrase of the model direction: see *R* v *Vosper* (1990) The Times 26 February: *R* v *Melwani* [1989] Crim LR 565; *R* v *O'Connell* (1992) 94 Cr App R 39; and *R* v *Lightfoot* (1993) 97 Cr App R 24.

Intention to permanently deprive.

Section 15(3) of the 1968 Act provides:

> 'Section 6 above shall apply for purposes of this section, with the necessary adaptation of the reference to appropriating, as it applies for purposes of section 1.'

Hence a defendant charged under s15 may be deemed to have intention to permanently deprive in those situations outlined in Chapter 7, section 7.7.

8.2 Section 16

Section 16(1) creates the offence of obtaining a pecuniary advantage by deception; as amended it provides:

> 'A person who by any deception dishonestly obtains for himself or another any pecuniary advantage shall on conviction on indictment be liable to imprisonment for a term not exceeding five years.'

Actus reus

As with s15, the obtaining (in this case of a pecuniary advantage) must be as a result of a deception exercised by the defendant. Section 16(3) provides that for the purposes of s16 'deception' should have the same meaning as in s15. See generally, therefore, the preceding section.

Pecuniary advantage has a very precise meaning within s16. It would appear to cover the following:

1. Being allowed to borrow by way of overdraft: see *MPC* v *Charles* (above). Where D pays for goods or services by way of a cheque drawn on his own account having been instructed by his bank not to do so, he will not commit an offence under s16 unless the cheque is supported by his cheque guarantee card and the bank, as a result, has to debit the amount of the cheque from D's account, thus increasing his overdraft; see *R* v *Bevan* [1987] Crim LR 129. If no cheque guarantee card is used, the bank will not increase D's overdraft because it will refuse to honour his cheque. A charge of attempt may be sustainable on such facts.

2. Taking out a policy of insurance or annuity contract, or obtaining an improvement of the terms on which the defendant is allowed to do so. Liability would arise if D were to lie about his age or health to P, an insurance company. Should D receive a payment under any subsequent policy, he could not be charged under s15 because the deception is too remote from his obtaining of property, hence the existence of this form of liability under s16.

3. Being given an opportunity to earn remuneration or greater remuneration in an office or employment. Again this is a situation that would fall outside s15. If D lies about his qualifications, and secures a job as a result, the money he receives is paid because of the work he does, not because of the lies he has told; the deception is too remote from the obtaining of property. The job is, therefore, the pecuniary advantage obtained by deception. There has been some debate as to whether this provision applied to those obtaining remunerative work as independent contractors. It was thought, for example, that if D falsely claimed to be a tree surgeon and was paid to remove P's tree, he did not obtain an 'office or employment' by deception: see further the prosecution's reliance on s15 in *R* v *King and Stockwell* [1987] Crim LR 398. Exactly what Parliament did intend in enacting this aspect of s16 may be unclear, as it was not included in the original draft Bill, but added as the legislation progressed through Parliament. Hence the matter is not adverted to in the Criminal Law Revision Committee's Report that led to the enactment of the 1968 Act.

Some clarification is provided, however, by the Court of Appeal's decision in *R* v *Callender* [1992] 3 All ER 51. The appellant agreed to prepare accounts for a number of small businessmen, having falsely held himself out as being professionally qualified to do so. In dismissing his appeal against conviction under s16, Wright J, on behalf of the Court of Appeal, observed:

'We have come to the clear conclusion that Parliament, in adopting the phrase "office or employment", intended section 16(1) of the Act of 1968 to have a wider impact than one confined to the narrow limits of a contract of service. A small indication is

> the use of the word "remuneration", which is a wide term, and the absence of any
> reference to salary or wages ... It seems to us that it is a perfectly proper use of
> ordinary language and as such to be readily understood by ordinary literate men and
> women to say of a person in this appellant's position that his services as an accountant
> were "employed" by his customers, and that this state of affairs is properly to be
> described by the word "employment".'

The court seems to have been motivated by a desire not to create a gap in the
law which would permit dishonest people, by arranging their affairs so that they
could come within the definition of 'self-employed', to escape conviction and
punishment for their deceitful conduct.

4. Being given the opportunity to win money by betting. This brings within s16
   situations such as that in *R* v *Clucas* [1949] 2 KB 226.

Mens rea

Section 16 requires that the defendant should intend to deceive or be reckless as to
whether he deceives another. Note that the deception can be exercised on X,
although the pecuniary advantage is obtained from P. (See *Charles* and *Lambie*
above). The defendant must also be dishonest at the time of obtaining the pecuniary
advantage, as discussed in the preceding section.

8.3 Section 17

Section 17(1), which creates the offence of false accounting, provides:

> 'Where a person dishonestly, with a view to gain for himself or another or with intent to
> cause loss to another –
> a) destroys, defaces, conceals or falsifies any account or any record or document made or
> required for any accounting purpose; or
> b) in furnishing information for any purpose produces or makes use of any account, or
> any such record or document as aforesaid, which to his knowledge is or may be
> misleading, false or deceptive in a material particular;
> he shall, on conviction on indictment, be liable to imprisonment for a term not exceeding
> seven years.'

Actus reus

A document made or required for any accounting purpose is interpreted as one
required for financial accounting. Accounting need not be the sole purpose for
which the document is produced provided it is one of the purposes. Section 17(2)
provides further:

> 'For purposes of this section a person who makes or concurs in making in an account or
> other document an entry which is or may be misleading, false or deceptive in a material
> particular, or who omits or concurs in omitting a material particular from an account or
> other document, is to be treated as falsifying the account or document.'

In *Edwards* v *Toombs* [1983] Crim LR 43 it was held that a turnstile operator, who allowed two persons into a stadium whilst only recording the entry of one, had falsified a record for the purposes of the offence. Similarly, it is submitted, an offence under s17 would be committed by a cashier failing to ring up the full amount tendered by a customer, where the cashier intended to remove the amount under-rung sometime later when an opportunity presented itself: see *R* v *Monaghan* [1979] Crim LR 673 and *R* v *Golecha* [1989] 3 All ER 908.

In *R* v *Scott-Simmonds* [1994] Crim LR 933 the Court of Appeal confirmed that the word 'account' was to be given its ordinary meaning and, following *Attorney-General's Reference (No 1 of 1980)* (1980) 72 Cr App R 60, was to be interpreted widely, on the basis that it had been the intention of Parliament that the offence should extend to the preparation of accounts as well as the alteration of existing accounts. Examples of documents that have been held to fall within the scope of s17 are: a document required for a report on title in connection with a mortgage advance (see *R* v *Cummings-John* [1997] Crim LR 660); a housing benefit claim form on which an applicant furnished false details in order to substantiate his claim – the form was the only document referred to by the local authority in determining the amount to be paid to the applicant (see *Osinuga* v *DPP* [1998] Crim LR 216); and insurance cover notes: see *R* v *Manning* (1998) The Times 23 July.

On the other hand the courts have held that an insurance claim form could fall outside s17, on the basis that it would not have been obvious to a jury that it was required for an accounting purpose: see *R* v *Sundhers* [1998] Crim LR 497. In *R* v *Okanta* [1997] Crim LR 451 it was held that the offence did not extend to documents such as an accountant's letter confirming the earnings of a mortgage applicant, if the evidence indicated that the lender relied on the letter only for the purposes of deciding whether or not to make a loan, as opposed to computing the rate of repayments and interest to be paid.

In *R* v *Manning*, the court suggested that a proper test might be whether or not a reasonable juror looking at the document could conclude that it was required for an accounting purpose. It is incumbent upon the prosecution to adduce some (expert) evidence as to the use to which a given document would be put in order to assist the jury in determining whether or not it falls s17.

Mens rea

The prosecution must prove three elements. First, dishonesty, as in *R* v *Ghosh* (considered at Chapter 7, section 7.6). Second, that D acted with a view to gain for himself or another, or with intent to cause loss to another. By virtue of s34(2)(a) of the Theft Act 1968, 'gain' and 'loss' encompasses the gaining or loss of money or other property, and 'gain' includes a gain by keeping what one has, as well as a gain by getting what one has not; and 'loss' includes a loss by not getting what one might get, as well as a loss by parting with what one has: see further *R* v *Eden* (1971) 55 Cr App Rep 193. Finally, D must know that the document is or may be misleading, false or deceptive in a material detail, or he must be at least subjectively reckless in this regard. On the basis of *R* v *Graham and Others* [1997] 1 Cr App R 302, there would appear to be no need to prove that D knew the document in question was going to be used for an accounting purpose.

8.4 Section 20

Section 20(1) creates the offence of dishonestly destroying, defacing or concealing a valuable security with a view to gain or intent to cause loss to another. Section 20(2) creates the offence of dishonestly securing the execution of a valuable security by deception, with a view to gain or intent to cause loss to another. Both offences carry a maximum possible sentence of seven years' imprisonment. They can to some extent be seen as preparatory offences in that liability can arise without any advantage having been obtained. As indicated below the offence under s20(2) has been used in respect of two particularly common forms of criminal activity, namely mortgage fraud and unauthorised use of cheques and credit cards. Since the enactment of s12 of the Criminal Justice Act 1987 it may be preferable, where the evidence reveals an agreement to indulge in such activities, to proceed with a charge of common law conspiracy to defraud.

What is a valuable security?

Section 20(3) provides that:

> '... valuable security means any document creating, transferring, surrendering or releasing any right to, in or over property, or authorising the payment of money or delivery of any property, or evidencing the creation, transfer, surrender or release of any such right, or the payment of money or delivery of any property, or the satisfaction of any obligation.'

The term valuable security is wide enough to encompass cheques (whether crossed or not), see *R* v *Cooke* [1997] Crim LR 436, and bills of exchange, but there is doubt as to whether the offence extends to promissory notes and letters of credit. The problem of defendant who procures an electronic transfer of funds by deception has now been addressed by the enactment of the Theft (Amendment) Act 1996 (considered at section 8.1), hence the issue of whether or not a CHAPS transfer amounts to a valuable security may become largely academic once the cases based on events arising before the introduction of the 1996 Act work their way through the courts.

At present the matter is far from clear. In *R* v *King* [1991] Crim LR 906 the Court of Appeal held that a CHAPS order, once processed, did effect a transfer of intangible property (money in the paying customer's account) to the payee (and hence the execution of a valuable security). In addition, it created property, in that the payee now possessed a chose in action, and evidenced the creation and transfer of property. The Court's conclusion is, perhaps, questionable, as it appears to hold that there is at once the transfer and creation of property. The problem is that if the property in question is the right to sue the bank on the credit balance of the account, once the paying customer's CHAPS order is executed his right to sue his bank in respect of the sum specified in the order is destroyed, and a new right, belonging to the payee, to sue his bank in respect of the sum now credited to his account, is created.

The preferable view, it is submitted, is evidenced by decisions such as *R* v *Bolton* (1991) 94 Cr App R 74, where the court held that the term 'document' as it was used in s20(3) could not be construed to include a telegraphic transfer of mortgage funds by a building society. Whilst further rejecting the submission that the bank statement indicating that the transfer had taken place could be regarded as a valuable security, the court was willing to accept that a mortgage deed would fall within the scope of the subsection: see *R* v *IK Dhillon and GS Dhillon* [1992] Crim LR 889. The court in *R* v *Manjdadria* [1993] Crim LR 73, a case confirming that a telegraphic transfer of funds is not a valuable security, expressed the view that *King* was to be regarded as a decision defining the extreme limits of what could constitute a valuable security, a view more recently supported by *R* v *Cooke* [1997] Crim LR 436.

Note that s20(1) is wider in ambit than s20(2). In addition to dealing with valuable securities, it can be used to charge the defendant who destroys or defaces testamentary documents, or original documents filed with a court of law or government department.

What constitutes execution?

The Court of Appeal's ruling in *R* v *Beck* (1985) 80 Cr App R 355, to the effect that 'execution' was not to be construed in a restricted sense, has not been followed in subsequent decisions. In *R* v *Nanayakkara* (1987) 84 Cr App R 125, the trial judge's ruling, that execution in the form of 'acceptance' under s20(2) meant merely taking into possession, was rejected by Lord Lane CJ, on the ground that an examination of the legislative history of the provision revealed that 'acceptance' had been used in its technical sense in previous enactments, and there was no evidence to suggest that s20(2) was using the term in any different sense. This restrictive interpretation now has the approval of the House of Lords, following the decision in *R* v *Kassim* (1991) 93 Cr App R 391. In that case the appellant had opened a number of bank accounts having given false particulars to the bank, and subsequently used the cheque books and cheque cards with which he had been issued to obtain sums of money and goods from third parties. The prosecution could have tried to charge the appellant with offences contrary to s15 of the 1968 Act, but as Lord Ackner observed:

'... I fully appreciate that the current use of cheque guarantee cards and credit cards does give rise to problems where charges are brought under s15 in cases where the representation alleged is that the defendant was authorised to use his card, when he knew he was not because, for example, his account is overdrawn. However, since the whole object of the card is to relieve the tradesman from concerning himself with the relationship between the customer and his own bank, the tradesman may well not care whether or not the customer was exceeding the authority accorded to him by his own bank. All he will be concerned with is that the conditions on the card are satisfied. Such cases obviously give rise to the difficulty of establishing an operative deception. This problem cannot, however, be overcome by overstraining the meaning of the word "execution" as used in s20(2).'

Lord Ackner concluded that a defendant who presents a cheque for payment knowing he will not have funds to meet it falls outside the scope of s20(2) because, although he seeks financial gain for himself, the dishonest means by which he intends to achieve this is not by the cancellation or destruction of the cheque (ie the execution of it), since he will have achieved the sought after financial gain prior to the cheque's destruction or cancellation. As his Lordship succinctly put it:

'The subsection contemplates acts being done to or in connection with such documents. It does not contemplate and accordingly is not concerned with giving effect to the documents by the carrying out of the instruction which they may contain, such as the delivery of goods or the payment out of money.'

The mental element

The offences under s20 require proof of dishonesty, as to which see the guidelines in *R* v *Ghosh*; similarly, deception bears the meaning provided by s15(4). The proof of the defendant's 'view to gain' etc is governed by s34(2)(a).

8.5 Obtaining services by deception

Section 1(1) of the Theft Act 1978 creates the offence of obtaining services by deception. Services can clearly be of economic value, and it is right that they should be protected by criminal law. Section 1 provides:

'A person who by any deception dishonestly obtains services from another shall be guilty of an offence.'

Section 4(2)(a) states that a defendant convicted on indictment for this offence can be sentenced to a maximum of five years imprisonment. Note that a defendant who commits this offence may also incur liability under ss2 and 3 of the 1978 Act considered below.

Actus reus

The Act provides no detailed definition of services, although s1(2) does provide a partial definition where it states:

'It is an obtaining of services where the other is induced to confer a benefit by doing some act, or causing or permitting some act to be done, on the understanding that the benefit has been or will be paid for.'

Although the point is not expressly made in the subsection, it has been interpreted so as to encompass the situation where D obtains a service for the benefit of another: see *R* v *Nathan* (1997) (CA No 96/6899/24) (unreported).

The requirement that the provision of the service should be a 'benefit' to the defendant should not be construed too narrowly. Whether or not a service is beneficial is a matter of taste; for example tattooing, being given a 'mohican' haircut, or having one's car sprayed purple. It is submitted that a service is a benefit if it is something that an individual would be willing to pay for, or alternatively if it would be sufficient consideration to support a contract. The matter has produced little in the way of illuminating authority. In *R* v *Halai* [1983] Crim LR 624, D drew cheques on his bank account, in which there was only £28, to pay for a building society survey of a property he wished to buy and to open a savings account at the building society. He also misrepresented his employment status in order to try to obtain a mortgage advance from the building society. The Court of Appeal held that in respect of the property survey, the defendant had been rightly convicted under s1; the cheque was the deception (the defendant representing that it would be met on presentation, which was not true). The provision of the survey was a benefit to the defendant, not only because it was an essential step in his obtaining a mortgage but also because it was provided on the understanding that it would be paid for. The provision of a savings account was held not to be a service, however, because even if it was a benefit to D, it was not one for which the building society made any charge and was thus regarded as falling outside the scope of s1(2). The court's further finding that a mortgage advance was not a service, because it was a lending of money for the purchase of a property, was always regarded as dubious by most commentators. Such an advance is clearly to D's benefit, and there would have been no question of his not having to pay for it through interest payments. It was also difficult to reconcile with the later Court of Appeal decision in *R* v *Widdowson* [1986] Crim LR 233, wherein it was held that a hire-purchase agreement was a service within the terms of s1(1). Reflecting this growing criticism, the Court of Appeal, in *R* v *Teong Sun Chuah* [1991] Crim LR 463, went so far as to observe that *Halai* bore all the hallmarks of being per incuriam, a matter subsequently confirmed by the Court of Appeal in *R* v *Graham; R* v *Kansal; R* v *Ali; R* v *Marsh* [1997] 1 Cr App R 302.

For the avoidance of doubt Parliament has now enacted the Theft (Amendment) Act 1996, s4(1) of which provides that it is an obtaining of services where the other is induced to make a loan, or to cause or permit a loan to be made, on the understanding that any payment (whether by way of interest or otherwise) will be or has been made in respect of the loan.

The words 'on the understanding that the benefit has been or will be paid for' which appear in s1(2) have the effect of excluding gratuitous services from the scope of the offence. Clearly, a service provided free of charge is not one for which payment will have been made or be expected. Hence where D persuades a taxi driver P to give him a free ride after telling him a false 'hard luck' story, he will not be committing an offence within s1. The important point to bear in mind is that P is under no illusion as to whether he will be paid for providing the journey. Should he not wish to provide it for free, he can simply refuse. In such a case D may be guilty of an offence under s2(1)(c) (see below).

The requirement that the service should not be one that is gratuitous may have some interesting consequences. In *R* v *Atwal* [1989] Crim LR 293, for example, the trial judge directed the jury at Knightsbridge Crown Court that to obtain an American Express credit card by deception could be an offence under s1(1) of the 1978 Act, because an annual fee is charged in respect of membership, but no such offence would be made out where the defendant had exercised a deception in order to obtain a Visa or Access card, for which, at the time no charge was made. Note the difficulties inherent in charging the defendant with obtaining property (ie a card) by deception, given the need to establish intention to permanently deprive under s15 of the 1968 Act. Similarly, in *R* v *Shortland* [1995] Crim LR 893, D's appeal in respect of obtaining services by deception, where he had used false information to open a bank account, was allowed because there was no direct evidence adduced at the trial that the provision of banking services would, under the contract between D and the bank, have to be paid for by D. Hence there was no evidence that it was a service within s1(2). It remains a moot point whether or not a bank offering 'free banking' to those customers who maintain a credit balance in their current accounts is offering a service within the scope of s1(2).

There is nothing in s1(2) to expressly exclude from the definition of services acts which are contrary to law or against public policy, such as where D induces P to whip him in order to satisfy a particular sexual preference, or where D induces P, a prostitute, to have sex with him. In the absence of authority the point must remain open, although as a matter of construction, the fact that Parliament has expressly provided for this matter in relation to 'making off without payment' (see s3(3)) perhaps suggests that such acts are not to be excluded from the definition of services.

The obtaining of services must be by deception. The deception must therefore precede the obtaining of the service, and must be operative in the sense that it induces the provision of the service. Further, s5(1) of the 1978 Act provides:

> 'For the purposes of sections 1 and 2 above "deception" has the same meaning as in section 15 of the Theft Act 1968, that is to say, it means any deception (whether deliberate or reckless) by words or conduct as to fact or as to law, including a deception as to the present intentions of the persons using the deception or any other person; and section 18 of that Act (liability of company officers for offences by the company) shall apply in relation to sections 1 and 2 above as it applies in relation to section 15 of that Act.'

Any suggestion that the deception must relate to payment is to be rejected. In the majority of cases the deception will relate to payment, such as where D sits in a barber's chair having no intention of paying for his haircut, but by his conduct he induces the barber to provide the service. The situation where D produces a false driving licence in order to hire a car is also covered, even though D pays in full for the hire. The provision of car hire is a service within s1(2) because it is a benefit to D provided on the understanding that he will pay for it: see *R* v *Adams* [1993] Crim LR 525.

Mens rea

The defendant must be dishonest at the time of obtaining the service. The test in *R* v *Ghosh* is to be used. The defendant must have the mens rea for deception, which is intention or recklessness: see s15(4) of the 1968 Act, considered above. There is clearly no need here for any intention to permanently deprive, since once the service has been provided its economic value has been passed to the defendant.

8.6 Evasion of a liability by deception

Section 2 of the Theft Act 1978 creates three offences concerned with the defendant's evasion of a liability by deception. On the basis of *R* v *Holt and Lee* [1981] 2 All ER 834 (discussed below) it is submitted that the three offences are not mutually exclusive.

Section 2(1)(a)

Section 2(1)(a) provides:

> '... where a person by any deception dishonestly secures the remission of the whole or part of any existing liability to make a payment, whether his own liability or another's, he shall be guilty of an offence.'

The deception must precede the securing of the remission of liability, and must cause it: see above and s5(1) of the 1978 Act.

The liability referred to must be an existing legal liability to pay, in the sense that it is legally enforceable. Section 2(2) further provides that liability should not be interpreted as extending to a liability that has not been accepted or established to pay compensation for some wrongful act or omission, such as where D deceives P into believing that he cannot sue D for damages in respect of an accident caused by D's negligence. This restriction on the definition of liability applies equally to all three offences under s2(1). The fact that a liability to pay might only be enforced by a court order, such as one arising under an improperly executed credit agreement, does not prevent it from being an existing liability for the purposes of s2(1): see *R* v *Modupe* [1991] Crim LR 530.

The requirement in s2(1)(a) that the defendant must have 'secured the remission' of the liability in question means something more than that he has persuaded the creditor by deception to relieve him of liability, partly because such activity is amply catered for under s2(1)(b), but also because of the absence of the need to prove any intention to make permanent default under s2(1)(a). A defendant who secures the remission of a liability would therefore be one who succeeds in extinguishing his legal liability to pay, so that the creditor could not pursue him for payment. Such a situation can arise where D owes P £100 repayable on 23 June, and P agrees to accept £80 in full settlement of the debt on 20 June. The earlier repayment, albeit of a lesser sum, constitutes consideration which supports P's promise not to claim the remaining £20. D has here secured the remission of his liability to pay the £20. If D were to have induced such an agreement by P by falsely telling him that he was emigrating to Australia on 21 June and that if P waited until 23 June he would receive nothing, it might be contended that D had now committed an offence contrary to s2(1)(a) on the basis that he had now secured the remission of his liability to pay the remaining £20 by deception. The problem is whether, as a matter of civil law, D can ever have wiped out his legal liability to pay a debt where he has exercised a deception. It could be argued that his fraud renders P's agreement void and of no effect, or at least that P's agreement is voidable, and that as soon as P discovers the truth he can sue D for the remaining £20. If this interpretation is correct it becomes difficult to see to what situations, if any, s2(1)(a) can apply.

Notwithstanding this difficulty, the Court of Appeal in *R* v *Jackson* [1983] Crim LR 617 held that a defendant committed the offence where he paid for petrol with a stolen credit card. The existing liability was to pay for the petrol that he had put into the tank of his motorbike. The deception was the use of another person's card. The use of the card induced the petrol station to look to the credit card company for payment, not the defendant, and the credit card company would be contractually bound to reimburse the petrol station provided the conditions of using the card had been met. On this basis the court felt that Jackson had secured the remission of his liability to pay for the petrol. It is submitted that the defendant might have been more appropriately charged under s2(1)(b) or s3 of the 1978 Act (see below). He could not really be said to have wiped out his legal liability to pay for the petrol. If for any reason the credit card company had refused to reimburse the petrol station, the proprietors would have wanted, if at all possible, to recoup payment from the defendant.

The mens rea required for s2(1)(a), which is common to all three offences under s2, is that the defendant should be dishonest (see Chapter 7, section 7.6), and intend to deceive or be reckless as to whether he deceives, see above and s5(1) of the 1978 Act. Given that the section requires proof of the defendant securing the remission of a liability, any further requirement of proof that the defendant intended to make permanent default would be pointless.

Section 2(1)(b)

Section 2(1)(b) provides:

> 'Where a person by any deception with intent to make permanent default in whole or in part on any existing liability to make a payment, or with intent to let another do so, dishonestly induces the creditor or any person claiming payment on behalf of the creditor to wait for payment (whether or not the due date for payment is deferred) or to forgo payment, he shall be guilty of an offence.'

The observations concerning deception and dishonesty made above in relation to s2(1)(a) apply equally to the offence under s2(1)(b). It is aimed at the defendant who seeks to delay repayment of a debt by lying to his creditor, whilst not having any real intention of ever repaying the money. Where D owes P £20, the date for repayment having passed, and D falsely tells P that he has been robbed and will not have the money to repay P until next week, D commits an offence under s2(1)(b) if P accepts this story and D never intends to repay. P has been induced by D's deception to wait for payment. Similarly if P were to be persuaded by D's lies to let him off the debt altogether, P would then have been induced to forgo payment. Note that the section also caters for the situation where D acts with intent to let another person make permanent default on an existing liability.

The Court of Appeal decision in *R* v *Holt and Lee* [1981] 2 All ER 834 illustrates the operation of the section. The defendants had consumed a meal in a restaurant and decided that when the waitress presented the bill for payment they would tell her that they had already paid another waitress (which was untrue) and on being left unattended would make good their escape. The defendants were overheard planning their crime by an off-duty policeman who was dining at a nearby table and he promptly arrested them. The court held that the defendants had been rightly convicted of an attempt to commit an offence under s2(1)(b). Had the plan succeeded, the waitress acting as agent of the creditor would have been induced by their deception to forgo payment for the meal, their mens rea being evident.

Section 2(3) provides:

> 'For purposes of subsection (1)(b) a person induced to take in payment a cheque or other security for money by way of conditional satisfaction of a pre-existing liability is to be treated not as being paid but as being induced to wait for payment.'

Thus where D induces P to take a cheque D knows to be worthless, in that it will be dishonoured on presentation, in payment for a liability, and D has the appropriate mens rea, D will be guilty of an offence under s2(1)(b). The purpose of s2(3) is to replace the common law rule that acceptance of a cheque amounts to a conditional payment, suspending the creditor's remedies until the cheque has been paid or dishonoured. Such a rule might make it difficult to show that P had been induced to wait for or forgo payment (but see also *R* v *Andrews and Hedges* [1981] Crim LR 106).

The mens rea required for s2(1)(b) is dishonesty and deception (see above) and in addition the defendant must have an intention to make permanent default on the existing liability, which in simple terms means an intention never to pay the debt. Where the charge alleges that D acted with intent to let another person default on their liability, the trial judge should be careful to direct the jury that the conduct of D that might be regarded as dishonest where he acted for his own benefit might not necessarily be so regarded where he acted for another: see *R* v *Attewell-Hughes* (1991) 93 Cr App R 132.

Section 2(1)(c)

Section 2(1)(c) states:

> 'Where any person by any deception dishonestly obtains any exemption from or abatement of liability to make a payment he shall be guilty of an offence.'

Liability has the same meaning here as it does for the other two offences under s2, but unlike them encompasses also future liabilities. This point was emphasised by the Court of Appeal in *R* v *Firth* (1989) 91 Cr App R 217. The appellant, a consultant gynaecologist/obstetrician who had treated both private and NHS patients at hospitals within the Mid Downs Area Health Authority, had an arrangement with the Authority under which he would inform them if an antenatal test, or hospital bed, was being provided for one of his private patients. In such cases the appellant would be responsible for paying the Authority and could recoup the charges from his patient at a later stage. A number of specimen charges had been brought against the appellant alleging that, contrary to s2(1)(c) of the Theft Act 1978, he had dishonestly by deception obtained exemption from a liability by not informing the Authority that certain patients receiving treatment in its hospitals were his private patients and not NHS patients. He appealed against conviction on the grounds, inter alia, that the offence contrary to s2(1)(c) could not be committed by omission, and that at the time of the alleged deception, there had been no existing liability to make a payment.

As to the first of those grounds, the court declared that it was satisfied that if, under the arrangement with the Authority, it had been incumbent upon the appellant to inform the hospital of the status of a particular patient, and as a result of his failure to do so he was not billed for treatment as he otherwise would have been, the requirements of the section were made out. This duty to inform the hospital of the status of his patients receiving treatment presumably arose from the appellant's contract with the hospital, but the point is not clearly explained in the course of the Lord Chief Justice's judgment. His Lordship appears to have been happy to accept the prosecution assertion that this was the case. Given that such a contractual duty did exist, there is no doubt that the offence could be committed by omission.

As to the second ground, the court regarded it as significant that ss2(1)(a), and 2(1)(b) of the 1978 Act expressly required the prosecution to establish an existing liability that a defendant had tried to evade whilst s2(1)(c) was silent on this point. Their Lordships did not think that this omission had been accidental, but was evidence that, in relation to s2(1)(c), Parliament had not intended that any existing liability need be shown at the time of the deception. The subsection applied equally, therefore, to future liabilities such as that in the present case. Deception should be interpreted in the same way here as it is under the other s2 offences.

By virtue of s2(4), 'obtains' in s2(1)(c) includes obtaining for another or enabling another to obtain. The mens rea required is dishonesty and deception; no intention to make permanent default need be established.

The major difficulty with s2(1)(c), as with s2(1)(a), is in determining its sphere of operation, since strictly construed, it is hard to see how a defendant would ever gain genuine exemption from a liability where he has exercised a deception. As soon as the deception is discovered he will become liable to pay the full amount due. It may be more sensible to view the offence as one of deceiving a prospective or actual creditor into believing that only a reduced payment, or even no payment at all, is due from the defendant. Such an interpretation is supported by the Court of Appeal decision in *R* v *Sibartie* [1983] Crim LR 470, where the defendant's conviction for attempted evasion of a liability by deception was upheld, following his showing of an invalid travel ticket to a London Underground ticket inspector in the hope that she would be tricked into letting the defendant pass on to the next stage of his journey. Had his scheme worked the defendant would not have gained exemption from his liability to pay the full fare but would have persuaded the inspector that no further payment was due from him. It is arguable that the defendant was also guilty of an attempt to commit an offence under s2(1)(b).

8.7 Forgery and Counterfeiting Act 1981

The Forgery and Counterfeiting Act 1981 (the 1981 Act) resulted largely from the Law Commission's Working Paper No 26 (1970) and the Commission's Report (No 55) (1973). Its purpose is to make fresh provision for the offence of forgery, and the offences related to the counterfeiting of notes and coins. Section 13 of the 1981 Act states that the offence of forgery at common law is abolished, hence pre-1981 authorities cease to be binding, but may still be regarded as persuasive in the interpretation of the new law. The 1981 Act also repealed the Forgery Act 1913 and the Coinage Offences Act 1936. It should be borne in mind that the use of forged and counterfeited articles will frequently involve D in liability for theft or obtaining property by deception. The 1981 Act introduces liability at an earlier stage, for example by imposing liability for the making or possession of such articles, behaviour that would be unlikely to amount to even an attempt to steal or obtain by deception.

The offence of forgery

Section 1 of the 1981 Act provides:

'A person is guilty of forgery if he makes a false instrument, with the intention that he or another shall use it to induce somebody to accept it as genuine, and by reason of so accepting it to do or not to do some act to his own or any other persons's prejudice.'

The maximum penalty that can be imposed following conviction on indictment is ten years' imprisonment.

Actus reus

Under s9(2) a person is to be 'treated as making a false instrument if he alters an instrument so as to make it false in any respect (whether or not it is false in some other respect apart from that alteration).' The change here from the previous law under the Forgery Act 1913 is that the alteration does not have to relate to a material particular, an alteration making the instrument false in any respect will suffice. The meaning of 'instrument' for the purposes of Part I of the 1981 Act is defined by s8(1) which provides that (subject to subsection (2)) the term covers: any document, whether of a formal or informal character; any stamp issued or sold by the Post Office; any Inland Revenue stamp; and any disc, tape, sound track or other device on or in which information is recorded or stored by mechanical, electronic or other means. Subsection (2) excludes currency notes from the meaning of instrument. The definition of 'instrument' does not, therefore, extend to include counterfeit goods such as imitation Cartier watches, or a fake Stradivarius, but would cover a document that purported to be a certificate stating that such items were genuine. With regard to the facts of *R* v *Donelly* (below), jewellery would not be an instrument, but a valuation certificate would be.

Although the activities of those who gain unauthorised access to computer systems for fraudulent purposes are likely to contravene the Computer Misuse Act 1990, if not the Theft Act 1968, it may also be possible to bring charges under the 1981 Act. Much depends on the nature of D's activities. If it involves a process whereby a number or password is held momentarily in a control segment of a computer for verification, prior to being irretrievably expunged, it will not involve the recording or storing of information such as to give rise to the creation of a false instrument for the purposes of s8(1): see *R* v *Gold and Shifreen* [1988] 2 All ER 186. By contrast, if it involves altering the data on a disk, it will fall within the scope of the 1981 Act: see *R* v *Governor of Brixton Prison, ex parte Levin* [1997] 1 Cr App Rep 335, where Beldam LJ observed that: 'the disc embraces the information stored as well as the medium on which it is stored, just as a document consists both of the paper and the printing upon it. Thus by entering false instructions onto the disc it was in our opinion falsified.'

The most complex element of the actus reus of the offence is that the instrument should be 'false'. An exhaustive definition is provided by subs9(1)(a)–(h) which provide that an instrument is false for these purposes of this Part of this Act if it purports to have been made in the:

1. form in which it is made by a person who did not in fact make it in that form (s9(1)(a));
2. form in which it is made on the authority of a person who did not in fact authorise its making in that form (s9(1)(b));
3. terms in which it is made by a person who did not in fact make it in those terms (s9(1)(c));
4. terms in which it is made on the authority of a person who did not in fact authorise its making in those terms (s9(1)(d)).

Alternatively an instrument can be false because it purports to have been:

1. altered in any respect by a person who did not in fact alter it in that respect (s9(1)(e));
2. altered in any respect on the authority of a person who did not in fact authorise the alteration in that respect (s9(1)(f));
3. made or altered on a date on which, or at a place at which, or otherwise in circumstances in which, it was not in fact made or altered (s9(1)(g)); or
4. made or altered by an existing person but he did not in fact exist (s9(1)(h)).

The Law Commission noted in its Report No 55 (para 43) that:

> 'The essential feature of a false instrument in relation to forgery is that it is an instrument which "tells a lie about itself" in the sense that it purports to be made by a person who did not make it (or altered by a person who did not alter it) or otherwise purports to be made or altered in circumstances in which it was not made or altered. Falsity needs to be defined in these terms to cover not only, for example, the obvious case of forging a testator's signature to a will, but also the case where the date of a genuine will is altered to make it appear that the will was executed later than it in fact was, and therefore after what in truth was the testator's last will.'

As Blackburn J stated in *R* v *Windsor* (1865) 10 Cox CC 118 at 123:

> 'Forgery is the false making of an instrument purporting to be that which it is not, it is not the making of an instrument which purports to be what it really is, but which contains false statements. Telling a lie does not become a forgery because it is reduced into writing.'

The following example illustrates the distinction. If D is applying for a means-tested welfare benefit and fills in an application form falsely stating that he has no savings, he may be attempting to obtain property by deception, but the application form does not thereby become a 'false' instrument. Were D to purchase a rent book, however, and register within it payments to his landlord for rent, which had never been paid, accompanied by an imitation of his landlord's signature, then the rent book would be 'telling a lie about itself', and would constitute a false instrument within Part I of the 1981 Act: see further *R* v *Winston* (below).

Subsections 9(1)(a)–(h) would appear to cover the following situations: D applies for a job and produces a reference which purports to have been written by his previous employer, but which has in fact been written by D, or some other person, without the employer's authority (s9(1)(a)); where the reference purports to have been written on the authority of the previous employer it would fall under subsection (b). Subsections (c) and (d) would cover a reference that had been made by D's previous employer, but which had been altered in some respect by D, for example by substituting a much higher figure as his leaving salary. Subsections (e) and (f) would relate to unauthorised alterations: for example where D, having enjoyed a meal in a restaurant, receives a bill from the waiter which he alters to a lower amount. The bill would purport to have been altered by a person who did not in fact alter it. It would be different had the waiter been deliberately failing to enter items at the correct price on the bill so that an accomplice D could receive a cheap meal. Here the bill would simply have been inaccurate, not false (subject to s9(1)(g) considered below), because it would have been made by the person authorised to do so. Similarly, if the waiter were to alter a correctly totalled bill in D's favour.

The ambit of subs9(1)(g) was considered by the Court of Appeal in *R* v *Donelly* (1984) 79 Cr App R 76. The appellant, the manager of a jewellery store, had drawn up a valuation certificate in relation to jewellery that did not exist, the purpose being to enable another man, with whom he was collaborating, to defraud an insurance company. The appellant contended that the document was not false within the meaning of the Act. The Court held that the certificate came within s9(1)(g) because it purported to have been made 'otherwise in circumstances in which it was not in fact made'. On the facts it purported to have been made following the examination of certain jewellery which did not in fact exist; therefore, it told a lie about itself, the circumstances in which it had been made. Had the jewellery in fact existed and the appellant simply overvalued it for insurance purposes, the document would not have been false, simply inaccurate.

Despite being subject to considerable academic criticism the decision *Donelly* was applied in *R* v *Jeraj* [1994] Crim LR 595. The appellant, the manager of a branch of an Indian bank, met two men at a London hotel and, following discussions, signed a document on bank notepaper. The prosecution alleged that the letter amounted to verification of his bank's endorsement of a letter of credit drawn by the Banco Unidyn de Bolivia, the prosecution case being that the letter of credit and the Banco Unidyn de Bolivia never existed and that the document signed by the appellant was part of a banking fraud that would be perpetrated in the United States. The appellant contended that he had been duped by the two men and had signed the document merely as confirmation that he had seen a letter of credit that had been drawn up in a form acceptable to his bank. Upholding his conviction, the Court ruled that the trial judge had rightly ruled that the document could amount to a forgery within s9(1)(g) of the Forgery and Counterfeiting Act 1981 on the basis that it purported to have been made in circumstances in which it was not in fact made: see further *R* v *Warneford and Gibbs* [1994] Crim LR 753.

Finally, s9(1)(h) brings within the definition of false instruments those that purport to have been made or altered by an existing person who does not in fact exist. The provision causes great difficulty where a person acts under an alias. If D fills out an application form using the alias 'Mickey Mouse', is the form a forgery? Mickey Mouse may be a fictitious character, but D (alias Mickey Mouse) is a real person. The problem arose under the old law in *R* v *Hassard and Devereux* [1970] 2 All ER 647, where the Court of Appeal held that the drawing of a cheque on an account opened in a false name (using a stolen cheque) was a forgery in that it purported to be made by a fictitious person. The decision has been criticised for the reasons given above, and now seems untenable in the light of the House of Lords' decision in *R* v *Moore* [1987] 3 All ER 825. Moore had come into possession of a cheque for £5,303.23, made payable to an 'M R Jessel'. He opened a building society account using the name 'M R Jessel', and ten days later withdrew £5,000, using a withdrawal form made out in the name of the payee. Moore was convicted of making a false instrument, namely the withdrawal form, and the point of law certified for the House of Lords was whether or not the instrument became false within s9(1) of the 1981 Act because Moore had used someone else's name to open the account, and complete the withdrawal form. The House of Lords held that the conviction would have to be quashed. The withdrawal form did not tell a lie about itself. It purported to have been made by the person who had opened the account, ie the defendant using the name 'M R Jessel', and in that respect it was entirely accurate. The withdrawal form did not purport to have been made by the original payee in whose name the cheque had been drawn to open the account.

Mens rea

Beyond a basic intention to make a false instrument, s1 requires a specific intent on the part of the defendant that the false instrument should be used to induce another to accept it as genuine and thereby act, or fail to act, to their own or another's prejudice. *R* v *Ondhia* [1998] Crim LR 339 confirms that this is satisfied even where D makes a false instrument with the intention of faxing it to P. The argument that the facsimile would not, in those circumstances, be a 'false instrument' was rejected. D's intention at the time of the making of the original false instrument was that the recipient would be induced, by means of a fax machine, to accept it as genuine.

The requirement that some other person be induced to accept the false instrument as genuine is given an extended meaning by s10(3) which provides that:

'... references to inducing somebody to accept a false instrument as genuine, or a copy of a false instrument as a copy of a genuine one, include references to inducing a machine to respond to the instrument or copy as if it were a genuine instrument or, as the case may be, a copy of a genuine one.'

Where the subsection applies, the act or omission intended to be induced by the machine responding to the instrument or copy shall be treated as an act or omission to a person's prejudice (s10(4)).

Section 10 provides an exhaustive definition of what, for the purposes of Part I of the Act, constitutes a person acting (or failing to act) to their prejudice. Subject to s10(2) and (4) an act or omission intended to be induced is to a person's prejudice if, and only if, it is one which, if it occurs will result in his:

1. temporary or permanent loss of property (s10(1)(a)(i));
2. being deprived of an opportunity to earn remuneration or greater remuneration (s10(1)(a)(ii));
3. being deprived of an opportunity to gain a financial advantage otherwise than by way of remuneration (s10(1)(a)(iii)).

'Loss' for the purposes of this section includes not getting what one might get as well as parting with what one has (s10(5)).

Alternatively, the act or omission is to a person's prejudice if it is one which, if it occurs, will result in somebody being given an opportunity:

1. to earn remuneration or greater remuneration from him (s10(1)(b)(i));
2. to gain a financial advantage from him otherwise than by way of remuneration (s10(1)(b)(ii)).

Lastly, the act or omission is to a person's prejudice if it is one which, if it occurs, will be the result of his having accepted a false instrument as genuine, or a copy of a false instrument as a copy of a genuine one, in connection with his performance of any duty. In *R* v *Utting* [1987] 1 WLR 1375 the defendant produced a false document with the intention that the police should accept it as genuine, and take no further steps to prosecute him for theft. He was convicted of forgery contrary to s1 and appealed on the basis that the act or omission that he intended the document to induce, namely his non-prosecution, was not within the meaning of 'an act or omission ... to a person's prejudice' in s10, and further that the offence was only made out where the victim of the forgery would have acted to his prejudice, or some person other than the perpetrator would have done so. The court held that these submissions were well founded. The forger could not be 'any other person' within s1, otherwise it would be an offence for the forger to make a false instrument with the intention of inducing someone to accept it as genuine and thereby do an act to the prejudice or harm of the forger himself. The court held that this cannot have been the intention of Parliament, and thought it remarkable that the non-prosecution should be regarded as being to the defendant's prejudice. The court went on to point out that the situation might have been different had the charge against the defendant proceeded on the basis that the act or omission would have been to the prejudice of the police within s10(1)(c), but that was not the basis of the charge here. See further *R* v *Garcia* (1987) 87 Cr App Rep 175.

As a matter of law, a person does not act to his own or another's prejudice simply by performing an enforceable duty, or refraining from an action which he is not entitled to take anyway. Section 10(2) provides that an 'act which a person has an enforceable duty to do and an omission to do an act which a person is not entitled to do shall be disregarded for the purposes of this Part of this Act.' Hence, if D is owned money by P and D forges a letter which puts pressure on P to repay, D does not induce P to act to his prejudice, as his duty to repay the money is enforceable at law: see *R* v *Parkes* (1910) 74 JP 210. The matter has been considered on a number of occasions by the Court of Appeal since 1981. First, in *R* v *Campbell (Mary)* (1985) 80 Cr App Rep 47, where the appellant endorsed a cheque for her friend by forging the payee's signature and paying it into her own account. She then took out an equivalent amount in cash from her account and gave it to her friend. The Court of Appeal, upholding the conviction under s1 of the 1981 Act, held that the appellant's argument in reliance on s10(2), to the effect that the bank was under a duty to pay out on the cheque, and that she had not, therefore, intended that the bank should act to its prejudice, was to be rejected. The bank only had a duty to pay out on a valid instrument, thus s10(2) was of no relevance. The actions of the appellant were to the bank's prejudice by reference to s10(1)(c), because the bank accepted the cheque in connection with the performance of a duty. It should be further noted that the appellant would have had mens rea even if she had believed her friend had a right to the amount of money represented by the cheque, because she must have known that in any event the bank would not be willing to pay out on a fraudulently endorsed cheque. Similarly, in *R* v *Winston* (1998) The Times 24 July, the Court of Appeal upheld a conviction under s1 where the appellant, who was entitled to Housing Benefit, had manufactured a letter and rent book in support of his claim. It was not sufficient that the objective criteria for payment of benefit were met. There was no enforceable duty to pay benefit unless the requisite evidence of entitlement was submitted.

Finally, in *R* v *Tobierre* [1986] Crim LR 243, the appellant was convicted under s3 of the 1981 Act (see below), having signed a child allowance book in his wife's name, failing to report the fact that his wife and children were abroad, living in St Lucia. The Court of Appeal quashed the conviction due to the trial judge's failure to give an adequate direction on intention. It was held that ss3 and 10 of the Act, when read together, required proof of two states of mind: an intention to induce another to accept an instrument as genuine, and an intention that the other person should act or omit to act to his own or some other person's prejudice. The jury should have been directed to consider whether the appellant believed that he had authority to sign on his wife's behalf, and if he did believe this, whether he believed as a consequence that the Secretary of State was under a duty to pay out within s10(2). Had the defendant so believed he would not have had the necessary intention to cause another to act to his own or some other person's prejudice. Such an interpretation, it is submitted, goes some way towards alleviating possible injustices under the Act, given the absence of any need to establish dishonesty.

The offences of copying and using false instruments

Section 2 of the 1981 Act creates the offence of copying a false instrument. It is an offence for a person to:

> '... make a copy of an instrument which is, and which he knows or believes to be, a false instrument, with the intention that he or another shall use it to induce somebody to accept it as a copy of a genuine instrument, and by reason of so accepting it to do or not to do some act to his own or any other person's prejudice.'

The maximum penalty following conviction on indictment is ten years' imprisonment. The section puts it beyond doubt that it is now an offence to photocopy a false instrument with the requisite mens rea. Section 3 makes it an offence for D to use 'an instrument which is, and which he knows or believes to be, false, with the intention of inducing somebody to accept it as genuine, and by reason of so accepting it to do or not to do some act to his own or any other person's prejudice.' Note that this offence was the subject of the charge in *R v Tobierre* (above). This offence also carries the possibility of ten years' imprisonment. Section 4 extends liability to D who uses 'a copy of an instrument which is, and which he knows or believes to be, a false instrument, with the intention of inducing somebody to accept it as a copy of a genuine instrument, and by reason of so accepting it to do or not to do some act to his own or any other person's prejudice.'

The offences of counterfeiting notes and coins

Section 14 of the 1981 Act makes it an offence for a person to make a counterfeit of a currency note or of a protected coin, with the intention of passing it or tendering it as genuine. Subsection (2) creates the offence of making a counterfeit of a currency note or of a protected coin without lawful authority or excuse. The offence under s14(1) is the more serious offence by virtue of the ulterior intent; it carries with it a maximum sentence of ten years' imprisonment following conviction on indictment. Section 14(2) carries a maximum of two years imprisonment following conviction on indictment.

Actus reus

Section 27(1) defines a 'currency note' as 'any note which has been lawfully issued in England and Wales, Scotland, Northern Ireland, any of the Channel Islands, the Isle of Man or the Republic of Ireland [that] is or has been customarily used as money in the country where it was issued and is payable on demand ...'. The definition also covers any note which has been lawfully issued in any other country that is customarily used as money in that country. 'Protected coin' is similarly defined.

A coin or note is a counterfeit for these purposes if, under s28(1), 'it is not a currency note or a protected coin but resembles a currency note or protected coin (whether on one side only or on both) to such an extent that it is reasonably capable of passing for a currency note or protected coin of that description ...'. The definition also extends to currency notes or protected coins altered so that they can reasonably be capable of passing for currency notes or protected coins of some other description.

Mens rea

Section 14(2) is arguably an offence of basic intent requiring only that the defendant intended to produce the prohibited articles. Section 14(1) requires a further, or ulterior, intent to pass such notes or coins as genuine.

Other offences relating to counterfeit notes and coins

Section 15 creates various offences relating to the passing of counterfeit notes and coins. Under s15(1) 'it is an offence for a person to pass or tender as genuine any thing which is, and which he knows or believes to be, a counterfeit of a currency note or of a protected coin ...'. The offence carries a maximum penalty of ten years' imprisonment.

Section 16 creates offences concerned with having custody of, or control over, counterfeit notes and coins. Section 16(1) provides for the more serious offence of possession of materials that D knows, or believes, to be a counterfeit of a currency note or of a protected coin, intending either to pass or tender it as genuine. Section 16(2) provides for the basic possession offence. Section 17 creates three offences relating to the making or possession of counterfeiting equipment, and s18 creates the offence of reproducing British currency notes. Section 19 creates two offences relating to the making and distribution of imitation British coins. Sections 20 and 21 create offences relating to the unlawful importation and exportation of counterfeit notes and coins.

9

Robbery, Blackmail and Burglary

9.1 Robbery

9.2 Blackmail

9.3 Burglary

9.4 Aggravated burglary

9.1 Robbery

Robbery is essentially an aggravated form of theft. The aggravating factor is the force used on the victim, or threats of force made, prior to or during the theft. Section 8(1) of the Theft Act 1968, which creates the offence, provides:

> 'A person is guilty of robbery if he steals, and immediately before or at the time of doing so, and in order to do so, he uses force on any person or puts or seeks to put any person in fear of being then and there subjected to force.'

It should be noted that a conviction for robbery will only be secured where all the elements of theft are established. In particular, a defendant charged with robbery can raise points of law by way of defence that would have been available had he been charged with theft. In *R* v *Robinson* [1977] Crim LR 173, the Court of Appeal held that a defendant should be found not guilty of robbery where he honestly believed he had a right in law to take the property, in other words, where the defendant came within s2(1)(a) of the 1968 Act.

The aggravated nature of robbery is also reflected in the punishment available to the court by s8(2) which provides:

> 'A person guilty of robbery, or of an assault with intent to rob, shall on conviction on indictment be liable to imprisonment for life.'

Use of force

The question of whether or not force has been used is one that should be left to the jury; the Court of Appeal so held in *R* v *Dawson* (1976) 64 Cr App R 170, where the defendant had nudged the victim and caused him to lose his balance so that his wallet could more easily be taken. As Lawton LJ observed:

'The choice of the word "force" is not without interest because under the Larceny Act 1916 the word "violence" had been used, but Parliament deliberately on the advice of the Criminal Law Revision Committee changed that word to "force". Whether there is any difference between "violence" or "force" is not relevant for the purposes of this case; but the word is "force". It is a word in ordinary use. It is a word which juries understand.'

The force can be used upon any person, not necessarily the owner or custodian of the property in question, thus confirming the decision of the House of Lords (under the previous law) in *Smith* v *Desmond Hall* [1965] AC 960, where the defendant was convicted of robbery after overpowering a night watchman in order to steal cash from an office some distance away.

The statute requires the force to be used 'on any person', but it may be sufficient for the defendant to use force on the victim's possessions in a way which affects the victim. In *R* v *Clouden* [1987] Crim LR 56 the defendant had pulled on the victim's handbag to wrench it from her hands. The Court of Appeal held that whilst a snatching of property without resistance from the owner, such as by a pickpocket, should not amount to robbery, the question of whether force had been used 'on any person' should be left to the jury. The defendant's appeal was dismissed.

There is no need for actual physical contact between robber and victim; it is sufficient that the victim is put in fear of immediate physical violence, or that some other person present is similarly put in fear. Were D to threaten P that, unless P handed over £100 immediately, P's child X would be beaten on the way home from school later that day, the appropriate charge would be blackmail and not robbery, because X is not put in fear of force being used as he is not present when the threat is made; conversely P, who *is* present, is not being threatened with force: see *R* v *Taylor* (1996) (CA transcript No 96/2587/X4). Presumably robbery is committed where D makes threats to P prior to stealing his property even though P is not frightened by them, as s8(1) covers the situation where D 'seeks to put any person in fear'.

The force must have been used by D, or he must be an accomplice to its use. Theft without knowledge of any violence having taken place is not robbery: see *R* v *Harris* (1988) The Times 4 March.

'In order to steal ...'

The force, or threats of force, must be used in order to steal, as was held by the Court of Appeal in *R* v *Shendley* [1970] Crim LR 49; there is no such thing as robbery without violence. Hence where D attacks P in order to settle an argument, and having hit P to the ground finds his wallet to have fallen out, D will not be guilty of robbery should he run off with the wallet, because the force was not used by him with the intention of stealing.

Coincidence of force and stealing

Section 8(1) clearly provides that the force must be used immediately before, or during the course of, the theft, raising the question of for how long theft continues.

Where force, or threats of force are used prior to stealing, the requirement of immediacy must be met. It is submitted that where a threat of force is made at some time before the appropriation of property, the jury must be satisfied that the threat was still affecting the mind of the victim immediately before or during the theft. In short, there must be a continuing threat.

The theft that the use of force must precede or accompany will continue for as long as appropriation continues; this can be for a split-second, or an indeterminate length of time. In *Corcoran* v *Anderton* [1980] Crim LR 385 the defendant's appeal against conviction was dismissed by the Divisional Court on the ground that even though the victim had only been momentarily dispossessed of her property, where the defendant had tugged at her bag causing it to fall to the ground, there had been an appropriation accompanied by force. At the other extreme, the Court of Appeal in *R* v *Hale* (1978) 68 Cr App R 415 held that appropriation could be a continuing act; the point at which it ceased was to be determined by the jury on the facts of each case. Where, therefore, D steals property belonging to P, is discovered by P, and threatens P that unless he is allowed to escape without the police being called he will assault P, D will be guilty of robbery. The threats to P are made whilst the theft (appropriation) is continuing, and are made in order to accomplish the theft: see further *R* v *Atakpu* [1993] 3 WLR 812 (considered at Chapter 7, section 7.7) and *R* v *Lockley* [1995] Crim LR 656.

9.2 Blackmail

The offence of blackmail existed before 1968 in a variety of offences under the Larceny Act 1916. The essence of the offence is that the defendant makes an unwarranted demand with menaces. Section 21(1) of the Theft Act 1968 provides:

> 'A person is guilty of blackmail if, with a view to gain for himself or another or with intent to cause loss to another, he makes any unwarranted demand with menaces; and for this purpose a demand with menaces is unwarranted unless the person making it does so in the belief:
> a) that he has reasonable grounds for making the demand; and
> b) that the use of the menaces is a proper means of reinforcing the demand.'

A defendant convicted of blackmail on indictment may be sentenced to up to 14 years' imprisonment.

Demand

The demand, which lies at the heart of blackmail, can be in the form of words, actions or omissions, and can be express or implied. In *R* v *Collister and Warhurst* (1955) 39 Cr App R 100 two police officers discussed, within earshot of the victim, that payment of some money might lead them to drop what were in any event bogus indecency charges against the victim. It was obvious to the victim, and would have been obvious to a reasonable man, that a demand was being made even though it was never directly addressed to the victim.

It should be remembered that the offence does not require proof that the demand ever reaches the victim. Blackmail is, in a sense, an inchoate offence, raising the nice question of whether there is such an offence as attempted blackmail. Such an offence may exist in theory but will, it is submitted, be of slight practical importance.

The question of demands made by way of letter delivered by the Post Office was considered by the House of Lords in *Treacy* v *DPP* [1971] AC 537. The defendant had posted a letter containing unwarranted demands with menaces to a woman in Germany. By a majority their Lordships took the view that the demand, for the purposes of blackmail, had been made when the letter was posted in England, and thus the English courts had jurisdiction over the offence. Lord Diplock was willing to go further and suggest that had the letter been posted in Germany and received by a victim in England, then the English courts would still have had jurisdiction on the basis that the demand continued to be made once the letter had been sent, and would thus be 'made' in England as well as Germany.

With menaces

It has been suggested, by Cairns LJ in *R* v *Lawrence* (1971) 57 Cr App R 64, that 'menaces' is an ordinary English word which would normally call for no elaboration on the part of a trial judge, unless there were exceptional circumstances where what would not normally be menacing to an ordinary person, was menacing to the victim. Lord Wright in *Thorne* v *Motor Trade Association* [1937] AC 797 stated that:

> 'I think the word "menace" is to be liberally construed and not as limited to threats of violence but as including threats of any action detrimental to or unpleasant to the person addressed. It may also include a warning that in certain events such action is intended.'

It is submitted that this is wide enough to include threats to reveal a person's criminal record, adultery, medical details, or to adversely affect an individual's business or property.

The test applied to determine whether or not menaces have been established, is that laid down by the Court of Appeal in *R* v *Clear* [1968] 1 QB 670 (a case decided under the Larceny Act 1916). It was suggested that the actions of the defendant should be considered in the light of the effect they would have on the ordinary person of reasonable fortitude. This test may have to be modified, however, where the victim is unusually timorous or brave. In *R* v *Garwood* [1987] 1 All ER 1032 Lord Lane CJ held that if the victim was not influenced by the menaces, but the evidence was that an ordinary person of normal stability would have been, then the menaces were made out. On the other hand, where the threats did affect the victim, but would not have so influenced the reasonable person of normal stability, menaces were made out where the defendant nevertheless realised the effect of his actions on the victim.

Again, regard should be had to s21(2) which provides (inter alia) that it is immaterial whether the menaces relate to action to be taken by the person making the demand. Common sense dictates that there will be some demands which are of such a trivial or lighthearted nature that no menaces can sensibly be implied. Such a situation arose in *R v Harry* [1974] Crim LR 32 where a student had suggested to a shopkeeper that if he were to make a £50 contribution to the college's Rag Week fund, the shop would be 'immune' from Rag Week activities. The trial judge ruled that he was not satisfied that there were any menaces within the meaning of the Act.

'With a view to gain or loss ...'

Although s21(2) provides that the nature of the act or omission demanded is immaterial, s21(1) clearly states that the demand must be made by the defendant either with a view to gain for himself or another, or with intent to cause loss to another. Thus were D to say to P, 'let me have sex with you or I will tell your mother that you secretly had an abortion', D would not be committing an offence of blackmail because his demand would not be made with a view to gain or causing another loss. (Although if he proceeds with the plan and has intercourse with P he may be guilty of rape.) The concept of 'gain' and 'loss' is given an artificially wide meaning by s34(2)(a) of the Theft Act 1968 which provides:

> 'For purposes of this Act –
> a) "gain" and "loss" are to be construed as extending only to gain or loss in money or other property, but as extending to any such gain or loss whether temporary or permanent; and
> i) "gain" includes a gain by keeping what one has, as well as a gain by getting what one has not; and
> ii) "loss" includes a loss by not getting what one might get, as well as a loss by parting with what one has.'

The effect of s34(2)(a) is to bring within the scope of blackmail situations such as where D threatens to reveal P's adultery to P's wife, unless P repays D the £100 which he owes him; this demand is made by D with a view to 'gain' even though D is trying to recover that to which he had a right in any event. Similarly an offence may be committed where D makes such a threat to P unless P relinquishes his right to sue D for money owed by D to P; here P's 'loss' is not getting what he might get: see *R v Parkes* [1973] Crim LR 358. In *R v Bevans* (1988) 87 Cr App R 64, D was convicted of blackmail, after he had threatened to shoot a doctor if he did not provide D with a pain-killing morphine injection, on the basis that his demand had been made with a view to gain. As Jones J observed:

> 'It seems difficult, if not impossible, to argue that the liquid which constituted the substance which was to be injected into the appellant's body was not property. It clearly was. There has been no dispute but that if an ampoule containing the liquid had been handed over to the appellant instead of being transferred to a syringe and injected into his body, he would have got property in that sense. This Court can see no difference between

the liquid being contained in the syringe before it is passed into his body and the liquid being contained in an ampoule. There can be no question but that that morphine was property ... It is nothing to the point that his ultimate motive was the relief of pain through the effect which that morphine would have upon his bodily processes. It was pointed out in the course of argument that someone may very well demand a bottle of whisky. His ultimate motive may simply be to get drunk, that is to drink it all himself and to get drunk. That does not detract in any way from the proposition that in fact he would be demanding property in the form of the bottle of whisky and in particular the bottle's contents. By analogy exactly the same argument must apply here. This demand, which was a demand for an injection of morphine, involved two things: first of all it involved the passing of a drug to him, and secondly it involved the service by the doctor of actually carrying out the injection. The fact that he was gaining the service does not in any way mean that he was not gaining the property which consisted of the morphine. There is no suggestion anywhere in the Act that the gain must be exclusively directed to one particular object.'

Unwarranted

A demand will be unwarranted unless the defendant makes it in the belief that he has reasonable grounds for so doing, and in the belief that the use of the menaces is a proper means of reinforcing the demand. The test is prima facie subjective, in that the defendant's belief does not have to be reasonable, although the more unreasonable it is the less likely the jury are to believe him. Further, note that both states of mind have to be established.

The defendant may honestly believe that there are grounds for making the demand for any number of reasons. He does not have to establish any particular legal, moral or factual basis for his belief; he will nevertheless have to provide evidence upon which a jury can act, that he honestly believed such grounds to exist. The fact that the defendant was owed money by the victim, or had been in some other way disadvantaged by the victim, might provide such evidence. The nature of what is demanded by the defendant may be relevant here.

The subjective nature of this provision, particularly as regards the defendant's belief that menaces were appropriate in the circumstances, may be problematic. Where the defendant has very low moral standards he may regard as 'proper means' methods which a reasonable person would find outrageous. Perhaps the problem is more theoretical than real in that the jury would convict in such a situation. In any event, an important limitation was introduced by the Court of Appeal in *R* v *Harvey* (1980) 72 Cr App R 139. The defendant had threatened to kill, maim, and rape members of the victim's family if he did not return £20,000 that he had obtained from D by deception. The trial judge directed the jury that as a matter of law such threats could not be a 'proper' means of enforcing his demand for the return of the money. The Court of Appeal upheld this ruling, emphasising that a defendant could not claim that the means adopted were 'proper' whilst he also knew that they would involve the commission of serious criminal offences. On the facts there was little doubt that D had been aware that the means adopted would have involved the commission of serious crimes, and although the court did feel that the trial judge had erred in leaving this issue to the jury, the proviso was applied. As Bingham J observed:

> 'In order to exonerate a defendant from liability his belief must be that the use of the menaces is a "proper" means of reinforcing the demand. "Proper" is an unusual expression to find in a criminal statute. It is not defined in the Act, and no definition need be attempted here. It is, however, plainly a word of wide meaning, certainly wider than (for example) "lawful". But the greater includes the less and no act which was not believed to be lawful could be believed to be proper within the meaning of the subsection. Thus no assistance is given to any defendant, even a fanatic or a deranged idealist, who knows or suspects that his threat, or the act threatened, is criminal, but believes it to be justified by his end or his peculiar circumstances. The test is not what he regards as justified, but what he believes to be proper. And where, as here, the threats were to do acts which any sane man knows to be against the laws of every civilised country no jury would hesitate long before dismissing the contention that the defendant genuinely believed the threats to be a proper means of reinforcing even a legitimate demand.'

Blackmail and robbery

In some situations there may be an overlap between robbery and blackmail. The highwayman who points his gun at the victim and declares 'your money or your life' and thus induces him to hand over valuables doubtless commits robbery contrary to s8 of the Theft Act 1968, but also blackmail. What separates the two offences, amongst other things, is that s8 requires a person to be put in fear of being 'then and there subjected to force': see *R* v *Taylor* (above). As indicated above, if D demands money from P saying that if it is not paid P's child will be beaten up leaving school that day, D will be guilty of blackmail, but not robbery, no one is put in fear of being then and there subjected to violence.

Blackmail and handling

Note that, for the purposes of s24(4) of the Theft Act 1968, goods obtained as a result of blackmail are regarded as stolen for the purposes of handling stolen goods.

9.3 Burglary

The offence of burglary created by s9 of the Theft Act 1968 replaces the old offences of 'breaking and entering', and much of the complexity that went with them. The section creates two forms of burglary: the first where the defendant enters as a trespasser with intent to commit one of four specified offences; the second where the defendant has entered as a trespasser and gone on to commit theft or grievous bodily harm. A person found guilty of burglary can be imprisoned for up to 14 years where the offence is committed in a building or part of a building used as a dwelling, or in other cases for a maximum of ten years: s9(3)(a) and (b).

Common features of both forms of burglary are that the defendant must enter a building as a trespasser; these matters will be considered, therefore, before the two offences are considered separately.

'Building ... or part of a building'

Byles J, in *Stevens* v *Gourley* (1859) 7 CBNS 99 at 112, stated that a building was

> 'a structure of considerable size and intended to be permanent or at least to endure for a considerable length of time'.

There is no requirement that the premises should be used for human occupation; in *B and S* v *Leathley* [1979] Crim LR 314 (a decision of Carlisle Crown Court) a large freezer container standing in a farmyard without foundations was held to be a building. In each case, whether or not a structure constitutes a building is a mixed question of law and fact to be determined by the jury after guidance from the trial judge. In *Norfolk Constabulary* v *Seekings and Gould* [1986] Crim LR 167, a lorry trailer which was used for storage, and to this end supplied with mains electricity, was held not to constitute a building. In this respect note also s9(4) which provides:

> '(4) References in subsections (1) and (2) above to a building, and the reference in subsection (3) above to a building which is a dwelling shall apply also to an inhabited vehicle or vessel, and shall apply to any such vehicle or vessel at times when the person having a habitation in it is not there as well as at times when he is.'

Reference to 'part of a building' covers the situation where D enters P's house with permission, but then enters P's bedroom, which he does not have permission to do. D would not have committed burglary on first entering the house, but may have done so, subject to what follows below, on entering the bedroom. The Court of Appeal decision in *R* v *Walkington* (1979) 68 Cr App R 427 further illustrates the point. The defendant had entered a department store during opening hours, and had approached a three-sided partition that surrounded a till on the middle of the shop floor. He proceeded to stand inside the partitioned area and opened the till drawer to see if it contained any money for him to steal. The Court of Appeal held that the area inside the partition represented a 'part of a building' from which the public had been impliedly excluded. The defendant being aware of this had been correctly convicted under s9(1)(a) of entering part of a building as a trespasser with intent to steal.

'Enters ... or ... having entered'

The defendant must enter, or have entered, a building in order to be guilty of the completed offence of burglary – failure to enter may still leave the possibility of an attempt charge. Placing a key in a lock, or the blade of a knife inside a window, will not be enough for the completed offence. The view of Edmund-Davies LJ, expressed in *R* v *Collins* [1973] QB 100 at 106, to the effect that an entry must be 'substantial' and 'effective', must considered in the light of more recent decisions such as *R* v *Brown* [1985] Crim LR 212 and *R* v *Ryan* [1996] Crim LR 320. In the former case the Court of Appeal held that leaning into a broken shop window to extract goods was enough to constitute an entry for burglary. In *Ryan*, D was found trapped with his head and right arm wedged in the window of a house. Following *Brown* the court held that it was irrelevant that D had become trapped and was thus unable to proceed to stealing anything from within the building.

' ... as a trespasser'

In civil law A commits a trespass upon B's land, where he enters upon that land without B's permission. B will of course only be able to recover damages where A actually causes him some loss. The civil law concept of trespass is at the heart of the crime of burglary, and in simple terms it could be said that D enters a building owned by P as a trespasser, either where D has no express or implied permission from P to do so, or where D exceeds the express or implied permission granted by P.

In *R* v *Collins* (above), the Court of Appeal confirmed that trespass, for the purposes of the Theft Act 1968, does require proof of mens rea. The appellant sought to challenge his conviction for burglary contrary to s9(1)(a), on the ground that he believed that he had been given permission to enter the house in question by the owner's daughter. Edmund-Davies LJ observed that:

'... there cannot be a conviction for entering premises "as a trespasser" within the meaning of section 9 of the Theft Act unless the person entering does so knowing that he is a trespasser and nevertheless deliberately enters, or, at the very least, is reckless as to whether or not he is entering the premises of another without the other party's consent.'

It is submitted that the recklessness envisaged here is 'subjective' as in *R* v *Cunningham* [1957] 2 QB 396, and not 'objective' as in *R* v *Caldwell* [1982] AC 341, hence D might escape liability where he stopped to consider the risk that he might be trespassing, but went on to dismiss it as negligible.

The court went on to reject the proposition that a defendant could enter a building with permission, but then become a trespasser within s9 simply by exceeding the permission that he had been given, for example by deciding *after* entry to rape or steal. As Edmund-Davies LJ observed:

'... we are entirely in agreement with the view ... that the common law doctrine of trespass ab initio has no application to burglary under the Theft Act 1968.'

See further in this regard *R* v *Laing* [1995] Crim LR 395.

It might be different, of course, where D is invited into P's house for tea, and D accepts the invitation, intending to steal silverware from P's lounge whilst P is out of the room. Provided that D has this secret dishonest intent at the time of his entry into P's house, he will be trespassing, as he will be entering for a purpose in excess of his permission to do so. In *R* v *Smith and Jones* [1976] 3 All ER 54, the appellants, who had visited the house of Smith's father and stolen his television set, were convicted under s9(1)(b) and appealed on the basis that they had permission to go into the house and thus could not have been trespassing. The court held that the defendants were rightly convicted under s9(1)(b), on the basis that a person enters a building as a trespasser where he realises he has exceeded his permission, or is reckless as to whether he has done so. The defendants might have had permission to enter the house for normal domestic purposes, but not to enter in the middle of the night to steal. Confirming that the decision in *R v Collins* (above) had added to the concept of trespass as a civil wrong the mental element of mens rea, James LJ observed:

> '... it is our view that a person is a trespasser for the purpose of section 9(1)(b) of the Theft Act 1968, if he enters premises of another knowing that he is entering in excess of the permission that has been given to him, or being reckless as to whether he is entering in excess of the permission that has been given to him to enter, providing the facts are known to the accused which enable him to realise that he is acting in excess of the permission given or that he is acting recklessly as to whether he exceeds that permission ...'

In *R v Collins* a further point was raised by the prosecution, to the effect that the daughter, not being the tenant or occupier of the dwelling-house and her mother being apparently in occupation, could not have extended an effective invitation to the appellant to enter. Regardless of the position in the law of tort, the court regarded the application of such a proposition in criminal law as 'unthinkable'.

Section 9(1)(a)

Section 9(1)(a), which creates the first form of burglary, provides:

> 'A person is guilty of burglary if –
> he enters any building or part of a building as a trespasser and with intent to commit any such offence as is mentioned in subsection (2) below.'

Subsection (2) (as amended by the Criminal Justice and Public Order Act 1994, Sch 10, para 26) further provides:

> 'The offences referred to in subsection (1)(a) above are offences of stealing anything in the building or part of a building in question, of inflicting on any person therein any grievous bodily harm or raping any person therein, and of doing unlawful damage to the building or anything therein.'

A defendant can incur liability under s9(1)(a) for entering as a trespasser with intent to steal, regardless of whether there is any property to steal in the building. The Court of Appeal's ruling in *Attorney-General's References (Nos 1 & 2 of 1979)* [1979] 2 WLR 578 establishes that the essence of the offence is the defendant's state of mind at the time of entry; the intent to steal can exist quite independently of any property that he can, or wants to, steal.

The offence of inflicting grievous bodily referred to in s9(2) is assumed to be that under s18 of the Offences Against the Person Act 1861, given that the defendant is required to have a specific intent to commit the offence.

Section 9(1)(b)

Section 9(1)(b) provides:

> 'A person is guilty of burglary if having entered any building or part of a building as a trespasser he steals or attempts to steal anything in the building or that part of it or inflicts or attempts to inflict on any person therein any grievous bodily harm.'

Note that the defendant does not need to have had the intention to steal or inflict grievous bodily harm when he entered the building as a trespasser; such intent can be formed subsequent to entry. Curiously, the infliction of grievous bodily harm under s9(1)(b) does not have to constitute an offence, it simply requires D to have inflicted or attempted to inflict grievous bodily harm upon P. The Court of Appeal in *R* v *Jenkins* [1983] 1 All ER 1000 contemplated that a defendant would be guilty under s9(1)(b) where he entered a house as a trespasser and was observed by an occupant of whose presence he was unaware. Should the occupant suffer a stroke as a result of this shock, the defendant would have inflicted grievous bodily harm regardless of his lack of mens rea. The House of Lords, although allowing the defendant's appeal in *R* v *Jenkins* [1983] 3 All ER 448, did not dissent from the above analysis of s9(1)(b).

This unsatisfactory state of affairs is adverted to in the Law Commission's Draft Code, which restates, in code terminology, the offence of burglary. Clause 147 provides (inter alia) that a person commits burglary if, having entered a building as a trespasser, he commits in the building an offence of causing serious personal harm. The causing of such harm, as indicated by clauses 70 and 71 of the Code, would require proof of either intention or recklessness. As the commentary upon cl 147 explained:

> 'This clause takes the opportunity to correct a plain and unintended error in s9 of the Theft Act 1968. Section 9(l)(a) expressly requires entry as a trespasser with intent to commit an "offence". But s9(l)(b) does not expressly require the infliction of grievous bodily harm, which may convert a trespassory entry into burglary, to be an offence; if paragraph (b) were taken literally, burglary could be committed accidentally by someone in a building as a trespasser. This anomaly is an accident of the parliamentary proceedings on the Theft Bill. Our draft eliminates the error, consistently with known parliamentary intention and, we believe, uncontroversially.' (Vol II, para 16.8)

9.4 Aggravated burglary

The offence of aggravated burglary is created by s10(1) of the 1968 Act which provides:

> 'A person is guilty of aggravated burglary if he commits any burglary and at the time has with him any firearm or imitation firearm, any weapon of offence, or any explosive; and for this purpose –
> a) "firearm" includes an airgun or air pistol, and "imitation firearm" means anything which has the appearance of being a firearm, whether capable of being discharged or not; and

b) "weapon of offence" means any article made or adapted for use for causing injury to or incapacitating a person or intended by the person having it with him for such use; and
c) "explosive" means any article manufactured for the purpose of producing a practical effect by explosion, or intended by the person having it with him for that purpose.'

A defendant convicted of the offence on indictment may be sentenced to a maximum of life imprisonment.

The definition of firearm seems to be largely in line with that given under the Firearms Act 1968. Weapon of offence would cover a wide range of articles such as knuckle dusters, coshes, flick knives, razors, pickaxe handles and so on: see *Gibson* v *Wales* [1983] 1 All ER 869 and *R* v *Simpson* [1984] Crim LR 39. Explosives can be defined with reference to the Explosives Act 1875.

The defendant must be proved to have had the weapon with him at the time the burglary is committed. In the case of a s9(1)(a) burglary this is the moment of entry as a trespasser with intent. In the case of s9(1)(b), it is the moment when the offence of theft or grievous bodily harm is attempted or committed: see *R* v *Francis* [1982] Crim LR 363 and *R* v *Klass* (1997) The Times 17 December.

Following *R* v *Stones* [1989] 1 WLR 156 it appears that it will not avail a defendant charged under s10 to contend that, despite his possession of a weapon at the time of the burglary, it had not been his intention to use it. The Court of Appeal held that s10 merely required that the appellant had with him a weapon of offence at the time of the burglary. Applying the mischief rule, the court felt that what Parliament sought to prevent was the commission of burglary by a defendant who might be tempted to use any weapon of offence in his possession if challenged or opposed during the course of a burglary.

These matters were reviewed in *R* v *Kelly* (1992) 97 Cr App R 245. The prosecution case was that the appellant had used a screwdriver to gain access to the house in question, and on being disturbed by the occupant had ordered him to unplug a video recorder. It was further alleged that the appellant had then pushed the screwdriver into the occupant's ribcage and made off. The appellant was subsequently apprehended and stated in evidence that he had never taken the screwdriver out of his pocket during the burglary. Rejecting a submission of 'no case', the trial judge ruled that the key question was whether or not the appellant had had the screwdriver with him as a weapon of offence at the time of the burglary (that is, under s9(1)(b), at the time the video recorder was stolen). On this basis he was satisfied that the appellant had induced the occupant to unplug the video recorder by taking out his screwdriver. In summing up, the trial judge directed the jury that the offence was made out if the appellant had with him at the time of the burglary a weapon with which he intended to inflict injury should the need arise. Dismissing the appeal, the Court of Appeal held that s10(1) of the 1968 Act was specifically concerned with the use of a weapon which made the offence of burglary more serious. The screwdriver was a weapon of offence if the appellant intended to use it to injure the occupant. Given that the burglary occurred at the moment when the appellant stole the video recorder, the only remaining issue was whether or not the appellant had the weapon with him at this time. It would seem that, on the basis of *Kelly*, D could incur liability under s10(1) where he enters a building unarmed, steals property, is disturbed by the occupant, and picks up an ashtray and assaults the occupant with it. One might ask if this was what Parliament intended? D might argue that the offence of burglary is in fact made out under s9(1)(b) once he has attempted to steal property, thus in the example given, use of the weapon is not 'at the time' of the burglary. The decision in *Hale* (above) suggests, however, that the court would regard the burglary as continuing for at least as long as D was appropriating the property within the building.

10

Handling Stolen Goods

10.1 Introduction

10.2 Stolen goods

10.3 Modes of handling

10.4 Mens rea

10.5 Innocent receipt and subsequent mens rea

10.1 Introduction

Section 22(1) of the Theft Act 1968 creates the offence of handling stolen goods, replacing offences under the Larceny Acts of 1861 and 1916 which had previously represented the law. As may be seen from what follows, the 1968 Act may have replaced the old law, but it is an area that still bristles with complexities due in no small part to the form in which the offence is drafted. Section 22(1) provides:

> 'A person handles stolen goods if (otherwise than in the course of the stealing) knowing or believing them to be stolen goods he dishonestly receives the goods, or dishonestly undertakes or assists in their retention, removal, disposal or realisation by or for the benefit of another.'

The maximum punishment for handling following conviction on indictment is 14 years' imprisonment. The rationale behind punishing handlers more severely than thieves is that were it not for the existence of handlers (or 'fences') there would be little theft of an organised nature.

10.2 Stolen goods

The combined effect of a number of provisions in the 1968 Act is that the term 'stolen goods' has acquired a meaning peculiar to the offence.

Goods
Section 34(2)(b) provides:

289

' "Goods", except in so far as the context otherwise requires, includes money and every other description of property except land, and includes things severed from the land by stealing.'

The phrase 'and every other description of property' is presumed to encompass choses in action as well as tangible property. Were it to be otherwise it might prove impossible to convict a defendant of handling stolen goods where money had been stolen by the thief, paid into the thief's bank account, and then transferred via a bank credit to the defendant's bank account. The chose in action, the bank balance, clearly represents the original stolen money: see further *R* v *Pitchley* (1973) 57 Cr App R 30; *Attorney-General's Reference (No 4 of 1979)* (1980) 71 Cr App R 341.

Stolen

The question of whether or not goods are 'stolen' for the purposes of s22(1) is best approached in stages. Section 24(4) provides:

'For purposes of the provisions of this Act relating to goods which have been stolen (including subsections (1) to (3) above) goods obtained in England or Wales or elsewhere either by blackmail or in the circumstances described in s15(1) of this Act shall be regarded as stolen; and "steal", "theft" and "thief" shall be construed accordingly.'

Note that the goods must have been obtained as a result of one of the three offences (theft, obtaining property by deception, or blackmail) having been committed. It is not enough that the defendant believes the goods to have been stolen: see *R* v *Porter* [1976] Crim LR 58. In such a case, however, the defendant might still be convicted of attempting to handle stolen goods on the basis that he believes them to have been stolen, even though they have not: see below.

If s24(4) is satisfied, it is necessary to ensure that the goods have not ceased to be stolen for the purposes of s22(1) by operation of s24(3), which provides:

'But no goods shall be regarded as having continued to be stolen goods after they have been restored to the person from whom they were stolen or to other lawful possession or custody, or after that person and any other person claiming through him have otherwise ceased as regards those goods to have any right to restitution in respect of the theft.'

Hence if goods are restored to the possession of the person entitled to possess them they cease to be stolen. There is a similar result if they are placed in police custody, but this in itself raises the difficult question of what constitutes police custody. In *Haughton* v *Smith* [1975] AC 476, a lorry loaded with tins of meat ceased to be stolen when police stopped the vehicle, and climbed aboard, hiding themselves in the trailer, intending to ambush other members of a criminal gang when they came to unload the contents of the lorry. On the other hand, in *Attorney-General's Reference (No 1 of 1974)* [1974] 1 QB 744 the Court of Appeal were unwilling to conclude that a police officer who had spotted what he thought might be stolen goods inside a car, and who as a consequence had removed the car's rotor arm, thus immobilising the car, had taken lawful possession and custody of the car. He had kept it under observation so that he could question the driver when he returned, but the court ruled that the matter was one that should have been left to the jury on the facts. Essentially it was a question of what the police officer had intended at the time.

Where goods cease to be stolen because of the operation of s24(3), but the defendant fails to realise this and handles goods believing them to be stolen, he can be charged with attempting to handle stolen goods, contrary to s1(1) Criminal Attempts Act 1981. The House of Lords' decision in *Anderton* v *Ryan* [1985] 2 WLR 968, which had suggested that there could be no charge of attempted handling in the absence of proof that goods were actually stolen, has been overruled by a more recent decision of their Lordships in *R* v *Shivpuri* [1986] 2 WLR 988. The problem should now be dealt with by asking: 'Did the defendant take steps that he believed were more than merely preparatory to the commission of the offence of handling stolen goods?' Such a belief can exist regardless of whether or not the goods are stolen.

Further, s24(3) refers to goods ceasing to be stolen for the purposes of s22(1) where the owner ceases to have any right of restitution in respect of those goods. The law relating to restitution is a large and complex topic, an explanation of which would be neither suitable or practical in a work of this nature. A relatively simple illustration of the subsection's operation can, however, be given by the following example: A obtains property by deception from P, for example having purchased goods by drawing a worthless cheque. A obtains voidable title to the goods. Now suppose that before P takes any effective steps to avoid this transaction, A sells the goods on to B, a bona fide purchaser for value without notice. It is submitted that in such a case P would have lost his right to restitution, and even if B later discovers the origin of the goods, B cannot be guilty of handling because the goods cease to be stolen by virtue of s24(3).

Section 24(2) is the third provision that may need satisfying in determining when goods are stolen. It deals with the situation where stolen property has changed hands and been exchanged for other forms of property. It states:

'For purposes of those provisions references to stolen goods shall include, in addition to the goods originally stolen and parts of them (whether in their original state or not) –
a) any other goods which directly or indirectly represent or have at any time represented the stolen goods in the hands of the thief as being the proceeds of any disposal or realisation of the whole or part of the goods stolen or of goods so representing the stolen goods; and
b) any other goods which directly or indirectly represent or have at any time represented the stolen goods in the hands of a handler of the stolen goods or any part of them as being the proceeds of any disposal or realisation of the whole or part of the stolen goods handled by him or of goods so representing them.'

Despite appearances, the aim and effect of s24(2) is to limit the scope of handling stolen goods. For goods to be stolen they must be, or have been, in the hands of a thief or handler and directly or indirectly represent the stolen goods in whole or part. The original stolen property will remain stolen throughout any scheme of handling until the provisions of s24(3) come into play. Section 24(2) is of more significance where a defendant knowingly deals with the proceeds of the original stolen goods. The extent to which s24(2) can actually restrict the scope of handling is illustrated by the following example.

A steals a car from P and sells it to B for £500. A then gives £100 of this money to C, who is innocent as to its origin. C spends the £100 on a watch, then discovers the truth and resolves to keep it. The complexities of innocent receipt and subsequent mens rea are considered later, but for present purposes it should be noted that the watch purchased by C is not stolen property. It does indirectly represent the stolen car (the original stolen property) but it has not been in the hands of a thief or a handler, and is not in the hands of a thief or handler. It would be otherwise had C realised the source of the money before buying the watch.

Some uncertainty has in the past surrounded the situation where stolen money is put into a bank account. In *Pitchley* (above) D's son stole £150, which D placed in his Post Office savings account. D later learnt of the source of the money and after a few days informed the police. D was convicted of assisting in the retention of the money for the benefit of his son, a decision upheld by the Court of Appeal. The decision has been criticised on the basis that when the money was paid into the account it became a different type of property, namely a debt, or chose in action, and as such ceased to be stolen because it had not been and was not in the hands of a thief or handler in that form; see further *Attorney-General's Reference (No 4 of 1979)* (1980) 71 Cr App R 341. It is likely that these uncertainties will have been removed with the enactment of the Theft (Amendment) Act 1996, which creates a new offence of dishonestly retaining a wrongful credit by inserting a new s24A in the 1968 Act. Under this section a person is guilty of an offence if:

1. a wrongful credit has been made to an account kept by him or in respect of which he has any right or interest;
2. he knows or believes that the credit is wrongful; and
3. he dishonestly fails to take such steps as are reasonable in the circumstances to secure that the credit is cancelled.

A wrongful credit to an account is one that is to the credit side of a money transfer obtained contrary to s15A or one derived from an offence under s15A, or by blackmail, or from stolen goods. Note that under s24A(5), in determining whether a credit to an account is wrongful, it is immaterial (in particular) whether the account is overdrawn before or after the credit is made.

10.3 Modes of handling

Section 22(1) creates several different modes of handling such as receiving, removing, retaining and so on. The Court of Appeal held in *R* v *Nicklin* [1977] 2

All ER 444 that a defendant could be charged on an indictment which simply alleged handling without particularising the mode. Where an indictment does particularise a mode of handling, however, such as receiving, the defendant cannot be convicted of a different form, such as assisting in the removal of goods.

Receiving

Receiving, and arranging to receive, are the only modes of handling that can be charged where the defendant does not act for the benefit of another or assist another to deal with the property. The most obvious instances are where the defendant takes stolen property into his possession or control for his own use. It is not necessary to show, however, that the receiving is for the benefit of the defendant, and *Haughton* v *Smith* [1975] AC 476 is evidence that it is sufficient for the defendant to have taken control of goods.

The two forms of handling

It is apparent from the decision of the House of Lords in *R* v *Bloxham* [1982] 1 All ER 582 that the modes of handling fall into two forms: on the one hand the defendant might receive, or arrange to receive; on the other hand the defendant might undertake the retention, removal, disposal, or realisation of stolen goods for another's benefit or assist in the retention, removal, disposal, or realisation of stolen goods by another person, or for the benefit of another.

Removal would simply involve transportation or movement of the stolen goods from one point to another. For example, D entrusts stolen goods to X, who does not know they are stolen. Later D informs X of the truth and requests X to take the goods to Y's house, which X does. X cannot be charged with receiving stolen property because he lacked mens rea at the time of receipt, but he clearly undertakes the removal of stolen goods for another's benefit with mens rea.

Realisation involves the defendant in the sale or exchanging of stolen property. Placing stolen cash in a bank account is arguably the realisation of stolen property on the basis that tangible property has been changed into intangible property, a debt. Disposal would encompass such activity as burying or destroying stolen property.

Retention, according to the Court of Appeal in *R* v *Pitchley* (above) should be given its ordinary dictionary meaning of 'keep possession … not lose, continue to have', and the court proceeded to hold that the defendant had assisted in the retention of money stolen by his son, by permitting it to remain in his savings account. The decision raises the question of to what extent a defendant may be guilty of retention by omission. In *R* v *Brown* [1970] 1 QB 105, the Court of Appeal held that a defendant, who had told police searching for stolen property in his flat that he knew nothing of any stolen property and that they should 'get lost' might not necessarily be guilty of assisting in the retention of stolen goods. The failure of the defendant to reveal the presence of stolen goods was evidence of his guilt but not conclusive proof. Given that the defendant is not under a legal duty to inform the police of such matters, the decision is clearly correct. The situation might be rather different where the defendant deliberately misleads the police. In *R v Kanwar* [1982] Crim LR 532, the Court of Appeal held that the defendant who had lied to the police as to the origin of goods in her house that had in fact been stolen and stored there by her husband, was held to have assisted in their retention by him.

Strange as it may seem, although a defendant can be guilty of retention by misleading the police, he or she will not necessarily incur liability simply by using goods known to be stolen. In *R v Sanders* (1982) 75 Cr App R 84 the defendant had used a fan heater and battery charger at premises owned by his father, knowing that his father had stolen the items. The Court of Appeal allowed his appeal against conviction for handling the stolen goods by assisting in their retention, on the basis that mere use of the goods knowing them to be stolen was not enough; it had to be proved that the defendant had assisted in the retention in some way, for instance by making them more difficult to identify or holding them pending their ultimate disposal.

Arranging

Section 22(1) creates yet further modes of handling by making it an offence to arrange to receive, arrange to undertake the removal, realisation, disposal, retention of stolen goods for another's benefit, or arrange to assist in the removal, realisation, disposal or retention of stolen goods by another person. The effect is to create an inchoate form of handling akin to conspiracy, which is indeed what it will become if 'another party' to the arrangement has the requisite mens rea. Liability depends upon the goods being stolen when the arrangement is made, although as with other forms of inchoate liability, there is no need for the arrangement to be carried out. The need for the goods to have been stolen before any such arrangement can found a conviction was reiterated by the Court of Appeal in *R v Park* [1988] Crim LR 238.

'For the benefit of another'

From the above it will have been seen that the so-called second form of handling requires the defendant to act in the assistance of another person or undertake action for another's benefit. It is this latter provision which has caused some uncertainty. The principal authority on the point is the House of Lords' decision in *R v Bloxham* (above). The defendant bought a car at a bargain price. He later discovered that it was stolen, and sold it on cheaply to an unknown person. The defendant was charged with assisting or undertaking the realisation of stolen property by another person or for another's benefit. In holding that this activity fell outside the scope of handling as defined by s22, Lord Bridge observed:

> 'The critical words to be construed are "undertakes ... their ... disposal or realisation ... for the benefit of another person". Considering these words first in isolation, it seems to

me that, if A sells his own goods to B, it is a somewhat strained use of language to describe this as a disposal or realisation of the goods for the benefit of B. True it is that B obtains a benefit from the transaction, but it is surely more natural to say that the disposal or realisation is for A's benefit than for B's. It is the purchase, not the sale, that is for the benefit of B. It is only when A is selling as agent for a third party C that it would be entirely natural to describe the sale as a disposal or realisation for the benefit of another person ... the words cannot ... be construed in isolation. They must be construed in their context, bearing in mind ... that the second half of the subsection creates a single offence which can be committed in various ways ... the ... words contemplate four activities (retention, removal, disposal, realisation). The offence can be committed in relation to any one of these activities in one or other of two ways. First, the offender may himself undertake the activity *for the benefit of* another person. Secondly, the activity may be undertaken *by* another person and the offender may assist him. Of course, if the thief or an original receiver and his friend act together in, say, removing the stolen goods, the friend may be committing the offence in both ways. But this does not invalidate the analysis and if the analysis holds good, it must follow, I think, that the category of other persons contemplated by the subsection is subject to the same limitations in whichever way the offence is committed. Accordingly, a purchaser, as such, of stolen goods, cannot, in my opinion, be "another person" within the subsection, since his act of purchase could not sensibly be described as a disposal or realisation of the stolen goods *by* him. Equally, therefore, even if the sale to him could be described as a disposal or realisation for his benefit, the transaction is not, in my view, within the ambit of the subsection.'

On this basis Bloxham would, presumably, have been guilty had he instructed the purchaser to pay over the purchase money direct to some third party, as this would have been a realisation for another's benefit. Although Bloxham would have been protected from any liability for theft, in relation to the car, by s3(2) of the 1968 Act, it is conceivable that he might have been charged with obtaining the proceeds of the sale by deception, if the purchaser bought the car on the basis that it had not been the subject of a theft.

'Otherwise than in the course of stealing'

This phrase appears in parenthesis in s22(1) and is there in order to avoid, to some extent, an overlap in liability between thieves and handlers, bearing in mind the greater maximum penalty that might be imposed on the latter. The provision nevertheless creates two particular difficulties.

When does stealing end and handling commence? If A picks P's pocket and immediately hands the contents to B who is standing next to him, is A guilty of theft and B of handling, or is B an accomplice to A's theft? The answer rather depends on the approach taken to appropriation. In *R v Pitham and Hehl* (1977) 65 Cr App R 45, the view was taken that appropriation was an instantaneous act; thus if A offered to sell P's goods to B, both A and B knowing that they had no right to be dealing with P's goods in this way, A would be guilty of theft as soon as the offer to sell was made, and B would be guilty of arranging to receive as soon as he accepted. The theft by A would be complete on the making of the offer, thus B's acceptance would be otherwise than in the course of stealing. The contrary view of appropriation is illustrated in the Court of Appeal's decision in *R* v *Hale* (1978) 68 Cr App R 415, wherein it was held that appropriation was a 'continuing act' that began when the defendant assumed the rights of the owner; where it ended was a matter to be determined on the facts by the jury. It is generally agreed that unless this latter interpretation is adopted, the 'otherwise than in the course of dealing' provision becomes of little use.

The second difficulty is in determining to whom the phrase applies. Clearly the original thief, but what of those who knowingly deal with the stolen property subsequently? The problem arises from the fact that nearly all those who handle stolen property also commit theft of it, in the sense that they dishonestly assume the rights of the owner with intention to permanently deprive the owner of it. Were the provision to be applied strictly it would be virtually impossible to convict anyone of handling stolen goods because they would be acting *within* the course of stealing. The problem may be, however, more apparent than real. The decision of the Court of Appeal in *R* v *Sainthouse* [1980] Crim LR 506 suggests that the 'course of stealing' should be restricted to the initial theft by which the goods become 'stolen'. Thus subsequent handlers can also be charged as thieves and vice-versa, the limitation having no application to them: see also *R* v *Dolan* (1976) 62 Cr App R 36. The prosecution does not have a positive duty to prove that a (subsequent) handling is otherwise than in the course of stealing: see *R* v *Cash* [1985] Crim LR 311 and *Attorney-General for Hong Kong* v *Yip Kai Foon* [1988] 1 All ER 153.

10.4 Mens rea

Dishonesty

The defendant's dishonesty must coincide with and relate to his mode of handling. There are no particular provisions in s22 relating to dishonesty (unlike theft), hence the question is one for the jury to decide on the facts. The Court of Appeal decision in *R* v *Roberts* [1986] Crim LR 122 suggests that whilst the test in *R* v *Ghosh* can be used, it should only be resorted to when there is a real case for so doing, ie the defendant must have raised the defence that he did not realise that anybody would regard what he was doing as dishonest. See further to the same effect in *R* v *Brennen* [1990] Crim LR 118.

'Knowledge or belief that the goods are stolen'

In addition to dishonesty, the prosecution must prove that the defendant knew or believed the goods to be stolen at the time of handling, and the moment of handling should be particularised in the direction to the jury: see *R* v *Brook* [1993] Crim LR 455. In *Atwal* v *Massey* (1971) 56 Cr App R 6, the Court of Appeal sought to make clear that the correct approach to 'belief' was to apply a subjective test. As Lord Widgery CJ observed:

'If when the justices said that the appellant ought to have known that the kettle was stolen they meant that any reasonable man would have realised that it was stolen, then that was not the right test. It is not sufficient to establish an offence under section 22 that the goods were received in circumstances which would have put a reasonable man on his enquiry. The question is a subjective one: was the appellant aware of the theft or did he believe the goods to be stolen or did he, suspecting the goods to be stolen, deliberately shut his eyes to the consequences?'

As James LJ pointed out, however, in *R* v *Griffiths* (1974) 60 Cr App R 14, great care should be taken by a trial judge, directing a jury on the basis of *Atwal* v *Massey*, to avoid confusion between the mental element of knowledge or belief and the approach by which the jury may arrive at a conclusion as to knowledge or belief. He commented:

'To direct the jury that the offence is committed if the defendant, suspecting that the goods were stolen, deliberately shut his eyes to the circumstances as an alternative to knowing or believing the goods were stolen is a misdirection. To direct the jury that, in common sense and in law, they may find that the defendant knew or believed the goods to be stolen, because he deliberately closed his eyes to the circumstances, is a perfectly proper direction.'

The question, therefore, is not whether a reasonable man in the circumstances would have believed the goods to be stolen, but whether the defendant actually did so. Where there was evidence that should have made the defendant suspicious, and it appeared that he deliberately turned a blind eye to this, the jury could infer from this that he believed the goods to be stolen, but it is not to be equated with such belief. It is certainly a misdirection to tell a jury that a defendant can be treated as having 'belief' where he thinks goods are probably stolen: see *R* v *Reader* (1978) 66 Cr App R 33; *R* v *Lincoln* [1980] Crim LR 575; *R* v *Stagg* [1978] Crim LR 227; *R* v *Grainge* [1974] 1 All ER 928; *R* v *Toor* [1987] Crim LR 122; and *R* v *Forsyth* (1997) (CA No 96/02860/X2).

R v *Brook* (above) indicates the dangers where the trial judge seeks to embellish the standard 'subjective' direction. In that case the trial judge had directed that jury that the fact that there was no reasonable conclusion other than that the contents of a bag in the appellant's possession comprised stolen goods was a factor that might assist them in deciding whether or not the appellant knew or believed the goods to be stolen. The Court of Appeal held that the trial judge had erred in introducing an unwarranted element of objectivity in relation to the mens rea to be proved. The fact that an objective observer would have concluded that the goods were undoubtedly stolen was irrelevant given that the test for mens rea was subjective. In the light of the above one might be tempted to ask whether or not the law should be amended to permit the jury to consider evidence as to whether or not it was reasonable for such a belief to be held. By way of analogy consider the approach in rape to the defendant's honest belief that a woman was consenting to sexual intercourse: see s1(2) Sexual Offences (Amendment) Act 1976.

Recent possession

Where a defendant is found to have been in possession of stolen property and gives no explanation or at least no satisfactory explanation for its presence, the jury will be told of the short passage of time between the reporting of the theft and the finding of the defendant in possession of the stolen goods, and is entitled to infer from this evidence that the defendant acquired the goods knowing or believing them to be ' stolen.

10.5 Innocent receipt and subsequent mens rea

Where a defendant receives stolen property innocently but later discovers it to have been stolen, he cannot be charged with receiving stolen property because he was innocent at the time of receipt; non-coincidence of mens rea and actus reus. Whether he will incur liability subsequent to his discovering the truth depends upon whether he gave value for the property, and what he does with it.

Where the defendant receives stolen property innocently as a gift and then discovers the truth, he is likely to incur liability of some sort if he does anything other than restore it to lawful custody. If he decides to keep the property for himself, he cannot be guilty of handling, for although the goods are stolen he does not assist in or undertake the retention of the goods by another, or for another's benefit. He would, however, be guilty of theft by virtue of s3(1) Theft Act 1968, in that he has come by the property innocently and later assumed the rights of the owner by keeping it. If he decides to sell or dispose of the property he will not be guilty of handling, see *R* v *Bloxham* (above) because this will not be 'by another' or 'for another's' benefit. He will be guilty of theft as above in that the sale or disposal will be an appropriation of another's property.

Where the defendant gives value for the property and then discovers the truth, he will be protected from liability for theft regardless of how he deals with the property, on the basis of s3(2) Theft Act 1968 which provides that:

> 'Where property or a right or interest in property is or purports to be transferred for value to a person acting in good faith no later assumption by him of rights which he believed himself to be acquiring shall, by reason of any defect in the transferor's title, amount to theft of the property.'

Given *R* v *Bloxham* (above) the defendant should also escape liability for handling in that his removal, retention, disposal, or realisation of the property will not be 'by or for the benefit of another': see further *R* v *Wheeler* (1990) 92 Cr App R 279.

11

Criminal Damage

11.1 Introduction

11.2 The basic offence

11.3 Actus reus

11.4 Mens rea

11.5 The 'aggravated' offence

11.6 'Without lawful excuse'

11.1 Introduction

The Criminal Damage Act 1971 was introduced to replace the old complex law relating to damage and destruction of property based on the Malicious Damage Act 1861. The 1971 Act creates two different types of liability for criminal damage; s1(1) creates the 'basic' or 'simple' offence of damaging/destroying property belonging to another, s1(2) creates the aggravated offence of damaging or destroying property with either intention to endanger life, or recklessness as to whether life is endangered. Under s1(3) the offence committed by destroying or damaging property by fire should be charged as arson. The need to maintain a clear distinction between criminal damage caused by fire and criminal damage otherwise caused is signified by s4(1) which provides for a higher penalty in the case of arson: see *R* v *Cooper (G) and Cooper (Y)* [1991] Crim LR 524.

It should be noted that, to some extent, the offence of criminal damage complements the offence of theft. Indeed some situations may give rise to the possibility of charging a defendant with either theft or criminal damage, eg where D takes P's car and destroys it by driving it into a brick wall.

Section 2 of the 1971 Act creates the offence of making threats to damage or destroy another's property, intending to cause fear thereby, or making threats to damage his own property in a way which he knows is likely to endanger life, again intending to cause fear as a result.

Section 3 makes it an offence for any person, without lawful excuse, to have in his control anything he intends to use to damage another's property, or which he intends to use to damage his own property in a way which he knows is likely to endanger life.

Conviction for offences under the Act carries the possibility of ten years imprisonment, with the exception of ss1(2) and 1(3) where the maximum sentence available is life imprisonment. Section 46 of the Criminal Justice and Public Order Act 1994 amends s22(1) of the Magistrates' Courts Act 1980 with the effect that magistrates can try summarily any criminal damage case where the value involved does not exceed £5,000 (an increase from £2,000).

Section 30 of the Crime and Disorder Act 1998 introduces a new offence of 'racially aggravated' criminal damage. The offence comprises criminal damage contrary to s1(1) of the Criminal Damage Act 1971 (destroying or damaging property belonging to another) which is racially aggravated, as defined in s28 (see Chapter 5, section 5.1 for an explanation of this concept as it applies to assault). Note that s30(3) provides that, for the purposes of the aggravated criminal damage offence, s28 has effect 'as if the person to whom the property belongs or is treated as belonging for the purposes of that Act were the victim of the offence.' The maximum penalty where the offence is tried on indictment is increased to 14 years.

11.2 The basic offence

Section 1(1) of the Criminal Damage Act 1971 provides:

> 'A person who without lawful excuse destroys or damages any property belonging to another intending to destroy or damage any such property or being reckless as to whether any such property would be destroyed or damaged shall be guilty of an offence.'

11.3 Actus reus

'Property'

The basic definition of property, for the purposes of this offence, is provided by s10(1) of the Act which states:

> 'In this Act "property" means property of a tangible nature, whether real or personal, including money and:
> a) including wild creatures which have been tamed or are ordinarily kept in captivity, and any other wild creatures or their carcasses if, but only if, they have been reduced into possession which has not been lost or abandoned or are in the course of being reduced into possession; but
> b) not including mushrooms growing wild on any land or flowers, fruit or foliage of a plant growing wild on any land.
> For the purposes of this subsection "mushroom" includes any fungus and "plant" includes any shrub or tree.'

Similarities with the definition of property provided by s4 of the Theft Act 1968 are evident, except that criminal damage may be committed in relation to land, whilst land cannot be stolen; conversely intangible property can be stolen, but cannot be the subject of a criminal damage charge.

Whilst a computer program might not be regarded as tangible property, the material on which the program is stored certainly will be. In *Cox* v *Riley* [1986] Crim LR 460, the Divisional Court held that a defendant who had damaged a plastic circuit card used to operate a computerised saw so that the card would require reprogramming before it could be used, had damaged tangible property within the scope of s10(1).

This decision has been followed by *R* v *Whiteley* (1991) 93 Cr App R 25, a case in which the appellant gained unauthorised access to a computer network, the Joint Academic Network (JANET), and proceeded to create and delete files, change the passwords of authorised users, and delete the user file to remove evidence of his own use of the system. In seeking to have his convictions for criminal damage quashed the appellant had contended that the magnetic disks on which the system's files were stored had not themselves been damaged by his activities, hence the only damage was to the information stored on the disks, and this fell outside the scope of the offence as it was intangible property. The Court of Appeal rejected this argument, holding that the magnetic disks on which files were stored were clearly tangible property, and by deleting files, the appellant had interfered with the configuration of magnetic particles on the disks. Lord Lane CJ pointed out that it was wrong to conclude that, because the offence of criminal damage required interference with tangible property, the damage itself had to be tangible, in the sense that it had to be observable to the naked eye, or perceptible by touch. Any alteration to the physical nature of the property would suffice. It is interesting to note that the jury acquitted the appellant in respect of the prosecution's other allegations of criminal damage, which had been based on the premise that the appellant had damaged the computer system itself as his activities caused it to be shut down for long periods whilst the effects of his interference were rectified.

In its report, *Computer Misuse* (Cm 189), the Law Commission recommended the introduction of a new offence specifically to deal with the problems of computer misuse. The need for such legislation was further emphasised by the prosecution's failure to sustain charges under the Forgery and Counterfeiting Act 1981 against computer hackers: see *R* v *Gold*; *R* v *Schifreen* [1988] AC 1063. The result of this pressure for reform was the Computer Misuse Act 1990 which creates, inter alia, three new offences, namely: 'unauthorised access to computer material (s1)'; 'unauthorised access with intent to commit or facilitate commission of further offences' (s2); and 'unauthorised modification of computer equipment' (s3). In this respect it is interesting to note that s3(6) of the 1990 Act provides that:

> 'For the purposes of the Criminal Damage Act 1971 a modification of the contents of a computer shall not be regarded as damaging any computer or computer storage medium unless its effects on that computer or computer storage medium impairs its physical condition.'

On the basis of this provision, it is submitted that were the circumstances in *Cox* v *Riley* and *R* v *Whiteley* to re-occur, neither defendant would be guilty of criminal damage. The offence under s3 of the 1990 Act carries up to five years imprisonment. For an illustration of the 1990 Act's potential usefulness in providing ancillary offences, see *Attorney-General's Reference (No 1 of 1991)* [1992] 3 WLR 432.

'Belonging to another'

Section 10(2) provides the basic definition of belonging to another. It states:

'Property shall be treated for the purposes of this Act as belonging to any person:
a) having the custody or control of it;
b) having in it any proprietary right or interest (not being an equitable interest arising only from an agreement to transfer or grant an interest); or
c) having a charge on it.'

Section 10(3) provides that where property is 'subject to a trust, the persons to whom it belongs will be taken to include any person having a right to enforce the trust'. Section 10(4) provides that the property of a corporation sole shall be treated as belonging to the corporation, notwithstanding a vacancy in the corporation.

Note that the requirement that the property in question should belong to another is not an element of offences under ss1(2), 2(b), or 3(a) of the Act.

'Damages or destroys'

Whilst the offence contemplates total destruction to property, damage will be sufficient. In *Samuel* v *Stubbs* [1972] 4 SASR 200, the court held that criminal damage had been done to a policeman's helmet when it had been jumped upon, causing 'a temporary functional derangement'. It seems clear that spoiling, polluting, rearranging, dismantling or otherwise physically interfering with an individual's property can constitute criminal damage, the decision to prosecute perhaps being determined by the extent to which property has been reduced in value (eg a priceless painting being slashed with a knife), or the cost to the owner of restoring the property to its original state. For example in *R* v *Henderson and Battley* (1984) 29 November (unreported) unauthorised dumping of waste on a building site which cost £2,000 to remove was held to constitute criminal damage.

Some care may need to be taken in the drafting of the information or indictment. In *Morphitis* v *Salmon* [1990] Crim LR 48, the respondent, S, had erected a barrier, consisting of uprights, a scaffolding bar and a clip, across an access road leading to premises used by both himself and M. M had removed the bar and clip and taken them to his garage. The bar was found to have been scratched but it was not proved that M had caused this. M was convicted of criminal damage to the bar and clip. M appealed by way of case stated alleging that the property had not been damaged within the terms of the 1971 Act. The Divisional Court, quashing the conviction, held that even if M had scratched the bar it would not have amounted to criminal damage as it did not interfere with its usefulness. The dismantling of machinery could amount to criminal damage where this interfered with the working of the machine as a whole, but the information in the present case alleged damage to the individual parts of the barrier, hence the prosecution should not have succeeded. It would appear that the appellant may have been successfully prosecuted had he been charged with criminal damage to the barrier as a whole.

In *Hardman and Others* v *Chief Constable of Avon and Somerset Constabulary* [1986] Crim LR 330, Bristol Crown Court held, on an appeal from justices, that human silhouettes sprayed onto pavements by CND supporters to indicate vaporised human remains following the dropping of an atomic bomb did constitute damage within the Act, even though the figures would be washed away by the next rainfall. The local authority had been put to the expense of cleaning away the figures. The court expressly approved of the approach taken by Walters J in *Samuel* v *Stubbs* (above) where he stated (at p203):

> 'It seems to me that it is difficult to lay down any very general and, at the same time, precise and absolute rule as to what constitutes "damage". One must be guided in a great degree by the circumstances of each case, the nature of the article, and the mode in which it is affected or treated. Moreover, the meaning of the word "damage" must as I have already said, be controlled by its context. The word may be used in the sense of "mischief done to property".'

Whether graffiti as such will amount to criminal damage is a question of fact and degree in each case. In *Roe* v *Kingerlee* [1986] Crim LR 735 the Divisional Court held that the application of a brown substance to the walls of a cell, which cost £7 to remove, could constitute criminal damage.

The damage or destruction in issue will normally arise from the defendant's freely willed act; it should be remembered however, that a defendant may be held responsible for failing to halt the spread of harm started accidentally. See further *R* v *Miller* [1983] 2 WLR 539.

11.4 Mens rea

Intention

The defendant must be proved not only to have intended the act which causes the damage but also to have intended that the act should cause the damage. For example, D may intend to light a fire, but will not be held to have intended criminal damage unless he intended that fire to consume property belonging to others.

It is submitted that a defendant will have the necessary intention for criminal damage where he has the damage or destruction of another's property as his purpose, or where he foresees it as an inevitable consequence of his actions.

The defendant's motive, for example, a belief that his additions or alterations to property make it look more attractive, will normally be irrelevant: see *R* v *Fancy* [1980] Crim LR 171.

Recklessness

The prosecution, in securing a conviction for criminal damage, does not have to establish intention; it will suffice if it can be shown that the defendant was reckless. The meaning of recklessness in the context of criminal damage has as its basis the decision of the House of Lords in *R* v *Caldwell* [1981] 1 All ER 961.

Prior to the *Caldwell* decision, the recklessness involved in criminal damage was understood to be subjective in nature. A defendant would only be regarded as having been reckless if he took an unjustifiable risk, and was aware at the time that the risk (of criminal damage) might materialise. Decisions such as *R* v *Stephenson* [1979] QB 695 are evidence of this approach.

The 'revolution' introduced by *Caldwell* was the addition of an alternative form of recklessness, one based on the defendant having failed to give any thought to an obvious risk that property would be damaged or destroyed. This type of recklessness is frequently referred to as being 'objective' in nature in that it imposes liability upon the defendant for not adverting to a risk which would have been 'obvious' to the reasonable man. Any doubts as to the objective nature of this liability were dispelled by the Divisional Court's decision in *Elliot* v *C* [1983] 2 All ER 1005 wherein it was held that a defendant could still be regarded as reckless, notwithstanding her inability to recognize a risk due to low intelligence, where a reasonable person would nevertheless have perceived the risk of criminal damage as obvious. This type of recklessness applies equally to the 'basic' offence of criminal damage under s1(1) and to 'aggravated' criminal damage under s1(2). See further the Court of Appeal decision in *R* v *Sangha* [1988] 1 WLR 519, and the detailed consideration of recklessness at Chapter 3, section 3.3.

'Belonging to another'

Mens rea must extend to this element of actus reus for there to be liability under s1(1). Where, as in *R* v *Smith* [1974] QB 354, a defendant damages property in the mistaken belief that it is his, he will not be guilty of an offence provided the mistake is a honest one. The defendant is judged on the facts as he believes them to be, his mistake in civil law relating to the ownership of property amounting to a defence.

11.5 The 'aggravated' offence

Section 1(2) of the 1971 Act provides:

> 'A person who without lawful excuse destroys or damages any property, whether belonging to himself or another:
> a) intending to destroy or damage any property or being reckless as to whether any property would be destroyed or damaged; and
> b) intending by the destruction or damage to endanger the life of another or being reckless as to whether the life of another would be thereby endangered;
> shall be guilty of an offence.'

The 'aggravating' factor is clearly that supplied by s1(2)(b), of the intention to endanger life, or recklessness as to whether this occurs. Note that no lives actually have to have been endangered in order for there to be liability here; the defendant's state of mind is what is in issue. Whilst intention and recklessness have the meanings considered above, it should be noted that the words 'by' and 'thereby' are crucial in s1(2), as is illustrated by the House of Lords' decision in *R v Steer* [1987] 3 WLR 205. The defendant fired an automatic rifle at the bedroom window of his business partner's house. The bedroom was occupied at the time. The defendant, who had pleaded guilty to a charge under s1(2)(b), causing criminal damage being reckless as to whether life would be endangered, following a ruling by the trial judge, appealed on the ground that he had not intended that the criminal damage to the window should endanger life, and therefore lacked the mens rea for the aggravated offence. The defendant was successful before the Court of Appeal and, on appeal by the prosecution, the House of Lords answered the certified question by holding that upon the true construction of s1(2)(b) of the 1971 Act the prosecution were required to prove that the danger to life resulted from the destruction of or damage to property; it was not sufficient for the prosecution to prove that it resulted from the act of the defendant which caused the destruction or damage. In other words the prosecution would have had to show that the defendant intended that the damage to the window would endanger life, or at least be reckless to this possibility. For evidence that the distinction is a fine one, which continues to give the courts difficulties, see *R v Webster and Others; R v Warwick* [1995] 2 All ER 168, where Lord Taylor CJ explaining the operation of s1(2), and adverting to what he said some would regard as a 'dismal distinction', observed:

'... if a defendant throws a brick at the windscreen of a moving vehicle, given that he causes some damage to the vehicle, whether he is guilty under s1(2) does not depend on whether the brick hits or misses the windscreen, but whether he intended to hit it and intended that the damage therefrom should endanger life or whether he was reckless as to that outcome. As to the dropping of stones from bridges, the effect of the statute may be thought strange. If the defendant's intention is that the stone itself should crash through the roof of a train or a motor vehicle and thereby directly injure a passenger, or if he was reckless ... as to that outcome, the section would not bite ... If, however, the defendant intended or was reckless that the stone would smash the roof of the train or vehicle so that metal or wood struts from the roof would or obviously might descend upon a passenger endangering life, he would surely be guilty.'

A defendant can still be guilty of the aggravated offence even though the damage actually caused is not as great as he may have foreseen. In *R v Dudley* [1989] Crim LR 57 the appellant had thrown a fire-bomb at a house causing a small fire that was quickly extinguished, the damage caused being relatively slight. In response to the appellant's contention that there was no evidence upon which the jury could find that the actual damage caused was intended to endanger life, the Court of Appeal held that the intention to endanger life, or recklessness as to whether life would be endangered, should be looked at in the light of the harm he intended to cause, and not by reference to that which he actually caused: see further *R* v *Parker* [1993] Crim LR 856.

Hence, in *Dudley*, if D's petrol bomb had been aimed at the house, but had missed and set fire to a nearby car causing damage to it, he could still have been convicted of the aggravated offence on the basis that he caused criminal damage and was reckless as to whether it (ie the damage he actually intended) would endanger life.

11.6 'Without lawful excuse'

Section 5 of the Criminal Damage Act 1971 provides some elaboration of what is meant by the expression 'lawful excuse' within the scope of criminal damage. Section 5 applies to ss1(1), 2(a) and 3(b) only. Section 5(5) makes it clear that these provisions operate without prejudice to any other defence available in criminal law.

Belief in owner's consent

A person is treated as having a lawful excuse under the 1971 Act where, as provided by s5(2)(a):

'At the time of the act or acts alleged to constitute the offence he believed that the person or persons whom he believed to be entitled to consent to the destruction of or damage to the property in question had so consented, or would have so consented to it if he or they had known of the destruction or damage and its circumstances.'

Section 5(3) further provides that '... it is immaterial whether a belief is justified or not if it is honestly held'. In *R* v *Denton* (1982) 74 Cr App R 81 it was held that no offence was committed where an employee destroyed his employer's property after being ordered to do so, even though the defendant believed that his employer intended to make a bogus insurance claim in respect of the property. Note that the defendant's belief in the employer's authority to order such destruction was sufficient. Whether an employer can in law issue such instructions is more questionable. In *R* v *Appleyard* [1985] Crim LR 723 the Court of Appeal held that a managing director, who had set fire to a store belonging to the company for whom he worked, was guilty of criminal damage. The court rejected his argument that he must have been entitled to consent to such damage on behalf of the company under a 'self-authorisation' principle.

'Defence of property'

Section 5(2)(b) provides that a defendant has a lawful excuse for his destruction of property:

'... if he destroyed or damaged or threatened to destroy or damage the property in question or, in the case of a charge of an offence under section 3 intended to use or cause or permit the use of something to destroy or damage it, in order to protect property belonging to himself or another or a right or interest in property which was or which he believed to be vested in himself or another, and at the time of the act or acts alleged to constitute the offence he believed:

i) that the property right or interest was in immediate need of protection; and

ii) that the means of protection adopted or proposed to be adopted were or would be reasonable having regard to all the circumstances.'

This provision almost amounts to a statutory defence of necessity. Note that the defendant must believe his actions to be reasonable in the circumstances; however s5(3) again provides that his belief that his actions are reasonable does not itself have to be reasonable! Further, the defendant's actions must be taken in order to protect property, and it is for the court to determine whether or not this was the case. In *R v Hunt* (1977) 66 Cr App R 105, where the warden of a block of flats deliberately set fire to some bedding to illustrate the inadequacies of the fire alarm system, it was held that he had been rightly convicted, as his purpose had not been the protection of any other property. The decision raises a number of interesting issues. The defendant could, in a sense, be described as acting to save property, in that the building would be damaged if there was a fire which was not extinguished promptly due to the defective alarm system, although there would obviously be difficulties in his establishing his belief as to the immediacy of this threat. A defendant destroying property with a view to preserving life cannot invoke s5(2)(b), but may perhaps seek to rely on s5(2)(a), considered above.

The decision in *R v Hunt* has subsequently been relied upon by the Court of Appeal in *R v Ashford and Smith* [1988] Crim LR 682 and *R v Hill; R v Hall* (1989) 89 Cr App R 74. Both cases involved defendants who sought to rely upon the provisions of s5(2)(b) in relation to damage to perimeter fencing at air bases. The basis for invoking the subsection was that by cutting the perimeter fence of the base they might have persuaded those responsible for the armed forces that such sites were no longer secure, leading to the removal of military hardware, with the result that the bases and surrounding properties might cease to be regarded as targets by Soviet forces. In *R v Hill; R v Hall*, the Court of Appeal indicated that the correct approach to the lawful excuse provisions of s5(2) was first to ascertain what the accused had had in mind, secondly to ascertain whether as a matter of law, on the facts as the accused believed them to be, the actions contemplated could amount to steps taken to protect property in immediate danger. The court felt that the trial judge had correctly proceeded on the basis that the cutting of the wire fence would have been too remote from the protection of property to come within the terms of s5(2), and further, on the evidence, there was no ground for believing that the appellants thought that any property was in immediate danger.

R v Blake [1993] Crim LR 586 reaffirms the objective gloss placed on s5(2)(a) and (b) by *Hunt* and *Hall*. The appellant had participated in a demonstration, in the vicinity of the Houses of Parliament, against the involvement of Allied troops in the Gulf War. Following his arrest for writing a biblical quotation on a pillar, he contended that he had a lawful excuse for the criminal damage to the pillar, either because he had the consent of God as the owner of the property (s5(2)(a)), or because he had acted to protect other property (s5(2)(b)). Dismissing his appeal against conviction the court held that belief that God was the person entitled to consent to the damage would not form the basis of a valid defence, no matter how genuine that belief was. Even if the appellant genuinely believed that property in the Gulf states could be protected by his protest, it was for the court, applying an objective test, to determine whether or not his action did, or could, protect property as he had contended. There was no sufficiently immediate threat to the appellant or others to found a more general defence of duress of circumstances. It is submitted that, on a strict application of s5(2)(a) and (b) the test should be should be subjective, but the uncertainty introduced by permitting a defendant to rely on honest belief in divine commands is self-evident. See further *Johnson* v *DPP* [1994] Crim LR 673.

The defendant who, ignoring warning signs about the wheel clamping of illegally parked cars, returns to find his vehicle has been immobilised by a clamp cannot rely on the lawful excuse provision if he uses force to remove the wheel clamp and damages it in the process: see *Lloyd* v *DPP* [1991] Crim LR 904. If, however, he returns to find his car about to be set alight by vandals, and destroys the wheel clamp so as to move his car to safety, s5(2)(b) presumably would provide an escape route, if not s5(2)(a).

Similarly, it can be relied upon by D who demolishes a wall built to prevent him exercising his right of way (a form of property) across another's land: see *Chamberlain* v *Lindon* [1998] 2 All ER 538. The fact that D had also chosen to demolish the wall rather than engage in lengthy litigation did not mean that his act was not done to protect his right of way on the facts as he saw them. See Chapter 16, section 16.4, for further details.

Note that the section will not avail D who destroys property in order to protect another person: see *R* v *Baker and Wilkins* [1997] Crim LR 497 where D was convicted of criminal damage having broken down the door of a house where she believed her child was being illegally detained.

Honesty and reasonableness

It has been noted above that s5(3) requires the defendant's belief to be honest, but not necessarily reasonable. Further evidence of this is supplied by the decision of *Jaggard* v *Dickinson* [1981] QB 527, where the defendant, who was very drunk, caused damage when breaking into a house which she wrongly thought to be owned by her friend who had given her permission to enter at any time. The defendant successfully relied on s5(2)(a) in that she honestly believed she had the consent of the owner to enter the house in that way. Section 5(3) does not state that such belief must be honest *and* sober.

Where s5 does not apply

As noted above, the statutory concept of lawful excuse does not apply to cases of aggravated criminal damage contrary to s1(2), yet curiously that offence does refer to the defendant acting 'without lawful excuse', thus suggesting that there is some residual common law concept of reasonable excuse that could negate liability. Situations where this might arise are:

1. where D acts out of necessity – see *R* v *Pommell* [1995] 2 Cr App Rep 607;
2. where D acts under duress;
3. where D acts in self-defence, or defence of others;
4. where D acts in the belief that he has the actual consent of the owner of the property – see *R* v *Merrick* [1996] 1 Cr App R 130.

12

Inchoate Offences

12.1 Introduction

Inchoate liability can be imposed upon a defendant who progresses some way towards committing a criminal offence, but does not necessarily succeed in completing the commission of the offence. The earliest stage at which liability can arise is where the defendant commits incitement by suggesting the commission of an offence to another person. This might be followed by conspiracy, where two or more parties agree on a course of conduct which will result in the commission of an offence, and finally a defendant who actually progresses beyond merely preparing to commit an offence may be guilty of attempt. It should be borne in mind that the prosecution is at liberty to charge a defendant with an inchoate form of an offence, even though he appears to have actually committed the completed crime. Frequently this occurs where there is some evidential difficulty with pursuing a prosecution for the full offence. Equally, a defendant cannot be charged with both inchoate and complete offences in respect of the same criminal act, as to do so would amount to 'overloading' the indictment.

12.2 Incitement

Incitement occurs where a defendant suggests the commission of a criminal offence to another person. What follows is an account of incitement at common law, but it

310

should be noted that there are many statutory forms of the offence, such as incitement to racial hatred, or incitement to murder.

Actus reus

The actus reus of incitement is committed where a defendant suggests the commission of an offence to another person. It has to be shown that the suggestion from the incitor has reached the mind of the incitee, but there is no need to provide evidence that the incitee acted on the suggestion. The nature of the actus reus was considered by Lord Denning MR in *Race Relations Board* v *Applin* [1973] QB 815. The defendant had conducted a campaign against a white family's fostering of black children, and he had been charged with inciting the commission of an offence under the Race Relations Act 1968. In concluding that the defendant was guilty of incitement, Lord Denning MR observed:

> '[It was suggested before us] that to "incite" means to urge or spur on by advice, encouragement or persuasion, and not otherwise. I do not think the word is so limited, at any rate in the present context. A person may "incite" another to do an act by threatening or by pressure, as well as by persuasion.'

In theory, therefore, it is possible for a defendant to incite millions of others to commit offences, for example via a television broadcast. In *R* v *Most* (1881) 7 QBD 244 the defendant was convicted of incitement to murder after publishing a newspaper article inciting certain readers to rise up in revolutionary ferment and kill their respective heads of state. Similarly, where D publishes a book explaining how to cultivate and produce cannabis: see *R* v *Marlow* [1997] Crim LR 897.

Where the incitement does not actually reach the mind of the incitee, perhaps because he is deaf, out of earshot, or because a letter containing the incitement is never delivered, the incitor can still, in theory be charged with attempted incitement: see *R* v *Ransford* (1874) 13 Cox CC 9 and *R* v *Rowley* (1992) 94 Cr App R 95.

Generally, the incitee must know of the facts that make the conduct incited criminal. Hence a defendant can only be guilty of incitement to handle stolen goods if the incitee knew or believed the goods in question to be stolen. (Again the incitor might still be guilty of attempted incitement here.) In *R* v *Curr* [1968] 2 QB 944, the defendant ran a loan business whereby he would lend money to women with children in return for their handing over their signed family allowance books. He would then use other women to cash the family allowance vouchers. He was convicted of inciting the commission of offences under s9(b) of the Family Allowance Act 1945, which made it an offence for any person to receive any sum by way of family allowance knowing it was not properly payable, but appealed successfully to the Court of Appeal, where it was held that the trial judge had erred in not directing the jury to consider whether those women, who were being incited to use the signed allowance books to collect money on behalf of the defendant, had actually known that what they were being asked to do was unlawful. It would have been more appropriate to have charged the defendant as the principal offender, relying on the doctrine of innocent agency.

Inciting incitement

Although such cases will necessarily be rare, an indictment can lie at common law for the doubly inchoate offence of inciting incitement. In *R* v *Sirat* [1986] Crim LR 245, where it was alleged, inter alia, that the appellant had incited a middle man to procure someone who would carry out an attack on the appellant's wife, the Court of Appeal confirmed that liability for inciting incitement could arise, but in so doing recognised the difficulty created by the abolition of liability for inciting conspiracy brought about by s5(7) of the Criminal Law Act 1977. Arguably what the defendant was alleged to have done was to incite the middle man to enter into an agreement which would result in an attack being carried out on the appellant's wife, ie an incitement to conspire. He may thus have been convicted of an offence no longer known to law. This was one of several reasons why the appellant's conviction was quashed by the court. It is submitted that a distinction has to be drawn between the situation where D suggests to X that he arranges with Y for Y to attack P; and the situation where D suggests to X that X pressurises Y into carrying out an attack on P. In the former case there will clearly have to be some agreement between X and Y, and thus D cannot be charged with inciting their conspiracy. In the latter case, however, there need be no agreement as such between X and Y, Y will simply be choosing to respond to what X has said. Here D can be charged with inciting X to incite Y to attack P. Support for this proposition is to be found in the Court of Appeal's decision in *R* v *Evans* [1986] Crim LR 470.

Mens rea

D must know of the circumstances that would make the course of conduct incited a criminal offence if the incitement were acted upon. For example, if D incites X to store certain goods in his (P's) garden shed, D cannot be guilty of inciting X to handle stole goods unless he knows or believes the goods to be stolen. Further, D must intend to persuade or encourage X to commit the offence. In addition, it must be D's intention that the incitement will be acted upon by the incitee, hence if D is making the suggestion as a practical joke he should escape liability

In many cases mens rea will have to be established as a necessary inference from the circumstances. If D markets a product, such as a police radar speed-trap detector, that will result in motorists committing criminal offences if they use it as advertised, he will be guilty of inciting the commission of that offence: see *Invicta Plastics Ltd* v *Clare* [1976] RTR 251. Similarly, where D publishes a book explaining how to make bombs or produce Class A drugs: see again *Marlow* (above).

In the absence of 'purpose' type intent it is submitted that D could be guilty if there was evidence that he foresaw it as virtually certain that his incitement would be acted upon by the incitee. On the basis of *Curr* (above), D must also be proved to have knowledge that the incitee knows that what is being incited is unlawful. However where the incitee lacks such knowledge and acts on the basis of the incitement D could be charged as a principal offender acting through an innocent agent.

Inciting the commission of offences outside the jurisdiction

At common law liability for incitement will only arise where D incites another to commit an offence that would be triable in England and Wales, ie an offence in respect of which the courts in England and Wales would have jurisdiction. Where, therefore, D incites another to commit an offence overseas, no liability (at common law) will arise. With the enactment of the Sexual Offences (Conspiracy and Incitement) Act 1996 D may be charged with incitement if he does an act that would amount to the offence of incitement to commit a listed sexual offence, but for the fact that what he had in view would not be an offence triable in England and Wales, provided: (a) the whole or part of what he had in view was intended to take place in a country or territory outside the United Kingdom; and (b) what he had in view would involve the commission of an offence under the law in force in that country. The listed sexual offences for these purposes are: rape; sexual intercourse with a girl under the age of 13; sexual intercourse with a girl under the age of 16; buggery; indecent assault on a girl; indecent assault on a boy; and activity that contravenes s1 of the Indecency with Children Act 1960. Any act of incitement by means of a message (however communicated) is to be treated as done in England and Wales if the message is sent or received in England and Wales. The 1996 Act was introduced, primarily, by way of response to the activities of those organising trips for 'sex tourists' (ie those who exploit children for sexual purposes in developing countries). Note that the territoriality provisions of the more recent Sex Offenders Act 1997 allow the courts of the United Kingdom to prosecute United Kingdom residents and citizens if they commit any listed sexual offences (see Schedule 2), notwithstanding that the prohibited acts take place outside the jurisdiction of the United Kingdom courts. It may transpire that the offences created by the 1997 Act effectively make the 1996 Act redundant, as the 1997 Act will allow the prosecution of organisers of trips for 'sex tourists' as accomplices.

12.3 Conspiracy: statutory

Until 1977 conspiracy was a common law offence, defined in *R* v *Mulcahy* (1868) LR 3 HL 306 as an agreement between two or more people to do an unlawful act. The difficulty with this definition was that it left open the possibility of a defendant being charged with the criminal offence of conspiring to commit acts which were unlawful merely because they were tortious, eg trespass to land.

The primary purpose of the Criminal Law Act 1977 was to place the offence of conspiracy on a statutory footing, and to limit liability for conspiracy to those situations where there was an agreement to commit a criminal offence, and to this end s5(1) abolishes the common law offence of conspiracy. The Act does, however, expressly preserve two forms of common law conspiracy. Section 5(2) states that conspiracy to defraud is to be retained, and s5(3) states that conspiracy to corrupt public morals is to be preserved. The surviving forms of common law conspiracy are considered below.

The statutory offence of conspiracy is created by s1(1) of the Criminal Law Act 1977, as amended by s5 of the Criminal Attempts Act 1981, which provides:

> 'Subject to the following provision of this part of this Act if a person agrees with any other person or persons that a course of conduct shall be pursued which, if the agreement is carried out in accordance with their intentions, either:
> a) will necessarily amount to or involve the commission of any offence or offences by one or more of the parties to the agreement, or
> b) would do so but for the existence of facts which render the commission of the offence or any of the offences impossible,
> he is guilty of conspiracy to commit the offence or offences in question.'

Actus reus

Agreement

The parties to a conspiracy must be proved to have agreed on a course of conduct. Only rarely will the prosecution have direct evidence of an agreement, perhaps in the form of letters or tapes of telephone conversations, most conspirators wishing to avoid any permanent record of their plans coming into existence. In the majority of conspiracy trials it appears that the existence of an agreement is a matter to be inferred by the jury from the evidence of the parties' conduct. For example, if three men wearing stocking masks and carrying sawn-off shot-guns are arrested by the police whilst sitting in the back of a van parked by a bank, there is an almost irresistible inference that they must have agreed to rob the bank. It can hardly be coincidence that they are all there at the same time with similar clothes and equipment.

The jury should be warned against confusing the term 'agreement' with any notions of contract law. There is no need for the prosecution to prove anything equating to an 'intention to create (il)legal relations' on the part of the conspirators. On the other hand, as stated in a decision on the old common law offence, *R v O'Brien* [1974] 3 All ER 663, conspiracy is not committed simply by talking about the possibility of committing an offence. It seems from this case that the parties must reach a stage where they agree to carry out the commission of the offence so far as it lies within their power to do so. Once agreement is reached it must be communicated between parties to the conspiracy; it cannot be tacit agreement: see *R v Scott* (1979) 68 Cr App R 164.

Form of the conspiracy

In a typical conspiracy involving, say, four parties, it would be normal for them all to have met together and agreed on a plan. It should be noted, however, that it is not necessary for every party to a conspiracy to be aware of the existence of every other party. In 'chain' conspiracies, the sequence of agreements might look as follows:

A agrees with B who agrees with C who agrees with D who agrees with E and so on ...

In such a scheme A might be completely unaware of the involvement of C, D and E, yet they are all parties to the same conspiracy.

An alternative arrangement illustrating the same possibility arises with what are known as 'wheel' conspiracies. Here there may be numerous parties, but each agrees with one central figure, eg:

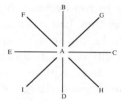

Again, B may be unaware of the existence of C, D, and E, etc, but they can all be charged as parties to the same conspiracy.

Parties

Section 2 of the 1977 Act does place certain restrictions upon those who can become parties to a conspiracy. Section 2(1) provides that a person cannot be charged with conspiracy if he is the intended victim of the crime, and s2(2) provides that a person cannot be charged with conspiracy if the only other party or parties to the conspiracy comprise that person's spouse, or a person under the age of ten.

The provision was considered by the Court of Appeal in *R* v *Chrastny* [1991] 1 WLR 1381 where the appellant had been convicted of conspiracy to supply a Class A drug, and sought to challenge her conviction on the ground that the trial judge had erred in law in directing the jury that, although the appellant had only agreed with her husband that the offence should be committed, s2(2)(a) of the Criminal Law Act 1977 provided no protection where she had nevertheless known of the existence of the other conspirators. In dismissing the appeal, Glidewell LJ pointed out that the provision does not enable a wife to escape liability simply by taking care only to agree with her spouse, even though she knows of the existence of other parties to the conspiracy. Only where she remained genuinely ignorant of other parties to such a conspiracy would s2(2)(a) protect her.

'... necessarily amount to ... the commission of any offence'

If these words, which appear in s1(1) of the 1977 Act, were construed strictly, as criminal statutes are supposed to be, it would be extremely difficult to secure any convictions for conspiracy. How is the prosecution to prove beyond all reasonable doubt that the defendants' plan, if carried out, would *necessarily* have resulted in the commission of a particular criminal offence? For example, suppose that D1 and D2 agree to dig a pit so that P will fall into it and be injured when he walks by. Prima facie this appears to be a conspiracy to cause at least actual bodily harm, but can it be shown that P would necessarily have taken the route in question, that he would have failed to notice the pit, or that he would necessarily have suffered actual bodily harm?

Donaldson LJ adverted to these difficulties in *R v Reed* [1982] Crim LR 819, where he suggested that a jury should be directed to consider the conspirators' 'plan', and to ask themselves whether an offence would necessarily be committed if the plan is carried out as the conspirators intend. Hence where D1 and D2 agree to rob a bank, provided there are no police officers in the area when they arrive, they should be convicted of conspiracy to rob because that is the offence that they would have committed had events gone as they had wished.

As suggested above, this has to be the sensible approach to the problem because, in a sense, all conspiracies are conditional in as much as the parties agree to commit an offence, provided they can get away with it. Common sense dictates that such conditionality cannot be allowed to defeat a charge of conspiracy.

Mens rea

Essentially, the mens rea of conspiracy requires proof that the defendant intended to agree on the commission of a particular offence, and proof of an intention that the offence should be committed. Even if the completed offence is one in respect of which a defendant can be convicted without knowledge of the facts constituting the offence, he will not be at risk of conspiring to commit such an offence unless he actually knows of the facts or circumstances necessary for its commission; see s1(2) of the 1977 Act. The point is illustrated by the Court of Appeal's decision in *R v Siracusa* (1989) 90 Cr App R 340. The appellants had been convicted of conspiring to import cannabis resin from Kashmir, and heroin from Thailand. In dismissing their appeals, the court held that the mens rea for conspiring to commit an offence was not necessarily to be equated with that required for the completed offence. In the case of murder, intention to kill or do grievous bodily harm was sufficient, whereas for conspiracy to murder an intention to kill had to be established. In the present case, whilst a defendant charged with the completed offence of being knowingly concerned in the prohibited importation of controlled drugs, did not have to be shown to have known what class of controlled drug he was dealing in, a defendant charged with conspiring to commit such an offence had to be shown to have known precisely the class of drugs involved. On the facts the court was satisfied that the judge had made this requirement abundantly clear in his summing up.

Does D have to intend to play an active part in the carrying out of the agreement?
If A agrees with B that B will steal C's car, are A and B guilty of conspiracy to

steal? Prima facie the answer would appear to be affirmative, even though A does no more than agree that the crime should take place and desire that it should be committed by B. Such a simple solution has to be considered, however, in the light of the House of Lords' decision in *R* v *Anderson* [1986] AC 27. The defendant, who had been convicted of conspiring to effect the escape of a prisoner, appealed to the House of Lords contending that he had lacked the mens rea for conspiracy because, although he had received £2,000 as an advance payment for his part in planning the escape and he had admitted intending to acquire some diamond cutting wire that could be used to cut through prison bars, he had never intended the escape plan to be carried into effect and had not believed that it could actually succeed.

In dismissing his appeal the House of Lords held that it was sufficient, on a charge of statutory conspiracy, for the prosecution to establish, by way of mens rea, that the defendant had agreed on a course of conduct which he knew would involve the commission of an offence and, as Lord Bridge stated (at p39):

> '... beyond the mere fact of agreement, the necessary mens rea of the crime is, in my opinion, established if, and only if, it is shown that the accused, when he entered into the agreement, intended to play some part in the agreed course of conduct in furtherance of the criminal purpose which the agreed course of conduct was intended to achieve. Nothing less will suffice; nothing more is required.'

The decision confirms views expressed in earlier cases, such as *R* v *Allsop* (1976) 64 Cr App R 29, to the effect that a defendant can be convicted of conspiracy regardless of whether he desires the commission of the offence agreed upon. He may be quite indifferent as to whether the object of the conspiracy is achieved, yet it is sufficient that he knows that an offence will be committed if the agreement is carried out in accordance with the wishes of the other parties to the conspiracy. Hence if D1 and D2 agree to kill P, and D3 agrees to supply them with a gun that cannot be traced, with which they can shoot P, D3 can be charged with conspiracy to murder, even though he may be quite disinterested in whether P lives or dies. To paraphrase the words of Lord Bridge (above), D3 will have assented to a course of conduct which he must know will result in the death of P, and he intends to play some part in the furtherance of the criminal purpose which the agreed course of conduct was intended to achieve.

Lord Bridge's words would seem to suggest, however, that in the example of the theft of the car by B, cited above, A could not be guilty of conspiracy to steal because he does not intend to play some part in the commission of the offence. The passage cited has, perhaps not surprisingly, attracted some trenchant criticisms. For example, the authors of *Smith & Hogan* state (8th ed, 1996, pp281–282):

> 'It was clear in that case that two or more of the alleged conspirators did intend to carry out the agreement, so [Anderson's] conviction could have been upheld on the ground that he aided and abetted that conspiracy ... [B]ut, if no intention need be proved on the part of one alleged principal offender in conspiracy, it need not be proved on the part of another. A conspiracy which no one intends to carry out is an absurdity, if not an impossibility.'

The Court of Appeal in *R* v *Siracusa* (above) attempted to clarify Lord Bridge's comments by stating that his speech had to be read as a whole. It was said that his Lordship had not meant that a defendant could only be guilty of conspiracy if it was shown that he intended to play some part in executing the agreement, simply that when the defendant agreed to the course of conduct he knew that it involved the commission of an offence. It would thus appear that a conspirator can now play his part simply by agreeing that others should carry out the commission of an offence. In fact the court goes as far as to state that:

'intention to participate in the furtherance of the criminal purpose [can be] established by his failure to stop the unlawful activity'.

One particular problem thrown up by this approach to the mens rea of conspiracy is that of the police officer who is working under cover with a members of a criminal gang in order to collect evidence that can be used to ensure their eventual conviction. He or she will necessarily agree to the commission of various offences, despite having no desire that the agreement should succeed, and may even intend to take some steps short of committing the completed crime. Subject to the discretion to prosecute not being exercised, how can such a person escape liability for conspiracy? The matter was adverted to by Lord Bridge in *R* v *Anderson* (above), where he stated that:

'The mens rea implicit in the offence of statutory conspiracy must clearly be such as to recognise the innocence of such a person, notwithstanding that he will, in literal terms, be obliged to agree that a course of conduct be pursued involving the commission of an offence.'

Short of recognising a public policy exemption for such a defendant, he or she would be caught by Lord Bridge's assertion, elsewhere in his speech, to the effect that a conspirator could be guilty of the offence even if he was indifferent as to whether the other conspirators actually carried out the agreement.

A more rational approach is demonstrated in the Privy Council's decision in *Yip Chiu-Cheung* v *R* [1994] 3 WLR 514, where the appellant had entered into an agreement with N, an undercover police officer, whereby N would fly from Australia to Hong Kong, collect a consignment of heroin from the appellant, and return with it to Australia. N kept the Australian and Hong Kong authorities fully informed of the agreement, and they undertook to allow him free passage from Hong Kong and into Australia. The purpose of N's mission was to identify not only the suppliers of the drug in Hong Kong, but also the dealers in Australia. N in fact missed his flight to Hong Kong and proceeded no further with the plan to meet the appellant. In due course, however, the appellant was charged with, and convicted of, conspiring to traffic in dangerous drugs. He appealed on the ground that there could be no conspiracy given that his co-conspirator, N, had been acting to promote law enforcement, and that N's purpose had been to expose drug trafficking. Dismissing the appeal, the Privy Council, held that even though N would have been acting courageously and from the best of motives, it had nevertheless been his intention, at the time the agreement was made, to take prohibited drugs from Hong Kong to Australia. If the agreement had been executed he would have committed a serious criminal offence. N, therefore, had possessed the necessary mens rea for the conspiracy, and the appellant's conviction could be sustained.

One assumes that the law enforcement authorities in Hong Kong and Australia had no intention of prosecuting N had he actually imported the heroin into Australia but, as Lord Griffiths indicated, that was not the relevant point in this appeal. The authorities would not have had the power to suspend the relevant laws relating to drug trafficking so as to de-criminalise the activities of N. Hence when N agreed to import the drugs he did have the mens rea for conspiracy.

Jurisdictional issues

Section 1(4) of the 1977 Act, as originally enacted, provided that the offence of conspiracy was concerned with agreements to commit offences that would be triable in England and Wales. Hence, in general terms, an agreement between D1 and D2 to commit theft in France would not have been triable as a conspiracy in England and Wales. The only exception to this rule was in respect of conspiracy to commit murder where the actus reus was to take place abroad. Both the Computer Misuse Act 1990 and the Sexual Offences (Conspiracy and Incitement) Act 1996 extended the jurisdiction of the courts in England and Wales in respect of specific types of conspiracy to commit offences outside the jurisdiction, but the matter is now regulated by s5 of the Criminal Justice (Terrorism and Conspiracy) Act 1998, which adds a new s1A to the 1977 Act. Under s1A liability for conspiracy to commit offences outside the jurisdiction can arise where there is an agreement between two or more persons on a course of conduct that would, at some stage, involve an act by one or more of the parties, or the happening of some other event, intended to take place in a country or territory outside the United Kingdom, provided that the act or other event constituted an offence under the law in force in that country or territory. The conspiracy alleged must also be one that would have been triable under s1 of the 1977 Act but for the fact that the offence agreed upon would have been committed outside the jurisdiction. The prosecution must also establish that a party to the agreement, or a party's agent, did something in England and Wales in relation to the agreement before its formation, or that a party to the agreement became a party in England and Wales (by joining it either in person or through an agent), or that a party to the agreement, or a party's agent, did or omitted to do anything in England and Wales in pursuance of the agreement.

If D1 and D2 agree, whilst in France, to commit theft in London, it seems likely that they could be charged with conspiracy to steal, on the basis that the effect of the conspiracy would be felt within the jurisdiction. This was certainly the case at common law (see *DPP* v *Doot* [1973] AC 807) and, it is submitted, remains the case, given that the 1977 Act is silent on this point.

12.4 Conspiracy: common law

As stated above, the 1977 Act did not entirely sweep away all forms of common law conspiracy. Conspiracy to defraud was expressly preserved by s5(2). Conspiracy to corrupt public morals also survives: see *Shaw* v *DPP* [1962] AC 220 and *Knuller* v *DPP* [1973] AC 435.

Conspiracy to defraud

The offence was defined, by Viscount Dilhorne in *Scott* v *MPC* [1975] AC 819, as involving:

> '... an agreement by two or more by dishonesty to deprive a person of something which is his or to which he is or would be or might be entitled and an agreement by two or more by dishonesty to injure some proprietary right [of the victim's].'

Although agreement is the essence of the offence, the prosecution do not need to identify the party that D is alleged to have agreed with, and can charge him with conspiring with another or others unknown. The offence is triable on indictment only and attracts a maximum penalty of ten years' imprisonment: see s12(3) Criminal Justice Act 1987.

In *Adams* v *R* [1995] 1 WLR 52 the Privy Council upheld the appellant's conviction for conspiracy to defraud on the basis of his agreeing to dishonestly use a complex system of offshore companies and accounts to disguise that fact that he would be using the assets of a company, of which he was a director, to make a secret profit. The failure to account for the profits could have been culpable as the appellant, being a director, would have been under a legal duty to disclose such information. The Privy Council appeared to draw a distinction between an agreement to make a secret profit – which on the basis of previous decisions such as *R* v *Tarling* [1979] Crim LR 220 would not result in liability for conspiracy to defraud – and an agreement to conceal the making of such profits. The rationale for the distinction being, perhaps, that if the profit was concealed the company would have been unable to exercise its right to recover the money.

Defraud, in the context of this offence, does not require proof that anyone would have been deceived. As Viscount Dilhorne went on to explain in *Scott* (at p839):

> '... the words "fraudulently" and "defraud" must ordinarily have a very similar meaning. If "fraudulently" means "dishonestly", then to "defraud" ordinarily means, in my opinion, to deprive a person dishonestly of something which is his or of something to which he is or would or might but for the perpetration of the fraud be entitled.'

Some uncertainty surrounds the issue of whether D must intend to defraud, or whether recklessness as to the adverse affects of the agreement on a third party's interests would be enough. In *R* v *Allsop* (1976) 64 Cr App R 29 the Court of Appeal held that liability for conspiracy to defraud could arise even though D was not certain that his actions would have an adverse effect upon P's economic interests. As Shaw LJ stated (at p31):

'Generally the primary objective of fraudsmen is to advantage themselves. The detriment that results to their victims is secondary to that purpose, and incidental. It is "intended" only in the sense that it is a contemplated outcome of the fraud that is perpetrated. If the deceit which is employed imperils the economic interest of the person deceived, this is sufficient to constitute fraud even though in the event no actual loss is suffered and notwithstanding that the deceiver did not desire to bring about an actual loss.'

Against this, in *Attorney-General's Reference (No 1 of 1982)* [1983] QB 751, the Court of Appeal expressed the view that D could not be guilty of conspiracy to defraud unless it was his 'true object' to inflict such damage.

Despite academic criticism of *Allsop* (see *Smith & Hogan* (8th ed, 1996) pp297–298) on the ground that it confuses the issue of the mens rea required by possibly blurring the distinction between intention and recklessness, it has subsequently been approved of by the Privy Council in *Wai Yu-Tsang* v *R* [1991] 3 WLR 1006. D was convicted of conspiring to defraud a bank, of which he was the chief accountant, of US$124 million. The allegation was that he had conspired with the managing director, the general manager and others to dishonestly conceal the dishonouring of certain cheques by not recording them in the bank's account. D contended that he was not guilty as he had been acting on the instructions of the managing director, and had acted in good faith to prevent a run on the bank. The trial judge's direction to the jury, with which the Privy Council agreed, was to the effect that for conspiracy to defraud, no desire to cause loss on the part of D need be shown, it being sufficient that he had imperilled the economic or proprietary interests of another party. As to the nature of the mental element to be established, Lord Goff commented:

'Their Lordships are ... reluctant to allow this part of the law to become enmeshed in a distinction, sometimes artificially drawn, between intention and recklessness. The question whether particular facts reveal a conspiracy to defraud depends upon what the conspirators have dishonestly agreed to do, and in particular whether they have agreed to practise a fraud on somebody ... it is enough ... that ... the conspirators have dishonestly agreed to bring about a state of affairs which they realise will or may deceive the victim into so acting, or failing to act, that he will suffer economic loss or his economic interests will be put at risk. It is however important ... to distinguish a conspirator's intention (or immediate purpose) dishonestly to bring about such a state of affairs from his motive (or underlying purpose). The latter may be benign to the extent that he does not wish the victim or potential victim to suffer harm; but the mere fact that it is benign will not of itself prevent the agreement from constituting a conspiracy to defraud.'

Where the intended victim of the conspiracy is a public servant, it is sufficient that D intends to deceive him into contravening that duty. There is no need in such cases to show any 'purpose' of causing economic loss to another: see *R* v *Moses and Ansbro* [1991] Crim LR 617.

The offence requires prof that D acted dishonestly. Despite views expressed by the court in *R* v *McIvor* [1982] 1 WLR 409, the approach to be taken is the same as that applicable to Theft Act offences, which involves adherence to the Court of Appeal's guidelines in *R v Ghosh* [1982] 1 QB 1053.

The significance of conspiracy to defraud lies in the fact that the agreement may involve following a course of conduct which, if pursued, might not necessarily result in the commission of a substantive criminal offence. Whilst it is possible to criticise the continued existence of such an offence on grounds of uncertainty and vagueness, the Law Commission has recognised that it fulfils an important role as a residual form of criminal liability where D's dishonesty does not fall within the terms of any other substantive offence, and that the abolition of the common law offence might leave an unacceptable number of gaps in the law.

The usefulness of conspiracy to defraud as a residual offence which can be charged in the event of a lacuna in the law is illustrated by *R v Hollinshead* [1985] AC 975. The defendants agreed to supply black boxes (devices which caused electricity meters to under-record the amount of electricity used by a consumer) to a middle man who would then sell them on to customers of various electricity boards. The defendants were charged on two counts: count one alleging a statutory conspiracy to aid, abet, counsel or procure an offence under s2(1)(b) of the Theft Act 1978; and count two which alleged a common law conspiracy to defraud. They were convicted on the second count, and appealed successfully to the Court of Appeal on the ground that there could be no conspiracy to defraud where the dishonest conduct contemplated was to be carried out by a third party (the user of the black box), as opposed to the conspirators. The Crown appealed to the House of Lords, which was asked to consider first, whether such activity could be the subject of a common law conspiracy charge, and second, if it could not, whether it could be charged as a statutory conspiracy to participate in the commission of an offence under the Theft Act 1978. It was held that the first question should be answered in the affirmative, because the sole purpose of the agreement was the causing of loss to the electricity boards (the black boxes have no other use). Having answered the first question in this way, their Lordships felt that it was not necessary for them to deal with the second question, but it is perhaps worth noting that the defendants would have to have been charged with conspiring to supply the black boxes to a person who would in turn supply them to the principal offender. It is submitted that it is most unlikely that such a charge could have been sustained. Note that in this case it could be said that the defendants' 'purpose' had not been to defraud the electricity supplier, but to obtain money for the black boxes. They may have been quite indifferent as to whether the boxes were ever used or not.

When should common law conspiracy be charged?

Can the prosecution choose which form of conspiracy to charge? Prior to the enactment of s12 Criminal Justice Act 1987, prosecutors ran the risk of being wrong-footed if they charged D with common law conspiracy to defraud on facts that revealed conspiracy to commit a substantive criminal offence. In *R v Ayers*

[1984] AC 447, the House of Lords held that common law conspiracy to defraud should only be charged where the agreement was one which, if carried out, would not necessarily result in the commission of a substantive criminal offence by any of the conspirators, but the matter is now governed by s12 of the 1987 Act which provides:

'(1) If –

a) a person agrees with any other person or persons that a course of conduct shall be pursued; and

b) that course of conduct will necessarily amount to or involve the commission of any offence or offences by one or more of the parties to the agreement if the agreement is carried out in accordance with their intentions,

the fact that it will do so shall not preclude a charge of conspiracy to defraud being brought against any of them in respect of the agreement.'

The provision effectively reverses the decision in *Ayers* and creates a potentially wide overlap between the statutory and common law offences.

12.5 Attempt under the pre-1981 law

Until the enactment of the Criminal Attempts Act 1981, the crime of attempt was a creation of the common law. Despite the fact that the 1981 Act had the effect of abolishing entirely the common law offence of attempt, some knowledge of the pre-1981 law is necessary for a proper understanding of the new law.

Actus reus of common law attempt

One of the difficulties associated with the old law on criminal attempts was the question of how far a defendant would have to progress towards the commission of the completed crime for it to be said that he had committed the actus reus of attempt. A number of tests were propounded by the courts.

In *R* v *Eagleton* (1855) Dears CCR 515, the defendant was convicted of attempting to obtain money by false pretences on the basis that he had committed the 'last act' towards being paid the money. This test was applied more recently in *DPP* v *Stonehouse* [1978] AC 55, where the defendant had faked his suicide, and was subsequently charged with attempting to obtain money (benefits under insurance policies) by deception for another, his wife. The fact that the defendant's wife had taken no steps herself towards claiming the money under the policies was regarded as irrelevant to the question of the defendant's liability. The House of Lords was satisfied that he had committed the last act that lay within his power, towards the commission of the offence.

An alternative test, applied in a number of other authorities, was to ask whether or not the defendant had committed an act which was sufficiently proximate to the commission of the completed crime. On this basis a defendant would be acquitted where his actions were regarded as being no more than merely preparatory to the commission of an offence. Hence in *R v Robinson* [1915] 2 KB 342, the defendant, a jeweller who had tied himself up and hidden some of his stock in order to create the impression that he had been robbed, was acquitted of attempting to obtain monies under an insurance policy by false pretences, on the basis that as he had not even made a claim under the policy, he had not gone far enough towards the commission of the completed crime to be convicted of attempt. On the basis of *Comer v Bloomfield* (1970) 55 Cr App R 305, a defendant did not incur liability under the common law even where he faked the theft of his motor vehicle and wrote to his insurers to inquire as to whether a claim for theft would be covered by his policy, again the reasoning being that he had done nothing towards the commission of the completed offence that went beyond mere preparation. See further *R v Ilyas* (1983) 78 Cr App R 17.

Mens rea of common law attempt

At common law a defendant could only be convicted of attempt if he was shown to have an intent to commit the completed crime. Thus in *R v Whybrow* (1951) 35 Cr App R 141, the Court of Appeal held that it had been a misdirection for a trial judge to direct a jury, on a charge of attempted murder, that they should convict if the defendant had intended to kill or do grievous bodily harm. Only an intention to kill would suffice. Similarly in *R v Mohan* [1976] QB 1, where the defendant was charged with attempting, by wanton driving, to cause bodily harm to a police officer, the Court of Appeal held that recklessness as to consequences could play no part in the mens rea of attempt; there had to be proof that the defendant intended to bring about the full offence. In short, it had to be the defendant's purpose to commit the completed crime.

12.6 The Criminal Attempts Act 1981

The aim of the 1981 Act was to amend the law relating to criminal attempts. What it in fact achieved was a wholesale replacement of the common law with a new statutory offence of attempt. For the avoidance of doubt, s6(1) of the Act provides:

'The offence of attempt at common law and any offence at common law of procuring materials for crime are hereby abolished for all purposes not relating to acts done before the commencement of this Act.'

Section 1(4) also abolishes liability for attempting to aid, abet, counsel or procure the commission of any offence, attempted conspiracy, attempting to assist an offender contrary to s4(1) of the Criminal Law Act 1967, and attempting to commit a summary offence. The exclusion of liability for attempting to commit summary offences applies to offences that are summary by classification, not simply because of the mode of trial adopted in any given case. For example, in *R* v *Bristol Magistrates' Court, ex parte E* [1998] 3 All ER 798, D contended that he could not be charged with attempting to commit criminal damage to a pane of glass in a bus shelter because the value of the property involved was below £5,000. He relied on the fact that s22 of and Sch 2 to the Magistrates' Court Act 1980 provided that in such circumstances an offence of criminal damage had to be tried summarily, hence s1(4) of the Criminal Attempts Act 1981 precluded any charge of attempt. Upholding the justices' decision not to stay the proceedings on the basis of this argument, the Divisional Court held that the value of the property involved determined the mode of trial, not the nature of the offence. If D's contention had been correct a police officer would not know whether an offence had been committed until a court ruled on the value of the property involved.

The actus reus of statutory attempt

Section 1(1) of the 1981 Act provides:

> 'If, with intent to commit an offence to which this section applies, a person does an act which is more than merely preparatory to the commission of the offence, he is guilty of attempting to commit the offence.'

and s4(3) provides:

> 'Where, in proceedings against a person for an offence under section 1 above, there is evidence sufficient in law to support a finding that he did an act falling within subsection (1) of that section, the question of whether or not his act fell within that subsection is a question of fact.'

In seeking to produce an acceptable formula for the actus reus of the new statutory offence of attempt, the Law Commission stated in its *Report on Attempt, and Impossibility in Relation to Attempt, Conspiracy and Incitement* (1980 No 102) at para 2.47:

> 'The definition of sufficient proximity must be wide enough to cover two varieties of cases; first, those in which a person has taken all the steps towards the commission of a crime which he believes to be necessary as far as he is concerned for that crime to result, such as firing a gun at another and missing. Normally such cases cause no difficulty. Secondly. however, the definition must cover those instances where a person has to take some further step to complete the crime, assuming that there is evidence of the necessary mental element on his part to commit it; for example, when the defendant has raised the gun to take aim at another but has not yet squeezed the trigger. We have reached the conclusion that, in regard to these cases, it is undesirable to recommend anything more complex than a rationalisation of the present law.'

And in para 2.48 it stated:

> 'The literal meaning of "proximate" is "nearest, next before or after (in place, order, time, connection of thought, causation, et cetera)." Thus, were this term part of a statutory description of the actus reus of attempt, it would clearly be capable of being

interpreted to exclude all but the "final act"; this would not be in accordance with the policy outlined above.'

Some of the first decisions under the 1981 Act seemed to have been decided in ignorance of this policy. For example, in *R v Widdowson* (1986) 82 Cr App R 314, D had filled in an application form for credit facilities using a false name and was charged with attempting to obtain services by deception. The Court of Appeal quashed his conviction on the ground, inter alia, that he had not committed any acts more than merely preparatory to the obtaining of the service in question. In the view of the court, D could not incur liability for attempt until he received a favourable response to his request for credit and decided to act upon it. In this respect the court seemed to be applying a type of 'last act' test to determine the defendant's liability which, as noted above, was a feature of the common law offence that the 1981 Act purported to abolish.

Gradually, by opting to develop the law on a case by case basis, the Court of Appeal has developed a more satisfactory approach to the determining whether or not D has committed acts more than merely preparatory to the commission of an offence. In *R v Gullefer* (1990) 91 Cr App R 356 (Note) D visited a greyhound race meeting and, during the last race, climbed the fence on to the track in front of the dogs, waving his arms and attempting to distract them. He was unsuccessful, and the stewards decided that it was unnecessary to declare 'no race'. Had they made such a declaration, the bookmakers would have been obliged to repay the appellant's stake money. He was convicted of attempted theft of the stake money and appealed successfully to the Court of Appeal. As the Lord Chief Justice observed (at p358):

'Might it properly be said that when he jumped on to the track he was trying to steal £18 from the bookmaker? Our view is that it could not properly be said that at that stage he was in the process of committing theft. What he was doing was jumping on to the track in an effort to distract the dogs, which in its turn, he hoped, would have the effect of forcing the stewards to declare "no race", which would in its turn give him the opportunity to go back to the bookmaker and demand the £18 he had staked. In our view there was insufficient evidence for it to be said that he had, when he jumped on to the track, gone beyond mere preparation.'

Given its ruling on the absence of any attempt, it was not necessary for the court to consider whether or not, if D had succeeded and had collected his stake money, he would have committed theft of the £18, although this in itself would have been a vexed question.

In *R v Jones* (1990) 91 Cr App R 351, D had bought some guns, shortened the barrel of one of them and gone to the place where his intended victim dropped his daughter off for school. As the girl left the car, D jumped in and took the gun from a bag, pointing it at the victim from a range of 10–12 inches. The intended victim was able to grab the gun and throw it from the car window before D could fire it. It was significant that the gun's safety catch had been on throughout the struggle, and that the intended victim could not state categorically that D's finger had been on the trigger. In dismissing D's appeal against his conviction for attempted murder,

Taylor LJ, considering how the courts should interpret the statutory formulation of the actus reus of attempt, expressed the view that, as the 1981 Act was a codifying statute, seeking to amend and set out completely the law relating to attempt, the correct approach was to look first at the natural meaning of the statutory words, not to turn back to earlier case law and seek to fit some previous test to the words of the section. His Lordship then cited with approval passages from the judgment of Lord Lane CJ in *Gullefer* (above) wherein he stated:

> 'The first task of the Court is to apply the words of the Act of 1981 to the facts of the case. Was the appellant still in the stage of preparation to commit the substantive offence, or was there a basis of fact which would entitle the jury to say that he had embarked on the theft itself? So far at least as the present case is concerned, we do not think that it is necessary to examine the authorities which preceded the Act of 1981 save to say that the sections we have already quoted in this judgment seem to be a blend of various decisions, some of which were not easy to reconcile with others. It seems to us that the words of the Act of 1981 seek to steer a midway course. They do not provide, as they might have done, that the *Eagleton* test is to be followed, or that, as Lord Diplock suggested, the defendant must have reached a point from which it was impossible for him to retreat before the actus reus of an attempt is proved. On the other hand the words give perhaps as clear a guidance as is possible in the circumstances on the point of time at which Stephen's "series of acts" begin. It begins when the merely preparatory acts come to an end and the defendant embarks upon the crime proper. When that is will depend of course upon the facts in any particular case.'

On the facts before him, Taylor LJ felt that there was evidence from which a reasonable jury, properly directed, could conclude that D had done acts which were more than merely preparatory to murder. The court regarded D's acts in obtaining the gun, in shortening it, in loading it, in putting on his disguise, and in going to the school, as merely preparatory to the killing, but his actions in getting into the car, taking out the loaded gun and pointing it at the victim provided sufficient evidence of acts more than merely preparatory to the killing for the jury to consider.

Adopting this approach in relation to a charge of attempted rape Lord Taylor CJ, in *Attorney-General's Reference (No 1 of 1992)* (1993) 96 Cr App R 298 observed:

> 'It is not, in our judgment, necessary, in order to raise a prima facie case of attempted rape, to prove that the defendant with the requisite intent had necessarily gone as far as to attempt physical penetration of the vagina. It is sufficient if there is evidence from which the intent can be inferred and there are proved acts which a jury could properly regard as more than merely preparatory to the commission of the offence. For example, and merely as an example, in the present case the evidence of the young woman's distress, of the state of her clothing, and the position in which she was seen, together with the respondent's acts of dragging her up the steps, lowering his trousers and interfering with her private parts, and his answers to the police, left it open to a jury to conclude that the respondent had the necessary intent and had done acts which were more than merely preparatory. In short that he had embarked on committing the offence itself.'

The decision again underlines the point that, provided that there is evidence upon which they can act, the issue is one of fact for the jury, to be resolved by the members exercising their collective common sense in the light of evidence as to D's intent at the time of the acts alleged. Watkins LJ noted in *R* v *Campbell* (1991) 93 Cr App R 350 that it would be unwise for any trial judge directing a jury on a charge of attempt to embark discursively upon what the law was previously, and to provide a jury with elaborate instances of what can and what cannot constitute an attempt. It would be permissible, however, for a trial judge to put a gloss on the wording of s1(1) of the 1981 Act to the effect that an attempt will have been committed if it could be shown that D had done an act which showed that he was actually trying to commit the act in question, rather than merely putting himself in a position, or equipping himself, in order to do so: see *R* v *Geddes* [1996] Crim LR 894; *R* v *Tosti* [1997] Crim LR 746; *R* v *Toothill* [1998] Crim LR 876; and *R* v *Nash* (1998) (CA No 9706719/X5).

The mens rea of statutory attempt

Section 1(1) of the 1981 Act (above) refers to a defendant acting with 'intent' to commit an offence. This rather suggests that far from amending the law in this area, the Act has in fact codified the common law. This view is borne out by the Court of Appeal's decision in *R* v *Pearman* (1985) 80 Cr App R 259, where the defendant's conviction for attempted grievous bodily harm was quashed, following the trial judge's direction to the jury that it was sufficient for the defendant to have foreseen grievous bodily harm as a probable consequence of his actions. Stuart-Smith J, delivering the judgment of the court, stated that it had not been the purpose of the 1981 Act to alter the law relating to the mens rea of attempt, and that as a result, the court regarded itself as still bound by decisions such as *R* v *Whybrow* (1951) 35 Cr App R 141, and *R* v *Mohan* [1976] QB 1. Consequently, whilst it would be permissible for a judge to direct a jury to consider what the defendant had foreseen as evidence of what he had intended, it was a clear misdirection to equate such foresight with mens rea itself. On the nature of intent: see Chapter 3, section 3.2.

In *R* v *Walker & Hayles* (1990) 90 Cr App R 226, the Court of Appeal confirmed that whilst a defendant charged with murder had to be proved to have intended to kill, such intent could be inferred by the jury from evidence of the defendant's foresight that death was a virtually certain consequence of his actions.

The position is now that 'purpose' type intent, involving proof of the defendant's desire to bring about the prohibited consequence, would clearly be sufficient to secure a conviction on a charge of attempt. Indeed, the Court of Appeal in *R* v *Walker & Hayles* (above) expressed the view that a jury, considering a charge of attempted murder, could be directed that 'trying to kill' was synonymous with the defendant having the death of the victim as his purpose. Oblique intent, based on evidence of what the defendant foresaw, would also suffice, provided there was evidence, upon which a jury could act, that the defendant foresaw a consequence as virtually certain. It has been cogently argued (see J C Smith [1990] Crim LR 48), that trying to bring about a result and foreseeing a result as virtually certain will frequently be indistinguishable states of mind.

Where the elements of an offence specify that recklessness will suffice in respect of matters other than the prohibited consequence, the courts will not require proof of intent or knowledge simply because the defendant is charged with attempting to commit such an offence. In *R v Khan & Others* (1990) 91 Cr App R 29, the Court of Appeal considered the mens rea for attempted rape and referred to the earlier decision of *R v Millard and Vernon* [1987] Crim LR 393, wherein Mustill LJ had raised the matter in the following terms:

> 'Must the prosecution prove not only that the defendant intended the act [ie sexual intercourse], but also that he intended it to be non-consensual? Or should the jury be directed to consider two different states of mind, intent as to the act and recklessness as to the circumstance?'

The court concluded that a defendant could be convicted of attempted rape provided that he intended to have sexual intercourse with a woman, in circumstances where the woman did not consent; he knew that she was not consenting or was reckless as to whether she consented, and had committed some act which was more than merely preparatory to sexual intercourse.

The court stressed that the attempt related to the physical activity; the mental state of a defendant charged with attempt was the same as one charged with the completed crime. It did not make sense to talk of a defendant being reckless as to whether he had sexual intercourse, but it did make sense to talk of his recklessness in relation to circumstances, such as the presence or absence of the woman's consent. The words 'with intent to commit an offence' meant, when applied to rape, 'with intent to have sexual intercourse with a woman in circumstances where she does not consent and the defendant knows or could not care less about her absence of consent'.

The rationale of *Khan* has subsequently been applied to attempted aggravated criminal damage, being reckless as to whether life would be endangered thereby, by the Court of Appeal in *Attorney-General's Reference (No 3 of 1992)* [1994] 1 WLR 409. The trial judge directed that the respondents be acquitted on the ground that the endangering of life was a consequence of criminal damage under the aggravated offence, and thus recklessness was not sufficient mens rea where the charge was one of attempt. The Court of Appeal confirmed that reckless as to whether life would thereby be endangered would be sufficient mens rea on a charge of attempt, provided the defendant had taken steps more than merely preparatory to causing criminal damage, with intent to cause criminal damage. In drawing an analogy with *Khan*, Schiemann J observed:

> '... what was missing [in *Khan*] ... was the act of sexual intercourse, without which the offence was not complete. What was missing in the present case was damage to [the car] without which the offence was not complete. The mental state of the defendant in each case contained everything which was required to render him guilty of the full offence ...

> The prosecution had to show an intention to damage the [car], and the remaining state of mind required for the aggravated offence of arson.'

Notwithstanding this ruling, it has been cogently argued (see D W Elliot 'Endangering Life by Destroying Property or Damaging Property' [1997] Crim LR 382 at 392) that it is inappropriate to apply the rationale of *Khan* to the aggravated offence under s1(2) of the Criminal Damage Act 1971, as in *Khan* the matter in respect of which D was found to have been reckless as an objectively substantiated fact (ie the absence of consent). In cases of attempted aggravated criminal damage there is no requirement for the prosecution to prove that any lives were actually endangered. The aggravating factor is D's intention to endanger life or his recklessness as to whether any life is so endangered. In short it is a mens rea requirement. Logically, liability for an attempt to commit an offence contrary to s1(2) should require proof that D intended to cause criminal damage and proof that he intended that the damage should endanger life.

Going equipped

When considering liability for attempted theft, obtaining by deception or burglary, consideration ought to be given to the specific preparatory offence created under s25 of the Theft Act 1968, which provides:

> 'A person shall be guilty of an offence if, when not at his place of abode, he has with him any article for use in the course of or in connection with any burglary, theft or cheat.'

The offence carries a maximum sentence of three years' imprisonment following conviction on indictment. The offence is clearly designed to cover situations where a defendant is searched and found to have a collection of skeleton keys in his possession for which he cannot provide a satisfactory explanation, a number of credit cards or cheque books the names upon which do not correspond to his own, and the defendant whose car is found to contain housebreaking implements such as a crowbar, 'jemmy' or other such items.

It should be noted that the offence is aimed at the defendant who has such items intending to use them in the course of committing offences outlined below. It is not an offence within the section to be in possession of such items merely because they have been used in the course of committing such offences: see *R* v *Ellames* [1974] 3 All ER 130.

In theory, s12 could be charged as an alternative to attempted theft or deception where D is in possession of the relevant equipment at the time of the attempt: see *DPP* v *Minor* [1988] Crim LR 55.

'When not at his place of abode ...'

The offence is preparatory in its nature, nevertheless the defendant does not commit any offence where he has the relevant articles at his dwelling place, regardless of his mens rea. As soon as the defendant leaves his home with the tools and has the necessary mens rea, an offence within the section may be committed. A defendant having such articles at his place of work might, therefore, incur liability.

In *R* v *Bundy* [1977] 1 WLR 914, the Court of Appeal considered the case of a defendant found to have housebreaking tools in his car, but who claimed not to be guilty under s25, since the car was also his 'place of abode', the defendant having no other house. The court held that whilst the car might be his place of abode when he was using it as such (eg sleeping in it), when he was using it as a car, he was committing an offence within the section.

'Has with him ...'

This expression implies that the defendant has an article within his possession or control. A defendant has an article in his control if he is able to gain access to it quickly, for example, the driver of a vehicle who has tools in the boot of his car. Note that s25(3) provides:

> 'Where a person is charged with an offence under this section, proof that he had with him any article made or adapted for use in committing a burglary, theft or cheat shall be evidence that he had it with him for such use.'

In *R* v *McAngus* [1994] Crim LR 602 the applicant took two undercover fraud investigators to a bonded warehouse and showed them a number of shirts which falsely purported to be of a brand manufactured in the United States. The prosecution case was that he had agreed to sell the shirts to the officers. The applicant, who was due to be extradited to the United States on a charge of going equipped, applied unsuccessfully for a writ of habeus corpus on the ground, inter alia, that he had not had the shirts 'with him' as required by the wording of s25 of the Theft Act 1968. There might, it is submitted, be some debate as to whether the applicant, although obviously not at his place of abode, was actually *going* equipped on these facts. The Criminal Law Revision Committee report that presaged the 1968 Act envisages an offence being committed where D starts out on his journey to commit one of the specified offences whilst in possession of the prohibited articles. On the basis that any ambiguities should be construed in favour of the accused it is submitted that there is an arguable case that the present decision offends at least the spirit of s25 if not the letter.

'Any article for use in the course of or in connection with any burglary theft or cheat'

The offence is potentially very wide given the use of the phrase 'any article'. Its effect is narrowed, however, by reference to the offences that the defendant must be proved to have had in mind. Some common sense should also be exercised in the application of the section. For example, a defendant on his way to commit a burglary may be wearing a shirt and trousers. He intends to wear them (it is hoped!) whilst committing the burglary, but it would seem to be straining the wording of the section to say that they are 'articles for use in the course of the burglary'. The point is that the defendant would have been wearing the clothes anyway. A more difficult question arises where the defendant is wearing gloves, or a balaclava helmet. Is he wearing these items because he is cold, or to avoid detection?

The section contemplates that the articles are to be used in connection with the following offences:

1. burglary;
2. theft: a typical example is provided by *R* v *Goodwin* [1996] Crim LR 262, where D was convicted of going equipped to steal on the basis of his using foreign coins to operate gaming machines. The Court of Appeal held that the property in any prize money paid out as a result of using the coins would not pass to the appellant. Note that, for the purposes of s25, theft includes an offence under s12 of the Theft Act 1968;
3. cheat.

For these purposes 'cheat' means an offence under s15 Theft Act 1968. Considerable difficulties have arisen as to what approach should be taken by the courts in determining whether a defendant in possession of certain items would have actually deceived another person by use of the items. In *R* v *Rashid* [1977] 2 All ER 237, the Court of Appeal held that a defendant British Rail steward who was caught boarding a train in possession of bread and tomatoes that he intended to sell to passengers as his own, pocketing the proceeds, was not going equipped to 'cheat' on the basis that it could not be said that the British Rail passengers could not have bought his food had they known the truth. In short, the court was not satisfied that Rashid's deception would have been operative on the passengers – a point it was necessary for the prosecution to establish for liability under s15 (the 'cheat').

Conversely in *R* v *Doukas* [1978] 1 All ER 1061, the Court of Appeal held that the defendant hotel wine waiter was guilty of going equipped to cheat where he was stopped entering the hotel for work, carrying two bottles of wine that he intended to sell to hotel diners as being the hotel's and pocketing the proceeds. The evidence was that the hotel diners would not have knowingly participated with Doukas in a fraud on the hotel; his deception as to the origin of the wine would have been operative. This decision was subsequently followed by the Court of Appeal in *R* v *Corboz* [1984] Crim LR 629, on facts very similar to those arising in *R* v *Rashid* (above).

More recently the matter has come before the House of Lords as a subsidiary issue in *R* v *Cooke* [1986] AC 909, which concerned an alleged agreement between the defendant and others to supply British Rail passengers with their own food; the facts again being very similar to *R* v *Rashid* and *R* v *Corboz* (above). Regarding the question of whether the defendant should have been charged with conspiracy to commit an offence contrary to s25, it was held that there was no evidence to show that British Rail passengers would have refused to purchase the food supplied by the defendant had they known of its origin. In the view of Lord Mackay, whether or not the 'cheat' element of the s25 offence is made out is a question for the jury based on the evidence of the attitude and understanding of those receiving the supplies.

Difficulties remain, however, as exemplified by the Court of Appeal's decision in *R v Whiteside and Antoniou* [1989] Crim LR 436. The appellants were arrested selling 'pirate' cassette tapes of popular recording artists, and convicted of going equipped for cheating. The appellants claimed in evidence that if any customer had enquired into the provenance of the tapes they would have admitted that they were not authorised copies. Before the Court of Appeal they contended first, that there was no direct evidence that they had intended to cheat any member of the public, secondly that the trial judge had been wrong to raise issues relating to the Copyright Act when directing the jury on dishonesty, and thirdly that the trial judge had erred in directing the jury that the obtaining of property by deception (the cheat) could be wholly or partly as a result of the appellants' actions.

Whilst the court allowed the appeal by concurring with the second and third contentions, it held that the tapes bore a close resemblance to the 'genuine' article, and the appellants had done nothing to indicate to the public generally that they were not authorised copies, hence the jury had been entitled to infer the intention to 'cheat' the public. This conclusion is perhaps debatable, since potential customers would not have been deceived as to the nature of the music recorded on the tapes, and there was no evidence that the quality of the recordings was any worse than that of the authorised versions. The only deception, therefore, would have been as to whether the permission of the copyright owner had been obtained prior to making the copies. Such a deception could only become operative if it could be shown that a potential customer would not have bought one of the tapes had he known that its production had involved breaches of the Copyright Act, thus raising exactly the same problem as that in *R v Doukas* and *R v Cooke*.

Mens rea

The defendant must know he is not at his place of abode, and must know that he has the relevant articles 'with him'. It is in the nature of the offence that the defendant will almost invariably know the nature of the articles. That knowledge of the presence of the articles is necessary is, it is submitted, evidenced by *R v Lester and Byast* (1955) 39 Cr App R 157, a decision under the former law. Further, the defendant must intend to use the said articles in the course of one of the offences discussed above. If, therefore, a defendant intends to use a stolen membership card to obtain services by deception, contrary to s1 Theft Act 1978, he would not be guilty under s25.

In *R v Ellames* (above) the Court of Appeal held that a defendant could be convicted under s25 even though he does not have a specific theft or burglary in mind. Any theft or burglary will suffice. Further, in *R v Hargreaves* [1985] Crim LR 243, the Court of Appeal held that an intention to use an article in the course of a theft, cheat or burglary, should the opportunity present itself, would also be sufficient mens rea. The defendant's appeal was allowed however, on the basis that the jury might have been misled by the judge's direction into thinking that a defendant had the necessary mens rea even where he had not decided whether or not to use the article should the opportunity to commit one of the above offences present itself.

12.7 Impossibility

To what extent, if at all, should the fact that D is suggesting, agreeing to or attempting the commission of an offence that, for reasons beyond his control, it is impossible to carry out be a factor having a bearing on whether or not he should be convicted of an inchoate offence? On the one hand there is the argument that if D tries to commit an offence that it is impossible to carry out, no liability should arise as he has not caused any harm, and indeed could not have done so. On the other hand it is argued that D should incur liability, notwithstanding the issue of impossibility, because he was morally culpable in the sense that he was willing to commit the offence. In many cases it will be a matter of pure luck that D is prevented from carrying out the completed offence; for example D intends to stab P to death whilst P is asleep, but, unknown to D, P dies five minutes before D carries out his attack.

Prior to the enactment of the 1981 Act, a defendant charged with attempt could raise the issue of impossibility in circumstances outlined by the House of Lords in *Haughton* v *Smith* [1975] AC 476. A lorry-load of stolen meat travelling from Liverpool to London was repossessed by the police, and thereby ceased to be stolen property for the purposes of handling stolen goods under s22 of the Theft Act 1968. The lorry was allowed to continue south, where it was met by the defendants who had intended to unload the meat. They were charged with attempting to handle stolen goods, but the House of Lords held that they could not be guilty of attempting to commit a crime which, in the circumstances, it was impossible to carry out. This was viewed as a case of legal impossibility; in other words, although there were cases of meat that could be handled, as a matter of law they had ceased to be stolen by the time the defendants took possession of them.

It was Parliament's intention to reverse the effect of this decision, and deal more generally with the confusion that surrounded cases of factual impossibility, by enacting s1(2) and (3) of the 1981 Act which provide as follows:

'(2) A person may be guilty of attempting to commit an offence to which this section applies even though the facts are such that the commission of the offence is impossible.
(3) In any case where –
a) apart from this subsection a person's intention would not be regarded as having amounted to an intent to commit an offence; but
b) if the facts of the case had been as he believed them to be, his intention would be so regarded,
then, for the purposes of subsection (1) above, he shall be regarded as having had an intent to commit that offence.'

Initially, the House of Lords was reluctant to interpret these provisions in a manner that would produce the result intended by Parliament. In *Anderton* v *Ryan* [1985] AC 560, D had bought a video recorder for £110, but later confessed to the police that she believed it to have been stolen property when she bought it. She was charged, inter alia, with attempting to handle stolen goods, although the prosecution was unable to prove that the video recorder had in fact been stolen property. The House of Lords (Lord Edmund-Davies dissenting) quashed D's conviction on the ground that she could not be guilty of attempting to handle stolen goods unless such property was shown to have existed. A majority of their Lordships refused to accept that D's belief that the goods were stolen was sufficient of itself to result in liability. Such a result may have been the aim of the 1981 Act, but their Lordships felt that Parliament would have to express its intentions more clearly before the courts would be willing to impose liability solely on the basis of what D had thought she was doing, as opposed to what she was actually doing.

The effect of this decision was short-lived, however. Given the facts of *R* v *Shivpuri* [1986] 2 WLR 988, the House of Lords had little choice but to overrule its previous decision in *Anderton* v *Ryan*. Shivpuri, whilst in India, was paid £1,000 to act as a drugs courier. He was required to collect a package containing a consignment of drugs which would be delivered to him in England, and distribute its contents according to instructions which would be given to him. On collecting the package he was arrested by police officers, and he confessed to them that he believed its contents to be either heroin or cannabis. In due course, further analysis revealed the contents of the package to be not drugs but a harmless vegetable substance. His appeal to the House of Lords against his conviction for attempting to be knowingly concerned in dealing with and harbouring a controlled drug, namely heroin, was dismissed. It was held that s1 of the 1981 Act was to be interpreted as requiring D to be judged on the facts as he believed them to be. On this basis he had taken steps that he believed to be more than merely preparatory towards dealing with a controlled drug.

The decision effectively lays to rest the ghost of *Haughton* v *Smith* and gives effect to s1 of the 1981 Act in the manner intended by Parliament. Nevertheless, it does open up a number of interesting, if somewhat hypothetical, possibilities, such as D who commits attempted unlawful sexual intercourse by having consensual sexual intercourse with a girl aged 17, believing her to be only 14; similarly, D who stabs at a pillow placed under some bedclothes, believing it to be the sleeping figure of his enemy, could now be charged with attempted murder; see further *R* v *Tulloch* [1986] Crim LR 50.

As far as the statutory offence of conspiracy is concerned, impossibility is similarly no longer a bar to liability. Section 5 of the Criminal Attempts Act 1981 amends s1(1) of the 1977 Act to the effect that D can be guilty of conspiracy if he agrees with another that a course of conduct shall be pursued which, if the agreement were carried out in accordance with their intentions, would necessarily involve the commission of any offence but for the existence of facts which render the commission of the offence impossible. Hence D1 and D2 can be indicted for conspiracy, even where the agreement is to assassinate Queen Victoria. The fact that she is already dead appears to be no bar to liability, provided that the defendants honestly believe that she is still alive. The effect of the amendment is to judge D on the facts as he honestly believes them to be.

As noted above, certain common law forms of conspiracy have survived the enactment of the Criminal Law Act 1977, notably conspiracy to defraud and conspiracy to corrupt public morals. As regards these forms of conspiracy, the issue of impossibility is still governed by the pre-Criminal Attempts Act 1981 law as stated in the House of Lords' decision in *DPP* v *Nock* [1978] AC 979. D1 and D2 were convicted of conspiring to produce cocaine, contrary to s4(2) of the Misuse of Drugs Act 1971, on the basis that they had agreed together to obtain cocaine by separating it from the other substance or substances contained in a powder which they had obtained from one of their co-defendants. They believed that the powder was a mixture of cocaine and lignocaine, and that they would be able to produce cocaine from it. In fact the powder was lignocaine hydrochloride, an anaesthetic used in dentistry, containing no cocaine, which made it impossible to produce cocaine by separation or otherwise. Allowing their appeals, the House of Lords held that the principles expounded in *Haughton* v *Smith* in relation to attempt at common law were equally applicable to conspiracy at common law; hence their Lordships recognised a distinction between agreements which were 'conspiracies at large' and agreements which were 'limited' or more specific in nature. In the case of the former, impossibility would not normally be a bar to liability, but it would be as regards the latter. As Lord Scarman observed:

'Counsel for the appellants concedes that, if two or more persons decide to go into business as cocaine producers, or, to take another example, as assassins for hire (eg Murder Incorporated), the mere fact that in the course of performing their agreement they attempt to produce cocaine from a raw material which could not possibly yield it or (in the second example) stab a corpse, believing it to be the body of a living man, would not avail them as a defence: for the performance of their general agreement would not be rendered impossible by such transient frustrations. But performance of the limited agreement [ie to produce cocaine from specific substances] proved in this case could not in any circumstances have involved the commission of the offence created by the statute ... common sense and justice combine to require of the law that no man should be punished criminally for the intention with which he enters an agreement unless it can also be shown that what he has agreed to do is unlawful.'

In essence the distinction drawn is between, on the one hand, an agreement to commit a crime capable of being committed in the way agreed upon, but frustrated by a supervening event making its completion impossible, and, on the other, an agreement to embark upon a course of conduct which could not in any circumstances result in the commission of the statutory offence alleged by any person at any time.

Unlike attempt and the vast majority of conspiracy charges, incitement remains a common law offence. It is submitted that Parliament did not take the opportunity to codify the law relating to incitement and impossibility when enacting the Criminal Attempts Act 1981 because, at the time, there did not appear to be any need to do so. In effect Parliament believed that the 1981 Act was simply bringing attempt and conspiracy in line with what was already the approach at common law to incitement and impossibility. The basis for this is the Court of Appeal's decision in *R v McDonough* (1962) 47 Cr App R 37. D was convicted of inciting a number of butchers to receive stolen meat carcasses. On appeal he had contended, unsuccessfully, that at the time of the incitement the meat carcasses had not been stolen, or possibly had not existed at all, and thus he should have been acquitted. The Court of Appeal took the view that his conviction should stand, as the essence of the offence lay in the making of the suggestion accompanied by mens rea. Both of these matters could be established quite independently of whether there were actually any stolen meat carcasses in existence. The decision represented a very straightforward approach to the problem of impossibility, and ensured that no distinction was drawn between legal ad factual impossibility, or between general and specific incitements (see comments on *DPP v Nock* above).

It was somewhat surprising therefore when, in its decision in *R v Fitzmaurice* [1983] 2 WLR 227, the Court of Appeal effectively introduced into the law of incitement the very complexities that Parliament had but two years previously legislated to excise from the law relating to attempt and statutory conspiracy. In *Fitzmaurice* D, acting on false information given to him by his father, arranged for three men to carry out a wages snatch on a woman delivering money to a bank at Bow in East London. The three men were arrested in a van parked outside the bank by the police who had been tipped off by D's father, whose only motive in all this had been to receive some reward money. As there was, in reality, no woman carrying wages to be robbed, the three men arrested outside the bank were acquitted of attempted robbery on the ground of impossibility (note these events took place before the Criminal Attempts Act 1981 came into effect). D was convicted of inciting the robbery, and his conviction was upheld on appeal. Notwithstanding that, in his speech in *DPP v Nock*, Lord Scarman appeared to be expressing the view that what was being said about impossibility and the offence of common law conspiracy in that case should not necessarily have any bearing on other common law inchoate offences, such as incitement, the Court of Appeal proceeded to hold that the right approach in a case of incitement was the same as that adopted in *DPP v Nock* as regards common law conspiracy. According to the Court of Appeal it would be necessary in every case to analyse the evidence with care to decide the precise offence which D was alleged to have incited. As Neill J observed:

> 'In some cases the evidence may establish that the persuasion by the inciter was in quite general terms whereas the subsequent agreement of the conspirators was directed to a specific crime and specific target. In such cases where the committal of the specific offence is shown to be impossible it may be quite logical for the inciter to be convicted even though the alleged conspirators (if not caught by section 5 of the Criminal Attempts

Act 1981) may be acquitted. On the other hand, if B and C agree to kill D, and A, standing beside B and C, though not intending to take any active part whatever in the crime, encourages them to do so, we can see no satisfactory reason, if it turns out later that D was already dead, why A should be convicted of incitement to murder whereas B and C at common law would be entitled to an acquittal on a charge of conspiracy. The crucial question is to establish on the evidence the course of conduct which the alleged inciter was encouraging.'

The court saw no inconsistency between its ruling and the earlier decision in *McDonough* on the basis that, in the latter, although there might have been no stolen goods or no goods at all which were available to be received at the time of the incitement, the offence of incitement to receive stolen goods could nevertheless be proved because it was not impossible that at the relevant time in the future the necessary goods would be there.

Despite the somewhat perverse nature of the decision in *Fitzmaurice* it has subsequently received implicit approval from a differently constituted Court of Appeal in *R* v *Sirat* (above).

12.8 Reform of inchoate offences

Incitement

Unlike conspiracy (*Conspiracy and Criminal Law Reform* (1976), Law Com No 76), and attempt (*Attempt, and Impossibility in Relation to Attempt, Conspiracy and Incitement* (1980), Law Com No 102), the substantive offence of incitement has not been the subject of a Law Commission report in its own right. As will be seen below, the Law Commission currently favours the abolition of the offence of incitement and in its stead, as a part of a reform of accessorial liability generally, a new offence of encouraging crime: see Consultation Paper No 131. It is instructive, nevertheless, to consider the original proposals that were put forward by the Code team regarding the retention and reform of incitement. At a general level the team saw the major problem with the existing state of the law relating to inchoate offences (or 'preliminary offences', as the Draft Code terms them) as the inconsistencies between the offences themselves. The aim of the Draft Code in this respect is stated in the commentary thereon:

'We believe that as far as possible there should be consistency between these offences. They share a common rationale concerned with the prevention of substantive offences and they frequently overlap. When two or more persons engage in conduct preliminary to a substantive offence more than one of these offences may well be involved. It would be illogical and confusing to a court or jury if similar problems were provided with significantly different solutions. Therefore we have regarded the policy concerning those issues in the offence of incitement which arise also in conspiracy and attempt as generally having been settled in the way recently provided by Parliament for conspiracy and attempt. On issues peculiar to incitement we have followed the general principle of restatement of the existing law ...' (Vol II, para 13.3)

In attempting to codify and rationalise the law relating to incitement, as with other inchoate offences, a number of issues arise. How should the elements of the offence be defined? What should be the relationship between the inchoate offence, other inchoate offences, and participation? How should the issue of impossibility be dealt with? Each of these issues is considered in turn below.

In terms of codification of incitement, cl 47(1) of the Draft Code proposes the following :

'A person is guilty of incitement to commit an offence or offences if
(a) he incites another to do or cause to be done an act or acts which, if done, will involve the commission of the offence or offences by the other; and
(b) he intends or believes that the other, if he acts as incited, shall or will do so with the fault required for the offence or offences.'

An 'offence' for the purposes of this provision means any offence triable in England and Wales; in other words, it includes incitement to commit summary offences. The retention of such a wide-ranging offence is justified for the following reasons:

'At common law incitement to commit an indictable or a summary offence is itself an offence. [The Draft Code] restates the general principle. However, it should be noted that in this respect the draft ... departs from the principle of consistency among the preliminary offences. There is no liability for attempting to commit a summary offence (Criminal Attempts Act 1981, s1(4)) but there is liability for conspiracy to commit a summary offence (Criminal Law Act 1977, s1). Parliament, in enacting the rule for attempt, rejected our recommendation that an attempt to commit a summary offence should itself be an offence [Law Com No 102, para 2.105]. The view was taken that there was no need to extend the ambit of attempt to summary offences. Any such extension might, it was felt, result in more time being taken up in magistrates' courts with complicated questions of attempts to commit minor offences than would be justified by any advantage of the extra reach of the law. In the absence of evidence of any need to extend the criminal law on this point we accept the decision. We maintain, nevertheless, that a different rule can be justified for conspiracy and incitement. These offences, which ex hypothesi concern more than one person, enable the promoters and organisers of large-scale minor offences to be brought within the reach of the law. Admittedly prosecutions may be appropriate in practice only on rare occasions. It was for this reason that we recommended in our Report on conspiracy that prosecutions for conspiracy to commit summary offences should only be brought with the consent of the Director of Public Prosecutions. We now make a similar recommendation in respect of incitement to commit a summary offence. The requirement of the Director's consent will ensure that the offence is not misused while keeping open the possibility of using such a charge to deal with cases where an element of social danger is involved in the deliberate promotion of offences on a widespread scale.' (Vol II, para 13.12)

In considering the terminology of the offence of incitement, the Law Commission preferred to retain the term 'incite' to describe the actus reus of the offence, rather than a term such as 'encourage'. It was persuaded by arguments that the latter word might mislead juries into thinking that there was a need for proof of actual encouragement; they would thus miss the point that the inciter may be liable for incitement even though the incitee is not in fact encouraged, indeed may have been quite indifferent to the incitement. As the commentary concludes, the word 'incite':

'... sufficiently conveys, without the need for an explanatory provision, that the person incited need not be influenced by whatever it is that constitutes the incitement.' (Vol II, para 13.6)

Note that under subs(4) of the proposed clause a person may be convicted of incitement to commit an offence although the identity of the person incited is unknown, thus preserving the effect of decisions such as *R* v *Most* (1881) 7 QBD 244. In relation to the mental element, the Code proposes that intention or belief on the part of the defendant that the incitee will commit the offence if he acts as incited should be sufficient. Whilst it is no surprise to see intention specified as the fault element, the Law Commission felt that some explanation of the inclusion of belief was required:

'It should ... be sufficient if the inciter believes that the person incited, if he acts at all, will do so with the fault required. For example, if D seeks to persuade E to have sexual intercourse with Mrs D, D believing that E knows that Mrs D does not consent to it, there seems to be a clear case of incitement to rape. It should not be necessary to prove that it was D's intention that E should have such knowledge. Whenever the fault required for a substantive offence includes knowledge of or recklessness as to circumstances (such as the absence of consent), it is likely to be more appropriate for the purposes of incitement to refer to the inciter's belief that such knowledge or recklessness exists rather than to his intention that it should.' (Vol II, para 13.9)

Note that cl 47 does not restate the common law requirement established in the much criticised case of *R* v *Curr* [1968] 2 QB 944; [1967] 1 All ER 478 that the incitee must have known that what was incited was unlawful. As the commentary observes

'... it is not necessary that any offence should be committed or even intended by the person incited, therefore it is irrelevant and confusing to ask whether that person had the mental element for the offence.' (Vol II, para 13.11)

Where the incitee is a child, or other innocent person, and the inciter is aware of the incitee's innocence, he may be charged with attempting to commit the relevant offence through an innocent agent. An example is provided in Appendix B to Volume I:

'D tells E, aged nine, to put a certain powder in P's drink to make him feel ill. D is not guilty of inciting E to administer a substance without consent (cl 73); even if E does this act with the fault required (knowledge that the substance is capable of interfering substantially with the other's bodily functions) he will not commit the offence because he is under ten (cl 32(1)). D may be guilty of attempting to commit the offence by an innocent agent. (Example 47(i))

Subsection (3) incorporates the rule in *R* v *Tyrell* [1894] 1 QB 710 to the effect that a member of a class of persons whom it is the purpose of the enactment creating the offence to protect is exempt from liability for incitement to commit such an offence.

Subsection (5)(b) proposes the retention of liability for inciting incitement, and inciting attempt, but interestingly proposes the reintroduction of liability for incitement to conspire. As the commentary explains:

'A number of problems arise concerning the use of preliminary offences in combination. In relation to incitement the present law has reached the point of absurdity. Incitement to conspire was abolished as an offence known to the law by s5(7) of the Criminal Law Act 1977. Recently the Court of Appeal has twice held that incitement to incite is an offence known to the law. It seems, however, that this is so only when the first person incited is to incite, but not to agree with, a second person to commit an offence. If the evidence shows that D incited E to agree with F to wound G, s5(7) of the Criminal Law Act 1977 apparently prevents a charge against D of incitement to conspire or of incitement to incite. But if D incites E to incite F (perhaps by a command, or a letter not requiring an answer) to wound G, D can be charged with incitement to incite. Such an absurd distinction cannot be restated in the Code ... Unlike other provisions of Part I of the Criminal Law Act 1977, s5(7) was not based on a recommendation in our Report, which did not deal with the point. Abolition of incitement to conspire had, however, been recommended by the Working Party. They had argued that to allow an offence of incitement to conspire would be to take the law "further back in the course of conduct to be penalised than is necessary or justifiable". [Working Paper No 50, paras 44,45]. The Working Party did not make any express reference to possible charges of incitement to incite, although it may be presumed that logically they would have wished to exclude this possibility also. The Code team's draft Bill followed the Criminal Law Act 1977 in excluding conspiracy from the scope of incitement, but did not exclude incitement itself thereby allowing for the possibility of charges of incitement to incite. The Scrutiny Group on preliminary offences invited us to look again at this problem, indicating that in their view it should be possible to indict for inciting to conspire ... Recent Court of Appeal decisions that incitement to incite is an offence known to the law have produced a clear anomaly. It would be illogical, and would bring the law into disrepute, to restate both the effect of these cases and s5(7) of the Criminal Law Act 1977. It would not be right, within the scope of this project, to attempt to overturn the recent decisions. Such a course would require much fuller discussion and consultation. We therefore recommend that neither incitement nor conspiracy should be excluded from the scope of incitement. In this way the anomaly will be eliminated without, we believe, a significant increase in the scope of criminal liability ... [It] is unclear whether an offence of incitement to attempt is known to the law. Virtually all possible instances of incitement are incitements to commit substantive offences, and it is difficult to conceive of a case where a charge of incitement to attempt (to commit an indictable offence) would not be inept. Smith and Hogan, however, suggest one possibility, namely where in the circumstances known to the inciter, but not to the person incited, the completed act will amount only to an attempt. The existence of this, admittedly, rare case, together with the general principle we referred to above of consistency of approach to the preliminary offences, persuade us that it would be preferable not to exclude attempt from the scope of incitement. Accordingly, our draft Bill makes no special provision with regard to incitement to attempt.' (Vol II, paras 13.13–13.16)

Subsection (5)(b) proposes that D could be an accomplice to an offence of incitement, but could not incur liability for inciting another to participate in the commission of an offence, as participation per se is not a crime. Consider further the reforms of accessorial liability, outlined in Chapter 13, section 13.7.

As noted above, impossibility is an issue that has continued to create confusion and controversy in the area of incitement, and in cl 50 the Draft Code aims to introduce a measure of consistency amongst the inchoate offences. It provides:

> '(1) A person may be guilty of incitement, conspiracy or attempt to commit an offence although the commission of the offence is impossible, if it would be possible in the circumstances which he believes or hopes exist or will exist at the relevant time.'

In referring to the absence of any provision dealing with incitement and impossibility in the Criminal Attempts Act 1981, the commentary on cl 50 notes:

> 'In relation to incitement we had taken the view that legislation was unnecessary. It appeared that the common law, as stated in *McDonough* ... and *DPP* v *Nock* ... was already in accordance with the position recommended for conspiracy and attempt. Subsequently, however, the Court of Appeal held in *Fitzmaurice* ... that the common law principles relating to impossibility, which it had been our concern to reverse as regards conspiracy and attempt, applied to the offence of incitement. The result, therefore, is that impossibility may in some cases be a defence to incitement but not to conspiracy or attempt ... [W]e agree with the Code team that it would be absurd to perpetuate this distinction. The same principle should apply to all the preliminary offences. This means that the position for incitement must be brought into line with that for conspiracy and attempt. We accept the Code team's view that it is unnecessary to make separate provision for each offence. Only one provision is needed to rule out impossibility as a defence to any of the preliminary offences.' (Vol II, paras 13.50–51)

Conspiracy

Clause 48 of the Draft Code restates the law relating to statutory conspiracy. The problem of common law conspiracy is considered in a separate report (see below). The Law Commission remains committed, however, to its view that all forms of common law liability should eventually be replaced with statutory provisions. The proposals concerning statutory conspiracy are necessarily complex. In the interests of clarity the external elements (actus reus) and fault elements (mens rea) need to be considered separately.

In relation to the external elements cl 48 provides:

> '(1) A person is guilty of conspiracy to commit an offence or offences if
> (a) he agrees with another or others that an act or acts shall be done which, if done, will involve the commission of the offence or offences by one or more of the parties to the agreement ...'

Subsection (5) goes on to state that a conspiracy continues '... until the agreed act or acts is or are done, or until all or all save one of the parties to the agreement have abandoned the intention that such act or acts shall be done'. This reflects the position at common law as established in *DPP* v *Doot* [1973] AC 807. Other subsections, largely for the avoidance of doubt, provide that a person may become a party to a continuing conspiracy by joining the agreement constituting the offence (subs(6)), and that a person may be convicted of conspiracy even though the other conspirators are unknown, have not been charged, have been acquitted, or cannot be convicted because of the availability of some defence (subs(8)).

It is significant that two exceptions to liability currently to be found in s2(2) of the Criminal Law Act 1977 – that a person cannot be guilty of conspiracy if the only other party is his spouse, or a child under the age of ten – are not reproduced in the Draft Code. The commentary on clause 48 explains the reasoning behind this proposed change:

'At common law the offence of conspiracy did not extend to agreements between spouses. The origins of this rule lay in the ancient notion of the unity of husband and wife. Because husband and wife were deemed to be one person they could not form the agreement which is the essence of the offence. It hardly needs to be said that in view of changed attitudes to marriage in modern society this "antique fiction" cannot sustain the rule. In our earlier Report on conspiracy [Law Com No 76, para 1.49], we recommended retention of the exemption for alternative reasons, principally the importance of maintaining the stability of marriage by non-interference with the confidential relationship of husband and wife. We are now persuaded, particularly having regard to subsequent developments in the law, that this argument is insufficient to sustain the rule. First, the exemption is an anomaly. Husbands and wives are capable in law of being accessories to each other's offences. Where, say, a wife agrees that her husband shall commit an offence, that agreement cannot ground liability for conspiracy by either party, but it will ground liability in the wife for aiding and abetting if the husband actually commits the offence. The distinction makes no sense. Secondly, as a result of section 80 of the Police and Criminal Evidence Act 1984, husbands and wives are now competent witnesses for the prosecution against each other in all cases and the privilege against disclosure of marital communications has been abolished. Thirdly the exemption was criticised on consultation. The Scrutiny Group on preliminary offences said that they saw no reasons of social policy for maintaining the rule relating to spouses. In the light of these considerations we recommend that the exemption for agreements with spouses should not be retained … In our conspiracy Report we proposed that a person agreeing with a child under the age of criminal responsibility to commit an offence should not be liable for conspiracy [ibid, paras 1.51 and 1.58]. This reflected the majority view on consultation on our Working Paper No 50 which had expressed the opinion that the law did permit a conviction for conspiracy in such a case. We are inclined to think now that the exemption is unjustified. The justification of conspiracy as a means of enabling early intervention to prevent crime applies as much to this case as to any other. We would now prefer to leave such cases to be dealt with according to general principles of conspiracy in the same way as cases of agreements with mentally disordered persons. That is, if the child understands the nature of the agreement and intends that the offence be committed, his own immunity from prosecution should not affect the liability for conspiracy of the person who is over the age of criminal responsibility. Accordingly, we recommend that the exemption for agreements with children should not be retained.' (Vol 2, paras 13.30–31)

In relation to the mental element in conspiracy, cl 48 provides:

'(1) A person is guilty of conspiracy to commit an offence or offences if
(a) he agrees [etc, see above]; and
(b) he and at least one other party to the agreement intend that the offence or offences shall be committed.

(2) For the purposes of subsection (1) an intention that an offence shall be committed is an intention with respect to all the elements of the offence (other than fault elements), except that recklessness with respect to a circumstance suffices where it suffices for the offence itself.'

The view of the Law Commission (as expressed in Vol II, para 13.22) is that the purpose of the existing law stating the mental element in statutory conspiracy (s1(1) of the Criminal Law Act 1977) had been to express a concept of conspiracy as involving agreement between two or more people, both or all of whom intend that the offence shall be committed. In drafting cl 48, the Commission considered the effect of the House of Lords' decision in *Anderson*, and noted that:

'... [the defendant] was treated by the House of Lords as a principal offender, not simply as an accessory to a conspiracy between the others involved. Their Lordships did not require by way of mens rea for any conspirator more than an intention to play some part in the agreed course of conduct. The implication of this is that there may be a conspiracy although no conspirator actually intends that the offence agreed upon shall be committed. This implication is, in our view, at odds with the plain meaning of the section [ie s1(1) of the 1977 Act]. We think, with respect, that the conviction in *Anderson* is better supported on the ground that the accused was an accessory to a conspiracy between others. He clearly assisted and encouraged the plan, knowing of the circumstances (that the plan was to effect an escape from prison) and of the conspirators' intention to commit that offence. A similar analysis can be applied to the hypothetical case put by Lord Bridge in *Anderson* [at p38]. The proprietor of a car hire firm who agrees to supply a car to a gang for a robbery is equally an accessory to the gang's conspiracy even though he may have no interest in whether the robbery is in fact committed ... A further point arises concerning a dictum in *Anderson* that each conspirator should intend to play some part in furtherance of the agreed course of conduct [at p39]. This contradicts the traditional view of conspiracy that it is necessary, and also sufficient, that each conspirator should intend that the agreed course of conduct be carried out whether by himself or other members of the conspiracy. If A and B agree that B shall murder C, A taking no part in the killing, the law has always taken the view that that is a conspiracy to murder. But, following this dictum, A would not be guilty of conspiracy and therefore B could not be guilty of conspiracy either since no other parties are involved. This seems to us to be contrary to public policy. Our clause does not therefore give effect to the dictum.' (Vol II, paras 13.24–13.25)

Note that under subs(2) recklessness will suffice as the fault element in conspiracy where the same is true of the completed offence. As the commentary illustrates:

'... if A and B agree to have sexual intercourse with C being aware that she may not consent they are guilty of conspiracy to rape. Because their awareness of the risk of her non-consent is sufficient fault in respect of that element of rape it is also sufficient for conspiracy to rape. The rule qualifies the general principle that intention is the characteristic fault requirement of the preliminary offences.' (Vol II, para 13.26)

The subsections that follow include provisions broadly similar to those relating to incitement: the extension of conspiracy to summary offences (subs(3)), and the exclusion from liability of those belonging to a class of persons intended to be protected by an enactment creating an offence (subs(4)). Subsection (7) provides that a person cannot conspire to assist in the commission of an offence, see *Hollinshead* [1985] AC 975; [1985] 2 All ER 769, but can assist in the commission of a conspiracy, see *Anderson* (above). As regards the relationship between conspiracy and the other forms of inchoate liability, subs(7)(b) expressly preserves the possibility of a charge of conspiring to incite. The commentary explains the reasons for this:

> 'We commented in our conspiracy Report that conspiracy to incite was a potentially useful offence [Law Com No 72 para 1.44] ... [W]e do not find it necessary to make any express provision concerning charges of conspiracy to conspire and conspiracy to attempt. We cannot envisage any circumstances in which it would be necessary to bring such charges in preference to charges of conspiracy to commit a substantive offence.' (Vol II, para 13.36)

The Law Commission has published a separate report dealing with the issue of conspiracy to defraud (Law Com 228) as part of a larger programme of review of offences of dishonesty. It has recommended the retention of the offence pending the completion of that review.

Attempt

Clause 49 of the Draft Code largely reflects the current law as stated in the Criminal Attempts Act 1981 by providing that:

> '(1) A person who, intending to commit an indictable offence, does an act that is more than merely preparatory to the commission of the offence is guilty of attempt to commit the offence.
> (2) For the purposes of subsection (1), an intention to commit an offence is an intention with respect to all the elements of the offence other than fault elements, except that recklessness with respect to a circumstance suffices where it suffices for the offence itself.
> (3) Act in this section includes an omission only where the offence intended is capable of being committed by an omission.
> (4) Where there is evidence to support a finding that an act was more than merely preparatory to the commission of the offence intended, the question whether that act was more than merely preparatory is a question of fact.'

The proposed offence of attempt would (with a number of minor exceptions) only relate to indictable offences. Liability would not extend to a person attempting to procure, assist or encourage as an accessory the commission of an offence by another, but a person could be charged as an accomplice to an attempt: see subs(6). A charge of attempting to attempt would clearly be otiose, but subs(6)(b) expressly preserves the possibility of a person being charged with attempting to incite, and attempting to conspire. Two further specific points should be noted, however.

The first is the Law Commission's acceptance that recklessness as to circumstances should be sufficient mens rea for attempt where this is sufficient for the completed crime: see *Khan* [1990] Crim LR 519; (1990) 91 Cr App R 29. As the Commission conceded in the commentary on cl 49:

> '[This] represents a change from the policy we formerly recommended of requiring for attempt an intention to bring about each of the constituent elements of the offence

attempted. That recommendation was at least partly based on the belief that the decision of the Court of Appeal in *Mohan* [1976] QB 1 to the effect that attempt is a crime of specific intent, applied equally in respect of consequences and circumstances specified in the definition of the offence attempted. However, in *Pigg* [1982] 1 WLR 762, a case on the common law decided after the Criminal Attempts Act 1981 had come into force, the Court of Appeal upheld a conviction for attempted rape on the basis that the accused was reckless whether the woman consented to intercourse ... In their Report the Code team ... sought to clarify the point by providing expressly that the intention required for an attempt was an intention in respect of all the elements of the offence attempted. An illustration was included of the application of the requirement to a case of attempted rape. On consultation the requirement and the illustration were strongly attacked by the Scrutiny Group on preliminary offences. The Group argued with force that the policy involved was undesirably narrow in relation to circumstantial elements of substantive offences, particularly in cases where intoxication was involved. They recommended that the Code should make clear that the principle of *Pigg* applied to the statutory offence of attempt ... In view of the decision in *Pigg* it is plain that some clarification is required. Section 1(1) of the Criminal Attempts Act 1981 leaves the matter in doubt. We ourselves have no doubt that the criticisms expressed by the Scrutiny Group reflect widely-held social judgments about the need to protect potential victims against certain types of drunken and violent offender. We find the Group's criticisms persuasive and take the view that we should depart from our previous recommendation to the extent provided for in the subsection. A minor complication of the proposed rule is that it erects a distinction between circumstances and other elements of the substantive offence attempted. This distinction may occasionally be difficult to apply. We are prepared to tolerate the difficulty because in the mainstream cases where the rule is likely to operate, namely, rape and obtaining property by deception, the rule appears to work well. The distinction between act (sexual intercourse) and circumstance (non-consent) or between result (obtaining) and circumstance (the falsity of the representation) is plain on the face of the definitions of the offences.' (Vol II, paras 13.44–45)

The second point is the possibility of attempt by omission. As has been noted above, subs(3) expressly states that 'act' in this section includes an omission only where the offence intended is capable of being committed by an omission, but the wording of clause 16 (which deals with the meaning to be given to the term 'act' within the Code) envisages offences such as murder and manslaughter being committed by omission. As far as these offences are concerned, a charge of attempting to commit such crimes based upon a failure to act could be sustained.

13

Accessorial and Vicarious Liability

13.1 Introduction

13.2 Modes of participation

13.3 Mens rea

13.4 'Joint enterprise'

13.5 Withdrawal from the common design

13.6 Problems with liability

13.7 Reform

13.8 Vicarious liability

13.1 Introduction

The commission of a criminal offence will often result from the planning and co-operation of a number of individuals. Provided the individual committing the offence has the requisite mens rea there should be no difficulty in establishing the elements of liability, but problems can arise as regards those who help in the commission of the offence. What sort of activities should be regarded as assistance? How much must the assistant know about the intended offence in order to be convicted as an accomplice? In theory the law does not distinguish between those who commit crimes themselves, and those who help in some way. The basis for this approach is s8 of the Accessories and Abettors Act 1861 (as amended by the Criminal Law Act 1977) which provides:

> 'Whosoever shall aid, abet, counsel, or procure the commission of any indictable offence whether the same be an offence at common law or by virtue of any Act passed or to be passed, shall be liable to be tried, indicted, and punished as a principal offender.'

Similar provision is made in respect of summary trial by the Magistrates' Courts Act 1980. Unless Parliament expressly indicates to the contrary, the common law doctrine of accessorial liability will apply to any statutory offences: see *R* v *Jefferson*; *R* v *Keogh* [1993] Crim LR 880.

Some confusion can arise because of the variety of terms used to describe different types of participation; many cases refer to 'accessories before the fact', 'accessories after the fact', and 'principals in the second degree', etc. For ease of reference, the following terms will be used: '*Principal*', the defendant who has actually committed the offence in question; '*Accomplice*', the defendant who has helped in some way. Accomplices are further subdivided into aiders, abettors, counsellors, and procurers, as detailed below. Reality is never as simple, however, as the theory would suggest and it should be noted that there may be cases where it is not possible to distinguish between principals and accomplices, for example, where there is evidence at a murder trial that the three defendants had each stabbed the victim, but it is not clear which of them actually dealt the fatal blow. In such cases, the defendants can, however, be charged as joint principals: see further *Abbott* v *R* [1977] AC 755.

Whilst the principles of accessorial liability are to be found in the common law, it will be noted that a large number of statutes also create specific offences of participation; for example, the Sexual Offences Act 1956 s28(1) states:

'It is an offence for a person to encourage ... the commission of unlawful sexual intercourse with ... a girl under the age of sixteen for whom he is responsible.'

The creation of such offences is largely for the avoidance of doubt, as at common law the activity prohibited by s28 would presumably come within the scope of abetting unlawful sexual intercourse.

13.2 Modes of participation

The broad distinction between counselling and procuring on the one hand, and aiding and abetting on the other, is that the former are thought to occur prior to the commission of the offence, whilst the latter, typically, will occur at the scene of the crime. Whilst this distinction will largely hold true, it should not be regarded as a rule. An accomplice may aid the commission of an offence by supplying the necessary equipment, notwithstanding that he is not at the scene of the crime: see the discussion of this issue in *Gillick* v *West Norfolk and Wisbech Area Health Authority* [1986] AC 112. It might seem logical to assume that each mode of participation requires proof that the accomplice caused the commission of the offence by the principal, and that there must be evidence of a plan or agreement between the parties. As indicated below, the law actually requires these issues to be addressed separately in relation to each mode of participation.

To counsel the commission of an offence involves an accomplice in advising, encouraging, persuading, instructing, pressurising, or even threatening the principal into committing the offence. In *R* v *Calhaem* [1985] 2 WLR 826, Parker LJ described this mode of participation in the following terms:

'There is no implication in the word itself that there should be any causal connection between the counselling and the offence ... [but] there must be a connection between the counselling and the [offence committed by the principal]. Equally, the act done must, we think, be done within the scope of the authority or advice ...'

It would suffice, therefore, that the principal offender knew of the advice, threats, encouragement or instructions of the accomplice, and that his actions were within those terms of reference. It would seem that counselling implicitly involves a degree of understanding between the parties, although to describe this as consensus may be inappropriate in those cases where the accomplice orders the principal to commit an offence under duress.

The leading authority as regards the meaning of procuring is *Attorney-General's Reference (No 1 of 1975)* (1975) 61 Cr App R 118. The accused had surreptitiously laced a friend's drinks with double measures of alcohol knowing the friend would shortly afterwards be driving home. The friend was convicted of drunken driving. The accused was charged as an accomplice to this offence, but was acquitted following a successful submission of no case. The trial judge took the view that there had to be evidence of some agreement between the accomplice and the principal for liability to be imposed. The Court of Appeal held that the submission of no case ought not to have been allowed to succeed. Lord Widgery CJ held that to procure meant to produce by endeavour, observing:

'You procure a thing by setting out to see that it happens and taking the appropriate steps to produce that happening.'

The accomplice's acts of procuration must be the cause in fact of the commission of the offence by the principal, ie in this case the amount of alcohol supplied by the accused must be shown to have taken the principal's blood/alcohol level over the legal limit for driving. The court went on to hold that, as regards procuring, there was no requirement to prove any agreement or consensus regarding the commission of the offence.

Aiding involves helping in the commission of an offence. For example if X is committing a burglary, and Y is standing in the grounds of the building keeping a eye out for police officers, Y would be described as aiding in the commission of the burglary by X. Similarly if a man, X, commits the offence of rape upon P, whilst Y, a woman holds P down, Y could be guilty of aiding the rape. Whilst the principal offender may not have committed the offence 'but for' the assistance given by the accomplice, it would perhaps be an over-generalisation to say that the aiding must cause the commission of the offence. There may be instances where the principal would have committed the offence anyway, the involvement of the accomplice simply making it easier, or less risky. In such cases much will depend upon the accomplice's state of mind, ie the extent to which he intended to facilitate the commission of the offence. Further, it should not be assumed that aiding necessarily requires proof of consensus between accomplice and principal. Whilst such cases will frequently involve some pre-planning, an accomplice could incur liability where, for example, he finds the principal about to assault P and, of his own accord, intervenes by holding P down.

Abetting implies encouragement and, as with counselling, it is sufficient that the principal should be aware of the encouragement; there is no need to prove that the principal would not have committed the crime but for being abetted by the accomplice. Equally there is no need to prove any consensus between the parties. Hence in *Wilcox* v *Jeffery* [1951] 1 All ER 464, the defendant, Wilcox, the proprietor of a publication entitled *Jazz Illustrated*, who had written reports of the musician Coleman Hawkins' arrival in the United Kingdom, attended a concert at which Hawkins delighted the crowd by getting up on stage and playing his instrument, a glowing account of which appeared in *Jazz Illustrated*. Hawkins had been forbidden, under the Aliens Order 1920, from taking any employment in the United Kingdom. The defendant was convicted of aiding and abetting Hawkins in the contravention of the Aliens Order 1920, and appealed unsuccessfully to the Divisional Court, where it was held that, as it had been an illegal act for Hawkins to play, and as the appellant had clearly known that this was illegal, his payment for a ticket and presence at the concert was an encouragement to commit this illegal act. In a memorable passage from his judgment Lord Goddard CJ stated:

> 'The appellant did not get up and protest in the name of the musicians of England that Mr Hawkins ought not to be here competing with them and taking the bread out of their mouths or the wind out of their instruments ... It might have been entirely different ... if he had gone there and protested, saying, "The musicians union do not like you foreigners coming here and playing and you ought to get off the stage." If he had booed it might have been some evidence that he was not aiding and abetting ...'

Similarly, where D has the right to control the actions of another, his failure to intervene can be construed as evidence of encouraging the criminal activities of that other person. As Kennedy LJ explained in *R* v *J F Alford Transport Ltd* [1997] 2 Cr App R 326, regarding the liability of the defendant company, its managing director and transport manager for aiding and abetting the company's drivers' falsification of their tachograph records, it would have to be shown that:

> '... the individual defendants, or either of them, knew that the drivers were illegally falsifying tachograph records, and if it could be shown that the individual defendants took no steps to prevent misconduct it was open to the jury in the absence of any alternative explanation, to infer that the individual defendant whom they happened to be considering, and thus the company, was positively encouraging what was going on ... [counsel for the appellant] submitted that in [previous cases, such as *Tuck* v *Robson* [1970] 1 WLR 741 and *Du Cros* v *Lambourne* [1907] 1 KB 40] it was critical that the aider and abettor was present at the time of the commission of the principal offence. In our judgment nothing turned on actual presence. What mattered was knowledge of the principal offence, the ability to control the action of the offender, and the deliberate decision to refrain from doing so ...'

A duty to prevent crime?

At common law a defendant can only incur criminal liability for failing to act if he is under a legal duty to act in a particular way. Similarly, in terms of accessorial liability, D may incur criminal liability for failing to prevent the commission of an offence by another if he is under a duty to prevent such activities. If A sees his wife, B, torturing their child, his failure to intervene could result in his being charged as an accomplice to her criminal acts. By contrast, if A becomes aware that B, a passenger in his car, is in possession of heroin, he does not, without more, become an accomplice to the possession offence as such.

In general, therefore, mere presence at the scene of a crime will not be sufficient to give rise to accessorial liability: see *R* v *Coney* (1882) 8 QBD 534. In *R* v *Clarkson* [1971] 1 WLR 1402 the defendants, two soldiers who had been present in a room whilst other soldiers raped a young woman, appealed successfully against their convictions for abetting rape. It was held that the jury should have been directed that there could only be a conviction if: the presence of the defendants at the scene of the crime actually encouraged its commission; and the accused had intended their presence to offer such encouragement.

What if D orders a shotgun from A's store and, in the interval between the ordering and delivery of the gun to D, A learns that D intends to use the gun to murder X? If A proceeds to sell the gun to D there seems little doubt that A could be convicted as an accomplice to the murder of P: see *National Coal Board* v *Gamble* [1959] QB 11. But what if D pays for the gun in advance, the contract of sale being completed, and A learns of the intended use of the gun shortly before D is due to take possession of what is, in law, now D's property? On the basis of *R* v *Lomas* (1913) 110 LT 239, it would appear that A could escape liability. In that case D had returned a crowbar to its rightful owner, knowing that it would be used by him to commit further burglaries. The court held that despite D's knowledge, his action could not be regarded as criminal, since if he had deliberately retained the crowbar he could have been liable for the tort of conversion, if not guilty of theft. The principle seems almost perverse. Suppose that X has lent his air rifle to Y, so that Y can scare cats from his garden, and one day, following a furious row with his wife, X rushes into Y's house demanding the return of the gun because he wants to use it to kill his wife. Can Y be absolved of all liability when he calmly hands the gun back to X who proceeds to kill his wife? Despite these arguments there is implied support for the *Lomas* approach in the obiter comments of Devlin J in *National Coal Board* v *Gamble*, and in the ruling in *R* v *Salford Health Authority, ex parte Janaway* [1988] 3 WLR 1350. In the latter case the applicant, a secretary at a doctor's surgery, had refused to type a letter referring a patient to a hospital for an abortion on the ground that, as a Roman Catholic, she did not want to aid the carrying out of an abortion. On her application for judicial review of her dismissal by the Area Health Authority the Court of Appeal held, inter alia, that as she was carrying out an obligation of her employment she could not be described as counselling or procuring an abortion.

13.3 Mens rea

Strict liability offences

A defendant cannot incur liability as an accomplice unless the prosecution can establish some degree of mens rea. This general proposition applies even where the offence committed by the principal is one of strict or absolute liability. It will obviously not be an excuse for the accomplice to state that he did not know that what the principal was doing was prohibited by the criminal law, but it will negate liability if the accomplice can show that he was unaware of the facts that constituted the offence. The relevant authority is *Johnson* v *Youden* [1950] 1 KB 544. The principal offender in this case was a builder who had been granted a licence to build a house by the local authority, subject to a condition limiting the maximum price at which it could be sold to £1,025. It was an offence of strict liability to sell a house in excess of any such condition. The builder induced another person to buy it from him for £1,275 and instructed the defendant solicitors to act for him in respect of the necessary conveyancing. The court held that of the three solicitors charged with aiding and abetting the builder, two had to be acquitted because they at no time knew what price the house was being sold at. The third would be convicted because he had been aware of the selling price and therefore did know of the facts which constituted the offence: see further *Callow* v *Tillstone* (1900) 83 LT 411. Similarly, in respect of drunken driving offences, it is necessary for the prosecution to prove that the accomplice either knew or was reckless as to whether the driver was unfit to drive through drink: see *Smith* v *Mellors* [1987] RTR 210.

Offences requiring proof of fault

If an accomplice can be shown to have had the mens rea required to justify conviction as a principal offender, for example intention to kill or to do grievous bodily harm in the case of murder, there should normally be little difficulty in imposing accessorial liability. Frequently, however, the degree of knowledge possessed by an accomplice regarding the nature of the offence to be committed by the principal offender falls someway short of certainty. It is fair to say that the common law has not fully resolved the question of what 'lesser' degree of fault will suffice. As a starting point it can be agreed that an accomplice must be shown to have intended to commit the relevant accessorial acts, but how precise must his knowledge be as to what the principal offender is going to do? As a matter of public policy it would be unacceptable to acquit an accomplice who supplies equipment in the belief that it will be used in the course of a robbery, when in fact it is used in the course of a burglary, but how are the limits of liability to be designated? A useful 'rule of thumb' for establishing the mens rea of accomplices who aid and abet the commission of offences is contained in the Court of Appeal's decision in *R* v *Bainbridge* [1959] 3 WLR 356, where D supplied cutting equipment which was subsequently used to break into the Midland Bank in Stoke Newington. He claimed that he had thought the equipment might be used for some illegal purpose, such as breaking up stolen property, but that he had not known that it was to be used to break into a bank. D appealed unsuccessfully against his conviction for being an accomplice to the break-in, the Court of Appeal endorsing the trial judge's direction to the jury, to the effect that the prosecution was not required to prove that D knew exactly what crime was going to be committed by the principal. As Lord Parker CJ stated:

> '... there must be not merely suspicion but knowledge that a crime of the type in question was intended, and that the equipment was bought with that in view.'

This approach can be summarised by stating that one who aids and abets must have contemplated the type of crime committed by the principal. If this is to be equated with a form of recklessness, it is clear from *Blakely, Sutton* v *DPP* [1991] Crim LR 763 that it is advertent (ie *Cunningham*) recklessness that has to be established, although it is perhaps best to avoid reference to recklessness altogether in this area: see *Chan Wing Siu* v *R* (below). D may be indifferent as to whether the principal offender commits the offence or not, either way it is sufficient that he knows that his acts (or omissions) will assist and encourage the commission of the offence by others: see again *National Coal Board* v *Gamble* (above). For example, on the facts of *R* v *J F Alford Transport Ltd* (above), whilst it had to be proved that the defendants had intended to do the acts which they knew to be capable of assisting or encouraging the drivers to falsify their tachograph records, liability did not turn upon the prosecution establishing that the defendants intended that the drivers should commit the offences. As Kennedy LJ explained :

> '... in the context of the present case ... if the management's reason for turning a blind eye was to keep the drivers happy rather than to encourage the production of false tachograph records that would afford no defence.'

Difficult to reconcile with this view, however, is the decision of the House of Lords in *Gillick* v *West Norfolk and Wisbech Area Health Authority* (above), where the majority (Lord Brandon dissenting) held that a doctor, prescribing contraceptives to a girl under the age of 16, would not be guilty of aiding the commission of the offence of unlawful sexual intercourse, provided he was exercising his clinical judgment in good faith, even if he knew that the girl wanted the prescription so that she could have under age sex without fear of pregnancy. The difficulty arises because the doctor would know of all the facts constituting the offence, and the fact that he acts from the best of motives should have no bearing on his liability, being a matter going to mitigation only. From the speeches of the majority one could assume that it must be the doctor's purpose that unlawful sexual intercourse takes place before he can incur liability.

In *R* v *Powell and Daniels*; *R* v *English* (considered below), Lord Hutton noted that the ruling in *Gillick* appeared anomalous, but was prepared to distinguish it on the grounds that the case involved a civil claim for a declaration, a situation remote from, for example, a case involving a common enterprise culminating in murder. Perhaps the decision is best distinguished on the grounds of the difficult and unusual issues of public policy to which it gave rise.

As regards one who counsels or procures the commission of an offence, the Court of Appeal in *Attorney-General's Reference (No 1 of 1975)* (above), appears to support a narrower approach, Lord Widgery commenting that to procure meant setting out to see that the desired consequence happens and taking the appropriate steps to produce that happening. His words are suggestive of more than mere contemplation of a consequence on the part of the procurer, perhaps requiring proof of something closer to intention, a view that receives support from the Divisional Court's ruling in *Blakely, Sutton* v *DPP* (above).

What if the accomplice gives the principal a blank cheque?

If, as stated above, the prosecution generally has to prove that the accomplice contemplated the type of crime the principal actually commits, can an accomplice escape liability by claiming that there were so many different crimes the principal might have committed that he was unable to have any clear idea as to what his liability might have been? On the basis of *DPP for Northern Ireland* v *Maxwell* (1978) 68 Cr App R 128 it would appear that such an accomplice will be a party to all the offences committed by the principal provided that they are amongst those contemplated by him. As Lord Scarman stated:

'An accessory who leaves it to his principal to choose is liable, provided always the choice is made from the range of offences from which the accessory contemplates the choice will be made.'

13.4 'Joint enterprise'

In many cases involving accessorial liability the courts refer to a defendant being a party to a 'joint enterprise'. Although this is not a term of art, it does seem to refer to those situations where the principal and accomplice are acting in pursuance of some pre-determined plan. In *R* v *Stewart and Scholfield* [1995] 1 Cr App R 441 Hobhouse LJ observed that:

'The allegation that a defendant took part in the execution of a crime as a joint enterprise is not the same as an allegation that he aided, abetted, counselled or procured the commission of that crime. A person who is a mere aider or abettor, etc, is truly a secondary party to the commission of whatever crime it is that the principal has committed although he may be charged as a principal. If the principal has committed the crime of murder, the liability of the secondary party can only be a liability for aiding and abetting murder. In contrast where the allegation is joint enterprise, the allegation is that one defendant participated in the criminal act of another. This is a different principle. It renders each of the parties to a joint enterprise criminally liable for the acts done in the course of carrying out the joint enterprise. Where the criminal liability of any given defendant depends upon the further proof that he had a certain state of mind, that state of mind must be proved against that defendant. Even though several defendants may, as a result of having engaged in a joint enterprise, be each criminally responsible for the criminal act of one of those defendants done in the course of carrying out the joint enterprise, their individual criminal responsibility will, in such a case, depend upon what individual state of mind or intention has been proved against them. Thus, each may be a party to the unlawful act which caused the victim's death. But one may have had the intent either to kill him or to cause him serious harm and be guilty of murder, whereas another may not have had that intent and may be guilty only of manslaughter.'

As will be seen below, the alleged existence of a joint enterprise will sometimes lead the courts to invoke particular principles, especially as regards the mental element in participation. Notwithstanding the fact that much of what follows cannot be easily understood without some explanation of the joint enterprise doctrine, it is nevertheless submitted that it is often difficult to see any concept of joint enterprise that is distinct from the general principles of accessorial liability. As can be imagined the vast majority of offences involving principles and accomplices do involve a degree of planning and agreement beforehand, even if it is tacit and occurs only seconds before the commission of the offence. All in that sense, involve what is sometimes called a joint enterprise or 'common design'. It is the cases that do not that are the exception, such as where A is engaged in lone criminal activity and B, unknown to A and without A seeking or perhaps wanting B to become involved, offers assistance to A.

Whether or not a joint enterprise exists will largely be a matter of fact for a jury to determine following an appropriate direction. Thus in *R* v *Petters and Parfitt* [1995] Crim LR 501, the Court of Appeal held that where there was uncertainty concerning the existence of a joint enterprise, a trial judge should direct the jury to consider whether the parties shared a common purpose and had, by their conduct, intimated to each other that they were acting in concert.

The point at which a joint enterprise materialises will obviously vary enormously depending on the facts of any given case. Even though a joint enterprise can emerge spontaneously, at the scene of the crime, there must be some communication between the parties, or at least an awareness and acceptance of each other's role, in the sense that they are authorising and encouraging each other to act.

An examination of the way in which accessorial liability would be dealt with by the courts in cases of joint enterprise is perhaps best illustrated by considering a number of examples.

Death or grievous bodily harm foreseen by the accomplice

Suppose that A (accomplice) and P (principal) agree to carry out a robbery on V (the intended victim). P is armed with a loaded gun and A knows that P might use it on V if necessary to achieve their objective. During the robbery V offers resistance resulting in P deliberately shooting V dead. If A, when formulating the plan with P, contemplated that V might suffer death or grievous bodily harm, he can be convicted of murder, on the basis of the principles developed by the Privy Council in *Chan Wing Siu* v *R* [1984] 3 All ER 877, *Hui Chi-Ming* v *R* [1991] 3 WLR 495, and the House of Lords in *R* v *Powell and Daniels*; *R* v *English* [1997] 3 WLR 959. In *R* v *Powell and Daniels*, the appellants, along with a third man who had not been apprehended, visited an address in South London in order to buy drugs. The prosecution evidence was that when the deceased opened the door to the group he was shot dead at point blank range by one of them. Following *R* v *Hyde* [1991] 1 QB 134 and *Chan Wing Siu* v *R*, the trial judge had directed the jury that they could convict the appellants as accessories to murder if they were satisfied that they had foreseen the possibility of death or grievous bodily harm as a possible incident of the common design being carried out. The appellants were convicted and appealed unsuccessfully to the Court of Appeal. The following question was certified for consideration by the House of Lords:

> 'Is it sufficient to found a conviction for murder for a secondary party to a killing to have realised that the primary party might kill with intent to do so or must the secondary party have held such intention himself?'

Answering the question in the affirmative, the House of Lords held that, in cases of joint enterprise where the victim of an unlawful attack is killed, an accomplice can incur liability for murder where he realises that, in the course of pursuing the joint enterprise, the principal offender might kill or cause grievous bodily harm with intent to produce either of those consequences.

In the course of his speech Lord Steyn rejected criticism that this approach involved the imposition of constructive liability on accomplices. As he argued:

> 'The accessory principle requires proof of a subjective state of mind on the party of a participant in a criminal enterprise, viz foresight that the primary offender might commit a different and more serious offence. ...The foresight of the secondary party must be directed to a real possibility of the commission by the primary offender in the course of the criminal enterprise of the greater offence. The liability is imposed because the secondary party is assisting in and encouraging a criminal enterprise which he is aware might result in the commission of a greater offence. The liability of an accessory is predicated on his culpability in respect of the greater offence as defined in law. It is undoubtedly a lesser form of mens rea. But it is unrealistic to say that the accessory principle as such imposes constructive criminal liability.'

Regarding the criticism that the disparity between the fault element required on the part of the principal when compared to the accomplice was anomalous, he went on to observe:

> 'The answer to this supposed anomaly, and other similar cases across the spectrum of criminal law, is to be found in practical and policy considerations. If the law required proof of the specific intention on the part of a secondary party, the utility of the accessory principle would be gravely undermined ... a secondary party who foresees that the primary offender might kill with the intent sufficient for murder, and assists and encourages the primary offender in the criminal enterprise ... ought to be criminally liable

for harm which he foresaw and which in fact resulted from the crime he assisted and encouraged. But it would in practice almost invariably be impossible for a jury to say that the secondary party wanted death to be caused or that he regarded it as virtually certain. In the real world proof of an intention sufficient for murder would be well nigh impossible in the vast majority of joint enterprise cases. Moreover, the proposed change in the law must be put in context. The criminal justice system exists to control crime. A prime function of that system must be to deal justly but effectively with those who join with others in criminal enterprises. Experience has shown that joint criminal enterprises only too readily escalate into the commission of greater offences. In order to deal with this important social problem the accessory principle is needed and cannot be abolished or relaxed.'

Lord Hutton was more prepared to recognise the anomalous nature of the distinction, but he too was persuaded by the overriding policy considerations in favour of maintaining the current rules. He observed that:

'... as a matter of logic there is force in the argument ... that ... it is anomalous that if foreseeability of death or really serious harm is not sufficient to constitute mens rea for murder in the party who actually carries out the killing, it is sufficient to constitute mens rea in a secondary party. But the rules of the common law are not based solely on logic but relate to practical concerns and, in relation to crimes committed in the course of joint enterprises, to the need to give effective protection to the public against criminals operating in gangs. ... In my opinion there are practical considerations of weight and importance related to considerations of public policy which justify the principle stated in *Chan Wing-Siu* and which prevail over considerations of strict logic ... unlike the principal party who carries out the killing with a deadly weapon, the secondary party will not be placed in the situation in which he suddenly has to decide whether to shoot or stab the third person with intent to kill or cause really serious harm. There is, in my opinion, an argument of considerable force that the secondary party who takes part in a criminal enterprise (for example, the robbery of a bank) with foresight that a deadly weapon may be used, should not escape liability for murder because he, unlike the principal party, is not suddenly confronted by the security officer so that he has to decide whether to use the gun or knife or have the enterprise thwarted and face arrest ...'

As Lord Hutton also noted, given the reaffirmation of *Chan Wing Siu*, the decision of the Court of Appeal in *R* v *Smith* [1988] Crim LR 616, to the effect that a party to a joint enterprise that culminated in grievous bodily harm being caused to the victim could not be convicted as such, unless he intended the commission of grievous bodily harm, was erroneous and should not be followed. *R* v *Powell and Daniels* has since been applied in cases such as *R* v *Reardon* (1998) (CA No 96011499/Z4). In that case the principal offender shot two men in a bar and dragged them outside. He then returned to the bar and asked the appellant for his knife because one of the victims was still alive. In fact both victims were still alive and the principal offender used the knife supplied by the appellant to stab both to death. In concluding that the appellant was a party to both murders the Court noted that, whichever victim the principal killed first, the appellant had contemplated death or grievous bodily harm being committed. The Court rejected the contention that the killing of a second victim was outside the scope of the actions contemplated by the appellant on the basis that if he was willing to let the principal 'finish off' one victim with the knife, it was open to the jury to infer that he had contemplated the principal doing the same to the second victim if he was still alive. Using the knife as contemplated twice, rather than once, did not go beyond the scope of the common design (although see *R* v *Saunders and Archer* (1573) 2 Plowd 473).

What of the secondary party who contemplates death or grievous bodily harm only to reject it as a possible outcome of the joint enterprise? On the basis of Sir Robin Cooke's comments in *Chan Wing Siu* v *R*, he should escape liability for murder:

> 'What has to be brought home to the jury is that occasionally a risk may have occurred to an accused's mind, fleetingly or even causing him some deliberation, but may genuinely have been dismissed by him as altogether negligible. If they think there is a reasonable possibility that the case is in that class, taking the risk should not make that accused a party to such a crime of intention as murder or wounding with intent to cause grievous bodily harm.'

See further *R* v *Roberts* (1993) 96 Cr App R 291, where Lord Taylor CJ also expressed the view that the secondary party, who fleetingly thinks of the risk of the principal using violence with murderous intent in the course of a joint enterprise only to dismiss it from his mind, cannot be described as having the necessary foresight or realisation at the time he lends himself to the venture because he has banished the risk from his mind: see further *R* v *Rook* [1993] 1 WLR 1005. Lord Hutton in *R* v *Powell and Daniels*; *R* v *English* concluded that (subject to his observations in relation to the second certified question in the case of the appellant English) only in those cases where the jury concluded that the secondary party genuinely dismissed the risk of death or grievous bodily harm as 'altogether negligible' should he escape liability for murder.

What of the secondary party who, whilst foreseeing that the principal offender might kill or cause grievous bodily harm with intent, hopes that he will not and is a 'reluctant' participant?

In *R* v *Powell and Daniels*; *R* v *English* (above), Lord Hutton, having reviewed the authorities – in particular *R* v *Smith (Wesley)* [1963] 1 WLR 1200 and *R* v *Anderson*; *R* v *Morris* [1966] 2 QB 110 – noted that in *Anderson* the court addressed the accomplice's mens rea in terms of what he had tacitly agreed to, whilst in *Smith* the emphasis had been placed on what the accomplice had contemplated, a term more suggestive of foresight of consequences. The distinction may be important in cases where a party to a joint enterprise foresees that the principal offender may commit a particular offence, but has not actually agreed that he should, indeed he may be a reluctant participant in that respect. In such cases Lord Hutton's expressed preference is that judges should direct juries by reference to the foresight of the accomplice:

> '... in many cases there would be no difference in result between applying the [tacit agreement] test ... and the test of foresight, and if there would be a difference the test of

foresight is the proper one to apply. I consider that the test of foresight is a simpler and more practicable test for a jury to apply than the test of whether the act causing the death goes beyond what had been tacitly agreed as part of the joint enterprise. Therefore, in cases where an issue arises as to whether an action was within the scope of the joint venture, I would suggest that it might be preferable for a trial judge in charging a jury to base his direction on the test of foresight …'

Liability where, unknown to the accomplice, the principal offender is armed, or the principal takes a more dangerous weapon than that contemplated by the accomplice

Let us vary the above robbery scenario by supposing that A and P agree to rob V, that A contemplates that P may cause grievous bodily harm if necessary, but that P will not use any sort of weapon during the attack. Unknown to A, P arms himself with a machete which he uses to kill V during the robbery.

If A did not know that P had the machete, or indeed did not agree to its use beforehand, he should escape all liability in relation to the death of V. P's action in using the weapon will have constituted a deliberate departure from the agreement between A and P, and as such P will have been acting independently of A. The leading authority in support of this conclusion is now the House of Lords' decision in *R* v *Powell and Daniels*; *R* v *English* (above). In *R* v *English* police officers were called to a house, occupied by a man named Weddle, in connection with an alleged assault by him on his girlfriend. The appellant English, and Weddle, had been drinking and had consumed temazepam tablets. They became involved in a fight with the police officers during which the appellant attacked Sgt Forth, one of the officers, with a fencing stave, and was then chased from the premises and arrested 100 yards away by PC Hay. Whilst the appellant was being handcuffed by PC Hay, Weddle pulled a knife on Sgt Forth and stabbed him to death. Weddle was convicted of murder and the appellant was convicted of murder as an accomplice. The additional question certified for consideration by the House of Lords in respect of this appeal was:

'Is it sufficient for murder that the secondary party intends or foresees that the primary party would or may act with intent to cause grievous bodily harm, if the lethal act carried out by the primary party is fundamentally different from the acts foreseen or intended by the secondary party?'

The House of Lords allowed the appeal on the basis that the trial judge had erred in not qualifying his direction to the jury on the foresight that had to be established, on the part of an accomplice in a joint enterprise, by stressing that an accomplice who did not foresee the use of a deadly weapon, in this case a knife, by the principal offender should not be convicted of murder.

The effect of the decision is that, in our given scenario, A should escape liability for both murder and manslaughter where death results from an act of a type not contemplated by P, in this case the use of a machete. The doctrine applies regardless of the fact that A may have contemplated death or grievous bodily harm. The crucial factor is that he has not foreseen the way in which the death would be caused: see further *Davies* v *DPP* [1954] AC 378.

Presumably the doctrine would extend to instances where A and P agree to use an unloaded gun to frighten V, but P deliberately departs from the plan by taking a loaded gun which he then uses to kill, although in such cases it may be the case that it would be impossible to establish that A had foreseen death or grievous bodily harm in any event: see *R* v *Perman* (below).

Again, on the basis of *R* v *Powell and Daniels*; *R* v *English*, if A, in the robbery scenario, had contemplated P using a baseball bat to beat V so severely that he would suffer grievous bodily harm, and during the robbery P had fired a gun shooting V dead, A should escape liability for both murder and manslaughter because death results from a type of act not contemplated by P.

One qualification that it might be wise to make here relates to the situation where P suddenly produces a deadly weapon during the course of an attack on V, the use of which has not been contemplated by A, where A continues to participate in the attack. It seems sensible that in such cases A becomes a party to the use of the deadly weapon, on the basis that he has consciously decided to carry on in the knowledge that it is being used: see *R* v *Uddin* [1998] 2 All ER 744 in Chapter 16, section 16.5.

Where the accomplice contemplates the use of a 'deadly weapon' but the principal uses a different type of 'deadly weapon', or uses it in a manner not contemplated by the accomplice?

In this variant A contemplates P using a knife to stab V during the robbery, but P uses a gun to kill V, A being unaware that P had thus armed himself. Conversely the scenario could be that A agrees that P should shoot V with a gun, but P decides to arm himself with a knife, which he uses to stab V to death.

In *R* v *Bamborough* [1996] Crim LR 744 the appellant, B, and T, the principal offender, entered P's dwelling intent on committing a robbery therein. T had a gun that was loaded. B knew that T had a gun but claimed that he believed it to be unloaded. P suffered serious head injuries during the robbery consistent with his having been 'pistol-whipped', and was also shot in the thigh by T. P bled to death from the gunshot wound shortly thereafter. B and T were convicted of the murder of P. B appealed on the ground that, although he had contemplated T causing grievous bodily harm to P (by striking him about the head with an unloaded pistol), he had not contemplated P being shot (ie he had not contemplated grievous bodily harm that might be life threatening). On this basis B contended that he should have been convicted of manslaughter. Dismissing the appeal, the Court of Appeal confirmed that it was sufficient, in order to substantiate B's conviction for murder as an accomplice, that he had contemplated grievous bodily harm as a possible incident of the common design, ie the Court was not overly concerned at how the accomplice might have foreseen the grievous bodily harm being caused.

Whilst the decision may be understandable on its facts – the Court of Appeal doubted B's claim that he did not know that the gun was loaded – it may be more questionable on the level of principle. On the one hand it could be argued that if A agrees to assist in an attack on V where P, the principal offender, is going to smash V's hand with a sledge hammer (undoubtedly grievous bodily harm), and P actually proceeds to shoot V in the leg, causing a fatal wound, A should not be regarded as a party to murder or manslaughter. P has used a different weapon to cause harm that is obviously much more life threatening. On the other hand, the rationale for the enlarged scope of the mens rea for murder (ie that intention to kill or cause grievous bodily harm should be sufficient) rests (in part) on the notion that any defendant willing to cause grievous bodily harm must be regarded as being willing to take the risk that those injuries might cause the death of the victim (possibly because of some physical peculiarity on the part of the victim).

The House of Lords' decision in *R v Powell and Daniels*; *R v English* (above) lends support to the view that the use of a different weapon, or the use of a contemplated weapon in an uncontemplated manner, can relieve the accomplice of liability for the death caused by the principal offender. In seeking to support his conclusion that Weddle, in using a knife to kill Sgt Forth, had acted in a manner and committed an offence not contemplated by the appellant English, Lord Hutton cited, with approval, the ruling of Carswell J in *R v Gamble* [1989] NI 268 (a decision of the Crown Court sitting without a jury). The appellant in that case had agreed to assist in the 'kneecapping' of a victim, a plan that would have involved the victim being shot through the back of the knee joint. During the attack the principal offender killed the victim by slitting his throat with a knife. Carswell J ruled that the principal offender had gone beyond the scope of the joint enterprise and that the appellant was therefore not a party to the killing. Crucial to this decision was the acceptance that it would be wrong to fix an accessory with liability for consequences that stemmed from an action on the part of the principal offender that he neither intended nor contemplated.

Again, this conclusion rests on the doctrine that accessorial liability only extends to those acts of the principal that are within the contemplation of the accomplice. Lord Hutton concludes on this point by observing that:

'... having regard to the differing circumstances in which the issue [raised by the second certified question in the appeal of *English*] may arise I think it undesirable to seek to formulate a more precise answer to the question in case such an answer might appear to prescribe too rigid a formula for use by trial judges. However I would wish to make this observation: if the weapon used by the primary party is different to, but as dangerous as, the weapon which the secondary party contemplated he might use, the secondary party should not escape liability for murder because of the difference in the weapon, for example, if he foresaw that the primary party might use a gun to kill and the latter used a knife to kill, or vice versa.'

Whether the weapon used by the principal is 'different enough' to that contemplated by the accomplice to justify a conclusion that the principal has exceeded the common design will be a matter of fact and degree in each case. In *R* v *Uddin* (above) Beldam LJ regarded the propensity of the weapon to cause death as a significant factor. On this basis a jury might, for example, decide that the use of a knife by a principal was sufficiently different from the agreed acts of hitting the victim with clubs and kicking him with shod feet to justify the conclusion that the principal had exceed the scope of the common design. See also *R* v *Greatrex* (1998) The Times 2 April, where the Court of Appeal appeared willing to accept that striking a victim with an iron bar and kicking him with a shod foot would not necessarily be 'fundamentally different' acts.

In the light of this, the position would appear to be, therefore, that a secondary party charged with murder can escape liability where he:

1. does not contemplate the use of a weapon, and the principal offender kills by using a weapon;
2. contemplates that the principle offender will use a gun to wound the victim, but the principal offender kills the victim by slitting his throat with a knife (or even perhaps by strangling the victim with his bare hands);
3. contemplates that the principal offender will use a gun to wound the victim (eg kneecapping) and the principal offender deliberately shoots the victim through the head killing him.

By contrast, a secondary party charged with murder will not escape liability where he contemplates:

1. that the principal offender will kill the victim by using a gun, when in fact the principal offender kills using a knife;
2. that the principal offender will kill the victim by using a knife and he in fact does so by using a gun.

Where the principal chooses a victim other than that agreed with the accomplice

Suppose that A agrees to act as a lookout whilst P shoots V dead. P approaches V who is walking down the street with W, his wife. P decides to kill W instead of V. Clearly P has deliberately chosen a different victim, albeit he has committed the agreed crime, ie murder. Surprisingly, perhaps, on the basis of *R* v *Saunders and Archer* (1573) 2 Plowd 473, no accessorial liability should attach to A, as P has deliberately selected a different victim. Such a result may seem odd given that, under the doctrine of transferred malice, a defendant can be held guilty of murdering X, even though when he fired his gun, he was aiming at, and intending to kill, Y: see *R* v *Pembliton*; *R* v *Latimer* etc considered at Chapter 3, section 3.8. In *Saunders and Archer* John Saunders wanted to kill his wife so that he could marry his mistress. Alexander Archer provided him with poison in the form of a roasted apple containing arsenic and roseacre. Saunders gave the apple to his wife, but she ate very little of it, handing it instead to their daughter, Eleanor, who subsequently died. Saunders was found guilty of the murder of his daughter on the basis of transferred malice. Archer was held not to be a party to the murder because Saunders had wilfully exceeded the common design in allowing the child to eat the apple. In effect the court held that Saunders' inactivity in standing by and allowing the child to consume the poisoned apple amounted to a deliberate departure from the common design, which had been to kill his wife, but it is clear that the court refused to apply the doctrine of transferred malice to Archer. A rationale for the decision can be found if one accepts that the doctrine of transferred malice is invoked where D accidentally kills the wrong victim, or damages the wrong property. In *Saunders and Archer* the death of the child results from a conscious decision of the principal offender that a victim other than that originally chosen should die. If Saunders been absent from the room when the apple was given to the child it is submitted that Archer would have been an accomplice to the death, as it would have been an accidental consequence of the common design being carried out.

Despite its antiquity, the decision in *Saunders and Archer* has received implicit support from *R v Leahy* [1985] Crim LR 99. In that case a person named Horsman had been in a fight with a man called Pearson and had received some injuries. Horsman told the defendant, Leahy, of this, and the defendant advised Horsman to 'glass him', meaning Pearson. Horsman then picked up a glass and pushed it into the neck of a man named Gallagher. Horsman was convicted of grievous bodily harm, contrary to s18 Offences Against the Person Act 1861, in respect of this attack, but Leahy, who had been charged with counselling it, succeeded on a submission of no case, the court accepting the argument that the actions of Horsman were a deliberate departure from the common design as contemplated by the defendant, ie an attack on Pearson.

It is submitted that the approach taken by the courts in the above two cases will only be appropriate where the common design is very narrow in its scope, ie the accomplice contemplates a specific named victim being attacked, or specific identified property being stolen or destroyed. Hence, where A supplies P with a gun and instructs him to prove his skill as an assassin by killing someone, the scope of the common design is very wide, and in theory A could be an accomplice to the killing of any victim chosen by P. Even here, however, there is an argument that A might not be guilty if P chooses A's only child as the victim. A would presumably contend that he had not contemplated P demonstrating his skills on a member of his own family. Note that in *R v Reardon* (considered above) the appellant was convicted as an accomplice to two murders notwithstanding that he had lent his knife to the principal in order to 'finish off' one of his two victims. On the facts the court was satisfied that the appellant had contemplated that the knife might be used on either, or both, of the men that the principal offender had shortly before shot and dumped outside the bar. If the principal offender had taken the knife and chosen to stab a passer-by outside the bar instead, the appellant could have relied on the ruling in *Saunders and Archer* to the effect that he only contemplated deliberate harm being caused to the two victims lying outside dying from gunshot wounds.

If the principal offender kills and is convicted of murder, when can an accomplice be guilty of manslaughter?

The above analysis suggests something of an 'all or nothing' approach to liability. Either the accomplice comes within the *Chan Wing Siu* principle and is guilty of murder, or he escapes liability for the death altogether on the basis that the principal was acting independently. The reality is that there are circumstances where the accomplice can be convicted of manslaughter.

Again, taking the robbery scenario, suppose that A and P agree to carry out a robbery on V, the plan being that P should threaten V with a baseball bat. If V offers resistance, P is to hit V with the bat. A is to act as a lookout throughout the operation. Now suppose that when P threatens V, V dies of shock because of a previously undiagnosed heart defect. P will be guilty of manslaughter as a principal offender; A as an accomplice. The general rule is that an accomplice will be liable for all the accidental, or unforeseen consequences that flow from the joint enterprise being carried out. The plan was to rob V using the baseball bat, which is precisely what A did. There were no actions by P that involved a deliberate departure from the common design on his part. A number of authorities support this conclusion. For example, *R v Baldessare* (1930) 22 Cr App R 70, in which the two defendants took a car to go joyriding. The driver killed another road user and was convicted of manslaughter. Baldessare was convicted as an accomplice to the manslaughter, as the death was an unforeseen consequence of the common design (driving the car in a reckless manner without headlights) being carried out. See also *R v Betts and Ridley* (1930) 22 Cr App R 148.

Using the same example as above, consider the case where the robbery is carried out as planned but V offers resistance. Suppose that P strikes V on the head intending to scare him into submission, but due to V having a thin skull V suffers head injuries that prove fatal. P would obviously still be guilty of manslaughter as a principal; A as an accomplice. Again, there would have been no deliberate departure from the common design.

The same reasoning could apply where the parties agree to rob using loaded weapons, but agree not to fire them. What if a weapon is discharged by accident, killing the victim? On the basis of *R v Reid* (1976) 62 Cr App R 109 the secondary party will be guilty of manslaughter. In a sense the death of the victim is, again, an accidental consequence of an activity that was within the scope of the joint enterprise. As Lawton LJ observed (at p112):

> 'When two or more men go out together in joint possession of offensive weapons such as revolvers and knives and the circumstances are such as to justify an inference that the very least they intend to do with them is to cause fear in another, there is, in our judgment, always a likelihood that, in the excitement and tensions of the occasion, one of

them will use his weapon in some way which will cause death or serious injury. If such injury was not intended by the others [ie the accomplices], they must be acquitted of murder; but having started out on an enterprise which envisaged some degree of violence, albeit nothing more than causing fright, they [the accomplices] will be guilty of manslaughter.'

Where A contemplates the acts of P that cause death, but not the mens rea with which P acts

Such situations will, perhaps, be rare, but an example might arise where A and P agree that P is to place some drugs in V's food, with the object of making V violently sick. Suppose that P knows that V has a fatal allergy to the drug, but this fact is not known to A. V dies as a result of the drug being administered by P. In such a case P will be guilty of murder. A will not be a party to murder on the basis that he does not foresee death or grievous bodily harm, but can it be right that he should escape liability for the death altogether? P has performed precisely those acts agreed to and contemplated by A. All that distinguishes the two is their mens rea. There is some force in the argument that A should be guilty of manslaughter because the death results from an unlawful criminal act by P (the poisoning) that was foreseen by A. Alternatively, it could be said that by acting with intent to kill, P is deliberately departing from the common design. The matter was considered by the Court of Appeal in *R* v *Stewart and Scholfield* [1995] 1 Cr App R 441. The appellants were charged with the murder of Dada, a shopkeeper. Stewart had suggested that they should rob Dada in his shop and armed herself with a knife for this purpose. Lambert, another member of the group, armed himself with a piece of scaffolding, and Scholfield kept watch outside the premises. Once at the scene, Lambert beat Dada to death with the pole and subsequently pleaded guilty to murder and robbery. Stewart and Scholfield were convicted of manslaughter. On appeal they contended that, with reference (inter alia) to *R* v *Anderson and Morris* (above), they could not be convicted of manslaughter where the principal offender, in committing murder, deliberately exceeded the bounds of the joint enterprise (ie the robbery). Their evidence was that in carrying out the murderous attack, Lambert had been motivated by racial hatred and not his desire to effect the robbery. The Court held that a party to a joint enterprise who was charged with murder, could only escape liability for manslaughter (in cases where the principal offender was convicted of the murder), if the killing was not actually committed in the course of the joint enterprise – a question of fact not law. The Court of Appeal seems to be saying that if the common design is to rob, and to be armed in order to do so, the accomplice can be guilty of manslaughter if the principal deliberately kills in the course of carrying out the actus reus of the joint enterprise (eg assaulting the victim), since all that distinguishes the accomplice from the principal is the degree of fault.

Note that the Court acknowledged the conflict of authority on this point and certified the following point of law of general public importance:

'Where participant "A" in a criminal joint enterprise contemplates that the carrying out of the joint enterprise may involve the victim suffering some bodily injury, but not a serious injury, and "B", another participant in that joint enterprise, forms, independently of the others, an intention to kill or do serious bodily harm to the victim and, with that intention, "B" does an act which causes the death of the victim: Are the jury precluded, as a matter of law, from finding as a fact that that act was done in the course of carrying out the joint enterprise and convicting "A" of manslaughter?'

It is submitted that the certified question should be answered in the affirmative.

Where the accomplice contemplates some harm, short of grievous bodily harm, occurring to the victim, and the principal offender deliberately kills the victim

Suppose that A agrees with P to rob V, the agreement being to use an unloaded gun to threaten V. P, unknown to A, arms himself with a loaded gun that he uses to shot V dead during the robbery. In this category of case the accomplice should not incur liability for manslaughter, albeit that he foresaw some harm being caused to the victim. The death is caused by a deliberate departure from the common design. As Roch LJ observed in *R v Perman* [1996] 1 Cr App R 24 (at pp35–36):

'... if the appellant did not know that the gun was loaded, and believed that it was unloaded, the scope of the joint enterprise in which he joined was the robbery of those in the shop by the putting of such persons as were in the shop in fear by the use of an unloaded and therefore innocuous gun ... [A] joint enterprise to cause fright or hysteria through threats being made with an unloaded and innocuous gun was not sufficient to found a conviction of manslaughter in the circumstances of this case.'

In *Davies* v *DPP* (above) a gang fight took place on Clapham Common, during which the principal offender killed an opponent with a knife. The defendant was acquitted of being an accomplice to either murder or manslaughter because the use of a knife during the attack was beyond the scope of what had been contemplated by him. The decision on the part of the principal offender to take a knife involved a deliberate departure from the common design. Had the victim died from blows to the head from the principal's fist or boot, then Davies could have been guilty as an accomplice to manslaughter, because such a mode of attack was contemplated by him, and the death of the victim would have been an unforeseen consequence of its being carried out. Similarly, in *R v Anderson and Morris* (above), where the defendants had agreed to 'rough up' a victim named Welch, Anderson, unknown to Morris, took a knife with him, which he used to deliberately stab Welch to death during the fight. Anderson was convicted of murder, but Morris' conviction for manslaughter was quashed on the ground that the cause of the victim's death was an action by Anderson that involved a deliberate departure by him from the common design, ie the use of the knife. Again, if Welch had died from a punch thrown by Anderson, Morris would have been an accomplice to manslaughter.

13.5 Withdrawal from the common design

If D1 supplies D2 with a gun with which he is to kill X on Christmas Day, and on Christmas Eve D1 tells D2 not to carry out the killing, but D2 still does so, can D1 be indicted as an accomplice to the murder of X? The question posed raises the problem of withdrawal from the common design by the accomplice. At what stage must withdrawal take place in order to be effective, and what actions are required on the part of the accomplice?

In *R* v *Becerra and Cooper* (1975) 62 Cr App R 212, the defendants agreed to burgle a house, and Becerra gave Cooper a knife to use in case there was any trouble. When they were disturbed by the householder, Becerra jumped out of a window and ran off, shouting 'Let's go'. Cooper remained behind and murdered the householder. Becerra was convicted as an accomplice to the murder despite his contention that he had withdrawn from the enterprise. In dismissing his appeal the Court of Appeal held that the withdrawal must effectively let the others know that they are now on their own. What is required will vary with the facts of each case. If the defendant had taken reasonable steps to prevent the commission of further offences by the principal that might have been enough for his actions to have constituted a withdrawal. As Roskill LJ stated:

'... there must be timely communication of the intention to abandon the common purpose from those who wish to dissociate themselves from the contemplated crime to those who desire to continue in it.'

or as Dunn LJ expressed the matter in *R* v *Whitefield* (1983) 79 Cr App R 36:

'If a person has counselled another to commit a crime, he may escape liability by withdrawal before the crime is committed, but it is not sufficient that he should merely repent or change his mind. If his participation is confined to advice or encouragement, he must at least communicate his change of mind to the other, and the communication must be such as will serve "unequivocal notice upon the other party to the common unlawful cause that if he proceeds upon it he does so without the aid and assistance of those who withdraw".'

The emphasis on communication of withdrawal to the other parties was re-affirmed by the Court of Appeal in *R* v *Rook* [1993] 1 WLR 1005, where, citing McDermott J in *Eldredge* v *United States* (1932) 62 F 2d 449, 451, Lloyd LJ agreed with the view that

'A declared intent to withdraw from a conspiracy to dynamite a building is not enough, if the fuse has been set; D must step on the fuse',

save only that his Lordship thought that it would be enough that the defendant should have done his best to step on the fuse.

Hence, in the above example of the murder planned for Christmas Day, it is submitted that, in order to have any hope of persuading the court that he had effectively withdrawn from the plan, D1 would have had to have expressly revoked the authority and support that he had previously given to the scheme: see further *R v Grundy* [1977] Crim LR 543 (pulling out two weeks before a burglary probably adequate for withdrawal).

13.6 Problems with liability

No actus reus committed by the principal

If the principal has not committed an actus reus, there will be no unlawful act for the accomplice to be a party to. In *Thornton v Mitchell* [1940] 1 All ER 339, the defendant, a bus conductor who had given inadequate hand signals to the driver of his bus (who had been attempting to reverse it), with the result that two pedestrians were hit and injured, one of them fatally, was acquitted of abetting the offence of careless driving. The driver had been acquitted of the offence on the basis that he had not been careless, thus an element of the actus reus in respect of the principal's liability had not been proved (the offence charged was one requiring only proof of an intention to drive). In short, there had been no *careless* driving to abet.

Similarly, in *R v Loukes* [1996] 1 Cr App R 444, where the Court of Appeal quashed the conviction of the defendant as an accomplice to causing death by dangerous driving given that the principal offender, one of the defendant's employees, had been acquitted of the offence. The acquittal of the principal offender effectively meant that no actus reus had been committed, the issue of dangerousness in respect of the driving falling to be determined by reference to what a competent and careful driver would have contemplated.

It should be borne in mind, however, that even though a principal offender might not successfully complete the commission of an offence, he may be guilty of an attempt, contrary to the Criminal Attempts Act 1981. Consequently, an accomplice may be charged with aiding and abetting the attempt: see *R v Dunnington* [1984] QB 472.

No mens rea on the part of the principal

In a situation where an accomplice causes or assists in the commission of an actus reus by a principal offender, but the principal acts innocently due to his not having mens rea, the accomplice can be charged as if he were the principal offender by virtue of the doctrine of innocent agency. For example, where D hands X a tablet containing a deadly poison, and tells X to place it in P's drink, telling X that it is a headache tablet, with the result that P is killed. Assuming that X has not been reckless (or possibly grossly negligent) in not realising that the tablet was poison, he will not incur any liability for P's death. X would be regarded as the innocent agent of D, and D would in fact be charged as the principal offender: see *R v Michael* (1840) 9 C & P 356.

Difficulties arise, however, where the actus reus of the relevant offence is one that cannot realistically be committed via an innocent agent, in the sense that it requires the personal intervention of the defendant, as is typically the case with offences requiring proof of sexual intercourse, or conduct such as driving.

In *R* v *Cogan and Leak* (1975) 61 Cr App R 217, Leak persuaded Cogan to have sexual intercourse with Mrs Leak, telling him that she liked being forced to have sex against her will, and that if she struggled it was merely evidence of her enjoyment. Cogan was convicted of raping Mrs Leak, but appealed successfully against his conviction, on the basis that he had honestly thought she was consenting to sexual intercourse. Leak appealed against his conviction for aiding and abetting the rape, on the basis that if the principal had been acquitted, there was no offence to which he could have been an accomplice. In dismissing his appeal, the Court of Appeal held that the actus reus of rape had been committed by Cogan in that Mrs Leak had been forced to submit to sexual intercourse without her consent. Leak had known that she was not consenting, and thus had possessed the necessary mens rea to be an accomplice. Alternatively, the court was willing to view Cogan as an innocent agent through whom Leak had committed the offence of rape (even though as the law then stood a husband could not be guilty of raping his wife), but this is an unsatisfactory analysis for reasons mentioned above.

The problems raised by *Cogan and Leak* stem largely from the fact that English criminal law follows the derivative approach to accessorial liability, in the sense that the accomplice's liability is seen as being dependant upon that of the principal. Looked at independently, Leak intended his wife to be raped and encouraged Cogan to perform the necessary acts. The fact that Cogan believed the victim to be consenting should have been irrelevant. Some indication that the courts are beginning to recognise the limitations created by the derivative approach are provided by decisions such as *R* v *Millward* [1994] Crim LR 527. The appellant instructed H, his employee, to tow a trailer by means of a tractor on a main road but, because of the defective condition of the hitch mechanism, the trailer became detached and collided with a car, killing a passenger. H was acquitted on a charge of causing death by reckless driving. The appellant contended that, without a conviction of the principal offender, he could not be convicted of procuring the offence, and further, given that the offence was one of recklessness, the acquittal of the principal offender implied that the actus reus had not been committed. The case may be significant in that the Court of Appeal, dismissing the appeal, held that a defendant could be convicted of procuring the actus reus of an offence, in this case taking the vehicle on the road in its defective condition, regardless of the fact that the principal offender had been acquitted due to lack of mens rea. In this respect the case arguably goes further than *Cogan and Leak* (above), although one might query whether Millward had sufficient mens rea to sustain a conviction. He clearly knew of the defective state of the trailer hitch, but did not intend the death of another, or (apparently) foresee such an eventuality. On the one hand it could be argued that, for liability as a procurer to be sustained, D should be shown to have intended to produce the offence by endeavour: see *Attorney-General's Reference (No 1 of 1975)* (1975) 61 Cr App R 118. On the other hand it could be argued that D is liable for all the unforeseen consequences of the common design: see *R v Betts and Ridley* (1930) 22 Cr App R 148. The difficulty with this latter argument, however, is that procuring does not require any evidence of an agreement between the parties involved, merely that the procuring caused the commission of the offence. See further *R v Taylor* [1986] Crim LR 680 and *DPP v K and C* [1997] 1 Cr App R 36 (considered below).

Principal has less mens rea than the accomplice

In the past, problems arose where the principal offender possessed some mens rea but less than the accomplice. In *R v Richards* [1974] 1 QB 776, the Court of Appeal held that unless an accomplice was at the scene of the crime, he (or she as it was in this case), could not be charged with a more serious offence than that brought against the principal offender. Hence in that case, the liability of the defendant, who had hired two men to beat up her husband, was limited to the liability of the principals who carried out the attack for her. The decision has been the subject of considerable academic criticism (see *Smith & Hogan* (8th ed, 1996) p154). If taken to its logical conclusion the decision would produce some grotesque results. Suppose that D1 gives a box containing a time-bomb to D2, telling him that it contains smoke bombs, and asking him to place it in a crowded shop. The liability of D2, in the event of the bomb going off and causing death, would be limited to manslaughter, and as a result D1 could only be charged as an accomplice to the manslaughter. Fortunately the House of Lords' decision in *R v Howe* [1987] AC 417 effectively overrules *R v Richards*, thus opening up the possibility of an accomplice being charged with a more serious offence than the principal.

Principal has a defence not available to the accomplice

The respective liabilities of principals and accomplices may vary where the principal can avail himself of some defence not available to the accomplice. Hence a principal suffering from diminished responsibility may be convicted of manslaughter instead of murder, whilst the accomplice to the killing may still be convicted of murder, provided he is proved to have had the necessary mens rea. This holds true even where the principal succeeds with a defence which results in his being acquitted of all liability, such as mistake, or self-defence. As an example, consider *R v Bourne* (1952) 36 Cr App R 125, wherein the defendant was convicted of aiding and abetting the offence of buggery, having forced his wife to have connection with an alsatian dog. His liability remained unaffected despite the assumption by the court that she would have been acquitted on the grounds of coercion.

See also *DPP v K and C* [1997] 1 Cr App R 36 where the Court of Appeal upheld convictions for procuring rape despite the fact that the principal offender was under the age of 14 and the prosecution had failed to discharge the presumption that he had been doli incapax at the time of the offence. On this view, even if the principal offender had been under the age of ten, the appellants could still have been convicted as accomplices.

Victims as accomplices

On the basis of *R v Tyrell* [1894] 1 QB 710, an individual cannot incur liability as an accomplice if the offence in which he or she is alleged to have participated is one created for their protection. Hence, in the above case, the defendant, a girl below the age of 16, was acquitted of aiding and abetting a man to have unlawful sexual intercourse with her. This proposition has been reaffirmed more recently by the Court of Appeal in *R v Whitehouse* [1977] QB 868. The defendant had pleaded guilty to the offence of inciting his 15-year-old daughter to commit an act of incest with him. The court took the view that the defendant had in fact pleaded guilty to an offence unknown to law, since although s11 of the Sexual Offences Act 1956 made it an offence for a girl above the age of 16 to commit an act of incest (given that she would be old enough to consent to intercourse), it was not an offence for a girl below that age to permit an act of incest to take place. He could not be guilty of inciting her to aid and abet an act of incest by him upon her since, on the basis of *R v Tyrell*, she could not be guilty as an accomplice to an offence created for her protection.

Liability following the commission of an offence

The four modes of participation considered in this chapter all concern an accomplice's liability before or at the time of the commission of an offence. It should be noted that a defendant can become criminally liable for assisting an offender after the commission of an offence. The relevant statutory provision is s4(1) of the Criminal Law Act 1967:

> 'Where a person has committed an arrestable offence, any other person who, knowing or believing him to be guilty of the offence or of some other arrestable offence, does without lawful authority or reasonable excuse any act with intent to impede his apprehension or prosecution shall be guilty of an offence.'

Note that, on the basis of *R v Donald* (1986) 83 Cr App R 49, a defendant can be convicted of this offence before the principal has been convicted of the main offence.

13.7 Reform

Reform of the law relating to accessorial liability has been considered by the Law Commission in Working Papers Nos 43 and 50, and in the proposed codification of the common law in the DCCB in 1989. Its most recent review of this area of criminal liability is to be found in its Consultation Paper No 131, *Assisting and Encouraging Crime – A Consultation Paper*.

The thrust of the provisional proposals contained in the Commission's paper is that English criminal law should move away from the essentially derivative approach to accessorial lability, whereby the liability of the accomplice is contingent upon that of the principal offender. The paper endorses the view of Professor Sandford Kadish to the effect that any move towards reform had to be based on a recognition that complicity has two basic natures:

'... intentionally influencing the decision of the primary party to commit a crime, and intentionally helping the principal actor commit the crime, where the helping actions themselves constitute no part of the actions prohibited by the definition of the crime'.

The Commission invites comment on two new distinct offences of 'assisting' and 'encouraging' crime. Both offences would be 'inchoate' in the sense that liability would arise as soon as the acts of assistance or encouragement were committed, regardless of whether or not the principal committed the relevant completed crime. The proposed offence of encouragement would encompass activity currently falling within the crime of incitement. Justifying the inchoate nature of the proposed offences the paper notes:

'... under the present law ... the requirement that the principal crime should actually be committed adds nothing to the analysis of accessory liability and does not serve as any sort of principled limitation on that liability. Rather, it serves as an additional condition for liability, that may, however, enable some "assisters" to escape conviction, possibly in a quite erratic and unmeritorious fashion.' (para 4.25)

The provisional definition of the offence of assisting crime, at para 4.99, provides:

'(1) A person commits the offence of assisting crime if he
(a) knows or believes that another ("the principal") is doing or causing to be done, or will do or cause to be done, acts that do or will involve the commission of an offence by the principal; and
(b) knows or believes that the principal, in so acting, does or will do so with the fault required for the offence in question; and
(c) does any act that he knows or believes assists or will assist the principal in committing that offence.
(2) Assistance includes giving the principal advice as to [how to] commit the offence, or as to how to avoid detection or apprehension before or during the commission of the offence.
(3) A person does not assist the commission of an offence for the purposes of this section if all that he does is to fail to prevent or impede the commission of that offence.
(4) "Offence" in sub-paragraphs (a)–(c) of subsection (1) above means the breach of a specified prohibition laid down by statute or the common law; but, provided the defendant knows or believes sufficient facts to show that such a breach is taking place or will take place, he need not know the time, place or other details of the offence.
(5) A person also commits an offence under this section if he knows or believes that the principal intends to commit one of a number of offences and does any act that he knows or believes will assist the principal in committing whichever of those offences the principal in fact intends.'

The proposed formulation of assisting in crime would go some way towards resolving the problems posed by decisions such as *R* v *Bainbridge* (above), in the sense that the accomplice could only incur liability for assisting crimes committed by the principal if, at the time he gave his assistance, the offence committed by the principal was sufficiently identified by the accomplice as the object of that assistance.

Regarding liability for failing to prevent crime, the paper rejects the approach of the DCCB (that is, that liability should arise where the accomplice had a right to prevent the crime, or was under a duty to do so) on the ground that it would extend the proposed offence of assisting too far: see para 4.73.

The paper recognises that some provision would still have to be made for the accomplice who claims to have withdrawn from a common design, but proposes that:

'... a defence should only be available if the assister takes all reasonable steps to prevent the commission of the crime towards which he has assisted' (para 4.135).

As indicated above, the proposed offence of encouraging crime is envisaged by the Commission as

'... covering the ground that at the moment is addressed not only by the "counselling" element in aiding and abetting but also by the present law of incitement ...'.

The rationale for the offence is stated as being that the law should extend to:

'... all those who give encouragement and moral support to the commission of a crime, whether or not that encouragement has the effect of changing the principal's mind, or is intended to change the principal's mind, in the direction of the commission of that crime'. (para 4.148)

The proposed offence is stated in para 4.163 as follows:

'1(1) A person commits the offence of encouraging crime if he
(a) solicits, commands or encourages another ("the principal") to do or cause to be done an act or acts which, if done, will involve the commission of an offence by the principal; and
(b) intends that that act or those acts should be done by the principal; and
(c) knows or believes that the principal, in so acting, will do so with the fault required for the offence in question.
(2) The solicitation, command or encouragement must be brought to the attention of the principal, but it is irrelevant to the person's guilt whether or not the principal reacts to or is influenced by the solicitation, command or encouragement.
(3) The defendant need not know the identity of the principal, nor have any particular principal or group of principals in mind, provided that he intends his communication to be acted on by any person to whose attention it comes.
(4) "Offence" in sub-paragraphs (a)–(c) of subsection (1) above means the breach of a specified prohibition laid down by statute or the common law; but for the purposes of this section the defendant may solicit, command or encourage the commission of such an offence without intending that it should be committed at a specific time or place.'

The paper sees no objection in principle to liability for encouraging crime being based on a failure to act, but doubts whether such cases are likely to arise in practice. As with the proposed offence of assisting, the paper envisages an accomplice escaping liability where he has withdrawn from the criminal enterprise if, having encouraged the commission of the crime, he either countermands the encouragement with a view to preventing the commission of the crime, or he takes reasonable steps to prevent its commission.

A number of general issues arising from these proposals were also considered in the paper, and comments were invited on the following suggestions:

1. Given the inchoate nature of the proposed forms of complicity, impossibility, in the sense that the principal cannot commit the offence encouraged or assisted (or, indeed, unknown to the accomplice, does not have the mens rea for the offence), should be no bar to the accomplice's liability.
2. There should not be liability for assisting or encouraging an inchoate offence.
3. There should not be liability for assisting another to assist or encourage the commission of crime.
4. There should be provision for liability for attempting to assist or encourage crime.
5. There may be a residual role for an offence of procuring where there is no communication between accomplice and principal, and the principal commits the offence without fault. As the paper states:

    '... [such cases] can be met by a provision to the effect that where an offence can be committed without fault on the part of the principal, a person commits the offence of procurement if he does any act with the intent that it should bring about, or being reckless whether that act will bring about, the commission of that offence by another.' (para 4.196)

6. The problems arising in cases such as *Cogan and Leak* (above – principal acquitted due to lack of mens rea) and *Bourne* (above – principal has a defence that would result in acquittal) could be addressed by a specific offence of encouragement:

    '... where D solicits etc, acts on P's part which if performed will only fail to involve the commission of an offence by P because either (i) P can adduce a defence of duress based on threats made to him by D; or (ii) P is acting under a mistake of fact and that mistake has been intentionally brought about by D'.

13.8 Vicarious liability

Vicarious liability involves holding A responsible in law for the actions of B. As a general principle the courts will not hold one defendant criminally liable for the actions of another, but this is subject to a number of exceptions. If D gives X a tablet to place in P's tea, telling him that it is an aspirin when in fact it is cyanide, with the result that P dies of poisoning, D will be held responsible in law for the death, and X will escape liability as an innocent agent. In a sense D is vicariously liable for the criminal acts of X, but it is perhaps better to view X as simply the means by which D achieves his ends.

As will have been seen above, a defendant can be charged with an offence, despite the fact that he has only played out some accessorial role in its commission. One who counsels or procures the commission of an offence could be described as incurring a form of vicarious liability for the criminal acts committed by the principal offender, in the sense that his liability is derived from that of the person who commits the actus reus of the completed crime. What distinguishes such cases from the usual instances of vicarious liability, however, is that the counsellor or procurer will have some degree of mens rea; see further on this distinction *Ferguson* v *Weaving* [1951] 1 KB 814.

It is well known that employers can be held vicariously liable in civil law for torts committed by their employees in the course of employment. Where an employee commits criminal offences in the course of his employment, for example a solicitor's clerk defrauding a client of her property (see *Lloyd* v *Grace, Smith & Co* [1912] AC 716), there is no reason per se why the employer should also incur criminal liability, unless he can be shown to have actively participated in the commission of the offence, in which case the normal rules of accessorial liability will apply.

There are sound policy reasons, however, for recognising that in certain situations the law ought to impose vicarious criminal liability on an employer, particularly where a statute creates criminal liability of a regulatory or 'quasi-criminal nature'. Much depends on whether the court regards the imposition of vicarious liability as having been intended by Parliament as a necessary means of ensuring the effective operation of the law in question. Three situations in particular needs to be noted.

Statutory duty placed on an employer

Where a statute creates and imposes a legal duty upon a particular person, he will normally be liable for the failure of those acting on his behalf to ensure the performance of that duty. As Atkin J observed in *Mousell Brothers Ltd* v *London & North Western Railway Co* [1917] 2 KB 836:

'I think that the authorities cited ... make it plain that while prima facie a principal is not to be made criminally responsible for the acts of his servants, yet the legislature may prohibit an act or enforce a duty in such words as to make the prohibition or the duty absolute; in which case the principal is liable if the act is in fact done by his servants. To ascertain whether a particular Act of Parliament has that effect or not regard must be had to the object of the Statute, the words used, the nature of the duty laid down, the person upon whom it is imposed, the person by whom it would in ordinary circumstances be performed, and the person upon whom the penalty is imposed.'

The courts may, however, be willing to recognise a relaxation of this principle where the offence places D under a personal duty and goes on to provide for a 'due diligence' defence. For example in *Seaboard Offshore* v *Secretary of State for Transport* [1994] 1 WLR 541, the House of Lords held that the owner of a vessel could be criminally liable for a failing to ensure that it was operated in a safe manner, contrary to s31 of the Merchant Shipping Act 1988, but could not be criminally liable if this circumstance arose through the acts or omissions of his employees, if he himself had taken all reasonable steps to prevent its occurrence.

Act of the servant imputed to the employer

Cases such as *Griffiths* v *Studebakers Ltd* [1924] 1 KB 102 suggest that an employer can be vicariously liable in respect of strict liability offences committed by an employee during the course of his employment provided the wording of the offence is appropriate. In that case, an employee of the defendant company had taken a number of prospective purchasers for a trial run in one of the company's cars. The company was charged with using the vehicle contrary to the Road Vehicles (Trade Licences) Regulations 1922, on the ground that more than two passengers were carried on the trial run. In upholding the conviction, the Divisional Court held that the company could be said to be using the vehicle through its employee. As the offence was one of strict liability, there was no conceptual difficulty in holding the company liable as the principal offender, and the employee liable as an aider and abettor (although note that there can be no accessorial liability without fault). Similarly employers have been found guilty of 'selling' goods in contravention of what is now the trades descriptions legislation (see *Coppen* v *Moore (No 2)* [1898] 2 QB 306), and of 'keeping' a vehicle without a licence (see *Strutt* v *Cliff* [1911] 1 KB 1).

National Rivers Authority v *Alfred McAlpine Homes East Ltd* [1994] 4 All ER 286 concerned pollution of the River Medway during the construction of a housing estate by the respondent company. The pollution had been caused by wet cement being discharged into a culvert running through the site into the river. The company, charged with contravention of s85 Water Resources Act 1991, conceded that its employees had caused this pollution whilst constructing a water feature on the site, but the justices dismissed the information as disclosing no case to answer on the basis that those responsible for the discharge, the site agent and manager, were not sufficiently senior to be identified with the 'controlling mind' of the company. On appeal the court held that the pollution had been caused by employees of the respondent company who were actively responsible for the operation of the site whilst acting in the course of their employment. Only if the pollution could be shown to have been caused by the intervention of some third party would the company be relieved of liability. Simon Brown LJ seemed to regard the case one involving vicarious corporate liability, thus falling within the same category as *Alphacell Ltd* v *Woodward* [1972] AC 824, in the sense that the company should be criminally liable for the pollution resulting from its authorised procedures. Morland J also approached the offence as one that imposed vicarious liability, despite the absence of any clear words to that effect in the statute, and his justification for adopting such an approach is instructive. He stated:

> 'In my judgment, to make the offence an effective weapon in the defence of environmental protection, a company must by necessary implication be criminally liable for the acts or omissions of its servants or agents during activities being done for the company. I do not find that this offends our concept of a just or fair criminal justice system, having regard to the magnitude of environmental pollution, even though no due diligence defence was provided for ... [I]t can be strongly argued that the respondents by their activities directly caused the flow of polluting matter into the stream. It is difficult to see in principle why it should matter whether those activities are essentially mechanical by their plant or essentially manual by their servants or agents.'

Given that, in the cases considered above, it is the employer who is regarded in law as having committed the actus reus of the offence, not the employee, there are two situations where the application of this principle may prove difficult: first where the wording of the given offence requires proof of some physical activity, such as 'driving', that cannot be performed by an artificial legal entity such as a corporation; see further *Richmond upon Thames London Borough Council* v *Pinn and Wheeler Ltd* [1989] Crim LR 510. The second is where the wording of the offence implies proof of knowledge that cannot be established on the part of the employer. Thus in *James & Son Ltd* v *Smee* [1955] 1 QB 78 the defendant employers were charged with permitting a vehicle to be driven with defective brakes, contrary to vehicle use regulations. The Divisional Court quashed the conviction, holding that the use of the word 'permitting' in the statute implied some degree of mens rea, in that one could only permit something if one knew of it. There was no evidence to suggest that the defendants had known of the vehicle's defective brakes, and hence they had not had the mens rea necessary for a conviction. Similarly in *Readhead Freight Ltd* v *Shulman* [1988] Crim LR 696, the Divisional Court held that although the defendant company had, through its transport manager, caused an offence to be committed by the company's drivers not filling in their time sheets as required by law, there could be no liability in the absence of any evidence that the it had issued any instruction or mandate to this effect.

The delegation principle

In *Vane* v *Yiannopoullos* [1965] AC 486, Lord Morris expressed the view that:

> '... the principle "respondeat superior" finds no place in our criminal law. If a master tells or authorises his servant to do some particular act any criminal liability in the master that might result, either as a principal or as an accessory, springs from the authorisation and not simply from the relationship of master and servant ... I am not prepared to accept that there are any canons of construction which are specially applicable to legislation dealing with licensing, or that in such legislation the principle "respondeat superior" commands some exceptional yet general acceptance.'

Despite the force of these comments, the evidence is that the courts will not necessarily permit an employer or licensee to escape liability, even for offences requiring proof of mens rea, by delegating the management of an establishment to his servants. Thus in *Allen* v *Whitehead* [1930] 1 KB 211, D was convicted of permitting a café, which he owned but which was managed on his behalf by a servant, to be used as a place of resort by prostitutes, the knowledge of D's manager being imputed to the owner; see also *Linnet* v *Metropolitan Police Commissioner* [1946] KB 290. The rationale for the 'delegation' principle is to ensure that individuals cannot escape legal liability simply by placing the running of their businesses in the hands of others. If it were otherwise, a licensee could, for example, flout the licensing laws with impunity by installing a manager to operate his public house. The legislation stipulates that only the licensee can be punished as a principal offender, and the licensee would be able to deny any mens rea on account of his absence at the time the offence was committed.

In *R* v *Winson* [1969] 1 QB 371, the appellant, who held a justices' on-licence under the terms of which he was prohibited from selling alcohol to persons who had been members of the club for less than 48 hours, visited the bar infrequently, and had effectively delegated the running of the bar to a manager. Following evidence that alcohol had been sold at the club in breach of the terms of the licence, he was convicted under s161(1) of the Licensing Act 1964 of knowingly selling liquor to persons to whom he was not permitted to sell. Dismissing his appeal, Lord Parker CJ observed:

> 'The principle of delegation comes into play, and only comes into play, in cases where, although the statute uses words which import knowledge or intent such as in this case "knowingly" or in some other cases "permitting" or "suffering" and the like, cases to which knowledge is inherent, nevertheless it has been held that a man cannot get out of his responsibilities which have been put upon him by delegating those responsibilities to another ... If one licensee chooses to say to his co-licensee, although not his servant: "We are both licensees and both keepers of this house, but I am not going to take any part in the management of this house, I leave the management to you", he is putting his co-licensee into his own place to exercise his own powers and duties and he must, therefore, accept responsibility for what is done or known by his co-licensee in that exercise.'

It is possible that the doctrine can work to the defendant's advantage. In *DPP* v *Rogers* [1992] Crim LR 51 the licensee of a public house had been dismissed by the brewery and was on suspension pending an appeal against his dismissal. The respondent, the area manager for the brewery, appointed relief managers to run the business. The prosecution's claim that the respondent was aiding and abetting the unlicensed sale of alcohol by the relief managers was rejected by the Divisional Court on the basis that they were acting as delegates of the dismissed manager, and therefore had his authority to sell liquor. The problem with this interpretation, however, is that the dismissed manager had not consented to the appointment of relief managers, and would presumably have incurred vicarious liability for any breaches of the Licensing Act 1964 by the relief managers, unless the courts were willing to distinguish between wilful delegation, and enforced delegation.

The problem will often be one of degree; has there been delegation of management or not? In *Vane* v *Yiannopoullos* the defendant licensee, who was licensed to sell alcohol to those of his patrons who ordered meals, was charged under s22(1) of the Licensing Act 1961, of knowingly selling alcohol to persons to whom he was not permitted to sell, after one of his waitresses had sold alcohol to two youths in contravention of the terms of the licence. The defendant had been on the premises at the time, but on another floor. The magistrates had dismissed the case against the defendant on the basis that he had not had any mens rea, and the prosecutor's appeal was dismissed by the House of Lords on the basis that there had not been complete delegation of management to the servants of the licensee, or alternatively because the licensee had not absented himself. Whether or not there has been any such delegation will often be a nice question of fact and law; see further *Howker* v *Robinson* [1973] 1 QB 178.

Reform

The Draft Code contains the following restatement of vicarious criminal liability in cl 29:

'(1) Subject to subsection (3), an element of an offence (other than a fault element) may be attributed to a person by reason of an act done by another only if that other is –
(a) specified in the definition of the offence as a person whose act may be so attributed; or
(b) acting within the scope of his employment or authority and the definition of the offence specifies the element in terms which apply to both persons.
(2) Subject to subsection (3), a fault element of an offence may be attributed to a person by reason of the fault of another only if the terms of the enactment creating the offence so provide.
(3) This section does not affect the application in relation to any pre-Code offence (as defined in section 6) of any existing rule whereby a person who has delegated to another the management of premises or of a business or activity may, in consequence of the acts and fault of the other, have the elements of the offence attributed to him.'

The limits that cl 29 would impose upon the scope of vicarious liability are considered in the commentary:

'Subsection (1)(b) provides for two conditions to be satisfied before an offence may be interpreted as applying to a person who did not himself do the prohibited act. The relevant element of the offence must be expressed in terms which are apt for the defendant as well as for the person who in fact acted Secondly, the person who in fact acted must have done so within the scope of his employment or authority (that is, as the defendant's agent). These conditions are in accordance with the results reached in the great majority of cases. In their absence there can be no justification for imposing vicarious liability (unless, of course, Parliament has expressly provided for it). Under existing law an employee may disobey an express instruction from his employer and yet still be held to be acting within the scope of his employment [see *Coppen v Moore (No 2)* [1898] 2 QB 306].
    The reference in paragraph (b) to a person's "acting within the scope of his authority" extends, of course, to a case in which the person who does the prohibited act is acting for

the defendant not as an employee but as an independent contractor. It was proposed in Working Paper No 43 to exclude such persons from the range of agents whose acts may give rise to vicarious liability. As this proposal would change the law without a clear case being made for doing so, clause 29 does not adopt it. The clause does not distinguish between the person who "uses" the defendant's vehicle as his employee and the person who "uses" the defendant's vehicle on a single occasion because the defendant has asked him to do so, whether or not for payment. This does not mean that a person will necessarily be liable for the act of his independent contractor even where the offence employs a verb like "uses". The matter remains one for judicial interpretation. It is one thing to hold that a person carrying on a business of supplying milk or heavy building materials "uses" a vehicle if he employs an independent contractor to supply those things in the contractor's vehicle. It would be quite another thing to hold that a householder "uses" the removal van owned by the firm of removers whom he engages to carry his furniture to a new residence. Paragraph (b) also leaves open the possibility that, where an independent contractor does an act incidental to the act he was engaged to do, he will be held not to have acted within the scope of his authority. The courts have interpreted some offences requiring knowledge (notably licensees' offences) so as to permit a person's conviction on the basis of the act and knowledge of one to whom he has delegated management of premises or of an activity. This "delegation principle" was regarded as anomalous by members of the House of Lords in *Vane* v *Yiannopoullos* and our Working Party proposed its abolition. Subsection (2) gives effect to this proposal so far as concerns offences created by the Code itself or by subsequent legislation. Parliament will have to provide clearly for the attribution to one person of the fault of another if it wishes this to occur. There can be no question, however, of proposing the abolition of the delegation principle as it has been held to apply to existing legislation. Some legislation is so drafted that abolition would seriously affect its enforceability. Subsection (3) therefore expressly preserves the application of the principle to pre-Code offences.' (Vol II, paras 9.48–9.50)

The effect of the enacting cl 29 is illustrated in the examples contained in Appendix B to C Volume I:

'A statute provides that it is an offence for the holder of a justices' licence whether by himself, his servant or agent to supply intoxicating liquor on licensed premises outside permitted hours. No fault is required for this offence. D is the licensee of a public house. E, his barman, serves a drink to a friend outside the permitted hours. In the absence of any special defence D is guilty of the offence as a principal. Assuming fault on E s part, E is guilty as an accessory.' (example 29(i))

'A statute provides that it is an offence for a person to sell goods to which a false trade description is applied. No fault is required for this offence. E, an assistant employed in D's shop, sells a ham as a "Scotch" ham. D has previously given instructions that such hams are not to be sold under any specific name of place of origin. The ham is in fact an American ham. Both D and E are guilty of the offence as principals.' (example 29(ii))

14

General Defences: Where the Mental Element is Affected

14.1 Insanity

14.2 Intoxication

14.1 Insanity

The law has, for centuries, recognised that allowances ought to be made as regards the criminality of those who commit offences whilst criminally insane. As Serjeant Pollard contended in *Reniger* v *Forgossa* (1548) 1 Plow 1 at 19:

> '... if a man non sanae memoriae kills another, he has broken the words of the law, yet he has not broken the law because he has no memory or understanding, but mere ignorance which came to him by the hand of God.'

The modern basis of the law is provided by the rules laid down in *McNaghten's Case* (1843) 10 C & F 20. Following the acquittal of Daniel McNaghten, for shooting Sir Robert Peel's secretary whilst suffering from paranoia, the issue of insanity and criminal responsibility was debated in the House of Lords, subsequent to which the judges of the courts of common law were invited to answer a number of questions on the subject of insanity as a defence to criminal charges. On the basis of the McNaghten Rules jurors are to be told that D is to be presumed to be sane, and to possess a sufficient degree of reason to be responsible for his crimes, until the contrary be proved to their satisfaction; and that to establish a defence on the ground of insanity, it must be clearly proved that, at the time of the committing of the act, D was labouring under a defect of reason, from disease of the mind, as not to know the nature and quality of the act he was doing, or, if he did know it, that he did not know he was doing what was wrong.

The defence can be raised in respect of any offence that requires proof of mens rea, hence in *DPP* v *H* (1997) The Times 2 May the Divisional Court ruled that it could not be raised to as a defence to a strict liability offence such as driving with excess alcohol. The availability of insanity as a defence to summary offences requiring proof of mens rea was confirmed in *R* v *Horseferry Road Magistrates' Court, ex parte K* [1997] Crim LR 129.

Disease of the mind

The expression 'disease of the mind' has been interpreted by the courts to encompass both defects and injuries of the brain per se and also physical conditions that affect the working of the brain. In *R v Kemp* [1957] 1 QB 399 D suffered a blackout during which he attacked his wife with a hammer, causing her grievous bodily harm. The evidence showed that he suffered from arterial sclerosis, a condition that restricted the flow of blood to the brain. Devlin J, the trial judge, ruled that, for the purposes of the defence of insanity, no distinction was to be drawn between diseases of the mind and diseases of the body affecting the operation of the mind. As he observed:

> 'Hardening of the arteries is a disease which is shown on the evidence to be capable of affecting the mind in such a way as to cause a defect, temporarily or permanently, of its reasoning, understanding and so on, and so is in my judgment a disease of the mind which comes within the meaning of the Rules.'

In determining whether a physical condition should be classified as a 'disease of the mind' for these purposes the courts will also be looking at how the affliction manifests itself. Where D suffers from a disease of the body which affects the mind in a manner which, to paraphrase Lord Denning in *Bratty* v *Attorney-General for Northern Ireland* [1963] AC 386, manifests itself in violence and is likely to recur, it will be classified as giving rise to insanity, thus enabling the courts to order the detention of D if it is in the public interest to do so. The defendant Bratty in fact suffered from psychomotor epilepsy, strictly speaking a disease of the nervous system. Yet the House of Lords held that it had not been a misdirection for the trial judge to leave the defence of insanity to the jury rather than automatism.

The House of Lords has subsequently had occasion to reaffirm this approach to the concept of disease of the mind in *R v Sullivan* [1984] AC 156. D had inflicted grievous bodily harm contrary to s20 of the Offences Against the Person Act 1861 whilst suffering from a minor epileptic fit. During the course of the trial the judge had ruled that he would be willing to direct the jury on the defence of insanity, but not that of automatism, whereupon D changed his plea to one of guilty, and appealed on the ground that the trial judge had wrongly denied him the opportunity of raising the defence of automatism. In dismissing the appeal, Lord Diplock, with whom all of their Lordships were in agreement, recognised the natural reluctance that many sensible people would feel in labelling an epileptic as 'criminally insane', but went on to explain that:

> 'If the effect of a disease is to impair [the faculties of reason, memory and understanding] so severely as to have either of the consequences referred to in the later part of the [McNaghten] Rules, it matters not whether the aetiology of the impairment is organic, as in epilepsy, or functional, or whether the impairment itself is permanent or is transient and intermittent, provided that it subsisted at the time of commission of the act. The purpose of the legislation relating to the defence of insanity, ever since its origin in 1800, has been to protect society against recurrence of the dangerous conduct.'

How often the condition must be likely to recur in order for the courts to regard it as constituting a disease of the mind is open to question, but the more violence used by D, the more likely the court will be to take a cautious approach and regard his condition as amounting to insanity. Hence, in *R v Burgess* [1991] 2 WLR 1206, D attacked P causing cuts and bruises. At his trial he adduced expert medical evidence to the effect that he had been sleepwalking at the time of the attack and contended that the defence of automatism should be put before the jury. The trial judge ruled that the only defence the evidence revealed was that of insanity, and the jury in due course found him not guilty by reason of insanity. Confirming the approach taken by the court below, Lord Lane CJ observed:

'It seems to us that if there is a danger of recurrence that may be an added reason for categorising the condition as a disease of the mind. On the other hand, the absence of the danger of recurrence is not a reason for saying that it cannot be a disease of the mind ... Dr Eames in cross-examination ... accepted that there is a liability to recurrence of sleepwalking. He could not go so far as to say that there is no liability of recurrence of serious violence but he agreed with the other medical witnesses that there is no recorded case of violence of this sort recurring. The prosecution, as already indicated, called Dr Fenwick, whose opinion was that this was not a sleepwalking episode at all. If it was a case where the appellant was unconscious of what he was doing, the most likely explanation was that he was in what is described as an hysterical dissociative state. That is a state in which, for psychological reasons, such as being overwhelmed by his emotions, the person s brain works in a different way. He carries out acts of which he has no knowledge and for which he has no memory. It is quite different from sleep-walking. ... It seems to us that on this evidence the judge was right to conclude that this was an abnormality or disorder, albeit transitory, due to an internal factor, whether functional or organic, which had manifested itself in violence. It was a disorder or abnormality which might recur, though the possibility of it recurring in the form of serious violence was unlikely.'

An alternative rationale for the distinction between insane and non-insane automatism might be that suggested at Chapter 2, section 2.4; the fact that automatism will generally be caused by the effect of external factors operating upon the body, whilst insanity arises from internal defects. While it is submitted that to pursue such a distinction is likely to lead to a somewhat arbitrary classification of defendants, it would appear to be supported by a number of decisions. In *R v Quick* [1973] QB 910 D was charged with assaulting a patient whilst employed as a nurse in a psychiatric hospital. D was a diabetic and contended that the assault had occurred whilst he had been in a hypoglycaemia state (low blood sugar level due to an excess of insulin). Following the trial judge's direction that the evidence did not disclose the defence of automatism, D changed his plea to guilty, and appealed. Allowing his appeal, Lawton LJ observed that:

'In this case Quick's alleged mental condition, if it ever existed, was not caused by his diabetes but by his use of the insulin prescribed by his doctor. Such malfunctioning of the mind as there was, was caused by an external factor and not a bodily disorder in the nature of a disease which disturbed the working of his mind. It follows in our judgment that Quick was entitled to have his defence of automatism left to the jury ...'

Contrast this with the approach of the Court of Appeal in *R* v *Hennessy* [1989] 1 WLR 287. D, a diabetic who failed to take the insulin necessary to stabilise his metabolism, was stopped by police officers whilst driving a stolen car. Medical evidence suggested that D had been in a state of hyperglycaemia (high blood sugar level) at the time the car was taken. D was not permitted to put the defence of automatism before the jury, the trial judge having indicated that he would only be prepared to direct the jury on the defence of insanity. The Court of Appeal, in confirming the correctness of the trial judge's ruling, held that as D's loss of awareness had not resulted from the operation of external factors upon his body, such as the injection of insulin (as in *Quick*), but rather had resulted from an inherent physical defect, ie diabetes, D was to be regarded as suffering from a disease of the body which affected the mind for the purposes of the McNaghten Rules.

Despite the arbitrariness involved, the distinction between hypoglycaemia (too little sugar in the blood caused by treatment with insulin or by inadequate quantities of food) and hyperglycaemia continues to be used as the basis for distinguishing between sane and non-insane automatism: see further *R* v *Bingham* [1991] Crim LR 43.

'So as not to know the nature and quality of his act'

One of the two grounds upon which insanity can be established is that D's disease of the mind caused him to be unaware of his actions. It has been seen that in *Kemp* D was unaware of his actions because of a 'blackout'. Similarly, the defence would be made out where, due to a disease of the mind, D killed P believing himself to be chopping down a tree, or where D placed a baby on a fire believing the child to be a log. Were an apparently sane defendant to act in this fashion he would be entitled to rely on the defence of mistake (see Chapter 3, section 3.6), but it should be noted that the more outlandish his mistake, the less likely the jury are to conclude that D honestly believed the facts to be as he claims them to have been. Further, on the basis of *Bratty*, such a defence might entitle the prosecution to introduce any evidence of insanity.

'Actions were wrong'

The alternative basis upon which the defence can be made out is for D to be shown not to have known that his actions were wrong due to his disease of the mind. 'Wrong' in this context has been interpreted to mean wrong in law, as opposed to simply immoral: see *R* v *Windle* [1952] 2 QB 826. Hence, the defence of insanity offers one of the very few situations where ignorance of the criminal law can be relied upon to avoid liability.

The limited nature of the defence

The defence of insanity has been the subject of prolonged and cogent academic criticism on a number of grounds, but primarily in relation to its limited scope. It will be apparent from the above that, whilst the defence can cater for D who is unaware of his actions, or their illegality, there is no provision for D who is aware of his actions, and knows them to be unlawful, yet cannot prevent himself from committing offences. Where D kills as a result of such a condition, he can at least avail himself of the defence of diminished responsibility which recognises impairment of responsibility as a partial defence, but in relation to all other offences there exists a serious gap in the provision of defences. This problem is illustrated by the decision in *R v Bell* [1984] Crim LR 685, where D had been charged with reckless driving, having used a van as a battering ram to drive through the entrance gates of a Butlins' holiday camp. When interviewed he told the police: 'It was like a secret society in there, I wanted to do my bit against it.' D contended that he had not driven recklessly because, although he knew there was a risk of his causing damage, he felt that he was able to cope with it because he was being instructed to act by God. Following the rejection of his submission of 'no case' on this basis, he changed his plea to one of guilty. The Court of Appeal held, dismissing the appeal, that as he had been aware of his actions he could not have been in a state of automatism, and the fact that he believed himself to be driven by God could not provide an excuse, but merely an explanation for what he had done. In other words he could not rely on the defence of insanity either because the evidence was that he had known what he was doing, or had known that what he was doing was illegal.

Fitness to plead

Prior to 1991 D could be found to be unfit to plead before the issue of liability was investigated, sometimes resulting in his being detained in a secure hospital simply on the basis of unfitness to plead. The Criminal Procedure (Insanity and Unfitness to Plead) Act 1991 was enacted to improve the situation of such defendants by requiring a court, which has found D unfit to plead, to continue with a trial of the facts to the extent of ascertaining whether or not he committed the acts reus of the offence alleged. If the court concludes that he did not, he defendant should be acquitted. Whilst this development is to be welcomed, it should be remembered that the distinction between actus reus and mens rea is somewhat illusory in many cases, and it may be that in practice the court has no option but to investigate both elements.

Who raises the issue of insanity?

It will normally be for D to establish, on the balance of probabilities, that he was insane at the time of the offence. The trial judge can withdraw the issue from the jury if he feels that this burden has not been discharged. Alternatively, the prosecution can lead evidence of insanity if D conducts his defence in such a manner as to put his state of mind in issue, for example by relying on an implausible mistake of fact to deny mens rea. Even if D has not raised the issue of his mental responsibility at all, it appears that the trial judge may, in exceptional circumstances, leave the option of the special verdict to the jury if he thinks fit: see *R* v *Dickie* [1984] 3 All ER 173.

The special verdict

It is, strictly speaking, inaccurate to describe insanity as a defence. Under the provisions of s2 of the Trial of Lunatics Act 1883, as amended by the Criminal Procedure (Insanity) Act 1964, the jury will return the special verdict under which D is found to be 'not guilty by reason of insanity'. The real significance of this verdict is that it leaves D under the control of the court. Section 5 of the 1964 Act provides that where a special verdict is returned, the court 'shall make an order that the accused be admitted to such hospital as may be specified by the Secretary of State.' The range of options open to the court in respect of D, provided he has not been charged with an offence to which a mandatory penalty is prescribed, has been increased by the Criminal Procedure (Insanity and Unfitness to Plead) Act 1991. The court can now make a supervision and treatment order, a guardianship order, order D's admission to hospital for a limited or unlimited period, or discharge D completely.

Alternative strategies

Defendants are likely to find the prospect of the special verdict, with the possibility of hospitalisation, and the stigma of being declared criminally insane, unattractive. Coupled with the narrowness of the actual terms of the defence of insanity, this perhaps goes some way to explaining why relatively little use is made of the defence in modern day trials. Where D is charged with murder, which carries a mandatory penalty of life imprisonment, the flexibility introduced by the 1991 Act will not be available to the court dealing with his case. He will almost certainly rely on the defence of diminished responsibility under s2 of the Homicide Act 1957 (see Chapter 4) in preference to a plea of insanity, the principal advantage being the greater discretion left to the trial judge following a finding of diminished responsibility by the jury. It should be noted, however, that those convicted of manslaughter on the grounds of diminished responsibility will invariably be sentenced to a term of imprisonment, sometimes for life, and in any event, under s6(1)(b) of the Criminal Procedure (Insanity) Act 1964, the prosecution can lead evidence of D's insanity where he has raised the defence of diminished responsibility, although the prosecution must establish this beyond all reasonable doubt.

Alternatively, if D does not wish to be made the subject of a special verdict, he can simply plead guilty to the offence as charged in the hope that he will be sentenced as would a sane defendant, this being perhaps more likely where less serious offences are involved. Again this tactic may prove counter-productive for D, because, following conviction, the prosecution has a duty to put before the court all relevant evidence for the purposes of sentencing, and this can include evidence as to D's insanity. Although he avoids the stigma of the special verdict, D can still find himself being made the subject of a hospital order.

Reform

The Butler Committee Report (Cmnd 6244) (1975) recommended the introduction of a new verdict of 'not guilty by reason of mental disorder' which could be returned in two situations:

1. where the defendant was unable to form the requisite mens rea due to mental disorder; or
2. where the defendant was aware of his actions but was at the time suffering from severe mental disorder.

The Report's recommendations have never been implemented and, with the passage of time, their implementation seems increasingly less likely.

The difficulty lies in producing a concept of insanity which is, on the one hand, simple enough for the averagely educated man or woman on a jury to understand, but which on the other hand is sufficiently sophisticated to encompass the varying types of mental abnormality with which other modern courts are likely to have to deal.

The Draft Code seeks to build upon the foundations laid by the Butler Committee. The commentary on the Code Report states:

'The necessity of incorporating in the projected Criminal Code an appropriate provision to replace the outdated "insanity" defence was one justification given by the [Butler] Committee for its review of the subject. We ourselves are persuaded that implementation of the Committee's proposals would greatly improve this area of the law. We have, however, found it necessary to suggest some important modifications of those proposals. Clauses 34 to 40 therefore aim to give effect to the policy of the Butler Committee as modified by us in ways that will be explained in the following paragraphs.' (Vol II, para 11.9)

Clauses 35 and 36 of the Draft Code detail the circumstances in which the proposed mental disorder verdict would be returned. Clause 35 provides:

'(1) A mental disorder verdict shall be returned if the defendant is proved to have committed an offence but it is proved on the balance of probabilities (whether by the prosecution or by the defendant) that he was at the time suffering from severe mental illness or severe mental handicap.

(2) Subsection (1) does not apply if the court or jury is satisfied beyond reasonable doubt

that the offence was not attributable to a severe mental illness or severe mental handicap. (3) A court or jury shall not, for the purposes of a verdict under subsection (1), find that the defendant was suffering from severe a mental illness or severe mental handicap unless two medical practitioners approved for the purposes of s12 of the Mental Health Act 1983 as having special experience in the diagnosis or treatment of mental disorder have given evidence that he was so suffering.'

This provision would cater for the defendant who currently comes within the second limb of the M'Naghten Rules, that is, the defendant who commits the actus reus of an offence with mens rea, but who is unaware that his actions are wrong in law.

Clause 36 seeks to provide for the defendant who, through mental disorder, acts without the requisite fault element. It states:

'A mental disorder verdict shall be returned if –
(a) the defendant is acquitted of an offence only because, by reason of evidence of mental disorder or a combination of mental disorder and intoxication, it is found that he acted or may have acted in a state of automatism, or without the fault required for the offence, or believing that an exempting circumstance existed; and
(b) it is proved on the balance of probabilities (whether by the prosecution or by the defendant) that he was suffering from mental disorder at the time of the act.'

As the commentary explains, under cl 36:

'... an acquittal is inevitable because the prosecution has failed to prove that the defendant acted with the required fault (or to disprove his defence of automatism or mistake); but the reason for that failure is evidence of mental disorder, and it is proved that the defendant was indeed suffering from mental disorder at the time of the act. This differs from [clause 35 cases] in casting no burden on the defendant of proving his innocence.' (Vol II, para 11.11)

The proposals under the Code envisage either the prosecution adducing evidence of the defendant's mental disorder, or the defendant himself pleading 'not guilty by reason of mental disorder' (cl 37). The prosecution would not be able to adduce such evidence unless the defendant has given or adduced evidence that he acted without the fault required for the offence, or believing that an exempting circumstance existed, or in a state of automatism, or (on a charge of murder) when suffering from mental abnormality as defined in cl 57(2). Whether or not evidence given was to be treated as evidence of mental disorder or automatism would be a question of law for the trial judge.

The definition of 'mental disorder' and associated terms is dealt with by cl 34. Mental disorder is defined as involving:

'... severe mental illness, ... a state of arrested or incomplete development of mind ... a state of automatism (not resulting only from intoxication) which is a feature of a disorder, whether organic or functional and whether continuing or recurring, that may cause a similar state on another occasion ...' The term 'severe mental illness' is itself further explained in clause 34 as involving one or more of the following characteristics:
'(a) lasting impairment of intellectual functions shown by failure of memory, orientation, comprehension and learning capacity;

(b) lasting alteration of mood of such degree as to give rise to delusional appraisal of the defendant's situation, his past or his future, or that of others, or lack of any appraisal;
(c) delusional beliefs, persecutory, jealous or grandiose;
(d) abnormal perceptions associated with delusional misinterpretation of events;
(e) thinking so disordered as to prevent reasonable appraisal of the defendant's situation or reasonable communication with others ...'

For an explanation of references to voluntary intoxication as that phrase is used in the Code, see cl 22, considered below.

14.2 Intoxication

A defendant can become intoxicated, as that term is understood by the criminal law, either through his own voluntary intake of drugs, or through his being forced or tricked into taking drugs. The former is referred to as self-induced intoxication, the latter as involuntary intoxication.

A state of intoxication can arise from the use of any number of stimulants, although those most frequently encountered by the courts are alcohol and hallucinogenics. The defendant seeking to rely on intoxication as a defence will have to provide some evidence that he did not form the necessary intent because of the effect of the intoxicant: see *R* v *O'Connor* [1991] Crim LR 115 and *R* v *Brown and Stratton* [1998] Crim LR 485. The fact that a defendant does something whilst drunk that he would not have done when sober, will not, of itself, give rise to the defence of intoxication. A drunken intent is nevertheless an intent: see *R* v *Bowden* [1993] Crim LR 380.

The problem for the criminal law is in developing a defence of intoxication which recognises the defendant's reduced responsibility for his actions, but which also ensures that the defendant is adequately punished, so as not to encourage the irresponsible use of drugs. As will be seen, the solution developed at common law is not without its shortcomings.

The specific intent/basic intent dichotomy

Self-induced intoxication is not a general defence in criminal law. On the basis of two House of Lords decisions, *DPP* v *Beard* [1920] AC 479 and *DPP* v *Majewski* [1977] AC 142, self-induced intoxication can be raised as a defence where a defendant is charged with a crime of specific intent, but not where the charge involves a crime of basic intent. It is thus essential to be able to distinguish between crimes of specific and basic intent in order to be able to understand the operation of intoxication as a defence.

A basic intent crime is sometimes described as one where the mens rea does not exceed the actus reus. In simple terms this means that the defendant does not have to have foreseen any consequence, or harm, beyond that laid down in the definition of the actus reus. The offence of malicious wounding, contrary to s20 of the Offences

Against the Person Act 1861, provides an example. The actus reus of the offence is obviously wounding. The mens rea, denoted by the term 'malicious', was defined by Diplock LJ, in *R v Mowatt* [1968] 1 QB 421, as involving proof that the defendant foresaw the possibility of some physical harm occurring to the victim, albeit slight. Thus the defendant charged under s20 can be convicted without proof of his having intended to do anything more than wound the victim. Indeed the defendant can be convicted under s20 even if his mens rea falls some considerable way short of intending to wound, eg foresight of the victim being bruised is sufficient.

A specific intent crime, by contrast, is one where in theory the mens rea goes beyond the actus reus. The offence of wounding with intent to do some grievous bodily harm, contrary to s18 of the Offences Against the Person Act 1861, provides an example of such a crime. As with the s20 offence considered above, the actus reus is 'wounding', but by contrast, the defendant must be shown not only to have had the mens rea for wounding, but also a further or 'specific' mens rea, in the form of an intention to do some grievous bodily harm. Hence the reference to the 'mens rea going beyond the actus reus'.

Unfortunately, one cannot apply the above theory to every criminal offence as a determinant of whether it should be classified as one of basic or specific intent, because the law in this area is as much moulded by public policy as it is by coherent legal theory. The result is that some crimes, which in accordance with the above theory should be classified as specific intent crimes, are in fact classified as basic intent, and vice versa. The offence of murder provides a glaring example of this inconsistent approach. The actus reus of the offence is essentially to cause the death of another human being, yet the mens rea does not 'go beyond' this in any way; in fact it is sufficient for the prosecution to prove that the defendant intended grievous bodily harm, ie the mens rea does not even have to go as far as the actus reus, yet murder is treated as a specific intent crime for the purposes of self-induced intoxication. Conversely, the offence of rape contrary to the Sexual Offences (Amendment) Act 1976, might be thought to be one of specific intent, in that it requires proof not only that the defendant intended to have sexual intercourse, but also that he knew that the woman was not consenting or was at least reckless as to this fact. Given the number of rapists who would raise the issue of self-induced intoxication, however, it is not surprising that the courts have dealt with the offence as one of basic intent: see *R v Woods* [1982] Crim LR 42.

The present position might be summarised as follows:

Basic intent crimes
1. common law assault and battery;
2. sections 47, 20 and 23 of the Offences Against the Person Act 1861;
3. manslaughter;
4. rape;
5. 'reckless' criminal damage contrary to s1(1) and (2) of the Criminal Damage Act 1971.

Specific intent crimes
1. murder;
2. sections 18 and 24 of the Offences Against the Person Act 1861;
3. criminal damage with intent to endanger life, contrary to s1(2) of the Criminal Damage Act 1971;
4. sections 1, 8, 9(1)(a), 15, 16, 21, 22 and 25 of the Theft Act 1968;
5. sections 2(1)(b) and 3 of the Theft Act 1978;
6. inchoate offences.

The above is intended as a general guide only, as it will be realised that in the case of certain offences a degree of subtlety is required to determine the distinction. For example, in respect of indecent assault, if the assault is unambiguously indecent, there is no need to prove any mens rea in relation to the indecency, thus the offence would be one of basic intent: see *R* v *C* [1992] Crim LR 642 (D's defence of intoxication disregarded where he had inserted his finger into a child's vagina). Where, however, there is ambiguity regarding the indecent nature of the assault, proof of the defendant's purpose may be relevant: see *R* v *Court* [1989] AC 28. If the defendant's mens rea is sufficiently affected by intoxication his liability should be reduced to that of common assault.

Self-induced intoxication as a defence to crimes of specific intent

Self-induced intoxication will operate as a partial or complete defence to a crime of specific intent, if a defendant can show that he lacked the necessary specific intent due to drink or drugs. The burden rests on the defendant to provide some evidence of intoxication which can be put before the jury; the onus will then be on the Crown to establish beyond all reasonable doubt, that despite such evidence, the defendant still had the necessary mens rea. The effect of a defendant successfully relying on the defence will depend on the nature of the offence with which he is charged.

In the case of murder, the defendant's liability will be reduced to that of the 'lesser included' basic intent crime of manslaughter; similarly wounding with intent reduces to malicious wounding, and s1(2) criminal damage to the s1(1) offence. Where there is no 'lesser included' offence, however, the defendant should be completely acquitted, as would be the case with theft, burglary with intent to steal, and obtaining property by deception.

Self-induced intoxication and basic intent crimes

Where a defendant commits a basic intent crime and there is evidence that he lacked the necessary mens rea through his voluntary taking of drugs, he will not, subject to possible exceptions considered below, be permitted to rely on the evidence of intoxication as negativing his mens rea. The authority for this proposition is the

House of Lords' decision in *DPP* v *Majewski* (above) approving the earlier Court of Appeal decision in *R* v *Lipman* [1970] 1 QB 152.

If a defendant does not have the mens rea required for a basic intent crime, how can the courts justify his conviction and punishment? As Lord Elwyn-Jones LC explained in *DPP* v *Majewski* the 'fault' element is supplied by the defendant's recklessness in becoming intoxicated, this recklessness being substituted for the mens rea that the prosecution would otherwise have to establish.

This approach has had a number of significant consequences. The first is that it is now accepted that where a defendant is charged with a basic intent crime and leads evidence of self-induced intoxication, there is no need for the prosecution to prove that he had mens rea at the time the offence was committed, the defendant's evidence normally being in itself conclusive proof of recklessness. The evidence of self-induced intoxication cannot be relied upon by the defendant to deny intention or foresight because, as a matter of law, it is not relevant evidence within s8 of the Criminal Justice Act 1967 (although see the somewhat exceptional case of *Jaggard* v *Dickinson* [1981] 2 WLR 118).

The second consequence has been the classification of any crime for which 'recklessness' is sufficient mens rea as one of basic intent. The House of Lords' decision in *Commissioner of Police of the Metropolis* v *Caldwell* [1982] AC 341, raised, inter alia, the question of whether self-induced intoxication could be a defence to a charge of causing criminal damage, being reckless as to whether the life of another would be endangered thereby, contrary to s1(2) of the Criminal Damage Act 1971. It was held, by a majority, that whereas self-induced intoxication could be relevant evidence negativing an intention to endanger life by means of criminal damage, it was not relevant where such a charge proceeded on the basis of the defendant's alleged recklessness. It was Lord Diplock's view that the rule in *DPP* v *Majewski* (that the defendant's recklessness in becoming intoxicated supplied the necessary mens rea for the offence in question), applied not only to the recklessness in causing criminal damage, but also the further recklessness as regards the endangering of life. Lord Edmund-Davies, in a powerful dissenting speech, did not seek to detract from the decision in *DPP* v *Majewski*, but saw in it no justification for the extension of its principles to the 'further' intent in crimes such as aggravated criminal damage: see further *R* v *Cullen* [1993] Crim LR 936.

The emphasis in both *Majewski* and *Caldwell*, is on the assumption that the defendant was reckless in voluntarily consuming intoxicants. Such an assumption may be justified in the case of alcohol and other substances which are commonly known to reduce an individual's responsibility for his actions. It would now appear, however, that a distinction should be drawn between such cases, and situations where the defendant has been affected by a substance, voluntarily consumed by him, that would not normally have been expected to have had an adverse effect on his self-control. In *R* v *Hardie* [1985] 1 WLR 64, the Court of Appeal quashed the conviction of the defendant, who had been charged with causing aggravated criminal damage whilst under the influence of valium, following the trial judge's direction to the jury that evidence of such self-induced intoxication was irrelevant to a charge involving a basic intent crime. The court held that the trial judge should have distinguished valium, a sedative, from other types of drugs, such as alcohol, which were widely known to have socially unacceptable side effects. Whilst the voluntary consumption of dangerous drugs might be conclusive proof of recklessness, no such presumption was justified in the case of non-dangerous drugs. The jury should have been directed to consider whether the defendant had been reckless in consuming the valium, in the sense that he had been aware of the risks associated with its consumption, although not necessarily aware of the risk that he would actually commit aggravated criminal damage.

'Dutch courage'

On the basis of Lord Denning's speech in *Attorney-General for Northern Ireland* v *Gallagher* [1963] AC 349 at 382, a defendant who deliberately gets himself drunk in order to overcome his nerves or inhibitions in committing a specific intent crime, cannot later rely on his intoxicated state at the time of the offence as evidence negativing his mens rea. As his Lordship stated:

> 'The wickedness of his mind before he got drunk is enough to condemn him, coupled with the act which he intended to do and did do.'

The decision can be criticised on the ground that mens rea requires proof of a present intention to commit an offence, as opposed to an intention to commit an offence at some time in the future. If, due to his intoxicated state, the defendant did not have the necessary mens rea for murder at the time of the killing, he should have been afforded the defence of intoxication. Conversely, if the defendant was still acting with the purpose of killing his victim, the defence of intoxication would not have been made out, and the defendant could have been convicted of murder.

Drunken mistake

As outlined above, where D is charged with a basic intent crime the jury will be directed that evidence of self-induced intoxication is normally irrelevant to the question of what D believed to be happening. Inevitably this results in the jury having to indulge in some rather artificial mental exercises, as the intoxication may be only too relevant to the commission of the offence. In *R* v *Woods* (1981) 74 Cr App Rep 312 the appellant sought unsuccessfully to appeal against his conviction for rape, following the trial judge's direction to the jury to the effect that self-induced intoxication afforded no defence to the allegation that he was reckless as to whether the complainant consented to sexual intercourse. Despite the fact that s1(2) of the Sexual Offences (Amendment) Act 1976 provides that the jury at a trial for rape has to consider all relevant matters in deciding whether a man believed that a woman was consenting to sexual intercourse, the Court of Appeal held that evidence of self-induced intoxication was to be ignored because it was not relevant evidence. Observing that prior to the enactment of the 1976 Act self-induced intoxication had not been recognised as a defence to rape, Griffiths J continued:

'If Parliament had intended to provide in future that a man whose lust was so inflamed by drink that he ravished a woman, should nevertheless be able to pray in aid his drunken state to avoid the consequences we would have expected them to have used the clearest words to excise such a surprising result which we believe would be utterly repugnant to the great majority of people. We are satisfied that Parliament had no such intention and that this is clear from the use of the word "relevant" [which means] ... in this context, legally relevant. The law, as a matter of social policy, has declared that self-induced intoxication is not a legally relevant matter to be taken into account in deciding as to whether or not a woman consents to intercourse. Accordingly, the appellant's drunkenness was not a matter that the jury were entitled to take into consideration in deciding whether or not reasonable grounds existed for the appellant's belief that the woman consented to intercourse.'

The decision prompts the conclusion that the jury must, therefore, determine the issue by asking whether or not the defendant would have made the mistake in question even if he had been sober, presumably only acquitting if the prosecution fail to disprove this beyond all reasonable doubt. The *Woods* line of reasoning has since been applied to a defendant who drunkenly mistook a woman for his wife and proceeded to have sexual intercourse with her: see *R v Fotheringham* [1988] Crim LR 846.

It would appear that evidence of self-induced intoxication is also irrelevant as regards a defendant's honest belief as to the availability of a common law defence, such as self-defence. In *R v O'Grady* [1987] 3 WLR 321, D had spent a day drinking with P prior to their returning to D's flat where they fell asleep. D was later woken by blows to his head being administered by P and retaliated with what he thought were a few mild blows, after which he fell asleep again. When D woke up again, some time later, he found the body of P who had died from blows to the head. When tried for murder, D claimed that he had been mistaken as to the amount of force that he had needed to use to defend himself because he had been drinking. The trial judge directed the jury that D was entitled to rely on the defence of self-defence, and was to be judged on the facts as he believed them to be, but he was not entitled to go beyond what was reasonable by way of self-defence, and the fact that he might have mistakenly done so due to the effect of drink did not afford him a defence. Rejecting his appeal against conviction for manslaughter, Lord Lane CJ observed:

'[In] ... *R v Williams (Gladstone)* ... the court was ... considering what the situation might be where the mistake was due to voluntary intoxication by alcohol or some other drug. We have come to the conclusion that where the jury are satisfied that the defendant was mistaken in his belief that any force or the force which he in fact used was necessary to defend himself and are further satisfied that the mistake was caused by voluntarily induced intoxication, the defence must fail. We do not consider that any distinction should be drawn on this aspect of the matter between offences involving what is called specific intent, such as murder, and offences of so called basic intent, such as manslaughter ... Though the problem of violent conduct by intoxicated persons is not new to society, it has been rendered more acute and menacing by the more widespread use of hallucinatory drugs ... in *R* v *Lipman* [1970] 1 QB 152 ... the defence ... was put on the grounds that the defendant, because of the hallucinatory drug which he had taken, had not formed the necessary intent to found a conviction for murder, thus resulting in his conviction for manslaughter. If the appellant's contentions here are correct, Lipman could successfully have escaped conviction altogether by raising the issue that he believed he was defending himself legitimately from an attack by serpents. It is significant that no one seems to have considered that possibility.'

In relation to statutory defences based on the defendant's honest, albeit drunken, belief, see *Jaggard* v *Dickinson* (above) and Chapter 11.

Involuntary intoxication

A defendant may seek to raise the defence of intoxication on the basis of his having been forced to ingest intoxicants, or having been deceived into consuming them. If the result is to reduce the defendant to a state of automatism, he should (assuming no prior fault) be able to raise this as a defence to whatever crimes he is alleged to have committed whilst in this state. Where, despite the involuntary or unwitting consumption of intoxicants, the defendant is still aware of his actions, but does not form the necessary intent, he could, in theory, still rely on the defence of intoxication in respect of specific intent crimes, but this might not absolve him from liability completely where the defence operates only to reduce liability to the lesser included basic intent crime. It might be contended that the decision in *Hardie* (above) provides a possible solution, in the sense that where a defendant's intoxication is involuntary he will not have been reckless in consuming the intoxicant, and will thus not have the necessary degree of prior fault for the application of the *Majewski* rule. Notwithstanding the decision of the Court of Appeal in *R* v *Allen* [1988] Crim LR 698, to the effect that the appellant, who consumed a quantity of wine without realising that it had an exceptionally high alcoholic content, could not contend that his resulting intoxication was involuntary, it is submitted that a defendant who honestly, but mistakenly, believes that he is consuming a low, or non-alcoholic drink, should be able to contend that he did not act recklessly in consuming it.

Subject to these observations, the law has, historically, provided little allowance for the victim of involuntary intoxication charged with a basic intent crime, where the effect of involuntary intoxication has been merely to interfere with the defendant's inhibitions, or perception of circumstances and consequences, but not to prevent him from possessing the necessary mens rea for the offence. The leading authority on this issue is now the House of Lords' decision in *R* v *Kingston* [1994] 3 WLR 519. The respondent, a homosexual paedophile who had committed an indecent assault on a 15-year-old boy, claimed that prior to these acts he had been drugged by his co-defendant, and could not recall the incident. There was a difference of medical opinion as to the extent to which the drugs, believed to have been consumed by the respondent, would have affected his ability to recall the incident. However, there was no evidence to suggest that the drugs would have made the respondent do anything he would not have done under normal circumstances. The trial judge ruled that whilst it was not open to the jury to acquit the respondent if they found that his intent to commit the indecent assault had been induced by the surreptitious administration of drugs by his co-defendant, it was open to them to find that secretly administered drugs could negative the respondent's mens rea. The respondent appealed successfully to the Court of Appeal, where it was held that if there was evidence that his inhibitions had been affected by drugs surreptitiously administered by a third party, with the result that he acted upon an intention to commit an act that he might not have had but for the effect of the drugs, he should not bear criminal responsibility for his actions. Lord Taylor CJ expressed the view that the problem was one that could be addressed by turning to first principles. He observed:

> 'The importance of ensuring, under a system of law, that members of the community are safeguarded in their persons and property is obvious and was firmly stated in *DPP* v *Majewski* ... However, the purpose of the criminal law is to inhibit, by proscription and by penal sanction, antisocial acts which individuals may otherwise commit. Its unspoken premise is that people may have tendencies and impulses to do things which are considered sufficiently objectionable to be forbidden. Having paedophiliac inclinations and desires is not proscribed; putting them into practice is. If the sole reason why the threshold between the two has been crossed is or may have been that the inhibition which the law requires has been removed by the clandestine act of a third party, the purposes of the criminal law are not served by nevertheless holding that the person performing the act is guilty of an offence. A man is not responsible for a condition produced "by stratagem, or the fraud of another". If therefore drink or a drug, surreptitiously administered, causes a person to lose his self-control and for that reason to form an intent that he would not otherwise have formed, it is consistent with the principle that the law should exculpate him because the operative fault is not his. The law permits a finding that the intent formed was not a criminal intent or, in other words, that the involuntary intoxication negatives the mens rea.'

Allowing the appeal by the prosecution, the House of Lords treated the case as effectively being one of disinhibition. The drug did not create a desire that had not previously existed, but enabled an existing desire to be released and acted upon. Lord Mustill, with whom the Law Lords agreed, stated that there was no authority for the Court of Appeal's assertion that mens rea was absent where there was no evidence that the respondent was to blame for his intoxicated condition. In his Lordship's view the epithet 'rea' in the expression 'mens rea' referred to the criminality of the respondent's act not its moral blameworthiness. More generally, he felt that there would be difficulties in attempting to reconcile the new defence asserted in the court below with the continued rejection at common law of any defence of irresistible impulse, and expressed fears as to the possibility of spurious defences being raised. In his view justice could be achieved by an appropriate line being taken on sentencing, rather than the creation of a novel defence, although he conceded that difficulties could arise in relation to the mandatory sentence for murder.

The Court of Appeal fell into error by suggesting that an intent induced by the surreptitious administration of narcotics is not mens rea. The Lord Chief Justice regarded the situation as analogous to the defence of duress, ie the defendant does in fact have mens rea, but because of certain circumstances shown to exist should be excused from criminal liability. It is submitted that there should be little surprise that the House of Lords has held back from recognising what would effectively be a new defence (described by Glanville Williams in *Archbold News* 28 May 1993 as a form of exculpatory excuse), given that, as put forward by the respondent, it would be a complete answer to any charge (save perhaps offences of absolute liability), would be subjective in nature, and would require considerable expert evidence as to the effect of the narcotics administered and the psychology of the respondent; see also *R* v *Leslie Davies* [1983] Crim LR 741.

Reform: the Consultation Paper

The Law Commission has devoted considerable time and energy to an examination of proposals for reform of the law relating to intoxication and criminal liability. Its current recommendations are to found in its report *Legislating the Criminal Code: Intoxication and Criminal Liability* (Law Com No 229), but it is also instructive to consider the options for reform that were investigated in the Consultation Paper *Intoxication and Criminal Liability* (Consultation Paper No 127) issued by the Commission prior to the publication of its report.

The Commission's Consultation Paper was critical of the existing law, based upon the House of Lords' decision in *Majewski* (above), on the ground that the examination of the intoxicated defendant's culpability should centre around the issue of whether or not he had mens rea. By contrast, under *Majewski*, the law tries to ensure that the jury does not take into account D's voluntary intoxication when assessing fault for basic intent crimes, despite the fact that most defendants who have taken intoxicants are still capable of performing acts requiring a degree of cognition, usually enough to satisfy the minimum requirements for subjective forms of mens rea. More specific criticisms of the *Majewski* approach were:

1. The decision purports to promote a policy of protecting the innocent citizen against the drunkard, but is patchy in its coverage of offences because the split between specific and basic intent offences is not based on a coherent policy, and not all specific intent offences have a lesser included offence so as to ensure a conviction of D.
2. The inconsistency in the treatment of offences and defences. It was seen as illogical that a jury should consider intoxication in determining whether or not D had the mens rea for murder, but not in relation to whether or not he thought

himself to be acting in self-defence. Similarly, in relation to criminal damage – compare the approach taken by the law to a drunken mistake as to the owner's consent regarding the destruction of the property, and a drunken mistake as to ownership.

3. The impossible task handed to the jury in relation to basic intent crimes if required to assess whether or not D had mens rea *disregarding* evidence relating to his intoxicated state.

The Consultation Paper reviewed the various options for change and rejected the following:

1. The retention or modified codification of *Majewski* because of its stated shortcoming and complexities.
2. The suggestion of the CLRC contained in its 14th Report (1980) (Cmnd 7884) that the *Majewski* principle be limited to offences that can be committed recklessly; ie that D should still be convicted if he would have been aware of a given risk had he been sober. Also rejected was the American Model Penal Code approach which is closely linked to the CLRC proposals.
3. The suggestion that the law should be amended so as to prevent the defendant from putting forward any evidence of voluntary intoxication to negative an element of an offence, with or without the provision of a statutory defence.

The two options favoured by the Commission in its Consultation Paper were:

1. Abolition of the *Majewski* principle without replacement.
   Under this scheme there would be no defence of intoxication, simply an investigation into what mens rea, if any, D had. This is currently the position at common law in Australia and New Zealand. The ordinary rules of mens rea would secure the conviction of all but a very small number of offenders. Underlying this approach is the question of why the existence of evidence of intoxication should reduce the burden on the prosecution of proving all the elements of the offence? Research in Australia conducted subsequent to the adoption of such a rule indicates that there has not been a massive increase in acquittals based on intoxication.
2. A new offence of causing harm whilst deliberately intoxicated that could be charged on its own or as an alternative to an existing offence. If D were charged with, for example, unlawful wounding, the jury would (assuming proof of the external elements) consider whether or not D had the mens rea for the offence. If mens rea was proved D would be convicted of the substantive offence. If fault was not established the jury could consider an alternative verdict in respect of the proposed 'intoxication' offence.
   Liability for the new offence would require proof that D, whilst deliberately intoxicated, committed an act or omission that constituted or caused a listed type of harm. These harms would include homicide, rape, buggery, criminal damage,

indecent assault, causing danger to road users, assaults upon constables and certain public order offences. Inchoate offences such as attempt, and offences of dishonesty would be excluded from the list.

The absence of mens rea in relation to the listed harm would be irrelevant, even if this lack of awareness amounted to automatism.

The term 'intoxicated' in this context would involve proof that D had taken an intoxicant that caused his awareness, understanding or control to be substantially impaired. The requirement of substantial impairment would operate to rule out the coincidental consumption of intoxicants, for example where D commits an offence having consumed one pint of beer at lunchtime.

Intoxication would be deliberate where D took the intoxicant of his own will, and was aware that the quantity involved would or might cause him to become intoxicated, provided that D had not taken the intoxicant solely for medicinal, sedative, or soporific purposes.

A consequence of creating such an offence would be that D should only be permitted to rely on an intoxicated mistake where, viewed objectively, the mistake is one that would have been made by a reasonable person not in a state of intoxication, but otherwise circumstanced as the defendant was.

The paper envisaged a defendant convicted of the intoxicated harm offence being subject to a lower maximum sentence than would have been the case had he not been intoxicated. The imposition of imprisonment would be on the basis that a defendant convicted of the intoxicated harm offence would not be sentenced to a term exceeding two-thirds of what could be imposed for the standard offence, subject to a maximum of ten years' imprisonment.

Reform: the Law Commission's Report

In the light of the above, the recommendations that have emerged in the Law Commission's Report (Law Com No 229) *Legislating the Criminal Code: Intoxication and Criminal Liability* (1995) represent something of a volte-face. The report expresses the view that the *Majewski* approach operates fairly and without undue difficulty, and the main thrust of the report is that the principles in *Majewski* should be codified, subject to some minor clarifications. The Commission states that this change of heart results from the findings of the consultation process, but it is submitted that an ideal opportunity for root and branch reform of an unsatisfactory area of the law has been missed.

If the Commission's proposals were adopted, voluntary intoxication could be relied upon to rebut allegations of specific types of fault, namely intent, purpose, knowledge, belief, fraud and dishonesty. By a process of elimination, therefore, it becomes clear that evidence of voluntary intoxication would not be admissible to rebut allegations of other types of fault (ie recklessness). Clause 1(3) of the proposed draft Bill provides that a person will be treated as having been aware of anything he would have been aware of had he not been voluntarily intoxicated. In a sense this represents an expanded concept of recklessness. D is either aware of a risk, or he would have been aware of it but for the intoxication.

Hence the proposals would abolish the concept of basic and specific intent offences, switching attention to the fault element alleged. This could prove interesting if D were charged on a indictment alleging two counts, one of intentional assault and one of reckless assault. D would be able to plead intoxication as a defence to the intentional assault but not the reckless assault, whereas at present it is regarded as a basic intent crime. In practical terms, however, prosecutors are likely to draft only one count.

Voluntary intoxication is defined in the report as an impairment of awareness understanding or control resulting from the use of a drug or any other substance which has a capacity, when taken into the body, to impair awareness, understanding or control.

The intoxication is to be regarded as voluntary unless:

1. D is unaware of the properties of the substance, or its effects upon him in particular.
2. D takes the substance under duress.
3. D takes the substance as prescribed by a GP.

Where D has taken a mixture of intoxicants, some of which he was aware of and some of which he was unaware of, the report proposes that a court would have to separate out the substances and ask if D, intoxicated only by the 'unknown' substances, would have been aware of the relevant risk. It is submitted that, in the admittedly small number of cases where this problem might arise, it would prove to be a very difficult task for the jury.

In cases of mistaken belief induced by voluntary intoxication, the report proposes that D should not be permitted a defence where the offence with which he is charged is one that can be committed with a fault element of awareness of risk, and he would have been aware of that risk had he not been intoxicated. Note that this would involve a departure from *R* v *O'Grady* (above).

Where D's voluntary intoxication causes automatism, he would (assuming the offence in question is one of recklessness) still be caught under the proposals if, but for the intoxication, he would have been conscious of his actions and aware of the relevant risk.

15

General Defences: Compulsion

15.1 Compulsion – duress of circumstances

15.2 Compulsion – duress per minas and coercion

15.3 Justification – self-defence, prevention of crime and lawful chastisement

15.4 Challenging the validity of the law

15.1 Compulsion – duress of circumstances

Where D pleads the defence of necessity he is in effect saying that he was justified in committing the offence with which he has been charged, because he was acting to prevent a greater evil from transpiring. This type of necessity is sometimes referred to as duress of circumstances because the threat arises from the non-criminal behaviour of a third party, or from some natural cause.

R v *Rodger and Another* [1998] 1 Cr App R 143 confirms that in each case of duress of circumstances the causative feature giving rise to the plea must be something extraneous to D, ie not D's own suicidal tendencies. As Sir Patrick Russell observed, having reviewed the recent authorities on duress of circumstance:

'The feature which was causative of the defendants committing the offence was in all the authorities extraneous to the offender himself. In contrast, in these appeals it was solely the suicidal tendencies, the thought processes and the emotions of the offenders themselves which operated as duress. That factor introduced an entirely subjective element not present in the authorities. ... We do not consider such a development of the law would be justified, nor do we think that such an extension would be in the public interest. If allowed it could amount to a licence to commit crime dependent on the personal characteristics and vulnerability of the offender. As a matter of policy that is undesirable and in our view it is not the law and should not be the law.'

Hence this plea might be raised by the prisoner who escapes from prison because it is on fire, in the belief that he will die if he remains in his cell. It might be raised by D, who does not hold a full driving licence, where he takes control of the car to convey P, the driver who has suffered a heart attack, to a nearby hospital. Whilst all would sympathise with the person who is placed in such a dilemma, the problem for the criminal law is in laying down the boundaries of this excuse. How is the choice between evils to be made? Can the excuse be raised in relation to all offences? A key problem here is the extent to which the approach should be subjective. Is it realistic to allow D to rely on his judgment of what action was warranted by the circumstances? To give way to arguments based on expediency would undermine any attempt by the criminal law to lay down a moral code as to what behaviour is to be expected from adult individuals.

The problem could be resolved by administrative means. Rather than develop a principled defence of necessity, the Crown Prosecution Service (CPS) could develop a policy of not prosecuting in cases where, because of the compelling circumstances under which D acted, it does not feel that a jury would convict. Such a possibility was adverted to by Lord Denning in *Buckoke* v *GLC* [1971] 1 Ch 655, where he observed that, whilst the driver of an emergency vehicle would not be able to plead a defence of necessity if he drove through a red light whilst answering an alarm call, such a person ought to be congratulated rather than prosecuted. In *R* v *Howe* [1987] 2 WLR 568 at 591, Lord Griffiths regarded it as 'inconceivable' that a hijacked woman motorist forced to act as a getaway driver, or a witness forced to give misleading information to the police concerning a robbery or murder, would be prosecuted. In his view they would be the principal witnesses for the prosecution.

The obvious shortcomings of the administrative solution to the problem of duress of circumstances are that justice is not seen to be done, in the sense that the matters are not tried in open court, and there is also the possibility of inconsistency in the application of policy. From an academic perspective, it is also open to criticism on the ground that the courts would be denied the opportunity to develop a coherent set of principles on an important moral issue. To pretend that the problem does not exist is not the proper response from a mature system of criminal law.

The emergence of a common law defence

The English common law has traditionally set its face against the recognition of a defence of necessity, the decision in *R* v *Dudley and Stephens* (1884) 14 QBD 273 (considered below) casting a long shadow in this respect. In cases where the discretion to prosecute was exercised, the courts showed leniency to deserving defendants by resorting to generalised concepts of 'unlawfulness'. Hence in *R* v *Bourne* [1939] 1 KB 687, the defendant gynaecologist, who had performed an abortion on a young girl who had been the victim of a group rape, was found not guilty of the offence under s58 Offences Against the Person Act 1861 (unlawfully procuring a miscarriage), following a direction from the trial judge to the jury that a defendant did not act 'unlawfully' for the purposes of s58, where he acted in good faith, in the exercise of his clinical judgment. It should be noted in this regard that the operation was performed in a public hospital, with the consent of the girl's parents, and without any fee being paid. The case does not provide an authority as such, the jury's verdict having no value as a precedent, but it does stand as an endorsement of the defendant's choice between the prospective life of the foetus and the actual life of the mother.

Since 1986, however, the courts have gradually relaxed the law on the availability of duress of circumstances, to the point where it can now be said that there is a recognised, albeit partial, common law defence of necessity. In *R* v *Willer* (1986) 83 Cr App Rep 225 D had driven recklessly to escape from a crowd of youths who appeared intent upon causing physical harm to the passengers in his car; in *R* v *Conway* [1988] 3 All ER 1025 D had driven recklessly to protect his passenger from what he had honestly believed was an assassination attempt; in *R* v *Backshall* (1998) The Times 10 April D had been convicted of driving without due care and attention in whilst trying to escape from a pedestrian he believed was about to attack him; and in *DPP* v *Bell* [1992] Crim LR 176 D drove his car to escape from pursuers threatening violence despite the fact that he was over the blood-alcohol limit. In each of these cases the Court of Appeal ruled that the appellants should have been permitted to put the defence of necessity before the jury, given the apparent threat of death or bodily harm created by the circumstances.

In *Conway* the court appeared to reject the extension of the defence to offences such as causing death by reckless driving, but this perhaps only serves to raise other questions, such as whether a defendant who causes grievous bodily harm as a result of his reckless driving would be allowed to rely on necessity.

In both *Willer* and *Conway*, the threat of death or serious harm arose from the unlawful acts of a third party. That necessity could arise from the actions of a third party that did not in themselves involve the commission of an offence was subsequently recognised by the Court of Appeal in *R* v *Martin* (1988) 88 Cr App R 343. D drove whilst disqualified following his wife's threats that she would commit suicide if he did not get their son to work on time. In allowing his appeal against conviction the Court of Appeal, following *Conway*, recognised that a defence of necessity could exist if the accused was acting reasonably and proportionately in order to avoid a threat of death or serious injury. If the court was satisfied that this evidential basis existed, the jury should be directed to determine two questions:

1. Was the accused, or may he have been, impelled to act as he did because as a result of what he reasonably believed to be the situation he had good cause to fear that otherwise death or serious physical injury would result? If so;
2. Might a sober person of reasonable firmness, sharing the characteristics of the accused, have responded to that situation by acting as the accused acted? If yes, the jury should acquit.

Some confusion has been created by *DPP* v *Rogers* [1998] Crim LR 202, in which the Court of Appeal (claiming to apply *R* v *Baker and Wilkins* [1997] Crim LR 497) held that the correct approach was reflected in the restatement of the law proposed in cl 26(2) of the Draft Bill annexed to the Law Commissionís Report on Offences Against the Person (Law Com 218) (considered below). But it is submitted that this does not accord with the approach to defences of duress established by the Court of Appeal in *R* v *Graham* and the House of Lords in *R* v *Howe* (both considered below), and for that reason should not be followed.

Baker and Wilkins also rejected the notion that the defence of necessity could be raised in circumstances where the harm that D contemplated and sought to prevent was psychological, as opposed to physical, but this seems overly cautious in the light of the House of Lords' ruling in *R v Ireland; R v Burstow* [1997] 3 WLR 534, to the effect that psychiatric harm could amount to grievous bodily harm: see also *R v Chan-Fook* (1994) 99 Cr App R 147) and comments of Brooke LJ in *DPP v Rogers*.

It will be noted that the development of the defence in the above cases centres exclusively around road traffic offences, and the question inevitably arose as to whether the principles enunciated in these cases could or should be of wider application. The view of Sir John Smith ([1992] Crim LR 176), to the effect that the defence of duress of circumstances should be co-terminus with the defence of duress per minas, has now been vindicated by the Court of Appeal's decision in *R v Pommell* [1995] 2 Cr App R 607. D's house was entered by police officers executing a search warrant. They discovered D in possession of a loaded gun for which he did not possess a firearms certificate. At his trial D sought to raise the defence of duress of circumstance, on the basis that he had been visited in the small hours by a man who intended to carry out a revenge killing on another party. D claimed that he had taken custody of the gun and the ammunition in order to prevent the killing being carried out, and had intended handing over the gun to the police the following day. The trial judge ruled that, even assuming the defence of necessity had been available in such circumstances, D's failure to hand the gun over to the police immediately robbed him of the right to raise the defence, and he was convicted of possessing a prohibited weapon and ammunition without a certificate. Allowing his appeal and ordering a retrial, the Court of Appeal held that the defence of duress of circumstance, as defined in *Martin* (above), was available in relation to all offences with the exception of murder, attempted murder and treason. The continued availability of the defence did depend, however, on D desisting from the commission of the offence as soon as he reasonably could. Whether or not D had done so would be a question for the jury, unless the trial judge was of the view that there was no evidence (ie indicating that the defendant had acted as soon as he reasonably could have) upon which a reasonable jury could act. As to the characteristics of D that will be taken into account in applying the objective test for duress of circumstances: see section 15.2 below.

Homicide and necessity

It will be noted that one of the exceptions concerning the availability of the defence of duress highlighted by the Court of Appeal concerns murder. This exception is based upon the long-standing principle established in *R v Dudley and Stephens*. The defendants, a third man, and a cabin boy, were cast adrift in a boat following a shipwreck. They were some 1,600 miles from land, and had endured over a week without food and water. Dudley and Stephens agreed that as the cabin boy was already weak, and looked likely to die soon, they would kill him and live off his flesh and blood for as long as they could, in the hope that they would be rescued before they themselves died of starvation. Dudley carried out the killing, and all three surviving crew members ate the boy's flesh. A few days later they were rescued by a passing ship. On returning to England, the defendants were charged with murder, the jury returning a special verdict to the effect that if the defendants had not eaten the boy they would probably have died; that the boy would have died in any event, and that at the time of the killing the defendants had had no reasonable prospect of being rescued; but that there had been no greater reason to take the life of the cabin boy than that of any other member of the crew. The special verdict was referred for consideration by the judges of the Queen's Bench Division, where it was held that the defendants were guilty of murder in killing the cabin boy.

Lord Coleridge CJ, having referred to Hale's assertion (1 Hale PC 54) that a man was not to be acquitted of theft of food on account of his extreme hunger, doubted that the defence of necessity could ever be extended to a defendant who killed another to save his own life. After referring to the Christian doctrine of actually giving up one's own life to save others, rather than taking another's life to save one's own, he referred to the impossibility of choosing between the value of one person's life as against another's:

> 'Who is to be the judge of this sort of necessity? By what measure is the comparative value of lives to be measured? Is it to be strength, or intellect, or what? It is plain that the principle leaves to him who is to profit by it to determine the necessity which will justify him in deliberately taking another's life to save his own. In [the present case] the weakest, the youngest, the most unresisting life was chosen. Was it more necessary to kill him than one of the grown men? The answer be, No ...'

The defendants were sentenced to death, but this was commuted to six months' imprisonment.

Whilst the decision reflects a principled moral stance, it is open to criticism for not taking into account the utilitarian arguments that reflect the 'lesser of two evils' approach. Thus, if a motorist driving on a mountain road sees a huge boulder rolling towards his car in which there are four small children, and to avoid the certain death of himself and his passengers he deliberately swerves his car to one side, knowing that he will hit and kill an elderly man standing at the roadside, it will not avail him, when charged with murder, to say that he acted to save five lives at the cost of one, even if the hypothetical reasonable person would have acted in the same way.

Statutory exceptions

In addition to the common law position as now stated in *Pommell* (above), one can also find a number of statutory provisions that have the effect of providing D with a necessity based defence. For example, under s5(2)(b) Criminal Damage Act 1971, a defendant is to be treated as having a lawful excuse for damaging and destroying another's property, contrary to s1(1) of the Criminal Damage Act 1971, if he does so in order to protect other property belonging to himself, or that of another, in the belief that such action must be taken immediately, and that it constitutes reasonable steps by way of protection of the property. An obvious example of where such a provision might be invoked is provided by the fire fighters dealing with a blaze spreading along a row of terraced houses. The only way to stop the fire spreading, and thus causing further harm, might be to dynamite one house in the terrace which is as yet untouched by the fire, so as to form a gap which it is hoped the fire will not cross. The fire fighters would be excused under s5(2)(b), on the basis that they had honestly chosen between the lesser of two evils. Similarly the Infant Life (Preservation) Act 1929, which creates the offence of 'child destruction' in the proviso to s1(1), states:

> 'No person shall be found guilty of an offence under this section unless it is proved that the act which caused the death of the child was not done in good faith for the purpose only of preserving the life of the mother.'

Although the defendant in *R* v *Bourne* (above) was not charged under the 1929 Act, this proviso was referred to the jury as an indication as to how it might deal with the question of whether he had acted unlawfully, and it seems reasonable to assume that a defendant in similar circumstances who was charged under the 1929 Act would also succeed in avoiding liability. Again the defendant's justifiable choice between two evils seems to be the basis of the statutory defence.

Note that s1(4) of the Abortion Act 1967 expressly states that a qualified medical practitioner acting alone can lawfully terminate a pregnancy where:

> '... he is of the opinion, formed in good faith, that the termination is immediately *necessary* to save the life or to prevent grave permanent injury to the physical or mental health of the pregnant woman'.

Reform

The Law Commission's Report *Offences Against the Person and General Principles* (Law Com No 218) contains proposals for reforming and codifying the law relating to duress of circumstances, duress by threats, and the use of force in public or private defence. The DCLB, if enacted, would replace the current common law relevant to these defences. The duress of circumstances defence, illustrated in cases such as *R* v *Pommell* (above), is limited to what the defendant reasonably believed the danger to be, and is assessed by reference to what a person of reasonable firmness would have done. The commentary on the DCLB recognises that, notwithstanding the codification of this defence, there might still be a common law concept of necessity that was more widely drawn, for example where a defendant simply has to make a difficult choice between two courses of action. His will to resist is not 'overborne' as is the case with duress by threats, but the issue still arises as to whether he should be punished because of the choice he has made: see *Smith & Hogan* (8th ed, 1996) p253. To this end, cl 36(2) of the DCLB provides that the defence of duress, whether by threats or of circumstances, is abrogated, but without prejudice to any distinct defence of necessity. It is the Commission's view that a general defence of necessity could be codified if a more detailed and certain common law definition is developed.

Clause 26 of the DCLB proposes the following defence of duress of circumstances:

'(1) No act of a person constitutes an offence if the act is done under duress of circumstances.

(2) A person does an act under duress of circumstance if –

(a) he does it because he knows or believes that it is immediately necessary to avoid death or serious injury to himself or another, and

(b) the danger that he knows or believes to exist is such that in all the circumstances (including any of his personal characteristics that affect its gravity) he cannot reasonably be expected to act otherwise.

It is for the defendant to show that the reason for his act was such knowledge or belief as is mentioned in paragraph (a).

(3) This section applies in relation to omissions as it applies in relation to acts.

(4) This section does not apply to a person who knowingly and without reasonable excuse exposed himself to the danger known or believed to exist.

If the question arises whether a person knowingly and without reasonable excuse exposed himself to that danger, it is for him to show that he did not.

(5) This section does not apply to –

(a) any act done in the knowledge or belief that a threat has been made to cause death or serious injury to himself or another ... or

(b) the use of force within the meaning of [clause 27 or 28] or an act immediately preparatory to the use of force, for the purposes mentioned in [clause 27 or 28].'

Significantly, the proposal envisages a departure from *R* v *Dudley and Stephens*, a move which is inevitable given the Commission's proposals for reforming the law of duress by threats, considered below. Were the case to come before a court following the enactment of cl 26, it would be for the jury to assess the reasonableness of the defendant's action in the circumstances as they believed them to be.

Note that threats to property would not provide a sufficient basis for the defence.

15.2 Compulsion – duress per minas and coercion

Duress per minas and duress of circumstances distinguished

Whereas necessity, or duress of circumstance, is characterised by circumstances such as D driving dangerously to avoid the falling tree, escape from the rapidly spreading fire, or exceeding the speed limit in order to rush an injured child to hospital, duress per minas is characterised by D feeling compelled to commit a particular offence for fear that death or serious injury will be caused by the threatener if he does not comply. Drawing the dividing line between situations that fall within the scope of duress of circumstances, and those that fall within duress per minas, may not always be straightforward. In *R v Cole* [1994] Crim LR 582, D was convicted of committing a number of robberies at building societies, having unsuccessfully sought to adduce evidence that he had acted under duress. His evidence was that he had owed money to men who had threatened him, his girlfriend, and their child with violence if it was not repaid. Dismissing his appeal, the Court of Appeal held that the defence of duress per minas was only made out where the threatener nominated the crime to be committed by D. In D's case the threatener had indicated that he wanted the appellant to repay the debt, an action that, if carried out, would not necessarily involve the commission of an offence. For the appellant to have relied on the defence of duress of circumstances, as that defence had been developed in cases such as *R v Martin* and *R v Pommell* (above), there would have to be a greater degree of directness and immediacy between the danger to the appellant or others and the offence charged. What was required was evidence that the commission of the offence had been a spontaneous reaction to the prospect of death or serious injury.

What does duress involve?

An immediate threat

A defendant wishing to succeed with the defence of duress must provide evidence that he had no reasonable opportunity to avoid having to comply with the demands made upon him. In this sense it is said that the threat that forms the basis of the alleged duress must be immediate. Hence, the bank manager who is told that his wife will be attacked if he does not provide a team of bank robbers with the details of his bank's security system within the next four days, would be unlikely to succeed with the defence of duress, there being at least prima facie evidence that there was a four-day period in which he could have alerted the police. Failure to avail oneself of such protection will not necessarily be fatal to reliance on duress, however. In *R v Hudson and Taylor* [1971] 2 QB 202, the defendants were two young women who gave perjured evidence during a criminal trial after threats had been made to them as to the harm they would suffer if they told the truth. The defendants were convicted of perjury following the trial judge's direction to the jury that the defence of duress was not available because the threat was not sufficiently immediate. Allowing the appeals, Lord Widgery LJ stated that although the law would only permit the defence of duress where the threat was effective at the moment the crime was committed, the fact that the women could have gone to the police before giving evidence did not mean that as a matter of law the defence was not available. The matter should have been left to the jury with a direction that, whilst it was always open to the Crown to show that the defendants had not availed themselves of some opportunity to neutralise the threats, and that this might negate the immediacy of the threat, regard had to be had to the age and circumstances of the accused.

Of what?

It would appear that the defence of duress must be based on threats to kill or do serious bodily harm: see *R* v *Hudson and Taylor* (above). In *DPP for Northern Ireland* v *Lynch* [1975] AC 653, Lord Simon stated obiter, that the law would not regard threats to a person's property as a sufficient basis for the defence. Similarly in *R* v *Valderrama-Vega* [1985] Crim LR 220, threats to reveal the defendant's homosexuality were rejected as insufficiently compelling.

To whom?

Threats to kill or seriously injure the defendant himself will obviously suffice for these purposes. There is authority suggesting that the defence will be available where the threats are made to the defendant's wife and immediate family: see *R* v *Hurley and Murray* [1967] VR 526. It is submitted that provided the threat is sufficiently immediate and compelling, it should not matter whether it is made to the defendant, his family and friends, or a complete stranger. To ration the availability of the defence depending on the defendant's family or social connection with the person threatened would not only introduce unjustified uncertainty, but would involve an assumption that some lives are more worthy of protection than others, contrary to the dicta in *R* v *Dudley and Stephens* (above).

The direction to the jury

The model direction to be given to a jury where the defendant has raised the defence of duress, is that laid down by the Court of Appeal in *R* v *Graham* (1982) 74 Cr App R 235, as subsequently approved by the House of Lords in *R* v *Howe* [1987] 2 WLR 568 (considered below).

The jury should first consider whether or not the defendant was compelled to act as he did because, on the basis of the circumstances as he honestly and reasonably believed them to be, he thought his life was in immediate danger. If the jury concludes that this was not the case, then the defence falls at this stage. If, however, they are of the opinion that the defendant has satisfied this first subjective test, they should then consider the second, more objective test; would a sober person of reasonable firmness sharing the defendant's characteristics have responded in the same way to the threats? The jury should be directed to disregard any evidence of the defendant's intoxicated state when assessing whether he acted under duress, although he may be permitted to raise intoxication as a separate defence in its own right.

The extent to which other factors personal to D may amount to 'characteristics' for the purposes of the objective test has been considered on a number of occasions by the Court of Appeal. On the basis of these decisions it would seem that where the characteristic has no bearing on the defendant's will to resist threats, or is a susceptibility to threats that has been self-induced, or is one that simply makes the defendant more pliable or timid than the person of reasonable fortitude, it will not be taken into account.

In *R* v *Flatt* [1996] Crim LR 576 D, a drug addict, was convicted of possession of prohibited drugs with intent to supply. He claimed that he had been forced to look after the consignment of drugs by a drug dealer to whom he owed money, and who had threatened to shoot members of D's family if he did not cooperate. The trial judge's decision, when dealing with the objective element of the test for duress, not to direct the jury to consider how the reasonable drug addict would have responded to the threats was upheld by the Court of Appeal, either: because there was no reason to suppose that a drug addict would display less fortitude that any other person; or because the mental abnormality induced by addiction was self-induced and therefore excluded on policy grounds. This latter point, whilst consistent with provocation, may seem harsh when compared to the approach taken to drug addiction that causes a permanent condition of mental impairment, eg prolonged alcohol abuse and diminished responsibility, in cases such as *R* v *Tandy* (1988) 87 Cr App R 45.

In *R* v *Bowen* [1996] 2 Cr App R 157 D, who had been charged with a number of offences relating to the obtaining of goods on credit by deception, contended by way of defence that he had been compelled to commit the offences by two men who had threatened to attack his family home with petrol bombs if he did not comply. In directing the jury on the issue of duress per minas the trial judge followed the model direction in *Graham*, but in relation to the characteristics of D to be attributed to the reasonable person refused to accede to defence counsel's argument that D's low intelligence quotient of 69 was a characteristic that could be said to have affected his ability to withstand the threats, or that it was one that might inhibit him in seeking police protection in respect of the threats. Dismissing the appeal, Stuart-Smith LJ for the Court of Appeal observed that, whilst the age and sex of an appellant would be taken into account, and his physical health or disability might be taken into account, mere pliability, timidity or vulnerability (short of a recognised psychiatric impairment) would not of themselves amount to characteristics for the purposes of a *Graham* direction. The decision is largely consistent with the earlier case of *R* v *Hegarty* [1994] Crim LR 353, where D's conviction for robbery was upheld following the trial judge's refusal to admit evidence from two medical witnesses to the effect that D suffered from a 'grossly elevated neurotic state'.

Although comparisons are often drawn between the objective tests for provocation on the one hand and duress on the other, the law in its current state reveals certain key differences. Simply because a characteristic is relevant for the purposes of the objective test in relation to provocation does not mean that it will necessarily be relevant for the purposes of the test for duress. For example, a man might be provoked by taunts relating to his homosexual proclivities and have his homosexuality taken into account as a characteristic, but his homosexuality would be irrelevant in respect of his ability to withstand threatening behaviour for the purposes of the test for duress.

If the Privy Council's ruling in *Luc Thiet Than* v *R* [1996] 3 WLR 45 correctly represents the law (see Chapter 4, section 4.4), mental abnormality such as might affect D's ability to exercise self-control cannot be taken into account as a characteristic for the purposes of provocation. As regards duress, the court in *Hegarty* (above) also doubted whether such characteristics could be attributed to the 'sober person of reasonable firmness' when assessing the second (objective) stage of the *Graham* test, as to do so indicated an inherent contradiction between the assumptions made about the reasonable person, and the personality of D: see further *R* v *Emery* (1993) 14 Cr App Rep (S) 394. In *Bowen* (above), however, Stuart-Smith LJ was willing to accept that a recognised psychiatric impairment could be taken into account if it was such as would generally render those suffering from it more susceptible to pressure and threats, and thus assist a jury in determining whether a reasonable person suffering from such a condition would have been impelled to act as D had. Thus, whilst the defendant relying on provocation is expected (according to the Privy Council) to display the self-control to be expected of the reasonable person, even if he is not capable of achieving this, the defendant relying on duress could be judged according to whether he resisted the threats as well as he could reasonably be expected to given any 'recognised psychiatric impairment' that he was suffering from.

Availability of duress

Duress is considered to be a general defence in criminal law, but there are a number of offences in relation to which it cannot be raised as a defence. On the basis of the Privy Council decision in *Abbott* v *R* [1977] AC 755, duress was not available to a defendant charged with murder as principal, but on the basis of the House of Lords' decision in *DPP for Northern Ireland* v *Lynch* [1975] AC 653, duress was available to a defendant charged as an accomplice to murder. The matter is now governed by the House of Lords' decision in *R* v *Howe* (above), in which it was held (overruling *DPP for Northern Ireland* v *Lynch*) that duress would not be available to a defendant who committed murder either as principal or accomplice. Lord Hailsham expressed the view, which was shared by his fellow judges, that to permit a defendant to kill an innocent person because of the threats that had been made to his own life, would involve the House in overruling *R* v *Dudley and Stephens*, which it was not prepared to do.

The removal of the plainly illogical distinction between principals and accomplices to murder as regards the availability of duress is clearly to be welcomed, but the decision does bring within its wake a number of other anomalies. Duress is still available to a defendant charged with grievous bodily harm contrary to s18 of the Offences Against the Person Act 1861. Such a defendant may have acted with sufficient mens rea for murder, yet if he succeeds with the defence of duress he will be completely acquitted. The difference between the victim living or dying could depend on a whole range of arbitrary factors beyond the control of the defendant, such as the speed with which medical assistance can be summoned, or the availability of a particular blood type for transfusion.

The House of Lords appeared unsure as to whether duress would be available on a charge of attempted murder, but the matter has since been considered by the House of Lords in *R* v *Gotts* [1992] 2 AC 412. In upholding the trial judge's ruling a majority of their Lordships (Lord Keith and Lowry dissenting) held that there was little or no justification for allowing to a defendant charged with attempted murder a defence not available to one charged with the completed crime. The mens rea required for attempted murder was a more culpable state of mind than that required for the completed crime. In most cases, whether the victim lived or died was dependent on arbitrary factors beyond the control of the accused. Despite this ruling, it would appear that duress remains a defence to a defendant charged with wounding with intent contrary to s18 of the 1861 Act, despite the parity of mens rea with the completed offence of murder. By this decision the House of Lords is arguably extending criminal liability in a manner best suited to Parliament; see, in particular, obiter comments by Lord Lowry on this issue (pp439–41).

The decision does not directly address the issue of the availability of duress to a defendant charged with conspiracy to murder, or incitement to commit murder, but the Court of Appeal ([1991] 2 WLR 878) implied that a legitimate distinction could be drawn between the various inchoate forms of liability, in that conspiracy and incitement would be likely to occur at some distance from the completed offence. It is submitted that in such cases, even if the defence of duress is permitted in theory, it may not be established on the facts if there is evidence that the defendant had an opportunity to contact the police and alert them as to the threat that had been made to him.

Criminal association voluntarily joined

In *R* v *Fitzpatrick* [1977] NI 20 the defendant, who had voluntarily joined the IRA, tried to raise the defence of duress to a charge of robbery. He claimed that he had committed the offence following threats that had been made to him by other IRA members if he did not take part. The appeal court held that the trial judge had been correct in withdrawing the defence of duress from the jury. As a matter of public policy the defence could not be made available to those who voluntarily joined violent criminal associations, and then found themselves forced to commit offences by their fellow criminals. To do so would positively encourage terrorist acts, in that the actual perpetrators could escape liability on the ground of duress, and further, it would result in a situation where the more violent and terrifying the criminal gang the defendant chose to join, the more compelling would be his evidence of the duress under which he had committed the offences charged.

Whilst the above was, strictly, only a persuasive authority in English law, it has since been endorsed by the Court of Appeal in decisions such as *R* v *Sharp* [1987] Crim LR 566, and *R* v *Shepard* [1987] Crim LR 686, subject to the proviso that, where D cannot have been expected to foresee that he would be forced to commit offences by his criminal associates, the defence of duress may still be available. The most recent restatement of this principle is to be found in *R* v *Ali* [1995] Crim LR 303. D, who had been was charged with robbing a building society, claimed that he had become addicted to heroin and owed money to X, his supplier, a man he knew to be of a violent disposition. When D had failed to pay X for a consignment of heroin, X had supplied him with a gun and instructed him to get the money the following day by robbing a bank or a building society. X made it clear that a failure to obtain the money would result in D being killed or seriously injured. The Court of Appeal endorsed the trial judge's direction to the effect that, by obtaining heroin from X, D might have put himself in a position where he knew that he was likely to be forced to commit a crime by X. Presumably the act of X in supplying a gun, and specifying that D should obtain the money owed by robbing a bank or building society, was sufficient to substantiate D's case that he had been ordered to commit an offence by X, ie duress per minas. *R* v *Cole* [1994] Crim LR 582 suggests how the court might have dealt with the case if the evidence had been that X had supplied the gun and stated 'get the money!'.

Superior orders

In English criminal law the absence of any general defence of superior orders means that D cannot rely on the fact that his commission of an offence resulted from his carrying out the instructions of his employer, a police officer, or a military officer of higher rank. The authorities may decide not to prosecute in such cases, but that is a matter of administrative justice, rather than substantive law. It is conceivable that one acting under superior orders might be induced to make a genuine mistake of civil law, such as a claim of right, that might negative the mens rea of an offence, but any acquittal would result from the absence of fault, not a substantive defence. In *Yip Chiu-Cheung* v *R* [1994] 3 WLR 514, Lord Griffiths, denying the existence of a defence based upon superior orders at common law, cited with approval the dictum of Gibbs CJ in the Australian case of *A* v *Hayden (No 2)* (1984) 156 CLR 552, to the effect that:

> 'It is fundamental to our legal system that the executive has no power to authorise a breach of the law and that it is no excuse for an offender to say that he acted under the orders of a superior officer.'

Lord Griffiths was of the view that this statement was of equal validity as regards the laws of Hong Kong and England.

Coercion

At common law a wife was permitted to raise the defence of marital coercion in respect of some crimes committed in the presence of her husband. The presumption was that she had acted under the orders of her husband. Although that presumption was abolished by s47 of the Criminal Justice Act 1925, the defence is still available. On the basis of *R* v *Shortland* [1995] Crim LR 893, the defence of marital coercion can be said to be wider in its ambit than duress per minas, in that it encompasses situations where D is subject to moral pressure, as well as threats of physical harm. D was acquitted, on appeal, of offences of making false statements in order to procure a passport, following the trial judge's failure to distinguish adequately between marital coercion and duress per minas. The court held that the defence of marital coercion did not require proof of any physical force having been used or threatened against D. The court endorsed the approach taken in *R* v *Richman and Richman* [1982] Crim LR 507, where Hutton J had stated that:

> 'Coercion did not necessarily mean physical force or the threat of physical force, it could be physical, or moral, [the wife raising the defence] had to prove that her will was overborne by the wishes of her husband ... coercion was different from persuading someone out of loyalty ...'

Reform

The proposals contained in the DCLB relating to duress by threats are based on cl 42 of the Draft Code, although the matter has been under consideration by the Law Commission since 1974 (Working Paper No 55). The Commission proposes that duress by threats should remain as a 'true' defence (in other words, not a factor that simply mitigates punishment) and relieve the defendant of all liability (that is, not reduce murder to manslaughter), and that the defendant should be required to establish duress on the balance of probabilities. The codified defence would have as its guiding principle

> 'the reasonable reaction of the defendant in the circumstances as he or she believed them to be' (Law Com No 218, para 29.7).

The proposal does not specify to whom the threats must be made, but the closer the connection between the defendant and the person threatened, the greater the evidence of compulsion to act.

Clause 25 of the DCLB provides:

> '(1) No act of a person constitutes an offence if the act is done under duress by threats.
> (2) A person does an act under duress by threats if he does it because he knows or believes –
> (a) that a threat has been made to cause death or serious injury to himself or another if the act is not done, and
> (b) that the threat will be carried out immediately if he does not do the act or, if not immediately, before he or that other can obtain official protection; and
> (c) that there is no other way of preventing the threat being carried out,
> and the threat is one which in all the circumstances (including any of his personal circumstances that affect its gravity) he cannot reasonably be expected to resist.
> It is for the defendant to show that the reasons for his act was such knowledge or belief as is mentioned in paragraphs (a) to (c).

(3) This section applied in relation to omissions as it applies in relation to acts.
(4) This section does not apply to a person who knowingly and without reasonable excuse exposed himself to the risk of the threat made or believed to have been made.
If the question arises whether a person knowingly and without reasonable excuse exposed himself to such a risk, it is for him to show that he did not.'

As to the state of mind of a defendant seeking to bring himself within the scope of the restated defence, the Code Report commentary on what was cl 42 of the Draft Code provides this explanation:

'The emphasis in ... [what is now clause 25(2) of the DCLB] on the actor's knowledge or belief reflects the fact that a defence of duress depends essentially upon a state of mind. In this respect the clause somewhat departs from the prevailing judicial view, according to which a person's belief in the existence of a threat must be "reasonably" held if it is to found the defence. This requirement would, we believe, be inconsistent with the tendency of judicial developments in other contexts [See especially in the context of defences: *Gladstone Williams* (1983) 78 Cr App R 276; *Beckford* v *The Queen* [1988] AC 130]. It would also be at odds with the general policy of the Code, in keeping with those developments, of assigning the reasonableness of a person's asserted belief to the domain of evidence.' (Vol II, para 12.15)

The Commission remains convinced that the defence of duress should reflect the subjectivist approach to defences (Law Com No 218, paras 29.8–29.10).

The Commission has re-affirmed its view that a person's 'firmness' is itself one of his characteristics that may affect the gravity of the threat to him, and remains unconvinced that personal characteristics can be separated in the way that the *Graham* test suggests (Law Com No 218, paras 29.11–29.14).

The most significant departure from the common law signalled by cl 25 is the availability of duress by threats where the defendant is charged with murder. Enactment of the clause would clearly nullify the effect of *Abbott* v *R, R* v *Howe* and *R* v *Gotts.*

The Commission was aware of the cogent arguments against such a change, namely that the State should not sanction deliberate killing, and that the defence might be used in terrorist or organised crime cases, but felt that the counter-arguments outweighed these objections. In particular the Commission felt that:

1. The defendant's failure to attain an heroic level of behaviour should not justify punishment by the state.
2. The simple moral equation derived from *Dudley and Stephens* broke down where the defendant sought to avoid the implementation of threats to a third party, for example where D threatens to kill X unless Z kills Y. In such cases Z is not taking a life in order to preserve his own, but is being forced to choose between the lives of others.
3. Fairness to the defendant who kills under duress by threats could not be achieved by executive discretion regarding the decision to prosecute.
4. The defence should not be denied to the innocent simply because terrorists might seek to rely on it.

15.3 Justification – self-defence, prevention of crime and lawful chastisement

Both the common law and statute recognise that there are situations where D may be justified in using reasonable force. These situations are normally examined under the all embracing heading of self-defence but, as will be explained, such a generic term is likely to give a misleading impression of the scope of the defence.

The protection of oneself at common law

The basic proposition is that an individual can use force that is reasonable in the circumstances to defend himself from an attack by another. The concept of reasonableness is obviously somewhat flexible, and will clearly vary with the circumstances. Commenting on the need for some degree of proportionality between the attack and the response, Lord Morris in *Palmer* v *R* [1971] AC 814 observed:

'It may in some cases be only sensible and clearly possible to take some simple avoiding action. Some attacks may be serious and dangerous. Others may not be. If there is some relatively minor attack, it would not be common sense to permit some action of retaliation which was wholly out of proportion to the necessities of the situation.'

The courts will not permit a defendant to rely on the defence where the danger has ceased to exist. The law distinguishes between self-defence and revenge. In assessing the reasonableness of D's actions, Lord Morris observed that the jury might have to be prepared to permit him some margin of appreciation:

'If there has been attack so that defence is reasonably necessary, it will be recognised that a person defending himself cannot weigh to a nicety the exact measure of his necessary defensive action. If a jury thought that in a moment of unexpected anguish a person attacked had only done what he honestly and instinctively thought was necessary, that would be most potent evidence that only reasonable defensive action had been taken. A jury will be told that the defence of self-defence, where the evidence makes its raising possible, will fail only if the prosecution show beyond doubt that what the accused did was not by way of self-defence.'

It is clear that there is an evidential burden on D, to the extent that he will have to provide the court with evidence indicating that he was threatened, but to what extent must he show that he did everything within his power to avoid having to use force, for example, by seeking to escape from the perceived threat? The matter was considered in *R* v *Julien* [1969] 1 WLR 839, 843 by Widgery LJ, who commented that:

'It is not, as we understand it, the law that a person threatened must take to his heels and run ... but what is necessary is that he should demonstrate by his actions that he does not want to fight. He must demonstrate that he is prepared to temporise and disengage and perhaps to make some physical withdrawal; and that that is necessary as a feature of the justification of self-defence is true, in our opinion, whether the charge is a homicide charge or something less serious.'

These comments were subsequently cited with approval in *R* v *McInnes* [1971] 1 WLR 1600 by Edmund-Davies LJ, who added that:

> '... a failure to retreat is only an element in the considerations upon which the reasonableness of an accused's conduct is to be judged ... a factor to be taken into account in deciding whether it was necessary to use force, and whether the force used was reasonable ...'

Where the attack upon D involves the commission of a criminal offence, as it will normally do, D may also rely on the statutory right to use reasonable force to prevent the commission of a offence: see s3(1) Criminal Law Act 1967 (below).

The protection of others at common law

The common law principle extends to a defendant who uses reasonable force to protect others from physical attack; see by way of illustration *R* v *Rose* (1884) 15 Cox CC 540, where D was acquitted of murder on the grounds of self-defence, having shot dead his father who had launched a murderous attack on D's mother. Any uncertainty as to whether the common law defence was limited to defendants who acted to protect those they were closely related to was removed by the decision in *R* v *Duffy* [1967] 1 QB 63.

Again, where the attack involves the commission of a criminal offence, D may also rely on the statutory right to use reasonable force to prevent the commission of an offence: see s3(1) Criminal law Act 1967 (below).

The protection of one's property at common law

An individual could, at common law, use reasonable force to defend his property. At one time (eg *R* v *Hussey* (1924) 18 Cr App R 160) it was thought that D could use lethal force to prevent P from dispossessing him of his property. The modern view is, however, that this would probably exceed what was reasonable. The situation has in any event been altered by the intervention of Parliament. Once again the Criminal Law Act 1967 will be relevant, as in most cases that come before the courts D will be acting to prevent a criminal offence in relation to his property, namely theft, criminal damage, or burglary. Note that if a householder decides that he is going to use force to prevent a burglary from being committed, he might, unwittingly, be entitling the burglar to use reasonable force to defend himself, if the householder uses excessive force; but see *R* v *Mason* (1756) Fost 123.

D may also rely on provisions of the Criminal Damage Act 1971 (see Chapter 11) where he destroys property belonging to another in the honest belief that such destruction is necessary in order to protect his own property – for example, where D breaks the window of P's car so that D can retrieve his dog which has been locked inside and is suffering from the effects of heat.

The Criminal Law Act 1967

Section 3(1) of the 1967 Act states that a person may use such force as is reasonable in the circumstances to prevent crime, assist in or effect the lawful arrest of suspected offenders or others unlawfully at large. The effect of the defence succeeding is that D escapes both civil and criminal liability in respect of his actions; they cease to be unlawful.

As has been noted above, s3(1) covers much of the ground previously covered by the common law, and s3(2) goes on to state that subs(1) 'shall replace the rules of the common law on the question of when force used for a purpose mentioned in the subsection is justified by that purpose.'

The effect is that s3(1) provides a justification for the use of force in circumstances where the common law might not have applied. For example, in relation to 'victimless' crimes D can now use reasonable force to prevent the commission of drugs offences, offences related to the possession and distribution of pornography and offences related to public morality. Further, D can use force to prevent criminal damage being caused to public property, such as bus shelters, or street furniture, even though he has no direct interest as an owner.

It is assumed that the statutory concept of reasonable force does not differ in any material respects from that developed at common law.

Availability and effect of the defences

Self-defence, whether in its common law form, or under s3 of the 1967 Act, can be raised by way of defence to any offence, including murder. At first blush this may seem anomalous, in light of the case law dealing with duress, given that if D is faced with a murderous attack being launched by P, and D kills P to prevent it, D has chosen to save his own life at the cost of P's. The distinction, or course, is that in the self-defence situation, the life taken is not 'innocent' in the sense that P is engaged in criminal activity. Nevertheless an interesting academic question arises where P is a child under the age of ten, or an adult in a state of automatism.

If D successfully relies on the defence of self-defence he will be acquitted, not on the basis that he did not commit the actus reus, or possess the mens rea for the offence, but on the basis that his actions were justified. If D is entitled to use force but uses more than is reasonably necessary in the circumstances the defence fails entirely. Hence, where D kills intentionally and is found to have used excessive force in circumstances where reasonable force would have been permitted, he will be guilty of murder, not manslaughter. Given that murder carries a mandatory life sentence the law may be thought to be somewhat inflexible, if not harsh in its operation. It becomes an 'all or nothing' situation for the defendant. The House of Lords, in *R v Clegg* [1995] 2 WLR 80, reaffirming that where the use of excessive force resulted in death the correct conviction was one for murder, expressed the view that no valid distinction was to be drawn between death resulting from excessive force used in self-defence and similar force used in the prevention of crime, and no exception could be recognised in the case of soldiers or police officers acting in the course of duty. The House recognised the weight of the arguments in favour of recognising a partial defence based upon the use of excessive force, that would reduce D's liability to manslaughter, but declined the opportunity to change the law on this point on the ground that to do so would involve a usurpation of the role of the legislature.

Where D mistakenly acts in self-defence or to prevent crime

In *R* v *Williams (Gladstone)* (1983) 78 Cr App R 276 a man named Mason had seen a youth trying to rob a woman in the street, and had chased him, eventually knocking him to the ground. The appellant, who had not witnessed the robbery, then came on the scene and was told by Mason that he was a police officer (which was untrue). When Mason failed to produce a warrant card a struggle ensued, the appellant being charged with an offence under s47 of the Offences Against the Person Act 1861. At his trial he claimed that he had mistakenly believed that Mason was unlawfully assaulting the youth and had intervened to prevent any further harm, but was convicted following the trial judge's direction to the jury that his mistake could only afford a defence if it was both honest and reasonable. The Court of Appeal held that *DPP* v *Morgan* [1976] AC 172 should be followed in such cases, and quashed the conviction on the basis that the jury should have been directed to consider the facts as the appellant believed them to be, no matter how unreasonable his belief might have been. One might question the extent to which the Court of Appeal was justified in taking a doctrine developed to deal with mistake as to an element of an offence and applying it without modification to mistakes relating to the availability of defences, but the decision was subsequently approved by the Privy Council in *Beckford* v *R* [1987] 3 WLR 611, where the defendant police officer who had shot dead a suspect, having been told that he was armed and dangerous, was held to be entitled to be judged on the facts as he honestly perceived them to be. Lord Griffiths (having referred to *DPP* v *Morgan*) observed:

> 'There may be a fear that the abandonment of the objective standard demanded by the existence of reasonable grounds for belief will result in the success of too many spurious claims of self-defence. The English experience has not shown this to be the case. The ... model direction on self-defence which is now widely used by judges when summing up to juries contains the following guidance:
>
>> "Whether the plea is self-defence or defence of another, if the defendant may have been labouring under a mistake as to the facts, he must be judged according to his mistaken belief of the facts: that is so whether the mistake was, on an objective view, a reasonable mistake or not."'

Even though the test for mistaken belief is subjective there must still be adequate evidence of such a belief for the matter to be left before the jury. Where the defendant's explanations are too fanciful to be seriously considered the trial judge may decline to direct the jury on the matter: see *R* v *Oatridge* [1992] Crim LR 205. In extreme cases it may be that the defendant's evidence of mistaken belief indicates the possibility of insanity, an issue that the prosecution would be entitled to raise since the defendant would have put his state of mind in question.

The decisions in *Williams* and *Beckford* are primarily concerned with situations where D is mistaken as to the circumstances giving rise to the need to use force, as for example where D's son unexpectedly returns home in the middle of the night and D attacks him wrongly believing him to be a burglar. An alternative possibility is that D does have legitimate grounds for using force, but is mistaken as to the amount of force that is needed to deal with the situation. Beldam J, giving the judgment of the Court of Appeal in *R* v *Scarlett* [1993] 4 All ER 629, seemed to suggest that a mistake as to the amount of force required, albeit an unreasonable one, ought to relieve D of liability. As he put it:

> '[The jury] ought not to convict him unless they are satisfied that the degree of force used was plainly more than was called for by the circumstances as he believed them to be and, provided he believed the circumstances called for the degree of force used, he is not to be convicted even if his belief was unreasonable.'

Taken at face value this is a rather alarming assertion, appearing as it does to remove any objective element from the test for self-defence. It should, however, be considered in the light of the subsequent ruling in *R* v *Owino* [1996] Cr App R 128 where Collins J explained the decision in these terms:

> 'What [Beldam J] was not saying, in our view ... was that the belief, however ill-founded, of the defendant that the degree of force he was using was reasonable, will enable him to do what he did ... if that argument was correct, then it would justify, for example, the shooting of someone who was merely threatening to throw a punch, on the basis that the defendant honestly believed, although unreasonably and mistakenly, that it was justifiable for him to use that degree of force. That clearly is not, and cannot be, the law.'

Given the decisions in respect of D who mistakenly believes in circumstances that, if true, would justify the use of reasonable force by way of self-defence, it should be the case that D is permitted to use reasonable force to prevent what he honestly, albeit unreasonably, believes to be the commission of a criminal offence. The Court of Appeal's decision in *R* v *Baker and Wilkins* [1997] Crim LR 497, however, suggests that s3 cannot be relied upon unless there is some objective evidence that an offence is being committed. If this view is followed unfairness could result. For example, suppose D sees P breaking into a house. Unknown to D it is in fact P's own house and he is breaking in because he has lost his key. If D uses force to restrain P is he to be denied reliance on s3 in answer to an assault charge because no offence was actually being committed by P? Surely his honest belief that an offence was being committed provides the basis for the defence?

Reform

Clause 27 of the DCLB provides:

'(1) The use of force by a person for any of the following purposes, if only such as is reasonable in the circumstances as he believes them to be, does not constitute an offence –
(a) to protect himself or another from injury, assault or detention caused by a criminal act;
(b) to protect himself or (with the authority of that other) another from trespass to the person;
(c) to protect his property from appropriation, destruction or damage caused by a criminal act or from trespass or infringement;
(d) to protect property belonging to another from appropriation, destruction or damage caused by a criminal act or (with the authority of the other) from trespass or infringement; or
(e) to prevent a crime or a breach of the peace.
(2) The expressions "use of force" and "property" in subsection (1) are defined and extended by sections 29 and 30 respectively.
(3) For the purposes of this section, an act involves a "crime" or is "criminal" although the person committing it, if charged with an offence in respect of it, would be acquitted on the ground that –
(a) he was under ten years of age, or
(b) he acted under duress, whether by threats or of circumstances, or
(c) his act was involuntary, or
(d) he was in a state of intoxication, or
(e) he was insane, so as not to be responsible, according to law, for his act.
(4) The references in subsection (1) to protecting a person or property from anything include protecting him or it from its continuing; and the reference to preventing crime or a breach of the peace shall be similarly construed.
(5) For the purposes of this section the question whether the act against which force is used is of a kind mentioned in any of paragraphs (a) to (e) of subsection (1) shall be determined according to the circumstances as the person using the force ("D") believes them to be.
In the following provisions of this section references to unlawful or lawful acts are to acts which are or are not of such a kind
(6) Where an act is lawful by reason only of a belief or suspicion which is mistaken, the defence provided by this section applies as in the case of an unlawful act, unless –
(a) D knows or believes that the force is used against a constable or a person assisting a constable; and
(b) the constable is acting in the execution of his duty,
in which case the defence applies only if d believes the force to be immediately necessary to prevent injury to himself or another.
(7) The defence provided by this section does not apply to a person who causes conduct or a state of affairs with a view to using force to resist or terminate it.
But the defence may apply although the occasion for the use of force arises only because he does something he may lawfully do, knowing that such an occasion may arise.'

In addition cl 28 provides:

'(1) The use of force by a person in effecting or assisting in a lawful arrest, if only such as is reasonable in the circumstances as he believes them to be, does not constitute an offence.
(2) The expression "use of force" in subsection (1) is defined and extended by section 29.

(3) For the purposes of this section the question whether the arrest is lawful shall be determined according to the circumstances as the person using the force believed them to be.'

The use of force is defined by cl 29, which provides:

'(1) For the purposes of sections 27 and 28 –
(a) a person uses force in relation to another person or property not only where he applies force to, but also where he causes an impact on, the body of that person or that property;
(b) a person shall be treated as using force in relation to another person if –
(i) he threatens him with its use, or
(ii) he detains him without actually using it; and
(c) a person shall be treated as using force in relation to property if he threatens a person with its use in relation to property.'

The clause goes on to provide that its provisions apply equally to acts immediately preparatory to the use of force, and states that a threat of force may be reasonable although the actual use of force would not be. The possibility of retreat prior to the use of force is a factor to be taken into account when determining whether the use of force was reasonable. Clause 30 defines property, for the purposes of the defence, in terms similar to those used in s10 of the Criminal Damage Act 1971.

Lawful chastisement

At common law parents or those in loco parentis (such as a school teacher), can use reasonable force to control and discipline children, subject to the proviso that force should not be administered for the gratification of rage or passion: *R* v *Hopley* (1860) 2 F & F 202. Corporal punishment in schools has effectively been outlawed by the combined effect of s47 of the Education (No 2) Act 1986 and s293 of the Education Act 1993. A parent disciplining a child who is, as a result, charged with assault may be able to raise the common law defence of lawful chastisement, it being for the prosecution to prove that an assault exceeds what is required by way of lawful punishment. For how much longer this remains the case is open to question in the light of the ruling in *A* v *UK* (1998) The Times 1 October. The applicant had been beaten with a stick by his stepfather. At the stepfather's trial on a charge of causing actual bodily harm contrary to s47 of the Offences Against the Persons Act 1861 the jury returned a verdict of not guilty following the stepfather's assertion that his actions had been reasonable chastisement in the circumstances. The European Court of Human Rights held that UK law failed to provide sufficient protection to children in this regard, resulting in a violation of art 3 of the European Convention on Human Rights, which prohibits torture, inhuman and degrading treatment. Whether treatment reached the minimum level of severity necessary to trigger the operation of art 3 depended on the circumstances. Where the victim was a child, the minimum threshold would be more easily attained. The obligation to prevent this happening lay with the state. Whilst the Ccourt accepted that the United Kingdom could not be held responsible for the actions of the applicant's stepfather, it was responsible for a system of criminal law that allowed a person inflicting serious harm upon a child to be acquitted on the grounds that the harm was justifiable chastisement. On this basis the Court concluded that the United Kingdom had failed to adequately safeguard the applicant against treatment that was contrary to art 3.

15.4 Challenging the validity of the law

A defendant may seek to defend himself in criminal proceedings by contending that the law the prosecution seeks to enforce is invalid or at least incompatible with a supervening provision. Following the House of Lords' ruling in *Boddington* v *British Transport Police* [1998] 2 All ER 203, where the prosecution alleges that the defendant has committed an offence created by subordinate legislation, typically in the form of a bye-law, the defendant should be allowed to raise, by way of defence, the contention that the bye-law is ultra vires its parent Act, unless there is clear evidence in the relevant statute that some other procedure should be used to question the validity of the proceedings (see for example *R* v *Wicks* [1997] 2 All ER 801).

Reliance on EC law

The United Kingdom became a member of the European Communities with effect from 1 January 1973, by virtue of the Treaty of Accession 1972 as incorporated by the European Communities Act 1972. By virtue of s2(1) of the 1972 Act the provisions of the various Treaties 'are without further enactment to be given legal effect or used in the United Kingdom shall be recognised and available in law, and be enforced, allowed and followed accordingly ...'. In the event of an apparent incompatibility between domestic law and EC law, s2(4) applies to the effect that domestic law should be construed and have effect subject to directly applicable EC law: see further *Macarthys Ltd* v *Wendy Smith* [1979] 3 All ER 325: and *Garland* v *British Rail Engineering Ltd* [1983] 2 AC 751. The possibility arises, therefore, that a defendant might face prosecution for non-compliance with a domestic penal provision that is incompatible with EC law: see for example *Pubblico Ministero* v *Ratti* [1979] ECR 1629, where Ratti was allowed to rely on an EC directive when defending criminal proceedings regarding the correct labelling of dangerous solvents. If a court is in doubt as to whether the application of EC law provides a defendant with a lawful justification for his actions it can refer the matter to the European Court of Justice under art 234 (formerly 177) EC Treaty. In *Conegate Ltd* v *Customs & Excise* [1987] QB 254 the customs authorities relied upon art 30 EC Treaty (formerly art 36 – prohibition of imports on the grounds of public morality) to justify the seizure of a consignment of inflatable rubber women imported in to the United Kingdom by Conegate Ltd. On a reference under what is now art 234 EC

Treaty the European Court of Justice held that the seizure was not justified because the manufacture and supply of such items within the United Kingdom was not prohibited by domestic law.

EC law as a justification is further recognised in cl 45 of the DCCB, which provides, inter alia, that 'A person does not commit an offence by doing an act which is justified or excused by ... and "enforceable Community right" as defined in section 2(1) of the European Communities Act 1972 ...'.

Reliance on the European Convention on Human Rights

Towards the end of 1999, or early in the year 2000, the Human Rights Act 1998 will come into effect, incorporating certain of the rights provided for under the European Convention of Human Rights. Under s7(1)(b) of the 1998 Act litigants will be allowed to 'rely on the Convention right ... in any legal proceedings' including, for these purposes 'proceedings brought by or at the instigation of a public authority; and ... an appeal against the decision of a court or tribunal': s7(6)(a) and (b). A court or tribunal called upon to do so, must interpret primary legislation and subordinate legislation 'in a way which is compatible with the Convention rights': see s3(1). This duty applies whether the legislation was enacted before or after the coming into force of the Human Rights Act 1998. Section 2(1) of the 1998 Act makes it clear that any court or tribunal determining a question arising in connection with a Convention right must take into account: any judgment, decision, declaration or advisory opinion of the European Court of Human Rights; any opinion of the Commission given in a report adopted under art 31 of the Convention; any decision of the Commission in connection with arts 26 or 27(2) of the Convention; or any decision of the Committee of Ministers taken under art 46 of the Convention, 'whenever made or given, so far as, in the opinion of the court or tribunal, it is relevant to the proceedings in which that question has arisen.' A court, as a public body will be obliged to act in a manner that is consistent with the Convention rights and will be empowered to grant any remedy that is within its normal powers to ensure that this is the case. Hence a criminal court, having heard submission from a defendant based on the 1998 Act, will be able to stay proceedings if it is satisfied that this is appropriate and just. The court may adopt such a course of action where the defendant establishes that his actions were justified in terms of the rights protected by the 1998 Act, or where it is shown that the substantive criminal law is inconsistent with the Convention rights. Following incorporation it will be incumbent upon any defendant, seeking to take a case to Strasbourg, to show that he raised the issue of non-compliance in the relevant domestic criminal proceedings. If a defendant establishes that a provision in a domestic statute is incompatible with the rights protected under the 1998 Act the House of Lords, the Judicial Committee of the Privy Council, the Courts-Martial Appeal Court, or the High Court or the Court of Appeal, will be empowered to grant a declaration of incompatibility. Where such a declaration is made it does not 'affect the validity, continuing operation or enforcement of the provision in respect of which it is given; and … is not binding on the parties to the proceedings in which it is made': s4(6). The relevant minister may then, if he considers that there are compelling reasons for so doing, make orders to amend the relevant legislation to the extent that considers necessary to remove the incompatibility: see s10(1) and (2).

16

Recent Cases

16.1 The protection of life

16.2 Sexual offences and consent

16.3 Theft

16.4 Criminal damage

16.5 Accessorial and vicarious liability

16.1 The protection of life

R v Smith (Morgan) [1998] 4 All ER 387 Court of Appeal (Criminal Division) (Rose LJ, Potts and Douglas Brown JJ)

Provocation – characteristics to be taken into account when assessing the self-control expected from the reasonable person

Facts

The defendant argued with P and stabbed him a number of times. P died from his injuries and D was charged with murder. At his trial he put forward the defence of provocation and sought to have his severe depression taken into account for the purposes of assessing how a reasonable person sharing the characteristics of the accused would have reacted. The trial judge ruled that the reasonable person could only be imbued with the characteristic of severe depression for the purposes of assessing the gravity of the provocation to the defendant, not for the purposes of assessing whether the reasonable person would have lost his self-control. The defendant was convicted of murder and appealed.

Held

The appeal was allowed. The defendant's conviction for murder was quashed and a conviction for manslaughter substituted. The Court of Appeal confirmed that when attributing characteristics of the accused to the reasonable person for the purposes of the objective test in provocation, no distinction was to be drawn between characteristics that related to the gravity of the provocation and those that related to reasonable person's reaction to the provocation. Potts J expressed the view that this conclusion was not inconsistent with the speech of Lord Diplock in *DPP* v *Camplin* [1978] AC 705. In particular, he cited Lord Diplock's comments at p718 to the effect that:

'... a proper direction to a jury ... would be on the following lines. The judge should state what the question is, using the very terms of the section. He should then explain to them that the reasonable man referred to in the question is a person having the power of self-control to be expected of an ordinary person of the sex and age of the accused, but in other respects sharing such of the accused's characteristics as they think would affect the gravity of the provocation to him and that the question is not merely whether such a person would in like circumstances be provoked to lose his self-control *but also would react to the provocation as the accused did* ...' (emphasis added by Potts J).

Potts J also sought support from the dissenting advice of Lord Steyn in *Luc Thiet Thuan* v *R* [1997] AC 131, who in turn cited from Lord Simon's speech in *Camplin* where (at pp724–725) he observed:

'... it is one thing to invoke the reasonable man for the standard of self-control which the law requires; it is quite another to substitute some hypothetical being from whom all mental and physical attributes (except perhaps sex) have been abstracted.'

Potts J agreed with the view expressed by Lord Steyn in *Luc* to the effect that Lord Simon's views were inconsistent with the notion that youthful immaturity was the only mental characteristic that could be taken into account when applying the objective limb of the test for provocation.

Having referred to the line of Court of Appeal decisions from *R* v *Ahluwalia* [1992] 4 All ER 889 to *R* v *Thornton (No 2)* [1996] 2 All ER 1023, Potts J continued:

'In our judgment, Lord Taylor CJ in *R* v *Thornton (No 2)* did no more than adapt Lord Diplock's formulation in *Camplin*'s case to the facts of the case then under appeal. In our opinion, the decisions of the Court of Appeal cited are in accordance with, and are a logical extension of, the decision in *DPP* v *Camplin*. They are binding on this court. In origin, the defence of provocation saved from the gallows those who would otherwise have been guilty of murder. Its incremental development over the years has been marked not by logic but by a slowly changing sense of what is fair. Words have been added to conduct as a possible trigger and the number of characteristics with which a reasonable man is deemed to be endowed, when having his theoretical response assessed by a jury, have been increased. The essential question raised by this appeal is whether, on the authorities binding on this court, any distinction can now properly be drawn, when attributing such characteristics for the purposes of the objective part of the test imposed by s3 of the Homicide Act 1957, between their relevance to the gravity of the provocation to a reasonable man and his reaction to it. It seems to us that in *Camplin*'s case Lord Diplock drew no such distinction, nor did other divisions of this court in the cases to which reference has been made. In our judgment the minority advice of Lord Steyn in *Luc Thiet Thuan* ... accurately states the law of England. We emphasise here that we have not overlooked the speech of Lord Goff in *R* v *Morhall*. But the House of Lords in *Morhall* was, as Lord Steyn pointed out in *Luc Thiet Thuan*, concerned with a different problem altogether – the characteristic supplying the sting of provocative conduct. There is nothing in Lord Goff's speech in that case inconsistent with Lord Taylor CJ's reasoning in *R* v *Thornton (No 2)* or of this court in the other decisions cited.'

Comment

The court does seem to have acted upon the basis of Lord Steyn's comments in *Luc* (at p131) to the effect that the dictates of justice were more important than the promptings of legal logic. One might ask why the Court of Appeal was so keen to embrace a dissenting advice in a decision that was not binding upon it in any event. The answer may of course be that Lord Steyn's views were simply consistent with the previous decisions of the Court of Appeal itself. The matter needs to be resolved once and for all by the House of Lords and in this respect it is worth noting that leave to appeal to the House of Lords was granted by the Court of Appeal. Note that the appellant, who had previous convictions for a number of offences of violence, was sentenced to seven years' imprisonment.

The present decision is consistent with *R* v *Parker* [1997] Crim LR 760, where the Court of Appeal quashed a murder conviction and ordered a retrial in the case of a defendant who had stabbed his neighbour to death. The Court of Appeal held that the evidence of the defendant's chronic alcoholism that had damaged the left temporal lobe of his brain ought to have been taken into account when assessing his defence of provocation.

16.2 Sexual offences and consent

B v *DPP* [1998] 4 All ER 265 Queen's Bench Division (Brooke LJ, Tucker and Rougier JJ)

Indecency with Children Act 1960 – whether mens rea as to age of the child required

Facts

B, aged 15 at the time, incited P (a 13-year-old girl) to perform oral sex on him. He was charged under s1(1) of the Indecency with Children Act 1960, which provides:

> 'Any person who commits an act of gross indecency with or towards a child under the age of fourteen, or who incites a child under that age to such an act with him or another, shall be liable on conviction on indictment to imprisonment for a term not exceeding two years ...'

Following a ruling by the youth court that the offence was one of strict liability, B was convicted of inciting an act of gross indecency and appealed by way of case stated. The essence of his appeal was the contention that he had honestly believed P to be over the age of 14.

Held

The appeal was dismissed. Ignorance as to the age of the victim was no excuse. Rougier J observed that the court would start from the position that even if the statute in question was silent as to mens rea, there was a presumption that

Parliament intended some mens rea to be established as a precondition to any conviction, unless the prosecution could show that Parliament had intended otherwise. He further noted that in *Sweet* v *Parsley* [1970] AC 132 the House of Lords had held that truly criminal offences, ie those in respect of which a conviction carried considerable social stigma, would not normally be treated as strict liability offences. Against this, the courts were willing to treat an offence as one of strict liability where the danger to society posed by the defendant's conduct justified such an approach. The present case presented both features. It was a truly criminal offence as it involved sexual abuse of children, but also involved a grave social danger.

Rougier J adverted to the legislative history of the 1960 Act. He explained that, whilst the Sexual Offences Act 1956 provided for offences of indecent assault in ss14 and 15, both offences required proof of an assault. It quickly became apparent that a loophole existed where a defendant persuaded a child to commit an act of indecency without using force (for example out of affection or obedience). The 1960 Act sought to close that loophole, as no proof of assault was required. Protection was extended to children up to the age of 14 on the assumption that children over the age of 14 would be able to refuse to engage in such behaviour (thus creating a loophole in relation to those aged between 14 and 16). Because the 1960 Act was enacted to close a loophole in the 1956 Act Rougier J felt that it was appropriate to regard the 1960 Act as effectively being an appendix to the 1956 Act, and that the 1960 Act should be construed on that basis. As he stated (at p270):

'To my mind, the significance of this history is that it is quite plain that the 1960 Act, or at least s1, was only omitted from the 1956 Act by oversight and should be regarded as an appendix to that Act, in effect to s14. From that it follows that the principles of construction which are applicable to the 1956 Act should also apply to the 1960 Act.'

Rougier J noted that some provisions in the 1956 Act expressly required proof of mens rea, as denoted by reference to the defendant acting 'knowingly' in regard to some aspect of the actus reus. Elsewhere there were provisions in the 1956 Act that were silent as to mens rea, but in relation to which Parliament had created statutory defences. In particular, he noted that s5 of the 1956 Act (sexual intercourse with a girl under the age of 13) provided for no excuses as to a mistaken belief that the girl might be older, whilst the less serious offence under s6 (sexual intercourse with a girl under the age of 16) did provide for the so-called 'young man's defence' (ie a man under 24 could contend that he had reasonable believed the girl to be older than 16). As Rougier J observed (at p274e–h):

'To my mind, the inclusion of the specific statutory defence in the two sections which I have mentioned demonstrates conclusively that Parliament did not intend that defence to be available to those other offences where there is no such provision. For instance, the comparison between the terms of ss5 and 6 to my mind is deadly. How could it possibly be said that, having expressly provided for a limited defence to the less serious offence, Parliament must be assumed to have intended that a similar defence should be available for the more serious *without* express provision? And this takes no account of the fact that if the appellant's contention is right, the suggested implied defence would be available to a person of any age with a number of previous convictions for similar offences behind him, whether or not there were reasonable grounds for his mistaken belief. If I am correct in believing that the principles governing the construction of the 1956 Act apply also to s1 of the 1960 Act, then it follows that there is no room for implying what I have called the basic principle defence founded on a mistaken belief or lack of knowledge of the victim's age.'

Hence the absence of any express mens rea requirement under s1(1) of the 1960 Act, and the absence of any statutory defence, persuaded him to the conclusion that a mistake as to the age of the victim under s1(1) would be irrelevant, regardless of whether it was honest or reasonable.

B contended that an analogy should be drawn with the offence of rape, as enacted under s1 of the Sexual Offences Act 1956, which had also been silent as to mens rea. He relied in particular on *DPP* v *Morgan* [1976] AC 182, where the House of Lords had held that a defendant could be acquitted of rape if he mistakenly but honestly believed the complainant to have been consenting. Rejecting this analogy, Rougier J pointed out that it had never been suggested in *Morgan* that rape might be a strict liability offence. The issue was whether a mistake as to consent had to be reasonable, or merely honest.

Tucker J agreed with Rougier J, and referred to a range of other offences where mistake as to age would not be regarded as providing any defence, notably incest and possession of indecent pictures of children. He added, somewhat tellingly (at p276e–f):

'I deduce from all these statutory provisions that it is the clear intention of Parliament to protect young children and to make it an offence to commit offences against children under a certain age, whether or not the defendant knows of the age of the victims, and that it was intended that, save where expressly provided, a mistaken or honest belief in the victim's age should not afford a defence. In my judgment it is not open to the courts to create a defence in circumstances such as the present where Parliament clearly intended that no such defence should be available. The effect of [counsel for the appellant's] submissions would be that a defendant charged with an offence under s1(1) of the Indecency with Children Act 1960 would be in a better position than if he were charged with an offence under s6(1) of the Sexual Offences Act 1956. This is because, according to [his] submission, in the first case the onus of proof would be on the prosecution, whereas in the second case proof of the exception lies on the person relying on it. Such a result would offend common sense, and cannot have been intended by Parliament.'

Comment

Note that Brooke LJ took the opportunity to criticise the failure of Parliament to clarify this and other aspects of the criminal law. He stated (at p276g–j):

'G K Chesterton told us how the rolling English drunkard made the rolling English road long before the importation to these islands of more efficient road making techniques. The rolling English criminal law was not made by the rolling English drunkard – much though he has contributed to the overload of our criminal justice system – but to a student of history who is not concerned with the efficient and fair administration of the law, parts of it must have much the same old-fashioned charm as some of our winding country lanes. How the more incoherent parts of our criminal law will stand up to the rigorous standards required by the European Court of Human Rights, by which the citizen must have an adequate indication of the legal rules which are to be applied in any given case, remains to be seen as we prepare to receive the Convention for the Protection of Human Rights and Fundamental Freedoms ... into our national law in the millennium year.'

Leave to appeal to the House of Lords was refused, but the Divisional Court did certify the following point of law of general public importance were involved in the decision:

'(1) is a defendant entitled to be acquitted of the offence of inciting a child aged under 14 to commit an act of gross indecency, contrary to s1(1) of the Indecency with Children Act 1960, if he may hold an honest belief that the child in question was aged 14 years or over? (2) If Yes, (a) must the belief be held on reasonable grounds? (b) on whom does the burden of proof lie?'

16.3 Theft

R v *Kelly* [1998] 3 All ER 741 Court of Appeal (Criminal Division) (Rose LJ, Ognall and Sullivan JJ)

Theft – property – whether parts of a corpse capable of being stolen

Facts
The defendant was an artist who had been granted access to the Royal College of Surgeons so that he could draw anatomical specimens. Working in conjunction with L, a junior technician at the College, the defendant removed between 30 and 40 body parts from the College, making casts of some of them. Police investigating the disappearance of the body parts found some at the defendant's flat, some at the house of his friends, and other parts buried in a field. The defendant and L were convicted of theft of the body parts and appealed contending: (i) that the body parts were not capable of constituting property for the purposes of s4(1) of the Theft Act 1968; and (ii) the body parts had not been in the lawful possession of the Royal College of Surgeons (having been retained by the College for more than the two years permitted under the Anatomy Act 1832) and hence could no longer be regarded as belonging to the College for the purposes of s5(1) of the Theft Act 1968.

Held
The appeals were dismissed. The body parts were property and the issue of whether or not the College's possession was lawful was irrelevant.

Considering the question of whether or not the body parts were property Rose LJ observed (pp749c–750c):

'The status of the holder of the thing is irrelevant to determination of whether it is property or not ... The common law doctrine as to who has the right to possession or control is irrelevant to whether a thing is property. Parts of a corpse have all the properties of a thing; the common law relates to rights not things. In the 1968 Act, Parliament did not declare that a corpse was not property and could not be stolen. As a matter of statutory construction, a corpse or part of a corpse is within the definition of property in s4 ... the draftsmen of the 1968 Act must presumably have been well aware of the state of the common law for the last 150 years or more, and they do not appear to have made any exception in the 1968 Act by reference to it ... To address the point as it was addressed before the trial judge and to which his certificate relates, in our judgment, parts of a corpse are capable of being property within s4 of the Theft Act, if they have acquired different attributes by virtue of the application of skill such as dissection or preservation techniques, for exhibition or teaching purposes ... Furthermore, the common law does not stand still. It may be that if, on some future occasion, the question arises, the courts will hold that human body parts are capable of being property for the purposes of s4, even without the acquisition of different attributes, if they have a use or significance beyond their mere existence. This may be so if, for example, they are intended for use in an organ transplant operation, for the extraction of DNA or, for that matter, as an exhibit in a trial.'

Regarding the question of whether the property had ceased to belong to the College (and thus had ceased to be property belonging to another) Rose LJ observed:

'So far as the question of possession by the Royal College of Surgeons is concerned, in our judgment the learned judge was correct to rule that the College had possession, sufficiently for the purposes of and within s5(1) of the Theft Act 1968. We are unable to accept that possession, for the purposes of that section, is in any way dependent on the period of possession, ie whether it is for a limited time, or an indefinite time. In our judgment, the evidence, so far as it was material, before the jury, was to the effect that factually, the parts were in the custody of the Royal College of Surgeons. They were, as it seems to us, in their control and possession within the meaning of s5(1). That conclusion is, as it seems to us, reinforced by the judgment of the Court of Appeal in *R v Turner (No 2)*. We do not accept that the passage in Lord Parker CJ's judgment which we have read is to be regarded as limited to the facts of that particular case. In expressing the view that no other word such as "lawful" was to be read into s5(1), by reference to possession, that court was construing s5 entirely consonantly with the construction which we now place upon it for the purposes of this appeal ... it was not necessary for the judge to direct the jury that the College was in lawful possession rather than merely in possession.'

Comment

On the basis of this decision it seems clear that A can be guilty of theft where he steals property from B that B has just stolen from C. The lawfulness of B's possession is irrelevant – he is in possession as a matter of fact.

16.4 Criminal damage

Chamberlain v *Lindon* [1998] 2 All ER 538 Queen's Bench Division (Rose LJ and Sullivan J)

Criminal Damage Act 1971 – demolition of a wall to gain access to land – whether any lawful excuse within s5(2)(b) Criminal Damage Act 1971

Facts

L purchased land from C, but could only access this property by crossing land still owned by C. A right of way was granted to L by C, which L exercised by driving diagonally across C's land. C objected to L's behaviour and built a brick wall across his land to prevent the right of way being exercised in this way. L demolished the wall in order to access his property. C brought a private prosecution for criminal damage, which was dismissed by the justices. On appeal by C, the following question was stated for the opinion of the Divisional Court: were the justices, on the facts as found, entitled to find that L had a lawful excuse for the purposes of s5(2)(b) of the Criminal Damage Act 1971?

Held

The appeal was dismissed. Following *R v Hill; R v Hall* (1989) 89 Cr App R 74, it was significant that L had believed that he was acting to protect his property (his right of way), and it could be said, viewing the matter objectively, that his action had had that purpose. The fact that he had also chosen to demolish the wall rather than engage in lengthy litigation did not mean that his purpose had not been to protect his property.

Regarding the issue of whether or not the property had been in need of immediate protection, the court noted that this was not a case of the defendant engaged in a pre-emptive strike – the threat to the property had already materialised. As Sullivan J observed (p543d–g):

'In *R v Hill, R v Hall* Lord Lane CJ clarified the nature of the two stage test in cases such as this. First one decides what was in the respondent's own mind; the subjective stage. Second one decides, objectively, whether it can be said that on those facts, as believed by the respondent, demolishing the wall could amount to something done to protect his right of way. Mr Dean [for the appellant] concedes that demolishing the wall was capable of protecting property, but he says it was done for an additional purpose, to avoid litigation and if there is a dual purpose then the objective test is not met.

I agree with Mr Forde [for the respondent] that it is plain, on the facts as found by the justices, that what the respondent did, namely demolishing the wall, could on the facts, as believed by him (namely that he was entitled to exercise a right of way which was being obstructed by the wall) amount to something which was done to protect his right of way ... No doubt he hoped to avoid litigation. He could have sought to protect his right of way either by recourse to litigation or by way of abatement. The fact that he chose the latter does not mean that his act of destroying the wall was not done to protect his right of way on the facts as he saw them. His purpose was to protect the right of way. He chose the means of abatement because he hoped to avoid litigation. That does not convert the avoidance of litigation into his purpose.'

Comment

The longer the wall remained in place the greater the urgency regarding the need to remove it, lest the appellant contend that the respondent had acquiesced in the nuisance.

16.5 Accessorial and vicarious liability

R v *Uddin* [1998] 2 All ER 744 Court of Appeal (Criminal Division)
(Beldam LJ, Johnson and Wright JJ)

Accessorial liability – group attack on victim – proper direction

Facts

The appellant was involved in a group attack on S. Some members of the group
were armed with poles and bars. During the attack another member of the group, T,
produced a flick-knife that he used to stab S to death. The appellant and T were
convicted of murder. Other members of the group were convicted of manslaughter.
The appellant appealed against his conviction on the ground that he had not known
that T had been armed with a knife and alleged that there were deficiencies in the
trial judge's direction to the jury on the extent to which the principal offender's use
of a knife constituted a deliberate departure from the common design.

Held

The appeal was allowed and a retrial ordered. A defendant can only be guilty of
murder as an accomplice if the principal's acts causing death are a type that the
defendant foresees (even if he does not intend that death or grievous bodily harm
should result). Where the principal's actions are of an 'entirely different' type to that
contemplated by the accomplice, the accomplice will not incur accessorial liability.
This holds true even where the accomplice foresees death or grievous bodily harm
being caused by the principal, albeit by different means. Hence, if the accomplice
does not foresee the use of any weapon by the principal, and the principal kills using
a gun, the accomplice will not be a party to the killing. Difficulties arise in those
cases where the accomplice does contemplate the use of a weapon, but the principal
uses a different weapon. Where the principal uses a different, but equally lethal,
weapon, liability will still ensue. In other cases it may be less clear cut. As Beldam
LJ observed (at p751):

> 'In deciding whether the actions [of the principal are of an entirely different type to those
> contemplated by the accomplice] the use by [the principal] of a weapon is a significant
> factor. If the character of the weapon, eg its propensity to cause death, is different from
> any weapon used or contemplated by the others and if it is used with specific intent to
> kill, the others are not responsible for the death unless it is proved that they knew or
> foresaw the likelihood of the use of such a weapon.'

On the facts Beldam LJ expressed the view that it was for the jury to decide if the
use of a knife was 'so different' from the concerted actions of hitting the victim with
clubs and kicking him with a shod foot.

If there is an agreement not to use any deadly weapons in an attack, but during
the attack one of the participants produces such a weapon, the others can incur
accessorial liability for the harm caused by the use of such a weapon if they continue

to participate in the attack in the knowledge that such a weapon is being used by one of their number.

Comment

Note that the summing up at the appellant's trial predated the House of Lords' ruling in *R* v *Powell and Daniels; R* v *English* [1997] 3 WLR 959 by almost a year. Note, also, that *R* v *Greatrex* (1998) The Times 2 April, another Court of Appeal decision concerning accessorial liability for murder arising out of a group attack, was decided on the same day as *R* v *Uddin*. The appellant appealed successfully against his conviction for murder on the basis that he had not known that the principal offender had armed himself with an iron bar before carrying out the attack. The appeal was allowed because of deficiencies in the trial judge's direction on this point, but it should be noted that the Court of Appeal was willing to accept that striking a victim with a iron bar and kicking him with a shod foot would not necessarily be fundamentally different acts. Whether there is a sufficient difference between the contemplated and actual acts of the principal offender to those actions outside the scope of the 'common purpose' was a matter of degree.

Index

437

Law Update 2000

Law Update 2001 edition – due February 2001

An annual review of the most recent developments in specific legal subject areas, useful for law students at degree and professional levels, others with law elements in their courses and also practitioners seeking a quick update.

Published around February every year, the Law Update summarises the major legal developments during the course of the previous year. In conjunction with Old Bailey Press textbooks it gives the student a significant advantage when revising for examinations.

Contents

Administrative Law • Civil and Criminal Procedure • Commercial Law • Company Law • Conflict of Laws • Constitutional Law • Contract Law • Conveyancing • Criminal Law • Criminology • English Legal System • Equity and Trusts • European Union Law • Evidence • Family Law • Jurisprudence • Land Law • Law of International Trade • Public International Law • Revenue Law • Succession • Tort

For further information on contents or to place an order, please contact:

Mail Order
Old Bailey Press
200 Greyhound Road
London
W14 9RY

Telephone No: 020 7385 3377
Fax No: 020 7381 3377

ISBN 1 85836 347 0
Soft cover 246 x 175 mm
392 pages £9.95
Published February 2000

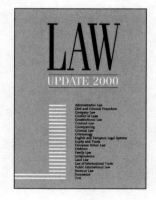

Old Bailey Press

The Old Bailey Press integrated student law library is tailor-made to help you at every stage of your studies from the preliminaries of each subject through to the final examination. The series of Textbooks, Revision WorkBooks, 150 Leading Cases/Casebooks and Cracknell's Statutes are interrelated to provide you with a comprehensive set of study materials.

You can buy Old Bailey Press books from your University Bookshop, your local Bookshop, direct using this form, or you can order a free catalogue of our titles from the address shown overleaf.

The following subjects each have a Textbook, 150 Leading Cases/Casebook, Revision WorkBook and Cracknell's Statutes unless otherwise stated.

Administrative Law
Commercial Law
Company Law
Conflict of Laws
Constitutional Law
Conveyancing (Textbook and Casebook)
Criminal Law
Criminology (Textbook and Sourcebook)
English and European Legal Systems
Equity and Trusts
Evidence
Family Law
Jurisprudence: The Philosophy of Law (Textbook, Sourcebook and
    Revision WorkBook)
Land: The Law of Real Property
Law of International Trade
Law of the European Union
Legal Skills and System
Obligations: Contract Law
Obligations: The Law of Tort
Public International Law
Revenue Law (Textbook,
    Sourcebook and Revision
    WorkBook)
Succession

Mail order prices:	
Textbook	£11.95
150 Leading Cases/Casebook	£9.95
Revision WorkBook	£7.95
Cracknell's Statutes	£9.95
Suggested Solutions 1998–1999	£6.95
Law Update 2000	£9.95
The Practitioner's Handbook 2000	£54.95

To complete your order, please fill in the form below:

Module	Books required	Quantity	Price	Cost
		Postage		
		TOTAL		

For Europe, add 15% postage and packing (£20 maximum).
For the rest of the world, add 40% for airmail.

ORDERING

By telephone to Mail Order at 020 7385 3377, with your credit card to hand.

By fax to 020 7381 3377 (giving your credit card details).

By post to:

Mail Order, Old Bailey Press, 200 Greyhound Road, London W14 9RY.

When ordering by post, please enclose full payment by cheque or banker's draft, or complete the credit card details below. You may also order a free catalogue of our complete range of titles from this address.

We aim to despatch your books within 3 working days of receiving your order.

Name

Address

Postcode   Telephone

Total value of order, including postage: £

I enclose a cheque/banker's draft for the above sum, or

charge my   ☐ Access/Mastercard   ☐ Visa   ☐ American Express
Card number

☐☐☐☐☐ ☐☐☐☐☐ ☐☐☐☐☐ ☐☐☐☐☐

Expiry date   ☐☐☐☐

Signature: ....Date: ....